Public Speaking

Theory into Practice

Second
Edition

Public Speaking

Theory into Practice

Second Edition

John J. Makay

Professor and Chair,
Department of Interpersonal
and Public Communication

Bowling Green State University

Harcourt Brace College Publishers

Fort Worth   Philadelphia   San Diego   New York   Orlando   Austin   San Antonio
Toronto   Montreal   London   Sydney   Tokyo

Publisher Ted Buchholz
Senior Acquisitions Editor Carol Wada
Developmental Editor Laurie Runion
Senior Project Editor Steve Welch
Senior Production Manager Ken Dunaway
Art Director Priscilla Mingus/Vicki Whistler
Photo Permissions Editor Lili Weiner

Cover Image: Hans Staartjes

ISBN: 0-15-501626-1

Library of Congress Catalog Card Number: 94-75158

Address for Editorial Correspondence: Harcourt Brace College Publishers, 301 Commerce Street, Suite 3700, Fort Worth, TX 76102.

Address for Orders: Harcourt Brace & Company, 6277 Sea Harbor Drive, Orlando, FL 32887-6777. 1-800-782-4479, or 1-800-433-0001 (in Florida).

I have enjoyed the opportunity to prepare a second edition of *Public Speaking: Theory into Practice,* and I am both pleased and grateful for its widespread use in colleges and universities across the United States.

In preparing this edition I examined the first edition carefully to ascertain ways in which it could be strengthened without compromising the style of writing and the emphasis on putting theory into practice. I also received valuable suggestions from reviewers and from a focus group conducted at one of the Speech Communication Association's national conventions. Certainly much of the information in this edition is what was presented in the first edition, but I believe the changes made are substantive rather than cosmetic.

ABOUT THE SECOND EDITION

Complete and thorough coverage. Public Speaking, Second Edition, continues to offer students complete and thorough coverage. It blends theory and practical skills, analyzing public speaking as a form of reciprocal communication between speaker and audience. The focus on the needs of the audiences helps make this textbook unique.

The depth of coverage in the text makes it distinctive. For example, in no other public speaking text will students find as complete, up-to-date information on computerized library research or on a practical library search strategy. Similarly, the coverage of statistics as a form of support is more extensive than in any other textbook, and two chapters are devoted to persuasive speaking.

Early first speech chapter. Chapter Two, "Preparing Your First Speech," recognizes that students must speak in class before completing the entire textbook. This chapter gives students an overview of the process of public speaking and many of the ideas introduced here are developed fully in subsequent chapters. Chapter Two pays special attention to the concept of speaker as spokesperson and to helping students channel speech tension into positive behavior.

Interviews with well-known speakers conducted especially for this book. Among the special features of this textbook are interviews with nationally known public speakers and others involved in the field of public address. Subjects include Vickee Jordan Adams, Vice-President, Director, Ketchum Communications Training Center; Dr. Bob Arnot, CBS News medical correspondent; Sarah Brady, chair of Handgun Control, Inc.; Joe Clark, controversial educator and public speaker; Peter Davis, award-winning writer, producer, and director; Sarah Weddington, feminist attorney and women's advocate; and Edith Weiner, president of Weiner, Edrich, Brown.

In addition, there are five new interviews: John V. Esposito, attorney and author; Dr. Alberto Gonzalez, an outstanding Latino professor of communication; Curt Smith, author, journalist, and former presidential speech writer; Gerry Tausch, the co-owner of a successful international speakers bureau and public speaker; and General Myrna Williamson, the first woman to become a brigadier general in the United States Army.

The interviews examine the art of public speaking by linking substance and technique, by focusing on public speaking ethics and motives for speaking, and by analyzing individual styles and preferences. What emerges from the reflections of these professional speakers is the recognition that each speaker must define his or her own personal speaking style—work that should begin in this course.

Focus on Research. Public speaking is supported by extensive research. Many chapters contain a *Focus on Research* feature, which may examine either a qualitative or quantitative study of communication. Research findings, in traditional rhetorical studies and in modern social sciences, are blended within the text to introduce students to important concepts and techniques that may be useful to them as speakers.

There are two new *Focus on Research* boxes: a rhetorical criticism that looks at ethics and a major speech by President Nixon on the Vietnam War, and a quantitative study that looks at the effects of gestures and speech rate on effective public speaking.

Speak Easy. How should speakers handle audience questions? How do they avoid plagiarism? How do they make transparencies for overhead projectors? These questions are addressed in the *Speak Easy* feature that accompanies many chapters.

Focus on public speaking ethics. With ethical concerns becoming prominent in government and business, audiences are often skeptical about the integrity of public speakers. In many cases, audiences do not believe what they hear, or they question the motives of the speaker. This is the first public speaking textbook to feature an entire chapter on the ethics of public address early in the textbook.

Chapter Four, "The Ethics of Responsible Speech" includes a new discussion on Karl Wallace's four habits for promoting ethical communication. In addition, eleven unethical speech practices have been added. There are also new discussions of ethics in Chapters Fourteen and Fifteen on speaking ethically in informative and persuasive public speaking settings.

Focus on the "voice" of effective speeches. The second edition continues to include numerous excerpts from actual speeches in each chapter. Many were delivered by experienced speakers, while others are the products of students learning their craft. Students will begin to "hear" the "voice" of effective public address. By hearing the language and rhythm of effective speeches, they will be more attuned to the importance of language and its effective use.

There are now four complete speeches in the second edition. There is a speech given by the late Cesar Chavez in which he tries to persuade his audience to support the United Farm Workers and boycott California products. There is an annotated commencement speech given by Dr. John Kuo Wei Tchen, Associate Director of the Asian American Center at Queens College, City University of New York, on race and cultural democracy. There is also a student speech on suicide and an annotated student speech on environmental discrimination.

Focus on the history and social impact of public speaking. Throughout the text, examples of famous public speakers are used to illustrate ideas. Students learn, for example, about Eleanor Roosevelt's problems with a high-pitched, falsetto voice; how Ronald Reagan edited the language of a presidential address; how Harry Truman faltered reading a speech but delivered an inspiring extemporaneous address; how author and filmmaker Peter Davis adjusted the speech he delivered about Nicaragua to a group of IBM executives on the day the stock market crashed; and how Mary Fisher stood before the 1992 Republican National Convention to speak about being HIV-positive and to enlist support for those with AIDS. These current and historical examples add interest and texture as they help clarify concepts.

Discussion Questions and Activities. Each chapter contains discussion questions and activities designed to reinforce chapter concepts and help students put these concepts into practical application.

Other new features. In addition to the changes mentioned above, *Public Speaking: Theories into Practice, Second Edition* also includes the following revisions:

- New four-color interior design and photographs enhance readability and student interest.
- Chapter Fifteen has additional materials on reasoning for logical appeal, reasoning from sign, appeal to audience emotions, and ethics and persuasive speaking.
- Chapter Fourteen has new material on Monroe's motivated sequence, which is illustrated by a student speech.
- Chapter Eight, "Using Visual Aids," is now Chapter Eleven—a change suggested by users of the first edition that visual aids need to precede the chapter on speech delivery.
- New examples throughout to illustrate theories and principles of public speaking.

In addition to the textbook, the following materials are available:

ANCILLARY PACKAGE

- *Instructor's Manual/Test Bank* The instructor's manual/test bank has been completely revised. It includes sample syllabi and objectives for semester and quarter courses; speaking assignments and critique sheets; outlines, objectives, and activities for each textbook chapter; and a test bank.
- *Public Speeches for Analysis Video* A new videotape for public speaking courses includes many professional public speeches, but has an emphasis on student and business speeches. Each speech is chosen for its illustration of a particular concept or technique. Many of the speeches are shown in two versions as a way to demonstrate changes made for audience or for improvement.
- *Understanding Public Speaking Apprehension Video* This new videotape is designed to help students minimize their fear of public speaking. This

videotape features a lecture by Ron Adler on minimizing fear and shows students practicing techniques that help to minimize speech apprehension.

✂ *Computerized Test Bank* The test questions found in the instructor's manual are also available as IBM or Macintosh software.

✂ *Overhead Transparencies* A set of four-color overhead transparencies that illustrate textbook principles is available to adopters.

✂ *Speech-On-Line Software* This revised and improved software has been developed to help students develop their speech topics and outlines. This software features a step-by-step approach to refining a speech topic, gathering information and ideas, and coalescing this information into a powerful speech outline. It also includes models of other speeches at each step in the process for the student to refer to.

ACKNOWLEDG-MENTS

This new edition would not be possible without the special assistance of a number of individuals who provided support and encouragement along the way. Dr. Leigh Makay has given me time, ideas, and criticism in the development of this edition and, as a user, has offered insightful ideas about what works with her students. Leigh also prepared the instructor's manual and test bank, provided the studies for the *Focus on Research* feature in Chapter Ten, and wrote the script for the software. I am indeed grateful for all of her professional contributions.

Gerry Tausch, co-owner of the Speaker's Connection, a highly successful international speaker's bureau, invited me to address the International Platform Association, became a new friend, allowed me to interview her for this edition, and provided me with introductions and phone numbers of professional speakers whose interviews appear in this edition. I am grateful to Gerry and I anticipate learning more from her in the future.

My friend, Curt Smith, a former presidential speech writer and always an outstanding baseball writer, offered me the opportunity to interview him a second time and his insights and observations again make an important contribution to Chapter Ten.

I am pleased that John Esposito allowed me to interview him and offered a great deal of encouragement.

My colleague and special friend, Dr. Alberto Gonzalez, agreed to an interview on intercultural communication with an eye toward the speaker-audience connection, and Chapter Five is considerably stronger in this edition because of his views.

The library feature in Chapter Six was examined carefully by R. Errol Lam, Reference Librarian and Assistant Professor at Bowling Green State University. I am grateful for his comments and suggestions for strengthening and upgrading my work.

As a department chair, my professional life is more complicated than other faculty in our department and to help me meet deadlines and polish portions of my work, my secretary, Janet Swartzlander, was always available to respond to requests I made while rushing from one task to another.

While there are a number of persons at Harcourt Brace to acknowledge in helping me bring the second edition into print, I want to particularly thank my "phone pals" Laurie Runion, Developmental Editor, and Steve Welch, Senior Project Editor. Both of them offered me skillful advice, sound judgment, and welcome listening when I needed to talk and worked to meet deadlines. I also appreciate the support of Carol Wada, who came on board as Senior Acquisitions Editor while this project was under way. Senior Production Manager Ken Dunaway and Art Directors Priscilla Mingus and Vicki Whistler helped ensure that this book was both attractive and on schedule.

I would also like to thank the reviewers of the first edition whose comments continue to impact this edition:

Marcee Andersen, University of Wisconsin-Stout; James Brooks, Middle Tennessee State University; Tom Burkholder, Southwest Texas State; Liz Coughlin, Northern Virginia Community College; Virginia Covington, University of Southern Mississippi; Jerry Ferguson, South Dakota State University; Ken Frandsen, University of New Mexico; Fred Garbowitz, Grand Rapids Junior College; J. Douglas Gibb, Brigham Young University; Fran Hassencahl, Old Dominion University; Anne Holmquest, University of Louisville; David McLennan, Texas Christian University; Don Ochs, University of Iowa; David Ralph, Michigan State University; Robley Rhine, University of Colorado at Denver; Edwin Rowley, Indiana University; Richard Rowley, Normandale Community College; Gwenn Schultze, Portland Community College; Anita Vangelisti, University of Iowa; David Walker, Middle Tennessee State University; Joseph Wenzel, University of Illinois; Donald Williams, University of Florida; and Jon Winterton, University of Colorado at Denver.

I would also like to thank the following reviewers whose comments helped improve the second edition:

Bobby Bell, Seminole Community College; Jacquelyn Buckrop, Ball State University; Risa Dixon, California State University-San Bernadino; John Ellsworth, Nassau Community College; David McLennan, Texas Christian University; Scott Rodriguez, California State University-San Bernardino; Deborah Smith-Howell, University of Nebraska-Omaha.

CONTENTS

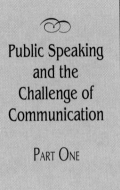

Public Speaking
and the
Challenge of
Communication

PART ONE

CHAPTER   THREE

C H A P T E R   F O U R

C H A P T E R   F I V E

C H A P T E R   S I X

Preparing and
Presenting Your
Speech

Part Two

RESEARCHING YOUR SPEECH   130

CHAPTER ELEVEN

CHAPTER   TWELVE

C H A P T E R   T H I R T E E N

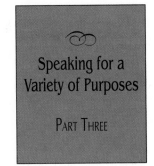

Speaking for a
Variety of Purposes

PART THREE

C H A P T E R   F O U R T E E N

CHAPTER SEVENTEEN

INTERVIEWS

FOCUS ON RESEARCH

Public Speaking
and the
Challenge of
Communication

PART ONE

"There is an elemental power in having a living breathing human being—right here, right now—interacting with other human beings. And when that living, breathing human being is a skilled communicator, he or she possesses real power. The power to change the way people feel, to change the way they think, and even to change the way they act."[1]

Rex Kelly, General Manager, Corporate Communications, Mississippi Power Company.

INTRODUCTION TO PUBLIC SPEAKING

ften nothing is more powerful than the spoken word delivered to an audience gathered to hear it. Timothy Donohue, a Vietnam veteran who in 1990 was a senior at Clark University, tapped into this power when he invited six World War II veterans from the Ex-P.O.W. Speakers Bureau in Boston to address his classmates about a war they knew little about.

This invitation was not unusual for the members of the Speakers Bureau, who have delivered presentations at nearly fifty schools to more than 8,000 students since 1986. Motivating the veterans is the desire to tell students about the horror of war. Through the art of public speaking, the veterans present what Donohue describes as "a living, breathing history lesson" that centers on the speakers' personal experiences in the war.

Philip Toland talks about being held prisoner by the Japanese for nearly four years and being forced to march more than seventy miles with 7,000 other prisoners. He explains how six of every seven soldiers died along the way.

Students may have read about the atrocities of World War II, but the emotion of these speeches affects them more powerfully. "I was moved by how tense [the speakers] were," said student John Gilman. "This was more effective than just reading about it or hearing about it in class," added student Jennifer Hines.

"There are students who can't relate to what happened," said Michael Salem, who described his trip to Stalag 7A in a railroad boxcar so packed that prisoners had to stand for days without food or water. "We are trying in our own humble way to educate them. I'm going to keep on talking . . . until they understand."[2]

At the University of California at Santa Barbara, hundreds of students enroll each semester in the most popular course on campus—a course dedicated to testimonials about the Vietnam War. Speakers tell of their personal experiences during the war as soldiers, antiwar protesters, families of veterans, and Vietnamese civilians caught in the middle of the conflict.

Something tangible happens to the audience during these accounts. Student Lisa Frankenburg explains: "I don't know how to describe it, unless you're sitting there. It's an emotional release. You can just feel it." "Every time I walk out of there," adds student Laura Pitter, "I want to work harder to prevent a war from ever happening again."[3]

This text begins with these examples to demonstrate the power you hold as a public speaker—power to communicate facts and emotions, convictions and attitudes, values and beliefs in a way that leaves a lasting—and often unequalled—

1. Rex Kelly, "Speakers and the Bottom Line: The Character of the Speaker," speech delivered to the Utility Speakers Activities Committee of the Edison Electric Institute, August 7, 1987. Reprinted in *Vital Speeches of the Day,* November 1, 1987, p. 48.
2. "Clark University: Enlivening History Through Veterans of World War II," *The New York Times,* December 10, 1989, p. 67.
3. "U.C., Santa Barbara: In Popular Class, Lessons Concern the Vietnam War," *The New York Times,* February 25, 1990, p. 43.

impression on your audience. These speakers told of the war, but the potential for communication is the same for whatever topic you choose as long as you have the skill to communicate and an understanding that public speaking involves person-to-person connections.

Our goal is to help you learn the art of public speaking as we introduce you to a sampling of American speeches. We want you and your audience to achieve the kind of understanding Michael Salem describes—an understanding based on genuine, effective communication. Throughout this text, and especially in the interviews we conducted with some of the nation's most accomplished public speakers, public speaking begins to appear broader than any set of skills we can teach. It is an art that must be defined and fine-tuned by every person who addresses an audience. It is an art that centers on a message; indeed, its soul is in the message. It is an art that involves ethics, stage presence, and the intangible relationship each speaker has with the audience.

Before we examine the nature of public speaking, let's address its value in your everyday life.

PUBLIC SPEAKING IN YOUR LIFE

At the start of this public speaking course, it is fair to ask what value public speaking has in your life. We answer, at least in part, using two examples:

⌘ A young, talented, and ambitious woman sidetracked her career at a Washington, DC-based trade association at the very time her supervisor was giving her a glowing job rating. After praising the woman for her performance during the past year, the supervisor explained that he wanted her to give speeches about the industry to consumer groups across the country. The more specific he became about her future public speaking responsibilities, the more uneasy the woman grew. After several minutes, she said that she had never spoken in public before and that she was not about to start now—even if it meant losing her job.

⌘ A student proudly announced to her class that what she was learning in her public speaking course had been instrumental in raising her level of personal achievement. For example, she said, she had been asked to help obtain corporate sponsors for her sorority's fund-raiser to aid a nearby children's hospital. Her speech to an audience of executives at a local corporation persuaded them to make a contribution of $1,000. A company spokesperson told the student that hers was the best presentation the executives had heard from a college student. Her announcement moved her classmates to applause. Several students told the instructor that they were also finding their public-speaking skills increasingly valuable.

Public speaking skills can be important in many different ways. How you choose to use them depends on your educational, career, and life-style choices.

F O C U S   O N   R E S E A R C H

DO REAL PEOPLE EVER GIVE SPEECHES?

Who are today's public speakers? Most people would answer Ross Perot, Dr. Joycelyn Elders, Connie Chung, and Elizabeth Taylor. But most people do not consider themselves—or other ordinary mortals—to be part of this group. According to communication professor Kathleen Edgerton Kendall, some rethinking may be in order.

To find out whether "real people ever give speeches," Kendall examined the public speaking experience of a group of 202 randomly selected subjects and found that a surprising number of noncelebrities speak to audiences, many on a regular basis. Here are some of Kendall's findings:

⌘ Fifty-five percent of the respondents had spoken to a group of ten or more at least once during the past two years. According to Kendall, seven of ten speakers had delivered four or more speeches during the period—an indication that once people feel comfortable speaking in public they are likely to do so on a regular basis.

⌘ The speakers reported that their speaking was often work-related. More than a third used their public speaking skills "to teach or instruct." Included in this group were classroom teachers, nurses, fire officials, and parents. Only seven subjects cited instances of speaking to persuade, which included speaking as a court defendant and engaging in public relations.

⌘ In general, women are more likely to speak out than men.

⌘ People with higher incomes do more public speaking than people who earn less money.

⌘ Kendall found that younger people, both men and women, are more likely to engage in public speaking than older, more experienced people.

⌘ Educational level affects willingness to speak in public: The more education we have, the more likely we are to be public speakers. According to Kendall, "The implications of this fact for the college-educated may be that they should expect to give speeches—and would probably benefit from training."[4]

Public Speaking Often Begins in College

How comfortable and competent you are as a public speaker can influence your success in college—not only in this communication course, but in many other courses. Every time you make an oral presentation in English or Philosophy or Political Science you use these skills. Your involvement in extracurricular activities may also be influenced by your ability to speak in public. If you are uncomfortable or lack the skills to address an audience, it will be impossible to run for student body president, to present your point of view at a PTA meeting, or to be part of a film criticism workshop.

---

4.   Kathleen Edgerton Kendall, "Does the Public Speak Publicly? A Survey," *World Communication 17*, no. 2, (Spring 1988): 279–90, Kathleen Edgerton Kendall, "Do Real People Ever Give Speeches?" *Central States Speech Journal* (1974): 233–35.

No Matter Your Career Choice, You May Also Be a Public Speaker

As you read in the first example, how far you go in a corporation often depends on your ability to speak to groups—at business conferences and at public presentations. According to management consultant Nelson Lees, "Corporate America is all about visibility. The people who get ahead are those who don't shirk from the opportunity to convey their thoughts and ideas to management."[5] Recent business studies have concluded that public speaking will be even more important in the years ahead.[6] Public speaking skills are an essential part of almost all professional interactions, including sales presentations, campaigns for public office, teaching and training programs, the presentation of research findings at conventions, regulatory and consumer meetings, annual stockholders' meetings, and employee recruitment campaigns and awards ceremonies. Few executives know more about the importance of public speaking in business than corporate consultant Edith Weiner. In the interview on pp. 8–9, Weiner explains the eight elements of a successful speech.

At a time when lifetime loyalty to one company is uncommon and when corporate mergers and acquisitions result in mass layoffs, being an accomplished and confident public speaker may help you find—and keep—a job. According to *The New York Times,* "Total avoidance [of public speaking] is a luxury many Americans no longer have. The proliferation of . . . business conferences and other activities has exponentially increased the demand for competent speakers."[7]

Public Speaking in Your Role as a Citizen

Unexpected events in our lives often catapult us into the public arena. We become public speakers because we believe we must. After an escaped convict shot and killed Lois Hess' twenty-four-year-old son in 1975, she conducted a one-woman lobbying campaign in support of gun control in her home state of Maryland. To help pass legislation in 1988 banning the sale of handguns, Hess testified before the state legislature.[8]

Lucie McKinney was also a private person before tragedy struck. After her husband, Congressman Stewart B. McKinney, died of AIDS in 1987, Mrs. McKinney devoted her energies to setting up a foundation to provide group homes in suburban

---

5. Alison Leigh Cowan, "Meek and Mumblers Learn Ways of Getting a Word In," *The New York Times,* May 29, 1989, p. 1.
6. According to Donald C. Hambrick and James W. Fredrickson, professors at Columbia University's Graduate School of Business and authors of a report on the qualifications needed by top managers in the year 2000, our corporate leaders will have to be accomplished public speakers who have learned the art of addressing small and large groups as well as the news media. Cited in Elizabeth M. Fowler, "Training 21st-Century Executives," *The New York Times,* June 20, 1989, p. D13.
7. Cowan, p. 24.
8. "A salute to everyday heroes," *Newsweek,* July 10, 1989, p. 63.

I N T E R V I E W

Edith Weiner
President, Weiner,
Edrich, Brown

Since she was twenty-three years old, Edith Weiner has been giving speeches in her field of strategic planning for major corporations and government institutions. She has spoken before Congress, served as a college guest lecturer at Harvard, Brown, and Wharton, and addressed industry groups and corporations. Weiner was the youngest woman ever elected to the board of directors of a major financial institution when she joined UNUM's board in 1978 at the age of twenty-nine.

Twenty-four years after her first speech, Weiner shares her opinions on what she considers the eight elements of a successful speech. She is as unconventional in her opinions as she is as a speaker:

Question: You've delivered hundreds of speeches in the past twenty-four years and listened to many more. What makes a successful speech?

Answer: At the top of my list is humor. I make some of my most important points with humor because I know that people will remember the jokes and that the jokes will connect them to the rest of my speech. If you take yourself too seriously, your audience may learn something, but it's the kind of learning that doesn't feel good. Think of it as the difference between having a tasty but heavy meal that fills you up after a few bites and a light, fantastically delicious meal you can't get enough of.

Humor also clears the air. I can tell you that it worked when I was pregnant with my son. I knew

that everyone was looking at me wondering whether I was pregnant or just fat. (There weren't too many pregnant women giving speeches in 1979.) So I made a few jokes about being pregnant, had everyone laughing, and went on to my message. My jokes told people that I was comfortable and that we could all get down to business.

Second, never read your speech. You'll lose your listeners within minutes. That's a guarantee.

Third, make some portion of what you say shocking, even if it means exaggerating your own beliefs or playing devil's advocate to the conventional view. It is important not to waste people's time by telling them things they already know—even if you tell it to them in an interesting way. You want them to come away with a new thought or something that jars them.

For example, in a speech I recently gave, I made the point that we're all getting tired of watching the super-rich show off their money. Instead of saying this (this was no surprise to anyone in the room), I decided to tell the story of how I encourage my son to read good literature—including the old standby *MAD* Magazine. I then told them how, in a recent issue, I found this statement, "Even the man with everything is envious of the man with two of everything." Now, within a space of minutes, I jarred my audience by telling them I consider *MAD* to be good literature and, through this statement, revealed an indisputable truth of human nature. They all laughed.

Fourth, fill your speeches with personalized anecdotes. Make your points in human terms, not textbook terms, either by referring to yourself, your friends, your family, or someone from the audience. People learn from examples that mean something to them, not from abstractions.

Fifth, go out of your way to actually name members of your audience during your speech. If you're speaking to a group in which you know only a few people, remember one or two things about them or something they told you when you were planning the speech. Then weave this information into your talk. Say something like, "And as Irene Chambers said . . ." Statements like this make you sound like you belong. You're one of the group because you know one of the group. These simple references make it possible for people to imagine themselves in conversation with you over breakfast.

Sixth, never give the same exact talk twice. It will bore you and when you're bored, your audience doesn't have a chance. Even if you're scheduled to repeat your 9:00 A.M. speech at 3:00 in the afternoon, you will learn something in the intervening hours that can change your talk. Making these changes is even easier if you have weeks or months between talks.

Point seven: Pretend you're talking to a roomful of friends instead of strangers. When you make a point, make it the way you would at a dinner party or during a political argument with your brother. Tell yourself that you've been given twenty minutes to tell Joe and Mary and John what you think without being interrupted. You'll feel like you've just been given a present and that you have the freedom to be natural.

Finally, think of your speech as the opportunity you always wanted to perform in public. I'm convinced that somewhere in every speaker's heart is the dream of being a rock star or even the host of "The Tonight Show." When you're asked to give a talk, realize that this is probably the closest you'll ever get to the cabaret. It's a dream come true, the chance to captivate an audience. When you're through, you'll find yourself saying, "Wow. If I can only do that again before I die . . . ."

(*Source:* Interview with Edith Weiner, October, 10, 1989.)

communities for AIDS victims. To promote her cause, Mrs. McKinney has spoken to Congress as well as to local community government and citizen action groups.

Your commitments, your interests, your hopes for the future may lead you to involvement in causes that involve public speaking. Your need may be as "ordinary" as addressing a parent teacher association meeting or as "extraordinary" as speaking out in public against the location of a hazardous waste disposal site near a residential community. Whatever your cause, the level of your personal involvement is often defined by your willingness and ability to speak in public.

Public Speaking Skills Are Important in Our High-Tech Age

Although we live in an age of electronic communication in which zapping messages back and forth via computers, facsimile machines, and closed-circuit cable TV is becoming as common as talking on the telephone, public speaking is no less important today than at any other time in our history. The more we are surrounded by technology, the more we want to hear and see someone talking to us about the issues that affect our lives. Peggy Noonan, former speechwriter for Ronald Reagan and George Bush, explains:

> Another reason speeches are important: because the biggest problem in America, the biggest problem in any modern industrialized society, is loneliness. A great speech from a leader to the people eases our isolation, breaks down the walls, includes people: It takes them inside a spinning thing and makes them part of the gravity.[9]

Communication via high technology prevents us from really touching one another and experiencing the empathy involved in the speaker-audience relationship. Psychologists define empathy as the capacity to understand, care about, and vicariously experience the feelings and thoughts of someone else. The following experience, described by speech consultant and author Ron Hoff, would not have been possible had it not involved a speaker talking to his audience. Hoff describes what he heard and saw:

> He was a young man, no more than twenty-five or twenty-six. He stood up before a small group of his coworkers, neatly dressed, but slender almost to the point of fragility.
>
> I can see him now—maybe six feet away from me, tall and thin—talking quietly, but with almost tangible intensity.
>
> "I have what is politely called a health problem," he said, "I have had it since I was a child. I started losing weight. One week I lost twenty pounds. The next week I lost fifteen. The doctor said I would never gain those pounds back again.
>
> "The doctor gave me one of these." He walked over to a nearby table and carefully removed a hypodermic syringe from its case. The barrel was empty. He reached into a sack and took out a blue vial. He punched the needle into the top of the vial and drew the plunger upward. It was then that I noticed his hands were shaking. I thought he was nervous, trembling from the experience of making a presentation before his peers.
>
> He returned to the center of the room. He held the hypodermic instrument up for all to see. "The reason I am shaking so badly is that I haven't had my insulin injection yet today. I usually take it when I first wake up—about seven o'clock—and now it is ten. I'm late. But I wanted to show you exactly what I have to do."
>
> He bent his right arm at the elbow and made a fist. I felt frightened for him. He positioned the needle halfway up his arm, then pushed it into his vein just above the elbow.
>
> Silence.
>
> "There," he said quietly. "It's really quite simple. Quite easy. Look." He extended his right arm and it was shaking slightly, but not nearly as uncontrollably as before. "I guess I am a little nervous," he said.
>
> He went on to tell how diabetes had changed his life. "I probably look at life a bit differently than you do," he said. "I see each new day as a gift, a bonus—and this needle is my friend."

---

9. Peggy Noonan, *What I Saw at the Revolution: A Political Life in the Reagan Era* (New York: Random House, 1990), p. 69.

His quiet, intense voice never faltered. "If you have diabetes, or have ever wondered about having it—I'd like to talk to you, to tell you what it's done for me. I don't think you'll fear it anymore."

The young man sat down. The audience was silent, stunned.

Suddenly my personal problems didn't seem nearly as serious. Then, there were murmurs of agreement, understanding. There was a feeling that we had shared something almost therapeutic. I felt different.[10]

Although technology has changed our lives, it can never bring to us this depth of human emotion nor the caring, concern, hope, and trust that spring from it.

Public Speaking Teaches Critical Thinking

Of all the skills you will learn in college, and throughout later life, none is more important than critical thinking—the application of the principles of reasoning to your ideas and the ideas of others. Critical thinking enables you to evaluate your world and make choices based upon what you learn. It gives you the intellectual tools you need to make critical decisions at work ("Do I recommend or discourage a new product line?"); at home ("Should I encourage my children to learn to read before kindergarten or wait until they are older?"); and in your roles as consumer and citizen. ("Should I believe everything the car dealer tells me or do my own independent research?")

The critical thinking skills required to answer these questions can be developed, in part, through public speaking. Here are some of the ways you use critical thinking every time you prepare a speech:

Choosing appropriate speech topics. Involved in this process is the evaluation of different subjects based on their meaning to you and your audience. You may decide, for example, that although a speech describing how to fix a car's transmission would be right for a group of auto mechanics, it would be too technical for your public speaking classmates.

Researching your topic. You must decide what kinds of supporting materials best enable you to express your views. Should you use quotations, examples, statistics, analogies, or a combination of these and other forms of support?

Organizing your presentation. The order in which you present your ideas reflects the clarity of your thinking.

Building, advancing, and assessing arguments. You must know how to construct lines of reasoning for both informative and persuasive purposes. The term *reason* is used here to mean movement from something known, or believed, to arrive at probable statements or claims declared to be accurate and truthful. Reasoning is the process of using known and believed information to explain or prove other statements less well understood or accepted. Thinking

---

10. Ron Hoff, *I Can See You Naked: A Fearless Guide to Making Great Presentations* (Kansas City, MO: Andrews and McMeel, 1988), p. 226.

critically requires thinking about the arguments in active, organized, and purposeful ways.

Choosing appropriate language and presentation level.   Language choices are based on an analysis of how much your audience already knows about your subject and its specialized vocabulary as well as on the needs of the occasion. It would be inappropriate, for example, to use slang in a speech while accepting a prestigious academic award.

Critical thinking and listening.   Critical thinking skills are essential as you listen to and evaluate the presentations of other speakers. As an audience member, your analysis will focus on several factors including the purpose and organization of the speech; whether the speakers have accomplished their goal to persuade, inform, or speak appropriately on a special occasion; whether they have satisfied your needs as an audience member, and so on. As your critical thinking skills develop, you will be able to say effectively exactly what you mean and be able to assess other speakers' effectiveness.

RHETORIC AND PUBLIC SPEAKING

A recognition of the power of speech to influence others goes back to ancient times. Aristotle wrote about the art of persuasion in his *Rhetoric.* Plato examined the way speech serves the search for truth, opposing speakers who manipulated their messages without concern for their audience. And Isocrates made the link between the citizen-orator and good government.[11] From this historical tradition the art and science of rhetoric emerged.

Rhetoric and Communication

Communication can be defined as the creation of shared meaning through symbolic processes. Through words, physical expression, visual displays, and even environmental cues, communicators seek to reach some level of understanding with their listeners.

Speakers achieve their goals through the use of well recognized stimuli that bring thoughts and feelings to listeners' minds. The spoken word is the primary symbol for the public speaker, but not the only one. When a paraplegic veteran who lost the use of his legs to a land mine in Vietnam sits in his wheelchair in full uniform before the black granite Vietnam Veterans' Memorial in Washington, DC, his presence serves as a rhetorical symbol of all who sacrificed during that terrible struggle. The wall itself is a symbol. With 58,156 names etched into its surface, it communicates a message honoring the dead, grieving over the enormity of the nation's loss. When the veteran wheels himself to center stage to address a Memorial Day audience, he extends the reach of these rhetorical symbols to include the words he speaks. In this case, as in all cases, both words and appearance communicate

---

11.   James L. Golden, Goodwin F. Berquist, and William E. Coleman, *The Rhetoric of Western Thought,* 4th ed. (Dubuque, IA: Kendall/Hunt, 1989), p. 4.

Every occasion for public speaking operates within a broad cultural context.

meaning. Communication is achieved when listeners understand these and other varied symbols and share the speaker's intended meaning.

If communication can be defined as the creation of shared meaning, we can define rhetoric as "an invitation to respond."[12] That is, in the act of addressing an audience, the public speaker invites the audience to respond to the speech. Rhetoric can thus be considered the process of communication in which a message is designed to achieve a desired response, which is the specific purpose of the message. (We go into more detail about the concept of specific purpose in Chapter Two.) Rhetorical communication, in the form of public speaking, is often used as an instrument for change by which speakers communicate their thoughts and feelings to listeners with the intent of generating knowledge, influencing values, beliefs, attitudes, and actions, and reaching mutual understanding.[13,14]

---

12.   Professor Dan Hahn, Florida Atlantic University. Point made in a lecture presented to communication majors at SUNY–Geneseo, February 20, 1990.

13.   John J. Makay, "Psychotherapy as a Rhetoric of Secular Grace," *Central States Speech Journal* (Fall 1980): 184–96; John J. Makay and William R. Brown, *The Rhetorical Dialog: Concepts and Cases* (Dubuque, IA: William C. Brown Co., Publishers, 1972), pp. 3–4.

14.   Although rhetoric may be oral or written, verbal or nonverbal, and can take the form of music or film, slogans or lengthy discourse, the roots of communication and rhetoric are grounded in public speaking, which continues to be one of its most important voices. For an example of the rhetorical potential of music, see Alberto Gonzalez and John J. Makay, "Rhetorical Ascription and the Gospel According to Dylan," *Quarterly Journal of Speech* (February 1983): 1–14; for an example of the rhetorical potential of a popular book, see John J. Makay, "Bad Things and Good People: A Rhetoric for a Misfortunate Audience," in *Rhetorical Studies Honoring James L. Golden,* Lawrence W. Hugenberg, ed. (Dubuque, IA: Kendall/Hunt Publishing Co., 1986), pp. 145–62.

As you present speeches, you will use the shared symbols of communication to achieve your specific rhetorical purpose. The messages you deliver fall into three general categories:

Speeches to inform.   These speeches share information with an audience. Your professors deliver informative speeches when they lecture in class. Doctors deliver informative speeches to disseminate AIDS prevention warnings.

Speeches to persuade.   These speeches attempt to convince listeners of the speaker's point of view. A sales manager delivering a pep talk to the company sales force is engaging in persuasion as is a political candidate trying to convince a group of voters to support her election.

For many years, rhetoric was defined solely in terms of persuasion. Although today the definition is broader, persuasion is still viewed as rhetorics' most powerful voice. Through rhetoric, speakers attempt to sway their audiences and, often as a result, bring about change. When you deliver a persuasive speech in class, you have no guarantee that change will take place. However, if you speak convincingly on a subject of importance to your audience, you can have an impact on the way listeners think, feel, and act.

Speeches to entertain or inspire, particularly on special occasions.   These speeches are appropriate for awards ceremonies, family celebrations, commemorative events such as funerals, and the introduction of other speakers. They share the goal of meeting the needs of a special occasion. When, for example, you deliver a humorous speech at your brother's wedding, your rhetorical goal is to entertain. When you accept an award for outstanding community service, your goal is to acknowledge the honor. In both situations, the speech must be appropriate for the time, setting, and situation.

Whatever the category or combination of categories, your speaking objective is to elicit a response from your audience—a response further defined by the specific purpose of your speech.

Public Speaking and the Democratic Tradition

Public speaking is the foundation of our democratic society. As an instrument for social activism, free speech defines us as a nation, setting us apart from countries like the People's Republic of China where voices of protest have been silenced by guns and tanks. Rhetoric is the cornerstone of leadership in America. Through the spoken word, the drive for change often begins. Throughout our history, we have heard the power of speech in the voices of civil rights leaders such as Martin Luther King, Jr.; advocate for women's suffrage Elizabeth Cady Stanton; former Presidents John F. Kennedy and George Bush; and in the thousands of other voices that have sought social change.

In our society, speakers rarely act alone. One speaker's voice is often heard in concert with the messages of other like-minded leaders. When actress Elizabeth

Taylor raises her voice to enlist international support in the fight against AIDS, she is joined by the voices of others such as rock superstar Elton John and health care practioners, physicians, and legislators who speak out and act against this fatal disease. When Betty Friedan raises her voice in protest against the unequal treatment of women, she is joined by the voices of feminist leaders Geraldine Ferarro and Gloria Steinem. Rhetorical sharing of this kind is evident throughout our society in politics, religion, business, government, education, and elsewhere.

Speech and Charismatic Authority.   Through their impassioned communication, leaders may achieve charismatic authority. They can inspire the passion, devotion, and personal loyalty of millions of people who support their views on social issues. Martin Luther King, Jr. used the charisma of his voice and delivery and the symbolism of nonviolence to awaken America to the suffering of African-Americans. Although leaders like Dr. King have worked for social good, dictators like Adolf Hitler have used the spoken word to usurp control and destroy individual freedoms.

Hitler, considered by many the most evil demagogue in history, practiced every aspect of his public appearances in order to take advantage of popular prejudices to gain and maintain power. He rehearsed words and gestures and carefully chose the symbols that would mark the Third Reich. He chose the sign of the swastika and even the clothing his troops would wear. The twisted, but nevertheless effective, genius of Hitler's rhetoric lay in his ability to mobilize the German people following their bitter defeat in World War I. Hitler understood his people's pathological need for revenge and a return to world power. Otto Strasser, one of the earliest members of the Nazi party, explains: "His words go like an arrow to their target. He touches each private wound on the raw, liberating the unconscious, exposing its innermost aspirations, telling it what it most wants to hear."[15]

Through his words Hitler galvanized Germany in its struggle to regain its national honor—a struggle that ultimately would lead to World War II. What the German people lacked during the years of Hitler's ascension to power was the ability critically to evaluate his rhetoric and realize that he was leading the world on a path of destruction. Though Hitler's example is extreme, it demonstrates how charismatic speakers can abuse their power through public speaking and why technique should never be separated from the content of the speaker's message. The example compels us to define and examine the ethics of public speaking, which we do in Chapter Four.

Public Speaking in the Classroom

As you present speeches to your classmates, keep in mind that you are part of a tradition that finds equality in the voice and message of every speaker. Although we may listen more carefully to well known leaders than anonymous citizens, obscure individuals can rise to national attention on the strength of their rhetoric.

---

15.   "Who Was Hitler?" *U.S. News & World Report,* August 28/September 4, 1989, p. 48.

If you define your classroom presentations as rhetorical opportunities to show your understanding of and commitment to an idea and your ability to communicate your thoughts and feelings to others, you will succeed in this course and as a public speaker. Use your public speaking class as a training ground to develop and refine these skills, for they will serve you well throughout your life.

THE RECIPROCAL NATURE OF PUBLIC SPEAKING

The lounge at the student union building was packed with angry freshmen who sat anywhere they could—on the floor, on the arms and backs of chairs, on each others' laps—to hear their protest leader. Those who could not find a place in the room crowded together in the adjacent hallway near a public address loudspeaker. The reason for the meeting—and for the anger—was a new college ruling, designating two freshman dormitories off-limits to students of the opposite sex. Most of the freshman class had come to the student union to decide what—if anything—they could do the protest this intrusion in their lives. Their spokesperson was the new freshman class president who was about to learn what it is like to be at the center of a conflict. The room grew quiet as she began to speak:

> We are here today as responsible adults, although the administration insists on treating us like children.
>
> We are here today because we do not want an anonymous college official behaving like our parent. And, ironically, our parents never asked for this either.
>
> We are all old enough—and wise enough—to know when others have stepped over the line that divides guidance from interference. As someone who has just been told that I cannot study with, or even talk with a male student in my room, I can tell you that guidance has nothing to do with what is happening to us now. Our lives are being interfered with and it is time it stopped.

Applause interrupted the speaker in a sign of support. When she began again, her voice was even stronger.

> What do we want? A simple choice is enough. We want to be given the choice of living in a dorm with visitation restrictions or living in one where there are none. We cannot be assigned this choice. We must make it ourselves.
>
> If we succeed in changing the administration's mind, we have won only a partial victory. Our victory will be complete only when we demonstrate, through our behavior, that we *are* responsible—that we will not take advantage of the privacy and values of our roommates and that we will not forget that we came to college to study and learn.

The interruption this time was not applause. Dissatisfied voices came from various parts of the room—voices that expressed an undercurrent of disagreement. The speaker continued, trying to regain her composure and speak above the low hum of dissent:

> Let us all sign the petition I am holding, demanding that this decision be put back in student hands where it belongs and insisting that we be treated like the adults we are.

This speech, like all speeches, is marked by a process of reciprocal communication—

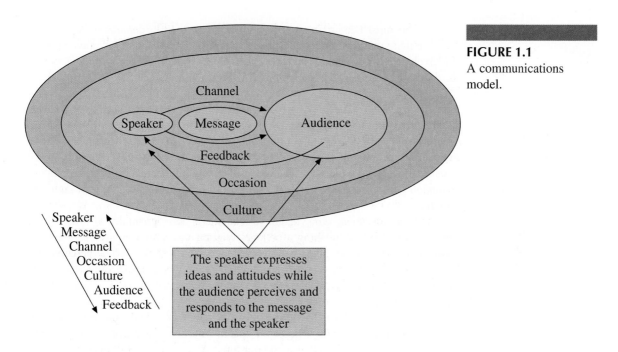

FIGURE 1.1
A communications model.

In the figure: Channel, Speaker, Message, Audience, Feedback, Occasion, Culture; Speaker, Message, Channel, Occasion, Culture, Audience, Feedback; "The speaker expresses ideas and attitudes while the audience perceives and responds to the message and the speaker"

a give and take between audience and speaker.[16] While the freshman class president spoke, members of her audience listened to her remarks, attributed meaning to them, and responded based upon their own values, attitudes, motives, needs, and experiences. Although the speaker was the central focus in this exchange, she was only one of the elements. She was part of a process of communication—a type of transaction—in which meaning is determined not only by what the speaker says but by what the listener perceives and creates. The success of this transaction determines the meaning and impact of a speech.

We examine public speaking as a communication transaction, looking at seven interrelated elements that affect a speech's meaning: the speaker, the message, the channel, the occasion, the culture, the audience, and the feedback (see Figure 1.1).

Element 1: The Speaker

As the students listened to their class president, they judged not only her remarks but also her appearance and other, less tangible qualities. They were deciding whether she was believable, trustworthy, ethical, competent, sincere, authoritative, and dynamic—qualities of character that determine public speaking success just as surely as the message the speaker delivers. As explained in Chapter Two, to succeed as a

16.   Gerald Phillips and Nancy Metzger, *Intimate Communication* (Boston: Allyn and Bacon, 1976), pp. 40–42.

speaker you must become a spokesperson for your cause, demonstrating to your audience that you are strongly committed to your message and to communicating it effectively. In this case, the speaker's involvement in her cause was evident as was her desire to share her plan of action with her audience.

Your Image Makes a Statement.   In class, the image your audience has of you will be shaped, in part, by the ideas and organizations with which you identify. If you are a member of the "goon squad" of the college athletic team, the label "jock" will be attached to you even before you open your mouth. If, on the other hand, you are captain of the chess team, you will be considered an intellectual. In both cases, your reputation will precede you to the lectern and determine, in part, how your audience responds.

Everything about you makes a statement. For example, if you are a nontraditional student finishing a college program you started many years earlier, your age and experience help shape your image. You are likely to be perceived as someone apart from the group until—and if—your words prove otherwise. As a public speaker, you must deal with your audience's preconceived notions. When these conclusions are wrong—which they often are—you must convince your listeners through your topic choice, delivery, and words that you are more—or different—than you seem. When you speak, your words and style of delivery communicate your involvement with your topic. Your listeners will need only a few moments to pass judgment on your sincerity, integrity, and competence. Once their opinions are formed, changing them will be difficult.

The Needs of the Speaker.   Through the communication transaction, speakers seek from their audience a response that can satisfy certain needs. Depending upon their goal, speakers need to be understood, to have influence, to bring about action, to be liked and respected, or hated and feared.[17]

Element 2: The Message

All public speakers have a message designed to elicit a response from an audience. The message of the speech delivered by the freshman class president was generally sympathetic to the group's cause. Like the members of her audience, she believed that the administration had overstepped its bounds, and her speech was an expression

---

17.   When Sigmund Freud made his only trip to the United States in 1909 to deliver a series of five lectures on psychoanalysis at the Clark University Celebrity Lecture Series, he understood that through these lectures his theories could gain acceptance in the U.S. medical community. Included in Freud's audience were the noted psychologists William James and Edward Tichner who listened, heard, evaluated, and responded to Freud's remarks and later helped promote his theories in the United States. According to historian William Koelsch, "If no Clark, then no Freud in America." See Martha Cooper and John J. Makay "Knowledge, Power, and Freud's Clark Conference Lectures," *Quarterly Journal of Speech* 74 (1988): 416–33; and Nathan G. Hale, Jr. *Freud and the Americans: The Beginning of Psychoanalysis in the United States, 1876-1917* (New York: Oxford University Press, 1971), pp. 3–4.

of her determination to force a change. Although she was generally encouraged when she completed her speech, she was also concerned about the rustling she heard in the room when she tied a student victory to responsible student behavior. Was she sounding too much like a parent herself? Although she did not intend to take a parental tone, she suspected that the message she meant to convey was not the one some of her listeners received.

Communication theorists have long recognized that public speaking is a meaning-centered process. That is, the essence of the message lies not only in what the speaker intends but also in the meaning the audience perceives. As explained in Chapter Three, although a hundred people may listen to the same speech, each person will come away with a different interpretation of what the speaker said. Although we share the same language, we do not share identical experiences nor the meanings that stem from them. In the class president's case, when she called upon her fellow students to respect the privacy and personal values of their roommates, some audience members interpreted her remarks as too authoritative and moralistic. Others questioned why she labeled the school's decision as parental—their own parents imposed few such rules.

To minimize misunderstanding, you must make your message as clear as possible—through your words and delivery. Depending upon the nature of your topic, you may have to do some extensive research to find supporting material to explain your message and, most importantly, make it relevant to your listeners. As explained in Chapter Seven, you can reinforce your meaning through examples and statistics, quotations and analogies. The repetition of key points and the precise use of language also help to communicate meaning. If your topic is complicated or novel, you must organize your ideas so that one thought follows logically from another. Finally, an appropriate delivery style is crucial. Your audience may not hear your message if you are apathetic, bombastic, or disorganized.

Element 3: The Channel

Every message is communicated through a medium or channel. In our example, the message was sent from speaker to listeners in two ways. For the students in the room, there was direct face-to-face communication. For those in the adjoining hallways, the message was delivered electronically through a public address system. A speaker's message can be sent via other channels as well, including radio and television and tape recordings. When the speaker's words are transcribed, the communicating channel is the printed word.

When you are in the same room with a speaker, you have the advantage of experiencing the speech and the speaker firsthand. You can react to a person rather than a televised image or a disembodied voice and make judgments that are not possible in other circumstances. You are in a better position to judge, for example, the intangible qualities, including the speaker's honesty, ethical stance, commitment to the topic, trustworthiness, and sincerity. These qualities are communicated through eye contact, gestures, and the speaker's delivery. When you are listening to a speech through a less direct channel, your ability to judge these qualities is diminished.

Element 4: The Occasion

Every speech occurs within the context of an occasion—the time, place, event, and traditions that define the moment. As people file into a room before a speech begins, they have expectations of what they will hear. For example, the students who came to listen to the freshman class president expected a call to arms and a course of action. A sense of occasion is critical to your success as a speaker. With this sense, you can begin the process of understanding what an audience wants and needs.

Physical surroundings help define the speaking occasion. As a speaker, you should know in advance whether you are speaking indoors or out; whether you are speaking to five people or several hundred; whether you will be speaking from an elevated platform or from an easy chair surrounded by an audience of listeners also seated in easy chairs. You must also be aware of the order of your speech in the day's events. Are you the first or last speaker? Is your speech scheduled right before or after lunch? Knowing the circumstances surrounding your speech, you will be better prepared to meet the needs of the occasion with an appropriate presentation. For example, if your speech is scheduled at the end of the day, a short speech is more appropriate than a long one.

Element 5: The Culture

Every occasion operates within a broader cultural context affecting the entire rhetorical experience. Culture determines, in part, the common ground between speaker and audience. The implied, unspoken language between people makes some things acceptable and others not. Culture is defined in terms of norms, the rules people follow in their relationships with one another; values, the feelings people share about what is right and wrong, good and bad, desirable and undesirable; customs, accepted community or institutional practices and expressions; institutions; and language.

Cultural differences exist not only between countries but between segments of our own population. These differences have the potential to make a comment appropriate for a sophisticated urban environment out of place in a conservative small town. In our earlier example, community values permitted unmarried male and female students to spend time alone in a dormitory room. In a highly conservative culture this discussion would never have taken place.

As a speaker, it is important to realize that cultural differences exist between audiences. If you are delivering a speech supporting English-only instruction in our nation's schools, you may get a far different response from an audience of recent immigrants who consider their native tongue a link to their homeland than from an audience of assimilated Americans.

As U.S. markets have expanded throughout the world, American business-women and men have been asked to give speeches in different countries. Most learn very quickly that their presentations will succeed only if they understand and acknowledge the cultures of their listeners.

Element 6: The Audience

As we mentioned earlier, listeners bring to the speech their own frames of reference that are the totals of their personalities and experiences. Everything they have experienced will influence how they respond to the speaker's message.

As explained in Chapter Three, although listeners may hear all the words a speaker says, they may miss shades of meaning or attribute meanings that have little or nothing to do with the speaker's intent. In our example, many listeners resented what they thought was the speaker's attitude when, in fact, the speaker never intended that meaning. Because the potential for misinterpretation always exists, it is critical to plan every speech with your audience in mind. In the classroom, use terms your classmates can understand. Use examples that touch their lives and choose language that is neither too sophisticated nor too elementary.

Just as the speaker needs affirmation, understanding, and approval during a speech, audience members also have needs. According to Ron Hoff, audience members often look to the speaker for help. Hoff explains: "By coming to your presentation, by simply showing up, your audience is expressing a need for help, counsel, wisdom, inspiration—maybe even something that can change its life . . . . If truth be told," Hoff contends, "the audience arrives on the scene with the ardent hope that the presenter knows something that it does not."[18]

Although you may not think your public speaking classmates need something from you, they actually seek your counsel on two levels. First, they hope they can learn something from your presentation that they can apply to their own speech making. You may, for example, use your hands in an effective way or modulate your voice to build emotion. Second, although they are a captive audience, they may be open to your message—if it touches their lives.

Element 7: The Feedback

In the public speaking transaction, feedback refers to the messages the audience sends back to the speaker. These can take the form of applause, boos, yawns, cheers, facial expressions, mumbling, movement, and the like. Although we generally think of the speaker as the sender and the listener as the receiver, both speaker and listener send and receive messages. According to communication professor Sarah Trenholm, by its nature, most audience feedback is nonverbal and difficult to interpret. Audience members rarely stop a speech to ask questions or express differences.[19] However, as we saw in our earlier example of the student class president's speech, audience feedback can clearly communicate to the speaker what listeners are thinking.

---

18.   Hoff, p. 9.
19.   Sarah Trenholm, *Human Communication Theory* (Englewood Cliffs, NJ: Prentice-Hall, 1986), pp. 201–02.

Reverend Jesse Jackson addresses the 1988 Democratic National Convention.

An Example: The Public Speaking Transaction

When Jesse Jackson addressed the 1988 Democratic National Convention, he delivered a speech many considered the most compelling of the Democratic campaign. Its effectiveness was largely the result of Jackson's understanding of public speaking as a communication transaction. Throughout his speech he anticipated and answered many of his listeners' questions, such as: Who is Jesse Jackson—really? How should I feel about him? Does he act presidential? Does he sound qualified to lead the nation? Is he concerned about all of the people or just his own constituency? Does he care about me? Here is how Jackson connected himself to the poor members of his audience—a connection that helped all his listeners receive his message.[20]

> I have a story. I wasn't always on television. Writers were not always outside my door. When I was born late one afternoon, October 8th, in Greenville, S.C., no writers asked my mother her name. Nobody chose to write down our address. My mama was not supposed to make it. And I was not supposed to make it. You see, I was born to a teenage mother who was born to a teenage mother.
>
> I understand. I know abandonment and people being mean to you, and saying you're nothing and nobody, and can never be anything. I understand. Jesse Jackson is my third name. I'm adopted. When I had no name, my grandmother gave me her name. My name was Jesse Burns until I was 12. So I wouldn't have a blank space, she gave me a name to hold me over. I understand when nobody knows your name. I understand when you have no name. I understand. . . .
>
> I understand work. I was not born with a silver spoon in my mouth. I had a shovel programmed for my hand. My mother, a working woman. So many days she went to work early with runs in her stockings. She knew better, but she wore runs in her stockings so that my brother and I could have matching socks and not be laughed at at school. . . .
>
> Every one of these funny labels they put on you, those of you who are watching this broadcast tonight in the projects, on the corners, I understand. Call you outcast, low down, you can't make it, you're nothing, you're from nobody, subclass, underclass— when you see Jesse Jackson, when my name goes in nomination, your name goes in nomination.

Jackson understood that the channels of communication affected the way his listeners would receive his message. He spoke not only to the thousands of people who sat before him at the convention in Atlanta, but also to those reached by the mass media. He spoke to the occasion and to the unique culture, traditions, and heritage of political conventions and the political process:

> My right and my privilege to stand here before you has been won—in my lifetime—by the blood and the sweat of the innocent.
>
> Twenty-four years ago, the late Fanny Lou Hamer and Aaron Henry—who sits here tonight from Mississippi—were locked out on the streets of Atlantic City, the head of the Mississippi Freedom Democratic Party.

---

20. Jesse Jackson, "Common Ground and Common Sense," speech delivered at the Democratic National Convention, Atlanta, Georgia, July 20, 1988, *Vital Speeches of the Day,* August 15, 1988, pp. 649–53.

But tonight a black and white delegation from Mississippi is headed by Ed Cole, a black man, from Mississippi, 24 years later.

Many were lost in the struggle for the right to vote. Jimmy Lee Jackson, a young student, gave his life. Viola Luizzo, a white mother from Detroit, called nigger lover, and had her brains blown out at point blank range.

Schwerner, Goodman and Chaney—two Jews and a black—found in a common grave, bodies riddled with bullets in Mississippi. The four darling little girls in the church in Birmingham, Alabama. They died that we might have a right to live.

Dr. Martin Luther King, Jr., lies only a few miles from us tonight.

Tonight he must feel good as he looks down upon us. We sit here together, a rainbow, a coalition—the sons and daughters of slave masters and the sons and daughters of slaves sitting together around a common table, to decide the direction of our party and our country. His heart would be full tonight.

As a testament to the struggles of those who have gone before; as a legacy for those who will come after; as a tribute to the endurance, the patience, the courage of our forefathers and mothers; as an assurance that their prayers are being answered, their work has not been in vain, and hope is eternal; tomorrow night my name will go into nomination for the presidency of the United States of America.

The thunderous applause that filled the auditorium during Jackson's speech was his feedback—his audience's audible sign of approval and connection. With this sign, the public speaking transaction was complete—and, at the same time, continuous between speaker and audience.

SUMMARY

Public speaking skills are important to your success in college, your post-college career, and your role as a citizen. Without these skills, you may be forced to limit your involvement in community and social causes. Public speaking continues to be important despite the reliance on high-tech communication. Nothing can replace the person-to-person contact that defines the relationship between speaker and audience. Public speaking also teaches critical thinking.

Communication involves the creation of shared meaning through symbolic processes. Meaning is communicated through the verbal and nonverbal symbols that surround speaker and audience. Rhetoric extends the concept of communication to include an invitation for the audience to respond to the speaker's message.

In public speaking, rhetorical messages fall into three categories: speeches to inform, speeches to persuade, and speeches to entertain or inspire on special occasions.

The free and open exchange of ideas in the form of public speaking forms the foundation of our democratic system. Some charismatic speakers, like Adolf Hitler, abuse the spoken word to gain and maintain power.

Public speaking involves reciprocal communication between audience and speaker. Seven elements are involved in the public speaking transaction: the speaker, the message, the channel, the occasion, the culture, the audience, and the feedback.

1. Considering your personal career goals, how are public speaking skills likely to QUESTIONS FOR STUDY AND DISCUSSION
    help you in the years ahead?
2. Why is public speaking considered an art, not a science?
3. Think of some of the major institutions in society including, among others, government, schools, and the judicial system. What role do public speakers play in each of these settings?

1. Design your own model of communication, identifying the key elements in ACTIVITIES
    public speaking. How does your model differ from the model in the text?
2. Prepare a 500-word essay on how you believe the study of public speaking will benefit you professionally and personally.
3. Think of someone you admire as a public speaker, and write an essay describing why you have chosen this person.

"Speech is a mirror of the soul:
as a man speaks, so is he."

Publilius Syrus (c. 42 B.C.)

PREPARING YOUR FIRST SPEECH

Step 1: Select a Topic You Care About
Start with Your Own Interests
How to Focus Your Choice

Step 2: Determine the Purposes and Core Idea of Your Speech
General Purposes
Specific Purpose
Choose Your Core Idea

Step 3: Consider Yourself a Spokesperson

Step 4: Analyze and Adapt to Your Audience

Step 5: Define Your Speech's Beginning, Middle, and End
Introduction
Body
Conclusion
Organizing Your First Speech

Step 6: Use Sound Reasoning and Firm Support
Rely on Expert Testimony
Use Statistics
Build Your Case Through Examples
Use Indisputable Facts
Construct Analogies

Step 7: Choose Your Words with Care

Step 8: Consider Your Ethical Responsibilities

Step 9: Make Your Nerves Work for You
What Is Speech Tension and Why Do Some People Suffer from It More Than Others?
How to Control Your Tension

Step 10: Perfect Your Delivery

Interview: Brigadier General Myrna H. Williamson, U.S. Army Retired

imothy Gallwey and Bob Kriegel are ski instructors of a different sort—their message has little to do with actual ski slopes. They help skiers by focusing on the relationship between mental attitude and athletic success—and by transforming the fear of falling (a negative fear they call *Fear 1*) into positive energy (a force they call *Fear 2*).

According to Gallwey and Kriegel, Fear 2 is the body's response to actual danger. You wake up from a sound sleep, smell smoke, realize your house is on fire and you have to escape. Almost instantaneously, your adrenaline soars, your heart races, the pupils of your eyes dilate, the volume of blood sent to your muscles and arms increases, giving you the strength—and determination—to get out safely.

Although Fear 2 empowers you, Fear 1 renders you helpless—even when no danger is present. It exaggerates your sense of danger, minimizes your ability to cope, and emphasizes your vulnerability—responses that guarantee failure. Gallwey and Kriegel explain how Fear 1 affects skiers:

> Standing at the head of a trail, the skier in the grip of Fear 1 looks down and begins to think how steep it looks. Feeling the anxiety churning in his stomach, he thinks of the times he has fallen on similar slopes or in similar conditions. He may remember a time when he was hurt and see it happening again. Instead of flexing slightly in readiness for action, his muscles react to his fear by becoming rigid and immobile. His courage ebbs, he feels weaker and his vision blurs.[1]

As you will learn in this chapter, Fear 1 has as much to do with public speaking as it does with skiing. It can make your knees shake and your mouth go dry; it can make uttering the simplest words seem the hardest thing you have ever done. It can make you want to drop this course before your first speech. How do you overcome this fear? One of the goals of this chapter is to help you channel your nervous energy—your Fear 1—into the specific, manageable skills that define public speaking. In the right frame of mind, you can transform your Fear 1 into Fear 2, enabling you to give speeches with confidence and self-assurance. Although your apprehension may never completely go away (even well known speakers get nervous), you can learn to harness your nervous energy to ensure a better performance.

As you read this chapter, think about being on top of a ski slope for the first time—nerves and all. Then keep in mind that public speaking is no different from any other acquirable skill, including skiing. That is, with understanding, practice, discipline, and a positive attitude, your ability will improve and your fear will subside.

We start with an overview of the steps involved in preparing and presenting a speech. This overview is particularly important for your first speech because you will be asked to make presentations before you have finished reading the text. Keep in mind that although the material in this chapter is presented as separate steps, you will move back and forth among the steps as you prepare and present your speech. The overview introduces you to principles and ideas discussed in depth in the

---

1.   Timothy Gallwey and Bob Kriegel, *Inner Skiing* (New York: Random House, 1977), pp. 58–59.

A public speaker, not unlike an accomplished skier, must transform fear or tension into positive energy.

remaining chapters. This chapter gives you information to get your public speaking under way. The chapters ahead will guide you to grow and improve in your knowledge about public speaking and in your skill as a speaker and as a listener.

STEP 1: SELECT A TOPIC YOU CARE ABOUT

Jim is causing a family crisis. At age twenty-five, he wants to move back home after being on his own since college. His reasons are economic: he doesn't earn enough to pay his rent and have any kind of social life. (When he went to the movies recently he had to borrow the money to get in.) From his point of view, his parents should be delighted to have him back. After all, he reasons, he lived in their house for eighteen years and is still their son. Jim's parents see things differently. His mother envisions piles of dirty laundry waiting for her at the foot of his bed; all his father can think of is yet another fight over the family car. Although they love their son, they don't want him living at home, a decision Jim can't accept. Needing an ally, he turns to his sister Adriane for help. As Adriane walks into public speaking class, all she can think of is how she is going to change her parents' minds. Her thoughts are interrupted by her professor's instructions to choose a topic for her first speech. She draws a blank.

Start with Your Own Interests

Without realizing it, Adriane is preoccupied with an ideal topic for her first speech. Because this topic springs from her own interests, she can bring to it the involvement, motivation, and information necessary for a good speech. Here are a few of her possible choices:

1. A persuasive speech on why an independent adult child should be permitted to return home.

2. An informative speech on the economic conditions recent college graduates face—conditions rendering it difficult for them to make ends meet.

3. An entertaining speech on why Empty Nesters don't want their young back home.

Learn from Adriane's experience and choose your first speech topic from the things you know best.

If you decide to expand beyond your personal experiences, don't make the mistake of ignoring your interests and feelings. Give a speech about the plight of the homeless only if you care about the topic. Talk about the need for corporate-sponsored day care only if you are convinced that corporations have been shirking their responsibility to help employees care for their preschoolers. To do otherwise is to handicap yourself before you begin.

For your first speech in class, you will probably be asked to deliver an informative message. In the remaining pages of this chapter, we look at examples of informative speeches to help you develop your own presentation. We also examine examples of persuasive speeches to acquaint you with this type of speech.

How to Focus Your Choice

Three questions will help you focus on your topic (see Figure 2.1):

1. *How much time do you have to speak?* If you only have three minutes, the clock will force you to limit the amount of detail you present.

2. *How much do you know about the topic?* After researching your subject, you have a wealth of information from which to draw. Now, your job will be to narrow your topic so that your audience will not be overwhelmed by too many details. As you will see in Chapter 5, an audience's ability to absorb information is limited by a number of different factors. If you bombard people with too much, they simply stop listening. On the other hand, if your research yields very little, that fact alone will limit the breadth of your speech.

3. *What are the needs of your audience?* Each audience has a unique personality, defined by the reason they are listening to your speech. In most cases, people come together because of their membership in a group or because of a shared interest in the topic of your speech.

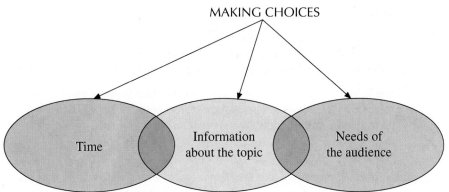

FIGURE 2.1
Making choices.

Mary Fisher, a forty-four-year-old mother of two who contracted the AIDS virus from her former husband, addressed the Republican National Convention in August, 1992. She believed the party members needed to put aside partisan political rhetoric and make a new and firmer commitment to the battle against this devastating disease. She told her audience:

> "Tonight I represent the AIDS community, whose members have been reluctantly drafted from every segment of American society. . . . Though I am white, I am one with the black infant struggling with tubes in a Philadelphia hospital. Though I am female, and contracted this disease in marriage and enjoy the warm support of my family, I am one with the lonely gay man sheltering a flickering candle from the cold wind of his family's rejection."[2]

She wanted her audience to grasp the sense of identification she now shared with others who were suffering and dying. She believed the audience needed to understand the disease and act with knowledge, compassion, and commitment.

A Topic Discovery System.   If no ideas come to you, try this simple method to find a topic. Write down two or three broad categories representing subjects of interest to you; then divide the categories into parts. You might begin, for example, with the broad areas of politics and sports. From these general topics, the following lists may emerge:

Politics
1. Political corruption
2. Campus politics
3. Political campaigning in an age of "sound bites"

---

2. John Nichols, "HIV-Infected Mother Asks Sympathy for AIDS Victims," *The Toldeo Blade* August 20, 1992, p. 1. See also "You Are At Risk," *U.S. News & World Report* August 31–September 7, 1992, p. 26.

Sports

1. How to improve your tennis game

2. The dangers of football for younger players

3. The pay scale of professional athletes

As you enlarge your list of choices, you will probably find yourself coming back to the same topic or a variation of it. For example, spinal cord injuries in young football players is a variation of item 2 on your sports list. Now you have your topic.

STEP 2: DETERMINE THE PURPOSES AND CORE IDEA OF YOUR SPEECH

The time you spend preparing your speech may be worth little if you do not define for yourself what you want your speech to accomplish. At the beginning, you should clarify the general and specific purposes and core idea of your speech.

General Purposes

As explained in Chapter One, speeches have three general purposes: to inform, to persuade, and to entertain or inspire, particularly on a special occasion. In speech class your instructor may assign you the type of speech to deliver. In other settings, this decision will be left to you, or the occasion will call for a particular kind of speech.

It is difficult to deliver a speech that is just persuasive, or just informative, or appropriate only to a special occasion. The more experience you have, the more you will realize that these general purposes often converge. For example, a speech informing your classmates about the problem of sexual harassment on campus or in the workplace may also persuade students to rally in support of harassment victims.

Specific Purpose

Once your general purpose is set, you need to define the specific purpose of your speech—that is, the response you want from your audience. Specific purpose statements should be expressed in clear, action-oriented sentences defining what you hope to accomplish in your speech. Here are two examples of specific purposes:

⌘ To inform an audience at a local political club about the problem of low voter turnout.

⌘ To persuade an audience of recent college graduates to support and join labor unions.

Because it focuses on the audience who will hear your speech, the specific purpose can help you decide what to say and how best to say it. You will deliver a different speech about labor union membership to a group of recent college graduates looking for their first jobs than to a group of longtime union members. Although you may have to resort to some hard persuasion in the first instance, your goal in the second will be to reinforce prevailing values.

Choose Your Core Idea

While the general and specific purpose statements set the goals for your speech, the core idea, or thesis statement, focuses on what you want to say. The core idea distills your speech to one sentence, which summarizes your main idea. According to James Humes, a corporate speech consultant, Winston Churchill once sent back a pudding because he said it had no theme. Similarly, a well-defined theme is critical to your speech's success.[3]

The following examples show how to move from your topic to general and specific purpose statements and core idea:

   I.   First choose your topic:
     A. Topic: Lyme disease
  II.   Then define your general purpose:
     A. To inform
 III.   Then indicate your specific purpose:
     A. To inform my classmates about what Lyme disease is and the common-sense precautions that can help prevent it.
 IV.   Finally, define your core idea:
     A. Lyme disease is a potentially debilitating disease carried by a tiny deer tick that has spread illness throughout forty-three states and changed the way millions of Americans spend time outdoors.

You can use your core idea in your speech to communicate your main point. It is the central message you want listeners to take with them after your speech is over.

STEP 3: CONSIDER YOURSELF A SPOKESPERSON

When Barbara C. Jordan delivered the keynote address to the 1976 Democratic National Convention, her job was to convince the thousands of listeners in the convention hall and the 75 million people who watched her on television that the Democratic party deserved voter support. As she spoke, Jordan became a spokesperson for the Democratic party's political ideals and, as such influenced the outcome of the national election. (In November 1976, Democrat Jimmy Carter became president of the United States.) In part, here is what Jordan said:

> What is it, what is it about the Democratic Party that makes it the instrument that people use when they search for ways to shape their future? Well I believe the answer to that question lies in our concept of governing. Our concept of governing is derived from our view of people. It is a concept deeply rooted in a set of beliefs firmly etched in the national conscience, of all of us. . . .
>
> We are a party of innovation. We do not reject our traditions, but we are willing to adapt to changing circumstances, when change we must. We are willing to suffer the discomfort of change in order to achieve a better future.

---

3. N. R. Kleinfield, "Teaching the 'Sir Winston' Method," *The New York Times,* March 11, 1990, Section 3, p. 7.

Barbara Jordan—a powerful spokesperson for human rights and responsible government.

> We have a positive vision of the future founded on the belief that the gap between the promise and reality of America can one day be finally closed. We believe that.
>
> This my friends, is the bedrock of our concept of governing. This is a part of the reason why Americans have turned to the Democratic Party. These are the foundations upon which a national community can be built.[4]

As this example demonstrates, a spokesperson is one who is motivated by a desire to speak and act for an idea, issue, or group. Spokespersons are motivated by their identification with the speech topic. When speakers effectively communicate their sense of the significance of their message to the audience, this identification broadens to include the audience itself. Speakers who perceive themselves as spokespersons "infect" their audiences with their enthusiasm. Management consultant Edith Weiner explains: "I don't think people should give speeches if they don't believe in what they are saying. Wimps won't sell *toothpaste* to an audience, let alone important ideas."[5]

This identification process is possible in speeches to inform, persuade, and entertain. Barbara C. Jordan achieved her purpose if she convinced her listeners of the worth of the Democratic party. Similarly, a lecturer teaching students about cardiovascular resuscitation achieves her purpose if she communicates how important she believes this technique is in saving lives.

---

4.   Barbara C. Jordan, "Democratic Convention Keynote Address: Delivered July 12, 1976," in *We Shall Be Heard: Women Speakers in America: 1828–Present,* Patricia Scileppi Kennedy and Gloria Hartmann O'Shields, eds. (Dubuque, IA: Kendall/Hunt, 1983), p. 333.
5.   Interview with Edith Weiner, October 10, 1990.

Identification creates a sense of shared meaning. This shared meaning does not imply that speaker and audience must agree on every point, but that they experience some level of common understanding. In the view of Kenneth Burke, one of the foremost social, literary, and rhetorical theorists of our era, a speech is most effective when the speaker and audience achieve a state of identification.[6]

As discussed in Chapter One, public speaking is an audience-centered activity. Your reason for presenting a speech is to communicate your message to others in the most convincing way. You must first understand who your listeners are, what they know and feel about you and your message, and the knowledge base they bring to your speech. Often, you can clarify these facts by asking yourself the following questions:

STEP 4: ANALYZE AND ADAPT TO YOUR AUDIENCE

1. *What does the audience know about me and the organization or cause I represent?*   If you are a spokesperson for the tobacco industry, your audience will respond to your message about the dangers of smoking very differently than if you are affiliated with the American Cancer Society. In most cases, it is safe to assume that your audience will have this basic information about your background before your speech begins.

2. *How much knowledge does the audience have and how does it feel about the specific purpose I have chosen?*   If you are addressing a group of doctors on the need to convince pregnant women to stop smoking, you can assume far greater audience knowledge than if you are delivering the same message to a group of pregnant high school dropouts.

3. *How does the audience feel about me and my topic?*   Attitudes can be more important than information in determining how your audience responds to your message. High school students who are forced to attend a stop-smoking lecture as a school requirement will be harder to reach than students who attend the lecture voluntarily because of their desire to quit.

4. *How do audience members define themselves?*   People who come together to try to stop smoking are bound by a common concern. They will be more receptive to your stop-smoking suggestions than an audience with no such common link.

5. *How does the audience feel about the setting and occasion?*   Give an antismoking speech to your public speaking classmates and you can be sure that many of your listeners will be thinking of other things. They may be focusing, for example, on their own speeches. The setting (a public speaking classroom) and the occasion (the presentation of first speeches) can have a dramatic effect on your ability to communicate.

6. *Is there anything I should know about this audience that is likely to affect the way it will respond to my speech?*   If you are the sixth speaker your

---

6.   Kenneth Burke, *A Rhetoric of Motives* (Berkley, CA: University of California Press, 1969), pp. 19–21.

audience has heard in a two-hour period, you will almost certainly receive a different response than if you are the first. Similarly, if you are the last speaker of the day, the last speaker before lunch, the first speaker after lunch, or the speaker immediately before or after the keynote address, you are likely to get less than the audience's full attention. It is important to know these facts while you are planning your speech, so that you can adapt your remarks to the needs of your listeners.

Your audience for your first speech consists of your classmates, a group bound by their interest in public speaking (or by a curriculum requirement) and because they are college students. Because of the diverse interests of the group (some may be physics majors, others psychology majors, others art majors), you cannot assume common knowledge or interest in the topic you choose. Your job is to create interest through the use of vivid language, clear organization, and supporting material that explains your subject and captures attention.

In one sense, it is harder to analyze a public speaking-class audience than an audience brought together for a specific purpose. Members of the former group have no clearly defined set of interests tying them together, but the latter group exists *because* of a common interest. However, a few common denominators will help you analyze the needs of your classmates. Because you are dealing with college students, you can assume that the group has shared many of the same college experiences. Nearly everyone will be able to relate to a speech describing the new student registration system, and, if your college has a successful football team, a speech on the pros and cons of paying salaries to college athletes is likely to arouse interest.

Whether you are delivering your first speech or are an accomplished public speaker, you must plan, develop, and deliver your speech with your audience in mind. As you will learn in greater detail in Chapter Five, audience analysis is essentially a process of inquiry. As a speaker you need to gather information that gives you a reasonably complete image of your audience. Donald C. Bryant, the late distinguished rhetorical scholar noted that rhetoric involves the adjusting of ideas to people so that people could adjust to ideas.[7] This adjustment cannot be made without a solid understanding of who the audience is and how its members are likely to think and feel about your specific purpose.

STEP 5: DEFINE YOUR SPEECH'S BEGINNING, MIDDLE, AND END
If you spend days researching your first speech, but only a few hours organizing your ideas, the result is likely to be a speech that fails to present your message in a focused way. Speeches, like written forms of communication, depend for their effectiveness on an easy-to-follow organizational plan that makes it possible for others to receive your message. As you will see in Chapter Eight, the most effective way to develop this plan is to divide your speech into three parts: the introduction, body, and conclusion.

---

7.   Donald C. Bryant, "Rhetoric: Its Function and Its Scope," *Quarterly Journal of Speech* 39 (December 1953). Reprinted in *The Province of Rhetoric,* Joseph Schwartz and John A. Rycenga, eds. (New York: The Ronald Press, 1965), p. 19.

Introduction

The purpose of the introduction is to capture the attention and interest of your audience, establish your credibility as a speaker, and introduce your speech topic. You can accomplish these aims in a number of different ways including humorous anecdotes or a dramatic or startling statement. Here is the way Jonathan Esslinger, a student at the University of Wisconsin, introduced his remarks when he spoke about the conditions and trends of U.S. national parks:

> Imagine yourself viewing the most beautiful landscape on earth. Surrounded by trees, you look ahead and see a deep blue lake shining. In it the reflection of beautiful, white-capped mountains—with only the chattering of the squirrels and the music of the birds to keep you company—you feel you could sit back and stay forever. Then darkness, and credits start to roll. What you have been watching, according to the *Audubon* of February 1990, is a movie promoting our nation's parks. But if current trends continue, this movie is all that will be left of the beauty our national parks have to offer.[8]

Body

The body of your speech presents your core idea, subordinate points, and supporting material. Following his introductory remarks, Esslinger clearly states his core idea and then continues with a series of subordinate points including the following:

> "With all these benefits being lost, we must examine the destruction and degradation of our nation's parks. We will first examine this destruction, then explore the causes of this destruction; and finally, explore some solutions to save our national treasures."[9]

Conclusion

Your concluding remarks have several purposes: They review your main ideas, summarize your subordinate points, and provide closure—a graceful, appropriate way to end your speech. Your final comment may take the form of a quotation, statement, or question that reinforces and perhaps broadens your speech's purpose as it relates your message to the concerns of your audience. The conclusion of a persuasive speech may also include a call to action, a statement describing the specific actions you want your listeners to take. Esslinger concluded his speech this way:

> Every flower picked, every piece of paper thrown carelessly in the bushes debilitates our parks. National parks exist to remind us of the beauty and complexity of nature. Realizing how parks are being ravaged for their resources, polluted, and enveloped by concrete "civilization" has illustrated the frailty and vulnerability of our national parks. National legislation, local development of buffer zones and our personal involvement can save them. Perhaps in the future it won't be a matter of walking down the movie

---

8. Jonathan J. Esslinger, "National Parks: A Scenery of Destruction and Degradation," *Winning Orations of the Interstate Oratorical Association* 1992. Mankato State University, 1992, p. 133.
9. Jonathan Esslinger, p. 133.

theater isle to see the beauty and benefits of our parks. It will simply be a matter of walking through the park gates.[10]

Organizing Your First Speech

Esslinger organized his material in a clear, effective way. There is no mystery to this approach. Whether you are preparing your first speech or your fiftieth, start by constructing a comprehensive full-sentence planning outline, which lays your speech out into its component parts and ties these parts into a coherent whole. Next, distill this outline into speaker's notes, an outline with key words and phrases to act as your guide when you deliver your speech. A well thought out, clearly constructed planning outline and speaker's notes will take you and your audience through the introduction, body, and conclusion of your speech. (For more information on constructing planning and key-word outlines, see Chapter Eight.)

STEP 6: USE SOUND REASONING AND FIRM SUPPORT   Speakers are claim makers. That is, every time you are up before an audience and express a point of view, you are making a claim that should be backed up by solid reasoning and supporting material. For example, if the purpose of your first speech is to persuade your classmates about the value of all-day, rather than half-day, classes for kindergarten students, concrete evidence is necessary to support your specific purpose. As addressed in Chapter Seven, you can provide this support in a number of different ways.

Rely on Expert Testimony

Everyone pays attention to an expert. For the preceding example, you strengthen your claim with the following statement:

> *Newsweek Magazine* recently evaluated the merits of all-day kindergarten programs. Among the supporters they quoted was Sarah Rice, an early-childhood specialist in Montgomery County, Maryland. According to Rice, "If you have developmentally appropriate pacing of activities, [children] don't need time out for rest."[11]

Use Statistics

Statistics convince. You can tell your classmates, for example, that

> More than 1.6 million kindergarten-aged youngsters now attend school all day. That's 40 percent of all kindergarten students. Six states and the District of Columbia believe so strongly in the benefits of these programs that they have passed laws requiring their local school districts to offer full-day programs.

---

10. Jonathan Esslinger, p. 135
11. Connie Leslie and Pat Wingert, "From Half Day to Full Day: How Long Should the Kindergarten?" *Newsweek* June 26, 1989, p. 62.

Build Your Case Through Examples

You can tell your listeners about your nephew's experience:

> I can tell you from observing my five-year-old nephew that children today are ready for all-day kindergarten programs. I think one important fact about my nephew's life will help convince you: His school career started at the age of two-and-a-half in preschool. In fact, he is so used to going to school that an all-day program is a natural extension of what he knows.
>
> Our generation was very different. The first day of kindergarten was our first day of school—we had never even seen the inside of a school building before—and what an adjustment that was.

Use Indisputable Facts

Some facts are so strong that they automatically add weight to your argument, as in the following example:

> Family life has changed considerably over the past twenty years. Although our mothers were home to take care of us when school ended at noon, many women now hold full-time jobs before their children set foot in a kindergarten class—a fact that makes all-day programs a necessity in modern American society.

Construct Analogies

Analogies clarify through comparison. They lend support by encouraging listeners to think of your point in a novel way. You can use figurative analogies, which compare different kinds of things, or literal analogies, which compare similar categories (for example, the system of kindergarten education in the United States to the system in Great Britain). Consider the following figurative analogy to support your position:

> Imagine taking a group of five-year-olds to the beach for the first time and showing them what fun the sand and water can be. Just when the children begin to enjoy themselves, imagine telling them that they are not old enough to be there for more than a few minutes and that they will have to go home. Although playing at the beach all day seems natural for the children, an arbitrary system says they aren't ready for this type of fun. In my view, sending five-year-olds home after a half day of kindergarten makes as much sense.

STEP 7: CHOOSE YOUR WORDS WITH CARE

The enthusiastic young woman looked out into the audience of almost 1,500 people on her graduation day and was overwhelmed with the spirit that marked this important occasion. A hush fell over the crowd as she began her address as president of the senior class: "You guys are all terrific," she declared. "This has been an awesome four years for us, right?" As she proceeded, reflecting on the events of the past four years, her comments were laced with the type of slang that may have been suitable for coffee shop conversation but not for this special occasion.

As this example demonstrates, the words you choose to convey your message reflect your personality; your attitude toward your subject, occasion, and audience; and your concern for avoiding misunderstanding. Words are your primary vehicle for creating meaning. They set forth ideas, spark visions, arouse concerns, elicit emotions, and, if not used carefully, produce confusion.

Once you define the general and specific purposes of your speech and gather the information to support your claim, the following guidelines will help you choose your words with care:

1. *Use plain English.*   The late author George Orwell was so irritated by the tendency of speakers to use big words when little ones would do that he revised a powerful passage from Ecclesiastes to show how language can be misused:

   The original:
   I returned and saw under the sun that the race is not to the swift, nor the battle to the strong, nor yet bread to the wise, nor yet riches to men of understanding, nor yet favor to men of skill; but time and chance happeneth to them all.

   Orwell's version:
   Objective consideration of contemporary phenomena compels the conclusion that success or failure in competitive activities exhibits no tendency to be commensurate with innate capacity, but that a considerable element of the unpredictable must invariably be taken into account.[12]

   Let simple, direct language convey your message.

2. *Keep in mind that although some words are effective on paper, they are awkward to the ear.*   In a written report the terms "edifice," "regulations," "in the eventuality of," "to effectuate," "implement," and "munitions" may be acceptable; in public speaking the words "building," "rules," "if," "to do," "tool," and "guns" are far more effective.

3. *Relate your language to your audience's level of knowledge.*   If you are delivering an informative speech describing drug testing in professional sports, don't assume your audience understands such terms as "false positives," "chain of custody," and "legal and individual safeguards." If you use them your speech should carefully define these terms in order to keep the message clear.

4. *Use language for specific effect.*   If you are delivering an informative speech sensitizing your audience to the plight of America's working poor, the first passage below is less effective than the second:

---

12.   Cited in Dorothy Sarnoff, *Speech Can Change Your Life* (New York: Dell, 1970), pp. 71–72.

Version One:

Although millions of Americans work a full day, they can't pay their bills or provide for their families.

Version Two:

Millions of Americans come home each day, exhausted and covered with a layer of factory filth. Yet they are too worried to sleep. Their backbreaking labor has given them few rewards: they can't pay their rent, buy shoes for their children, or feed them meat more than once a week. Too proud to go on welfare or even accept Food Stamps, they are America's working poor.

The effectiveness of version two stems from its detail that paints memorable word pictures. We explain more about the power of language to create meaning in Chapter Ten.

Perhaps at no other time in our history have ethics been discussed more than they are today. Unfortunately, the reason for this heightened awareness is an explosion in ethical abuses by government leaders, business executives, religious leaders, professionals, and ordinary citizens—an explosion that has touched all of us. Here are two examples:

STEP 8:
CONSIDER
YOUR ETHICAL
RESPONSIBILITIES

⌘ General Dynamics, the nation's third largest military supplier, charged the government more than $75 million for such "overhead" expenses as country club fees and personal travel for corporate executives.

⌘ Fraud and mismanagement at the Department of Housing and Urban Development during the Reagan administration resulted in the siphoning of billions of dollars from housing programs for the poor into the pockets of influence peddlers.

These and other abuses have heightened our sensitivity to the need for honesty from all sources, including public speakers. Although each of us comes to the speaker's platform with different values and beliefs based on our family, cultural, and educational backgrounds, certain ethical standards must be considered universal.

Although freedom of speech is a fundamental right in our democracy, implied in this freedom is the speaker's responsibility to avoid deceiving others. According to communication professor Bert Bradley, "Speakers have ethical responsibilities which must be accepted if rhetoric is to play its most meaningful role in communication."[13] Although our Constitution grants us the right to speak freely, implicit in this right is the responsibility to speak truthfully, which implies concern for the welfare of others; the use of accurate and current information; a reliance on sound reasoning; and a speech that is your own work, based on your own research and views. We examine the ethical responsibility of speakers in detail in Chapter Four.

---

13. Bert Bradley, *Fundamentals of Speech Communication,* 5th ed (Dubuque, IA: Wm. C. Brown, 1988), p. 47.

STEP 9: MAKE
YOUR NERVES
WORK FOR YOU

The one thing you undoubtedly share with many others in your class is an overwhelming feeling of nervousness about your first speech. Whether you attribute this feeling to a lack of self-confidence or to stage fright, or whether you call it "speech apprehension," "speech tension," or merely a "bad case of nerves," you realize intuitively and intellectually that it can diminish the effectiveness of your presentation.

> If the mere thought of public speaking makes you breathless, whether it's to a group of 5 or 500, or just a one-on-one chat with the boss, chances are you've got "speech phobia," a malady that afflicts at least 5 million Americans.
> As bad as it makes you feel, it's not fatal, and what's more, it's curable.
> But, ignoring it could be costly, because, experts say, being able to communicate effectively, which has always been important, is an absolute must for climbing the corporate ladder in the '90s. Or maybe just to keep from falling off.[14]

What Is Speech Tension and Why Do Some People Suffer from It More Than Others?

If you are outgoing and self-confident you may be born to speak in front of crowds. Those fortunate enough to be in this group view public speaking as an opportunity to convey their message to others. If, on the other hand, you have been shy since childhood, you have the added burden of overcoming your natural reticence that makes taking center stage difficult. Most people are somewhere between these two extremes. Although they have to work to control their tension, they will succeed if they try.

Speech tension is, among other things, a physiological reaction. According to speech communication Professor Michael T. Motley, most people experience three stages of physiological arousal immediately before a speech and during its initial stages.[15]

> In stage one—the anticipatory stage that takes place in the few minutes before the speech—heart rates zoom from a normal resting rate of about 70 to between 95 and 140 beats per minute.
> In stage two—the beginning of the speech—heart rates jump to between 110 and 190 beats per minute. This stage usually lasts no more than 30 seconds.
> In stage three—the postconfrontational stage—the heart rate returns to anticipation levels or lower. However, for many speakers, the feelings of confrontation they experienced in stage two are so strong that they do not perceive the drop-off.

In addition to an accelerated heart rate, you may have other physiological symptoms including a dry mouth caused by a reduced flow of saliva, sweaty palms, and heavy breathing. These symptoms are your body's "fight-or-flight" response.

---

14. Bill Hendrick, "SPEECH! SPEECH! Just the thought of it makes millions panic," *The Toledo Blade,* January 16, 1993. p. 27.
15. Michael T. Motley, "Taking the Terror Out of Talk," *Psychology Today* (January 1988): 46–49.

People who experience speech tension often feel the urge to withdraw.[16] We are not always aware of this desire. Even when we convince ourselves that we are not nervous, our nonverbal behavior may reveal our unconscious discomfort.

How to Control Your Tension

Several strategies are available for reducing anxiety. These strategies won't eliminate tension, but they will help you make it work for you. Your goal is to channel this nervous energy into effective communication:[17]

1. *Focus on your message, not yourself.*   Keep your mind on your message and the best way to convey it to your audience. Always think of your audience as being on your side.[18]

2. *Prepare! Prepare! Prepare!*   Preparation sharpens your presentation and builds confidence. Start with a sound speech plan and then rehearse the speech out loud to yourself. Then practice the speech in front of friends to get the feel and response of an audience.

3. *Take several deep breaths.*   Deep breathing has a calming effect on the body and mind.

4. *Realize that you are your own worst critic.*   Studies have shown that the amount of anxiety a speaker reports has little relationship to the amount of nervousness an audience detects. Even listeners trained to detect speech tension often fail to perceive it.[19]

5. *The more you do speak, the more proficient you will become.*   Because public speaking experiences of all kinds will build your confidence, take opportunities to give "mini-speeches" at meetings and oral reports in class. As you gain confidence, volunteer for longer, more demanding presentations. And take every opportunity to write—reports, speeches, fiction, poetry, even letters to friends. Although writing and speaking are distinct activities they share a foundation in the need for organization and precise use of language.

---

16.   See Franklin Knower and A. Craig Baird, *The Essentials of General Speech* (New York McGraw-Hill, 1960) p. 99.

17.   For more information on the control of speech tension, see Joe Ayres, "Coping with Speech Anxiety: The Power of Positive Thinking," *Communication Education* (October 1988): 289–96; Joe Ayres and Theodore S. Hopf, "Visualization: A Means of Reducing Speech Anxiety," *Communication Education* 34 (October 1985): 318–23; Robert S. Littlefield and Timothy L. Sellnow, "The Use of Self-Disclosure as a Means for Reducing Stage Fright in Beginning Speakers," *Communication Education* (January 1987): 62–64.

18.   According to television journalist Sam Donaldson, speech tension often occurs when you "pay too much attention to what other people think." People ask themselves whether others will like them or accept them and they are afraid that their views will be considered "crazy or not as smart." According to Donaldson, these feelings have no place in the public speaking arena where everyone's views are "as good as anyone else's." See Sam Donaldson. "Talk that works," *USA Weekend,* September 22–24, 1989, p. 4.

19.   Michael T. Motley, p. 47.

One way to reduce anxiety is to spend time preparing and rehearsing your speech.

6. *Try to be at your physical and mental best.* Getting a good night's sleep and eating the right food will help. Because most people are lethargic after a big meal, eating lightly before a speech is sensible. Avoid caffeine-filled beverages, and *never* drink alcohol or take tranquilizers to calm your nerves; they will dull your senses—and presentation.

7. *Act confident and you'll be confident.* Putting on a facade of self-confidence can lessen your nervous tension. Resist your desire to flee, briskly step up to the podium, stand tall, breathe deeply, look straight at your audience, smile, and begin speaking as if nothing were more important to you than giving this speech. The more you imagine yourself an accomplished speaker, and the more you make an effort to act that way, the more spontaneous, natural, and comfortable this behavior will become.

8. *Visualize your own success.* Mental imaging—the creation of a powerful mental picture of success—has been used for many years in tennis, golf, and skiing to create a mental image of success.[20] This technique can be

---

20. "In my mind I know I'm going to be a star," *U.S. News & World Report,* June 15, 1987, p. 58.

used in public speaking to help you deal with speech tension. As you prepare for your speech, visualize yourself speaking with confidence and self-assurance. Then imagine the sound of applause after your presentation.

9. *Use gestures and movements.* Nervous tension tends to freeze inexperienced speakers in place. Hands clutching the lectern, feet planted stiffly behind it, these speakers are unable to move out of fear. Ironically, at the moment your body feels frozen in space, an extra flow of adrenaline is supplying a boost of energy, which, if harnessed in gestures and movements, could improve your presentation. Begin simply. Punctuate important points with motions of your hand. And don't hesitate to take one or two steps away from the podium.

10. *Establish eye contact.* Find several friendly faces in the audience and establish eye contact. When you sense that people are on your side, you will speak with greater ease.

11. *Rely on visual aids.* Visual aids provide a vehicle that makes gesturing easier. If you draw a diagram on the board before you begin, you will need to walk over and point to it during your speech. If you outline the main points of your speech on a flip-chart (key words are enough), you can use a pointer to emphasize these points as you speak. We address visual aids in Chapter Eleven.

12. *Take mistakes in stride and learn adjustment techniques.* Don't expect your speech to be perfect. Virtually every speaker—even with years of experience—makes mistakes. If your mind goes blank, repeat your last point and keep going. Sometimes physically taking a step back or to the side of the podium will help relieve your memory lapse. If it doesn't, present another part of the speech you do remember. In all likelihood, your audience will never realize you made an adjustment. Flexibility is possible only if you know your material very well.

As explained in Chapter Twelve, delivery involves the quality of your voice as well as gestures, posture, eye contact, and facial expressions. But here's a brief preview for now:

STEP 10: PERFECT YOUR DELIVERY

Your Audience Must Hear You.   Hearing precedes appreciation. No matter how convincing or powerful your speech, if you speak unclearly or too softly, the audience cannot hear your message and will not be able to respond. How loudly you speak will depend on the size and acoustics of the room, the number of people you are addressing, the presence or absence of a microphone, and your rhetorical goals. If you are trying to arouse your audience to action, your voice will probably be louder than if you are trying to calm it or create a mood of sorrow.

INTERVIEW

Brigadier General Myrna H. Williamson
U.S. Army, retired

Myrna Williamson made her way from life on a rural South Dakota farm to become a brigadier general in the United States Army. During her military career she served in numerous executive positions, including service as the U.S. delegate to the Committee on Women in the NATO forces and an appointment as Deputy Director of Military Personnel Management. General Williamson, now retired from military service, serves on the boards of directors of several national associations and corporations. She is also a professional public speaker who addresses audiences and conducts seminars around the world. We asked General Williamson about her public speaking.

Question: Students are often required to complete a course in public speaking and some of them wonder whether the course is likely to be of value to them in their lives beyond college or the university. How would you respond?

Answer: No matter what students plan to do as they look ahead, once they get out into their career path they discover they have to do things they did not plan and often it is speaking in front of a group. I always stress, when I have the opportunity, the importance of mastering the art of effective communication. I do not believe I would have enjoyed as much success in my military career or been selected to serve on boards of directors without my speaking skills. I also serve as president of other organizations,

am a past president of my college foundation, and if I were not comfortable on the platform and could not articulate my thoughts and ideas I would not be making these contributions.

Question: We teach our students that three general purposes for speaking define three kinds of speeches: to inform, to persuade, and to speak for special occasions, or what we call ceremonial speaking. What kinds of speeches do you usually deliver? Do you see yourself as a persuader or as a person essentially trying to inform your audiences?

Answer: The speeches I give now I would say are a combination of both persuasive and informative messages. In motivational speeches, for example, I am "persuading" my listeners to be all that they can be, to have the courage of their convictions, to step out on their own, and to be unafraid to take risks. Rarely do I speak as a advocate of a particular position because that is not what people are hiring me to do. I know I have been effective because I have had a number of people tell me that my message has made a difference in their lives. To illustrate: I often challenge young listeners to study basic finance, to learn about investments, to take charge of their financial lives. I recall one young lady in an audience of mine who stood up and said "Please let me tell you that I heard General Williamson say this five years ago. I listened to her and I now have stocks, bonds, real estate and mutual funds that are profitable." How do you beat that for a testimonial?

Question: When you are getting ready to go out and speak to an audience do you have a particular way or method of preparation?

Answer: I like to know as far in advance as possible what my listeners are expecting. Speaking at a luncheon or banquet, keynoting, or conducting a seminar all present different challenges. Being the first or an early speaker on a program differs from having a number of speakers in front of you. Of course you need to consider the agenda and purpose of the program. I am a mental planner. I work out ideas in my mind, and finally sketch out an outline and make notes of anecdotes I might want to use. I gather things together in a folder and then as the speaking date draws near I sit down and work out a final outline and get my key words on paper. I finalize my speech the night before I am scheduled to speak and I adjust further to what I believe to be the general feeling of an audience once I arrive. I never speak from a script. Also, I never tell the latest jokes. I use only personal anecdotes, for illustrations or humor, that have happened to me—that makes my material unique.

Question: To what extent are you conscious of time?

Answer: The clock is king! I am very conscious of time. I have my own little clock I stand or tape on the lectern. If I am asked to speak thirty minutes and I begin at 9:15 I will note at the top of my outline that I must stop at 9:45. I will *never* go overtime. Being on time as a speaker is very, very important. If questions and answers are part of my presentation, they are included in my total time, and I will take back the presentation for my final closing, still ending on time.

Question: How about feedback? You mentioned people coming up to you a year or more after hearing you for the first time. Do you do anything generally

to get feedback? Do you ask those who invited you to give you information about how your speech was received? Do you value audience response?

Answer: You can learn a lot by paying attention to your audience's reaction. Attentiveness, eye contact, and laughter all provide me with meaningful information. I also choose to stick around after my speeches and greet people and talk with them. At many events evaluation forms are given to members of the audience and they are later summarized or forwarded to me by the meeting planner. I also take a small recorder to the lectern with me and I record my speeches. Later I listen to them carefully and critically. My speaking agent is also an excellent critic and she provides me with valuable feedback. Occasionally I obtain a video of myself speaking and I find that is extremely helpful, too.

Question: In teaching public speaking we frequently make distinctions between the "content" of a speech and the "delivery." How important do you think your delivery is in your speaking?

Answer: If one does not consider delivery important then why speak? Just hand out your text and let everyone read it. My delivery is certainly an integral part of my speaking. When I speak I also avoid relying on overhead transparencies, slides, and charts as crutches. There are so many things that can go wrong using visuals. I prefer to paint a picture in the minds of the audience. When I talk about taking the "slide for life"—going hand over hand up a ninety-foot ladder, crouching on top of a three-foot-square platform, grasping a small metal bar attached to a cable stretched across a lake, pushing off into the air and sliding on this cable across the water with the air going through my hair, and finally dropping in water near the shore—I paint a word picture that no vu-graph can equal. I use language to create images and to bring about visualization. This is the challenge of speaking—putting the words together and then delivering them in such a way as to create a memorable experience for your audience.

Interview with General Myrna Williamson, April 19, 1993.

Don't Lead a Race.   Many inexperienced speakers let their nervous tension control their rate of speech, leaving their audiences gasping. Although rapid speech may get the task behind you in record time, it will not help you communicate your message effectively.

Work on Your Articulation and Pronunciation.   Proper articulation involves the verbalization of distinct sounds. If you tell your audience that they "hafta" (have to) go horseback "ridin" (riding), you are forcing your listeners to focus on your articulation rather than your words. Poor articulation and pronunciation often start early and develop into ingrained habits that are hard to break. Although correcting these patterns takes work, dramatic change is possible.

Avoid Nervous Fillers.   When actor Tom Cruise was interviewed on the "Today" Show several years ago, he kept repeating the phrase "you know." During the five minute interview, he repeated the phrase dozens of times—an indication that even an accomplished actor can suffer from nervous tension. Cruise's response is not uncommon. Many speakers punctuate their speeches with nervous fillers such as "you know," "um," and "er." Change is possible with awareness and effort.

Be Enthusiastic and Be Yourself.   The more enthusiasm you feel as you deliver your speech, the greater your ability to involve your audience. Enthusiasm implies honesty and openness—qualities many speakers find difficult to communicate to an audience. Public speaking consultant Roger Ailes, who directed President George Bush's 1988 media campaign, explains the importance of sharing your "real" self with an audience:

> You must be able to "drop the mask" and share deeply felt emotion. Be open enough with your listeners so that they don't just hear your words: bring them close enough to catch the fire of your ideas.[21]

Let Nonverbal Cues Work For You.   Students about to deliver their first speech often make the mistake of focusing solely on the words of their speech as if communication occurs only verbally. Audiences respond to the "gestalt" of a presentation, that is, everything speakers do or say while they are on stage. Thus, even if your verbal message is well thought out and effectively articulated, if you are frozen behind the podium, if you slouch, if you never lift your eyes from your notes to make eye contact with your audience, or if your face is contorted in a grimace reflecting your conscious or unconscious discomfort, you may significantly weaken the impact of your words.

As you work on your delivery, keep in mind that technique cannot be separated from the content of your message. The most accomplished showmen will fail as public speakers if they have nothing to say to their audience or if their remarks are

---

21.   Roger Ailes, "The Fire of Your Ideas," *The Toastmaster* (June 1989): 13.

unsupported or disorganized. Audiences gather to hear the substance of your remarks—not to watch a show.

Because you will be asked to deliver a speech before you complete this text, this chapter describes ten steps to prepare and present an effective speech.

Step 1: Select a topic you care about. Topic selection should start with your own interests.

Step 2: Determine the purposes and core idea of your speech. Define your general and specific purposes and core idea.

Step 3: Consider yourself a spokesperson. Identify with your topic, and your audience will too.

Step 4: Analyze and adapt to your audience. Understand who your listeners are, what they know and feel about you and your message, and the knowledge they bring to the speech.

Step 5: Divide your speech into an introduction, body, and conclusion.

Step 6: Use sound reasoning and firm support. Support your core idea with testimony, statistics, examples, facts, and analogies.

Step 7: Choose your words with care. Use plain, simple English and tie your language to audience knowledge.

Step 8: Consider your ethical responsibilities.

Step 9: Make your nerves work for you. Speech tension can be minimized using several strategies.

Step 10: Perfect your delivery. Work on the quality of your voice, gestures, posture, eye contact, and facial expressions.

1. What factors should you keep in mind when choosing a topic and framing a purpose for speaking? What is the relationship between choice, time, amount of information, and the needs of the audience?
2. What does being a spokesperson mean to you?
3. Although the degree of speech tension varies from speaker to speaker, most inexperienced speakers share common feelings of discomfort. What can you do to minimize these feelings, and to make your nervouse energy work for you rather than against you?

1. Make an inventory of your own strengths and weaknesses as a public speaker. Then establish goals and expectations you intend to pursue as you participate in this course.
2. Make a list of the basic steps in preparing your first speech. Study the list carefully and compare it to the steps outlined in the chapter.
3. Prepare and deliver a five- to six-minute informative speech. Draw the topic from your own experiences or interests, not from one of your college courses.

"It is the disease of not listening, the malady of not marking, that I am troubled withal.

William Shakespeare

LISTENING TO AND EVALUATING SPEECHES

What could be simpler than listening—than sitting back and giving the speaker your attention? As the following interchange between the speaker (left-hand column) and the listener (right-hand column) suggests, listening is more complicated than it appears. As public speakers, we speak in the hope that our message and meaning will be understood; as audience members we may try to listen attentively but have other things on our minds—physical distractions, preconceived notions, prejudices, misunderstandings, and stress. The message we receive may be far different from the message sent:

Here I am again—listening to another speaker who says he stormed his college administration building more than twenty years ago. This must be a popular topic on the college speaking circuit. Maybe this guy will be different from the other three middle-aged radicals I heard, but I doubt it. . . The least they could do is turn up the air conditioning. It's so hot I can hardly breathe, let alone listen.

These guys keep talking about how they know the way and how we're all wrong. . . I wonder what he does for a living. I'll bet he hasn't saved any lives lately or helped the poor. He probably earns big bucks giving speeches on campus telling us how horrible we are. . . He looks like he spends a lot of time cultivating his hippie look. He must have slept in those clothes for a week. These guys all look the same.

He's harping on the same old issues. Doesn't he know the Vietnam War is ancient history; that African-Americans have more opportunities than they ever had—I wish *I* could earn as much as Eddie Murphy; that women are on the job along with men; I wish *I* could earn as much as Connie Chung . . . I guess I'll have a pizza for dinner. I should have eaten before I came. I'm really hungry.

Of course we're interested in business. Maybe he had a rich father who paid his tuition, but I don't. I need to earn money when I graduate so I can pay back my student loans.

Who does he think he is—calling us conservatives. I'm not a bigot. When I believe something is wrong, I fight to change it—like when I protested against ethnic cleansing overseas and flag burning right here.

I wonder when he'll finish. I've got to get back to the dorm to study for my marketing exam. He just goes on and on about the same old things.

Here he was again—still a kid at heart but speaking to a group of college students who considered him an old man. Maybe his topic turned them off. Maybe his 1960s radical-student look no longer "played well" on campus. Maybe students had simply forgotten how to listen. Whatever the reason, as he started his speech on the growing conservative trend on campus, the speaker hoped this time would be different. He began:

More than twenty years ago, at about this time of year, I—and a whole lot of other committed students—spent a solid week—day and night—in the offices of our college president. Needless to say we hadn't been invited.

We were protesters and proud of it. We were there because we believed the Vietnam War was wrong. We were there because we believed racism was wrong. We were there because we believed that women should be given the same opportunities as men.

Were we victorious? For about ten years, I thought so. Then something happened. The signs were subtle at first. Haircuts got shorter. The preppie look replaced torn jeans. Business became the major of choice.

In a flash—it happened that quickly—these subtle changes became a way of life. Campus life, as I knew it, disappeared. Revolution and concern for the oppressed were out, and conservatism and concern for the self were in.

From the point of view of someone who has seen both sides—the radical, tumultuous sixties and the calm, money-oriented eighties and nineties—students of today are really 40-year-olds in 20-year-old bodies. They are conservative to the core at the only time of life when they can choose to live free. I am here to help you see how wrong you are.

Let's look at the reasons audiences stop listening:

When Our Attention Drifts We Stop Listening.   Listeners drift in and out of the speech thinking about the heat, their next meal, and an impending exam. Studies have shown that few of us can pay attention to a single stimulus for more than twenty seconds without focusing, at least momentarily, on something else.[1]

When We Are Distracted We Stop Listening.   Our environment determines how well we can listen. In this case, the heat made it difficult to pay attention. Internal stresses—hunger and concern about exams—are also distractions.

When We have Preconceived Notions We Stop Listening.   Before the speaker opened his mouth, the listener had already decided what the speaker stood for. The listener based his impressions on the speaker's appearance and on a stereotype of what sixties radicals stood for. Although in this case he was right—the speaker's views conformed to the listener's preconceived notions—he may be wrong about others.

When We Disagree We Stop Listening.   Although the speaker identified continuing social ills, the listener did not share his concerns. From his point of view, much more was right with the world than the speaker admitted—a perspective that reduced the listener's willingness and ability to consider the speaker's message.

When We Are Prejudiced or Inflexible We Stop Listening.   Few African Americans are as successful as Eddie Murphy; all women do not earn as much as Connie Chung. Yet the listener based his reaction to the speaker's message on the premise that if one member of a group can succeed, all can. His prejudice prevented him from seeing the truth in the speaker's words.

When We Are Faced with Abstractions, We Form Our Own Opinions and Stop Listening.   The speaker never defined the term "conservative." As a result, the listener brought his own meaning to the term, equating it with bigotry. This meaning may or may not have coincided with the speaker's intent.

As discussed in Chapter One, public speaking is a process involving reciprocal communication between audience and speaker. You succeed as a speaker when you achieve the lowest level of misunderstanding with your listeners. *One way to improve the public speaking transaction is to approach it from the listening side—that is, to work at developing better listening skills. These skills are essential for two different but complementary reasons:*

WHY GOOD LISTENING SKILLS ARE IMPORTANT

1.   By understanding the listening needs of your audience, you will be able to develop and deliver speeches that have the greatest chance of communicating your intended meaning.

1.   N. Moray, *Listening and Attention* (Baltimore: Penguin Books, 1972).

2. By understanding the factors affecting listening, you will be able to monitor your own listening habits and more effectively evaluate and criticize the speeches of others, including those of your classmates. As you read in the opening example, without this awareness you may consciously or unconsciously tune the speaker out; you may focus on minor details at the expense of the main point; you may prejudge the speaker based on appearance; you may allow your own emotional needs and responses to distort the message, and so on. There is a direct relationship between the quality of your listening and the quality of your speaking. Good speakers use what they hear to analyze and respond to the needs of their audience and to present information in a way that promotes communication.

In a classic study of listening, Paul Tory Rankin found that adults spend about 42 percent of their total verbal communication time listening, compared to 32 percent talking, 15 percent reading, and 11 percent writing. College students in the classroom typically spend about 53 percent of their time listening to their professors, to fellow students, to audiovisual presentations, and so on.[2]

Despite the amount of time we spend listening, our ability to retain what we hear is limited. According to communication Professor Ralph G. Nichols, a pioneer in listening research, immediately after listening to a speech, we can recall only half of what was said. After several days, only about 25 percent of the speech stays with us, if we are lucky—often we forget the whole thing.[3]

We can illustrate Nichols' findings by examining what people remember about John F. Kennedy's 1960 inaugural address. Although all who heard it when it was first delivered, or later on tape, remember these words, "And so, my fellow Americans, ask not what your country can do for you—ask what you can do for your country," few focused on the militant nature of Kennedy's remarks: "Let all our neighbors know that we shall join with them to oppose aggression or subversion anywhere in the Americas. And let every other power know that this hemisphere intends to remain master of its own house."

Later, we provide specific tips for improving your listening skills. Now, we will analyze the elements of listening.

HOW LISTENING IS DEFINED

Although listening seems to be an instantaneous activity, it consists of several identifiable stages. Researchers have created models of the listening process. Lyman Steil analyzes and explains listening in terms of four progressive stages:

---

2. Paul Tory Rankin, "The Measurement of the Ability to Understand Spoken Language," unpublished Ph.D. dissertation. University of Michigan, 1926, *Dissertation Abstracts* 12 (1952), pp. 847–48; Larry Baker et al., "An Investigation of Proportional Time Spent in Various Communication Activities by College Students," *Journal of Applied Communications Research* 8 (November 1980): 101–09.
3. Ralph G. Nichols, "Do We Know How to listen? Practical Helps in a Modern Age," *Speech Teacher* (March 1961): 118–24; see also Lyman K. Steil. *Your Personal Listening Profile* (New York: Sperry Corp., 1980).

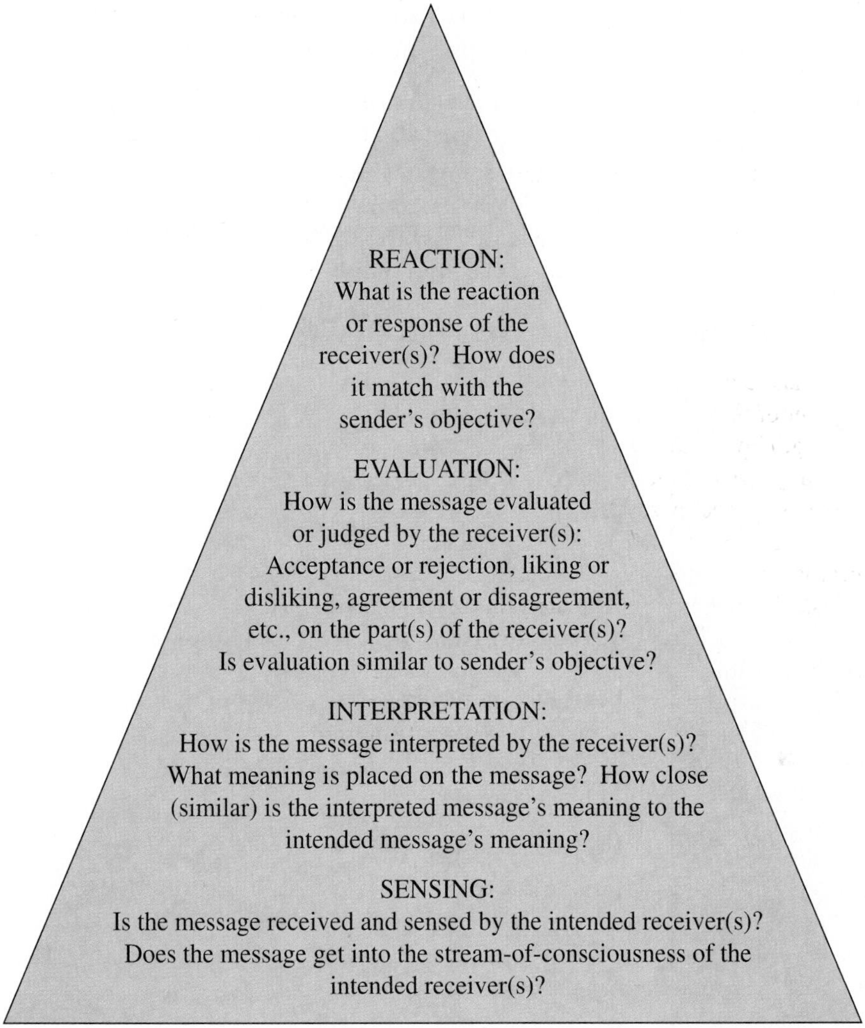

FIGURE 3.1
Four-stage
communication model.

REACTION:
What is the reaction
or response of the
receiver(s)? How does
it match with the
sender's objective?

EVALUATION:
How is the message evaluated
or judged by the receiver(s):
Acceptance or rejection, liking or
disliking, agreement or disagreement,
etc., on the part(s) of the receiver(s)?
Is evaluation similar to sender's objective?

INTERPRETATION:
How is the message interpreted by the receiver(s)?
What meaning is placed on the message? How close
(similar) is the interpreted message's meaning to the
intended message's meaning?

SENSING:
Is the message received and sensed by the intended receiver(s)?
Does the message get into the stream-of-consciousness of the
intended receiver(s)?

sensing, interpreting, evaluating, and responding (see Figure 3.1).[4] We move through these stages every time we listen to formal speeches or ordinary conversation. Listening can take place on several different levels characterized by different degrees of attention and emotional and intellectual involvement.[5] At times we only partially listen as we think about or do other things; other times we listen with complete commitment.

---

4.   Lyman K. Steil, *Listening: Key to Your Success* (New York: Random House, 1983).
5.   John J. Makay and Ronald C. Fetzer, *Business Communication Skills,* 2d ed. (Englewood Cliffs, NJ: Prentice-Hall, 1984), pp. 19–24.

Stage 1: Listening Starts When You
Sense the Information from Its Source

Listening begins with sensation, which requires the ability to hear what is said. (Sight is also involved because the speaker's gestures, facial expressions as well as the use of visual aids communicate intent.) Normally, the speaking voice is in the range of 55 to 80 decibels, a level that enables us comfortably to hear a speaker's words. Figure 3.2 shows how this level of sound compares with others in the environment.

FIGURE 3.2
How loud are the sounds around us?

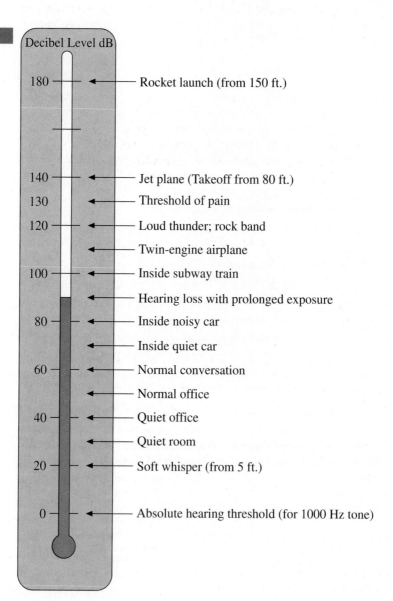

Decibel Level dB

180 ← Rocket launch (from 150 ft.)

140 ← Jet plane (Takeoff from 80 ft.)
130 ← Threshold of pain
120 ← Loud thunder; rock band
← Twin-engine airplane
100 ← Inside subway train
← Hearing loss with prolonged exposure
80 ← Inside noisy car
← Inside quiet car
60 ← Normal conversation
← Normal office
40 ← Quiet office
← Quiet room
20 ← Soft whisper (from 5 ft.)

0 ← Absolute hearing threshold (for 1000 Hz tone)

As anyone who has tried to listen to a speech over the din of a car siren realizes, obstacles can—and often do—interfere with reception. These obstacles are known to communication theorists as "noise." When your neighbor, in the seat to your left, starts coughing or when you are forced to sit at the back of a large, nonamplified auditorium, hearing is difficult, making concentrated listening impossible.

Noise takes other forms, such as environmental annoyances like smoke-filled rooms, uncomfortable chairs, or inadequate air-conditioning systems. At times a remedy is possible. The speaker, for example, can ask the audience to refrain from smoking, or audience members can find more comfortable seats. When nothing can be done about noise put yourself in the position of the speaker. Then work hard to listen to the message.

Stage 2: Listening Involves the Interpretation of Messages

A second critical element in listening is interpretation, the phase in which you attach meaning to the speaker's words. As a listener, it is important to keep in mind that words have different meanings to different people and that we interpret words based on our subjective experiences. According to communication professor Paul G. Friedman, "When listening we can only *hope* to know what a speaker actually is thinking and trying to convey. Often, our attempts at 'mind reading' . . . . are inaccurate."[6]

Emotional and Intellectual Barriers to Listening.   Our ability to interpret what we hear is influenced by emotional and intellectual barriers that get in the way of the speaker's intended message. We may stop paying attention or misinterpret a message when we encounter a barrier we cannot overcome. These barriers are forms of internal noise. Novelist David Leavitt explains how emotional barriers prevented him from dealing with the topic of AIDS. Leavitt, a homosexual, found any mention of AIDS so threatening that he shut off his ability to listen:

> The truth was that AIDS scared me so much I wanted to block it out of my mind. When AIDS came up in a conversation, I'd change the subject, when a frightening headline leaped out at me from the pages of the newspaper, I'd hurriedly skim the article, and, once assured that it described no symptoms I could claim to be suffering from myself, turn the page. Only later . . . did I recognize the extent to which I was masking denial with self-righteousness.[7]

In this case, the psychological mechanism of denial caused the listening obstruction. The list of other causes could go on and on. For example, the fact that you listen to a speech along with others may influence your ability to listen. According to a recent study, subjects who listen to instructional material alone comprehend significantly more than those who listen as a member of an audience.[8]

---

6.   Paul G. Friedman, *Listening Processes: Attention, Understanding, Evaluation,* 2d ed. (Washington, DC: National Education Association), quote from p. 12; pp. 6–15 used in writing this section.
7.   David Leavitt, "The Way I Live Now," *The New York Times Magazine,* July 9, 1989, p. 30.
8.   Michael J. Beatty and Steven K. Payne, "Effects of Social Facilitation on Listening Comprehension," *Communication Quarterly* 32, (Winter 1984): 37–40.

The following examples show that our ability to listen to and interpret messages may be influenced by many different conscious and unconscious thoughts:

⌘ A middle-aged woman who has never held a paying job and who has no idea how much her husband earns or how much savings the family has may unconsciously "tune out" when she hears a speaker delivering an informative speech on financial planning.

⌘ A rebellious teenager who has experimented with drugs may choose to stop listening to a speech on alcohol and drug abuse. In his mind, no adult has the experience necessary to relate to the pressure faced by modern teens.

⌘ An expert on public health can hardly sit still as he listens to a lecture on asbestos removal. After a few minutes he realizes that he and the speaker have completely different views on removal procedure safety. Instead of listening to the rest of the information, he fumes over this difference of opinion.

Whether emotional and intellectual barriers that influence interpretation are the result of an unwillingness to deal with real-world problems, a refusal to take advice, or a difference of opinion, the result is the same: Listening is obstructed, interpretation skewed, and communication prevented.

Understanding the listening needs of your audience will help you prepare and deliver meaningful speeches.

Stage 3: Listening Involves Evaluating What You Hear

Evaluation requires that you judge the worth of the speaker's ideas and decide their importance to you, particularly when listening to a persuasive message. You must decide whether you share the speaker's point of view and, if not, why not. Although we evaluate persuasive messages when, for example, choosing political candidates or deciding on college or community issues, it is a mistake to assume that we judge these messages solely on their own merits. Research has shown that we decide how these messages fit into our value system and judge them on that basis. According to Friedman, "This results from the human preference for maintaining internal consistency among personal beliefs, feelings, and actions."[9]

This tendency was first described by psychologist Leon Festinger in his theory of "cognitive dissonance," which states that all human beings seek consistency between related attitudes and between attitudes and related behaviors. When inconsistency exists, we experience mental stress. To reduce the stress, we're forced to change one or more of our attitudes or behaviors so that the inconsistency is reduced or eliminated. For example, if you have a high opinion of the president, but do not think his policy to rid the country of illegal drugs is effective, you may lower your overall opinion of the president somewhat, while simultaneously reassessing upward the value of his drug policy. Dissonance disappears when your overall impression is consistent with your impression of the specific policy. Thus, as listeners we seek information consistent with what we already know; we accept ideas more readily if they are linked to our values and commitments.[10]

Friedman explains what may happen when we confront new ideas that do not fit comfortably into our existing value system. To preserve psychological balance, we often reject these ideas and retain our original point of view. This rejection can take many forms, including the following:

1. *Shoot the messenger.*   If you are a member of a college fraternity, you may reject the notion that any fraternity found guilty of a hazing violation should be banned from campus. You may criticize the speaker as uninformed or as someone who was never able to get into a fraternity himself.

2. *Rally 'round the flag.*   Listeners who disagree with a speaker's message may seek the support of others who share their point of view—in this case, other fraternity members. Shared support provides comfort and reassurance. However, it does not necessarily mean that you are right.

3. *What the speaker says is not what you hear.*   Although the speaker may focus on hazing violations that put pledges in physical jeopardy, you hear

---

9.   Paul G. Friedman, *Listening Processes: Attention, Understanding, Evaluation,* 2d ed. (Washington, DC: National Education Association, 1986), p. 13.
10.   Leon Festinger, *A Theory of Cognitive Dissonance* (Stanford, CA: Stanford University Press, 1957).

him say that all violations—even minor infractions—should result in the fraternity being banned.

4. *Convincing yourself that the speaker's message has nothing to do with you.*   Even when opinions collide, you may convince yourself that you and the speaker are talking about two different things.

5. *Try to change the speaker's mind.*   You may approach the speaker to try to convince him that fraternity abuses have been blown out of proportion by the media. You argue that it is wrong to restrict fraternities based on a few isolated incidents.

6. *Don't think about it and it will go away.*   If as a fraternity member, you took part in several unpleasant hazing incidents, listening to the speech may force you to question what you have done. To avoid the emotional discomfort that goes with this soul-searching, you may unconsciously block messages with which you do not agree.

Although these methods of rejecting messages in conflict with our value systems may seem extreme, we all rely on one or more of them at one time or another. People who use them excessively—who are threatened by any difference of opinion—are considered dogmatic and authoritarian.[11]

Research has shown that when we perceive speakers as trustworthy, competent, reliable, highly regarded by others, dynamic and sociable, and similar to ourselves, we are more likely to evaluate them positively than when we see them in negative or less acceptable ways.[12]

Step 4: Listening Involves Responding to the Speaker's Message

If evaluation were the final stage in listening, the process could be described essentially as linear. To create a circular transaction, involving a give-and-take between audience and speaker, feedback is also necessary. As you can see in Figure 3.1, the fourth step in the listening process is responding, or reacting.

Listeners provide feedback in a variety of ways: clapping and smiling, nodding their heads in agreement, cheering or booing, questioning the speaker after the presentation is over. Often, listeners provide this feedback without realizing they are taking part in a transactional process. You may yawn during a particularly boring speech not to criticize the speaker, but simply because you are tired.

The best speakers rely on and encourage feedback from their audience. They watch carefully for messages of approval or disapproval and adjust their presentations accordingly. We discuss audience feedback in detail in Chapter Five.

---

11.   H.J. Ehrlich and D. Lee, "Dogmatism, Learning, and Resistance to Change: A Review and a New Paradigm," *Psychological Bulletin* 71 (1969): 249–60.
12.   D.K. Berlo, J.B. Lemert, and R. Mertz, "Dimensions for Evaluating the Acceptability of Message Sources," *Public Opinion Quarterly* 33 (1969): 563–76.

As a skill, listening is notoriously undervalued. Philosopher Mortimer J. Adler uses the following sports analogy to describe why the act of listening is as important as the act of speaking: "Catching is as much an activity as throwing and requires as much skill, though it is a skill of a different kind. Without the complementary efforts of both players, properly attuned to each other, the play cannot be completed."[13] The players involved in the act of communication are a speaker and listeners, all of whom have a role in the interaction. In this section, we explain how you can improve your listening skills—and, therefore, the chances of meaningful communication—by becoming conscious of your habits and, when necessary, redirecting your efforts. Listening is a multistage process that can be improved in many different ways.[14]

EIGHT WAYS TO FINE-TUNE YOUR LISTENING SKILLS

Step 1: Get Ready to Listen

Preparation is crucial, especially when you have other things on your mind. Plan to make the effort to listen even before the speech begins, deliberately clearing your mind of distractions to concentrate on the speech.

Step 2: Minimize Listening Barriers

This step is more difficult than it sounds, for it often involves overcoming the emotional and intellectual barriers to listening that we identified in preceding passages. Often, we need help in recognizing our listening blind spots. We need others to point out aspects of our own behavior we cannot see. In the public speaking course, your classmates can fill this role as you analyze each other's speeches. As you talk with your classmates, try to determine whether the message you received from a speaker was the same message they heard. If it was not, think about what the topic means to you; try to identify any reasons for your misunderstanding. (You also should consider the possibility that you are the only one who accurately understood the speaker's message. Sometimes an entire audience misses the point.) If a question-and-answer period follows the speech, you can question the speaker directly to make sure you have the right meaning.

Step 3: Leave Distractions Behind

Some distractions are more easily dealt with than others. You can change your seat to get away from the smell of perfume but you cannot make a head cold disappear. Although dealing with distractions is never easy, you can try to put them aside so you can focus on the speaker and the speech. This task will become easier if you view listening as a responsibility—and as work. By considering listening as more than a casual interaction, you will be more likely to hear the message being sent.

---

13.   Mortimer J. Adler, *How to Speak, How to Listen* (New York: Macmillan, 1983).
14.   For a perspective on the importance of listening to the community as well as the individuals, see Michael Purdy, "Why Listen? Speaking Creates Community, Doesn't It? The Role of Listening in Community Formation," *New York State Speech Communication Association: New Dimensions in Communication: Proceedings of the 47th Annual New York State Speech Communication Association,* III (October 13–15, 1989): 71–76.

F O C U S   O N   R E S E A R C H

THE DIFFERENCE BETWEEN GOOD AND BAD LISTENING

In an attempt to find ways to improve listening, Ralph G. Nichols, a pioneer in listening research, identified the hundred best and the hundred worst listeners in a University of Minnesota freshman class. He then subjected the entire group of two hundred to a series of objective tests and personal inventories and interviews. After nine months of studying the freshmen, Nichols identified ten factors differentiating good listeners from bad:

1. While bad listeners stop paying attention when they find a speaker's subject dry, good listeners acknowledge their lack of interest, realize that it would be difficult for them to leave during a speech, and commit themselves to paying attention in the hope that they might be able to learn something of value.

2. Poor listeners pay more attention to delivery than content. When they encounter an ineffective speaker, they stop listening. Good listeners look past poor delivery and focus on trying to learn something new.

3. Poor listeners are victims of overstimulation. As soon as the speaker says something that arouses their passions, they are overcome with the desire to take part in the argument. Nichols explains what happens when listeners disagree: "The aroused person usually becomes preoccupied by trying to do three things simultaneously: calculate what hurt is being done to his own pet idea; plot an embarrassing question to ask the speaker; enjoy mentally all the discomfiture visualized for the speaker once the devastating reply to him is launched. With these things going on,

subsequent passages go unheard." Effective listeners withhold evaluation until the speech is over.

4. Good listeners are able to focus on the central idea as they differentiate "between fact and principle, idea and example, evidence and argument." Poor listeners get bogged down in the minutiae of individual facts and fail to grasp the overall meaning of the speaker's message. Nichols points out that learning to focus on the central idea requires an ability to recognize organizational patterns, transitional language, and the speaker's use of summaries.

5. The hundred worst listeners always took notes in outline form regardless of whether the speech followed a clearly defined pattern of organization. The result was frustration and inattention when they encountered a poorly organized speech. The best listeners had developed four or five note-taking systems and applied the most effective system to each speech.

6. While the worst listeners spend little energy or effort in the listening situation, the best listeners make a conscious decision to work at listening.

7. The best listeners fight distractions through intense concentration. Poor listeners stop listening at the first sign of environmental noise.

8. While the most effective listeners are comfortable hearing difficult material in a speech and view comprehension as a mental challenge, poor listeners are uncomfortable listening to anything difficult

> or technical. They are inexperienced "recreational" listeners.
> 9. Poor listeners tend to stop listening when the speaker refers to a concept that has emotional meaning to the listener. Effective listeners try to get past their initial emotional responses and continue listening.
> 10. Because listeners think faster than speakers talk, the best listeners have learned to use their excess thinking time to analyze, anticipate, and summarize the speaker's message. Poor listeners frequently turn their thoughts to other things and, in the process, miss much of the speaker's message.[15]

Step 4: Don't Rush to Judgment

Soon after Republican presidential candidate George Bush chose Dan Quayle as his running mate in 1988, Quayle gained a reputation as a speaker whose words got him into trouble—an impression that persisted when he took office. Skeptics undervalued Quayle's speaking ability, discounting his speeches even before they were given—a tendency that ironically put the skeptics, rather than Quayle, at a disadvantage. Although Quayle was sometimes adept at uttering nonsense (for example, when addressing the United Negro College Fund, he mangled the group's slogan, "A mind is a terrible thing to waste" in the following way: "And you take the U.N.C.F. model that what a waste it is to lose one's mind or not to have a mind is being very wasteful. How true that is."), he was speaking as vice president, and his words had to be taken seriously. He matured under pressure as he learned to avoid some of the speaking pitfalls that were his undoing during the campaign.

Resist the temptation to prejudge speakers. As a listener, you have the responsibility to evaluate the content of the speech you are hearing and not jump to conclusions based on impressions of what you know about the speaker or how he or she looks.

Listeners have the tendency to prejudge topics as well as speakers. You may yawn at the thought of listening to one of your classmates deliver an informative speech about working at home until you realize that the topic is more interesting than you expect. Your ears perk up as you hear the speaker say:

> People who work at home are on the cutting edge of every technological change I know. They communicate via computer, facsimile machines, videotape and the ordinary telephone as they zap their work back and forth across the country and, if necessary, the world.

Some speakers save the best for last. They may start slowly and build a momentum of ideas and language. Your job is to listen and be patient.

---

15. Ralph G. Nichols, "Do We Know How to Listen? Practical Helps in a Modern Age," *Speech Teacher* (March 1961): 118–24.

Step 5: Listen First for Content, Second for Delivery

On April 30, 1973, President Richard M. Nixon tried to explain away White House involvement in the break-in of the Democratic National Committee headquarters at the Watergate Complex by delivering a dramatic television and radio address. The speech satisfied few, if any, of Nixon's critics. According to *The New York Times* columnist James Reston, "The President's speech was full of self-pity and unconvincing alibis . . . ."

Nixon's delivery also communicated a message. According to speech communication professor Waldo W. Braden, it "revealed Nixon's strain and worry. Tense and haggard, he was not as fluent as usual. In fact, in his introduction, he fumbled for words. Throughout the twenty-four minutes of the speech he had some difficulty following his manuscript. Unlike many of his other formal addresses, this speech gave the impression of complete seriousness . . . ."[16]

In all the speeches you will hear, both words and delivery impart meaning. Your job as a listener is to separate the two and to focus first on the ideas and second on the delivery.

Confronted with poor speakers, it is difficult to separate content from delivery and analyze each separately. The natural tendency is simply to stop listening when speakers drone on in a monotone, deliver speeches with their heads in their notes, or sway back and forth. Delivery often has little to do with the quality of the speaker's ideas. Many of the speakers you will hear over the years will be in the position to address you because of their accomplishments, not their speaking ability. While a Nobel Prize-winning scientist may be able to explain a breakthrough in cancer therapy, he or she may have no idea how to make contact with an audience. To avoid missing these speakers' points, look past poor delivery and focus on content.

Step 6: Become an Effective Note Taker

Each time a professor lectures or conducts a class discussion, you and your fellow students are expected to take notes. After years of note taking, this activity probably seems as natural as breathing; it is something you do to survive. Ironically, though you worked hard to develop this skill, it often disappears at graduation. Most people do not pull out a pad and pen when listening to a speech in the world outside the classroom. But, note taking is as appropriate and necessary for nonstudents as it is for students. When you listen to a speech at a political rally, in church or synagogue, or even on television, taking notes will help you listen more effectively.

The following guidelines will help you improve your note-taking—and listening—skills:

1. Divide a piece of paper with a vertical line down the middle. Write "Facts" at the top of the left-hand column; write "Personal reactions/questions" at

---

16.   Richard M. Nixon, "The Watergate Case," in *Representative American Speeches: 1972–1973*, Waldo W. Braden, ed., Vol. 45, no. 4 (New York: H.W. Wilson Co. 1973), p. 51.

The best listeners concentrate to analyze, summarize, and assess the speaker's message as they listen.

the top of the right-hand column. Keep these columns separate as you take notes. If the speaker does not answer your questions during the course of the speech, ask for clarification at the end.

2. Use a key-word outline instead of full sentences to document the speaker's essential points.

3. Use your own abbreviations or shorthand symbols to save time.

4. Use diagrams, charts, scales, and quick-sketch images to summarize thematic concepts or theories.

5. Use a numbering system to get down procedural, directional, or structural units of information.

6. If no matter how quickly you write you cannot keep up, ask the speaker—verbally or nonverbally—to slow down.

Step 7: Be an Active Listener

As listeners, we have the ability to process information at the rate of about 400 words per minute. However, because most people talk at only about 150 words per minute so we have a considerable amount of unused thinking time to spare.[17] This "extra

---

17.   Florence L. Wolff, Nadine C. Marsnik, William S. Tacey and Ralph G. Nichols, *Perceptive Listening,* (New York: Holt, Rinehart and Winston, 1983), p. 154.

time" often gets in the way of listening because we have the opportunity to take mental excursions away from the speaker's topic. To minimize this problem, listening experts suggest the following techniques:

1. Take notes to help you focus on the speech's important points.

2. Before the speech begins, write down any questions you have about the topic. As the speech progresses, determine whether the speaker has answered them.

3. If you know something about the topic, try to predict what the speaker will say next. If, for example, you are listening to a speech about children's TV viewing habits, you may speculate that the speaker will recommend a national policy to limit televised violence. You may also expect to hear about the good parts of children's television, including programs such as "Sesame Street" and "Mister Rogers' Neighborhood."

4. Apply the speaker's comments to your own experience and knowledge. Returning to the preceding example, you may think about how your brother starts throwing pillows after watching violent cartoons.

5. Define the speech's core idea and main supporting points. These will help you focus on the critical parts of the speech.

6. Decide whether you agree with the speaker's point of view and evaluate the general performance.

Step 8: Provide Feedback

Let speakers know what you think. Lean forward in your chair, nod your head, smile, frown. This kind of participation will force you to focus your attention on the speaker and the speech. Providing feedback at the various stages of a speech can be hard work, requiring total involvement and a commitment to fighting distractions.

EVALUATING
PUBLIC
SPEECHES

When you evaluate speeches, you engage in a form of feedback, a process that makes you a speech critic. As you consider the elements included in a speech and note the speech's strengths and weaknesses, you are taking part in a formal process of analysis and appraisal.

This formal process is not limited to the public speaking class. Even speeches given by the president of the United States are subject to being critiqued and "graded." After his inaugural address, President Clinton received a grade in a syndicated column written by William Safire, a political columnist and former speechwriter for Richard Nixon. Safire is the author of numerous books and has distinguished himself as an expert on language.

Safire gave the president's speech good marks in terms of its theme (simple, direct, fitting); use of metaphor ("a season of service," "we force the spring"); hint of policy in formation; anaphora (communications and commerce are global;

investment is mobile; technology is almost magical; and ambition for a better life universal); length (blessedly brief—14 minutes); historic resonance (echoes of Jefferson, Wilson, Roosevelt, Kennedy); turn of a phrase ("anyone who has ever watched a child's eyes wander into sleep"); and delivery (his best, strong voice, confident, demeanor, no flubs). The weaknesses he identified were with what he called "cheap shots" (The old "people are working harder for less"); "fuzzy sacrifice" ("We must invest more in our own people [i.e. raise taxes] . . . and at the same time cut our massive debt"); "applause lines" ("There is nothing wrong with America that can't be cured by what is right with America"); and "lift" (it never soared). Safire wrote: "I give it a B. Maybe he'll have another chance."[18]

Regardless of the political perspective that Safire may bring to a speech given by Bill Clinton, the point to keep in mind is that criteria are applied each time someone in an audience thinks about a speech, what it means, and what its value may be. About the same time Safire wrote about President Clinton's speech, media critic Jeff Greenfield wrote: "The central trouble with the inaugural was the same trouble that has afflicted 96.5 percent of American political speech since January 20, 1961. Everyone wants to sound like John Kennedy."[19]

As a participant in a public speaking course, you will be expected to criticize constructively your classmate's speeches. It is important that you note the constructive nature of this process, realizing that an entire tradition of speech criticism has been built on the qualitative analysis and assessment of public address.

As you criticize the strengths and weaknesses of speeches, keep in mind that your comments will help your classmates develop as speakers. Your remarks will help focus their attention on areas that need improvement as well as on areas that work effectively. All speakers need this feedback to improve the quality of their performance.

Unfortunately, many students feel like stone throwers when they criticize their classmates' speeches. Sometimes this reluctance is tied to camaraderie and self-interest—"Why should I find fault with her speech when I don't want people picking on my speech?" Other times the reluctance is related to a failure or unwillingness to work at listening. Reluctant students do not define rhetorical criticism as a skill in the same way they do public speaking. They do not realize that their success in this course is measured by their ability as a listener and critic as well as a speaker.

Criteria for Evaluating Public Speeches

Use the following guidelines to focus your criticism. These guidelines take the form of ten separate questions that analyze speeches in terms of their component parts. For our purposes here, and throughout the rest of the book, we examine content and

---

18.   William Safire, "No Spot on dean's list for Mr. Clinton," *The Toledo Blade,* January 22, 1993, p.13.
19.   Jeff Greenfield, "Let's Hear more Clinton, not rhetoric," *The Toledo Blade,* January 27, 1993, p. 7.

delivery separately. However, these elements are part of a unified whole that makes up the dynamic process of communication.

1. Was the topic appropriate for the assignment?
2. Were the general and specific purposes of the speech clear?
3. Did the speaker use strong supporting material to present the speech's core idea?
4. Did the speaker use clear, interesting, and accurate language?
5. Did the speaker make an effort to analyze the audience and adapt the speech to its needs?
6. Was the speech effectively organized?
7. Did the speaker appear confident and self-controlled?
8. Was the quality of the speaker's voice acceptable?
9. Were the speaker's movement and gestures meaningful?
10. Did the speaker look for and respond to feedback?

Learn the Art of Criticism

Use these ten questions as a guide as you evaluate your classmates' speeches. As you listen, remember that other members of the audience will be reacting to the speeches along with you. Although you should form your own opinions, you can take cues from your classmates that will tell you whether the speaker has effectively reached the audience.

When you begin to offer criticism, try to be as substantive and concrete as possible. Instead of saying, "She was great," or "I certainly did not like his topic," say, "I liked the way she linked her own experiences as a lifeguard to the need for greater water safety," or "His discussion of the way accounting students are trained was not appropriate for an audience of nonaccounting majors."

Because student speakers are likely to feel vulnerable and defensive in the face of their classmates' criticism, it is important to put them at ease by pointing out first what was right with their speech. Then you can offer suggestions for improving their presentation. Instead of saying, "Your views on the link between electromagnetic fields and cancer were completely unsupported," you might say: "I really enjoyed your explanation of how electromagnetic fields work. Your examples were clear and crisp, especially when you talked about how common electric appliances, including coffee makers, emit potentially dangerous fields. I may have let my mind wander, but I don't think you were as clear when you started talking about how these fields can produce changes in body cells. I suggest you use language and examples in the second portion of your speech that are as helpful as those in the first. While your voice was certainly conversational enough to help me listen with ease, you did not convey the sense of urgency that your topic implied. Although your words told us of possible cancer threats in our homes, your voice told us that there is nothing really to worry

---

Public Speaking Evaluation Form

Speaker_____   Date_____

Topic_____

Purpose (general and specific)

_____

Speech Critic_____

5 — *excellent* **4** — *very good* **3** — *satisfactory* **2** — *fair* **1** — *unsatisfactory*

1. Was the topic appropriate for the assignment?		5 4 3 2 1
2. Was the general and specific purpose of the speech clear?		5 4 3 2 1
3. Did the speaker use strong supporting material to present the speech's core idea?		5 4 3 2 1
4. Did the speaker use clear, interesting, and accurate language?		5 4 3 2 1
5. Did the speaker make an effort to analyze the audience and adapt the speech to its needs?		5 4 3 2 1
6. Was the speech effectively organized?		5 4 3 2 1
7. Did the speaker appear confident and self-controlled?		5 4 3 2 1
8. Was the quality of the speaker's voice acceptable?		5 4 3 2 1
9. Did the speaker's body language create meaning?		5 4 3 2 1
10. Did the speaker look for and respond to feedback?		5 4 3 2 1

Comments

FIGURE 3.3
Using a public speaking evaluation form like this one can help you give a speaker constructive and valuable criticism.

---

about. Also, try to look down at your notes less often. I found this behavior somewhat distracting."

To encourage this type of criticism, many instructors ask students to use a speech evaluation form, similar to that shown in Figure 3.3. Forms like this are used during the speech, and detailed comments are added after the speech is over. Try to provide as much written commentary as possible, for your explanations help speakers improve.

When communication professors Cassandra Book and Katrina Wynkoop Simmons studied the type of speech criticism most helpful to students, they found that students consistently criticized isolated elements of classmates' speeches rather than the overall performance of the speaker and that they used impersonal criticism that was not threatening to the speaker. According to the researchers, this pattern of criticism was perceived as most helpful to the speakers. This student-to-student feedback pattern is similar to that which characterizes student–teacher interactions.[20]

SUMMARY   Good listening skills are important for two reasons. First, by understanding the listening needs of your audience, you have a better chance of developing and delivering successful speeches. Second, an understanding of the factors affecting listening will enable you to monitor your own listening habits and help you evaluate the speeches of others. Studies have shown that although we spend a great deal of time listening, most of us are not good listeners. Listening is a complex activity that involves four separate stages. In stage 1, you sense the information from its source through the physiological process of hearing. In stage 2, you interpret the message by attaching your own meaning to the speaker's words. In stage 3, you evaluate what your hear by judging the worth of the speaker's message and deciding its importance to you. And in stage 4, you respond to the speaker's message through feedback.

You can improve your listening skills by preparing yourself to listen, by minimizing listening barriers, by leaving distractions behind, by not making snap judgments, by listening first for content and second for delivery, by becoming an effective note taker, by being an active listener, and by providing feedback.

In speech class, you will use your listening skills to evaluate the speeches of your classmates. It is important to learn the art of constructive criticism in order to encourage the speaker.

QUESTIONS FOR STUDY AND DISCUSSION

1. What role do our emotions play in listening, and how are they related to our ability to think about and analyze a message? Can we suspend our feelings while listening to a speaker? Why or why not?

2. Why is preparation important in listening? How would you prepare to listen to

    ✻ a speech on a topic about which you have strong, negative feelings?

    ✻ a political campaign speech delivered by a candidate you support?

    ✻ a speech on a crisis that affects your life?

    ✻ a lecture on a topic that interests but does not excite you?

3. From a listener's point of view, what is the relationship between the content and delivery of a speech? How does a dynamic delivery influence your opinion of the speaker's message? Compare this to your reaction to a flat, uninspired delivery.

---

20.   Cassandra Book and Katrina Wynkoop Simmons, "Dimensions and Perceived Helpfulness of Student Speech Criticism," *Communication Education* 29 (May 1980): 135–45.

4. Discuss the art of criticism as it pertains to public speaking. Why do so many people define criticism only in negative terms? Think of several well known public speakers and evaluate the content and delivery of their messages.

1. Attend a lecture, political event, or religious service with the intent of monitoring ACTIVITIES your own listening behavior. What barriers to listening do you notice as you attempt to follow the speaker's message?
2. Listen to a controversial speech in person or on a video cassette. Then, with the stages of listening in mind, jot down your thoughts and feelings at different times in the speech.
3. Write a brief paper (1 to 3 pages) about a successful listening experience. Be certain to explain what made the experience successful for you.
4. Examine the way you take notes in class as well as in other listening situations. Consider your note taking in light of the guidelines provided in this chapter.

"A speaker's honesty is intimately connected with his personal commitment. Neither one can be faked. If a speaker doesn't really believe what he is saying, the audience will sense it . . . . It is foolish, even dangerous, to think we can fool very many people even some of the time. Honesty is not only the best policy, it is the only policy."

From a speech delivered by Rex Kelly, General Manager, Corporate Communications, Mississippi Power Company[1]

THE ETHICS OF RESPONSIBLE SPEECH

*ebster's Ninth New Collegiate Dictionary* defines the term *oxymoron* as "a combination of contradictory or incongruous words, as in *cruel kindness.*" To an increasing number of people, the concept of *public speaking ethics* is an oxymoron, a term so contradictory that it fails to make sense. It is not hard to find reasons for this cynicism, including the following examples from the worlds of politics and the press:

⌘ As Ronald Reagan's press secretary, Larry Speakes on occasion made up statements the president never said. After Reagan met with Mikhail Gorbachev in 1985, for example, Speakes gave reporters the following presidential statement, which was pure fabrication: "There is much that divides us," said Speakes, purportedly quoting the president, "but I believe the world breathes easier because we are talking here together." This deceit was more shocking because of the commitment Speakes had made never to lie to the press.[2]

⌘ When Democrat David Dinkins and Republican Rudolph Giuliani ran for mayor of New York in 1989, neither focused on the problems tearing the city apart: crime, drugs, homelessness, AIDS, and a disturbingly large budget deficit. Instead they spent nearly the entire campaign engaged in a series of personal attacks. The voters learned, for example, how Dinkins had failed to file his income taxes twenty years earlier and how Giuliani neglected to include a cooperative apartment among his list of assets. The losers in this campaign were the voters who rarely heard the candidates talk about the issues.

⌘ A 1993 report on the "Dateline NBC" newsmagazine program alleged that some General Motors pickup trucks had a tendency to explode during collisions. It was later revealed that trucks shown in footage produced for the show had been rigged with incendiary devices to assure footage of an explosion. General Motors Corporation threatened litigation, resulting in the network issuing an on-air statement by journalist Stone Phillips to admit that NBC used the devices without informing the viewers.[3]

In these examples, speakers violated the moral principles and values that define public speaking ethics. By fabricating quotations, being arrogant and dishonest, and failing to deal with the issues of a political campaign, they said, in effect, that truth, integrity, and responsibility to the audience come after their own self-interest. According to Sissela Bok, professor of philosophy and author of *Lying: Moral Choice in Public and Private Life,* the result of these deceptions is the public's loss of trust in speakers and their messages. She uses the following story, told by a

1.   Rex Kelly, "Speakers and the Bottom Line: The Character of the Speaker," speech delivered to the Utility Speakers Activities Committee of the Edison Electric Institute, August 7, 1987. Reprinted in *Vital Speeches of the Day,* November 1, 1987, p. 49.
2.   Hugh Sidey, "Speaking out of Turn," *Time,* April 25, 1988, p. 36.
3.   Alan L. Adler, "GM Says Tests Part of NBC Plan to Poison Opinion." *The Toledo Blade.* February 9, 1993. p. 15.

university president who taught a Sunday school class for adults, to explain this erosion in public confidence:

> In that class there were bankers, business executives, and university professors. This was in the fall of '87, when the Iran-Contra scandal was still unfolding. He [the Sunday school teacher] posed the following question to his class: "We hear on the news that in the Persian Gulf an Iranian ship has sunk. The Iranian Government explains that this was done by American torpedoes. The United States Government says that the ship hit one of the Iranian mines, or perhaps several. Whom do you believe?" And all of these people, some quite conservative, some less so, thought and thought and thought. And finally, not a single one could answer one way or another. They all said that they wanted to hear more of the facts.
>
> Now what that means is that not a single one of those people trusted his own government to tell the truth. People in government sometimes think that this little lie and that little lie, told for short-term advantages, will just pass. But this is the kind of damage that is done in the long run.[4,5]

This erosion of trust in the ethics of speakers affects your presentation in class as much as it does the speeches given by government, political, and civil leaders in public forums. It affects your persuasive and informative speeches. Without an ethical roadmap (based on socially accepted values) to guide you, you might disregard your audience's need for truth, and engage in self-serving deceit, ambiguity, intellectual sloppiness, and emotional manipulation. If you do, your credibility as a speaker is lost as your listeners turn elsewhere for a message—and a speaker—they can trust. Because public speaking is a reciprocal process, audience mistrust can stand in the way of communication.

In this chapter, we emphasize the importance of meeting your ethical responsibilities to your listeners. We begin by examining the distinction between ethics and ethos, then turn to guidelines you can use to chart the ethics of your speeches.

WHAT ARE THE ETHICS OF PUBLIC SPEAKING?

Ethics are the socially accepted standards we use to determine right and wrong, good and evil. We live in a world defined and guided by many public and private ethical systems bound into the cultures in which our communities exist. To the Greek philosopher Aristotle, the study of ethics involved the systematic analysis of the

---

4.   Bill Moyers, *A World of Ideas: Conversations with Thoughtful Men and Women About American Life Today and the Ideas Shaping Our Future* (New York: Doubleday, 1989), p. 239.

5.   For background information on the ethics of public speaking, see S. Bok, *Lying: Moral Choice in Public and Private Life* (New York: Pantheon Books, 1978); Bok, *Secrets: On the Ethics of Concealment and Revelation* (New York; Pantheon Books, 1982); R.L. Johannesen, ed., *Ethics and Persuasion: Selected Readings* (New York: Random House, 1967); Johannesen, "Teaching Ethical Standards for Discourse," *Journal of Education* 162 (1980): 5–20; Johannesen, *Ethics in Human Communication*, 2d ed. (Prospect Heights, IL: Waveland Press, 1983); C.H. Sommers, "Ethics Without Virtue: Moral Education in America," *The American Scholar* 53 (1984): 381–89; L. Thayer, ed., *Ethics, Morality and the Media: Reflections on American Culture* (New York: Hastings House, 1980); R.M. Weaver, *The Ethics of Rhetoric* (Chicago: Regnery, 1953).

FOCUS ON RESEARCH

RICHARD NIXON'S SPEECH ON AMERICAN INVOLVEMENT IN THE WAR IN VIETNAM AND ETHICAL CONSIDERATIONS

In 1968 Richard M. Nixon, who suffered in defeat after losing the 1960 presidential race to John F. Kennedy, arrived at the White House after beating Minnesota Senator Hubert Humphrey. When Mr. Nixon took office, the United States was embroiled in an unpopular and costly war in Vietnam, a so-called "police action" that had become a major issue during the campaign. What should be the policy of the United States about the war in Vietnam? The country was torn by protest. Increasingly, Americans were killing—and dying—for reasons being questioned not only at home but also by the rest of the world. On November 3, 1969, as President of the United States, Richard Nixon delivered a televised address in which he provided his interpretation of the cause of the war, the present state of American as well as South Vietnamese activity, and the policy his administration would follow to achieve American disengagement from the conflict. Essentially he argued that most of the alternatives available to the nation were undesirable and dangerous with the exception of what he called "Vietnamization," a policy in which South Vietnamese soldiers would completely replace American troops according to an unannounced timetable for withdrawal. A number of research articles were published to provide studies of this speech and several of the essays raised serious ethical considerations.

Karlyn Kohrs Campbell, one of the foremost scholars in the field of communication, chose to assess the president's message in terms of criteria she believes were evident in Nixon's speech: truth, credibility, unity, and ethical responsibility. Campbell argued that the criteria suggested by President Nixon were also *violated* by him in a number of ways

and her argument calls attention to the ethics of responsible speech. First, she argued, the speaker did not tell the truth, by misrepresenting reality about the American resistance to the war and the threat of a defeat of South Vietnam by the North. Nixon's argument was that those opposed to the administration's policy were protestors who called for an immediate withdrawal of American forces, an action that would result in far more devastation than the protestors would admit. Campbell reminded her readers that the protestors did not constitute a homogenous group, that other alternatives were offered beside immediate withdrawal, and that most critics asked for a scheduled withdrawal according to an announced timetable. A second misrepresentation she cited was Nixon's assertion that fifteen years before his speech the North Vietnamese, supported by Communist China and the Soviet Union had launched an attack on South Vietnam to impose a communist government on its citizens. Campbell argued that the leader of the South Vietnamese government violated international agreements by avoiding elections to unify the country. She also pointed out that the South Vietnamese regime was supported by the United States. Campbell's study charges that the President failed as a "truth teller". If readers accept her analysis and assessment they have to admit that the White House created an ethical problem in communication.

Campbell also pointed out that the president maintained that his policy of "Vietnamization" was popular and easily supported by a vast, silent majority of citizens. However, the scope and intensity of the national debate at the time clearly indicated that the Nixon policy was not easily supported by most American citizens. A second contradiction she underlined was Nixon's assertion that to withdraw American forces would be to leave the South Vietnamese vulnerable to massacre by enemy forces. Campbell's research indicated that at the time of the speech the South Vietnamese had armed forces exceeding one million while the combined enemy forces totaled 210,000. Campbell contended that if a small army could defeat a much larger force, then the Nixon policy of "Vietnamization" was doomed. Finally, Campbell considered the Nixon speech in light of what she identified as reality rather than myth and charged that the president's message, while calling for unity, really contributed to national division over the war. She argued that the president's speech was a call for ethical responsibility while assigning no moral responsibility to American citizens. Americans were expected by the president simply to accept his credibility and judgment as well as his claim that the responsibility for the war was not due to U.S. actions but to the actions of North Vietnam, Communist China, and the Soviet Union. Campbell's study certainly suggests the United States' involvement in the policies and actions that fueled the war included some moral responsibility for the turmoil in Southeast Asia.

Essentially, then, the analysis of the speech by Richard M. Nixon raises serious ethical questions about whether the president was telling the truth, being credible, and promoting unity and ethical responsibility. The criteria are important to all of us if we choose to speak for the purpose of solving problems while bringing people together. Campbell's study finds the speaker suggested an important criteria he violated himself. While not everyone may be willing to accept the assessment of Professor Campbell, her argument is certainly profound, well developed, and highly appropriate for any consideration of the ethics of responsible speech. You may wish to form your own assessment by reviewing the situation, reading similar studies of Nixon's speech, and studying the speech itself. The speech and these studies can be found in a variety of places including *The Practice of Rhetorical Criticism* 2d edition, by James R. Andrews (Longman, 1990) pp. 91–150. The speech can also be found in *Vital Speeches of the Day,* XXXVI (November 15, 1969) pp. 66–60.[6]

"ultimate problems of human conduct." A. Craig Baird, the late distinguished professor of rhetoric, explains:

> The ultimate problems of human conduct to be studied are chiefly,
>
>   1.   What is the desirable life of the individual?
>
>   2.   What is the desirable end of society?
>
> Ethical inquiries are not so much searching for facts as they are dealing with values. Ethics is concerned not so much with behavior as it exists but as it ought to be. This branch of philosophy attempts to describe the ideal individual and the "good" society. It asks, "What is the highest good of human conduct and what is its ultimate aim?"[7]

---

6.   Karlyn Kohrs Campbell, "An Exercise in the Rhetoric of Mythical America," *Critiques of Contemporary Rhetoric,* Wadsworth Publishing Co. (1972). Reprinted in James R. Andrews' *The Practice of Rhetorical Criticism,* 2nd edition. N.Y: Longman, 1990, 121–126.

7.   A. Craig Baird, *Rhetoric: A Philosophical Inquiry* (New York: The Ronald Press Company, 1965), p. 95.

In contrast, *ethos,* a term Aristotle used in his references to rhetoric, refers to the notion of "ethical appeal." Aristotle defined ethos in terms of the intelligence, character, and goodwill a speaker communicates during a speech:

> Speakers are untrustworthy in what they say or advise from one or more of the following causes. Either through want of intelligence they form wrong opinions; or, while they form correct opinions, their rascality leads them to say what they do not think; or, while intelligent and honest enough, they are not well disposed [to the hearer, audience], and so perchance will fail to advise the best course, though they see it.[8]

Aristotle believed speakers can abuse their ethical relationship with their listeners when they misinterpret information or fail to collect all the information needed to give a complete and fair presentation; and when self-interest leads them to dishonesty and lack of goodwill.

Since Aristotle, scholars have made the distinction between intrinsic ethos and extrinsic ethos. While intrinsic ethos is the ethical appeal found in the actual speech, extrinsic ethos is a speaker's image in the mind of the audience. Both elements contribute to a speaker's credibility. According to communication theorists James C. McCroskey and Thomas J. Young, credibility is tied to the audience's perception of the speaker as an expert, as a person to trust, and as a person with positive and honest intent. These factors have an effect *before* speakers say a word.[9] The speeches you deliver during a semester establish your credibility. Although many students perceive each speech as an isolated exercise, the cumulative impact of each speech affects your credibility. If you take a casual, unprepared approach in your first three speeches, your audience will judge your fourth speech, in part, on the basis of your past performances. You will have a negative reputation to overcome.

The Communication of Values

Inherent in our explanation of public speaking ethics and speaker ethos is the communication of values, socially shared ideas about what is good, right, and desirable. Values propel us to speech and action, motivating much of our behavior. They determine what we consider important and what we ignore, how we regard our listeners, and how we approach the job of researching and developing a speech. Values are communicated through every word speakers say—and fail to say— through delivery, and through responsiveness to audience feedback. Even the titles of speeches reveal what speakers consider important:

> "To Be Conservative"—speech delivered by former conservative Republican Senator Barry M. Goldwater

> "In Pursuit of Equity, Ethics, and Excellence: The Challenge to Close the Gap"—speech delivered by Jesse Jackson to students at Howard University

---

8. Lane Cooper, *The Rhetoric of Aristotle* (New York: Appleton-Century-Crofts, 1960), pp. 91–92.
9. James C. McCroskey and Thomas J. Young, "Ethos and Credibility: The Construct and Its Measurement after Three Decades," *The Central States Speech Journal* 22 (Spring 1981): 24–34.

Freedom of speech provides opportunities to speak publicly with dramatic ethical responsibilities for both the speaker and the audience.

"Health Priorities for the Nineties"—speech delivered by former Surgeon General Antonia C. Novello

Although the link between values and ethics seems natural and inevitable, the two are often disconnected for the sake of expediency. Ethicist Michael Josephson explains why he once viewed values and ethics separately and what ultimately changed his mind:

> I was teaching law, and I was assigned to teach the course of ethics for the first time. You see, after Watergate, this became a mandatory course. . . . Like most law professors, I had not studied ethics myself in law, because that wasn't what I specialized in. I taught that ethics course the first year like I would teach a tax code—how to avoid it, how to evade it, how to see the ambiguities. After all, rules are just restrictions, just limitations. We've got to avoid them. Well, that same year, I had my child. And when I compared how I was approaching teaching ethics to the law students with how I wanted to teach my son ethics, and what I wanted him to be, I saw an enormous inconsistency. My

teaching of ethics to law students was not a value-based enterprise. But I wanted to teach my son values—the value of caring, the value of being trustworthy, the value of trying hard, the value of accountability.

And so you shift how you approach ethics. You think about it. You read about it. And then you make decisions about how you want to behave as a person.[10]

Why is it important to take a value-based approach to public speaking? The power that speakers have to influence public opinion and bring about change has focused attention on the values underlying spoken communication. We have seen how this power has been used to help people and how it has been used to further the speaker's self-interest. Here are two very different examples:

✶ Televangelist Jim Bakker abused the trust of millions of people when he asked for money to do the work of God and used it instead to build a personal fortune.

✶ Using speech rather than violence, Polish President Lech Walesa started a revolution that would ultimately change the face of Eastern Europe by bringing some degree of freedom to those under communist rule.

The value-based approach to public speaking applies equally to students on campus. You can speak out against anti-Semitism or remain silent. You can support, through public rhetoric, the university's right to displace poor families from their university-owned apartments to build another office tower or you can plead for a more humane solution.

ETHICAL GUIDELINES FOR PUBLIC SPEAKERS

Forty years ago rhetorical theorist Karl Wallace urged speakers to develop four habits that would promote ethical communication.[11] Wallace's insight is extremely relevant even today. Communication professor Donald K. Enholm comments on Wallace's "habits" for us:[12]

✶ *the "habit of search"* (that is, for information to confirm or dispute your point of view). We should develop the habit of search, stemming from recognition that, during the moments we are communicating, we are the primary if not the sole source of arguments and information on the subject at hand. Our message should reflect thorough knowledge of our subject, sensitivity to relevant issues and implications, and awareness that most public issues are complex rather than one-sided. As a test of this value, we should ask ourselves: Can I answer directly—without evasion—any relevant question a listener might ask?

---

10. Bill Moyers, *A World of Ideas: Conversations with Thoughtful Men and Women About American Life Today and the Ideas Shaping our Future* (New York: Doubleday, 1989), p. 19.
11. Karl R. Wallace, "An Ethical Basis of Communication," *The Speech Teacher* 4 (1955): 1–9. Cited in Ronald Arnett, "The Status of Communication Ethics Scholarship in Speech Communication Journals from 1915 to 1985," *Central States Speech Journal* (Spring 1987): 44–61.
12. Professor Donald Enholm teaches argumentation, rhetorical theory, and the ethics of persuasion at Bowling Green State University. His views on Wallace's "habits" were contributed April 19, 1993.

⌘ *The "habit of justice"* (be fair and open in your speech). We should cultivate the habit of justice by selecting fact and opinion fairly. The communicator, according to Wallace, should not distort or conceal evidence that the audience would need to justly evaluate the speech. The speaker should avoid substituting emotionally loaded language and guilt by association for sound argument. As a test of this value, we should ask ourselves: In the selection and presentation of materials, am I giving the audience the opportunity to make fair judgments?

⌘ *The "habit of preferring public to private motivation"* (help your audience rather than yourself). Speakers should habitually prefer public to private emotions. Responsible speakers should uniformly reveal the sources of their information and opinion. This will assist the audience in weighing any special bias, prejudices, and self-centered motivations in source materials. As a test question we can ask: Have I concealed information about either my source materials or my own motives which, if revealed, would damage my explanation or argument?

⌘ *The "habit of respect for dissent"* (see different points of view as a challenge, not a threat). Wallace urges us to cultivate the habit or respect for dissent by allowing and encouraging diversity of argument and opinion. A communicator will seek cooperation and compromise where appropriate and justified by conscience. But, Wallace feels we should not sacrifice principle to compromise" and we should "prefer facing conflict to accepting apeasement." He offers as a test question: Can I freely admit the force of opposing evidence and argument and still advocate a position which represents my convictions?

These habits are the foundation for the following guidelines.

Understand the Power of the Lectern

During the early 1950s, Senator Joseph R. McCarthy conducted a "witch hunt" for communists and communist sympathizers in the United States. Robert P. Newman, professor emeritus of rhetoric, explains how McCarthy preyed on fears of growing Soviet power:

> Joe McCarthy was probably the most successful peddler of devil insurance in U.S. history. At a time of great public anxiety, he produced simple and attractive answers to people's fears. The spread of communism in Europe and Asia, early Soviet acquisition of nuclear weapons . . . the arrest and conviction of high-level spies . . . all of these disasters he attributed to one simple cause: treason of the Democrats who has been in power so long. Eliminate these traitors, give his anticommunist crusade the green light, and all would be well. The country was ready for this gospel, and McCarthy had the skills to sell it.[13]

---

13.   Robert P. Newman, "Joseph Raymond McCarthy," in *American Orators of the Twentieth Century,* Bernard K. Duffy and Halford R. Ryan, eds. (Westport, CT: Greenwood Press, 1987), pp. 309–10. Remaining discussion based on pp. 309–15.

During the 1950s,
Senator Joseph
McCarthy conducted a
witch hunt for
communists and
communist supporters
in the United States.

In speech after speech from the Senate floor, McCarthy tried to expose subversives in and out of government. Indifferent to the facts, he charged high government officials with belonging to communist front organizations that sought to overthrow the U.S. government. Among his early targets was Judge Dorothy Kenyon of New York. In testimony before a Senate committee, McCarthy charged that Kenyon belonged to at least twenty-eight organizations with Soviet ties. In reality, Kenyon belonged to only one of the organizations McCarthy had named, the National Council of Soviet-American Friendship. Far from being subversive, the organization had a membership that included four U.S. senators and Albert Einstein.

Despite his lies and innuendo, McCarthy in his heyday was supported by more than half of the American people, as well as many prominent newspapers. The strength of his support made it difficult for critics to discredit his accusations. It took four years for the Senate to censure McCarthy's witch hunt and end his Senate career.

In the process, the reputations and careers of thousands of people were damaged—some irreparably—by McCarthy's attacks.

Although the McCarthy era occurred more than forty years ago, its lesson is valid today: *Through public speaking we wield enormous power for good—and for evil.* By taking advantage of people's fears, by using dramatic oratory, by manipulating facts, by lying, and by accusing critics of disloyalty, we can violate the ethics of responsible speech. Although few of us will have Senator McCarthy's position of influence, all public speakers have the power to persuade and the power to pass on information—powers that must be used for the common good.

Analyzing the common good is often complicated, for analysis often must be based, in part, on the needs of the situation. You may choose, for example, *not* to speak out against campus racism if your statement would compromise behind-the-scenes negotiations between African-American and white students and the college administration. Tempering your stand does not mean you have compromised your ethics, but that you are allowing others to help achieve your goal.

Speakers exercise the power of the podium for good causes on American campuses across the country. Speakers at Harvard, the University of Texas at Austin, and New York's Brooklyn College are protesting racism, sexism, and anti-Semitism. At Harvard, for example, student speakers protested the university's lack of commitment to the African-American studies department.[14] As a speaker, your goal is not to avoid controversy, but to deal with it in a responsible, ethical way.

Speak Truthfully and Be Certain of Your Facts

Whenever you speak before an audience, it is your ethical responsibility to be certain of your facts. If you present material as true when it is not, you will mislead your listeners and, in the process, diminish your credibility. When your listeners realize your facts are wrong, they will trust you less. If, for example, during a speech on campus thefts, you blame nonstudents for the majority of crimes when, in fact, most thefts are committed by students, you will lose credibility with listeners who have knowledge of the facts.

Too often we hear experienced, well known speakers—including presidents—present inaccurate statements. No one would deny, for example, former President Reagan's ability to reach the soul of the nation through his rhetoric. One story Reagan told involved a World War II Medal of Honor winner:

> The young ball-turret gunner was wounded, and they couldn't get him out of the B-17 turret there while flying . . . . . The last man to leave saw the commander sit down on the floor. He took the boy's hand and said, "Never mind, son, we'll ride it down together." Congressional Medal of Honor posthumously awarded.[15]

---

14.   "Dashed Hopes at Harvard," *Newsweek,* May 14, 1990, p. 56.
15.   Bob Schieffer and Gary Paul Gates, *The Acting President* (New York: E.P. Dutton, 1989), p. 178.

President Reagan confused facts and film. This is a scene from 20th Century Fox's *A Wing and a Prayer.*

The trouble was that when a newspaper reporter sifted through the files of all 434 World War II Medal of Honor winners, he could never find the man behind Reagan's story. He did find *A Wing and a Prayer,* a 1944 movie which included a Hollywood version of Reagan's account.[16] Although we will never know whether the former president purposely crossed the line between fact and fiction, it is certain that he did not check the accuracy of his comments—a mistake that put his listeners in the position of believing a story that wasn't true.

The audience believed the president's story because it was linked to its beliefs and values—a connection Reagan undoubtedly understood. Although as a speaker you can move your audience with false accounts, you must always ask the question of whether the end justifies the means.

We all rely on such secondary sources as books, newspapers, and news magazines for facts. When using these sources, it is your responsibility to be alert

16.   Ibid.

for inconsistencies, oversimplifications, and mistakes. If you have any doubt that these exist, read the editorial page in newspapers and magazines for retractions and corrections. The more research you do on your speech, the more likely it is that you will catch these mistakes and be able to correct them before passing them on to others.

Avoid Rumors and Innuendo.   It is also your ethical responsibility to avoid basing your speech on rumors. Rumors are unproven charges, usually about an individual, that are often untrue. By using them as facts, you can tarnish—or ruin—a reputation and convey misleading information to your audience.

Despite the negative implications of rumor mongering, political candidates sometimes spread rumors as they give speeches. During the 1988 presidential campaign, for example, George Bush was accused of having had an extramarital affair—a baseless rumor that caused the stock market to plunge more than twenty points in a temporary reaction. Rumors also spread about the state of Michael Dukakis' mental health. He was falsely accused of having received psychiatric treatment after his brother died in a hit-and-run automobile accident, an accusation that became more believable when President Reagan commented in a news conference that he was "not going to pick on an invalid," referring to Dukakis.

It is also ethically unacceptable to use innuendo to support a point. Hints or remarks that something is what it is not are veiled lies. President Eisenhower echoed these sentiments more than thirty years ago when in his final State of the Union address, he said: "We live in a storm of semantic disorder in which old labels no longer faithfully describe . . . . . We must use language to enlighten the mind, not as an instrument of the studied innuendo and distorter of truth. And we must live by what we say."[17]

George Wallace, once the segregationist governor of Alabama who ran for president on the American Independent party ticket in 1968, was a master of innuendo, especially when it came to arousing fears among whites about what the 1964 Civil Rights Law would *not* do. Wallace claimed, for example, that according to Title XI of the Act, civil rights violators would be thrown in jail without benefit of a jury trial. He warned:

> Remember all these things will be enforced without a trial by jury. And the folks who talk about civil rights—everybody believes in civil rights because they are guaranteed in the Constitution of the United States—these liberals and left-wingers they don't want you to have a jury trial.[18]

What Wallace failed to make clear is that the Civil Rights Act guaranteed trial by jury for anyone accused of a criminal violation, but not contempt of court. Further, except

---

17.   Richard E. Crable, "Dwight David Eisenhower," in *American Orators of the Twentieth Century: Critical Studies and Sources,* Bernard K. Duffy and Halford R. Ryan, eds. (Westport, CT: Greenwood Press, 1987), p. 119.

18.   John J. Makay, "The Rhetoric of George C. Wallace and the 1964 Civil Rights Law," *Today's Speech* 18 (Fall 1970).

I N T E R V I E W

Gerry Tausch
Co-owner,
The Speaker's
Connection

The Speaker's Connection Global Program Bureau, in Sarasota, Florida, is one of the nation's most widely used speakers bureaus. We asked Gerry Tausch, co-owner of The Speaker's Connection and a highly successful speaker as well, to discuss public speaking. We were particularly interested in how she views image and credibility as factors for a speaker's success. Early in this chapter we discuss the importance of ethos and credibility in a speaker's appeal to an audience. Mrs. Tausch talks about a speaker's image and credibility with regard to the appeal of a professional speaker. Today the term *image* is often used to describe the perception audiences have of the integrity, intelligence, goodwill, and communication skills of a speaker. The highly credible speaker with a positive image in the eyes of an audience is a speaker the listeners judge to be an ethical communicator. Mrs. Tausch also offers some important words about confidence and motivation to encourage us to work at becoming effective speakers.

Question: How would you describe *image* and *credibility* as factors for success for the speakers who work with your bureau?

Answer: Image is everything about us that makes a statement whether we want it to or not. Whether it is our voice, our appearance, or our choice of words, it all contributes to the overall impression we create. Image and credibility, as a matter of fact, provide powerful appeals to the audiences we face.

Question: I know that the speakers who work with you are authorities in their fields or professions. How does their expertise play a part in the selection of them for a speaking engagement?

Answer: It plays a tremendous part. We wouldn't accept Madonna or Phyllis Diller as newscasters, providing us with the evening news, because we would not assign to them the credibility or authority we would to Tom Brokaw or Peter Jennings. Those who select speakers are looking for expertise and authoritative speakers and they want an important message delivered in an interesting fashion.

Question: You seem to be implying that image, credibility, and delivery of nonverbal communication are interrelated. Am I right?

Answer: Yes. I think if a speaker gets up to address an audience and is not paying attention to his or her body language and appearance then the speaker is talking to himself or herself. For speakers I think the most important thing is to try to eliminate as many barriers as possible between yourself and your audience. I find, for instance, that when I have to speak from behind a lectern I do it. But the best connections I have had with an audience were when I have been able to use a battery pack mike and a clip so that I can move more freely and get close to the audience as I speak. I realize that environmental factors play a role in whether or not a speech is a success and sometimes we have little control over what we find when we stand before an audience to speak.

Question: In closing, let me ask how you would advise students about taking a class in public speaking?

Answer: I would advise students that public speaking is one of the most important courses offered in colleges. Why? Because everyone needs to learn to communicate well, both for personal and professional fulfillment. Through developing public speaking skills, you can learn to formulate your thoughts and messages, you can acquire discipline to formulate and implement well-developed plans of action, and, certainly one of the greatest benefits is your increased self-confidence. This naturally grows as you learn to be an effective communicator. I would also want to remind a student who is worried about speech "nerves," or has a fear of "seeming stupid,"

that all such concerns can be eliminated through speech education, commitment, practice, and experience. No one, in the history of the world, was ever an outstanding public speaker without first developing the necessary skills. As Emerson so aptly said, "All good speakers were, at one time, poor speakers." Students need to remember this when listening to a platform "pro" who seems highly confident, well organized, and polished. While many of us who have made a major personal investment of time and energy now command significant platform fees, each of us started out with similar worries to yours, the dry mouth, shaking knees and ice-cold hands. At first we may have faltered, felt nerve-racked, and felt sure we appeared inept. But one of the greatest thrills in life is overcoming such self-perceptions and moving out of one's personal comfort zone and into the exciting arena of personal challenge where life's real action and rewards await us.

in rare situations, contempt of court cases had never been subject to jury trials in federal, state, or local courts. Ironically, even Wallace's home state of Alabama offered no such jury trial guarantee.

Be Willing to Rock the Boat

Speaking in support of the public good implies a willingness to air a diversity of opinions, even when these opinions are unpopular. According to professor of communication, Roderick P. Hart, we must "accept boat-rocking, protests, and free speech as a necessary and desirable part of [our] tradition."[19] Your goal as a speaker should be to encourage the "ideal of the best ideas rising to the surface of debate."[20]

Despite the stature of free speech in Western society, taking an unpopular stand at the podium is not easy, especially when the speaker faces the threat of repercussions. Let's look at an example:[21]

Roger Boisjoly is an aerospace engineer with twenty years experience working on National Aeronautics and Space Administration (NASA) projects. In 1985

---

19.   Roderick P. Hart, "The Politics of Communication Studies: An Address to Undergraduates," *Communication Education* 34 (1985): 162.
20.   Ronald Arnett, "The Status of Communication Ethics Scholarship in Speech Communication Journals from 1915–1985," *Central States Speech Journal* (Spring 1987): 46.
21.   Whistle-blower," *Life,* March 1988, pp. 19–22.

Boisjoly warned his employer, Morton Thiokol, Inc., that the O-rings on the space shuttle *Challenger* would not work if the temperature at launch was too low. The day before the *Challenger* launch, with meteorologists predicting a nighttime temperature as low as 18°F, Boisjoly joined thirty-three other engineers and administrators in a teleconference linkup with NASA. After a two-hour heated discussion, the decision was made to scrap the launch because of the cold weather—a decision that was overruled by Morton Thiokol's top management.

After the explosion took the lives of the seven *Challenger* astronauts, Boisjoly told an investigatory commission about Thiokol's failure to heed early warning signs that pointed to the vulnerability of the O-rings. As he explains, his testimony changed his life:

> People I respected and trusted told me I would be a major player in the redesign effort. But [less than four months after the crash] I sensed that I was being isolated from NASA. When I made a technical presentation . . . for the first time in six years nobody questioned a single thing I said. Just total silence. It was devastating.
>
> The five of us who testified called ourselves the lepers. There was a tremendous morale breakdown at [Morton Thiokol]. We were getting blamed for it, though it was the company itself that pushed the self-destruct button. One guy actually went up to a colleague who testified and said, "You're ruining this company—and if it goes down the drain, I'm going to drop my kids on your front doorstep."

Although Boisjoly left his job one year after the *Challenger* explosion due to poor health, he believes that what he did in speaking the truth both before and after the disaster was right. He explains:

> If those with information don't bring it forth, how are you ever going to stop accidents from occurring again? I am not a loose cannon trying to get even with anybody—I keep speaking out because the space program is very important. I just can't stand to see crummy engineering.

Although the circumstances are extreme, this example demonstrates the need to place the interests of the group ahead of the interests of the individual. As a public speaker you may face this ethical test. Here are two examples:

⌘ You have just been offered the job on the public relations staff of a tobacco company. Although the money and benefits are good, you decide to turn the job down because it would require that you deliver speeches minimizing the dangers of smoking.

⌘ As the newly elected president of the student body, you are upset at how apathetic your classmates seem to be. Instead of being involved in social and intellectual issues (you keep remembering your mother's stories about the student protests of the 1960s), most students spend their spare time going to parties and drinking beer. Although it is unpopular to attack this social pattern, you feel obligated to make a statement. You decide to do so in your inaugural address.

In your analysis of the common good, never ignore the needs of minorities. It is appropriate to reject a program that suits the needs of the majority if minorities will suffer because of it. Thus, speaking in support of white supremacist students who want the university's African-American studies department abolished is as wrong today as speaking in support of segregated schools was in the 1950s.

Do the Ends Justify the Means?

Do the ends justify the means for a public speaker? Read the following example and decide.

Like many suburban communities throughout America, your community is in the grip of a severe real estate recession. Hundreds of homes are on the market but few people are buying. This problem is particularly difficult for real estate agents. You and dozens of other agents can no longer make a living and may be forced to leave the field unless conditions improve.

In order to attract potential home buyers to your community, you decide to give a series of speeches in a nearby city extolling the virtues of suburban life. Although much of what you say is true, you bend some facts to make your community seem more attractive. For example, you tell your listeners there are jobs for them in suburbia when, in fact, the job market is very small. (The rosy employment figures you mention are ten years old.) You tell them that the community schools are among the best in the state when, in fact, only one out of five community schools is ranked above the state average. With your goal of restoring your community to its former economic health, you feel justified in this manipulation.

In this case, though your intentions were good, your ethics were faulty. No matter how great your need to convince people to support your point of view, you have only one ethical choice: to present the strongest possible *legitimate* argument and let each listener decide whether to support your position.

Speakers who adopt an end-justifies-the-means philosophy usually do so for one of the following reasons:[22]

They believe that only they know best.   But you should remember that if your argument is sound, chances are good that you will be able to convince your audience to support your point of view.

They believe their audience lacks the knowledge to be persuaded by the truth.   If this premise were true, persuasion should start with education, not manipulation or deceit.

They believe that deceit is the only way to overcome the strength of the opposition.   A strong opposition may be a signal that your point of view is flawed (or it could be that you are the only one who understands the issues).

---

22. Bert E. Bradley, *Fundamentals of Speech Communication,* 5th ed. (Dubuque, IA: William C. Brown, 1988), p. 49.

When too many people feel differently from the way you do, it may be time to examine your premise.

They believe that the other speakers have a greater ability to persuade the audience.   Truth will prevail over falsehood only if you have the skill to present it. So if the other speakers are more persuasive than you are, your goal should be to improve your presentation skills, not deceive your listeners.

Avoid Excessive and Inappropriate Emotional Appeals

Aristotle believed that the speaker's first responsibility is to present ideas through sound evidence and reasoning, not through excessive and inappropriate appeals to emotions. To be ethical, emotional appeals must be built on a firm foundation of reason and should never be used to take advantage of susceptible listeners. (We examine the nature of emotional appeals in Chapter Fifteen.) Here are four circumstances when emotional appeals are especially troublesome.[23]

1.   *When your speech creates a need in your listeners and requires a response that will benefit you.*   It is manipulative and unethical to try to convince a group of parents that the only way their children will succeed in school is to buy the set of encyclopedias you are selling. Your speech takes advantage of the love of these parents for their children and their desire to see them succeed.

       An emotional appeal can benefit you and your listeners at the same time. If, as a new physician in a community, you deliver an emotion-filled lecture on the problems you've seen when preventive medical care is ignored, your appeal is ethical despite the fact that some audience members decide to use you as their personal physician.

2.   *When the emotional appeal is made when your listeners are susceptible to manipulation.*   If during a financial planning seminar for recent widows, you prey on the widows' fear of poverty ("If you don't follow the strategy I suggest, you will lose all the money your husband left you"), you are taking advantage of people too vulnerable to evaluate your presentation. According to *The New York Times* columnist Anthony Lewis, New York Governor Mario Cuomo used an unethical emotional appeal to a vulnerable audience when he addressed a dinner of the United Jewish Appeal on the subject of U.S. policy toward Israel. According to Cuomo, at the 1990 summit between George Bush and Mikhail Gorbachev, the presidents agreed "that the emigration of Jews from the Soviet Union to Israel might be contained or limited." This statement was "pure demagogic invention," said Lewis, intended to arouse the worst fears in those concerned with the survival of Russian Jews.[24]

---

23.   Jo Sprague and Douglas Stuart, *The Speaker's Handbook,* 3d ed. (Fort Worth: Harcourt Brace Jovanovich, 1992), p. 292.

24.   Anthony Lewis, "Cuomo Fumbles in His Speech on U.S.–Israel," *Democrat and Chronicle* (Rochester, NY), June 20, 1990, p. 8A.

3. *When emotional appeals are part of a sustained plan to confuse an audience and make them feel insecure and helpless.* If, as a community leader, you oppose the effort to establish group homes for the retarded by referring repeatedly to the threat the retarded pose to neighborhood children, you leave your listeners feeling vulnerable and frightened. The fear of your listeners is so great that they cannot hear the truth when others explain that retarded people in group homes are neither violent nor emotionally disturbed.

4. *When you realize that your logic will not hold up under scrutiny and you appeal to audience emotions to disguise the deficit.* Instead of relying on the facts to convince your listeners, you appeal to their emotional needs. This tactic can be accomplished in several unethical ways:[25]

Name Calling. Former Washington, DC, Mayor Marion Barry used name calling after he was indicted on fourteen criminal counts, including three felony charges of lying under oath to a federal grand jury and misdemeanors for possession of cocaine. Barry, a Democrat, labelled his accusers racists. He charged them with being part of a white conspiracy to refuse to tolerate black power.

When a word such as "racist" is used as Barry used it, the purpose may be emotional manipulation. Speakers who resort to name calling do so to hide a weakness in their ability to convince their listeners—through reasoning and logic—to support their point of view.

Glittering Generalities. During the 1988 presidential campaign, George Bush gave many speeches identifying himself with the American flag, the pledge of allegiance, and patriotism. As the campaign progressed, the flag became Bush's symbol of the America he would help build if he became president. In the process, Bush's appeal to patriotism drew attention away from the real issues facing this country: the budget deficit, education, and the balance of trade. When generalities are used to spread the aura of an abstract virtue like patriotism over unconnected issues or over the speaker himself, the speaker is attempting to sway the audience through emotional appeals that have little to do with rational arguments about unresolved issues. Although acceptable to talk about patriotism, manipulating the audience's response so that critical judgments are clouded in other areas is unethical.

Testimonials. When Jane Fonda protested America's involvement in Vietnam, she used her status as a movie star to generate support for her antiwar position. So did Marlon Brando when he spoke in support of the Native Americans. Although both speakers may have used sound reasoning in their speeches, the audiences responded first to their movie star status and second to the credibility of their remarks. Testimonials outside of the person's area of expertise manipulate the audience by

25. List from Alfred McClung Lee and Elizabeth Briant Lee, *The Art of Propaganda* (New York: Harcourt, Brace and Company and Institute for Propaganda Analysis, 1939), pp. 23–24; cited in Sprague and Stuart, pp. 324–26.

taking advantage of emotional reactions to the speaker. If you are well known for your expertise in one area but have been asked to speak on an unrelated topic, you can minimize this reaction by acknowledging at the start what you know and what you don't about the topic and the reasons you were chosen to speak. During a classroom speech, don't call yourself an expert if you have little experience with a subject. Instead, cite the opinions of recognized experts with the credentials to back up their positions.

Plain Folks.   Beware when a speaker tells an audience, "Believe me because I'm just like you," for the speaker's agenda may not be what it seems. Speakers who present themselves as "plain folks" may be building an identification with their audience—something speakers often want to do—or they may be manipulating their listeners to support a position that has no validity. Using this technique, speakers often make a distinction between the common sense of the audience and the hare-brained reasoning of experts.[26] Here is an example of how this manipulation works:

> I'm here because I believe what you do: Despite what those fancy psychologists say, there are times when a good spanking is the only thing that will teach a child to behave.
>
> We've all heard enough talk about building kids' self-esteem through praise and rewards. That's fine when it works. But anyone who has been a parent knows that there are times when you can talk yourself blue in the face but your child still won't listen. Then I say, it's time to teach them a lesson with a good spanking.
>
> As parents, we're all in the same boat. Let's decide together that we have the right and the authority to remain in charge.

As you can see, the speaker didn't use facts to support her argument; she relied on an anti-intellectual stance and the psychological ploy that "plain folks know best."

Bandwagoning.   Few of us are comfortable taking a position no one else supports. Realizing this reluctance, unethical speakers may convince their listeners to support their point of view by telling them that "everyone else" is already involved. In an attempt to organize a campus rally against paying Oliver North to speak on campus (in your view, North broke the law and should not be paid for an appearance), you tell your listeners that you already have five hundred signatures on an anti-North petition when you have only twenty. No matter the merit of your position, your bandwagoning is unethical.

Bandwagoning can influence speakers as well. When speakers feel their positions have little support, they may be tempted to abandon their convictions in order to be accepted by the group. Or they may privately question a claim, but stop pursuing the truth because of the presence of a consensus. Bandwagoning that affects speakers curtails—and sometimes derails—the inventive nature of rhetoric.

As a speaker, you should try to convince others on the weight of the facts—not on the popularity of your opinion.

---

26.   Sprague and Stuart, p. 281.

GIVE CREDIT WHERE CREDIT IS DUE

Henry Ford II was never graduated from Yale because he hired someone to write his thesis instead of writing it himself. (His deception came to light when he forgot to remove the ghostwriter's bill.) As head of the Ford Motor Company, he returned to Yale years later to give a speech. When he stumbled over a line in the script, he said, "I didn't write this one, either."[27]

When Senator Joe Biden was running for president in 1987, he stole the words of British Labor Party leader Neil Kinnock as his closing statement of a debate. He used Kinnock's words again in a tape he made three days later for the National Education Association. In neither case did he give Kinnock credit. Nor did he credit the late Robert Kennedy or Hubert Humphrey for the words he took from them in other speeches. Despite his competent performance in the Senate, Biden lost all hope of winning the Democratic nomination when his plagiarism was revealed.[28]

Whether you are a corporate leader, a presidential candidate, or a student taking an introductory public speaking course, the temptation to use the words of others can be strong, especially if you are under the pressure of a deadline to complete your assignment. Before you succumb, realize the seriousness of what you are doing:

Implications for Your Audience
Your audience expects to hear your ideas in your own words. When you plagiarize, you are deceiving your listeners.

Implications for the Person Whose Words You Plagiarized
Legally and ethically, when you use someone else's material, the source deserves credit. If enough material is involved, the law requires that you request permission for use and, if necessary, pay a usage fee.

Implications for You
If your audience finds out that you are a plagiarist, your credibility will be diminished. Plagiarism robs you of the opportunity to communicate your own thoughts in your own words and to grow intellectually as a result of your efforts.

It is not wrong to use the ideas or even the words of others if you give the sources credit in your presentation. By using quotation marks ("And I quote. . . . End quote") or vocal pauses indicating the beginning or end of a quotation, you tell your audience that an idea belongs to someone else.

It is also acceptable to use the services of a speechwriter when you reach a position of power and authority. No one expects the president of the United States to write all of his own speeches. Nor do we expect corporate leaders like Lee Iacocca to do so. But we do expect the speaker to work with the speechwriter so that the speaker is not merely mouthing the writer's words. What you say to an audience—even when the words are written by someone else—must be what you believe.

We expect that speeches given by local civic leaders are the products of the speakers' own efforts and that every speech delivered in a public speaking course contains the original words and ideas of the speaker. By buying a speech and presenting it as your own, you deceive your audience just as surely as Joe Biden did when he ran for president.

---

27. Ari Posner, "The Culture of Plagiarism," *The New Republic,* April 18, 1988, p. 20.
28. "Biden's Familiar Quotations," *Time,* September 28, 1987, p. 17.

Use Credible Sources

There is no difficulty in calling yourself an expert. Just hang out a shingle and proclaim your status. Unfortunately, the world is filled with charlatans who promote themselves as experts despite their lack of training or knowledge. In some cases, they may have a professional background but engage in sloppy research. When collecting supporting material for a speech, it is your ethical responsibility to determine whether you are quoting a professional who has done a professional research job or someone with less credibility. Often you can find this deceit out by digging a little deeper at the library.

Suppose, for example, in gathering material for a speech on women's attitudes toward men, you come across a book called *Women and Love: A Cultural Revolution in Progress* by Shere Hite. The findings of this book, based on a survey Hite sent out to 100,000 women in forty-three states, reveal women's extreme dissatisfaction with men. Hite asserts that seven of ten respondents who have been married more than ten years reported extramarital affairs. Fewer than one in five considered their relationship to be the central focus of their lives, she writes.

If you simply took Hite at her word and reported these results in a speech, you would be passing on flawed data. Although Hite couched her survey in precise, scientific terms, her critics reveal that her conclusions were baseless. By analyzing critical reactions to Hite's book, you would find that her survey was biased because of the small percentage of women who answered it. Only 4,500 of the 100,000 questionnaires were returned—a response rate considered unacceptably low. One way to be sure that you are presenting credible material is to research it thoroughly. In a case like this, you would have found critical journal and magazine articles that would make it impossible for you to take Hite at her word.

You can ensure credibility by preferring certain sources over others. For example, if you are researching a speech on the need for college students to update vaccinations against early childhood diseases with booster shots, an article in *New England Journal of Medicine* or *Science* would be preferable to an article in *Newsweek* or *Time*. Although the latter popular publications are generally reliable, scientific journals are the better source for this kind of information.

Never Try to Be Purposefully Ambiguous

If you are writing a speech on how far men have come in the past decade in sharing home and child care responsibilities with their wives, it is ambiguous and misleading to tell your audience this:

> Men are doing more today than ever before. Today's husband is in the kitchen along with his wife, preparing meals and keeping house. He is changing more diapers, doing more laundry, and reading more bedtime stories to the children. And in most homes, he still takes out the garbage.

Although your statements are true, you have omitted a few essential details that would cloud the accuracy of your comments. A less ambiguous version would add:

> Despite this transformation, research has shown that the average American working woman puts in roughly fifteen more hours of work each week than her husband. According to Arlie Hochschild, a sociologist at the University of California at Berkeley, women still do far more housework and child care than men. In a survey of couples in the San Francisco area, Hochschild found that only 18 percent of the men share housework equally with their wives while more than three out of five say they do little or nothing at home.[29]

Ambiguity often takes the form of oversimplification. Sometimes speakers eliminate details from their speeches supposedly to make it easier for their listeners to understand their messages—or at least that's their claim. But oversimplification may represent the speaker's attempt to control audience opinion. When details can make a difference in audience perception, it is your responsibility to present as complete a picture as possible.

Is ambiguity in pursuit of a rhetorical point fair? The answer is no, if the result is a distortion of the truth. Do speakers make ambiguous statements to prove their points? Yes, all the time. Just listen to a candidate at a political rally and you will hear ambiguous statements. A mayoral candidate, for example, may promise to hire hundreds of additional police officers and to increase social services for the poor while hedging on the issue of how the city will pay for these programs.

Your obligations as a speaker are clear: you should avoid ambiguity if it compromises your ethical responsibilities to your listeners. When giving speeches in class, choose your words carefully to communicate your point. Realize, for example, that references to "hazing abuses" may connote, in the minds of some listeners, images of death and bodily injury, while other listeners may think of harmless fraternity pranks. Ambiguities often stem from inadequate or sloppy research. Speakers who do not take the time to find out the facts may try to disguise their failure through ambiguous language.

Choose Current Sources

What do you do when you find supporting material to buttress your argument but realize it is out of date? Do you use it and fail to call attention to the problem or do you discard it and hope to find more current sources?

Suppose, for example, that you are giving a persuasive speech advocating the one couple-one child population control policy adopted in China during the 1970s. This policy was the Chinese government's attempt to lower the nation's exploding birth rate by rewarding couples who limited their family to one child and imposing

---

29. Jim Miller, "Women's Work Is Never Done," *Newsweek,* July 31, 1989, p. 65.

negative sanctions on couples with more than one child. (Positive and negative sanctions are given—or taken away—in the form of monthly bonuses, free health care, priority placement for housing and schooling, pension benefits, and so on.) It is your position that this policy makes sense, considering the survival needs of the roughly 1.1 billion Chinese. What you fail to mention are the changes you discovered while reading recent research. Although the Chinese are still attempting to control their population, these newer sources make clear that in the past several years enforcement has eased in many parts of China, and many couples voluntarily are deciding to limit their family size. By delivering this speech without mentioning the shifts in government policy and personal attitudes, you are misleading your listeners.[30]

With change a pervasive fact of life, old facts are often wrong facts, especially in such volatile social issues as population control. But the need for currency is also true for politics, economics, science, medicine, art—nearly every aspect of our society. Rely on the most recent data bases when you conduct your research. If you find evidence that undermines your position, be honest enough to evaluate it fairly and change your position if you must. Throughout this process, keep in mind your ethical obligation to your listeners to present accurate information.

USE THESE GUIDELINES TO ENGAGE IN A DIALOGUE WITH YOUR AUDIENCE

To speech communication Professor Richard L. Johannesen, certain clear signs indicate speaker sensitivity to ethical issues. The least sensitive speakers, says Johannesen, engage in a "monologue." They view the audience as an object to be manipulated and, in the process, display such qualities as deception, superiority, exploitation, dogmatism, domination, insincerity, pretense, coercion, distrust, and defensiveness—qualities Johannesen considers unethical. He explains:

> Focus is on the speaker's message, not on the audience's real needs. . . . Audience feedback is used only to further the speaker's purpose; an honest response from receivers is not wanted or is precluded. Often choices are narrowed and consequences obscured.

In contrast, sensitive speakers engage in a "dialogue" that demonstrates an honest concern for the welfare of their listeners. Their speech communicates trust, mutual respect and acceptance, open-mindedness, equality, empathy, directness, lack of pretense, and nonmanipulative intent—qualities Johannesen considers inherently ethical.

"Although the speaker in dialogue may offer advice or express disagreement, he does not aim to psychologically coerce an audience into accepting his view," explains Johannesen. "The speaker's aim is one of assisting the audience in making independent, self-determined decisions."[31]

---

30. See Nicholas D. Kristoff, "More in China Willingly Rear Just One Child," *The New York Times,* May 9, 1990, p. A1.
31. Richard L. Johannesen, "Attitude of Speaker Toward Audience: A Significant Concept for Contemporary Rhetorical Theory and Criticism," *Central States Speech Journal* (Summer 1974): 95.

In 1972, the Speech Communication Association endorsed a *Credo For Free and Responsible Communication in a Democratic Society.* This statement still serves as the association's ethical guide.[32] Although the credo is intended to apply to instructors of communication, its message linking free speech and ethics is meaningful to all public speakers. In part, the credo says:

THE LINK BETWEEN FREE SPEECH AND ETHICAL SPEECH

> We accept the responsibility of cultivating by precept and example, in our classrooms and in our communities, enlightened uses of communication; of developing in our students a respect for precision and accuracy in communication, and for reasoning based upon evidence and a judicious discrimination among values.

Thus, each speaker has an ethical responsibility to communicate accurately, to use sound reasoning, and to decide what is best said and not said based on well-thought-out values. This responsibility, combined with the privilege of free speech, is at the very heart of our democratic system.

Johannesen in his text, *Ethics in Human Communication,* lists eleven means that he has culled from a variety of texts, all of which advise against unethical practices:

1. Do not use false, fabricated, misrepresented, distorted, or irrelevant evidence to support arguments or claims.

2. Do not intentionally use unsupported, misleading, or illogical reasoning.

3. Do not represent yourself as informed or as an "expert" on a subject when you are not.

4. Do not use irrelevant appeals to divert attention or scrutiny from the issue at hand. Among the appeals that commonly serve such a purpose are "smear" attacks on an opponent's character—appeals to hatred and bigotry, derogatory insinuations—innuendos, God and Devil terms that cause intense but unreflective positive or negative reactions.

5. Do not ask your audience to link your idea or proposal to emotion-laden values, motives, or goals to which it actually is not related.

6. Do not deceive your audience by concealing your real purpose, by concealing self-interest, by concealing the group you represent, or by concealing your position as an advocate of a viewpoint.

7. Do not distort, hide, or misrepresent the number, scope, intensity, or undesirable features, consequences, or effects.

8. Do not use "emotional appeals" that lack a supporting basis of evidence or reasoning, or that would not be accepted if the audience had time and opportunity to examine the subject themselves.

---

32. Entire credo reprinted in Peter E. Kane, "Legal Constraints on Communication," in Gerald M. Phillips and Jilia T. Wood, eds, *Speech Communication: Essays To Commemorate the 75th Anniversary of the Speech Communication Association,* Carbondale, Il: Southern Illinois University Press, 1990, p. 254.

9. Do not oversimplify complex, gradation-laden situations into simplistic two-valued, either-or, polar views or choices.

10. Do not pretend certainty where tentativeness and degrees of probability would be more accurate.

11. Do not advocate something in which you do not believe yourself.[33]

SUMMARY   Because of the many ethical abuses that have taken place in recent years, audiences are skeptical about the ethics of public speakers. According to Aristotle, speakers abuse their ethical relationship with their listeners in two basic ways: (1) when they misinterpret information or fail to collect all the information to give a complete and fair presentation; (2) when self-interest leads to dishonesty and lack of goodwill.

Public speaking ethics are anchored in the values of the speaker, his or her audience, and the larger society. It is important to take a value-based approach to public speaking because of the power speakers have to influence public opinion and bring about change.

The following guidelines are offered to help you define your ethics as a public speaker:

Understand the power of the podium.

Speak truthfully and be certain of your facts.

Be willing to rock the boat.

Never allow the ends to justify the means.

Avoid excessive and inappropriate emotional appeals.

Use credible sources.

Never try to be purposefully ambiguous.

Choose current sources.

According to Richard L. Johannesen, ethical speakers engage in a "dialogue" with their audience, communicating qualities such as trust and directness, while unethical speakers engage in a "monologue" as they manipulate their audience to their own end.[34]

QUESTIONS FOR
STUDY AND
DISCUSSION

1. How would you define the ethical responsibilities of public speakers?
2. Can you think of speakers not mentioned in this chapter who have behaved ethically or unethically in addressing an audience?
3. What do you believe is the ethical relationship between self-interest and the needs and interests of the audience?

---

33. Richard L. Johannesen, *Ethics in Human Communication*. 3d ed., Prospect Heights: Waveland Press, 1990. 256. Used with permission.
34. Johannesen, "Attitude," 95.

4. What is the connection between truth and ethics in public speaking?
5. Are there differences between lying and deception, and are there instances to justify a speaker doing either before an audience?

1. Select a written or recorded speech and critically analyze it in terms of the ethics **ACTIVITIES** of responsible speech.
2. Select a speaker you believe possesses considerable ethical appeal. Based on a speech the speaker has delivered, write a brief paper analyzing the speaker's extrinsic and intrinsic ethos.
3. Write a short paper on the proposition that, "through public speaking we wield enormous power for good and for evil." Then meet in small groups to explore different points of view.

"Like hungry guests, a sitting
audience looks."

George Farquhar

THE SPEAKER-AUDIENCE CONNECTION

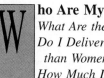

ho Are My Listeners?
What Are the Ages of My Listeners?
Do I Deliver a Different Speech to Men
  than Women?
How Much Do My Listeners Know About
  My Topic?
To Which Groups Do My Listeners Belong?
Should I Consider Life-style Choices?

Interview: with Alberto Gonzalez, Ph.D, Authority on Intercultural Communication

Why Is My Audience An Audience?
Define the Occasion
Define Audience Interest In Your Speech Topic
Determine How Much Your Audience Knows About You

How To Find Out What Your Audience Is Thinking Before You Speak
Analyze Your Audience With A Questionnaire
Observe and Interview

How To Make The Speaker–Audience Connection
Get to the Point Quickly
Have Confidence Your Audience Wants to Hear
  Your Speech
Be of the People Not Above the People
Make Personal Connections with Your Listeners
Make Your Speech a Participatory Event

Speakeasy: Physical Surroundings and Audience Response

Find Out What Your Audience Thought After Your Speech

Focus on Research: Adapting To Your Audience: Can You Go Too Far?

lthough Ross Perot certainly achieved considerable success as a public speaker during the 1992 presidential campaign, the Texas billionaire occasionally failed to achieve his goals as a speaker. On July 13, 1992, as an undeclared candidate for the presidency, Perot faced one of his toughest audiences of his campaign, delegates of the National Association for the Advancement of Colored People (N.A.A.C.P.) who were meeting in Nashville, Tennessee. His remarks were sprinkled with references to "you people" and "your people," words many African-Americans resent. The terms have often been regarded as being offensive to many black citizens because they lump all African-Americans together and "indicate a lack of appreciation for diversity." Even though Perot's audience was not noticeably angry, the impact of his message was seriously diminished and, of course, the media lost no time in highlighting his gaffes in national news reports. "It was a failed opportunity," said Milton Morris, vice president of the Joint Center for Political and Economic Studies, a research organization specializing in black-oriented issues. "He has not made direct contact with the black population thus far. He's just a vague image to them, and this was his first opportunity, using about the best platform or stage he's going to have, to talk to the black community."

H. Ross Perot was not a professional speaker and he wrote his own campaign speeches to create the message he believed needed to be heard in the 1992 campaign. His intention was certainly not to offend his audience but rather address them with ideas he believed were not being presented by candidates in both the Democratic and the Republican national parties. Nonetheless, by not addressing issues of primary concern to African-Americans and by making inappropriate references to his listeners, H. Ross Perot did not make the successful speaker–audience connection that could have strengthened his political campaign.[1]

Whether they are in a large auditorium, a corporate board room, or classroom, all audiences are self-centered. Listeners want to know what they can learn from your speech or how they can take action that will, in some way, enhance their lives. If you solve listeners' problems, show that you understand what their needs are, and help them to achieve their goals, they will listen. How do you prepare and deliver a speech that will mean enough to your audience to capture attention and convince its members to listen? Begin by learning as much as you can about your listeners so that you can focus on their concerns.

WHO ARE MY LISTENERS?

Peggy Noonan is known for crafting the speeches of presidents and presidential candidates. She wrote the speech George Bush delivered when he accepted the Republican nomination for president in 1988, Ronald Reagan's speech after the 1986 *Challenger* disaster, and the speech Reagan delivered on the fortieth anniversary of

---

1.   Steven A. Holmes, "Perot in Trouble," *The New York Times,* July 14, 1992, p. A17.

Ross Perot emerged in the 1992 presidential campaign as a widely popular and independent speaker.

D-Day in 1984. Noonan's images touch us all because they are deliberately connected to the audience. She explains:

> I strived to make each [speech] special. I thought about the audience. I would think how happy they were to be near the President and how each deserved something special, something personal . . . . I did not endear myself to the researchers when I asked them to go back again and again to find out who the leader of such and such an organization was and what his nickname was and has he ever met the President. And in the town where he's speaking, what are the people talking about, is there a local problem like a garbage scow nobody wants, does the local school have a winning team, what's the big local department store and are they hiring? Anything to make it seem as if someone had thought about this speech and these people.[2]

From these questions an audience profile emerges that enables Noonan to write speeches that mean something to the audience. Audiences listen and are captivated by Noonan's words because of her ability to let them know that the speaker cares about them.

You need not be a presidential speechwriter to understand your audiences in this way. All speakers can create a profile of their listeners by analyzing them in terms

---

2.   Peggy Noonan, "Confessions of a White House Speechwriter," *New York Times Magazine,* October 15, 1989, p. 72.

of key demographic and psychological characteristics: age, sex, level of knowledge, group membership, and shared values and life-styles. The information that emerges from this analysis is the raw material for a successful speaker–audience connection.[3]

What Are the Ages of My Listeners?

Is your audience filled with senior citizens or high school students, middle-aged executives or newly hired corporate recruits? By finding out the average age of your listeners, you can avoid being on one side of an age gap and having your audience on the other. Here is how one young speaker, delivering her first speech as a retirement counselor, alienated her audience by failing to consider the sensitivities of her older listeners:

> I am here to talk with you tonight about what to do now that you are retired. Sounds funny, doesn't it coming from me? I won't be retiring for at least thirty years—that is, not unless I win the lottery.
>
> Now that the productive years of your life are over and the alarm clock no longer rings, it is time to decide how you will spend the remaining years of your life. From my point of view, a life of leisure doesn't sound too bad. Listening to Bon Jovi instead of working is my idea of a good day.

The speaker was patronizing and condescending. After the speech, many people felt they had listened to a teenage brat.

Had the speaker delivered the following message, she would have gotten a far better response:

> Retirement isn't what is used to be. People are living longer, healthier lives and are looking for involvement that makes their future even brighter than their past.
>
> In my work as a retirement counselor, I've met seventy-year-olds with schedules that make my day look like a life of leisure. Instead of listening to Bing Crosby records or watching "I Love Lucy" reruns, they are working—many never said goodbye to their businesses—and volunteering.
>
> They are valuable members of extended families, taking care of their grandchildren with the energy of new parents and the wisdom of people who understand that time leaves little alone.

Here are some suggestions for eliminating the age gap:

1. *Avoid dating yourself through your references or language.*   If you are addressing a group of teenagers on the topic of popular culture, you talk about their current favorite rock group, not the New Kids on the Block. If you are addressing a group of middle-aged executives, don't assume that they know what college students are thinking. And don't use slang

---

3. For a philosophical look at the speaker and his audience, see C. Perelman and L. Olbrechts-Tyteca, *The New Rhetoric: A Treatise on Argumentation* (Notre Dame, IN: University of Notre Dame Press, 1969).

expressions that are likely to be unfamiliar to older people and nonstudents.

2. *Make sure your appearance is appropriate for the group.*   For example, if you are a junior executive making a presentation to senior management, dress in an appropriate business suit.

3. *Minimize attention to age differences.*   If you are older than your listeners, don't give them the impression that one day they will learn what you know. If you are younger, don't leave them feeling that the best years of their lives are over.

4. *Avoid assumptions about the average age of your audience.*   Not long ago, nearly all college students fit into the eighteen to twenty-two age group. Today, about six million nontraditional students twenty-three or older are enrolled in four-year colleges, representing 45 percent of current enrollments.[4] On any campus, you will meet forty-year-old sophomores seeking a new career, returning to school after their children are grown or sixty-year-old freshmen returning because they love learning.

    You can find out the average age of your listeners by using a questionnaire or observing the group before your speech. (We address these information-gathering techniques later in the chapter.)

5. *Focus on your speech, not your age.*   Business consultant Edith Weiner started to deliver speeches in the early 1970s at the age of twenty-three. Her audiences were senior level executives. "I was much younger than people thought I was going to be," said Weiner. "When I got up to speak, they didn't know what to make of me."

    Weiner's response was to focus on her message. "If I did well in the first three minutes, not only did I surprise the audience, I created fans. Expectations were so low that when I came across as confident and funny and comfortable, the audience was hooked into the rest of my speech."[5]

6. *Learn to deal with heterogeneous groups.*   When your audience is made up of listeners of all ages, deliver a message that includes, rather than excludes, any age group. Focus on subjects with universal appeal, avoiding references that mean a great deal to one group, but little or nothing to another.

Do I Deliver a Different Speech to Men than Women?

Not long ago, speakers were advised to talk to women about home decorating and cooking and to men about politics and cars. But times have changed and public speaking advice has changed as well. Women are now astronauts and dentists,

---

4.   "'College Age' Means Almost Any Age," *The New York Times,* October 25, 1989, p. B7.
5.   Interview with Edith Weiner, October 10, 1989.

members of the president's cabinet and members of Congress. Men are now elementary school teachers and nurses, secretaries and full-time, stay-at-home parents. To deliver a speech that implicitly or explicitly minimizes the impact of these changes is to risk offending many, if not all, your listeners.

Avoiding gender stereotypes starts with awareness that stereotypes exist in your own thinking. Ask yourself, for example, whether all carpenters and army officers are men or all nurses and grade school teachers are women. Look for hidden prejudices in your speech, which often show up in the form of sexist language, as in the following example:

> Being chosen First Captain of the Corps of Cadets is the highest honor the U.S. Military Academy at West Point offers. Although the responsibilities of being First Captain are enormous, the man appointed to the job is qualified to handle the pressure. He is chosen because of his ability to lead and because of his competence as a student and athlete.

Through the use of "he" and "his" and the reference to the appointment of a "man," the speaker implies this military honor is reserved for men. Theoretically, this has not been the case since 1976—the year women were first accepted to West Point. Today, this language is even more offensive, for in 1989, Kristin M. Baker was appointed first captain of the corps of cadets.

Gender role differences do exist and generalizations based on these differences are not necessarily wrong. Despite the fact that today the majority of mothers work outside the home, it is accurate to assume that in many families mothers remain primarily responsible for the care of children and fathers earn the larger share of the family income. It is also a fact that more men than women are sports fans. Therefore, if you are addressing a group of young men who you know are likely to enjoy professional sports, it is fair to use a sports analogy to make your point—not because you are a fan but because talking about the Minnesota Vikings will help you connect with your listeners. These references tie your speech in a concrete way to the interests of the group.

How Much Do My Listeners Know About My Topic?

Look at your listeners' educational backgrounds. Are they high school dropouts or college graduates, experts with doctorates in the field or freshmen taking their first course? Use this information to gear the level of your remarks to listeners' knowledge. In the classroom, the educational level of your listeners is defined for you, but this does not always reflect their knowledge of your subject. Your classmates may know more or less than you think.

Don't assume that expertise in one area necessarily means expertise in others. For example, if you are a stock broker delivering a speech to a group of scientists about investment opportunities, you may have to define the rules that govern even simple stock trades. Although the more educated your audience, the more sophisticated these explanations can be, explanations must be included for your speech to make sense.

Be careful about assuming what your audience knows—and does not know—about technical topics. Mention a modem to people who know nothing about computers and they may be baffled. Define it for a group of computer experts and they will wonder why you were asked to speak to them. In both cases, you run the risk of losing your audience; people who are confused or know much more about a subject may simply stop listening.

You can determine how much your listeners know about your topic by the nature of the occasion (Are you talking to your chess club or public speaking classmates); by their educational backgrounds (Are they high school or college graduates, professional workers or tradespeople?); and by a direct assessment of their knowledge in a questionnaire. (The use of questionnaires is discussed later in the chapter.)

To Which Groups Do My Listeners Belong?

Are the members of your audience predominantly blue-collar workers or white-collar executives? Are they politically liberal or conservative? Are they fundamentalist Christian or Orthodox Jews? Are they African-American or white? Hispanic or Oriental? Do they earn more than $100,000 a year or less than $25,000? The answers to these questions may influence the nature of your speech and help you create common ground with your audience.

Religion.   Your speech topic was in vitro fertilization, one of medicine's newest techniques to help infertile couples have children. Although your presentation went well, when you looked at the faces of your listeners you knew you had hit a nerve.

The post-speech audience comments told you why. "How can we respond positively to your ideas when the Catholic Church tells us that this technology is wrong?" asked one student. "Why didn't you acknowledge the Church's point of view?" asked another. Without realizing it, you had offended a predominantly Roman Catholic audience by failing to deal with the religious implications of this procedure.

Speakers rarely intend to offend their audiences, especially about religion. But when speakers fail to realize that religious beliefs may also define moral attitudes about issues like abortion, premarital sex, living together before marriage, homosexuality, birth control, and medical intervention in human reproduction, they risk alienating their audience.

Failing to acknowledge and address the religious beliefs of your listeners when your speech concerns a sensitive topic sets up barriers to communication that may be difficult to surmount. Instead of ignoring the religious implications of in vitro fertilization, you could deal with them like this in your presentation:

> I know that many of you may disagree with what I am about to say. But in vitro fertilization is a medical fact of life. Although your own religious convictions may condemn this technology and refuse its benefits, thousands of childless couples look to it with hope and expectation. For them, it is the answer to their prayers, for it brings the hope of giving birth to a child.

Racial and Ethnic Ties.   Long ago, the image of the United States as a melting pot gave way to the image of a rainbow of diversity—an image in which African-Americans and Hispanics, Orientals and Greeks, Arabs and Europeans define themselves by their racial and ethnic ties as well as by their ties to the United States. Within this diversity are cultural beliefs and traditions that may be different from your own. These differences must be considered as you prepare your speeches.

Here are two examples of how cultural differences can get in the way of communication:

⌘ If you are delivering a speech on crowd behavior and talk about pushing and shoving in public places as signs of rudeness, you may get puzzled looks from Arab members of your audience. In Middle Eastern cultures, these behaviors are perfectly acceptable.

⌘ If you are delivering a speech on career advancement and describe how changing jobs will help you get ahead, Japanese students may appear startled. In their culture, workers are often employed by the same company for life.

Though most of the people you address will have ties in America for several generations, you cannot assume that ethnic ties have been left behind. If you ask Americans about their backgrounds, they may tell you they are African-Americans, Russians, Vietnamese, Puerto Ricans, and Koreans. With these ties come traditions and beliefs that must be recognized as you speak—perhaps not explicitly but by being sensitive to potential misunderstandings that stem from cultural differences.

National surveys reveal differences between groups on important issues. According to a Gallup Poll commissioned by the Joint Center for Political Studies, while only 24 percent of the white population surveyed believed government should guarantee jobs, 65 percent of the African-American population held this view. The poll also showed that the majority of African-Americans believe white people have a greater chance of advancement in the workplace.[6] If you approach a speech on job opportunities without realizing how differently these races view this issue, you will make your presentation less acceptable to some of your listeners than it has to be. We are not suggesting that you change your views, if they are carefully conceived and supported, but that you acknowledge that many members of your audience may disagree with you on key points and that you need to consider, and address, differences of opinion.

Occupational Groups.   Talk to a group of union members about giving back some of the benefits they gained over the years, and you are likely to be jeered. Address a group of corporate executives about hiring workers for life and you may find members of your audience leaving in the middle of your speech.

Because people often identify themselves in terms of their work, it is important to know the types of jobs your listeners hold. Are they construction workers or

---

6.   "Facts and Figures: Divergent Views on Current Issues," *Black Enterprise* (March 1987): 32.

accountants, doctors or postal workers? The speaking occasion often makes this clear: You may be invited by a group of home builders to deliver a talk on the dangers of radon; or a group of insurance agents may ask you to talk about the weather conditions associated with hurricanes.

Occupational information can often tell you a great deal about listeners' attitudes. An audience of union electricians may be unwilling to give their union leader the support needed to negotiate a new contract because of their unwillingness to give back a benefit won in a previous contract. The speaker must find a way to convince the listeners that dropping the benefit is in their best interests. The speaker's tactic is to make listeners feel that, despite the concession, they have made major economic strides.

A knowledge of what your listeners do for a living may also tell you the type of vocabulary appropriate for the occasion. If you are addressing a group of newspaper editors you can use terms common to the newspaper business without bothering to define them. Engineers, firefighters, lawyers, teachers, police officers, speech therapists all have languages common to the group. We are not suggesting you use job-related words indiscriminately but that you use them to your advantage.

Because people often identify themselves in terms of their work, it is important to know the types of jobs or the nature of the work they do.

Political Affiliation.   If you are a fund-raiser for the homeless, you will probably give a different speech to a group with liberal beliefs than to a group of conservatives. Here are some variations:

Section of Speech to Group of Liberals

We are a nation of plenty—a nation in which begging seems as out of place as snow in July.

Yet our cities are filled with beggars who have no food or lodging. They are the have-nots in a nation of haves and, through their presence alone, they demand justice.

I ask for your help tonight because we are a nation built on helping one another escape from poverty. No matter how hard you work to cement your own success, you will never achieve the American Dream if one person is left on the streets without a home.

We share a vision of what this Dream is. Although equality for all may never be possible, a roof certainly is.

Section of Speech to a Group of Conservatives

It is in your best interest to help the homeless—to give money to homeless causes. I'm not talking about handouts on the street but money that goes into putting a roof over people's heads and into job training.

In the long run, giving people dignity by giving them a home and training them for productive work will mean fewer people on welfare and lower taxes. Is it a leap of faith to see this connection or just plain common business sense?

Acknowledging political differences has been important in America since its founding. You will not compromise your values when you accept the fact that political differences exist: rather, you will take the first step in using these differences as the starting point of communication.

Socio-Economic Group.   If the members of your audience earn less than $30,000 a year, they may not be able to respond to a speech demanding a change in the capital gains tax. In contrast, an audience with an annual income of $150,000 is likely to cheer you as you cite the reasons for lowering the tax. When Rabbi Harold S. Kushner talks to groups about his book, *When All You've Ever Wanted Isn't Enough,* he learns in advance the group's socioeconomic status. He explains:

Generally, if I'm addressing affluent business executives, I concentrate on the down side of economic success and on the spiritual nature of affluence. When the group is less affluent, I talk about learning to cope with economic failure and with the feeling of being left behind.[7]

Should I Consider Life-Style Choices?

Your life-style choices say a lot about you. If you choose to be a city dweller, living in a studio apartment twenty-two stories up, you probably have less inclination to experience nature than if you opt to live on a fifty-acre farm in Vermont. If you put

7.   Interview with Rabbi Harold S. Kushner, October 13, 1989.

in twelve-hour days at the office, your career is probably more important to you than if you choose to work only part-time.[8]

What do these choices tell public speakers? If you are addressing members of the Sierra Club, you can be sure the group has a keen sense of environmental issues. Similarly, if you are addressing an exercise class at the local Y, you can be sure that physical fitness is a priority of everyone in the room. If your listeners are hard-driving workaholics, they will be interested in what you say about business.

Life-style choices are linked to the attitudes, beliefs, and values of your listeners. *Attitudes* are predispositions to act in a particular way that influence our response to objects, events, and situations. Attitudes tend to be long-lasting, but can change under pressure. They are often, but not always, related to behavior.

Beliefs represent a mental and emotional acceptance of information. They are judgments about the truth or probability that a statement is correct. Beliefs are formed from experience and learning and are based on what we perceive to be accurate. To be an effective speaker, you must analyze the beliefs of your audience in the context of your message. For example, if you are dealing with people who believe that working hard is the only way to get ahead, you will have trouble convincing them to take time off between semesters. Your best hope is to persuade them that time off will make them more productive and goal-directed when they return. By citing authorities and providing examples of other students who have successfully followed this course, you have a chance of changing this belief.

Attitudes and beliefs are anchored in *values,* deep-seated abstract judgments about what is important to us. Values separate the worthwhile from the worthless and determine what we consider moral, desirable, important, beautiful, worth living or dying for. Free enterprise, free speech, hard work, and being part of a stable family are a few of the most important American values.

An audience of concerned students that values the importance of education might express this value in the belief that "a college education should be available to all qualified students" and in the attitude that "the state legislature should pass a tuition-reduction plan for every state college." If you address this audience, you can use this attitude as the basis for your plea that students picket the state capitol in support of the tuition-reduction plan. Understanding your listeners' attitudes, beliefs, and values will help you put your message in terms most likely to succeed.

Although an analysis of these demographic characteristics will give you some clue as to how your listeners are likely to respond to your speech, it will not tell you anything about the speaking occasion, why people have come together as an audience, how they feel about your topic, or about you as a speaker. This information emerges from the second stage of audience analysis, which centers on the speaking situation.

---

8. For years, advertisers have recognized the relationship between life-style choice and consumer demand. Arnold Mitchell, a researcher at SRI International who was at the forefront of values and life-style research, concluded that each stage of an individual's development is marked by a "particular pattern of priorities . . . a unique set of dominating values and needs." See Berkeley Rice, "The Selling of Life-styles," *Psychology Today* (March 1988):48; James Atlas, "Beyond Demographics," *Atlantic Monthly* (October 1984):49–58.

I N T E R V I E W

Alberto Gonzalez, Ph.D,
Authority on
Intercultural
Communication

Audiences' attitudes, beliefs, and values are culturally shaped, and the cultural context is part of the environment for public speaking. The speaker who intends to be effective needs to be sensitive to cultural and intercultural voices within the listeners who make up an audience. Dr. Alberto Gonzalez is a highly informed communication teacher and scholar who specializes in intercultural communication. His work appears in national, regional, and state journals in communication and he is the co-editor of the book *Our Voices: Essays in Culture, Ethnicity, and Communication.* We asked Dr. Gonzalez, an Associate Professor of Interpersonal Communication at Bowling Green State University, to speak with us about culture, intercultural communication, and public speaking with an eye toward having you think carefully about *cultural voices* and public speaking.

Question: You use the terms "culture" and "communication" throughout most of your working day. How do you define "culture" and the term you use frequently, "cultural voices?"

Answer: Raymond Williams, in a book called *Keywords: A Vocabulary of Culture and Society,* says that "culture" is one of the most complicated words in the English language! I'm sure that I'm guilty of both reducing and increasing its complexity.

I think of defining as a creative activity. Of a definition, I ask, "What new insight is revealed?"

and "What new thinking does the definition make possible?" I don't define things for all time because there are always new insights and new possibilities. So for now, when I approach "culture," I think of the following association: culture is to a community as personality is to the human being. Culture is like the personality of a community. In my usage, "culture" and "personality" are terms, *ideas,* that help us understand ourselves and the behaviors and events we see around us.

On the topic of "cultural voice," I'm heavily influenced by several sources. *Women's Ways of Knowing,* by Mary Belenky, and others contains an excellent discussion of the "voice" metaphor. A woman who speaks with her voice means speaking from her own experience. Chapter three of bell hooks' *Talking Back* addresses voice as well. Each of us has a "cultural voice." Each of us communicates in a way that places us in a unique cultural community.

Here's an example. When my brother died in 1988, I took a long cross-country flight to the memorial. Seated next to me was an eight- or nine-year-old girl who was traveling alone. Kids don't really take to me, but this one was delightful and unafraid. I was amazed at how comfortable she was with me. She kept me company for the entire trip. Seated next to her was a nun, whose presence was warm, though she never spoke. I recognized the nun as my mother, who died when I was a child. And the little girl I now recognize as my daughter who was born in 1991.

To the rational-scientific mind, my account describes a delusion brought on by intense grief. However, the mind open to spiritual rationality would see in this story the very natural power of *La familia* to shield and protect. My cultural voice reflects this mind. I speak it without confusion or shame.

The cultural voice reflects the shared meanings of our "home" communities. The complication arises when one community attempts to rob another of its knowledge and of its kind of talk. Speaking with one's voice entails the possibility of transformation and the practice of self-determination.

Question: We often advise students in public speaking courses to analyze audiences in terms of demographic factors that are inherent in any cultural context. What cultural factors or features of an audience should be understood and assessed by a speaker who is particularly concerned with being meaningful to an audience of a different culture?

Answer: That's a question of our times, isn't it? How do we understand one another? Why do we popularize certain meanings and not others? It takes a lot of work to discover the "unpopular" ways of living of cultural groups in the U.S.

In the United States, we've operated on the premise that everyone must conform to *one* language, *one* set of references. Standard American English operates as the prescribed language. Education that privileges European ideas and literature over, say, African or Asian ideas prescribes a certain past. But whose language is that? Whose past is that? Who decided upon only those prescriptions? Whose interests are served, and whose are diminished by these selections?

Some of us in communication argue that we should extend our awareness of the communicative styles and references of cultural communities other

than our own, rather than prescribe that all cultural groups conform to a single norm. What does this argument entail? It does not entail giving up one's own cultural values. It does mean a willingness on the part of the speaker to realize that, once you are removed from your own cultural community, you are an outsider, you are "the other."

So, the speaker might want to ask some questions. What is the social and historical relationship between my cultural community and the one I am addressing? What distinctive ways of knowing, valuing, and being do my listeners possess, and how am I respecting those ways? What values from my culture am I reproducing in my speech, both in content and delivery? What is the relationship between these values and the cultural values of the listeners? How will the listeners become active, equal participants in the telling of my message?

As you can see, these questions take a lot of work, perhaps years of work, to answer.

Question: What do you suspect might be the greatest problem in contemporary public speech that must be solved when speakers and audiences cross cultural boundaries to achieve mutual understanding and the resolution of conflict?

Answer: The greatest problem, and this is no great insight on my part, is ignorance. Just the other day a university professor who lives in the Southern U.S. told me that he knew nothing about Latino cultures. Why is that? As a society, we haven't placed any value in getting to know each other's cultural experiences. Some political commentators argue that people should be mirror images of one another. That sounds great—if you've made the mirror and you're holding it.

Question: The Latino population continues to grow dramatically in our society and brings its cultural presence into communities all across our country. You reflect this presence in your speaking, teaching, and writing. What do you do to try to communicate effectively that nurtures and sustains your Latino cultural identity and, at the same time, facilitates your efforts to communicate this identity with listeners centered in different cultures?

Answer: Sometimes I reflect that heritage and sometimes it gets reflected upon me. I remember several years ago a student telling me, "Dr. Gunzailus [her pronunciation removed me from the realm of Español], I don't think of you as a Mexican-American. I don't think of you as being anything." That comment was curious in itself, but anyway, when I later bought a red truck, this student immediately dubbed it "the Red Burrito." At a conscious level, this student related to that aspect of my identity that expressed values and practices that were very similar to her own. Yet at a deeper level, this student was very much aware of my difference; she reflexively associated me with the only Mexican domain she knew—food.

Mostly, I try to convey that being multicultural is cool. I point to my own bi-culturalism. The singer I recommend these days is Anna Gabriél. When someone shouts "cumbia!" at the baile, my wife and I move to the rhythm. I'm open to mystery, magic, and things generally impossible for the rational-scientific Euroamerican mind.

Question: Can you speculate on the role of public speaking in mediating change and serving other rhetorical functions as our country moves toward the next century?

Answer: I believe that public speaking will play a vital role in making us aware of this multicultural nation. The public readings of Maya Angelou and Maxine Hong Kingston, as well as the speeches of Henry Cisneros, Luis Valdez, and Toni Morrison work to reveal and validate the notion that there are multiple centers of interpretation. As people interested in the study and practice of communication we should allow ourselves to be informed and inspired by these voices.

Becoming familiar with the practices and references of another culture takes time—it can't happen, in any meaningful way, overnight. The speaker

should get informed now. Today's advocate can't afford to be like that person from down South who is in his middle age and knows nothing about his cultural neighbors!

I suggest two very broad projects. And, since I have a special interest in communication, these projects focus on the symbolic aspects of culture. The first involves an examination of your cultural self. To begin discovery of your cultural voice, answer the following: What adjectives do you use to describe your cultural community? What is an example of a "success" story you might tell someone? What is valuable "knowledge" and where does it come from? What metaphors do you use to describe the way you talk (is your talk "concrete" and "to the point")? What is the value of talk in your culture? What is the value of silence? What is the relationship between your culture and cultures around you? What are the signs of this relationship?

The second part of this project involves listening to the cultural voices speaking around you. Pertaining to Latinos, you might ask someone the following: How many Latino-authored books do you possess? Upon whom would you rely for a book recommendation? Is a Salvadoran an American? How do Latinos define "Latino"? What do Latinos think about the term "Hispanic"? How many Latino cultures can you identify and how are they different from one another? What are Latino influences in U.S. popular culture, politics, and economics? Who are the mythic heros and villians cited by Latinos with whom you work or go to school? What are some of the social priorities of Latinos and how are these priorities shaped by our sense(s) of cultural/historical identity?

Latinos are trying to engage in a dialogue with the peoples of both North and South American continents. This dialogue is not merely multi-national, it is multihemispheric. This dialogue is played out in national theatre, literature, critical theory, musical performance, and in how I walk down the sidewalk and raise my child. Are you listening?

Interview with Alberto Gonzalez, Ph.D., August 18, 1993.

Audiences are made of individuals drawn together in ways that create unity and a shared identity. This identity may be centered in roles, interests, group membership, ethnicity, or a combination of factors important enough to raise the question: Why is an audience an audience? In early July, 1992, more than 1,000 black Roman Catholics turned to their African heritage during three days of meetings about key issues they shared in common as representatives to the National Black Catholic Congress.

WHY IS MY AUDIENCE AN AUDIENCE?

Speakers who addressed the delegates knew why this audience was an audience—to strengthen "the African extended family and the spiritual dimension of African culture." One member of this unique audience put it this way: "The Church isn't responsive to black needs . . . There are many black people in our parish, but it is not reflected in the liturgy. It is good to be among people here because when I go to church . . . I don't see myself reflected on the alter."[9] This expression summarizes a view the speakers apparently recognized as a view likely to be shared by most members who gathered for the meetings. The audience was a composite of listeners gathered to experience unity, share needs, and pursue aspirations that could not be ignored by any speaker who addressed them.

Define the Occasion

Audience expectations are usually defined for you by the speaking invitation, which tells you the group you will address, the reason you were asked to speak, as well as the approximate length of your speech. If you are delivering a commencement address, your audience will expect you to talk about the college experience. Similarly, if you are a consumer advocate speaking before a Senate committee, your audience will expect your remarks to be political and consumer-oriented.

Here is the way Sydney H. Schanberg, newspaper columnist and author of *The Killing Fields* met the requirements of the occasion when he received an honorary degree and delivered a commencement speech at Nazareth College in Rochester, N.Y.[10]

> I am pleased and honored to have been invited here today. But I would be less than honest if I did not tell you that there are qualities about honorary degrees and other awards that make me uneasy.
>
> First, there is my general unease about our society's constant search for heroes, for celebrities, for royalty. We live in an age of instant human icons—which often means that we use them up quickly and discard them after a season or two. Then there is my specific disquiet about awards given to me. No, I'm not going to launch here into some exercise in false humility. My ego is much too hungry and needy to turn back honors that are extended to me. But I do not feel comfortable with official descriptions of me.

---

9.   Peter Steinfels, "Joyful Mood at Black Catholic Meeting," *The New York Times,* July 19, 1992, A16.

10.   Sydney H. Schanberg, "The Risk of Being Different: Stretch Yourself," speech delivered at Nazareth College, May 14, 1989. Reprinted in *Vital Speeches of the Day,* September 1, 1989, pp. 700 and 702.

Schanberg closed his speech by centering once more on the occasion:

> I leave you with a quote from Winston Churchill, who was speaking about his own young years and speaking to all young people. He said: "You will make all kinds of mistakes, but as long you are generous and true, and also fierce, you cannot hurt the world or even seriously distress her. She was made to be wooed and won by youth."

Although Schanberg chose to be controversial, his remarks were geared to the expectations of the audience and therefore were appropriate to the occasion.

Often, speaking invitations do not define the speech topic nor do they clarify the nature of your presentation. If, as an expert on first aid, you are invited to deliver a speech to a parents' group, it may be left to you to decide what is appropriate for the occasion. Put yourself in the position of your listeners and try to determine what would interest them. Are they more likely to be interested in hearing about first aid for common boating accidents (it's January in Michigan) or to see a demonstration of how to save a choking child?

Define Audience Interest in Your Speech Topic

Interest level often determines audience response. For example, if a former member of a religious cult using the following excerpt gave a speech to a class in public speaking soon after the explosive and controversial end to the Branch Davidian stand-off in Waco, Texas, in April, 1993, listener interest would have been assured:

> "The sun didn't blacken, nor did the moon turn red, but the world did come to an end, just as their prophet had promised. The end drove up to their doorstep in a tank, spitting gas, fulfilling prophecies."[11] These words from a report in *Time* are especially chilling to me, because for four years I was behind walls which housed a religious cult, devoted to the words and commands of the leader. I became quite ill and I was eventually taken to a hospital away from our temple-like compound. As I recovered I realized that I made a mistake by becoming a member of the cult. I ran away from the hospital, returned to my family, began to attend college again, and found a real reason to thank God.

Many topics do not guarantee the same degree of audience involvement, especially if they have been used by other speakers. Jenny Clanton, a student at Southeastern Illinois College, skirted this pitfall when she chose to speak on the *Challenger* disaster. She involved her audience through an unconventional approach:[12]

> On January 28, 1986, the American Space Program suffered the worst disaster in its more than 30 year history. The entire world was shocked when the space shuttle *Challenger* exploded seconds after lift-off, claiming the lives of seven brave astronauts and crippling our . . . space agenda. I suppose the oldest cliché in our culture, spoken on battlegrounds and indeed virtually anywhere Americans die, is "We must press

11. Information from "Bracing for the Big One," *Newsweek,* October 30, 1988, p. 28.
12. Jenny Clanton, "Title Unknown," *Winning Orations of the Interstate Oratorical Association,* 1988 (Mankato, MN: Interstate Oratorical Association, 1989), pp. 24–25.

forward so we can say they did not die in vain." Rest assured. They didn't. The deaths of our seven astronauts probably saved the lives of untold thousands of Americans.

For, you see, if the O-rings had not failed on January 28, 1986, but rather on May 20, 1987, the next scheduled shuttle launch, in the words of Dr. John Gofman, Professor Emeritus at the University of California at Berkeley, you could have "kissed Florida good-bye."

Because the next shuttle, the one that was to have explored the atmosphere of Jupiter was to carry 47 pounds of Plutonium 238, which is according to Dr. Gorman, the most toxic substance on the face of the earth.

Determine How Much Your Audience Knows About You

Most politicians have the experience every time they come up for reelection. They deliver a speech to voters solidly behind their opponent and no one bothers to listen to what they have to say. Their reputation has preceded them to the podium. Of course, this type of audience reaction can work *for* them as well as against them. Many politicians spend an entire campaign resting on their laurels, trying not to disturb voters' perception of them as a powerful and effective leader.

Although few of us are politicians running for office, our reputations may precede us and affect the way our audiences respond to our messages. If you are a restaurant critic invited to talk about your favorite eating spots, the response of your audience will be influenced by your credentials. Your reputation as a food critic is the reason you were invited to speak.

Your reputation can affect your classroom speeches as well. If you are known at school for your volunteer work on a literacy project, your audience is likely to perceive you as someone who understands the problem. If you run a part-time business trading baseball cards, your audience may be eager to hear your views on the value of these cards or to find out how you turned a hobby into a money-making business.

HOW TO FIND OUT WHAT YOUR AUDIENCE IS THINKING BEFORE YOU SPEAK

Stew Leonard, Jr. has delivered hundreds of speeches to corporate audiences about what makes his family's store in Norwalk, Connecticut, a success. Companies like AT&T, Marriott, and Union Carbide all want to hear what Stew Leonard, Jr. has to say about the unusual supermarket (with petting zoo, entertainment, and employees in costume) that looks more like an amusement park than a food store. Leonard intends to give his audiences what they need: "If I don't give them what they need I am not doing my job. That's why I spend so much time learning about an audience before I speak. I start by sending out a questionnaire that asks the goals and objectives of the meetings and the challenges facing the company. I also like to learn as much as I can about the audience—the age of the people attending, how many males, how many females, their educational backgrounds, and so on."[13]

---

13.   Interview with Stew Leonard, October 3, 1989.

Robert Waterman, Jr., coauthor of *In Search of Excellence,* spends a day or two before a speech observing his corporate audience at work. What he learns helps him address the specific concerns of his listeners.[14]

Although both men are professional speakers, they assume very little about the characteristics of their prospective audiences. They collect information that will tell them who their listeners are and what they want and expect from their presentations. To analyze their audiences, they use questionnaires and observation—techniques that can be used successfully in the classroom.

Analyze Your Audience with a Questionnaire

Public opinion polls are an American tradition—especially around election time. Pollsters Gallup, Harris, and Roper ask Americans for their views on the candidates and the issues. And when elections are over, pollsters try to find out what Americans think about such varied topics as U.S. foreign policy, church attendance, illegal drugs, and ice cream preferences. Their tool in these investigations is the questionnaire. Questionnaires also are used by market research companies to learn how the public might respond to a product and, every ten years, by the Bureau of the Census.

For your audience analysis, a questionnaire can help you determine the specific demographic characteristics of your listeners as well as their perceptions of you and your topic. It can also tell you how much knowledge your listeners have about your topic and the focus they would prefer in your speech.

You can use a questionnaire in several ways. By surveying all your classmates, by sampling every fourth person in your dorm, or by calling selected members of your audience and asking them questions, you can find out information about your audience in advance. These methods are simple—and effective.

The first step in using a questionnaire is designing specific questions that are likely to get you the information you need. Three basic types of questions are most helpful to public speakers: fixed-alternative questions, scale questions, and open-ended questions.[15]

Fixed-Alternative Questions.   Fixed-alternative questions limit responses to several choices, yielding valuable information about such demographic factors as age, education, and income. These questions can help you analyze the attitudes and knowledge of your prospective listeners. Here is an example of a fixed-alternative question focusing on attitudes:

Do You Think Professional Athletes Should Be Allowed to Take Part in the Olympics?

_____ Professionals should be allowed on all Olympic teams

---

14.   Walter Kiechel III, "How to Give a Speech," *Fortune,* June 8, 1987, p. 179.
15.   Material based on Gilbert A. Churchill, Jr., *Marketing Research: Methodological Foundations,* 3d ed. (Chicago: The Dryden Press, 1983), pp. 168–231.

_____ Professionals should be allowed to participate in selected sports

_____ Professionals should never be allowed to participate

_____ No opinion

This type of question is easy to tabulate and analyze and, from the point of view of your audience, easy to answer. In addition, you can be fairly sure that if you asked the same question a second time, you would get the same answer (assuming, of course, that attitudes had not changed). These questions also give you standardized responses. That is, for everyone answering the question, the frame of reference is the same. If you ask people, "How many times a week do you eat out?" and do not supply possible responses, you may receive answers like "regularly," "rarely," "every day," and "twice a day." These answers can be more difficult to interpret than answers guided by a fixed set of alternatives.

Fixed alternative questions help avoid confusion. Ask people to describe their marital status and they may reply "unhappy." If you want to know whether they are single, married, widowed, or divorced, ask them this instead:

What is Your Marital Status?

_____ single   _____ widowed

_____ married   _____ divorced

However, using fixed-alternative does have disadvantages: For example, you may be forcing people to respond to a question when they have no opinion or strong feelings, especially if you fail to include "no opinion" as a possible response. These questions also fail to indicate the intensity of a response. For example:

Do You Think Our Nation's Schools are Doing Their Job?

_____ They are doing an excellent job in educating children

_____ The system needs improvement

_____ No opinion

Someone who believes our educational system is in crisis would respond the same as someone who believes that, although the system needs improvement, it is basically in good shape.

Fixed-alternative questions can be multichotomous, offering many different alternative responses, or dichotomous, offering only two alternatives (yes/no questions fit into this category).

Scale Questions.   Scale questions are a type of fixed-alternative question that ask people to respond to questions set up along a continuum. For example:

How often do you vote?

Always   **Sometimes**   **Occasionally**   **Never**

Although these responses could have been asked in the form of an ordinary fixed alternative question, this format, placed at the top of a page, allows you to list different variables along the left margin. For example, you can ask people to use the scale to tell you how frequently they vote in presidential elections, congressional elections, state elections, and local elections.

Open-Ended Questions.   In an open-ended question, audience members can respond however they wish. For example:

How do you feel about a twelve-month school year?

Why do you think the Japanese sell so many cars in the United States?

A variety of answers is possible from these questions. In response to your question about extending the school year, one respondent may write "Keep the school year as it is," while another may suggest a workable plan for extending the year. Because the responses to open-ended questions are so different, they can be difficult to analyze. The advantage to these questions is that they allow you to probe for details; you give respondents the opportunity to tell you what is on their minds. Here are a few guidelines for constructing usable questions:

⌘ *Avoid leading questions.* Try not to lead people to the response you desire through the wording of your question. Here are two examples of leading questions:

Do you feel stricter handgun legislation would stop the wanton killing of innocent people?
Do you believe able-bodied men too lazy to work should be eligible for welfare?

These questions should be recast. For example, "Do you support stricter handgun legislation?" is no longer a leading question.

⌘ *Avoid ambiguity.* When you use words that can be interpreted in different ways, you reduce the value of a question. For example:

How often do you drink alcohol?

_____ Frequently   _____ Occasionally

_____ Sometimes   _____ Never

In this case one person's "sometimes" may be another person's "occasionally." To avoid ambiguity, rephrase the question:

How often do you drink alcohol?

_____ More than once a week

_____ At least once a month

_____ Not more than once every six months?

_____ Never

✻ *Ask everyone the same questions.* Because variations in the wording of questions can change responses, always ask questions in the same way. Don't ask one person, "Under what circumstances would you consider enlisting in the army?" but another, "If the United States were attacked by a foreign nation, would you consider joining the army?"

Observe and Interview

You may find that the best way to gather information about a prospective audience is to assume the role of an observer. If you are to deliver a speech on weight control to a former smokers' support group, attend a meeting to determine how many members are overweight and how much weight they have to lose. Then ask several people whether their weight problem is the result of their efforts to stop smoking or if they were overweight at other times in their lives. Similarly, if you are delivering a speech to corporate executives on ways to improve their written communication, ask for samples of letters, memos, and reports the executives have written so you can look at the problem firsthand.

The interviews you conduct during this process are likely to be less formal than the type you use to gather information about your speech topic (see Chapter Six). When questions occur as you watch a group in action, ask people their thoughts and feelings. Their responses will help you analyze audience need.

HOW TO MAKE THE SPEAKER–AUDIENCE CONNECTION

It takes your listeners only seconds to tune out your message unless they determine you have something relevant to say. You convince an audience your message has value, not by locking into a prepared script, but by centering your message on your listeners. The following suggestions will help you build the type of audience connection that defines the reciprocal nature of public speaking.

Get to the Point Quickly

Tell your listeners how you can help them first, not last. If you save this part of your presentation to the end, no one may be listening. In speech making, as in any interpersonal interaction, first impressions count. Although everything you say in a presentation is important, what you say in the first few minutes is critical. Experienced speakers try to make connections with their listeners as they open their speeches. And, more importantly, they try to convey to their listeners the idea that the speech will be important to them.

Have Confidence Your Audience Wants to Hear Your Speech

It happens all the time. Speakers with relatively little knowledge about a subject are asked to speak to a group of experts on the subject. An educator may talk to a group of athletes about intercollegiate sports. A lawyer may talk to a group of doctors about the doctor-patient relationship. A politician may talk to a group of drug counselors about the problem of crack cocaine. When you feel your listeners know more than you do about your topic, realize they have invited you for a reason. In most cases, they want your opinions. Despite their knowledge, you have a perspective they find interesting. Athletes may want to learn how the college sports program is viewed by a professor; doctors want to hear a lawyer's opinion about malpractice; and drug counselors want to know what a politician will do, if elected, to relieve the drug problem.

Be of the People, Not above the People

No one wants to listen to speakers who consider themselves more accomplished, smarter, or more sophisticated than their audience. If you convey even a hint of superiority, your listeners will tune you out. As a speaker you will learn that modesty inspires confidence. James D. Griffin endeared himself to his audience with his self-effacing modesty during a commencement speech at Moorpark College in California:

> When I received the call several months ago, that Moorpark College would like to have me as this year's commencement speaker, I was told that the school likes to choose a past graduate for this address, one who has gone on after graduation to achieve, perhaps, something great.
>
> I was also told at that time that I was in fact a world-famous professor of Medieval Literature at the University of California, Berkeley. That I was chosen for this address, as I said before, struck me as a very great honor. That I was a professor, however, struck me only as a very great surprise. I had studied at Berkeley; was admitted to Ph.D. program in classical and medieval languages; I even taught for a while, as a graduate student. But the sad truth is I am not now and never was a professor of anything, let alone world famous. From across the miles, it would seem, rumor had made me greater and more successful that I actually was.
>
> No problem! There was an alternate story floating around. According to this view, I had become a multi-millionaire and now gave generously to various charitable organizations. Ladies and gentlemen, I am indeed very sorry to report that this rumor is also false.
>
> In fact, only two things are definitely true. The first is that I did graduate in 1976 from this very school. The second is that I moved away.[16]

Later in his speech Griffin talked honestly about his accomplishments, but his earlier self-effacing remarks made it clear that he was not bragging. He mentioned his own success only in the context of the success of others.

Humor can help you make this connection with your audience. Opening your speech with a joke can put both you and your listeners at ease. Humor encourages people to think of you as approachable rather than remote. Effective humor should be related in some way to the subject of your speech, your audience, or the occasion. (See Chapter Ten for a discussion of humor in public speaking.)

---

16.   James D. Griffin, "To Snare the Feet of Greatness: The American Dream Is Alive," speech delivered at Moorpark College, Moorpark, California, June 16, 1989. Reprinted in *Vital Speeches of the Day,* September 15, 1989, pp. 735–36.

S P E A K   E A S Y

PHYSICAL SURROUNDINGS AND AUDIENCE RESPONSE

When speechwriter Robert B. Rackleff addressed his colleagues about the "art of speech writing," he offered this advice:

> The time of day affects the speech. In the morning, people are relatively fresh and can listen attentively. You can explain things more carefully.
>
> But in the late afternoon, after lunch . . ., the audience needs something more stimulating. And after dinner, you had better keep it short and have some fireworks handy.

Rackleff was reminding his listeners about the intimate connection between time of day and audience response. The relationship between physical surroundings and audience response is so strong that you should plan every speech with your surroundings in mind. In addition to time, the following factors are important.

Size of the Audience

Management consultant Edith Weiner says the vast difference between an audience of six people and an audience of dozens or even hundreds of people: In the first case, says Weiner, "I'm speaking *with* the audience" but in the second "I'm speaking *to* the audience." She explains:

> When I work with very small groups, I respond to individual faces. I wanted to give every listener as much as possible, so I try to be sensitive to individual reactions. When I work with larger groups, I respond to the feel of the group. If I see that everyone is taking notes, for example, but one person is sleeping, I'm not too concerned. On the other hand, if I see that everyone in the first three rows looks puzzled but yet there's one person in the middle of the auditorium nodding in agreement with what I just said, I stop and deal with the miscommunication.

The intimacy of a small group allows for a speaker–audience interchange not possible in larger groups. Small groups provide almost instantaneous feedback; large groups are more difficult to read.

Size of the Room

As a student, you will probably be speaking in a classroom. But in other speaking situations, you may find yourself in a convention hall, a small office, or an outdoor setting where only the lineup of chairs determines the size of the speaking space.

Room size is important because it influences how loudly you must speak and determines whether you need a microphone. If you are delivering an after-dinner speech in your own dining room to ten members of your Great Books club, you don't have to worry about projecting your voice to the back row of a large room. If, on the other hand, you are delivering a commencement address in your college auditorium to 1,000 graduates, you will need to use a microphone.

Proper mike technique takes practice. If you put your mouth too close to the mike, a popping sound will fill the room every time you pronounce the letter "p." If you are too far away, no one will hear you. The best solution is to practice using a mike, preferably in the auditorium in which you will speak.

The Seating Arrangement

Most speakers prefer to be in close contact with their audiences. Physical closeness encourages intimacy and feedback, both of which make for a good speech. Unfortunately, what is preferable is not always possible. What do you do, for example, when you are asked to speak in a hotel ballroom from a dais thirty feet away from your first row of listeners? Because there is little hope of intimacy, focus on content and delivery, not audience feedback.

Check out the Physical Surroundings in Advance

Take the time to look at the room before your speech. Sit in different areas to see how the speaking area appears. Find out the approximate time of day of your speech and who is scheduled to precede and follow you. And locate the light switch and thermostat so you can adjust the lighting and room temperature. Finally, make sure that if you are addressing a group of thirty, you are not placed in a room large enough for 250, and that if you are addressing an audience of 250, you are in a room large enough to accommodate everyone.

Make Personal Connections with Your Listeners

Before management consultant Edith Weiner gives a speech, she learns the names of several members of her audience as well as their roles in the company. During her speech, she refers to these people and the conversations she had with them, thereby creating a personal bond with her audience.[17] Connections are also made by linking yourself directly to the group you are addressing and by referring to your audience with the pronoun "you" rather than the third-person, "they." The word "you" inserts your listeners into the middle of your presentation and makes it clear that you are focusing your attention on them. Here is an example in a speech delivered by Jeffrey R. Holland, president of Brigham Young University, to a group of early childhood educators:

> You are offering more than technical expertise or professional advice when you meet with parents. You are demonstrating that you are an ally in their task of rearing the next generation. In all that you do . . . however good your work, and whatever quality of life parents provide, there is no comparable substitute for families. Your best opportunity to act in children's best interests is to strengthen parents, rather than think you can or will replace them.[18]

Make Your Speech a Participatory Event

When you ask your listeners to participate in your speech, they become partners in your success. Choose a member of your audience to take part in your talk and the rest of the group will feel like one of its own is up there at the podium. Involve the entire audience and they will hang on your every word. That's what Senator Edward M. Kennedy did in his "Where was George?" speech presented before the 1988 Democratic National Convention. With each seccessive refrain, the audience became more involved in the speech as they chanted along with the senator, "Where was George?"

---

17.   Interview with Edith Weiner, October 10, 1989.
18.   Jeffrey R. Holland, "Whose Children Are These? The Family Connection," speech delivered at the 1988 Conference of the Association for Childhood Education International, April 23, 1988. Reprinted in *Vital Speeches of the Day*, July 1, 1988, p. 559.

The Vice President says he wasn't there—or can't recall—or never heard—as the Administration secretly plotted to sell arms to Iran. So when the monumental mistake was being made, I think it is fair to ask—where was George?

The Vice President says he never saw—or can't remember—or didn't comprehend—the intelligence report on General Noriega's involvement in the cocaine cartel. So when that report was being prepared and discussed, I think it is fair to ask—where was George?

The Vice President claims he cares about the elderly—but evidently he didn't know, or wasn't there, when the Administration tried repeatedly to slash Social Security and Medicare. So when those decisions were being made, I think it is fair to ask—where was George?[19]

Consider the many ways to involve your audience: Ask someone to help demonstrate a point; use role playing. Although time constraints may limit your opportunity to use these techniques in the classroom, they can be invaluable in other settings.

FIND OUT WHAT YOUR AUDIENCE THOUGHT AFTER YOUR SPEECH

As you know from your classroom experience, hearing what your audience thought of your speech can help you give a better speech the next time around. Realizing the importance of feedback, some professional speakers hand out post-speech questionnaires, designed to find out where they succeeded and where they failed to meet audience needs. Valuable information often emerges from these responses that enables speakers to adjust their presentation for the next occasion. For example, if you have just delivered a speech to a civic organization on the increasing problem of drunk boating, you may learn that your audience would have preferred a speech with fewer statistics and more concrete advice on combating the problem. In addition, although they liked your suggestions for local legislation, one listener suggested a way to make current laws more effective. The suggestion is so good you may incorporate it into your next presentation.

How do you learn what your audience thought? Hand out a written questionnaire at the end of your speech and ask listeners to return it at a later time. (A self-addressed stamped envelope will encourage a large response.)

Here are some questions you can ask:

1. Did the speech answer your questions about the topic? If not, what questions remain?

2. Can you apply the information you learned in the presentation to your own situation?

3. Were you pleased that you attended the presentation?

4. How could the presentation have better met your needs?

---

19. Edward M. Kennedy, "Where was George?" speech delivered at the Democratic National Convention, July 19, 1988. Reprinted in *Vital Speeches of the Day,* August 15, 1988, pp. 654–55.

F O C U S   O N   R E S E A R C H

ADAPTING TO YOUR AUDIENCE:
CAN YOU GO TOO FAR?

Speech communication professor Craig R. Smith thinks speakers can go too far in adapting to an audience. As a case in point he analyzed the keynote speech Daniel J. Evans, governor of the state of Washington, delivered at the 1968 Republican National Convention. According to Smith, Daniel Evans, a liberal Republican, faced a diverse audience that included conservative convention delegates, a conservative American public, and voters in his home state who were more liberal than most Americans. In addition, Evans believed his keynote speech should embrace all the major presidential contenders including conservatives Richard M. Nixon and Ronald Reagan as well as liberal Nelson Rockefeller.

Smith comments about the choice Evans made: "To meet [the different factions in his audience] he devised a strategy of compromise which resulted in a speech which did not inspire great enthusiasms from any group. [Evans' speech] provided a good illustration of . . . too much adaptation."

According to profiles of the delegate audience (obtained through personal interviews) and the national audience (based on polls preceding the convention), the keynote address failed to reflect audience sentiment:

✼ Although Evans, conservative delegates, and the national audience agreed that Vietnam was the most important issue facing the nation, polls showed that the national audience was divided evenly between those who supported an escalation of the war and those who supported a pullout. However, the keynote address encouraged neither position, calling for a "Republican" solution to the war—73 percent of the

national audience was non-Republican, so Evans' stance left out the majority of the audience.

✼ Evans chose to avoid specific solutions, a strategy that encouraged listeners to reach their own conclusions. Even though he was personally in favor of "open housing" laws to help alleviate racial tension, he called for "individual involvement" in racial issues as a solution. "By avoiding a specific solution," said Smith, "Evans developed his idea in a way that did not correspond with the nation's perceptions and preferences. That is, he did not call for a repeal of 'open housing' laws nor did he endorse them."

✼ In an attempt to please his audience, Evans moved generally from a consensus on a problem to a vague or implied solution that satisfied no one. Smith points out that this strategy was unnecessary because keynote addresses often function as sparks for debate. Listeners have the option of accepting or rejecting individual positions proposed by the speaker.

What could Evans have done considering the varied audiences he faced? Smith believes Evans failed to advocate positions all his audiences held in common—positions he himself espoused. The result was an undramatic speech that created little enthusiasm in the convention hall or among the millions of American viewing the convention from their homes.

Evans' task of accommodating different audiences was not easy. But he made the job unnecessarily difficult by failing to understand and embrace areas of common ground.

To encourage an honest and complete response, indicate that people do not have to sign their names to the questionnaire.

Before reviewing these comments, be your own speech critic. Make a list of the strengths and weaknesses of your speech, as you perceived them. Decide the areas you will try to improve for your next presentation. Next, compare your criticisms with those of your listeners and reassess the areas where you and your audience disagree. By concentrating on the speech you have delivered instead of putting it immediately out of your mind, you will become more sensitive to your own performance.

The most important relationship in public speaking is the relationship between SUMMARY speaker and audience. Learn everything you can about your audience so you can meet its needs in your topic and your approach.

Start by developing a profile of your listeners based on demographic and psychological evaluations. Learn the average age of your listeners, whether they are predominantly male or female, their educational level and how much they know about your subject. Try to identify members of your audience in terms of their membership in religious, racial and ethnic, occupational, socioeconomic, and political groups. Life-style choices can tell you a great deal about audience attitudes, beliefs, and values.

Successful speakers define the expectations that surround the speaking occasion. They learn how much interest their audience has in their topic and how much their audience knows about it before they get up to speak.

Audience analysis is accomplished through the use of questionnaires based on fixed-alternative questions, scale questions, and open-ended questions. Audience analysis can also be conducted through observation and interviews.

To ensure a speaker-audience connection, show your listeners at the start of your speech how you will help them; have confidence your audience wants to hear you, even if they are more knowledgeable than you are; present yourself as fitting into the group, rather than superior to the group; refer to people in your audience; and involve your listeners in your speech.

When your speech is over, try to determine your audience's response through a post-speech evaluation-questionnaire.

1. Why will a speech fail in the absence of audience analysis?   QUESTIONS
2. Can speakers be ethical and adapt to their audiences at the same time? Does   FOR STUDY AND
   adaptation imply audience manipulation or meeting the audience's needs?   DISCUSSION
3. What underlying principles should you use to conduct an effective audience
   analysis?
4. From what you learned in Chapter Three about listening, what steps can you take
   to ensure a positive speaker-audience connection?

ACTIVITIES 1. Focusing on the core idea of your next speech, analyze the students in your public speaking class who will be your audience. Conduct several in-depth interviews with your classmates. Circulate a questionnaire. Based on the information you gather, develop an audience profile. Write a three-to-four-page paper in which you describe the attitudes, values, interests, and knowledge of your listeners as they relate to your topic and you. Finally, outline a strategy of audience adaptation that will serve your interests and the interests of your listeners.

2. Before another speech, give to every member of your class, including your instructor, an index card on which a seven-point scale is drawn, with 1 being the most negative point on the scale and 7 being the most positive. Ask your classmates to register the degree to which your speech was relevant to them. If most of the responses fall below the scale midpoint, analyze how you could have prepared a more successful speech.

3. Select a recent speech you have attended or a famous speech about which you have read that exemplifies a successful audience adaptation. In a written paper, analyze the factors that contributed to the audience's positive response and present findings to your class. Conduct the same analysis for a speech that failed to meet the audience's needs.

Preparing and
Presenting
Your Speech

PART TWO

"Knowledge is of two kinds: we know a subject ourselves, or we know where we can find information about it."

Samuel Johnson

RESEARCHING YOUR SPEECH

aul's speech was unique—or so it seemed. It was a persuasive speech, urging men, as well as women, to consider a career in nursing—a career dedicated to helping people in need. The basis for the speech, Paul said, was a visit he made to the intensive care ward of a university hospital where he spoke with nurses who cared for the terminally ill. Talking to these nurses and witnessing the conditions under which they worked gave his speech special significance—or so it seemed, until the post-speech questioning began.

Paul's first question came from a student whose mother was an intensive care nurse at a local hospital. Because the student knew so much about the field, she asked Paul to supply a few details he had neglected to mention in his speech—the name of the hospital he visited and the names and backgrounds of the nurses. To their surprise, Paul could not answer. After hesitating a few moments, he told his audience he had not expected these questions so had not prepared for them. Then he confessed that although the facts in his speech were true, they did not come from personal research. He had based the entire speech on an old magazine article.

Paul admitted he misled his listeners because he thought they would listen more closely if they believed he had visited a hospital and talked to the nursing staff. He admitted that he didn't give himself enough time for interviews or library research. Locating the magazine article in his files at home was all he could do to meet the speech deadline.

Although Paul's actions were unethical, his instincts about audience response were correct. The quality of a speaker's research, as well as the type of research, can affect the way people react. In this case, the personal interview would have been the most effective research tool, but other options were available. Paul could have conducted library research to supplement his outdated article; he could have contacted professional nursing organizations or scanned government sources. Paul's shortcut robbed his listeners of the opportunity to hear a well researched, carefully thought-out presentation and substituted an expedient solution unlikely to do justice to the topic, no matter how well it was developed or how effectively it was delivered.

According to speech communication researchers Helen Fleshler, Joseph Ilardo, and Joan Demoretcky, there is a link between the documentation you use in a speech and your credibility as a speaker, as well as the credibility of your message. The researchers define speaker credibility as the extent to which a speaker is perceived as a competent spokesperson; message credibility is the extent to which the speech is considered to be factual and well supported through documentation. The credibility-documentation link is especially strong when listeners know little about the speaker and have no strong attitudes toward the topic.[1]

In this chapter, we examine the research sources you can use to make sure that you will never find yourself in Paul's uncomfortable situation caused by sloppy or inadequate research. We analyze the process you can use to gather information from

1. Helen Fleshler, Joseph Ilardo, and Joan Demoretcky, "The Influence of Field Dependence, Speaker Credibility Set and Message Documentation on Evaluations of Speaker and Message Credibility," *The Southern Speech Communication Journal* (Summer 1974): 389–402.

interview subjects—including yourself—and introduce a library research strategy. As you research your topic, think of yourself as a detective, trying to find the most complete information without wasting time or energy. You will learn that some leads pay off while others go nowhere and that the greatest wealth of information often comes from the least expected source.

We live in an information society that produces far more information than we can use. With computers giving us access to ever larger data bases, one of your most important jobs will be to decide what is relevant and what is not; what you should incorporate into your speech and what you should discard. Setting limits on your own research requires that you use your core idea as a kind of mission statement: You will do what is required to give an effective presentation, but not allow yourself to be led down an interesting but unrelated path.

Research gives you the tools you need to expand your core idea into a full-length presentation. Often, it can lead you to deliver a slightly different type of speech than you expected. As facts emerge, you expand your speech here, streamline it there, take it apart to include new information, and, ultimately, piece it together in its final form.

Although research involves knowing where to look for information, it also involves an analytic process crucial to any kind of decision making. This chapter and the following investigate both the search and the analysis as the critical factors in successful research.

By the time you reach college, you have probably held one or more jobs, pursued hobbies like coin collecting, or sports like tennis, become an expert in repairing your 1978 Volkswagon, or joined a political club. You may know more about Woody Allen movies than anyone on campus or may be able to describe the customs that surround the celebration of the Chinese New Year.

BEGIN WITH YOUR OWN KNOWLEDGE AND SKILL

Can you use yourself as a credible source if you speak about any of these topics? Certainly, if your experience will make an impact on your audience. Randall Dale Adams spent thirteen years in a Texas prison, and three of them on death row for a murder he did not commit. Now he travels extensively to speak to audiences about his experiences and to offer advice about criminal justice, life in prison, and related topics centered in his personal knowledge gained from the day he was arrested in 1976. Shortly after his release from prison he began to accept invitations to speak about his experiences, usually on college campuses. Adams reports: "This was an indication that there was a great deal of interest in my story for, in truth, it could have happened to almost anyone."[2]

The most effective presentations start—but do not stop—with personal experiences. When Bill Clinton, as Governor of Arkansas, was asked to deliver a

---

2.   Randall Adams with William Hoffer and Marilyn Hoffer, *Adams V. Texas.* (New York: St. Martin's Paperbacks, 1991), p. 369.

I N T E R V I E W

John V. Esposito,
Attorney, Author, Professional Speaker

John V. Esposito is a nationally and internationally recognized attorney, with more than twenty years experience in the law, including civil and criminal litigation, in state and federal courts throughout the United States, and around the world. He has appeared on major television news and talk shows, addressing a variety of legal and social issues. His articles and lectures span a wide variety of topics and issues relative to U.S. and international law and jurisprudence. Mr. Esposito is the senior partner of the law offices of Esposito & Esposito, with offices located in Logan, West Virginia, Hilton Head Island, South Carolina, and Washington, DC. Because Mr. Esposito is a successful member of the legal profession and is in demand as a public speaker, we decided to ask him questions of interest to public speaking students. Our questions focused on the importance of research in public speaking. Frequently in front of the television camera, Mr. Esposito is also highly qualified to comment on the interplay of public speaking and television.

Question: How do you feel about the importance of research in supporting an argument, a line of reasoning, or a point of view?

Answer: Research is fundamental and paramount to any expression of thought in public speaking. When I enter a courtroom, or an auditorium to speak, or when I participate in an international symposium, or when I step before a television camera, I must know as much about the subject of my remarks as possible. While I certainly cannot be omnipotent . . . nevertheless, I do make every effort to know as much as I can about the subject. My success as a trial lawyer is based upon the principle that I know more about my case when I enter the courtroom than anyone else involved with it. As such, in all regards, research is fundamental to any type of presentation, especially with regard to public speaking.

Question: Do you have any particular way of doing research you favor?

Answer: I know that technology, such as computer research, offers access to a great deal of information; however, I am more traditional in this regard, and I prefer to go to the appropriate library, locate the books or source materials that I need, relative to the particular subject, and I read and study them very thoroughly. An illustration of this concept is in the area of litigation as a lawyer. In doing research for my briefs or memorandums of law in preparation for trial or argument in a case, I locate the cases that I need, and then I study them very thoroughly and, as such, when I stand before the judge to make a point, or to make a statement about the law, I refer specifically to the particular case, which may be reasonably appropriate, with great care and accuracy. I do not just read the highlights of a case in my preparation, but I study the entire case, and then I cast it into the form of a very cogent presentation. The same principles apply in public speaking. When you stand before an audience, you must communicate and speak about the subject with such intensity and with such a thorough understanding that the listeners will be convinced that you are an authority on that particular subject. To do otherwise is to deny the audience, as well as yourself, the benefit of a well reasoned and articulated discussion about the particular subject.

Question: Do you believe a person's attitude about doing research is a key to becoming an authority on the subject?

Answer: Attitude is an important factor in research. Personally, and professionally, I enjoy doing research because I find it to be an extension of my ability to employ the sense of reason. As such, I engage in my research, in the law or otherwise, with a certain amount of enthusiasm, and with a genuine quest for knowledge. You can never do enough research. I realize the limitations of the human mind and the frailties of human nature; however, given those limitations, the techniques of research are incredibly expansive today in our society, and we should take advantage of this abundance of information which is readily accessible to all of us at all levels. We should embark upon our research as though we were expanding our horizons and, likewise, those of our audience, whomever they may be.

Question: Let's turn to the use of television. You have spoken before television a great deal, and our students are interested in what a public speaker can suggest about expressing themselves through the medium of television.

Answer: As we move into the twenty-first century, television is clearly going to be the primary medium for public communication. Many of today's students will, more than likely, during the course of their career, irrespective of what it may be, appear before a television camera for one reason or another. In my opinion the same principles of public speaking apply, whether it is making a presentation on television, or appearing before a live audience. The techniques and basic principles of public speaking are adaptable to all forms of media presentation. Knowing the importance of effective communication, whether it be television or otherwise, I constantly study myself, in an attempt to ascertain my strengths and weaknesses as a speaker. We should all strive to improve our communicative skills, whether it be our voice, our manner of presentation, or delivery, our style, or any of the other aspects of communication. Also, I believe that public speaking and the communication of ideas and knowledge and information to others through the spoken word will be even more important in the twenty-first century,

as we reach beyond our local borders and communicate with others around the world. I find myself excited when I am invited to speak to an audience in our country or elsewhere in the world. I am honored to be asked to share my opinion. Perhaps the comment my father made to me when I graduated from law school is appropriate for this discussion in regard to public speaking. He advised me that I should be honored when someone seeks my legal counsel, and I am. I also follow that creed in regard to public speaking. Each of us, as public speakers, whether it be students or otherwise, should be honored to be asked to make an address and, as such, we should express ourselves to the best of our ability. We should make our presentation with the notion that our remarks could possibly alter the course of human history. The principles are the same, irrespective of the medium of presentation, to be the best public speaker we can be.

Question: You have certainly underscored the importance of research, command of the subject matter, and the adaptability of the principles of public speaking to television. As we close this interview, let me ask you if you have any final tip or statement you would like to share with the audience who studies this book.

Answer: I genuinely believe that every student, in a public speaking class, or elsewhere, should strive to be the very best that they can be. We should all take advantage of the opportunity to acquire knowledge in this age of communication and, as such, we should acquire as much knowledge as we can. When it is your turn to speak, whether it be to an audience of one, or to an audience of thousands, and whether it be in conversation with a king or a president, or just your next-door neighbor, you should strive to be the best speaker you can be. Each of us can, in fact, make a difference in the course of human affairs, and the difference is often dependent upon effective communication. I would offer a very simple formula for the students to follow. I believe that the keys to effective public speaking are as simple as the "three R's". However, for public speaking, I refer to it as the "six R's", which are, research it, "rite" it, read it, re-edit it, rehearse it, and recite it with eloquence and oratorical splendor.

Source: Interview with John Esposito, April 29, 1993.

An information-gathering interview can provide invaluable support for your speech.

nomination speech for Massachusetts Governor Michael Dukakis, who received the Democratic Party's nomination for President in 1988, he reached a low point as a speaker when he droned on for thirty-five minutes. Recognizing his error as his audience drifted away, he concluded his speech to applause signifying relief that it was coming to an end. On July 16, 1992, however, he used this experience to his advantage when he accepted the Democratic nomination for president by announcing: "I ran for President this year for one reason and one reason only: I wanted to come back to this convention and finish that speech I started in 1988." With a good laugh to his credit Mr. Clinton then proceeded to deliver a well received speech that was thick with biographical references and made extensive use of the research, including quotes from the Bible, John F. Kennedy, Mississippi civil rights activist Fannie Lou Hamer, and his grandfather."[3]

CONDUCTING PERSONAL INTERVIEWS

Look around you on campus and in your community. You'll find experts who can tell you as much as you need to know about thousands of subjects. You can get opinions about the stock market or about the effects of different types of running shoes on the development of shinsplints; on race relations and acid rain; on broadcast news simulations and the use of crack cocaine in the suburbs. This information is often available for the asking if you know how to conduct personal interviews.

---

3.   John Nichols, "Speech evolved after extensive study, 19 drafts," *The Toledo Blade,* Friday, Toledo, Ohio, July 17, 1992, p. 4.

By talking to an expert, you can clarify questions, fill in knowledge gaps, and learn more about a subject than you expected. In the process, you also gather opinions based on years of experience.

Interviews are especially useful if you want information too new to be found in published sources or if you want to give your listeners the views of an expert. If you are delivering a speech on a recent rule change in baseball, interviewing the manager of the Oakland Athletics will add authority as well as interest to your presentation.

Finding the Right Interview Subject

The first step is to find the right people to question.

Start With Your Family and Friends.   If you are preparing a speech comparing motherhood from the perspective of two groups of women—those who have children in their early twenties and those who wait till they're past thirty-five—you can start by interviewing your mother, who gave birth to you when she was twenty-three, and your aunt, who had her first child at the age of thirty-eight. You can speak to your best friend's father, an obstetrician, about childbirth in these two age groups.

Ask For Referrals.   Ask your interview subjects for the names of other people who might be willing to talk with you. The obstetrician, for example, may point you to one of his patients. Your mother may have a friend who had her first child at the age of twenty-one and her last at the age of forty-two.

Check Organizations.   If you have no friends or family who can act as experts or if you want a greater range of opinion, consider calling an organization that deals with your subject. In this case, you can contact the local medical society and ask for the name of an obstetrician who specializes in high-risk pregnancies (women over thirty-five fit into this group) or the director of a local nursery school with years of experience dealing with children and their mothers.

Spokespersons from trade associations and government agencies can also be good interview sources. For the latest statistics comparing the cost of childbirth in women under twenty-five and women over thirty-five, you can interview an expert at the Health Insurance Institute, a Washington, DC-based trade association, or a spokesperson for the U.S. National Center for Health Statistics, a government agency.

To learn the names, addresses, and phone numbers of special interest organizations, consult the *Encyclopedia of Associations*, available at your library. The latest edition of the *Washington Information Directory* (also available at the library) will help you find the government office with the information you need.

Corporations can also provide invaluable information. If you contact the public relations department of a retailer like Sears, you may learn, for example, that older women are more likely to buy business clothes when they are pregnant, an indication that they hope to continue working during their pregnancy and that they expect to return to work soon after their baby is born. Ask your librarian for a list of corporate addresses and phone numbers.

You may choose as interview subjects people who live far beyond your local community. Although you are not likely to do this for a college speech, long-distance interviews are common in business and civic speeches. You can write to these organizations for information. Students are often surprised at how many brochures, reports, pamphlets, and books they receive through simple written requests.

As you scan this material, keep in mind that healthy skepticism is in order. Believing everything you read from a corporation or a corporate trade association ignores the built-in bias of the material. A company is not likely to send you material that casts it or its products in a bad light. You'll get a presentation that may not necessarily be dishonest, but that will certainly be one-sided.

Check Published Sources.   Published sources, including books and magazine and newspaper articles, can provide excellent interview ideas. Because writers and reporters are trained to back their stories with the opinions of experts, you are likely to find citations you can use. If you are writing a speech on the hazards of asbestos, you may see the name Irving Selikoff, M.D. in many articles. Dr. Selikoff is an authority on asbestos whose interview would be invaluable for your speech. Similarly, if you are writing a speech on homelessness in your community, your local newspaper may have articles about advocates for the homeless.

Asking for an Interview

Regardless of whether people are well known, they may respond favorably to a request for an interview. Keep in mind that your request is a recognition of the individuals' knowledge and expertise.

You can ask for an interview by phone or letter. If you use the telephone, call the expert and introduce yourself. Then explain what your speech is about and why you would appreciate his or her cooperation. Honest flattery never hurts. Tell your interview subjects you chose them because of their expertise and reputation. If they agree to cooperate, set up an appointment at a place and time convenient to them. Busy people are rarely available the moment you call and appreciate notice to collect their thoughts. If you cannot get the person's phone number or want to introduce yourself in a more formal way, you can request an interview in writing.

Preparing for an Interview

Preparation is crucial to a successful interview.

Do Your Homework.   Learn all you can about your interview subjects and their special areas of expertise ahead of time through library research. Check for articles by or about them in newspapers, magazines, and professional journals. Review books they may have written. Ask them to send you a résumé and other background material.

Frame Your Questions.   Write down the most important questions you want answered. Try to avoid asking questions that can be answered "yes" or "no"; leading questions ("Don't you think that jury's decision was wrong?"); vague questions ("Is our jury system in good working order?"); or hostile questions, especially those attacking the person you are interviewing ("As one of this country's leading legal scholars, why aren't you doing more to save the American system of justice from ruin?"). Ask questions that will elicit a thoughtful response. Here, for example, are two questions we asked the public speakers interviewed for this text:

⌘ What is the hardest part of public speaking for you? The easiest?

⌘ How much do you learn about your audience before choosing your speech topic and writing your speech?

Write your questions in a logical order, one leading naturally to another. Place the most important questions at the top to guarantee that they will be answered before your time is up. Review the questions immediately before the interview begins so they are fresh in your mind and keep them with you during the interview. Although you may not necessarily adhere to them, they provide a framework.

During the Interview

Let things happen—within a structure:

Restate the Reason For the Interview.   Even if you have made your intentions clear in advance, it always helps to state the purpose of the interview.

Let the Person Do the Talking.   Try to intrude as little as possible. If the person digresses, politely but firmly ask questions to redirect the conversation. You can't afford to waste time or you'll leave without material for your speech.

Don't be too rigid in following the questions you framed before the interview. Ask follow-up questions based on the person's responses. Because you can't anticipate these in advance, try to be flexible. If you allow an interview to unfold, it may take a direction you never expected—one filled with information and interest.

Focus On the Person You are Interviewing, Not Yourself.   Listen to the responses your subject is giving. Interviewers often make the mistake of thinking about their next question while their previous question is being answered.

Make Sure You Understand What Is Said.   Ask the person to repeat anything that is unclear. You may have to do this several times if the expert uses technical language or thinks of you as a professional colleague instead of a layperson. Don't feel you will appear ignorant if you ask for clarification.

Ask for *specific* examples and anecdotes. Ask for the spellings of names and verify important facts and statistics by repeating them. If you are unsure of something that has been said, repeat the interview subject's words, summing up the points that have been made and reaffirming their correctness. Don't be afraid to ask a subject to slow down. Interviewers who are overly polite leave without usable information.

Be Sensitive to Nonverbal Clues.   Raised eyebrows, smiles, fidgeting, hesitations, arms hugging the body, and other nonverbal cues tell you a great deal about a person's thoughts. Use these clues to pursue the most productive questions.

Be Conscious of the Time.   If you promise the interview will take no longer than a half-hour, keep your word, if at all possible.

At the Close of the Interview

You can get information even as you say goodbye:

Ask This Parting Question.   "Is there any area we haven't touched on that you feel is important to this interview?" Although some people will say no, others will add vital comments.

Ask For Leads.   Many experts are so specialized that they are not able to respond to every question. For example, if you ask a general surgeon a question about a sports injury, he or she may lack the experience to provide the information. When this happens, ask for help. In this case, the surgeon may lead you to a colleague who specializes in sports medicine.

Ask For Written Materials.   Many experts can give you printed information that expresses their point of view including magazine or journal articles, press releases, and books. If these materials are not available, ask for a list of sources.

Ask For the Opportunity to Call With Questions.   As you review the interview, questions may occur to you. Ask the expert if you can call later for clarification.

After the Interview

While the conversation is still fresh in your mind, review your notes, recordings, as well as any written materials your interview subject may have given you. (If you put off the review, you may forget details and be unable to decipher the connections you made in your notes.) Your goal is to define the main points of the interview and see how they fit into the specific purpose of your speech. The review also enables you to identify usable quotations, statistics, and anecdotes and to note the areas that require additional research.

THE LIBRARY SEARCH STRATEGY

The library houses a variety of supporting materials for your speech including books; newspaper, magazine, and journal articles; and maps, charts, and other visual aids. Through a computer-linked electronic search, you can extend your search far beyond your campus or community library.

We suggest you follow a library search strategy in which you examine and evaluate materials from various sources to select the materials that will help you most. A search strategy moves from the general to the specific, enabling you to define—and refine—the approach you take to your topic. According to Virginia Tieffel, director of library user education at Ohio State University, "the decision to adopt the strategy is the most crucial part of the research process."[4]

As you work with the strategy, keep these things in mind: First, there is a distinction between primary and secondary sources. Primary sources are "original" materials, such as speeches, reports, and letters; secondary sources are interpretations and criticisms of the primary sources. If the U.S. surgeon general issues a report on the dangers of smoking, the report itself (available from the Surgeon General's Office) is the primary source; newspaper and magazine articles about the report are secondary source material.

Second, there is little relationship between the length of your speech and the amount of time you must spend in research. Many students learn the hard way that five minutes of research will not suffice for a five-minute speech. Whatever the length of the speech, you have to spend time uncovering facts and building a strong foundation of support.

Third, although the ten steps in the search strategy are presented in a logical order, you may have to move back and forth among the steps in order to get the information you need. You may learn something from an essay or a book (Step 5) that requires clarification in an encyclopedia or dictionary (Steps 1 and 2). Be flexible as you proceed—and be willing to ask the librarian for assistance. With experience, you will learn to focus on those steps most likely to give you the information you need.

The search strategy is one of the most useful things you will learn in college. Virginia Tieffel explains that we live in an age of information, and "information handling skills are crucial to your success" as a public speaker and as a professional. "Today, the challenge is not only to find information, but to evaluate it and focus on what is important."[5]

Before examining the search strategy, let's look at how the computer is changing the complexion of library research.

Computerized Research

Computerized research helps you in two ways: It reduces the amount of time needed to search for information and makes it possible to conduct new and different searches. The traditional card catalog and published indexes to journals offer limited search strategies, in general, allowing you to search by subject, author, and sometimes title. By contrast, you can use key words from titles and subject headings, instead of the exact full title or heading, to search computerized sources. For example, if you are

---

4.   Interview with Virginia Tieffel, December 4, 1989.
5.   Ibid.

interested in all books with the word "stepfamilies" in the title, you can conduct a computerized search using this word alone.

The ability to conduct a key word search is especially helpful when a library catalog or journal index lacks subject headings that precisely describe your topic. For example, if you are interested in legislation controlling semiautomatic weapons, you may find that the closest subject heading in the noncomputerized library catalog is "firearms—law and legislation." Using the computer, however, you can narrow your focus to law and legislation regarding semiautomatic weapons. The computer will identify all articles that deal with this specific topic.

The computer also allows you to narrow your search by examining the overlap between two or more general subject headings. If you are interested in the effects of child-rearing practices on self-esteem, traditional indexes will lead you to two separate subject headings: (1) child-rearing practices and (2) self-esteem. By contrast, the computer will lead you to the sources where these two headings intersect. Some computerized sources also allow you to restrict your search to certain types of materials (for example, books, government publications, or sound recordings); to materials published in a certain year or years; and to publications written in specific foreign languages.

What You Will Find on Computer.   Many familiar library sources have been computerized, including the library card catalog. In some systems, the catalog is linked with a computerized circulation system that tells you whether the library owns a particular book and whether it is currently on the shelves. Other computerized systems list all the books, periodicals, and other materials owned by several libraries, either within a limited geographic region or around the country. Virginia Tieffel explains how the computerized library system has changed the nature of research at Ohio State:

> Before computerization, if you wanted to use the common card catalog, you had to come to the main library. The catalog told you in which of our 26 libraries the book was shelved, but it didn't say anything about availability. If the book was in the undergraduate library, you had to walk three blocks to find out if it were there. Now, with the computer, you can see what is in the system from any library. Students sit down at computer work stations, type in their requests, and learn instantaneously what is available and where it can be found. If a book is on loan, the computer also tells them when it will be back in the system.[6]

Published indexes to magazine, journal, and newspaper articles have also been computerized. *The Readers' Guide to Periodical Literature* is now available on computer as well as in print. In some cases, the texts of entire journals or newspapers are available. You can read the *Harvard Business Review* on your computer screen. Even reference books are becoming available: Encyclopedias, dictionaries, and statistical compilations are some of the computerized sources you may find in

6.   Ibid.

libraries. The technology used to computerize these various sources takes several different forms.

On-Line Data Bases.   Many libraries have contractual arrangements with information providers enabling them to search providers' computer data bases. The library computer is connected to the information supplier's mainframe computer by way of communications software, a modem, and telephone lines. This technology is commonly referred to as on-line data base searching.

Among the most popular on-line data bases are Dialog, BRS Information Technologies, Orbit, and Wilson Line. Each gives you access to hundreds of different data bases in such fields as business, medicine, art, and the social sciences. Wilson Line, for example, provides access to all the indexes H. W. Wilson produces including *The Readers' Guide To Periodical Literature, Art Index,* and the *Social Sciences Index.*

Many of these on-line systems are expensive, with charges commonly based on the amount of time spent connected to the mainframe computer and the number of citations viewed or printed. A typical system charges $1 a minute and between fifty cents and $1 for every reference printed. The average cost of an on-line search is between $20 and $50. Many on-line systems are also difficult to use. These factors often make it necessary for libraries to impose restrictions on these services: they may require that all searches be done by librarians, limit the number or types of searches, or charge for searches.

Follow a library search strategy to discover the sources of information that will help you most.

Some information providers market their on-line data base services to individuals, who can obtain an account with the company and search from their home computers. Among the most popular on-line data bases used by individuals are CompuServe, EasyNet, Dialog's Knowledge Index, and BRS After Dark. Billing is done through a credit card.

Library Data Bases.   Libraries may own or lease data bases stored on magnetic computer tapes and mount them on their own mainframe computer or mini-computer. The data bases may then be searched from various terminals in a network similar to those found on many college campuses. Among these data bases are the library's own card catalog; ERIC (Educational Resources Information Center), which indexes sources relating to every aspect of education; and Medline, which accesses medical publications. Most of these data bases are user-friendly and less expensive than on-line systems. (Charges based on connect-time and number of citations viewed are eliminated.)

CD-ROM.   The most recent technology is the optical disc, used in a format called CD-ROM (*compact disc-read only memory*). As the name indicates, you can read information stored on the disc, but you cannot change the information in any way. CD-ROM data bases are stored on discs that look like audio compact discs, and they are searched and read using search software and a special disc drive connected to a microcomputer. Most CD-ROM data bases are user-friendly, although it still takes time and effort to learn to use them. Among the most popular CD-ROM data bases are Infotrack, which provides access to recent popular periodicals and newspapers; H.W. Wilson, which accesses the various Wilson indexes; and ERIC. (Many data bases are available in three different forms: CD-ROM, on-line, and magnetic computer tape.)

Change is Constant.   Information technology is advancing so rapidly that new technologies will probably be invented by the time you read this text.

While the computer is opening up new ways of gathering information, it is also making libraries seem more complex. An ever-increasing variety of computerized resources is available, operating in many different ways. It takes time and effort to learn to use each source effectively.

We now turn to the nine steps of the library search strategy, many of which involve the use of computers.

Step 1: Consult Encyclopedias

Encyclopedias are one or the other: general or specialized. The key to using any encyclopedia is to begin with the index, which usually refers you to the appropriate volume and page numbers.

Articles in both general and specialized encyclopedias often contain bibliographies that lead you to additional sources. Bibliographies may be found in many sources, including books, handbooks, journals, biographies, and essays. In addition to being part of other sources, bibliographies are also published as separate volumes. Sheehy's *Guide to Reference Books* is a good example of a single-volume general bibliography of reference titles. *Bibliographic Index: A Cumulative Bibliography of Bibliographies* (1937 to present) is a useful guide to bibliographies published separately or as parts of other books or journals.

Although encyclopedias can be a helpful basic source, they generally are not accepted on bibliographies for class speeches. Use them to lead to other information.

General Encyclopedias.   General encyclopedias cover a wide range of topics in a broad manner. You'll find coverage of topics as varied as the Vietnam War, rap music, riots at soccer games, and the history of television. The following are the most popular general encyclopedias:

The Encyclopedia Americana.   1991, thirty volumes. Extensive coverage of science and technology, excellent discussions of American History. Volume 30 is the index to the rest of the encyclopedia.

Encyclopedia Britannica.   1991, thirty volumes. Detailed scholarly articles with an international orientation. Strong in the arts, literature, and the humanities. Excellent bibliographies. The index, a series of volumes called the *Micropedia,* is arranged alphabetically by subject. The *Micropedia* provides quick information and cross-references to the more in-depth information in the *Macropedia.* Because most general encyclopedias are revised frequently, they are a source of current information.

Specialized Encyclopedias.   In contrast, specialized encyclopedias focus on particular areas of knowledge in more detail. Most disciplines have specialized encyclopedias; the following are examples of what is available. The title usually indicates the subject covered:

The Encyclopedia of Religion.   1986, sixteen volumes. Encompasses the theoretical, practical, and sociological aspects of the world's religions.

International Encyclopedia of the Social Sciences.   1968, seventeen volumes. Reflects the development of the social sciences, psychiatry, psychology, sociology, and statistics.

McGraw-Hill Encyclopedia of Science and Technology.   1992, twenty volumes. Covers the physical, natural, and applied sciences in nontechnical language.

Step 2: When Needed, Use a Dictionary

During your research, you may encounter an unfamiliar word or term. Consult a dictionary for a definition. Dictionaries also provide information on pronunciation, spelling, syllabication (word division), usage, and etymology (the origins and development of words). Like encyclopedias, dictionaries are classified as either general or special.

General Dictionaries.   General dictionaries define a broad range of terms. Unabridged dictionaries are comprehensive, while abridged dictionaries provide more limited coverage. Abridged dictionaries usually include only commonly used words; they are relatively small, revised frequently, and are a good source of information on new words.

Unabridged Dictionaries

Webster's Third New International Dictionary of the English Language.   Most recently revised in 1986. The standard general unabridged dictionary of the English language.

The Oxford English Dictionary.   1989, Twenty volumes. The most authoritative, scholarly, and complete English dictionary. The current *OED* traces and explains the historical development and meaning of all English words in use between 1150 and 1986. A supplement (published in four volumes between 1972 and 1986) is available. Words are illustrated with quotations from authors. The *OED* is also available in a two-volume version.

Abridged Dictionaries

The American Heritage Dictionary.   2d college ed., 1982.

Random House College Dictionary.   Rev. ed., 1980

Webster's Tenth New Collegiate Dictionary.   1993.

Webster's New World Dictionary of the American Language 2d college ed., 1982.

The distinctions between dictionaries, with a view toward strengths and weaknesses, are explained in William A. Katz's book *Introduction to Reference Work,* fifth edition, published in 1987 by McGraw-Hill Book Company. See especially pages 301–303. A second useful source is *The Reader's Adviser, A Layman's Guide to Literature,* thirteenth edition. This volume is edited by Barbara A. Chernow and George A. Vallaso and published by R. R. Bowler Company, 1986. See especially pages 25–29, Chapter two, "Dictionaries."

Webster's New World Dictionary of the American Language is the most prescriptive of the four dictionaries and is favored by *The New York Times,* The Associated Press and The United Press International. The definitions are in historical order and not by the most common current understanding. *The American Heritage Dictionary* first appeared in 1969 and a revision appeared in 1982. This dictionary stresses prescriptive entries, too, and has excellent usage notes. Of particular value are the illustrations (more than 4,000). *Webster's Tenth New Collegiate Dictionary,* another excellent source, emphasizes pronunciation and definitions and was one of the first dictionaries to include slang and vulgarities. *The Random House Collegiate Dictionary* is certainly a satisfactory reference source for word usage. Reference sources generally regard *Websters New World Dictionary of the American Language* to be the most useful reference in this group of four.

Special Dictionaries.   Rather than attempting to list all the words in the English language, special dictionaries cover only words associated with a specific subject or discipline. The dictionary's title usually indicates its coverage:

The American Political Dictionary.

Black's Law Dictionary.

Harvard Dictionary of Scientific and Technical Terms.

Webster's Sports Dictionary.

Step 3: Develop Questions by Reconsidering Your Audience

An important key to effective speaking we stress throughout this book is making an effective speaker–audience connection. Now that you have used general sources in your library search you need to return to a consideration of the needs of your audience in order to narrow your topic.

A careful audience analysis identifies the attitudes, beliefs, values, and needs of your audience as explained in the previous chapter. Understanding your audience helps you to develop specific questions which can be answered as you continue following the search strategy in your library. For example, suppose you were planning to speak on prenuptial agreements, the agreements couples often establish before a marriage. You could turn to a specialized encyclopedia such as *West's Guide to American Law,* in order to define the term "prenuptial" as the American Bar Association defines the term. In Step 2 of this search you probably would have consulted another general source, *The Family Law Dictionary.* This dictionary would give you additional information regarding whether anyone could construct a prenuptial agreement that would be valid or whether it would be necessary to consult an attorney. At this point you would have a clear idea about the general nature of the topic. However, in order to construct an effective speech that would achieve its specific purpose, you should return to your analysis of the audience and brainstorm some questions to guide you during the rest of your library search. Address the following questions as you consider the needs of your audience:

1. When do most people get married?
2. How many people get married each year?
3. How many marriages end in divorce?
4. What do most people think about prenuptial agreements?
5. What do experts think?
6. What happens to property in divorce?

7. How expensive is an agreement?

8. Can I draw this up myself?

Specific questions such as these provide you with a tool to manage the rest of your search. These questions could be placed on index cards with important terms put in the upper right-hand corner of each card. For example, "How expensive is an agreement?" could be labeled "cost." By constructing key terms you can avoid collecting every article that might have potential for your speech and you can develop a plan before you move further into the library. Question 4 might be answered by consulting periodicles that highlight specific cases of divorce where no prenuptial agreement was made. *By developing questions based on your understanding of the needs of your audience, you can increase the likelihood of establishing a most effective speaker–audience connection.*

Step 4: Use Journals and Newspapers

Your next step is to examine journal and newspaper indexes, which are the key to finding specific articles on a topic. Journals and magazines (also known as periodicals) and newspapers, provide up-to-the-minute information not yet published in books. Now that you have identified ideas to connect with the needs of the audience, you can look for specific information in journals and newspapers.

General Periodical and Newspaper Indexes.   General indexes cover such popular magazines and newspapers as *Time, Newsweek, U.S. News & World Report, The New York Times,* and *Los Angeles Times.* The following are among the most frequently used:

Readers' Guide to Periodical Literature—1915 to present. The most widely used index to general and popular periodicals. Organized according to author, subject, and fiction indexes. Included are reviews of motion pictures, television, plays, and books.

The New York Times Index. 1851 to present. Considered "the newspaper of record," *The New York Times* covers national and international news items, editorials, special feature articles, and critical commentaries. Also included are such primary sources as official reports, documents, and the texts of important speeches. The index is arranged under broad subject headings and then chronologically. Other newspapers with an index include the *Wall Street Journal* and the *Christian Science Monitor.*

Infotrac Academic Index. CD-ROM. A computerized index covering popular journals from 1985 to the present, selected psychology and sociology journals from 1987 to present, and *The New York Times* for the most recent six months.

Infotrac National Newspapers Index. CD-ROM. Computerized newspaper index covering five newspapers from 1985 to the present: *Christian Science Monitor, Los Angeles Times, The New York Times, Wall Street Journal,* and *Washington Post.*

The Education Index.   1929 to present. Focuses on all aspects of education. Covers journals, monographs, proceedings, and yearbooks in elementary, secondary, and higher education and includes both a subject and author index.

Humanities Index.   1974 to present (supercedes, in part, *Social Sciences and Humanities Index).* Covers classical studies, folklore, language and literature, philosophy, religion, and so on. Includes both an author and subject index.

Public Affairs Information Service Bulletin.   1915 to present. Indexes journals, books, pamphlets, and reports in economics, social conditions, public administration, international relations, political science, government, law, and legislation. Includes a subject index.

Social Sciences and Humanities Index.   1907 to 1974 (issued as *International Index,* 1907–1952; split into the *Social Sciences Index* and the *Humanities Index* in 1974).

Social Sciences Index.   June 1974 to present (supercedes, in part, *Social Sciences and Humanities Index).* Covers journals in such fields as anthropology, economics, geography, history, political science, law, criminology, and psychology. History is divided between this index and the *Humanities Index* where the coverage of history is more comprehensive. Includes author and subject index.

Step 5: Consult the Library Catalogs or On-Line Catalogs

Through the library catalogs you gain access to the library's collection of books, periodicals, government documents, newspapers, videotapes, recordings, and so on. Books are cataloged by either the Dewey Decimal System or the Library of Congress classification system.

To conduct an effective card catalog search, start by consulting the *Library of Congress Subject Headings* (LCSH) books, usually located near the card catalog. These books list the "correct" subject headings. Important indicators in this classification system include "BT" (broader term); "NT" (narrower term); "RT" (related term); and "UF" (used for), which can be considered another way of saying "see also." When you use LCSH, keep in mind that the boldface type indicates the correct subject headings.

Technology has spawned new types of library catalogs. In addition to the standard card catalog—and in some cases, in place of it—many libraries have transferred their complete list of publications onto computer discs. You can use an on-line catalog to search for material by author, title, and subject, according to LCSH headings.

Step 6: Consult Individual Works in Collections

Because not all works are published separately, an index to materials collected in a single volume is necessary. One of the most useful of these indexes is the *Essay and General Literature Index* (1900 to present). This index covers essays, articles, and symposiums in books published singly or in collections. It is a good source for biographical information and criticism of books. Indexed by author, subject, and title.

Step 7: Consult Biographical Sources

Biographical sources provide information on an individual's education, accomplishments, and professional activities. This information is useful in evaluating the credibility and reliability of remarks a person has made or the position he or she has taken on your topic.

Biographical sources may be either of two categories.

1. Biographical indexes indicate sources of biographical information in books and journals.

2. Biographical dictionaries list and describe the accomplishments of notable people.

Although the dictionary provides the information, the index refers to the source of the information. If you are looking for a brief background on a well known person, consult the biographical dictionary first. If you need an in depth profile of a less well known person, the biographical index is the better source.

These sources are divided further into the following types:

1. International (also known as general or universal) indexes that include people from all walks of life, regardless of nationality or profession.

2. National (also known as regional or geographic) indexes that include people from all walks of life on the basis of nationality (where they live or where they were born).

3. Specialized (also known as professional or subject) indexes that are organized by occupation or profession.

Each type may include material that is retrospective or current. As these classifications imply, restrospective indexes list deceased; current indexes list the living. Some indexes are both retrospective and current.

To start your search, consult the *Biography and Genealogy Master Index and Supplements,* 1980–1993. This volume serves as an index to more than 450,000 biographical sketches in more than 95 biographical dictionaries. Although it doesn't give the biographical citation, it refers you to the dictionary, encyclopedia, or literary criticism that has the citation.

If your library doesn't have this index or if it fails to cite your subject, ask yourself the following questions in order to identify the appropriate biographical source:

1. Is the person living or dead?

    If the person is dead, use a retrospective index.

    If the person is living, use a current source.

2. What is the person's nationality or date of birth?

> If the person's nationality is known, use the appropriate national or regional biographical source.

> If the person's nationality is not known, use an international or general biographical source.

3. What is the person's occupation or profession?

> If a person's occupation is known, use a specialized biographical source.

General Biographical Indexes (Furnish no biographical information as such.)

Author Biographies Master Index.   1984. Includes international, retrospective, and current biographical listings. A consolidated guide to the principal biographical dictionaries devoted to authors, poets, journalists, and other literary figures. Indexed by name.

Biography Index.   1946 to present. Covers international, retrospective, and current biographical references. Includes all occupations. Especially useful as an index to biographical materials in books, periodicals, letters, diaries, genealogies, and obituaries. Name and profession index.

The New York Times Index.   1851 to present. Covers international, retrospective, and current biographical information of people in all occupations. Look under person's name, or if deceased, look under "Deaths," then under the name. Not all obituaries are listed under "Deaths," or in *The New York Times Obituaries Index.* Sometimes obituaries will be found only by looking under a person's name.

The New York Times Obituaries Index. 1858–1968. A supplement covers 1969–1978. Includes international, retrospective, all occupations. Name index.

General Biographical Dictionaries.

Dictionary of American Biography.   1981. Covers notable Americans, retrospective, all occupations. Prestigious and scholarly bibliographies divided into six lists: (1) biographies; (2) authors of the biographies; (3) biographies, according to birthplace; (4) biographies, according to schools attended; (5) biographies, according to occupations; (6) subject index.

Dictionary of National Biography.   1981. Emphasis on national, noteworthy inhabitants of the British Isles and the colonies from the earliest historical period to the present. Retrospective, all occupations. Includes signed articles, followed by bibliographies. Volumes 1–21 cover persons deceased before 1901. Volume 22 contains biographies omitted from the first twenty-one volumes and spans the years 1901–1911. Most recent supplements cover 1901 to 1970. Each volume has a cumulative index.

Current Biography.   1940 to present. Lengthy coverage of international person-alities primarily influencing the American scene. Includes current biographies; lists all occupations. Short bibliographies follow coverage. Name and occupation; index.

Special Biographical Dictionaries: Authors.   When searching for information on authors, a good place to start is the *Author Biographies Master Index,* a guide to dictionaries and directories of authors. This will guide you to the appropriate index. Specific biographical dictionaries of authors include the following:

American Authors, 1600–1900: A Biographical Dictionary of American Literature. 1938. One volume with 1,300 biographies and 400 portraits. Biographies include brief bibliographies of writings by and about the authors.

Contemporary Authors.   1962 to present. A multivolume guide to current authors and their works. Contains biographical information and bibliographies listing each individual's publications. Cumulative name index.

European Authors.   1967. Includes brief biographies on European writers living between AD 1000 and 1925.

British Authors Before 1800: A Biographical Dictionary.   1952. Includes 650 biographies as well as bibliographies of works by and about the authors.

World Authors.   1950–1970 (supplements 1970–1975, 1975–1980). Covers more than 1,000 prominent authors between the dates covered. Lengthy biographies.

Special Biographical Dictionaries: Education.

Dictionary of American Scholars.   1982. Includes current U.S. and Canadian college professors and researchers. Each volume covers various professions: Volume 1, history; Volume 2, English, speech, and drama; Volume 3, foreign languages, linguistics, and philology; Volume 4, philosophy, religion, and law. Each volume contains a separate geographic index. Volume 4 includes a name index for the set.

Special Biographical Dictionaries: Science

American Men and Women of Science.   1982. Covers the physical and biological sciences and social and behavioral sciences. Current and international. Geographic and discipline index.

Step 8: Evaluate Your Sources with Book and Journal Reviews

Reviews of books and journals will help you evaluate and criticize a work, summarize its content, and learn something about the author. Book review indexes are divided into two categories: general and specialized book review indexes.

General Book Review Indexes.   If you need reviews for a popular fiction or nonfiction book or for a general interest book written during the past hundred years, begin your search with a general book review index.

Book Review Digest.   1905 to present. Covers popular and current interest magazines and book reviews. Provides brief summary of each book and three to four excerpts from selected reviews. Title and subject index.

Book Review Index.   1965 to present. Covers humanities, social sciences, fiction, poetry, juvenile literature, general nonfiction. Only citations for reviews are listed. Provides greater number of review citations than *Book Review Digest.* Title index.

Current Book Review Citations.   1976 to present. Includes fiction and nonfiction books, foreign language titles, new editions, juvenile and young adult literature. Author and title index.

Index to Book Reviews in the Humanities.   1960 to present. Covers art, architecture, biography, memoirs, drama, folklore, history, language, literature, music, philosophy, travel, and adventure.

The New York Times Book Review Index.   1896–1970. The five sections of the index provide access to book reviews by author, title, "byliner" (the reviewer, or author of essay, article, column, or letter), subject, and category (drama, anthologies, short stories, and so on). Only citations for reviews are given. Volumes for years following 1970 are also available.

The New York Times Index.   1913 to present. To locate book reviews in this index, find the subject heading "Book Reviews." Then scan the alphabetical listing of authors' last names for the books of your choice. Note the location of the review.

Readers' Guide to Periodical Literature.   1915 to present. Since 1976, book reviews have been indexed in the final section of each volume. Arranged alphabetically by author's last name. Only citations for reviews are given.

Specialized Book Review Indexes.   If your book is specialized, look for a review in a subject-specific periodical index that also has book reviews. Here are some examples.

Applied Science and Technology Index.

Art Index.

Biological and Agricultural Index.

Business Index.

Education Index.

Humanities Index.

Index to Religious Periodical Literature.

Philosophers' Index.

Social Science Index.

Reviews of Journals   Three helpful sources for these reviews are: Farber's *Classified List of Periodicals for College Libraries*, Katz' *Magazine for Libraries,* and *Book Review Index* (also references journals).

Step 9: Consider Statistical Sources

As you will see in Chapter Seven, facts and statistics can be used to give authority and credibility to research.

Almanacs.   Almanacs, also known as books of facts, are published annually and record a variety of facts and statistics. In addition to standard current and historic statistics, almanacs also provide facts about government, the economy, business, sports, the arts, current events, religious and other institutions. The following are the most important general almanacs:

World Almanac and Book of Facts.   1868 to present. American in its emphasis. Includes subject, occupation, and profession indexes.

Whitaker's Almanac.   1869 to present. Emphasis is on Great Britain and Europe. Includes subject, name, and profession indexes.

Specialized Statistical Sources.   These sources are published by government organizations.

Statistical Abstract of the United States.   1878 to present. Published by the U.S. Bureau of the Census. Best source for statistics about all aspects of the United States—politics, society, economics, industry, education, law, geography, and science. Gives original sources for most of the statistics cited. Subject index.

Statistical Yearbook: Annuaire Statistique.   1948 to present. Published by the United Nations. Presents statistical tables about every country in the world. Covers such topics as population, agriculture, mining, manufacturing, finance, trade, education, culture, housing, and social statistics. Gives original sources for the statistics cited so that you can locate further information. No index as such nor alphabetical arrangement. The geographic subdivision of most subjects is not strictly alphabetical by country. Countries are grouped by region (for example, Africa, Asia, USSR, Oceania) and are arranged alphabetically within the broad category. Scan the table of contents for the information you require.

Step 10: Consider Government Documents

The federal government is the largest publisher in the United States. Government publications are prepared by government agencies, bureaus, and departments that monitor the affairs and activities of the nation. Documents are issued by the Office of the President, the U.S. Congress, the departments of Commerce (included in this department is the Bureau of the Census), Agriculture, Education, Navy and Army, Indian Affairs, the Veterans' Administration, the Food and Drug Administration, and the FBI.

The U.S. Government Printing Office (GPO) is the primary publisher of federal government documents. Among the unique, authoritative, and timely materials issued by the GPO are detailed census materials, vital statistics, congressional papers and reports, presidential documents, military reports, and "impact statements" on energy, the environment, and pollution. To learn about current and past documents, consult *Monthly Catalog of United States Government Publications.* The catalog lists unclassified publications issued by every department and bureau of the federal government since 1905, listing books, pamphlets, maps, and serials. It contains monthly and cumulative annual indexes. Since 1974, each issue of the catalog has been divided into four parts: (1) the catalog, which lists new documents numerically; (2) a title index to those documents; (3) an author index; and (4) a subject index. Before 1974, the index was primarily organized by subject.

Government documents may also be listed in the library catalog.

If you have trouble finding a source or don't know where to look for a certain type of information, ask the librarian for help. Librarians are experts in finding information efficiently. They can help you learn to use the library's newest computer data base or to decide which of ten different source books on the same subject is most likely to have the information you need. **WHEN YOU NEED HELP, ASK THE LIBRARIAN**

Although librarians are helpful, they will not do your work for you. Before you approach a librarian, you should try to find the information yourself. If you are unsuccessful, phrase your question in specific terms. "I need a book that will give me the address and phone number of organizations for left-handers," is better than "I need information about being left-handed." With new reference sources being published every day, using the expertise of a librarian can make your job as a researcher a lot easier.

SUMMARY   Research gives you the tools you need to support your core idea. A solid research base helps increase your credibility.

Begin your research with your own knowledge and skill based on personal experience. You can then turn for information to experts you can interview. Interview

---

S P E A K   E A S Y

THE KEY TO RESEARCH: TAKING GOOD NOTES

Here are some note-taking techniques to help you organize your research. The key to using them successfully is consistency. Instead of scraps of paper, use 4 × 6 or 5 × 8 index cards as your basic organizer.

1. As you conduct your research, fill out a card for each publication (journal, book, and so on) that looks promising. These are preliminary cards, because you have not yet looked at the sources. Include on the card all the relevant bibliographic information.

2. Weed out the sources that lead nowhere. Then start taking notes on those that remain. Arrange each index card in the following way:

Topic: *The hazards of playing a musical instrument*

Source: Jane E. Brody, "For Artists and Musicians, Creativity Can Mean Illness and Injury," *The New York Times,* October 17, 1989. p. c1.

INFORMATION: As many as 75 percent of musicians are hurt playing instruments. They suffer neck and back pain, damage to the jaw, and hands as well as other musculoskeletal complaints. According to Dr. Richard J. Lederman, a neurologist at the Cleveland Clinic, these problems are often the result of poor habits developed years before. "Many later problems have their origins in the first decade of playing," explained the doctor.

The source card is arranged by topic rather than source. This gives you flexibility to rearrange your ideas as you organize your speech.

Although in this case we have included the entire source, you can include only the title and name of the article and refer to the original source card you completed for the full bibliographic listing. If you are taking notes on a book, include the pages from which the information came.

3. Make one point on each note card. You may have several different cards on a single source, each with different information. In this case, the Jane Brody source also talks about the hazards of art materials. If this information is relevant to your speech topic, make a separate card on it.

4. Use the same note-taking technique to organize the comments you gather in interviews. After the interview, write important comments on cards in the following way:

Topic: *Stress on Campus*

Source: Interview with Dr. Joan Smith, clinical psychologist, April 1, 1990.

INFORMATION: "Both good and bad events in a student's life can cause stress. For example, a new love interest may be even more stressful than increased workload. Evidence has shown that too much stress can lead to health problems."

---

subjects can be located through family and friends, by asking for referrals, by calling relevant organizations, and by checking published sources. Interviews require thorough preparation and careful attention while the interview is taking place. Some researchers take notes during the interview; others use a tape recorder or a combination of the two techniques.

The library search strategy moves you from the most general to the most specific information. Computerized research reduces the time needed to search for information and allows you to conduct different types of searches. During a computerized search, you may deal with on-line data bases, library data bases, and CD-ROM.

The following are the nine steps in the library search:

1. Consult encyclopedias

2. Use dictionaries

3. Reconsider your audience.

4. Use journals and newspapers

5. Consult the library catalog or "on-line catalogs"

6. Consult individual works in collections

7. Consult biographical sources

8. Evaluate your sources with book and journal reviews

9. Consider statistical sources

10. Consider government documents

QUESTIONS FOR STUDY AND DISCUSSION

1. In what ways is researching a topic for a written report similar to researching the same topic for a speech? How is it different?

2. How important is research in the preparation of most speeches? How can an audience tell whether a speech lacks a sound research base?

3. In this age of mass information, why is the search strategy described in this chapter becoming increasingly important?

4. How can you best use the services of a librarian?

ACTIVITIES

1. Tour the libraries at school and in your community. In a written report, compare the facilities and use your findings as a guide when you research your next speech.

2. Compare the electronic information services at your college library to the services described in this chapter. Ask the librarian what services have become available in the last year.

3. When you are given your next speech assignment, develop and follow a search strategy that includes both interviews and library research.

"There are a lot of people out there teaching how to read a speech, how to face a TV camera. But very few teach about the content of speeches. You can teach someone how to read the telephone directory like it's never been read before, but, let's face it, after it's all over, it's still the telephone directory."

James Humes, corporate speech consultant

SUPPORTING YOUR SPEECH

**Y**our public speaking professor has just given your class an assignment to deliver an informative speech on the problem of shoplifting. These two versions are among those presented:

Version 1:

Shoplifting is an enormous problem for American retailers who lose billions of dollars each year to customer theft. Not unexpectedly, retailers pass the cost of shoplifting onto consumers, which means that people like you and me pay dearly for the crimes of others.

Shoplifting is increasingly becoming a middle-class crime. Experts tell us that many people shoplift just for kicks—for the thrill of defying authority and for the excitement of getting away with something that is against the law. Whatever the reason, one in fifteen Americans is guilty of this crime.

Version 2:

What would you say if I told you that every year you and your family hand over $300 to storekeepers without getting anything in return?

I know what you're thinking. As a college student who has to account for every cent, there's no way you would allow $300 to slip through your fingers.

Yet that's exactly what you do. Every year, the average American family of four forks over this huge sum to make amends for the crimes of shoplifters.

Shoplifting is a big cost to big business. People who walk out of stores without first stopping at the cash register take with them between $8 billion and $50 billion annually. The spread between these figures is so large because it is impossible to calculate the exact amount.

FBI statistics tell us that one out of every fifteen of us is guilty of this crime. To bring this figure uncomfortably close to home, that's two students in a thirty-student class. Interestingly, shoplifting is no longer a poor person's crime. Hard as it is to imagine, many shoplifters can well afford to buy what they steal. We all heard about the case of Bess Myerson, a former Miss America, who was caught in the act of stealing variety store cosmetics.

Why do middle- and upper-income people steal? According to psychiatrist James Spikes, recently quoted in *Ms.* magazine, shoplifters are "defying authority. They're saying, 'The hell with them. I'll do it anyway . . . . I can get away with it . . . .'" Psychologist Stanton Samenow, quoted in *Life* magazine, agrees: "Shoplifters will not accept life as it is; they want to take shortcuts. They do it for kicks."[1]

SUPPORT STRENGTHENS YOUR SPEECH

Although both versions say essentially the same thing, they are not equally effective. The difference is in the supporting materials that buttress the main ideas—the information speakers use to build their case. Here is what we learn by comparing these two versions:

Support Should be Specific.   Version 2 gives listeners more details than version 1. We learn, for example, how much shoplifting costs each of us and the financial burden retailers must carry.

---

1. Susan G. Sawyer, "Psychology of a Middle-aged Shoplifter," *Ms.* magazine, September 1988, p. 46; Claudia Glenn Dowling, "Shoplifting," *Life* magazine, August 1, 1988, p. 33.

Support Should Clarify Ideas. We learn much more about the reasons for shoplifting from version 2. This clarification—from the mouths of experts—reduces the risk of misunderstanding.

Support Should Add Weight. The use of credible statistics and expert opinion adds support to version 2's main points. This type of support convinces through building a body of evidence that may be difficult to deny. The testimonies of Drs. Spikes and Samenow are convincing because they are authoritative. We believe what they say far more than we do unattributed facts.

Support Should Be Appropriate to Your Audience. Perhaps the most important difference between these two versions is version 2's attempt to gear the supporting material to the audience. It is a rare college student who would not care about a $300 overcharge or who cannot relate to the presence of two possible shoplifters in a class of thirty.

Support Should Create Interest. Although version 1 provides information, it arouses little or no interest. Listeners have a hard time caring about the problem or becoming emotionally or intellectually involved. Version 2, on the other hand, creates interest through the use of meaningful statistics, quotations, and an example. When used properly, supporting materials can transform ordinary details into a memorable presentation.

Effective support is used to develop the message you send to your listeners—a message that requires audience response. It is through this message that communication takes place between speaker and audience. In public speaking centers you cannot separate the act of speaking from the message the speaker delivers. Supporting your message is one of your most important tasks as you develop your speech.

FORMS OF SUPPORT

You can use a variety of supporting materials—including facts, statistics, examples, testimony and quotations, and analogies—to give your speeches greater weight and authority.

Facts

Nothing undermines a presentation faster than too few facts. Here is an example of a presentation that lacks factual information:

> An increasing number of women are choosing never to marry. They are making the decision that they would rather live alone than with a partner and many are happier for it.

Many questions come to mind. Why are more women choosing the single life? How do we know they are happy? Are more women remaining single today than fifteen or twenty years ago? These questions leave us uncomfortable with the amount of

FOCUS ON RESEARCH

DOES EVIDENCE REALLY CONVINCE?

Intuition tells us that there has to be a relationship between evidence and persuasion. That is, the more convincing the body of evidence a speaker offers in the form of examples, statistics, testimony, and analogies, the more likely we are to be persuaded that the speaker's point of view is correct. The problem with this commonsense approach is that for years researchers failed to prove it. Study after study could not find a conclusive link between the nature, quality, and quantity of support a speaker offers and the persuasiveness of a speech.

According to John C. Reinard, a professor of communication, intuition in this case makes a lot more sense than science.[2] After carefully examining two hundred studies on the use of evidence in persuasive messages given during a fifty-year period, Reinard concluded that evidence can persuade and that the inconclusive nature of the research is based, among other things, on problems in the study analysis and on inconsistent definitions of terms from study to study. Here are some of Reinard's conclusions:

There is a Direct Relationship Between the Credibility of the Speaker and the Persuasiveness of the Message

After reviewing the research, Reinard concluded that listeners are persuaded most by unbiased speakers who have nothing to gain by expressing a point of view; next by "reluctant" sources who take a position contrary to their own vested interest; and least by biased sources who advocate their own best interest.

High Quality Evidence is More Persuasive Than Low Quality Evidence

Among the studies Reinard cites is that conducted by Luchok and McCroskey (1978), which presents a message in five different ways: (1) a speech with no evidence; (2) a speech with solid, relevant evidence from qualified sources; (3) a speech based on unqualified sources; (4) a speech in which qualified sources were associated with irrelevant evidence; and (5) a speech in which the irrelevant evidence was attributed to unqualified sources. The researchers found that relevant, solid evidence produced greater attitude change than any other evidence form.[3]

Although No Magical Way Exists to Determine When Evidence is Sufficient to Persuade, Studies have Shown that the Continual Use of Strong Evidence has a Powerful Persuasive Effect

This is especially true if the audience knows nothing about the subject and if many different sources are used.

Evidence Increases the Persuasiveness of Credible Speakers Over the Long Term

Studies have shown that when a highly credible source—the president of the United States, for example—uses evidence in a speech, it does not increase the persuasiveness of the speech at the moment listeners hear it. In this case, the speaker's credibility—who he or she is and the position he or she holds—is the critical persuading element. However, when listeners are asked to evaluate the same speech after several weeks, strong evidence has a proven persuasive effect.

---

2. John C. Reinard, "The Empirical Study of the Persuasive Effects of Evidence: The Status After Fifty Years of Research," *Human Communication Research* (Fall 1988): 3–59.
3. J. A. Luchok and J. C. McCroskey, "The Effect of Quality of Evidence on Attitude Change and Source Credibility," *Southern Speech Communication Journal* 43 (1978): 371–83.

research the speaker has done. We feel very differently when the following facts are added:

> Thirty percent of American women will never marry—a figure that represents a 7 percent increase since 1972. Many of these women have made a conscious choice to remain single. No longer financially dependent on men, they can afford to live the good life on the money they earn. By remaining single, they also avoid what in their minds may be the near certainty of divorce. Having watched the marriages of their friends and relatives fall apart, they do not want to invest in a relationship that is likely to fail. According to a study done by sociologists Norval D. Glenn and Charles N. Weaver, these women are generally happy alone. Indeed, these researchers tell us that an increasing number of unmarried women and men report being very happy.[4]

Statistics and testimony are added here, both of which we will discuss in detail later in this section.

What Facts Do.   In the above example, facts serve many different purposes:

⌘ *They clarify your main point.*   They remove ambiguity, making it more likely the message you send is the message your audience will receive.

⌘ *They indicate your knowledge of the subject.*   An audience listening to version 2 is less likely to question your grasp of the topic than an audience listening to version 1.

⌘ *Facts also define.*   Facts may provide needed definitions that explain new concepts. (We examine the different types of definitions in Chapter Thirteen.)

If you are delivering a speech on "functional illiteracy," you may need to define the term for your listeners. Your definition should try to anticipate the potential confusion between the terms "illiteracy" and "functional illiteracy." You can differentiate between these terms in the following way:

> While an illiterate adult has no ability to read, write, or compute, relatively few Americans fall into this category. However, some 27 million Americans can't read, write, compute, speak, or listen effectively enough to function in society. They cannot read street signs, write out a check, apply for a job or ask a government bureaucrat about a Social Security check they never received. Although they may have minimal communications skills, for all intents and purposes, they are isolated from the rest of society. These people are considered functionally illiterate.

Definitions are crucial when your words have *connotative* meanings. Connotations are implications and suggestions, framed by our own personal experiences, that often lie in the realm of emotional responses. The emotional debate and other discourse in the controversy over abortion in this country have often centered in different definitions of an abortion. A dictionary provides a *denotative* definition of the word. But the heated arguments between factions—in this case, those opposed to abortion,

---

4. Laura Mansnerus, "In Happiness Quotient, the Unmarried Gain," *The New York Times,* June 15, 1988, pp. C1 and C8.

those who favor abortion, and those who favor leaving the choice to individuals—define *abortion* connotatively. Terms ranging from "baby killing" to "aborting a fetus" are surrounded by the speaker's language framed from personal experiences, perceptions, values, and emotions. If you choose to speak on issues centered in controversy, you need to define crucial terms: Whether the audience favors or disfavors your view, you should ensure that they understand what you mean and what you believe to be the facts that support your ideas.

Believed Facts Versus Facts That Require Verification.   Facts fall into two separate categories: "Believed facts" are facts that are common knowledge and, as such, require no explanation or proof. Many speakers build their presentations around believed facts as they refer to historic events, social conditions, natural disasters, and so on. According to the distinguished late communication professor Wayne N. Thompson, believed facts are the strongest of all forms of proof.

In contrast, other factual statements require verification. The need for verification is often tied to the nature of the audience rather than to the accuracy of the information. Thompson explains: "A medical missionary may find scientific fact less acceptable to ignorant natives than are the witch doctor's superstitions. Somewhat similarly, many experienced debaters and coaches can recall abandoning sound arguments because of their surface unbelievability.[5]

Therefore, your choice of facts should depend, in part, on your audience. Although some groups will readily accept your statements of fact and require little or no verification, other groups demand complete documentation.

Fact Versus Opinion.   Facts are verifiable and irrefutable but opinions are not. Opinions are points of view that may or may not be supported in fact. Too often, speakers confuse fact and opinion when adding supporting material to a speech. For example, although it is a fact to state that George Bush was the president of the United States, it is opinion to state that he was the best president America ever had.

Opinions are everywhere—even in such "unbiased" sources as newspapers, news magazines, and professional journals. Sometimes they are explicit—openly stated—while at other times they are implicit—unexpressed but understood. For example, while researching a speech on the escalating cost of college tuition, you may find an article that addresses only the financial difficulty low-income families have in sending their children to college. Although it isn't stated, the implication is that middle-income families should be able to afford an $80,000-plus expense over four years.

How do you avoid confusing opinion with fact? Awareness—and vigilance—are your best tools. Familiarity with your topic also helps. The more you read, the more you will be able to ferret out opinions and implications so that the supporting material you choose is factually strong.

---

5.   Wayne N. Thompson, *Modern Argumentation and Debate: Principles and Practices* (New York: Harper & Row, Publishers, 1971), pp. 102–04.

Guidelines For Using Facts.

1. *Carefully determine the number of facts to use.*   Too few facts will make clear that you spent little time at the library, while too many may overwhelm your listeners. To be effective, the number and complexity of your facts must be closely tied to the needs of your listeners, an acknowledgment of the reciprocal nature of public speaking. If you are delivering a speech to a group of hikers on poison ivy prevention, you may decide to focus on such practical issues as how to identify the plant and how to recognize, treat, and avoid the rash. A detailed explanation of the body's biochemical response to the plant is probably unnecessary for this audience. However, if you are delivering a speech on the same subject to a group of medical students, your audience will undoubtedly expect greater complexity.

2. *Make sure your connotations are clear.*   When running for re-election, President Bush told voters what he meant when he charged that Bill Clinton was just another "tax-and-spend Democrat." Bush also under-stood that voters would add their own meaning to the phrase. Depending on the purpose of your speech, this use of understood meanings can be an effective technique. However, if not used properly, it can lead to misunderstandings when your audience attributes meanings to terms you did not intend. The following, for example, can be interpreted differently and therefore are easily misunderstood: conservative, liberal, patriot, happiness, good, bad, smart, and success. Let's focus for a moment on the last term, *success*. While one person may define success in terms of material wealth, another may think of it in terms of family relationships, job satisfaction, and good health. When it is essential that your audience understand the meaning you intend, take the time to define it carefully as you speak.

3. *Define terms when they are first introduced.*   The first time you use a term that requires an explanation, define it so that your meaning is clear. If you are talking about the advantages of belonging to a health maintenance organization, define exactly what an HMO is (an organization that provides prepaid health care to patients by member physicians with limited access to specialists outside the group) the first time the term is used.

Statistics

The second form of supporting material is statistics, the collection, analysis, interpretation, and presentation of information in numerical form. The following example shows that statistics give us the information necessary to understand the magnitude of issues and to compare and contrast different points. In this speech, Herbert R. Temple, Jr., lieutenant general, chief, United States National Guard Bureau, cites many statistics as he talks about the pervasiveness of illegal drugs in America:

Drug abuse is everyone's problem: it is an all-consuming issue that brings destruction and danger to our cities, our communities, and our families.

Allow me, if you will, to present some rather sobering statistics that illustrate how prevalent drug use is throughout our society. Did you know that this very day it's estimated that:

⌘ 2,000 American will be arrested for drug related crimes;

⌘ 5,000 Americans will try cocaine for the first time;

⌘ 500,000 Americans are regular heroin users;

⌘ 6,000,000 Americans are regular cocaine users;

⌘ 23,000,000 Americans are regular marijuana users; and that

⌘ 38,000,000 Americans are using some illicit drug . . .?

The public opinion environment is one of frustration over the fact that the problem continues to plague our society. Last year, a survey was conducted which set out to assess what issues Americans felt were most vital to their security. It was revealed that 22 percent of those surveyed named "combatting international drug trafficking" as the United States' single most important national security goal. An overwhelming 83 percent of Americans feel the drug problem is out of control and 81 percent favored using military force to intercept illegal drugs coming across our borders.[6]

Perhaps because of the volume of data our society produces, statistics are more important today than ever. The more statistics we use, the more we seem to need. Some would say Americans have an insatiable appetite for statistics. We analyze our lives by the numbers—for information and curiosity. It seems as important to us—as it is to advertisers buying TV air time—to know how many people watch the Super Bowl each year. We demand quantifiable public opinion surveys, like the one cited in the previous speech, and we value statistical slots, that is, knowing how certain numbers or scores compare to others. Perhaps because we live in such a competitive society, learning that you scored in the 85th percentile on your college admission exam means as much, if not more, than simply knowing your score.[7]

How Statistics are Used in Speeches.   Public speakers commonly refer to the following statistical concepts: averages, correlations, and random samples.

Averages.   To the uninitiated, averages are calculated by adding all the numbers in a group and dividing by the number of items. If seven workers have the following yearly incomes: $12,500, $12,500, $32,000, $32,500, $41,250, $242,000 and $322,600, the total ($695,350) is divided by seven to get the average income of $99,335.71. This type of average, known as the arithmetic mean, is the most widely used statistical measure.

---

6.   Herbert R. Temple, Jr., "The Nation's War on Drugs," *Vital Speeches of the Day,* June 15, 1989, p. 517.

7.   Dr. Barbara Bailar, executive director of the American Statistical Association, puts the importance of statistics in perspective: "Statistics affect all aspects of our lives. Government economic statistics affect wages for workers; medical care is affected by health statistics. There really isn't a part of our lives that's not affected by statistics. See her "Statisticians Meet Where They Came of Age," *The New York Times,* August 7, 1989, p. A32.

However, it is not the only measurement for averages. Another average, the median, measures the middle score in the group. That is, half the values fall above it and half fall below it. Thus, the median income of these seven people is $32,500. The final measure of average is the mode—the value that occurs most frequently. In this case, the average as defined by the mode is $12,500.

Averages can be misleading. Here, for example, the mean income is high because of two large incomes: $242,000 and $322,000. These figures bring the average up so it does not represent the group. The mode of $12,500 is not representative, either. As a group average, it is too low. In many cases, the median has little meaning because it merely represents the midpoint of the range.

Therefore, when quoting statistical averages in your speeches, it is important to understand what these averages mean. While a union organizer might use the mode of $12,500 to encourage employees to band together for higher wages, management is more likely to quote the average salary in terms of the mean or median.

Correlations.   Many supporting materials refer to correlational studies, which express relationships between different variables—factors capable of change: For example, research has shown a high correlation between alcohol consumption during pregnancy and birth defects. In this case, the variables are alcohol consumption and birth defects. The conclusion is that women who drink while they are pregnant have a greater chance of giving birth to a malformed child than women who do not drink.

Although correlations express relationships, they do not necessarily explain why these relationships exist or whether one variable causes another. Although you may read about correlational studies between breast cancer and birth control pills, scientists are reluctant to tell women that taking birth control pills over a period of years *causes* breast cancer. Other factors may influence these results, including genetic predisposition, whether a woman has children, the age at which she has her first child, the age at which menstruation began, diet, smoking, and so on. Therefore, when citing a correlational study in a speech, you must be sure to cite it accurately, refraining from attributing cause when this attribution is not certain. Jumping to conclusions only confuses your audience.

Also, remember that some reported correlations have no basis in fact. For example, when correlations are suggested between a full moon and an increase in crime, you are forced to question the accuracy of these relationships.

Random Samples and Surveys.   Suppose you want to give a speech on the pros and cons of spanking children in school. Among the supporting materials you find are surveys asking people how they feel about this issue. (Surveys like these are often conducted by such polling organizations as Gallup, Harris, and Roper and published in popular newspapers and magazines.) A Harris survey may tell you, for example, that 53 percent of American parents are opposed to physical punishment in school, although 86 percent of parents approve of spanking at home.[8] How do you evaluate

---

8.   "Parents and Teachers Split on Spanking," *The New York Times,* August 16, 1989, p. B10.

these findings? As you recall from our discussion in Chapter Four of the credibility of supporting material, one way is to look at the nature of the survey sample.

Because surveying the entire U.S. population to ascertain attitudes is virtually impossible except in the U.S. census, researchers are forced to study a select group of people (known as *a sample*) who have the characteristics of the specific population being studied. In this case, the survey was based on a representative sample of American parents; people without children were excluded from this poll.

How do you know if a survey sample has been chosen properly? One way to judge is through the reputation of the journal, newspaper, or magazine that publishes the survey, as well as the survey source itself. You are much more likely to read the results of a scientific study in the *Journal of the American Medical Association* than in the *National Enquirer.* Similarly, when researchers have proper credentials (a doctorate in sociology, for example) and do not have a personal stake in what the survey reveals, they are much more likely to base their survey on an unbiased sample.

How to Judge the Value of Statistics.   In 1954 Darrell Huff published what was to become the classic study of statistical manipulation, *How to Lie with Statistics.* Huff suggests asking five questions to uncover statistical misrepresentations:

1. *Who says so?*   Look for conscious or unconscious bias that may distort the findings. You should tend not to believe statistics on smoking-related health problems that are issued by the tobacco industry. Look instead for statistics from such unbiased sources as the Centers for Disease Control.

2. *How do they know?*   Does the sample include misleading averages? Was it large enough and randomly chosen? If you read that four of five professors think today's college students are better informed than their predecessors, do more research before adding this information to your speech. If you learn that this statistic is based on a nationwide random survey of 1,500 college professors, you can feel comfortable about using it to support your point. If, on the other hand, you learn that the researcher talked to only ten professors, these findings are based on too small a sample to be useful.

3. *Did someone change the subject?*   Are the conclusions consistent with the data?

4. *What is missing?*   Unreported facts can change the meaning of any statistic.

5. *Does it make sense?*   Put all statistics to your own test of common sense.

The following guidelines will help you present statistical information in the most meaningful way:

Be Precise.   Be sure you understand the statistics before including them in your speech. Consider the difference between the following statements:

⌘ A 2-percent decrease was shown in the *rate of economic growth,* as measured by the gross national product, compared to the same period last year.

⌘ The gross national product *dropped* by 2 percent compared to the same period last year.

In the first case, the statistic refers to a drop in the *rate* of growth—it tells us that the economy is growing at a slower pace but that it is still ahead of last year—while in the second, it refers to an actual drop in the gross national product in comparison to the previous year. These statements say two very different things.

It is critical that you not misinterpret statistics when analyzing the data. If you have questions, refer to a basic statistics text or another source that further explains the data.

Provide Meaning Through Comparison.   If possible, use your statistics to create concrete images rather than just numbers. Here is how B. M. Thompson, executive vice president for Phillips Petroleum, made statistics understandable through comparison in a speech presented to the Coalition for Responsible Waste Incineration:

> Americans generate half a million tons of solid waste a day.
>   That's four pounds for every man, woman and child—every single day!
>   That's enough solid waste to fill a line of garbage trucks stretching from the White House to Boston Harbor—every single day! . . .
>   The largest U.S. landfill is New York City's Fresh Kills on Staten Island.
>   One business magazine (*Forbes*) pointed out that, by the turn of the century, Fresh Kills will become the highest point on the eastern seaboard south of Maine, rising 500 feet above New York Harbor.
>   That's about as high as the Statue of Liberty's waist.[9]

It is also effective to express statistics in terms that have meaning to audience members. Recall for a moment version 2 of the shoplifting example. These statistics are meaningful to students because they are expressed in terms of students' own financial budgets.

Avoid Using Too Many.   Too many statistics will confuse and bore your audience and blunt the impact of your most important statistical points. Save your statistics for the places in your speech where they will make the most impact.

Round Off Your Numbers.   Is it important for your audience to know that, according to the Census Bureau's daily population projection on July 28, 1989, the U.S. population reached 248, 451, 584? The figure will have greater impact—and your audience will be more likely to remember it—if you round it off to "more than 248,000,000."

Cite Your Sources.   Because statistics are rarely remembered for very long, it is easy for speakers to misquote and misuse them—often in a calculated way for their own ends. To make your audience believe that your statistics are correct, quote your sources.

---

9.   B.M. Thompson, "Good Riddance: Solving America's Hazardous Waste Problem," speech delivered before the Coalition for Responsible Waste Incineration, *Vital Speeches of the Day,* September 1, 1989, p. 683.

Use Visual Aids To Express Statistics.   Statistics become especially meaningful to listeners when they are put in visual form. Four types of graphic presentations are effective including the bar graph, line chart, pie chart, and pictograph. (For a discussion of these graphs, see Chapter Eleven.) Visual presentations of statistics free you from the need to repeat a litany of numbers that listeners will probably never remember. Instead, by transforming these numbers into visual presentations, you can highlight only the most important points, allowing your listeners to refer to the remaining statistics at any time.

Examples

Examples enliven speeches in a way that no other form of supporting material can. Grounding material in the specifics of everyday life has the power to create an empathic bond between speaker and audience, a bond strong enough to tie listeners to a speech and speaker even after the example is complete.

In this section, we examine five specific types of examples: brief, extended, narrative, hypothetical, and personal examples. Although examples differ in length, factual base, and source, their effectiveness lies in the extent to which they support the speaker's core idea.

Brief Examples.   Brief examples are short illustrations that clarify a general statement, as in the following:

> Since the beginning of time—or so it seems—baseball managers and baseball umpires have been less than the best of friends. Former New York Yankees manager Billy Martin was known to kick dirt in umpires' faces after bad calls. He would also scream at umpires from his spot in the dugout and have nose-to-nose shouting matches on the field. The result, on a regular basis, was Billy being ejected from the game.

Brief examples have the power to paint a panoramic picture. Linking a series of related brief examples can create a powerful impression. In a speech presented to the Interstate Oratorical Association, Katie Siplon of Boise State University, Idaho, used a series of brief examples to describe the reaction many people have to children with AIDS. Although she could have said something like this,

> Children with AIDS have been forced out of school, out of summer camp and, literally, out of town. Many have been left homeless and unloved in state and local institutions,

she chose instead to say this:

> One of the most widely publicized cases is that of the Ray family in Arcadia, Florida. All three of Clifford Ray's hemophiliac sons have tested positive for AIDS antibodies. The family had to obtain a court order to allow the boys to go to school and the public's response was brutal. A rally for citizens against AIDS was held with over 500 participants; over half the students boycotted school; and ultimately a suspicious fire in the Ray home forced the family to leave.
>   A two-year-old boy with AIDS named Rufus was well enough to be released in October of 1985 from Henry Ford hospital where he had spent his entire life, but not

Statistics can become especially meaningful when they are put in visual form. A bar graph can be effective in presenting complex statistical information.

one of the hundreds of foster families, nursing homes or hospices in the Detroit area would take him.

　Medical specialists attempted to start a summer camp for children with AIDS, but this plan was foiled when camp owners found out who their potential campers were.[10]

Brief examples can be used effectively throughout a speech. Your decision to use them will depend on serial factors including the needs of your audience, the nature of your material, and your approach.

Extended Examples.　Extended examples are longer and richer in detail than brief examples. They are used, most effectively, to build images and to create a lasting impression on the audience, as in the following example:

　Illegal drugs and alcohol abuse are big problems to big business. However, knowing how to treat drug and alcohol impaired workers can be an even bigger worry.

　In recent years, as on-the-job drugs have become more common, companies like Chemical Bank, General Motors, and Mobil have set up employee assistance programs (EAPs) to help impaired workers get back on their feet. At Mobil, for example, employees seek the help of trained EAP counselors who place them in approved hospital or outpatient drug clinics. During the rehabilitation period, sick leave pays at least part of the employee's salary and health insurance benefits cover the cost of treatment.

10.　Katie Siplon, "Children with AIDS," in *Winning Orations of the Interstate Oratorical Association:* 1988, p. 22.

According to experts, the success rate of this type of on-the-job intervention is extremely high. At Mobil, three out of four cases end with the employee returning to productivity on the job.

Because of their impact, extended examples should not be overused or used at inappropriate points. As with other forms of support, they should be reserved for the points at which they will have the greatest effect in clarifying the message, persuading listeners of your point of view, or establishing a speaker–audience relationship.

Narrative.   Narratives are stories within a speech, anecdotes that create visual images in listeners' minds. In many ways, they take extended examples a step further by involving listeners in a tale that captures attention and makes a point—a tale connected to the speaker's core idea. Speakers who rely on narrative understand that most listeners love a good yarn—often when the speech is over, the narrative is what they remember.

Here is how Dr. Gordon E. Gee, President of Ohio State University, used narrative in his 1992 commencement address to the graduating class at Bowling Green State University. President Gee's message was both a celebration of the success of completing the necessary work—especially that required for an undergraduate degree—and a reflection on the practical implications for the future for each graduate. To capture and maintain the audience's attention, he created a humorous narrative illustrating the change from college life to a life with a career beyond the campus in Northwest Ohio.

Yes, beginning today you will not be able to see "All My Children" in the afternoon. You will, instead, have to videotape the exploits of Erica Kane on your VCR while you are at work. You will not only miss seeing "The Young and the Restless," you will no longer be the young and the restless. You will be the mature and the rested. You will begin going to bed at about the same time you have been going out for the evening. Good-bye Arsenio Hall and David Letterman. Hello sunrise and "Good Morning America."

Having grown accustomed to doing your school work with background music supplied by the Cowboy Junkies or the Sugarcubes you will now join the world of work, with background music you have heretofore only heard in elevators and the dentist's office. You will no longer be able to wear a ball cap to cover "bed hair." And business attire means more than tucking your T-shirt into your Levis. Things will be changed after today. You have earned your degree. Really earned it, through hard work, financial sacrifice, long hours, and, for some of you, a great deal of luck!

On the way to getting your diploma, you have learned a lot. You have learned which grocery has macaroni and cheese three for a dollar, and which one of the pizza delivery places has the best deal—regular price, four bucks, four bucks, four bucks. You learned that, despite what Willard Scott says, the coldest place in America is not International Falls, Minnesota, but the plains of Bowling Green, Ohio, on a wind-swept winter day. You said good-bye to Mom's cooking, and learned that you can wear bright orange and brown and like it. You learned that a $40 physics book is only worth $10 after 10 weeks—even if you never opened it. You figured out that when the laundry bag is full, you can wear that shirt one more time—after you give it the smell test. You found that desk-top publishing could make a mediocre five-page paper into a good looking eight-page report.[11]

Once finished with the narrative of life and learning for the college student at the university, President Gee made an easy transition to idealistic but practical advice for the future. The audience concentrated on his reflections quite seriously because he began with a familiar narrative to make them laugh and to achieve a sense of identification with the life-style of many students. (We discuss humor more fully in Chapter 10.)

By their nature, narratives demand that listeners take an active part in linking the story to the speaker's main point. As the story builds from beginning, to middle, to end, listeners ask themselves how it illustrates the students' college experience. Even if the speaker supplies this link after the narrative, audience members still make the connections themselves as they listen.

Throughout his eight years in office, Ronald Reagan was the master of narrative. His story-telling ability was so great that it set the tone of his presidency. According to professor William F. Lewis, our perception of the Reagan presidency and our perception of his speeches are often very different, with Reagan's narrative abilities coming out ahead.[12]

A narrative can be used anywhere in a speech. No matter where it is placed, it assumes great importance to listeners as they become involved with the details. Through the narrative, speakers can establish a closeness with the audience that continues even after the story is over.

Hypothetical Examples. At times, it suits the speaker's purpose to create a fictional example to make a point: Although these examples are not based on facts, the circumstances they describe are often realistic and thus effective. Here is how Robert J. Aaronson, president of the Air Transport Association, used a hypothetical example to open his speech to the American Bar Association Forum on Air and Space Law:[13]

> It is not often that someone outside the legal profession has a chance to tell an audience of lawyers what he thinks about their line of work. So I will seize this opportunity, using the case study method to describe, in layman's terms, what legal practice is all about.
>
> The case I have chosen is that of an airport construction worker named Charlie. He is finishing work for the day on [an] airport expansion project. . . . He is aware of the OSHA [Occupational Safety and Health Administration] rule against leaving loose materials on a scaffold overnight. So when he notices some loose bricks on his scaffold, he grabs an empty barrel, hoists it up on the scaffold with a rope and pulley and puts the bricks inside of it.

11. Speech delivered by Dr. Gordon E. Gee at Bowling Green State University, May 9, 1992. Used with permission from Dr. Gee.
12. William F. Lewis, "Telling America's Story: Narrative Form and the Reagan Presidency," *Quarterly Journal of Speech* 73 (1987): 280–302.
13. Robert J. Aaronson, "Air Transportation: What Is Safe and Needed," *Vital Speeches of the Day,* July 15, 1989, p. 592.

Back on the ground, Charlie proceeds to lower the load. He has no trouble swinging the barrel free of the scaffolding. But the barrel, filled with bricks, is heavier than he is. So the barrel goes down, Charlie goes up, and along the way they collide, giving Charlie a severe bump on the head. Charlie somehow manages to hold on, but when he reaches the top, his fingers get mangled in the pulley, just as the barrel crashes to the ground and breaks open. With the bricks now disgorged, Charlie outweighs the barrel. So he goes down, the barrel goes up. Again they collide. This time Charlie breaks a few ribs. He hits the ground. He's stunned, and he lets go of the rope.

You probably can guess how this sorry tale ends. The barrel, no longer connected to Charlie, falls a second time. It lands on Charlie, and it breaks his leg. We all have our ups and downs in life, but certainly his falls in the category of a very bad day at the office.

I am sure all of you have identified the central legal question here: Does Charlie sue the airport, the construction firm, the brick company or the barrel maker? The answer, of course, is all four, PLUS the first grade teacher who made it possible for Charlie to read the OSHA handbook in the first place!

Hypothetical examples are useful when you want to exaggerate a point as Aaronson did. They are also useful when you cannot find a factual illustration for your speech. To be effective, they must be tied, in some way, to the point you are trying to illustrate. The previous example would not have worked if it did not illustrate the problems in the legal and regulatory systems.

Whether the hypothetical example you use is extended or brief, it is important that your listeners know when you are using a hypothetical example and when you are not. Avoid confusion by introducing these examples in a direct way, for instance:

⌘ Imagine that you live next door to a college professor we'll call Albert E. Simmons.

⌘ Let's talk about a hypothetical mother on welfare named Alice.

Personal Examples.   Sometimes the best examples come from within yourself. By revealing parts of your life that relate to your speech topic, you provide convincing evidence and, at the same time, potentially create a powerful bond between you and your audience. Here is how Carolyn Sue Mouttet, a student at the University of Nebraska at Omaha, used personal experience in a speech she gave to the Interstate Oratorical Association on the problems of being an older student:

From my personal experience—it's difficult to fit college classes and study time into a family schedule. Particularly when the family includes five children, a traveling father, track teams, soccer teams, Cub Scouts, Boy Scouts, paper routes. Then the Marine Corps sends my son home from California on leave—during finals. Yet none of these is the most damaging problem for non-traditional students. Robert Kastenbaum . . . tells of the problem most often cited by older students: negative attitudes toward age . . . . Accustomed to being the only ones in the classroom wearing the mantle of experience, [professors] often treat older students who make comments in class as though they were competitors.

Competitor sounds innocuous, doesn't it? Until you spend a class period having the instructor be kind and encouraging to everyone else, while attacking your every comment. Most people don't make encouraging comments to the competition. They don't offer to help THE COMPETITION. So when I asked what was wrong with my essay, the instructor said, "This just isn't very good work." When I asked how to improve it, the response was, "I don't know what to suggest." I didn't ask for help again. As we can see from this single example, negative attitudes because of age expose older students to double standards, cause them to receive less help than younger students, and make them less likely to ask for the help they need.[14]

The following suggestions will help you choose examples for your speeches:

⌘ *Choose representative examples.* Examples support your core idea only when they accurately represent the situation.

⌘ *Use examples frequently.* Examples are often the lifeblood of a speech. Use them to make your points—but only in appropriate places. If you are using examples to prove a point, more than one example generally is needed.

⌘ *Use only the amount of detail necessary to make your examples work and no more.* The detail you provide in examples should be based on the needs of your audience. If your listeners are familiar with a topic, you can simply mention what the audience already knows. If you are addressing a group of audiologists about the relationship of hearing loss to loud environmental noises, you need only say this:

> We have seen measurable hearing loss as a result of prolonged exposure to such environmental noises as the Sony Walkman, airplane, engines, garbage trucks, and even the common lawn mower.
>
> If you are addressing your classmates who have little knowledge of noise-related hearing loss, greater detail is necessary. In this case, the following sentence should be added:
>
> Users of the Walkman personal stereo, for example, blast their eardrums with more than 115 decibels of sound. As a point of comparison, this is louder than Evel Knievel's motorcycle and permanently damaging to the delicate ear.

⌘ *Vary example type and length.* Intersperse several long examples with short ones to vary the pace and detail of your discussion.

⌘ *Use examples to explain new concepts.* Difficult concepts become easier to handle when you clarify them with examples. Keep in mind that although you may be comfortable with the complexities of a topic, your listeners might be hearing these complexities for the first time. Appropriate examples can mean the difference between communicating with or losing your audience.

Testimony and Quotations

When most people think of testimony, they think of witnesses in a court of law giving sworn statements to a judge and jury to add credibility to a case. Although testimony in public speaking has nothing to do with jurisprudence, it has everything to do with

14. Carolyn Sue Mouttel, "Old Does Not Mean Stupid," in *Winning Orations of the Interstate Oratorical Association: 1988,* pp. 78–79.

credibility. When you cite the words of others, either directly or through paraphrase, in effect, you are attempting to strengthen your position by telling your audience that people with special knowledge support your position or take your side. Testimony can cite either experience or opinion.

Experience as Testimony.   The people you quote need not be recognized experts. Their credibility can stem from the fact that they are observers on the scene. For example, if the point of your speech is to convince people that your hometown of Orlando, Florida, is one of America's greatest cities, you can strengthen your position by adding the following testimony:

> Unlike many northern cities, Orlando has a low unemployment rate. As a result, it attracts people from all over the country in search of work. Former Iowans Christy Hill and her family came to Orlando for just this reason. What she found surpassed her wildest expectations: "There were no jobs in our town," says Hill. The first day in Orlando her husband was offered work in two different places. "I can't imagine leaving." said Hill. "We love life here." [15]

Although Christy Hill has no special credentials to make her an expert on Orlando, her family's job-hunting experiences make her worth quoting in your speech. Much of the testimony you gather may be from ordinary Americans like Hill whose credibility stems from the unique experiences of their lives.

Opinion as Testimony.   In many circumstances, the opinion of a recognized authority is needed to strengthen the information you present or to prove a point. For example, Heather Jamison, in her speech for the Interstate Oratorical Association, spoke about "the threat of AIDS-infected medical personnel, the challenges posed such as cost, privacy and preventative techniques, and the regulation that should be required." Her audience is likely to have wondered "What is the most reasonable position to take on what appears as another important and unpredicted problem tied to the AIDS epidemic?" The speaker used a variety of supporting materials but perhaps none was more powerful than her quotation from Kimberly Bergalis, the courageous young woman who lost a battle to AIDS contracted during a visit to her dentist. Jamison told her audience: "In an effort to avoid any future tragedies such as hers, Kimberly Bergalis wrote a letter to Florida state health officials April 6 of this past year. Within her letter lies the greatest evidence for the need for mandatory AIDS testing. She wrote,

> 'When I was diagnosed with AIDS, I was only 21 years old. I have lived to see my hair fall out, blisters on my sides. I've lived to go through nausea and vomiting . . . chronic fevers of 103 and 104 that don't go away anymore. I have cramping and diarrhea. I've had blood transfusions. I've lived to see white fungus grow all over the insides of my mouth, the back of my throat, my gums, and now my lips . . . I was infected by Dr. Acer in 1987. My life has been sheer hell . . . Do I blame myself? I sure don't. I blame Dr.

---

15.   "Coming Soon: Hollywood, the Sequel," *Newsweek,* February 6, 1989, p. 46.

> Acer and every single one of you . . . P.S. If laws are not formed to provide protection, then my suffering and my death were in vain.'"[16]

Short Quotations. Short quotations are a form of testimony, but their purpose is often different. Frequently they are used to set the tone for a speech, to provide humor, or to make important points more memorable. For example, in a speech on ethics in American business, you might contrast the following quotations:

> While the Bible tells us: "What shall it profit a man if he gains the whole world and loses his soul," convicted Wall Street financier Ivan Boesky tells us, "I think greed is healthy. You can be greedy and still feel good about yourself." Choose your source—the Bible or Boesky—in what promises to be a heated discussion over business ethics.

Guidelines for Using Testimony and Quotations

- *Use only recognizable or credible testimony and quotations.* At a time when media exposure is so great for experts of all kinds, it is easy to find someone who will support your point of view. Before citing this person as an authoritative source, be sure that he or she is an expert. If you are giving an informative speech on the declining birth rate in Western countries, it would be appropriate for you to quote Ben Wattenberg, senior fellow at the American Enterprises Institute and author of *The Birth Dearth,* a book describing this problem. Similarly, it would be appropriate to quote Gloria Steinem or Betty Friedan in a discussion of sexual harrassment on college campuses. However, none of these would be the proper choice for a speech on traffic congestion or for a speech on the joys of collecting and trading baseball cards.

  As you review expert testimony, keep in mind that nothing you read is the last word. The more research you do, the more opinions you will find. Ultimately, your choice should be guided by how useful the quote is to your speech and the credibility of the source. Your audience will respond to both elements. The fact that you quote Supreme Court Justice Sandra Day O'Connor in a speech on affirmative action is as important as the quote itself.

- *Choose unbiased experts.* How effective is the following testimony if its source is the owner of the Oakland Athletics?

  > There is no team in baseball as complete as the Athletics. The team has better pitching, fielding, hitting, and base running than any of its competitors in the National or American League.

  If the same quote came from a baseball writer for *Sports Illustrated* you would probably believe it more. Thus, when choosing expert testimony, bear in mind that opinions shaped by self-interest are less valuable, from the point of view of your audience, than those motivated by the merits of the issues.

- *Identify the source of your quote.* Because the names of many of the experts you quote will not be recognizable, it is important to tell your audience why

---

16. Heather Jamison, "Do No Harm," *Winning Orations of the Interstate Oratorical Association,* Mankato State University, Interstate Oratorical Association, 1992. p. 72.

they are qualified to give testimony. If you are delivering a speech on shopping in different cultures, the following expert testimony from Suzy Gershman will add little weight to your speech unless you tell your audience why Gershman's knowledge is special:

> According to Suzy Gershman, Americans shopping in Japan are often uncomfortable. "Americans don't know how to handle Japanese manners," said Gershman. "When you walk into a store in Japan, everyone greets you—in shouts. You can't help wondering what you did wrong.
>
> "All this attention makes most Americans nervous. Americans like to be invisible when they walk into a store. They want to touch everything and look around by themselves before asking for help. They don't want anyone intruding on their personal shopping space."[17]

By changing the first sentence in the following way, your audience is far more likely to value Gershman's testimony:

> According to Suzy Gershman, travel writer and author of *Born to Shop,* a worldwide series of insider shopping guides, Americans shopping in Japan are often uncomfortable . . . .

⌘ *Use all testimony in its proper context.*   Purposefully distorting the testimony of an expert to suit the needs of your speech is misleading and unethical. Be honest to your source as well as your audience.

⌘ *Know when to paraphrase.*   Sometimes quotations are too long or too complicated to present verbatim. At other times, your speech already has too many quotes. You can choose to cite the source but paraphrase the message. Instead of quoting the following description of the effect crack cocaine has on the body, it might be more effective to paraphrase:

Quote

According to Dr. Mark S. Gold, nationally known expert on cocaine abuse, founder of the 800-COCAINE helpline, and author of *The Facts About Drugs and Alcohol,* "as an anesthetic cocaine blocks the conduction of electrical impulses within the nerve cells involved in sensory transmissions, primarily pain. The body's motor impulses, those that control muscle function, for example, are not affected by low-dose use of cocaine. In this way cocaine creates a deadening blockage (known as a differential block) of pain, without interfering with body movement."[18]

Paraphrased Version

According to Dr. Mark S. Gold, nationally known expert on cocaine abuse, founder of the 800-COCAINE helpline and author of *The Facts About Drugs and Alcohol,* cocaine blocks pain without interfering with body movement.

The second version is more effective when speaking to a lay audience who knows little about medicine, while the former is appropriate for an audience of science students or physicians.

---

17.   Interview with Suzy Gershman, May 21, 1988.
18.   Mark S. Gold, *The Facts About Drugs and Alcohol* (New York: Bantam Books, 1986), p. 36

⌘ *Use your own testimony when you are an expert.* If you are writing a speech on what it is like to recover from a spinal cord injury, use your own expert testimony if you have suffered this injury. Similarly, if you are talking about the advantages and problems of being a female lifeguard, cite your own testimony if you are female and have spent summers saving lives at the beach. When you do not have the background necessary to convince your audience, use the testimony of those who do.

⌘ *Develop techniques to signal the beginning and end of each quotation.* How does your audience know when you are beginning or ending a quotation? Some speakers prefer to preface quotations with the words, "And I quote" and to end quotations with the phrase "end quote." Other speakers indicate the presence of quotations through pauses immediately before and immediately after the quotation or through a slight change of pace or inflection. It may be a good idea to use both techniques in your speech to satisfy your listeners' need for variety.

Analogies

At times, the most effective form of supporting material is the analogy, which points out similarities between what we know and understand and what we do not know or cannot accept. Analogies fall into two separate categories: figurative analogies and literal analogies.

Figurative Analogies. Figurative analogies draw comparisons between things that are distinctly different—the Concorde supersonic transport and a soaring American eagle, for example—in an attempt to clarify a concept or persuade. In the following example, biology professor and world-renowned environmentalist Paul Erlich uses an analogy of a globe holding and draining water to explain the problem of the world population explosion:

> As a model of the world demographic situation, think of the world as a globe, and think of a faucet being turned on into that globe as being the equivalent of the birth rate, the input into the population. Think of that drain at the base of that globe—water pouring out—as being the equivalent to the output, the death rate of the population. At the time of the Agricultural Revolution, the faucet was turned on full blast; there was a very high birth rate. The drain was wide open; there was a high death rate. There was very little water in the globe, very few people in the population—only above five million. When the Agricultural Revolution took place, we began to plug the drain, cut down the death rate, and the globe began to fill up.[19]

This analogy is effective because it helps the audience understand the population explosion. It explains the nature of the problem in a clear, graphic way. Listener understanding comes not from the presentation of new facts (these facts were presented elsewhere in the speech) but from a simple comparison. When you are dealing with difficult or emotionally charged concepts, your listeners benefit from this type of comparative supporting material.

---

19. Paul Erlich, speech delivered to First National Congress on Optimum Population and Environment, June 9, 1970.

Keep in mind that although figurative analogies may be helpful, they usually do not serve as sufficient proof in a persuasive argument. Erlich, for example, must back his analogy with facts, statistics, examples, and quotations to persuade his listeners that his analogy is accurate—that we are indeed in the midst of a population crisis.

Literal Analogy.   A literal analogy compares like things from similar classes—automaker General Motors with automaker Chrysler; a game of pro football with a game of college football. If, for example, you are delivering a speech to inform your classmates about Russia's involvement in the war in Afghanistan, the following literal analogy might be helpful:

> The war in Afghanistan was the former Soviet Union's Vietnam. Both wars were unwinnable from the start. Neither the Vietnamese nor the Afghans would tolerate foreign domination. Acting with the determination of the Biblical David, they waged a struggle against the Goliaths of Russia and the United States. In large part, the winning weapon in both wars was the collective might of village peasants who were determined to rid their countries of the Superpowers—no matter the odds.

Literal analogies serve as proof when the things compared are similar. When similarities are weak, the proof fails. The analogy, "As Rome fell because of moral decay, so will the United States," is valid only if the United States and Rome have similar economic and social systems, types of governments, and so on. The more the characteristics of the United States and Rome differ, the weaker the proof.

Guidelines For Using Analogies.

⌘ *Use them to build the power of your argument.*   Analogies convince through comparison to something the audience already knows. As mentioned in Chapter 3, it is psychologically comforting to your listeners to hear new ideas expressed in a familiar context. The result is greater understanding and possible acceptance of your point of view.

⌘ *Be certain the analogy is clear.*   Even when the concept of your analogy is solid, if the points of comparison are not effectively carried through from beginning to end, the analogy will fail. Suppose, for example, that you want to compare political campaigning with boxing. Your analogy must be as consistent and complete as it is here:

> In political campaigns, opponents square off against one another in an attempt to land the winning blow. Although after a close and grueling campaign that resembles a ten-round bout, one candidate may succeed by finding a soft spot in his opponent's record, the fight is hardly over. Even while the downed opponent is flat against the mat, the victor turns to the public and tells yet another distortion of the truth. "My opponent," he says, "never had a chance." Clearly, politicians and prize fighters share one goal in common: to knock their opponents senseless and to make the public believe that they did it with ease.

⌘ *Avoid using too many.*   A single effective analogy can communicate your point. Don't diminish its force by including several in a short presentation.

Supporting materials buttress the main points of your speech and make you a more   SUMMARY
credible speaker. Among the most important forms of support are facts—verifiable
information. Facts clarify your main points, indicate knowledge of your subject, and
serve as definitions. Opinions differ from facts in that they cannot be verified.

Statistical support involves the presentation of information in numerical form.
Statistics include averages, correlations, random samples, and survey findings.
Because statistics are easily manipulated, it is important to analyze carefully the data
you present.

Five different types of examples commonly are used as forms of support. Brief
examples are short illustrations that clarify a general statement. Longer and more
detailed, extended examples are used to create lasting images. Narratives are stories
within a speech that are linked to the speaker's core idea. Hypothetical examples are
fictional examples used to make a point. Personal examples are anecdotes related to
your topic that come from your own life.

When you use testimony and quotations, you cite the words of others to
increase the credibility of your message. Your sources gain expertise through
experience and authority.

Analogies focus on the similarities between the familiar and unfamiliar.
Figurative analogies compare things that are different, while liberal analogies
compare things from similar classes. Literal analogies can often be used as proof.

1. With the idea of a search strategy in mind, how will you determine the types and   QUESTIONS
   amount of support you will need to meet the specific purpose of your next   FOR STUDY AND
   speech?   DISCUSSION
2. Which supporting materials are most effective for clarifying a point and
   which are most appropriate for proof? Can some forms of support serve both
   aims? How?
3. In the hands of an unethical speaker, how can statistics and analogies mislead
   an audience? What is your ethical responsibility in choosing supporting
   materials?

1. Analyze the connection between your choice of topic and your choice of support.   ACTIVITIES
2. Select three different forms of support and assess the strengths and weaknesses
   of each as evidence in public speeches.
3. Include in your next persuasive speech as many different forms of support as
   possible. After your speech, hand out a questionnaire to determine which form
   of support had the most effect.
4. Develop your own guidelines for determining how much supporting material to
   include in each speech.

"Let our advance worrying
become advance thinking and
planning."

Winston Churchill

ORGANIZING AND OUTLINING YOUR IDEAS

t is easy to detect disorganized speakers. Their presentations ramble from topic to topic as they struggle to connect ideas. Here, a disorganized speaker addresses an audience on the topic of addictions:

> We are a nation of addicts. Not only are we addicted to drugs and alcohol—the substances usually associated with addiction—millions of us are also addicted to gambling, shopping, promiscuous sex, overeating, relationships that tear down our self-esteem, and even shoes. (Who can forget the cache of unworn shoes in Imelda Marcos' closets!)
>
> Before I explain how researchers view these addictions, I want to say something about the thousands of self-help groups that have sprung up across the nation to save addicts from themselves—groups like Messies Anonymous, Debtors Anonymous, Women Who Love Too Much, and Neurotics Anonymous.
>
> Well, maybe I should start with a discussion of what an addiction is. According to Florida State University researcher Alan Lang, quoted in *U.S. News & World Report,* "There is no single characteristic or constellation of traits that is inevitably associated with addiction." However, Lang states that certain traits predispose us to addiction including alienation, impulsivity, and a need for instant gratification.
>
> Those groups I was telling you about a moment ago, well, in total, there are about 2,000 of them that hold meetings each week, up 20 percent from a year ago.
>
> Now let's get back to the concept of addiction. Can someone really be addicted to soap operas in the same way they are addicted to cocaine? According to Harvey Milkman, professor of psychology at Metropolitan State College in Denver and co-author of *Craving for Ecstasy,* "The disease concept may be applied to the entire spectrum of compulsive problem behaviors."[1]

Listening to this speech is like watching a Ping-Pong ball bounce aimlessly across a table. You never know where the speaker will land next or what direction the speech will take.

ORGANIZE YOUR SPEECH TO HELP YOUR AUDIENCE

Organizing your ideas, you help your audience follow your points and understand your message—both of which are essential to the public speaking transaction. The organization of ideas in public speaking refers to the placement of lines of reasoning—and supporting materials—in a pattern that helps achieve your specific purpose.

A tight organization helps listeners pay attention to your message by connecting your main points and by maintaining a clear focus that leads listeners to a logical conclusion. An ordered speech contains an introduction, body, and conclusion. Your introduction and conclusion support the body of your speech. The introduction should capture your audience's attention, then the conclusion reinforces your message and brings your speech to a close. The body develops your core idea, so audiences expect you to spend the most time amplifying your main point.

---

1. Facts from "America's Addiction to Addictions," *U.S. News & World Report,* February 5, 1990, pp. 62–63.

F O C U S   O N   R E S E A R C H

DOES A WELL ORGANIZED SPEECH AID LEARNING?

Intuitively, we believe that a well organized speech helps the audience learn the material being presented. To test the strength of this assumption in the context of an informative speech, speech communication professors Christopher Spicer and Ronald E. Bassett conducted an experiment based on the following hypothesis.[2]

> Subjects who hear an organized informative message will achieve a significantly greater number of correct answers on a subsequent measure of learning than subjects who hear a disorganized version of the same message.

Involved in the experiment were ninety-five undergraduate speech communication students at the University of Texas in Austin who listened to a recording of a male graduate student reading the rules of *Risk,* a conquer-the-world board game. (None of the subjects was familiar with the game.) While half the students heard an organized, chronological presentation appropriate to the rules of the game, the other half heard an aimless, disorganized presentation that did not follow the chronological pattern presented in the rulebook.

After the subjects heard the presentations, Spicer and Bassett administered a twenty-five-item multiple-choice test to assess subjects' knowledge of game rules and to determine how well they were able to apply the facts they just learned to an actual game (a test of problem solving).

The results of the study support our intuitive belief that effectively organized speeches help listeners learn material presented in an informative speech. Subjects who heard the organized chronological message scored significantly higher on the test that measured understanding of the game's rules than those who heard the disorganized version of the same message. However, the effectiveness of the organization had no effect on subjects' ability to solve problems using the rules of the game. According to the researchers, "This condition may have resulted because, although subjects who heard the organized message learned the rules of the game significantly better than subjects receiving the disorganized message, they may not have learned the rules sufficiently well to use them appropriately in answering the problem-solving items."

Based on the findings of this study, the traditional emphasis on effective patterns of organization is warranted.

Spending ten minutes each on introduction and conclusion and only five minutes on the body of your speech will leave listeners confused about your message.

The main points in an organized speech follow a pattern of development. If, for example, you plan to develop three main points in the body of your speech, you can give equal time to each point or allot more or less time to each point as you proceed.

---

2.   Christopher Spicer and Ronald E. Bassett, "The Effect of Organization on Learning from an Informative Message," *The Southern Speech Communication Journal* 41 (Spring 1976): 290–99.

Equality Pattern

Total length of speech body: 12 minutes

⌘ Point 1: 4 minutes

⌘ Point 2: 4 minutes

⌘ Point 3: 4 minutes

Progressive Pattern

Total length of speech body: 12 minutes

⌘ Point 1: 2 minutes

⌘ Point 2: 4 minutes

⌘ Point 3: 6 minutes

(Using these patterns, the power of your speech builds as you proceed.)

or

Strongest Point Pattern

Total length of speech body: 12 minutes

⌘ Point 1: 6 minutes

⌘ Point 2: 4 minutes

⌘ Point 3: 2 minutes

(Using this pattern your presentation begins with your strongest point.)

The pattern you choose depends on your topic and audience. The effectiveness of your choice depends on the consistency and clarity of your presentation.

You can organize the body of your speech by following four steps: select the main points, support the main points, choose the best organizational pattern, and create unity throughout the speech.

STEP 1: SELECT YOUR MAIN POINTS

Usually you should limit your main points to no fewer than two and no more than five. If you add more, you are likely to confuse your listeners. Organization is the key to deciding which points to cover.

Start with Your Specific Purpose and Core Idea

As explained in Chapter 2, the specific purpose defines the response you hope to elicit from your audience, while the core idea summarizes the main idea of your speech. Both are critical to your organization, for they are constant reminders of the goals of your speech. Looking back at them as you determine your speech's main points will help prevent a misdirection.

If you are developing a speech on how family pets help children with psychological problems, you might define your specific purpose in this way:

> To inform an audience of college students that pets provide unexpected psychological benefits for children with emotional problems by helping bolster their self-esteem.

Your core idea might say this:

> A close relationship with a family pet can help children with emotional problems feel better about themselves, help therapists build rapport with difficult-to-reach patients, and encourage the development of important social skills.

With these statements as your guide, it would be difficult to justify including the following main points in your outline:

⌘ Pet grooming tips

⌘ Medical advances in the treatment of feline leukemia

⌘ How to choose a kennel when you go on vacation

These points suggest that your speech is on target:

⌘ Children who suffer from emotional neglect use their pet as a confidante when they are lonely and as a source of comfort when they are upset.

⌘ At Green Chimneys Children's Services in Brewster, NY, animals are part of the treatment of emotionally disturbed children.[3]

Generate and Cluster Ideas

With your specific purpose and core idea clearly in mind, your next step is to generate a list of ideas consistent with the goals of your speech. This stage is commonly known as brainstorming. Based on your research, write down ideas as they occur to you, using phrases or sentences. Another topic will demonstrate this process:

Specific Purpose.   To inform an audience of college students about the causes, symptoms, and treatment of shyness.

Core Idea.   Shyness, an anxiety response in social situations that makes individuals overly concerned with themselves and limits social interactions, may respond to appropriate treatment.

List of Possible Main Points

1. Symptoms of shyness
2. Is shyness hereditary?
3. Shyness as an anxiety response
4. Blushing, dry mouth, pounding heart, queasy stomach, trembling hands
5. Number of people affected by shyness
6. Shyness and self-esteem
7. How to handle a job interview if you're shy

---

3. Facts from Daniel Goleman, "Children and Their Pets: Unexpected Psychological Benefits," *The New York Times,* January 11, 1990, p. B10.

8.   Treatment for shyness

9.   Is shyness learned?

10.   What to do when your date is shy

As you look at this list more closely, you realize that several overlap. Item 4 is really an elaboration of item 1. Items 2 and 9 could be grouped under a single heading, "What causes shyness?" To narrow your list even more, assign priorities: Items 7 and 10 should be taken off the list because they don't deserve the same attention as the others.

Based on these changes, you make the following list of possible main points:

1.   Symptoms of shyness

2.   Causes of shyness

3.   Treatment for shyness

4.   Number of people affected by shyness

5.   Shyness as an anxiety response

6.   Shyness and self-esteem

With too many main points to develop still, examine your list more closely. You decide that "shyness as an anxiety response" describes a symptom of shyness and that "shyness and self-esteem" describes a cause. You decide that a discussion of the number of people affected by shyness belongs in your introduction.

Your final list of main points looks like this:

1.   Symptoms of shyness

2.   Causes of shyness

3.   Treatment for shyness

Through this process, you transform a random list into a focused list of idea clusters reflecting broad areas of your speech. As in this case, main points should be mutually exclusive. There should be clear distinctions between each point. In addition, your points should be considered equally important as an expression of your core idea.

STEP 2: SUPPORT YOUR MAIN POINTS   When this process is complete, use the supporting material you gathered in your research to strengthen each main point. Fitting each piece of research into its appropriate place may seem like you are completing a complex jigsaw puzzle. Patterns must be matched, rational links must be formed, common sense must prevail. When you finish, each subpoint should be an extension of the point it supports. If the connection seems forced, reconsider the match. Here, for example, is one way to develop the three main points of the speech on shyness. Many of the phrases are now full sentences, for now you can begin to think in terms of the language of your speech.

I. **The symptoms of shyness fall into two categories: those that can be seen and those that are felt.**
   A. Objective symptoms make it apparent to others that you are suffering from shyness.
      1. Blushing
      2. Cold clammy hands
      3. Dry mouth
      4. Trembling hands and knocking knees
      5. Excessive sweating
      6. An unsettled stomach
      7. Belligerence
         a. According to psychologist Philip Zimbardo, many shy people never develop the social skills necessary to deal with difficult situations.
         b. They overreact by becoming argumentative.
         c. The confrontation that results is proof to the shy person that he or she is socially inadequate.
   B. Internal symptoms make the experience horrible for the sufferer.
      1. Embarrassment
      2. Feelings of inferiority or inadequacy
      3. Feelings of self-consciousness
      4. An extreme discomfort in social situations
      5. A desire to flee
      6. Generalized anxiety
II. **Recent research has focused on three potential causes of shyness.**
   A. Heredity seems to play a large part.
      1. Psychologists at Yale and Harvard have found that 10 to 15 percent of all children are shy from birth.
         a. Dr. Jerome Kagan of Harvard found that shy children are wary and withdrawn even with people they know.
         b. These children seem to have sensitive nervous systems that are easily aroused. The result is that they are often uncomfortable in social situations.
      2. The heredity approach focuses on the innate qualities in a person rather than on environmental influences.
   B. Shyness is also the result of faulty learning that lowers self-esteem instead of boosting self-confidence.
      1. When parents criticize a child's ability or appearance or fail to praise the child's success, they plant the seeds of shyness by lowering self-esteem.
      2. Older siblings may destroy a child's self-image through bullying and belittlement.
   C. Shyness is also attributable to poor social skills that leave people in the uncomfortable position of never having learned how to interact with others.

III. Shyness is not necessarily a life sentence. Treatment is possible and so is change.

    A.   In a survey of 10,000 adults, Stanford University researchers found that 40 percent said that they had been shy in the past but no longer suffered from the problem.

    B.   People who are extremely shy may benefit from professional therapy offered by psychiatrists and psychologists.

As you weave together your main points and support, your speech should grow in substance and strength. It will be clear to your listeners that you have something to say and that you are saying it in a clear, organized way.

STEP 3: CHOOSE THE BEST PATTERN FOR ORGANIZING YOUR MAIN POINTS
The way you organize your main points depends on your specific purpose and core idea, the type of material you are presenting, and the needs of your audience. Following are five effective patterns of organization that can be used to structure speeches.

Arrange Your Ideas in Chronological Order

In a chronological speech, information is focused on relationships in time. Events are presented in the order in which they occur. Here a speaker describes the decade of the 1990s through a chronology of anniversaries:

> According to *Newsweek,* in 1990, the birth control pill is 30 years old; October 12, 1992 is the 500th anniversary of Columbus's voyage; in 1994 we celebrate the 30th anniversary of the Surgeon General's warning about the hazards of smoking. For some, January 8, 1995 is the biggest day of the decade since it marks the 60th anniversary of Elvis' birth. It has to compete for that title with July 16, 1995—the 50th anniversary of The Bomb.[4]

The speaker went on to explain the significance of these events and how this grouping of major anniversaries may influence our perception of the decade.

To show how different organizational patterns affect the content and emphasis of a speech, we will choose a topic, establish different purposes for speaking, and show how the presentation differs when the organizational pattern is changed. We choose the civil rights movement.

Specific Purpose.   To inform my audience of college students about certain crucial events that occurred in the civil rights movement between 1954 and 1988.

Core Idea.   The civil rights movement made dramatic progress from 1954 to 1988.

    I.   The impetus for change came in the 1954 U.S. Supreme Court decision, known as *Brown v. Board of Education,* stating that school segregation was unconstitutional.

---

4. Facts from "10s, 20s, 50s, and 100s," *Newsweek,* December 18, 1989, pp. 78–80.

II.   On December 1, 1955, Rosa Parks refused to give her seat to a white rider on a bus in Montgomery, AL. Her act resulted in a year-long boycott of city buses by African-Americans and a court ruling making bus segregation unconstitutional.

III. The most sweeping civil rights law in American history was passed in 1964 during the Johnson presidency.

IV.   For the first time in history, in 1984, an African-American—the Reverend Jesse Jackson—was a serious contender for the presidency of the United States.

V.   In 1988, Jackson ran a second time for the presidency and gathered enough delegate support to play a key role in the Democratic convention.

To be consistent, every event you analyze must be woven into the existing chronological outline.

Past–Present–Future.   Chronological order can also be used to construct a past–present–future organizational pattern:

I.   Before the movement for women's equality, women's opportunities in the workplace were limited.

II.   Today, greater opportunity is a reality, but women must now cope with the dual responsibilities of career and home.

III. We look forward to greater awareness from corporate America of women's dual roles and to accommodations that make the lives of working women easier.

Step By Step.   Finally, chronological patterns can be used to describe the steps in a process. Here is a step-by-step description of how college texts are produced. Like the other patterns, the process shows a movement in time:

I.   The author, having gathered permissions for use of copyrighted material, delivers a manuscript to the publisher.

II.   The manuscript is edited, a design and cover are chosen, photos are selected, illustrations are drawn.

III. The edited manuscript is sent to a compositor for typesetting and set in galley and page proof form.

IV.   The final proof stage is released to the printing plant where the book is printed and bound.

Use a Spatial Organizational Pattern

In speeches organized according to a spatial pattern, the sequence of ideas moves from one physical point to another—from East Berlin to West Berlin, from basement to attic, from end zone to end zone. To be effective, your speech must follow a consistent directional path. If you are presenting a new marketing strategy to the company sales force, you can arrange your presentation by geographic regions—first the East, then the South, then the Midwest, and finally the West. If, after completing

In speeches organized according to a spatial pattern, the sequence of ideas moves from one physical point to another.

the pattern, you begin talking about your plans for Boston, your listeners will be confused.

Using space as our organizational key, our speech on civil rights takes the following form. Although the central topic is the same, the pattern of organization is tied to a different specific purpose and core idea:

Specific Purpose.   To inform my audience of college students how the civil rights movement spread across the nation.

Core Idea.   The civil rights movement spread from the cities and rural areas of the South to the inner-city ghettos of the North and West.

    I.   In places like Selma and Montgomery, AL, and Nashville, TN, white brutality led to civil rights boycotts and protests.

    II.   Angry African Americans, pent up and hopeless in inner-city ghettos, rioted in Harlem, Newark, Chicago, and Detroit.

    III.   Rioting broke out in the Los Angeles ghetto of Watts, resulting in 35 deaths, 4,000 arrests, and enormous losses from arson and looting.

Follow a Pattern of Cause and Effect

Why are women having fewer children? Why do heart attacks strike middle-aged men? Why are there now more homeless in America? These questions lend themselves to an examination of cause and effect. If your topic is the birth dearth among modern American women, you might explain the cause in terms of certain social realities:

⌘ Most families need two incomes to survive, a reality that makes large families unlikely.

⌘ Women are better educated than their mothers, a fact that makes them less likely to have large families.

⌘ Many women postpone childbearing until their thirties, decreasing the likelihood of a large family.

A discussion of the effects is a logical outgrowth:

⌘ American women are having too few children to replace the current population.

⌘ With fewer births, the population is aging.

⌘ An aging population means fewer workers are available to fill jobs.

You can turn the cause and effect relationship around and describe the effect first and then the cause. If you are delivering a speech on air pollution, you can start with a description of how industrial pollution makes it difficult for the elderly and infirm to breathe. You can then move to the cause of the problem including relaxed government regulation, industrial abuse, criminal wrongdoing, and incompetence.

Here are the main points of our speech on civil rights arranged in a cause-and-effect pattern:

Specific Purpose.   To inform my audience of college students how the suffering experienced by African Americans in the 1950s and 1960s created the environment for social change.

Core Idea.   The racial discrimination in America during the 1950s and 1960s made sweeping social change inevitable.

I.   Through the 1950s and early 1960s, discrimination prevented African-Americans from using public accommodations, from being educated with whites, from riding in the front of buses, from exercising their constitutional right to vote, from being hired by corporations, or from working for equal pay.

II.   This pattern of discrimination resulted in such landmark Supreme Court cases as *Brown v. Board of Education,* making separate but equal schools unconstitutional; the hugely successful march on Washington in 1963; and the passage in 1964 of the Civil Rights Act.

Examine a Problem and Its Solution

A common strategy, especially in persuasive speeches, is to present an audience with a problem and then examine one or more likely solutions. For example, in a classroom speech, one student described a serious safety problem for women students walking alone on campus after dark. He cited incidents in which women were attacked and robbed. He also described unlighted areas along campus walkways where the attacks had taken place. Next, he turned to a series of proposals to eliminate, or at least minimize, the problem. His plan included a new escort service sponsored and maintained by various campus organizations. He suggested the installation of halogen lights along dark campus walks and the trimming of bushes where muggers could hide.

Occasionally, speakers reverse this order by presenting the solution before the problem. Had this student done so, he would have identified how to provide effective security before he described the reasons why these solutions were necessary. Many audiences have trouble with this type of reversal because they find it hard to accept solutions when they are not familiar with the problems that brought them about.

Let's turn, once again, to our speech on civil rights, this time arranging the material in a problem–solution pattern.

Specific Purpose.   To persuade my audience of college students that although the civil rights movement has reduced racial discrimination in many areas, the movement must continue to press for equality in education and employment.

Core Idea.   The civil rights movement in America must remain strong and active because discriminatory patterns still exist in education and employment.

  I.   Discrimination in education and employment has perpetuated a culture of poverty and joblessness for millions of African Americans who remain second-class citizens despite the gains of the civil rights movement.
 II.   Joblessness, and the poverty that results from it, must be addressed through job training programs and continuing pressure on corporations to hire minorities through affirmative action programs.

Here, the goal is to persuade an audience that a problem still exists and to have listeners agree about how it can be effectively handled.

Arrange Your Ideas in a Topical Pattern

The most frequently used organizational system is the most difficult to describe, a system not tied to time or space, problem or solution, cause or effect, but, instead, to the unique needs of your topic. The nature and scope of your topic dictate the pattern of your approach—a fact that makes it difficult to generalize from one topic to another.

Working within the confines of your topic, you determine a workable pattern. If you are delivering an after-dinner, humorous speech on the responses of children to their first week of preschool, you can arrange your topics according to their level of humor. For example:

  I.   The paraphernalia preschoolers think is necessary to survive at school.
 II.   How youngsters behave at school when they do not get their own way.

III.   Children's stories of their lives at home.
IV.   Why children believe their parents send them to school.

Let's see how our speech on the civil rights movement might be treated using a topical organizational pattern.

Specific Purpose.   To inform my audience of college students that the struggle for racial equality is continuing.

Core Idea.   The movement for civil rights is being waged from within the political establishment and from without the system in the form of organized protests.

    I.   Jesse Jackson became a leader in the Democratic party and succeeded in working within the system to register tens of thousands of African Americans to vote.
   II.   For the first time, an African American was elected the mayor of New York City and another is the governor of Virginia. Both have tried to guarantee the civil rights of all citizens.
  III.   When the system is unresponsive, African Americans continue to organize protests in places as diverse as Howard Beach, NY, in 1987 and Selma, AL, in 1990.

Without connections, your main points may be difficult to follow. Your audience may wonder what you are trying to say and why you have connected ideas that don't seem to have any clear relationship. To establish the necessary connections, use transitions, internal previews, and internal summaries.

STEP 4: CREATE UNITY THROUGH CONNECTIONS

Transitions

Transitions are the verbal bridges between ideas. They are words, phrases, or sentences that tell your audience how ideas relate. Transitions are crucial because they clarify the direction of your speech by giving your audience a means to follow your organization. With only one opportunity to hear your remarks, listeners depend on transitions to make sense of your ideas.

It helps to think of transitions as verbal signposts that signal the organization and structure of your speech. Here are several examples:

- ✿ The first proposal I would like to discuss. . . (you are telling your listeners that several more ideas will follow).
- ✿ Now that we've finished looking at the past, let's move to the future (these words indicate a movement in time).
- ✿ Next, I'll turn from a discussion of the problems to a discussion of the solutions (you are telling your listeners that you are following a problem-solution approach).

⌘ On the other hand, many people believe. . . (you are signaling an opposing viewpoint).

The following is a list of common transitional words and the speaker's purpose in using them.[5]

Speaker's purpose:	Suggested transitional words
to define. . .	that is to say; according to; in other words
to explain. . .	for example; specifically
to add. . .	furthermore; also; in addition; likewise
to change direction. . .	although; on the other hand; conversely
to show both sides. . .	nevertheless; equally
to contrast. . .	but; still; on the contrary
to indicate cause. . .	because; for this reason; since; on account of
to summarize. . .	recapping; finally; in retrospect; summing up
to conclude. . .	in conclusion; therefore; and so; finally

Internal Previews

Internal previews are extended transitions that tell the audience, in general terms, what you will say next. These are frequently used in the body of the speech to outline in advance the details of a main point. Here are two examples:

⌘ I am going to talk about the orientation you can expect to receive during your first few days on the job including a tour of the plant, a one-on-one meeting with your supervisor, and a second meeting with the personnel director, who will explain the benefits and responsibilities of working for our corporation.

⌘ Now that I've shown you that "junk" is the appropriate word to describe junk bonds, we will turn to an analysis of three secure financial instruments: bank certificates of deposit, Treasury bonds, and high quality corporate paper.

In the second example, the speaker combines a transition linking the material previously examined with the material to come with an internal preview. Previews are especially helpful when your main point is long and complex. They give listeners a set of expectations for what they will hear next.[6] Use them whenever it is necessary to set the stage for your ideas.

Internal Summaries

Internal summaries follow a main point and act as reminders. Summaries are especially useful if you are trying to clarify or emphasize what you have just said:

⌘ In short, the American family today is not what it was forty years ago. As we

---

5. From John J. Makay and Ronald C. Fetzer, *Business Communication Skills: Principles and Practice,* 2d ed. (Englewood Cliffs, NJ: Prentice-Hall, 1984), p. 68.
6. Frederick H. Turner, Jr., "The Effects of Speech Summaries on Audience Comprehension," *Central States Speech Journal* (Spring 1970): 24–39.

have seen, with the majority of women working outside the home and with divorce and remarriage bringing stepchildren into the family picture, the traditional family—made up of a working father, a nonworking mother, and 2.3 kids—may be a thing of the past.

⌘ In sum, the job market seems to be easing for health care professionals, including nurses, aides, medical technicians, physical therapists, and hospital administrators.

When summaries are combined with previews, they emphasize your previous point and make connections to the point to follow:

⌘ In sum, it is my view that cigarette advertising should not be targeted specifically at minority communities. As we have seen, R. J. Reynolds test marketed a cigarette for African-Americans known as "Uptown," only to see it come under a barrage of criticism. What is fair advertising for cigarette makers? We will discuss that next.

Organization plays an important role in effective communication. Five centuries ago, rhetoricians developed principles about the internal arrangement of ideas in public speaking. These ideas have been tested by time and have found support in modern research.[7]

Presenting your ideas in an organized way requires a carefully constructed planning outline and a key-word outline to be used as "speaker's notes." Both forms are critical to your success as an extemporaneous speaker—one who relies on notes rather than a written manuscript. Your outline is your diagram connecting the information you want to communicate in a rational, consistent way. It enables you to assemble the pieces of the information puzzle so that the puzzle makes sense to you and communicates your intended meaning to your audience. Think of outlining as a process of layering ideas on paper so that every statement supports your thesis.[8] It is a time-consuming process, but one that will pay off in a skillful, confident presentation.

The planning outline, also known as the full-content outline, includes most of the information you will present in your speech. It does not include every word you plan to say, but gives you the flexibility required in extemporaneous speaking. Let's examine the elements of an effective planning outline and discuss common mistakes and omissions in its preparation.

When developing a planning outline, it is important to use a traditional outline format that allows you to see the interconnections among ideas—how, for example,

THE PLANNING OUTLINE

7.   M.L. Clarke, *Rhetoric at Rome: Historical Survey* (New York: Barnes & Noble, 1963), pp. 23–37; Tom D. Daniels and Richard F. Witman, "The Effects of Message Structure in Verbal Organizing Ability upon Learning Information," *Human Communication Research* (Winter 1981): 147–60.
8.   Jo Sprague and Douglas Stuart, *The Speaker's Handbook,* 3d ed. (San Diego: Harcourt Brace Jovanovich, 1992), p. 92.

points are subordinated to one another and main ideas connected. In a traditional outline, roman numerals label the speech's main ideas. Subordinate points are labeled with letters and numbers. The following "boiler-plate" suggests the format for the body of a speech:

I.   Main point
    A.   Subordinate point (first subordination level)
        1.   Subordinate point (level 2)
            a.   Subordinate point (level 3)
            b.   Subordinate point (level 3)
                i.   Subordinate point (level 4)
                ii.   Subordinate point (level 4)
    B.   Subordinate point (level 1)
II.   Main point
    A.   Subordinate point (level 1)
    B.   Subordinate point (level 1)
        1.   Subordinate point (level 2)
        2.   Subordinate point (level 2)
III.   Main point

The proper positioning of the main and subordinate points with reference to the left margin is critical, for it provides a visual picture of the way your speech is organized. In all the outlines presented in this text, block indenting is used. In this form, you do not return to the left margin within a point, but begin immediately under the first letter of the previous line of text. These neat blocks of information are visual representations of the structure of your ideas. The traditional outline format implies a hierarchy in which broad, general points subsume more narrow points. This hierarchy expresses the internal logic of your ideas.

Many speakers include in their outlines labels for the introduction, body, and conclusion of their speech. These labels remind the speaker to give each section appropriate attention, focusing on the objectives of each section. These labels should be written in the left-hand margin of your outline.

A well constructed planning outline ensures a coherent, well-thought-out speech. It is important to use full sentences to define your ideas and guide your choice of language. Phrases and incomplete sentences will not state your points fluently, nor will they help you think in terms of the subtle interrelationships among ideas, transitions, and word choice. Although each unit of your outline should express a single idea, it may contain dependent clauses and may be more than one sentence.

Transitional sentences should also appear in your planning outline. They may be needed when you move from the introduction to the body to the conclusion of the speech. They may also be required to link various main points within the body and serve as internal previews and summaries. Put these sentences in parentheses between the points being linked and try to use the language you may actually speak. When appropriate, include internal summaries and previews of material yet to come.

Include at the end of your planning outline a bibliography listing all the sources used to prepare your speech, including books; magazine, journal, and newspaper articles; videos; speeches; and interviews. If you are unfamiliar with documentation requirements, check the style guide preferred by your instructor, such as *The Chicago Manual of Style* and *The MLA Handbook for Writers of Research Papers.*

Sample Planning Outline and Analysis

YOUNG WOMEN TAKE CONTROL OF THE MARRIAGE POOL

Stating your specific purpose and core idea will help keep your outline on track.

Specific Purpose: To inform my audience that for the first time in years marriageable young men outnumber young women.

Core Idea: Because there are far more unmarried men in their twenties than there are women in the same age group, young men today find it harder to meet eligible partners.

(Introduction)
This label should appear in the left margin. The introduction starts with provocative information to arouse audience interest.

I.   It wasn't that long ago that sociologists were telling us that there were far more women of marriageable age than men.

A.   A report issued by the University of California at Berkeley told us that if we tried to match each woman born in 1950 with a man three years older, we would have millions of women left over.

B.   Neil G. Bennett, Patricia H. Craig, and David E. Bloom, researchers at Yale, predicted a lifetime of singlehood for college-educated women who postponed marriage into their thirties and forties.

Then introduce new information that will be analyzed in the body of your speech.

II.   New data from the U.S. census bureau suggests this trend has reversed itself for people in their twenties.

A.   For every five single young women in their twenties, there are now six single young men.

B.   Young women now have the advantage.

This transition helps move you from the introduction to the body of your speech. Remember, although the word "transition" appears in the outline, it is not stated in your speech. This transition helps connect listeners, in a personal way, to the subject being discussed. It also states the core idea and previews the main points of the speech.

(Transition: Since I already see the men in my audience squirming and the women smiling, you must realize that the implications of this demographic shift are enormous. Because there are far more unmarried men in their twenties than there are women in the same age group, young men today find it harder to meet eligible partners.

We will look at the problem men face from a number of different perspectives including loneliness, pressure to marry from corporations, and the growing rivalry between older and younger men for the same women. At the end of the speech, we will examine some possible solutions.)

(Body)

The body of the speech is labeled in the left margin. Points A and B provide the details promised in main point III.

III. Before we begin, let's take a closer look at the hard data from the Bureau of Census.

A. There are 19.9 million men and 20.4 million women in their early twenties.

B. However, there are about 2.3 million more unmarried men in their twenties than unmarried women in the same age group.

1. In part, this statistic is explained by the fact that women tend to marry older men, thus eliminating themselves from the marriage pool.

2. Since the number of births in the United States fell by an average of 1.7 percent a year between 1957 and 1975, the men born in any given year outnumber the women born in the years that follow, making it even more difficult for men to find a mate.

The next main point analyzes the implications of this data.

IV. The result is that an increasing number of young men are finding themselves without a date on Saturday night.

A. These men are lonely.

B. Young male college graduates also feel pressure to marry in order to get the right job in corporate America.

1. According to career consultants, many corporations view unmarried men in their thirties as oddballs.

2. Corporations expect their young male managers to marry by the age of thirty.

C. Young men resent older men who date younger women.

1. According to William Beer, the deputy chairman of the sociology department at New York's Brooklyn College, young men feel that these "older men are poaching."

2. Older men claim they are just following a traditional pattern.

This transition moves you from a discussion of the implications for younger men to the reasons women find older men more suitable mates.

(Transition: Why are younger women attracted to older men, especially with a glut of younger men to choose from?)

V. Older men are perceived as more sophisticated.

A. They have had more time to explore the world and themselves.

Quotes are written word for word.

    B.   "The older men that I have met have done so much after college . . . that I haven't done," said Martha Catherine Dagenhart, then a senior at the University of North Carolina at Chapel Hill.

VI.   Older men have more money.

    A.   A thirty-year-old man may have worked eight years longer than a twenty-two-year-old college graduate.

    B.   Many older men have money in the bank.

As the outline proceeds from the first to the second to the third level headings, the specific details increase. Here and elsewhere, the outline proceeds from the general to the specific.

VII.   Older men are perceived as more powerful.

    A.   An attractive woman in her twenties may be willing to have a relationship with a man in his forties if he's achieved a certain status in society.

        1.   An executive may marry his young, attractive secretary.

        2.   This fits the stereotype of the May–September marriage.

    B.   Many older men cultivate an image of power and influence.

This transition takes the audience from the body of the speech to the conclusion by summarizing what has already been discussed and previewing what will come next.

(Transition: Now that we've examined the extent and implications of this phenomenon and looked at the reasons young women are attracted to older men, let's look at what eligible bachelors in their twenties can do.)

The speech concludes with a series of action-oriented suggestions.

VIII.   There are several possible solutions.

    A.   Young men in their twenties can consider dating older women.

        1.   Because unmarried women over thirty still outnumber men in the same age group, many women are available.

        2.   Women have traditionally dated older men. Demographic realities may force men to consider doing the same.

    B.   Men can be less selective in their choice of mates.

        1.   An "I'm not willing to settle" attitude may leave many men without a companion.

        2.   Standards should not be abandoned but they should be thoroughly examined to make sure they are meaningful.

    C.   Men must learn to accept the fact that they no longer have a ready supply of eligible partners—a fact older women have struggled with for years.

Sources are listed in alphabetical order.

Bibliography

Keith Bradsher, "For Every Five Young Women, Six Young Men," *The New York Times,* January 17, 1990, pp. C1 and C10.

Keith Bradsher, "Young Men Pressed to Wed for Success," *The New York Times,* December 13, 1989, pp. C1 and C12.

"Too Late for Prince Charming?" *Newsweek,* June 2, 1986, pp. 54–61.

SPEAKERS' NOTES

Speakers' notes are an abbreviated key-word outline lacking much of the detail of the planning outline. They function as a reminder of what you plan to say and the order in which you plan to say it. Speakers' notes follow exactly the pattern of your planning outline in a condensed format.

Here are guidelines for constructing your key-word outline:

Avoid overloading your outline. Many speakers feel the more information they have in front of them, the better prepared they will be to deliver their speech. The opposite is usually true. Speakers who load themselves with too many details are torn between focusing on their audience and focusing on their notes. Too often, as they bob their heads up and down, they lose their place. Include only the information you need to remind you of your planned points. Reduce your sentences to key phrases. Instead of writing: "The American Medical Association, an interest group for doctors, has lobbied against socialized medicine;" write: "The AMA and socialized medicine." Include transitions, but in an abbreviated form.

At times, of course, you must be certain of your facts and your words—when, for example, you quote an authority or present complex statistical data. In these cases, include all the information you need in your speaker's notes. Long quotes or lists of statistics can be placed on separate index cards or sheets of paper.

Your notes are useless if you cannot read them. Because you will be looking up and down at your notes as you speak, you must be able to find your place with ease at any point.

Here are some suggestions:

⌘ Place your notes on 5 × 8 index cards.

⌘ If you feel more comfortable using paper, write your outline in a notebook so that you cannot drop or inadvertently rearrange the pages as you speak.

⌘ Number the cards or pages and check to see that they are in sequence before speaking.

⌘ Leave space between the headings and in the margins. This technique helps you focus on the individual points in your outline as you proceed.

⌘ Use bold, dark, easy-to-read lettering. Consider using a highlighter for key points or circling important sections in red. Unless you have a typewriter with an extra-large typeface, do not type your key-word outline because it will be too small to read.

I N T E R V I E W

Dr. Bob Arnot
CBS News Medical Correspondent

In the past decade, we have witnessed an explosion of medical information about topics as varied as cancer, sports medicine, AIDS, environmental hazards, and stress. To help deal with the complexity—and volume—of data, we seek experts in the field of medicine and listen attentively to their speeches.

Dr. Bob Arnot is one of these experts. As the CBS News medical correspondent (Dr. Arnot has been seen on *CBS This Morning, CBS Nightly News with Dan Rather,* and *60 Minutes*), Dr. Arnot delivers about thirty speeches a year to varied audiences, from the American Diabetes Association to local wellness fairs. Among his topics are the revolution in biotechnology, relief from corporate stress, achieving your personal best, and television medicine.

We asked Dr. Arnot for his thoughts on public speaking about medicine. We were especially interested in how he translated scientific knowledge into everyday language and whether he speaks with an outline.

Question: Do most doctors have trouble speaking in language the public can understand?

Answer: Most physicians learn a complicated way of speaking as part of their initiation into medicine. Throughout their training, they are taught to use a kind of ritualistic medical language that is difficult for outsiders to understand. After years of relying on this language, they don't realize that when they use it with their patients or in front of a lay audience, they lose touch with their listeners. Ironically, in past centuries, doctors spoke and wrote beautifully. It's only been in the past fifty years that doctors started communicating in such an appalling way.

Question: How do you avoid this pattern of poor communication?

Answer: I try to listen to my audience. The wonderful thing about public speaking is that when you try a particular approach or even a choice of words, you get immediate feedback. You learn right away whether you've made a mistake, whether you're funny, whether people agree or disagree with you, and whether they understand you. These responses are important because merely getting your point across isn't enough; you have to engage people as you speak. When your audience perceives you as charming, funny, and knowledgeable in a way that means something to them, they are likely to believe you and trust your message.

Question: What do you consider yourself first: an informative speaker who translates complicated information into lay terms or a persuasive speaker who encourages attitude change and actions?

Answer: Implicit in what I do is the need to place the huge volume of scientific information people face into some meaningful context. I have to know what the thousands of research papers on a given topic say and be able to interpret them for the audience. But this is only the first step. Presenting facts without my perspective on what's important isn't helpful. I try to put information in the context of what will be important in the future as I explain to people how to take charge of their health. This is especially important since over the past five years the advice-giving role of the family doctor has diminished and many health insurance plans have taken away the freedom to choose doctors and seek opinions. People are forced to make many of their own medical choices and I try to help them make the best decisions.

Question: As a medical speaker, does part of your credibility come from the sources you cite? For example, does a research study from the prestigious *New England Journal of Medicine* give you more credibility than a study from an unknown source?

Answer: From my experience, if an audience thinks you're credible, you don't have to cite sources. Ironically, if you do cite them, you may be perceived as insecure. This reaction depends, of course, on the audience. When I address medical students at Harvard, the audience expects me to cite sources, and I do.

Question: How do you help your audience focus on your key points?

Answer: When I give a talk about personal health and fitness, for example, I organize my speech around four key points. I tell people that to stay young well into old age, they need to be athletic, they need to succeed, they need to beat stress, and they need to be optimistic about life. I repeat these points several times and make other minor points as well. The average person walks away remembering my focus.

I also weave stories into my speech. I tell, for example, about an eighty-six-year-old man who while running the last three miles of the Boston Marathon downed three beers. People enjoy hearing how he threw beer cans at the thirty-year-olds he passed and how he has remained vital enough to compete. The advantage of my work is that I come across anecdotes like this all the time.

Question: Do you use a prepared script or do you speak with an outline?

Answer: I use an outline. I grab points from it and then speak extemporaneously. I plug in anecdotes and cite statistics. Although I may read a line or two or recite statistics from my notes, I avoid a written script as much as possible.

I try to deliver a different speech to every audience. I'm convinced that audiences are impressed when speakers take the time to customize a speech, and I also believe that speakers are more interested in delivering a speech when they use fresh material.

Question: How do you define a successful speech?

Answer: The best speeches are anecdotal and humorous. Audiences always look for personal experiences and rules of thumb. The more you give them, the more real your speech will be. If all you do is quote statistics and cite journal articles, people will stop paying attention.

The best speeches are also conversational. We're so used to the informal conversation we hear on television that we expect the same when we listen to speakers. Television has also taught audiences how to spot a phony. Unless you're sincere, your audience won't get your message.

Source: Interview with Dr. Bob Arnot, June 6, 1990

⌘ Use only one side of the paper.

⌘ Never staple the cards or pages.

Follow the same indentation pattern you used in your planning outline to indicate your points and subpoints. Include notations for the introduction, body, and conclusion and indicate transitions. It is unnecessary to include the specific purpose and core idea statements since these statements will not be spoken during your presentation. However, it is helpful to include suggestions for an effective delivery. Remind yourself to slow down, gesture, pause, use visual aids, and so on. This will be helpful during your speech, especially if you experience speech tension.

Sample Speakers' Notes and Analysis

We will now transform the planning outline to a key-word outline form.

(Introduction)
The introduction is labeled. The exact number of women and year cited in the study are included to avoid a misstatement.

I. Sociology and the male/female dating ratio.
    A. Berkeley study: 3 million women born in 1950 will never have a mate.
    B. Yale study
II. New census bureau data
    A. Ratio five single women to six single men in their twenties.
    B. Advantage: women.

(Look around room. Make eye contact. Slow down.)
These delivery instructions help emphasize that your speech has implications to your listeners.
(Body)
The body of the speech is labeled.
(Slow down)
Delivery instructions help personalize the message.

(Men are finding it hard to meet mates. We will examine the problem and its implications.)

III. Closer look at data.
    A. 19.9 million men, 20.4 million women in their twenties.
    B. However, 2.3 million more unmarried men.
        1. Women marry older men.
        2. How declining birth rate affects pool of marriageable singles.

This outline follows exactly the pattern of the planning outline.

IV. Result for men: No dates.
    A. Loneliness
    B. Pressure to marry from corporate America.
        1. Unmarried "oddballs."
        2. Climb the corporate ladder: marry by thirty.

Exact quote is written as are name and qualifications of source.

    C. Young and old fight for same women.
        1. William Beer, Brooklyn College sociologist: "Older men are poaching."
        2. Men are following tradition.

This transition is in the form of a question that leads the audience to the next point.

(Why are younger women drawn to older men?)

Again the complete quote is written. Abbreviations are used whenever possible to shorten the outline.

V.   More sophisticated.
    A.   Time to explore themselves and the world.
    B.   "The older men that I have met have done so much after college that I haven't done." (Martha Catherine Dagenhart, senior at U. of NC at Chapel Hill.)
VI.   More money.
    A.   Working longer.
    B.   Money in the bank.
VII.   More powerful.
    A.   Relationships based on status of man.
        1.   E.g., secretary marries boss.
        2.   Stereotype: May–September marriages.
    B.   Older men cultivate the image of power.

This transitional statement acts as a summary and preview.

(Summarize, then lead into what eligible bachelors can do.)

(Conclusion)

Conclusion is labeled. (Make eye contact during list.)

VIII.   Several solutions.
    A.   Date older women.
        1.   Plenty of women over thirty.
        2.   Women have always dated older men.
    B.   Be less picky.
        1.   "I'm not willing to settle"
        2.   Examine but don't abandon your dating standards.
    C.   Accept and adjust.

The more experience you have as a speaker, the more you will come to rely on both your planning outline and speakers' notes, as both are indispensable to a successful presentation.

SUMMARY   The first step in organizing your speech is to determine your main points. Organize your efforts around your specific purpose and core idea, then brainstorm to generate specific ideas, finally group like ideas.

Your second step is to use supporting material to develop each main point. In step three choose an organizational pattern. Arrange your ideas in chronological order, use a spatial organizational pattern, follow a pattern of cause and effect, look at a problem and its solutions, or choose a topical pattern. Your final step is to connect your main ideas through transitions, internal previews, and internal summaries.

As you develop your speech, your primary organizational tool is the planning outline, which includes most of the information you will present. The outline uses a traditional outlining format, which establishes a hierarchy of ideas. The number of main points developed in your speech should be limited to between three and five. The planning outline also uses complete sentences, labels transitions, and includes a bibliography.

Speakers' notes, the notes you use during your presentation in an extemporaneous speech, are less detailed than the planning outline. They serve as brief reminders of what you want to say and the order in which you say it. They may include complete quotations and statistical data as well as important delivery suggestions. Speakers' notes are organized around phrases, not sentences, and they use the same format as the planning outline.

QUESTIONS FOR STUDY AND DISCUSSION

1. Match five speech topics with five different organizational patterns. Which pattern did you choose for each topic, and on what basis did you make your choice?
2. In public speaking, what functions are served by transitions and summaries? Can you think of several effective transitional statements to develop the speech topics from question 1?
3. Review the essential requirements for planning and key-word outlines. Why is it necessary to develop both outline forms, and why are both equally important in extemporaneous speaking? Explain the role each plays in different phases of a speech?

ACTIVITIES

1. Read a speech from *Vital Speeches of the Day* or from another collection. Outline the speech, identifying the specific organizational pattern or patterns the speaker has chosen. Write a paragraph examining whether the pattern chosen effectively communicates the core idea.
2. Write a specific purpose statement for a speech, then use three different organizational patterns to organize the speech.
3. Select a video from your library that contains a speech. Then listen to the speech to identify the organizational pattern. List the previews, transition, and summaries. Identify the core idea and its placement in the speech.

"The first ninety seconds: They're absolutely crucial."

Ron Hoff, public speaking consultant

INTRODUCING AND CONCLUDING YOUR SPEECH

INTRODUCING YOUR SPEECH

A s part of aconference she had for a group of business executives, management consultant Edith Weiner was scheduled to deliver a speech on the unequal distribution of world resources—a topic with the potential to put her listeners to sleep. Weiner was experienced enough as a speaker to realize that the last thing her listeners wanted to hear as a speech opener was a long list of statistics describing the bounty of North America compared to the failures of the distribution systems in other parts of the world. Her speech would never recover from such a dull start. The challenge she faced was to capture the audience's attention at the outset.

Arriving at the auditorium early on the morning of her speech, Weiner marked off different size sections of the hall to represent, proportionately, the various continents and allotted coffee, cake, and chairs according to the availability of food and income in each. Then she assigned audience members to these areas according to actual world population ratios.

What happened was predictable—and memorable. While thirty people in the area representing Africa had to divide three cups of coffee, two danish and two chairs, the seventeen people assigned to North America had more coffee and cake than they could eat in a week, surrounded by forty chairs. As participants took their quota of seats (with those in Asia and Africa standing most of the morning), they did so with a new perspective on world hunger and poverty and with a desire to listen to whatever Weiner had to say. She began:

> I wanted to speak with you today at this prestigious conference about a topic most people tire of, but you, being so important to the financial community, cannot ignore.
>
> I know that some of you are now hungry and some of you are stuffed, and I want you to take the next few minutes to look around you and observe the obvious.
>
> Hunger and poverty aren't comfortable, are they? Neither is bounty when you realize the waste and mismatch of people and resources.
>
> This is only a game, but it demonstrates what number, charts, and speeches cannot. The world's population is forced to live every day with overabundance and scarcity—realities that cost millions their lives as U.S. farmers and consumers throw away food and disposables.
>
> Can you, as a business, do anything to resolve these inequities and, ultimately, profit from your role? I intend to explore several options during the rest of my speech.[1]

What Your Introduction Should Accomplish

Weiner's introduction was effective because it accomplished several important objectives:

The Personal Greeting.   First, it communicated the speaker's personal greeting, which generally consists of your first words and can be considered the preamble to your introduction. Greeting your listeners sets a gracious tone for what is to follow. A personal greeting at the start of your speech tells your listeners that you are pleased

---

1.   Based on interview with Edith Weiner, October 10, 1989.

to be with them and that you see the speech as an opportunity to communicate your point of view. When Martin Luther King looked out over the sea of faces on the Washington Mall on August 28, 1964, he began by telling his audience, "I am happy to join with you today in what will go down in history as the greatest demonstration for freedom in the history of our nation." Then he delivered his "I Have A Dream" speech—his powerful and memorable civil rights address.[2] Personal greetings make the audience feel welcome and set the stage for the *real* introduction that follows.

Build Bridges.   Second, her introduction helped Weiner build a relationship with her listeners that is critical to the public speaking transaction. She wanted her listeners to care about what she was saying—to decide at the start that her message had meaning and importance. Although the introduction also helped make her point with its graphic demonstration of world food problems, its primary purpose was to build psychological bridges that would last throughout the speech.

Every introduction should seek to establish common ground with the audience. By focusing on something you and your audience can share and announcing it early, you will help people identify with your topic. When people perceive that your message is meant for them, they will listen attentively.

Capture Attention.   Every experienced speaker knows that the first few minutes are crucial to the success of the entire speech. It is within these minutes that your listeners decide whether they care enough to continue listening. You want your listeners to say to themselves, "Hey, this is interesting," or "I didn't know that," or "I never thought of it in quite that way," or "That was really funny." The common denominator in each of these responses is piqued audience interest. Weiner explains: "I know if I'm successful when I start a speech. I try to establish a rapport with the audience and sail from there. If you wait till the end to deliver the 'Big Bang,' you've already lost most of your audience—and there's no getting them back. I always start with some kind of hook, and from there on, the audience is in the palm of my hand."[3]

Build Credibility.   During your introduction, your listeners make important decisions about you. They decide whether they like you and whether you are credible. Your credibility as a speaker is judged, in large part, on the basis of what you say and how you say it during your introduction.

Edith Weiner became a credible speaker by demonstrating, in a graphic way, that she understood the problems of world food distribution and that she cared enough about her audience—and topic—to come up with a creative way to present her ideas. Credibility also increases as you describe, early in your speech, what qualifies you to speak about a topic. Weiner might have said, "I want to talk to you about world resources because for several years I have studied how your investments overseas can

2.   Dr. Martin Luther King, Jr., "I Have a Dream," speech delivered August 28, 1963, Washington DC. Reprinted in Richard L. Johannesen, R. R. Allen, and Wil A. Linkugel, *Contemporary American Speeches,* 6th ed. (Dubuque, IA: Kendall/Hunt Publishing Company, 1988), p. 301.
3.   Weiner interview.

have important impacts on your future economic well-being." When you use your introduction to tell your listeners the source of your expertise, you give them reason to listen attentively throughout your speech.

Preview Your Topic.   Finally, Weiner used her introduction to tell her audience what she would talk about during the rest of her speech. In a sentence, she previewed her focus. ("I intend to explore several options [for maximizing your role and gain] during the rest of my speech.") With this simple statement, she helped her listeners make the intellectual connections they needed to follow her speech. Instead of wondering, "What will she talk about?" or "What is her point of view?" they were ready for her speech to unfold.

What follows are specific techniques for capturing audience attention.

Make a Startling Statement

Some introductions seem to force listeners to pay attention. They make it difficult to think of other things because of the impact of what is being said. The effectiveness of these introductions comes, in part, from the audience's feeling that the speaker's message is directed at them.

Here is how Thomas K. Hearn, Jr, president of Wake Forest University, caught the attention of his audience of college football coaches:

> Your profession—college football coaching—is at risk. Paradoxically, the risk arises from the very success and influence of college football. Successful people in your profession are being given generous doses of the three most dangerous and addictive drugs known: fame, wealth and power. Big time sports has made football coaches into entertainment celebrities. The question is whether the pursuit of the rewards of victory will destroy the comfortable houses your game has made for you. "Impossible" you say? You are one scandal way.[4]

Hearn's audience was captivated by the drug addiction metaphor and the provocative comment, "You are one scandal away." Startling statements often challenge common misconceptions. Instead of revealing the expected, the speaker takes a slightly—or perhaps even a radically—different turn.

Use a Dramatic Story

Closely related to the startling statement is the dramatic story, which involves listeners in a tale from beginning to end. Shortly after returning from a winter vacation break, Shannon delivered a speech to her classmates that began this way:

> My friends and I were driving home from a day at the ski slope when suddenly, without warning, a pair of headlights appeared directly in front of our car.

---

4. Thomas K. Hearn, Jr., "Sports and Ethics: The University Response," speech delivered to the College Football Association, Dallas, TX, June 5, 1988. Reprinted in *Vital Speeches of the Day,* October 15, 1988, p. 20.

To avoid a collision, I swerved sharply to the right, forcing our car off the road into a snow-filled ditch.

It's funny what comes into your mind at moments like this. All I could think of was how New York Yankee manager Billy Martin had died in a ditch a few years ago after his car skidded off an icy road. I thought I was going to die too, just because of another driver's stupidity and carelessness.

Obviously, I didn't die or even suffer any serious injuries. And my friends are safe too, although my car was totalled. I'm convinced that we are all here today because we were locked into place by our seat belts. Billy Martin might have been here too had he bothered to buckle up.

Everyone in the audience knew what it was like to be driving home with friends—feeling safe and secure—only to be shocked into the realization that they were vulnerable to tragedy. Audience attention was riveted on the speaker as she launched into her speech on seat belt use.

Engage Your Audience with a Quotation

You can capture audience attention by citing the words of others. If you use an appropriate poem, the words themselves may be compelling enough to engage your listeners. E. Grady Bogue, chancellor of Louisiana State University, opened the commencement address he delivered at Memphis State University with the following quotation:

They deem me mad because I will not sell my days for gold;
And I deem them mad because they think my days have a price.

Gibran, Sand and Foam

As Bogue continued, he celebrated the "nobility" of a career in teaching:

Teaching is a journey of the heart, an opportunity to touch a life forever. It is an unselfish investment in the dignity and potential of one's student. The life of the master teacher honors all that is good and noble in mankind.[5]

Introducing a speech with a quote is also appropriate when you cite the words of a well known individual or a recognized authority whose reputation enhances your topic. Here for example is how Tisha Oehmen, a student at Lane Community College, began her speech to capture the attention of her audience. Quoting a knowledgable public figure she began:

"Each day the Columbia River dumps in the Pacific Ocean 90 billion gallons of fresh water. That is 3.7 billion gallons an hour, 61 million gallons a minute, and 1 million gallons a second. This is wasteful and sinful." These are the words of Los Angeles

---

5. E. Grady Bogue, "A Friend of Mine: Notes on the Gift of Teaching," speech delivered as commencement address, Memphis State University, May 7, 1988. Reprinted in *Vital Speeches of the Day,* August 1, 1988, p. 615.

County Superviser Kenneth Hahn, as quoted in *The Washington Post,* May 20, 1990. This is how Hahn prepared his Board of Supervisors for his proposal to siphon water out of the Columbia River to quench the thirst of his drought-stricken city. If he succeeds in building this aquaduct, the life and the environment in the Pacific Northwest and all who depend on its resources may be changed. The Columbia's diversion would not only scar the landscape, but the proposed diversion would slow shipping, cripple irrigation, harm the fragile salmon runs, and reduce the available electricity."[6]

In similar fashion, Andy Wood studying at St. Petersburg Junior College, captured his audience's attention when speaking about the nation's trauma centers by stating:

"If a criminal has a right to an attorney, don't you have a right to a doctor?" Democrat Harris Woffard used this slogan last year to win the Pennsylvania senate race. *The Washington Post,* November 24, 1991, reports that Woffard also sent an alarming wakeup call to President Bush and Congress to get serious about health care in America."[7]

Put Your Audience at Ease with Humor

Humor at the beginning of a speech helps break down the psychological barriers that exist between speaker and audience. (For more on the use of humor in public speaking, see Chapter 10.) Here is how a student used humor at the start of a classroom speech on the problem of divorce in America:

Janet and Lauren had been college roommates, but had not seen each other in the ten years since graduation. They were thrilled when they ran into each other at a college reunion and had a chance to talk.

"Tell me," asked Janet, "has your husband lived up to the promises he made when he was dating you in college?"

"He certainly has!" said Lauren. "He told me then that he wasn't good enough for me and he's proven it ever since."

The class laughed and Karen responded:

I laughed too when I heard that story. But the fact remains that about half the marriages in our country end in divorce and one of the major reasons for these failures is that one partner can't live up to the expectations of the other.

Humor works in this introduction for two reasons. First, the story is genuinely funny; we chuckle when we hear the punch line. And, second, the humor is tied directly to the subject of the speech; it is appropriate for the topic and the occasion. It also provides an effective transition into the speech body.

---

6. Tisha R. Oehmen, "Not A Drop To Drink," Winning Orations of the Interstate Oratorical Association. Mankato State University: The Interstate Oratorical Association, 1991. p. 96.
7. Andy Wood, "America's Trauma Crisis," Winning Orations of the Interstate Oratorical Association. Mankato State University, The Interstate Oratorical Association, 1992. p. 18.

Use Rhetorical Questions

When you ask a rhetorical question, you don't expect an answer. What you hope is that questions will cause your listeners to start thinking about the subject of your speech. This was the plan of Paula Pankow, a student at the Eau Claire campus of the University of Wisconsin, when she began her speech about sleep deprivation:

> Do you ever go through the day feeling like you're missing something? Well, what would you do if I said each one of you probably suffers directly from a deficit every day that you might not even realize? A loss that, according to the May 15, 1990, issue of *The New York Times,* affects 100 million Americans and 200 billion dollars a year in lost creativity and business productivity, industrial and vehicular accidents and medical costs.

The speaker linked these rhetorical questions and startling statistics firmly to her audience of students by connecting them with the life-style familiar to residential college students and to her core idea and to a preview of the main points in her speech:

> This loss is not our deprivation of national dollars, but a loss concerning deprivation of sleep. Now granted, we're in an academic setting and getting a full night's rest isn't as important to adults as getting our work done. Free from the nagging voices of parents who may order a nine o'clock bedtime, we now enjoy the freedom of going to bed when we want and sometimes where we want, whether it be 10 p.m., 1 a.m., or even 6 a.m. after pulling an all-nighter! Of course a mild loss of sleep once in awhile won't do that much harm to a person, but most of us would be more good-humored, productive, and satisfied with life in general if we got a full complement of sleep each night. Instead what we're finding in society today is that sleep deprivation is becoming chronic and extensive leading to serious consequences. So today I'd like to address the problem of sleep deprivation by explaining its nature and consequences, exploring why we don't get enough sleep and, finally, offering some things we can do to better our chances for a full night's rest.[8]

The best rhetorical questions are probing in a personal way. They mean something to every listener and encourage active participation throughout your speech.

How to Preview Your Main Points

Once you have captured audience attention, you are ready to preview the body of your speech. The preview is the final part of the introduction and has one primary purpose: to express what you intend to talk about in your speech. Paula Pankow previewed her points, and then discussed them as promised, in her speech on sleep deprivation. Here is how John E. Jacob, president and chief executive officer of the

---

8.   Paula K. Pankow, "Hours To Go Before I Sleep," *Winning Orations of the Interstate Oratorical Association.* Mankato State University, The Interstate Oratorical Association, 1991. p. 123.

National Urban League, previewed a speech he delivered to the Congressional Clearinghouse on the Future:

> Today I want to begin by briefly sketching what the Urban League is, and going on from there, to discuss the plight of black citizens. Along the way, I'd like to look back at some of the things America has done to deal with its racial problems. And I'd like to look ahead as well, to suggest some of the things we can do to secure the future for black people and for all Americans.[9]

When Jacob finished this statement, his audience had no doubt what his speech would cover.

How to Introduce the Same Speech in Different Ways

Many topics lend themselves to different types of introductions. A startling statement, a dramatic anecdote, a quotation, or a humorous story may each serve as an effective introduction to the same speech. Here, for example, is the same speech introduced in three different ways:

Startling Statement

Microwave cooking can be hazardous to your child's health. Children have been burned by opening bags of microwave-heated popcorn too close to their faces. Their throats have been scalded by jelly donuts that feel cool to the touch, but are hot enough inside to burn the esophagus. These and other hazards can transform your microwave into an oven of destruction in the hands of a child.

> What I would like to talk about today is how dangerous microwaves can be to young children and how you can safeguard your family from accidents.

Dramatic Story

Nine-year-old Jenny was one of those kids who managed quite well on her own. Every day she got home from school at 3:30 while her parents were still at work and made herself a snack in the microwave. She had been using the microwave since she was five and her parents never questioned its safety—that is, not until Jenny had her accident.

> It began innocently enough. Jenny heated a bag of microwave popcorn in the oven and opened it inches from her face. The bag was cool to the touch, hiding the danger within. Hot vapors blasted Jenny's face, leaving her with second and third degree burns.

> What I would like to talk about today is how dangerous microwaves can be to young children and how you can safeguard your family from accidents.

Quotation

Three out of every four American homes have microwave ovens and with them a potential for danger. Louis Slesin, editor of *Microwave News,* a health and safety

9.   John E. Jacob, "The Future of Black America: The Doomed Generation," speech delivered before the members of Congressional Clearinghouse on the Future, May 30, 1988. Reprinted in *Vital Speeches of the Day,* August 1, 1988, p. 616.

newsletter, explains how this common kitchen appliance can present potential hazards for young children:

> "On a rainy day," says Slesin, "a kid could climb up on a stool, put his face to the door and watch something cook for a long time. It's mesmerizing, like watching a fish tank, but his eye will be at the point of maximum microwave leakage. We don't know the threshold for cataract formation—the industry says you need tons of exposure, but some litigation and literature say you don't need much [for damage to occur]. Children younger than 10 or 12 shouldn't use the oven unsupervised. It's not a toy. It's a sophisticated, serious, adult appliance, and it shouldn't be marketed for kids."[10]

> I agree with Slesin, and what I want to talk about today is how dangerous the microwave can be to a young child.

Let's now look at how Peggy Noonan, author of *What I Saw at the Revolution: A Political life in the Reagan Era,* analyzed the introduction she wrote to a presidential speech.

An Analysis of the Introduction to a Presidential Speech

Peggy Noonan wrote the speech President Ronald Reagan delivered on June 6, 1984, the fortieth anniversary of D-Day. The president delivered the speech on the windswept cliffs of Pointe du Hoc where American soldiers had disembarked to speed the end to World War II. Here is the introduction and Noonan's description of the choices she made while writing:

> *Noonan:* I had decided on a plan. The first paragraph would be full of big, emotional words and images. . . . And so it began:

>> We are here to mark the day in history when the Allied Armies joined in battle to reclaim this continent to liberty. For four long years much of Europe had been under a terrible shadow. Free nations had fallen, Jews cried out in camps, millions cried out for liberation from conquerers. Europe was enslaved, and the world waited for its rescue. Here in Normandy the rescue began. Here on a lonely windswept point on the western shore of France.

> Then:

>> As we stand here today the air is soft and full of sunlight, and if we pause and listen we will hear the snap of flags and the click of cameras and the gentle murmur of people come to visit a place of great sanctity and meaning.
>>
>> But forty years ago at this moment the air was dense with smoke and the cries of men, the air was filled with the crack of rifle fire and the roar of cannons. . . .

> *Noonan:* What I was doing here was placing it all in time and space for myself and, by extension, for the audience. If we really listen to and hear the snap of the flags, the reality of that sound—snap. . . suhnapp—will help us imagine what is sounded like on D-Day. And that would help us imagine what D-Day itself was like. Then your head snaps back with remembered information. History is real.

---

10.   Laura Shapiro, "The Zap Generation," *Newsweek,* February 26, 1990, p. 56.

> "We are here to mark the day in history when the allied armies joined in battle to regain this continent to liberty."—President Ronald Reagan.

Noonan then describes how she moved from this point to the body of the speech:

Noonan: [The next part describes] what happened. [It] was a little for the average viewer but mostly for kids watching TV at home in the kitchen at breakfast:

> Before dawn on the morning of the sixth of June, 1944, two hundred American Rangers jumped off a British landing craft and ran to the bottom of these cliffs. Their mission was one of the most difficult and daring of the invasion: to climb these sheer and desolate cliffs and take out the enemy guns. The Allies had been told that here were concentrated the mightiest of those guns, which would be trained on the beaches to stop the Allied advance. Removing the guns was pivotal to the Normandy invasion, which itself was pivotal to the reclaiming of Europe and the end of the war.

Noonan: I wanted American teenagers to stop chewing their Rice Krispies for a minute and hear about the greatness of those tough kids who are now their grandfathers.

> The Rangers looked up and saw the big casements . . . . And the American Rangers began to climb. They shot their rope ladders into the face of these cliffs and they pulled themselves up. And when one Ranger would fall another would take his place, and when one rope was cut and a Ranger would hurtle to the bottom he would find another rope and begin his climb again. They climbed and shot back and held their footing—

Noonan: I wanted this to have the rhythm of a rough advance:

> —and in time the enemy guns were quieted, and in time the Rangers held the cliffs, in time the enemy pulled back and one by one the Rangers pulled themselves over the top—and in seizing the firm land at the top of these cliffs they seized back the continent of Europe.

Noonan: Pause, sink in, bring it back to now, history is real.

Forty years ago as I speak they were fighting to hold these cliffs. They had radioed back and asked for reinforcements and they were told: There aren't any. But they did not give up. It was not in them to give up. They would not be turned back; they held the cliffs.

Two hundred twenty-five came here. After a day of fighting only ninety could still bear arms.

Behind me is a memorial that symbolized the Ranger daggers that were thrust into the top of these cliffs. And before me are the men who put them there.

These are the boys of Pointe du Hoc. These are the men who took the cliffs. These are the champions who helped free a continent. These are the heroes who helped end a war.

Noonan: The day he gave the speech it was at this point that the cameras cut to the Rangers, all of them sitting there on their folding chairs, middle-aged, heavy, and gray. One of them began to weep.[11]

CONCLUDING YOUR SPEECH

After talking about the rebuilding and the reconciliation that took place at the end of the war and the reasons the American Rangers risked their lives at Normandy, Noonan concluded the Pointe du Hoc speech with these words:

We in America have learned the bitter lessons of two world wars: that it is better to be here and ready to preserve and protect the peace, than to take blind shelter in our homes across the sea, rushing to respond only after freedom has been threatened. We have learned that isolationism never was and never will be an acceptable response to tyrannical governments with expansionist intent.

Let our actions say to them the words for which Matthew Ridgway listened: "I will not fail thee nor forsake thee." Strengthened by their courage, heartened by their valor and borne by their memory, let us continue to stand for the ideals for which they lived and died.[12]

What Your Conclusion Should Accomplish

Communicate Closure.   This conclusion accomplished what all good conclusions must: It tied together the loose ends of the speech, leaving the audience with a sense of closure. A good conclusion tells your listeners your speech is over.

Communicate a Feeling.   Perhaps more importantly, it sets the psychological mood listeners carry with them from the hall.

Reinforce Your Message.   In the process, an effective conclusion also hammers home the main idea of the speech. The conclusion of the Pointe du Hoc speech, for

---

11.   Peggy Noonan, *What I Saw at the Revolution: A Political Life in the Reagan Era* (New York: Random House, 1990), pp. 85–86.
12.   Ibid. p. 88.

example, reinforced President Reagan's message that the liberties we fought for in World War II are the liberties we are still committed to today.

Summarize.   Depending upon the length and complexity of your speech, your conclusion can also act as a summary. Your review can be as simple as this:

> I would like to conclude by stating once more that our schools have done a dismal job teaching math and science. As we have seen, the results of standardized tests show that our high school and college students are well behind their counterparts in Japan and Western Europe. And, as we have also seen, the demands of business for skilled scientists and mathematicians are growing along with the complexity of technology.
>
> The hard truth is that businesses need many more students trained in math and science than our educational system is now producing. Generally, I don't like to make predictions, but I can say for certain that we face a crisis.

Using your conclusion to summarize your speech is a common technique. Many speakers believe that the best way to hammer home their point is to tell their audience what they are going to say in their introduction, say it in the body of their speech, and then remind their listeners of what they told them in the conclusion. According to speech communication professor John E. Baird, Jr., "Summaries may be effective when presented at the conclusion of a speech [because] they provide the audience with a general structure under which to subsume the more specific points of the speech."[13] Although research indicates that in some instances summaries are not essential, if your audience is unfamiliar with the content of your speech or if the speech is long or complex, a summary will help reinforce your main points.[14]

Relate Your Topic to Your Listeners' Lives.   Your speech will achieve the greatest success if your listeners feel that you have helped them in some concrete way. Consider making this connection in your conclusion. When Sarah Weddington, the lawyer who successfully argued *Roe* v. *Wade* before the Supreme Court in 1973— a case that guaranteed American women the right to abortion—spoke to students at Mercer University in Macon, Georgia, she used the conclusion of her speech to broaden her discussion to the lives of her listeners. Weddington said:

> I appreciate your willingness—at such a busy time—to give me some minutes to talk about the legal issue of *Roe* v. *Wade* and its implications.
>
> Obviously, many of you will not choose this issue to be your key issue, but I hope when you leave Mercer, you will pick some issue that you care about and that you will be involved in as a leader in deciding the path that society will travel.[15]

13. See John E. Baird, Jr., "The Effects of Speech Summaries upon Audience Comprehension of Expository Speeches of Varying Quality and Complexity," *Central States Speech Journal* (Summer 1974): 119–27.
14. For a study showing when summaries are not needed, see Frederick H. Turner, Jr., "Effects of Summaries on Audience Comprehension," *The Central States Speech Journal* 27 (Spring 1970): 24–29.
15. Sarah Weddington, speech delivered at Mercer University, Macon, Georgia, May 10, 1989.

Broaden Your Message.   Finally, the conclusion can be used to connect your topic to a broader context. If in your speech you talk about the responsibility of every adult to vote on election day, you can use your conclusion to tie the vote to the continuation of our democratic system. If your speech focuses on caring for aging parents, you can conclude with a plea to value rather than discard the wisdom of the elderly.

Here are several specific techniques for concluding your speech:

Call to Action

As you wrap up your speech you can make a direct appeal to your listeners, urging them to take a specific action or change their attitudes. In a persuasive speech, the conclusion is where you make your most forcible and most memorable plea to persuade.

Living in an age of mass media, we are bombarded by calls to action every time we turn on the television. Advertisers plead with us to drop everything and buy their products. We see 800-numbers flashed across the screen, urging us to order a magazine subscription. Televangelists urge us to contribute to their mission. The fact that we are all accustomed to these messages makes them a natural conclusion to a speech.

Reverend Billy Graham ends his sermons with a call to action for the audience to come forward to make a religious decision.

Realizing this, Thomas K. Hearn, Jr., concluded his speech to the College Football Association with these remarks:

> If there are values acquired by a life devoted to a game, even a game as violent as football, then those of you who coach this sport should be examples of the sport's ethical possibilities. Does playing football build ingredients of character? Does it make young men better? Whether team sports are good for people, people at any age, is always a question of coaching leadership. Your game has a noble heritage. All of you are guardians of your sport. . . .
>
> If football belongs in the university where young minds and character are being formed, and if being called "coach" is a title of honor among all coaches, football can lead the movement of reform, beginning today with all of us.[16]

Hearn is challenging his listeners to think and act in a more ethical way.

A call to action is an especially appropriate way to conclude a persuasive speech, but it can also be an effective end to an informative speech. Here is how a professor might conclude a lecture:

> I have explained my thoughts on the implications of the changes that are now taking place in Eastern Europe. As you review them, keep this in mind: What we are witnessing is nothing less than a sea change in world politics. In the days ahead, think about this change and about how it will affect each and every one of us in the free and communist worlds.

Use a Dramatic Illustration

Ending your speech with a dramatic story connected to your speech's main theme reinforces the theme in your listeners' minds. It is the last message of your speech the audience will hear and, as a story, it is the most likely to be remembered. Investigative reporter Dale Van Atta concluded a speech on international terrorism with the following story about the struggle for freedom:

> There was a woman in Laos who I will never forget. I was in the refugee camps along the border of the Mekong River. I was meeting with her and an interpreter and I asked her what happened when she escaped [from Laos]; she had come out about a week before.
>
> She said she was coming to the Mekong River with a group of about forty Laos citizens trying to flee from the communists. They were in the woods and began to hear the patrol and feared they would be caught. She had a four- or five-month-old baby who began to cry. As is common with the Lao people, they use opium for medicinal purposes. They always have some—they are not addicted; they use it like an herbal medicine. She decided that the only way she could silence the child and save the forty others was to blow a little of this opium into the child's nose so it would become very quiet. And it worked.
>
> And then she began to cry and the interpreter and the head of the camp did not know what had happened. He turned to me—the head of the camp—and said to me,

---

16. Thomas K. Hearn, Jr., "Sports and Ethics: The University Response," speech delivered to the College Football Association, June 5, 1988. Reprinted in *Vital Speeches of the Day,* October 15, 1988, p. 22.

"She doesn't have a baby with her." So I asked her what happened. She said by the time they got to the other side of the river, she found her baby was dead. She had blown too much opium into the baby's nose.

And then there was a long pause as we were all in tears. And I asked her "If you had to do it again, would you do it again?" And she said, "Yes. To come to America for freedom—for the sake of my other children."

We have a country that is so much [the country described by the] kindergarten child who got the Pledge of Allegiance wrong: "I pledge of allegiance to the flag of the United States of a miracle." He got it right.

Thank you very much.[17]

Close with a Quotation

Closing a speech with the words of others is an effective and memorable way to end your presentation. Here is how Charles Parnell concluded his remarks on speech writing to a group of business executives:

In conclusion, let me refer to some words of Dr. E. C. Nance, quoted in *Vital Speeches* more than 30 years ago:

Words can change the face of a city, build churches, schools, playgrounds, boys' clubs, scout troops, civic forums, civic clubs, little theaters, civic music organizations, garden clubs and better local governments.

We need words that will make us laugh, wonder, work, think, aspire, and hope. We need words that will leap and sing in our souls. We need words that will cause us to face up to life with a fighting faith and contend for those ideals that have made this the greatest nation on earth.

Ladies and gentlemen, with all the problems and challenges facing business, our country and the world, we are going to need words that can inspire us to do all these things.

You the communicators are the people who will give us these words.[18]

One of the most famous moments in recent oratory was the conclusion of President Ronald Reagan's eulogy to the crew of the space shuttle *Challenger.*

The crew of the space shuttle *Challenger* honored us by the manner in which they lived their lives. We will never forget them, nor the last time we saw them—this morning, as they prepared for their journey, and waved good-bye, and "slipped the surly bonds of earth" to "touch the face of God."

As in this example, quotations can be interwoven into the fabric of the speech without telling your listeners that you are speaking the words of others. If you use this technique, it is important that you use the quote exactly and attribute it to the writer if asked.

---

17.   Dale Van Atta, speech delivered at the 1989 convention of the International Platform Association.

18.   Charles Parnell, "Speechwriting: The Profession and the Practice," speech delivered to the International Association of Business Communicators Conference, October 9, 1989. Reprinted in *Vital Speeches of the Day,* January 15, 1990, p. 210.

Conclude with a Metaphor That Broadens the Meaning of Your Speech

You may want to broaden the meaning of your speech through the use of an appropriate metaphor—a symbol that tells your listeners that you are saying more. President Reagan used this technique several times at the conclusion of his State of the Union address by citing the heroism of a select group of individuals who were invited to sit in the balcony of the House of Representatives while the speech was being delivered. Here are Reagan's words:

> Tonight I have spoken of great plans and great dreams. They are dreams we can make come true. Two hundred years of American history should have taught us that nothing is impossible.
>
> Ten years ago a young girl left Vietnam with her family, part of the exodus that followed the fall of Saigon. They came to the United States with no possessions, and not knowing a word of English. The young girl studied hard, learned English and finished high school in the top of her class. This May is a big date on her calendar. Just ten years from the time she left Vietnam, she'll graduate from the United States Military Academy at West Point. I thought you might want to meet an American hero named Jean Nguyen.

(The young woman stood and bowed to the applause.)

> There's someone else here tonight. Born seventy-nine years ago, she lives in the inner city where she cares for infants born to mothers who are heroin addicts. The children, born in withdrawal, are sometimes even dropped at her doorstep. She heals them with love. Go to her house some night and maybe you'll see her silhouette against the window, as she walks the floor talking softly, soothing a child in her arms. Mother Hale of Harlem—she, too, is an American hero.

(Mrs. Hale stood to acknowledge the applause.)

> Your lives tell us that the oldest American saying is new again: Anything is possible in America if we have the faith, the will, and the heart. History is asking us, once again, to be a force for good in the world. Let us begin, in unity, with justice, and love.[19]

Presidential speechwriter Peggy Noonan explains the symbolic impact of this conclusion: "The heroes in the balcony was a metaphor for all the everyday heroism that never gets acknowledged. It was for kids, to show them what courage is."[20]

Conclude with Humor

If you leave your listeners with a humorous story, you will leave them laughing and with a reservoir of good feelings about you and your speech. To be effective, of course, the humor must be tied to your core idea.

---

19.   Peggy Noonan, op. cit., pp. 198–99.
20.   Ibid, p. 198.

A Hollywood screenwriter, invited to speak to students in a college writing course about the job of transforming a successful novel into a screenplay, concluded her speech with the following story:

> Two goats who often visited the set of a movie company found some discarded film next to where a camera crew was working. One of the goats began munching on the film.
>
> "How's it taste?" asked the other goat, trying to decide whether to start chomping himself.
>
> "Not so great," said the first goat. "I liked the book better."

The audience laughed in appreciation of the humor. When the room settled down, the speaker concluded her speech:

> I hope in my case the goat isn't right and that you've enjoy the films I've written even more than the books on which they were based.
>
> Thank you for inviting me to speak.

Encourage Thought with a Rhetorical Question

Rhetorical questions encourage thought. At the end of a speech, they leave listeners with a responsibility to think about the questions you raise after the speech is over. Your question can be as simple as, "Can our community afford to take the step of hiring fifty new police officers? Perhaps a better question is, can we afford not to?"

Rhetorical questions have the power to sway an audience with their emotional impact. Here, for example, is how a white candidate running for mayor of a large Midwestern city concluded his speech to a group of African-American voters. Fearing that his candidacy was being dismissed by African Americans simply because he was white (his opponent was black), the candidate delivered this impassioned conclusion:

> In conclusion, I want to urge the African-American community to see me as a candidate of all the people. Voting for my opponent just because he is black is self-defeating. Is segregation in the ballot box any better than segregation in any other form? Isn't it just as wrong for all the members of a group to set themselves apart and vote as a bloc, regardless of the merits of the candidates, as it would be for others to set them apart? Doesn't integration mean integration of all things?
>
> I urge you to think about these questions as you decide the best candidate to lead your community—and all the citizens of this great city—over the next four years.[21]

Refer to Your Introduction

Like matching bookends, closing your speech with a reference to your introduction provides intellectual and emotional symmetry to your remarks. You can refer to an opening story or quotation or answer the rhetorical questions you raised. Here is how

---

21. Based on John J. Makay and Thomas C. Sawyer, *Speech Communication Now!* (Columbus, OH: Charles E. Merrill Publishing Company, 1973), p. 160.

Shannon closed her speech on seat belt safety:

> One thing I didn't tell you at the beginning of my speech about my accident was that for years I resisted wearing my belt. I used to fight with my parents. I felt it was such a personal decision. How could they—or the state government, for that matter—dare tell me what to do?
>
> Thank goodness I had the sense to buckle up that day. And you can be sure that I will never get into a car without wrapping myself securely with my belt of life.
>
> I hope that my experience will be enough to convince you to buckle up too.

Make Your Last Words Your Most Memorable

Think of your conclusion as the climax of your speech—the words you want your listeners to remember as they leave the room. Too often, speakers waste the opportunity with endings like, "I guess I'm finished now," or "I'm through. Any questions?" Or they simply stop talking, giving the audience no indication that they have finished their speech. The best conclusions are also wrap-ups. They tell the audience that the speech is over.

Although saying thank you at the end of the speech indicates that you are finished, it is no substitute for a statement that brings your discussion to a close. You can, however, use the thank you statement as a transition into your concluding remarks. For example:

> And so, in summary, women certainly have more opportunity today than they ever had, but they also have more responsibility.
>
> Thank you for giving me the honor of being your keynote speaker. Sociologist Sylvia Ann Hewlett has described the gains of the women's liberation movement as a myth. She tells women that they have a "lesser life" than men—despite their considerable strides. She may be right today, but let's all do what we can to make sure she is wrong tomorrow.

How to Conclude the Same Speech in Different Ways

Just as many topics lend themselves to different types of introductions, they also lend themselves to various methods of conclusion. Here three different techniques are used to conclude a speech on learning to deal more compassionately with the elderly:

A Quotation That Personalizes Your Message
In 1878, in a poem entitled, "Somebody's Mother," poet Mary Dow Brine wrote these words:

> She's somebody's mother, boys, you know,
> For all she's aged and poor and slow.

Most of us are likely to be somebody's mother—or father—before we die. And further down the road, we're likely to be grandparents, sitting in a rocking chair, hoping that our children have figured out a more humane way to treat us than we've treated our elderly relatives.

BEGINNINGS AND ENDINGS
THAT DO NOT WORK

Knowing what *not* to do is almost as important as knowing what to do. Here is a list of approaches to avoid during your introduction:

Don't Promise Too Much
Some speakers, fearful that their speech says too little, promise more than they can deliver, in the hope that the promise alone will satisfy their listeners. It rarely does. Once you set expectations in the introduction, the body of your speech has to deliver or you will lose credibility.

Don't Rely on Shock Tactics
Your victory will be short-lived if you capture audience attention by screaming at the top of your lungs, pounding the table, telling bawdy jokes, or using material that has nothing to do with your speech. When you start talking about the real subject of your speech, your audience will trust you less because of the way you manipulated their attention. Using an innovative approach is effective as long as it is tied directly to the topic of your speech.

Don't Say Too Much in Your Preview
Don't give away the substance of your speech in your preview. Speakers who are forced to repeat their entire message when they reach the body of their speech lose their listeners. Use general terms to tell your audience what you expect to cover.

Don't Apologize
Even if you are a first-time speaker, don't use your introduction to apologize in advance for the mistakes you are likely to make. Similarly, don't apologize for what your speech will not cover.

Speakers face similar pitfalls in their conclusions.

Don't Use Your Conclusion
to Introduce a New Topic
Develop your core idea and subordinate points in the body of your speech, not in the conclusion.

Don't Apologize
Even if you are unhappy with your performance, don't apologize for your shortcomings when you reach the conclusion. Remarks like, "Well, I guess I didn't have that much to say," or "I'm sorry for taking so much of your time," are unnecessary and usually turn off the audience.

Don't Just Stop Talking
After Your Last Point
Just because you have made all your points does not mean that your speech is over. Your audience has no way of knowing you are finished unless you provide closure.

Don't Change the Mood
or Tone of Your Speech
If your speech was serious, don't shift moods at the end. A frivolous conclusion would be inappropriate and lessen the impact of your speech.

Don't Use the Phrases, "in Summary" or
"in Conclusion," Except when You Are
Actually at the End of Your Speech
Some speakers use these phrases at various points in their speech, confusing listeners who expect an ending rather than a transition to another point.

Don't Ignore Questions
Time and format permitting, be willing to answer questions.

Don't Ignore Applause
Graciously accept the praise of your audience by looking around the room and saying thank you.

A Dramatic Story That Also Serves as a Metaphor

Not too long ago, I had a conversation with a doctor who had recently hospitalized an eighty-two-year-old woman with pneumonia. A widow and the mother of three grown children, the woman had spent the last seven years of her life in a nursing home.

The doctor was called three times a day by these children. At first their calls seemed appropriate. They wanted to be sure their mother was getting the best possible medical care. Then, their tone changed. Their requests became demands; they were pushy and intrusive.

After several days of this, the doctor asked one of the children—a son—when he had last visited his mother before she was admitted to the hospital. He hesitated for a moment and then admitted that he had not seen her for two years.

I'm telling you this story to demonstrate that we can't act like these grown children and throw our elderly away only to feel guilty about them when they are in crisis.

Somehow we have to achieve a balance between our own needs and the needs of our frail and needy parents—one that places reasonable demands on ourselves and on the system that supports the elderly.

Some Difficult Rhetorical Questions

Imagine yourself old and sick, worried that your money will run out and that your family will no longer want you. You feel a pain in your chest. What could it be? You ask yourself whether your daughter will be able to leave work to take you to the hospital—whether your grandchildren will visit you there—whether your medical insurance will cover your bills—whether anyone will care if you live or die.

Imagine asking yourself these questions and then imagine the pain of not knowing the answers. We owe our elderly better than that.

SUMMARY   Speech introductions have several purposes: They extend the speaker's personal greeting to the audience, they help establish a relationship between speaker and audience, they capture attention, they build credibility, and they preview the topic of your speech.

Several techniques can be used to capture audience attention in the introduction. Among these are startling statements, dramatic stories, quotations, humor, rhetorical questions, and a reference to the title of your speech.

The conclusion of your speech should communicate closure and the mood you want your audience to carry with it from the hall. An effective conclusion reinforces your message, acts as a summary, relates your message to your listeners' lives, and connects your message to a broader context.

Among the techniques you can use to conclude your speech are a call to action, a dramatic story, a closing quotation, a metaphor that broadens meaning, humor, rhetorical questions, and a reference to the introduction.

1. What alternatives are available for capturing audience attention in an introduction? What alternatives are available for bringing closure to a speech?
2. What is the relationship between the effectiveness of a speech's introduction and conclusion and speaker credibility?
3. What mistakes do speakers commonly make in preparing the introduction and conclusion of a speech?
4. How do effective introductions and conclusions help meet the psychological needs of the audience?

1. Write a core idea for a speech, then use different techniques to draft several introductions and conclusions.
2. Examine the transcripts of several speeches in *Vital Speeches of the Day, Representative American Speeches,* or a similar collection. Analyze and assess the effectiveness of the speeches' introductions and conclusions. Consider the appropriateness of each for the topic, the audience, and the occasion.
3. Prepare a short persuasive speech with two different introductions and conclusions. Then deliver it in both forms to a small group. Ask the group which introduction and conclusion worked best. Find out how the choice influences your speech's specific purpose.

Maya Angelou reads a poem she composed for the 1993 inauguration of President Bill Clinton.

"A speech is poetry: cadence, rhythm, imagery, sweep! A speech reminds us that words, like children, have the power to make dance the dullest beanbag of a heart."[1]

Peggy Noonan, speechwriter for Ronald Reagan and George Bush

1. Peggy Noonan, *What I Saw at the Revolution: A Political Life in the Reagan Era* (New York: Random House, 1990), p. 68.

LANGUAGE, STYLE, AND HUMOR

231

hen politicians in Chicago make a speech everyone listens—not so much for the content of the speech (although this too may be interesting) but for the tangled rhetoric typical of Chicago politicians. The language is so unique that it sometimes takes a group effort to set it straight.

Take the case of A. A. (Sammy) Rayner, Jr., a former alderman, still active in Chicago politics. Recently he defended another politician by saying, "He is not the orgy some people think he is." Relying on the advice of Earl Bush, press secretary to longtime Chicago Mayor Richard Daley, to "Write what he means, not what he says," reporters who heard this comment translated "orgy" into "ogre," the word Rayner intended. For those not in the room when the sentence was spoken, logic prevailed.[2]

Public speakers are rarely met with such kindness when they mangle the English language. Don't count on anyone to tell others what you really mean. Your language will, in large part, determine the success of your speech. Your words create the vivid images that remain in people's minds after your speech is over.

Your choice of words and style of language influence your credibility as a speaker. By choosing language that appeals to your audience—by moving your audience intellectually and emotionally through the images of speech—you create a bond that encourages continued listening. Language must fit the needs of your audience or it will not advance your rhetorical purpose. General Dwight D. Eisenhower understood this during his 1952 presidential campaign. His opponent, Adlai Stevenson, favored an intellectual style with involved syntax, but Eisenhower appealed to the public through the simple, direct language of the common man— a style that helped win him the presidency.

In this chapter, we analyze how to use spoken language most effectively. We look at the differences between spoken and written language and emphasize the need for simplicity and precision in your choice of words. We also examine how your choice of language determines your speaking style and how it can capture the imaginations of your listeners. Finally, we examine how the use of humorous language can connect you with your listeners. Although much of the language you use in public speaking will be extemporaneous, it is important to train yourself to think about diction as you plan and develop your speech and how your specific words will affect your listeners.

SPOKEN LANGUAGE AND WRITTEN LANGUAGE ARE DIFFERENT

Don't try to convince yourself that a written report can be used as a speech. It cannot—at least not without major adjustments. The needs of written language and spoken language are different because listeners process information differently from the way readers do.

---

2. William E. Schmidt, "Syntax Is a Loser in Mayoral Race," *New York Times,* February 21, 1989, p. A14.

Spoken Language is Expanded Language

According to Jerry Tarver, professor of speech communication and professional speechwriter: "It takes more words per square idea to say something than to write it." Tarver explains: "I define conciseness the same way you do. Using no more words than necessary to express an idea well. It just happens that it takes more words to express an idea well in a speech than it does in an article."[3]

Redundancy is necessary in spoken language because of the time the brain needs to process information. We need the "padding" of extra words—not to carry the speaker's message—but to give us the time to understand the message. Speech communication experts tell us that only about half our words are necessary for meaning.[4] The rest are oratorical redundancies that help us transmit our verbal messages. Abraham Lincoln understood this when he wrote:

> A house divided against itself cannot stand. I believe this government cannot endure permanently half slave and half free. I do not expect the Union to be dissolved—I do not expect the house to fall—but I do expect it will cease to be divided.

Although these words contain Lincoln's entire thought, he chose to add seventy-eight more words to communicate meaning.

> It will become all one thing or the other. Either the opponents of slavery will arrest the further spread of it, and place it where the public mind shall rest in the belief that it is in the course of ultimate extinction; or its advocates will push it forward, till it shall become alike lawful in all the States, old as well as new—North as well as South.[5]

According to Tarver, "the need for an expanded style is imposed not by the message but by the medium" of the spoken word.

Spoken Language Affects the Order of Ideas

Spoken language also affects the order in which ideas should be arranged in a sentence, with the last idea presented being the most powerful. Consider this famous line spoken by John F. Kennedy at his inauguration:

> Ask not what your country can do for you, ask what you can do for your country.

Inverted the sentence loses its power:

> Ask what you can do for your country, ask not what your country can do for you.

---

3.   Jerry Tarver, "Words in Time: Some Reflections on the Language of Speech," speech delivered to the Chicago Speech Writer's Forum, March 2, 1988. Reprinted in *Vital Speeches of the Day,* April 15, 1988, p. 410. The following discussion is based on information from pp. 410–12 of the Tarver speech.
4.   For information on the importance of redundancy in communication, see David K. Berlo, *The Process of Communication* (New York: Holt, Rinehart and Winston, 1960), pp. 202–03.
5.   Abraham Lincoln, "A House Divided" (1858), in James Andrews and David Zarefsky, *American Voices—Significant Speeches in American History: 1640–1945* (New York: Longman, 1989), pp. 237–43.

Because speech is slower than silent reading, individual words take on more importance, especially those appearing at the end of the sentence.[6] The unusual arrangement of words or clauses within a sentence is known as *anastrophe.*

Spoken Language Demands Attention to Rhythm

In *The Rhetoric,* Aristotle states that when a speech has no rhythm, it is "unconfined," and the effect is "vague and unpleasing, as the indefinite always is." Rhythm refers to the ordered recurrent alternation of strong and weak elements in the flow of the sounds of speech. When speech is rhythmic, listeners feel that they are reaching some conclusion.[7]

Tarver uses Patrick Henry's famous line, "Give me liberty or give me death," to illustrate the importance of rhythm. By taking out one of the repetitive "give me" phrases, the rhythm—and impact—of the sentence changes. Read this modified version aloud:

> I know not what course
> Others may take.
> But as for me,
> Give me liberty
> Or death.

Now read the original, and notice the greater impact:

> I know not what course
> Others may take.
> But as for me,
> Give me liberty
> Or give me death.

The rhythm of speech is affected by variations in sentence length, by the use of figures of speech and parallel structure, and by the expression of images in groups of three.

Vary the Length of Your Sentences.   The rhythm of speech is affected by how well you combine sentences of varying lengths. Long sentences can be confusing and short sentences boring, but a combination of long and short sentences adds rhythmic interest. Franklin D. Roosevelt combined a two-word sentence with an eighteen-word sentence to increase the impact of the following message:

> Hostilities exist. There is no mincing the fact that our people, our territory and our interests are in great danger.

This combination is more interesting to *hear* than ten-word sentences.

---

6. Tarver, "Words in Time," p. 411.
7. Lane Cooper, *The Rhetoric of Aristotle* (New York: Appleton-Century-Crofts, 1960), p. 199.

Use Figures of Speech.   Figures of speech connect sentences by emphasizing the relationship among ideas and by repeating key sounds to establish a pleasing rhythm. The following are among the most popular figures of speech:

Anaphora is the repetition of the same word or phrase at the beginning of successive clauses or sentences. In the following example, Georgie Anne Geyer, foreign correspondent and syndicated columnist, uses this technique as she addresses students at Saint Mary-of-the-Woods College in Indiana.

> There is only one thing that I know to tell you graduates—only one thing—and that is to follow what you love! Follow it intellectually! Follow it sensuously! Follow it with generosity and nobility toward your fellow man! Don't deign to ask what "they" are looking for out there. Ask what you have inside.[8]

Epistrophe involves the repetition of a word or expression at the end of phrases, clauses, or sentences. Lincoln used this device in the phrase, "of the people, by the people, for the people."

Alliteration involves the repetition of initial sounds in series of words. Jesse Jackson frequently uses this device:

⌘ A mature person is one who can "produce, protect, and provide."

⌘ For blacks to achieve educational excellence, they "must contrast the politics of the five B's—blacks, browns, budgets, busing and balance—with the five A's—attention, attendance, atmosphere, attitude and achievement."[9]

Antithesis involves the use of contrast, within a parallel grammatical structure, to make a rhetorical point, as in these examples from Jesse Jackson:

⌘ Jackson told an audience of young African Americans. "We cannot be what we ought to be if we push dope in our veins, rather than hope in our brains."

⌘ Later, in the same speech, he told his listeners, "You are not a man because you can kill somebody. You are a man because you can heal somebody."

⌘ During his presidential campaigns, Jackson stated that African Americans were coming "from the outhouse to the White House."[10]

Use Parallel Structure.   Parallelism involves the arrangement of a series of words, phrases, or sentences in a similar form. Here are several examples:

⌘ *John F. Kennedy:* If a free society cannot help the many who are poor, it cannot save the few who are rich.

---

8.   Georgie Anne Geyer, "Joy in Our Times: I Am Responsible for My Own Fight," speech delivered as commencement address at Saint Mary-of-the-Woods College, May 7, 1989. Reprinted in *Vital Speeches of the Day,* August 15, 1989, p. 668.

9.   J. Justin Gustainis, "Jesse Louis Jackson," in Bernard K. Duffy and Halford R. Ryan, eds., *American Orators of the Twentieth Century: Critical Studies and Sources* (New York: Greenwood Press, 1987), p. 218.

10.   Ibid, p. 219.

⌘ *Richard M. Nixon:* Where peace is unknown, make it welcome, where peace is fragile, make it strong; where peace is temporary, make it permanent.

⌘ *A college president:* We expect to be around for a long time, and we expect to remain strong for a long time.[11]

Parallel structure emphasizes the rhythm of speech. When used effectively, it adds a harmony and balance to speech that verges on the poetic.

Three is a Magic Number.[12]   Winston Churchill once said, "If you have an important point to make, don't try to be subtle or clever. Use a pile driver. Hit the point once. Then come back and hit it again. Then hit it a third time—a tremendous whack." Experienced speakers know that saying things three times gets their point across in a way saying it once cannot—not simply because of repetition, but because of the rhythmic effect of the repetition. Here are examples from Abraham Lincoln and FDR:

⌘ Lincoln: "We cannot dedicate, we cannot consecrate, we cannot hallow this ground."

⌘ Roosevelt: "I see one-third of a nation, ill-housed, ill-clad, ill-nourished."

You can use this device in your classroom speeches: "I am here to honor, to praise, and to congratulate the members of the campus volunteer fire department."

Spoken Language Requires Signals

You may reread an important passage in a book to appreciate its meaning, but your audience hears your message only once—a fact that may make it necessary to signal critical passages in your speech. The following signals tell your listeners to pay close attention:

⌘ This can't be overemphasized

⌘ Let me get to the heart of the matter

⌘ The most significant point is this

⌘ I want to summarize

⌘ My five main points are

Although all speakers hope to capture and hold listeners' attention throughout their speech, you must draw people back to your message at critical points. Because of the nature of the medium, this is more necessary in spoken language than in print.

---

11.   Examples from Joan Detz, *How to Write and Give a Speech* (New York: St. Martin's Press, 1984), p. 69.
12.   Section based on ibid., pp. 67–68.

Throughout the text, we emphasize the importance of simplicity—in your choice of support, in the flow of ideas, in your delivery style. We also emphasize precision in your library research, in your choice of supporting material, in the building of your argument through logic and reason. Simplicity and precision are equally important in the language you choose to communicate meaning.

SIMPLICITY AND PRECISION HAVE NO SUBSTITUTE

Never Use a Long Word When a Short One Will Do

When Mark Twain wrote popular fiction, he was often paid by the word, a fee schedule that led him to this observation:

> By hard, honest labor, I've dug all the large words out of my vocabulary . . . I never write *metropolis* for seven cents because I can get the same price for *city.* I never write *policeman* because I can get the same price for *cop.*

The best speakers realize that attempting to impress an audience by using four- or five-syllable words usually backfires. Experience has taught them that short words are more effective in getting their points across. When Franklin Delano Roosevelt was given this sentence by a speechwriter—"We are endeavoring to construct a more inclusive society"—he simplified it this way: "We are going to make a country in which no one is left out."[13]

Here is a list of multisyllabic words and their simple alternatives.

Words to Impress	Words to Communicate
periodical	magazine
indisposed	sick
utilize	use
precipitation	rain
remunerate	pay
recapitulate	sum up
reiterate	repeat
enumerate	count
cognizant	aware
commence	begin
discourse	talk

Now compare a classroom teacher's sentence, using items from the left to one using items from the right:

Speech to Impress.   I would like to commence this discourse by reiterating my intention to utilize popular periodicals in my classroom lectures.

Speech to Communicate.   I would like to begin this talk by repeating my intention to use popular magazines in my classroom lectures.

---

13.   From ibid., pp. 50–53.

Avoid Language that Masks Meaning

This is an extension of the previous point. We've chosen to examine it separately because obfuscation—the use of obscure, confusing language that muddies rather than clarifies meaning—is the downfall of many speakers. Former Secretary of State Alexander Haig was a master of filling his speeches with unintelligible phrases. The *Wall Street Journal* once referred to his diction as "the strange tongue of Alexander Haig." Haig, a former general, combined the language of the military with the language of diplomacy to create phrases like these:

⌘ saddle myself with a statistical fence

⌘ caveat my response

⌘ epistemologicallywise

⌘ careful caution

⌘ definitizing an answer[14]

Here is one of his sentences: "At the moment we are subsumed in the vortex of criticality."[15] We are picking on Alexander Haig to make a point. Audiences listening to Haig often have no idea what he is saying, for his language obstructs, rather than facilitates, communication.

Although few speakers go as far as Haig in using incomprehensible language, obfuscation is more common than it should be. Euphemisms—inoffensive words or phrases substituted for more direct language—are particularly common. Consider, for instance, the number of ways corporate spokespersons refer to firing employees:

⌘ *Euphemism:* We are engaged in downsizing our operation.

⌘ *Meaning:* We are firing 5,000 employees.

⌘ *Euphemism:* We are offering employees over the age of fifty-five early retirement.

⌘ *Meaning:* If these older employees don't accept the deal, we'll fire them.

⌘ *Euphemism:* We are suggesting a career redirection.

⌘ *Meaning:* You no longer have a job here, so we suggest you find another type of work.

⌘ *Euphemism:* As of January 1, you will be separated from the company.

⌘ *Meaning:* You're fired on the first of the year.

Although euphemisms like these serve a purpose (they make it easier for speakers to deal with unpleasant topics), they can make it difficult, and sometimes impossible, for listeners to understand what is being said.

---

14.   Robert B. Rackleff, "The Art of Speech Writing: A Dramatic Event," speech delivered to the National Association of Bar Executives Section on Communications and Public Relations, September 26, 1987. Reprinted in *Vital Speeches of the Day,* March 1, 1988, p. 312.

15.   Morris K. Udall, "Stalking the Elusive Malaprop," *Saturday Evening Post,* October 1988, p. 40.

Use Jargon Only if You Are Sure
Your Audience Understands Your Meaning

Jargon is the technical terminology unique to a special activity or group. For example, the jargon of the publishing business includes such terms as "specs," "page proofs," "dummy stage," and "halftones." Although these terms are not five syllables long, they are difficult to understand if you are unfamiliar with publishing.

A special kind of jargon involves the use of abbreviations—the alphabet soup of an organization or profession. Instead of loading your speech with references to the FDA, PACs, the ACLI, or the AMA on the assumption that everyone knows what they mean, define these abbreviations the first time they are used. Tell your listeners that the FDA refers to the Food and Drug Administration; PACs, political action committees; the ACLI, the American Council of Life Insurance; and the AMA, the American Management Association.

Jargon can be used effectively when you are *sure* that everyone in your audience understands the reference. Therefore, if you are the editor-in-chief of a publishing company addressing your editorial and production staffs, publishing jargon requires no definition. However, if you are delivering a speech about the publishing business to a group of college seniors, definitions are needed.

Eliminate Unnecessary Words

Although, as we mentioned earlier, spoken language requires some redundancy, unnecessary repetition or directionless language is sloppy: its effect on listeners can be numbing. When people are forced to listen to a barrage of unnecessary words, they find it difficult to tell the difference between the important and the trivial. When the listening process becomes too difficult, they stop paying attention. Here is an example of unfocused rambling:

> Let me tell you what I did on my summer vacation. I drove down to Memphis in my car to take part in the dozens of memorial ceremonies marking the anniversary of the death of Elvis Presley. There were about 40,000 or 50,000 other people at the ceremony along with me.
>
> I took a tour of the mansion Elvis lived in before his death, known as Graceland, and I visited the new museum dedicated solely to his cars. The museum holds twenty different vehicles including the favorite of Elvis' mother: a pink 1955 Cadillac Fleetwood.

Here is the same thing, minus the verbiage:

> During summer vacation, I drove to Memphis to celebrate the anniversary of Elvis Presley's death. With about 40,000 or 50,000 other people I toured Graceland, Elvis' home, and visited the museum dedicated to his twenty vehicles, including his mother's favorite, a pink 1955 Cadillac Fleetwood.

Not only does the second version eliminate fifty of the original ninety-five words, it also sharpens the message and helps listeners focus on the important points.

Be Direct

Be Concrete.   Consider the differences between these two paragraphs:

Version 1:

On-the-job accidents take thousands of lives a year. Particularly hard hit are agricultural workers who suffer approximately 1,500 deaths and 140,000 disabling injuries a year. One fifth of all agricultural fatalities are children. These statistics make us wonder how safe farms are.

Version 2:

Farmers who want to get their children interested in agriculture often take them on tractors for a ride. About 150 children are killed each year when they fall off tractors and are crushed underneath. These children represent about half the children killed in farm accidents each year—a statistic that tells us that farms can be deadly. About 1,500 people die each year on farms and an additional 140,000 are injured seriously enough so they can no longer work.[16]

In version 2 the images and language are more concrete. Instead of wondering "how safe farms are," version 2 declares that "farms can be deadly." Instead of talking about "disabling injuries," it tells us that workers "are injured seriously enough so they can no longer work." More concrete language produces an emotional response in listeners that is likely to stay with them long after a speech is over.

Presidential speechwriter Peggy Noonan explains why she chose concrete language when she wrote for President Reagan:

It's not interesting to say, "America loves freedom," it's interesting to say, "Freedom to us is newspapers that everyone can buy on the street corner, newspapers that get to say just about anything about anybody—including me, and I'm supposedly the top man, and sometimes I don't like it a lot but I always know, all of us know, that bruised feelings and some anger are an inevitable part of the process as we look for, find, and publish the truth. . . ." Be specific, personalize. Make it real.[17]

On a continuum, words range from the most concrete to the most abstract. Concrete language is rooted in real-life experience—things we see, hear, taste, touch, and feel—while abstract language tells us little about what we experience, relying instead on more symbolic references. Compare the following:

Abstract	**Concrete**
Bad weather	Hail the size of golf balls
Capitalism	The New York Stock Exchange
Nervousnesss	Trembling hands; knocking knees
Ethics	A commitment to the truth; a refusal to lie
An interesting professor	When she started throwing paper airplanes around the room to teach us how air currents affect lift, I knew she was a winner.

---

16.   "Danger on the job," *Newsweek,* December 11, 1989, pp. 42–46.
17.   Noonan, *What I Saw at the Revolution,* p. 79.

Concrete words and phrases create pictures in listeners' minds and can turn a "ho-hum" speech into one that captures listener attention. Winston Churchill understood this premise when he said, during World War II, "We shall fight them on the beaches," instead of "Hostilities will be engaged on the coastal perimeter."[18]

Say Exactly What You Mean.   One of the chief causes of miscommunication is speakers' inability to say exactly what they mean and to say it in a direct way. Compare these two versions of the same idea:

Version 1:
I'm still thinking about the direction I want to take after college. A decision should be made in the next few months.

Version 2:
It is now December of my senior year and I still don't know what I'm going to do when I graduate in May. My parents are pressuring me either to work in the family jewelry business or to get my applications in for business school. (I'm late already.) If I don't decide soon, I'll be out of school, out of work, and, worse yet, out of money.

After reading version 1, listeners may wonder what the speaker is thinking of doing and why the speaker feels the urgency to decide. Version 2 answers these questions. In addition, because it is vivid and direct, version 2 encourages the listener to become involved with the speaker's plight.

Use the Active Voice.   A direct speaking style involves the use of the active rather than the passive voice as often as possible. The following examples demonstrate the use of the passive voice showing the subject of the sentence being acted upon:

- ✂ Students in an English class at Long Beach Community College were asked by their teacher to stand in line.

- ✂ After a few minutes, the line was broken by a student from Japan who walked a few yards away.

- ✂ The behavior demonstrated by the student shows how cultural differences can affect even the simple act of waiting on line.

- ✂ In this case, the need for greater personal space was felt by the student who considered it impolite to stand so close.

Here are the same sentences rephrased in the active voice, showing the subject of the sentence in action.

- ✂ An English teacher at Long Beach Community College asked the class to stand in line.

- ✂ After a few minutes, a Japanese student broke the line and walked a few yards away.

---

18.   N. R. Kleinfield, "Teaching the 'Sir Winston,' Method," *The New York Times,* March 11, 1990, p. 7.

⌘ The student's behavior demonstrated how cultural differences can affect even the simple act of waiting on line.

⌘ In this case, the student felt the need for more personal space because the Japanese culture considers it impolite to stand so close.

In addition to using fewer words, the active voice is more direct, easier to follow, and more vigorous.

Don't Exaggerate

Exaggerations are statements made to impress, not to report the facts accurately. Instead of telling your classmates that you "always" exercise an hour a day, tell them that you exercise an hour a day "as often" as you can. (Some of your classmates may know you well enough to realize that "always" is a lie.) Instead of saying that you would "never" consider double parking, tell your listeners that you would consider it "only as a last resort in an emergency." Obvious exaggerations diminish your credibility as a speaker.

SPEAK WITH STYLE AND SELF-ASSURANCE

Although your speaking style—the distinctive manner in which you speak to produce the effect you desire—like your style of dress, is personal, it is important to realize that some styles enhance communication while others act against you.

Don't Use Clichés

To speech communication professors Eugene Ehrlich and Gene R. Hawes, clichés are the "enemies of lively speech." They explain:

> They are deadwood: the shiny suits of your word wardrobe, the torn sandals, the frayed collars, the scuffed shoes, the bobby socks, the fur pieces, the Nehru jackets, the miniskirts—yesterday's chewing gum.[19]

Clichés can lull your listeners into a state of boredom as they suggest that both your vocabulary and imagination are limited. Here is a section of a slang and cliché-filled speech:

> *At this point in time,* the real estate market seems to be stronger than it was two years ago. In fact, you can say that now it's *super. At that point in time* I would *guesstimate* that there were 400 more houses on the market than there are today. For us, it was time to *hustle.* We *toughed it out* and *held onto the ball.*
>
> The *game plan* we should follow from now on is to convince potential buyers that we *have a good thing going* in this community—good schools, good libraries, a good transportation system. *By the same token,* we should also convince them that we're a *community with a heart.* We're here to help each other when we're *down and out.*

---

19. Eugene Ehrlich and Gene R. Hawes, *Speak for Success* (New York: Bantam Books, 1984), p. 48.

F O C U S   O N   R E S E A R C H

POWERLESS TALK

What makes some people powerful and dynamic while they speak and others seem less effective, even when the content of the message is similar? The answer to this question is important to anyone who wants to convince others, but is crucial to others who work in the legal setting. Studies have shown that speaking style of witnesses who testify in court can affect jurors' decisions. Often these jurors must decide the guilt or innocence of defendants in court.

Legal experts and communication researchers have studied speaking style. In 1974, William O'Barr studied factors affecting juror's perceptions through a grant for the Law and Language Project at Duke University.[20] He and his colleagues observed ten weeks of courtroom activity in Durham, North Carolina. They audiotaped 150 hours of testimony and took notes on nonverbal displays and other data that could not be audiotaped. After listening to the tapes they found a correlation between language use and the perceived credibility, competence, and intelligence of witnesses.

Powerful speech affected jurors' decisions positively, while powerless speech had a negative effect. Powerless speech includes some or all of the following elements. (generally, the more often these factors were included in speech, the less effective the speakers were perceived by jurors):

Intensifiers

To emphasize the impact of what they said, speakers interspersed words like "very," "quite," "so," and "really" in their speech. Instead of stating, "That movie is scary. You should go," powerless speakers said, "That movie was *so* scary. You *really* should go."

Hedges

These phrases communicated uncertainty, for example: "Well, I *sort of* thought you *might* like to go out tonight."

Hesitation Forms

Speakers sometimes used phrases and meaningless particles of speech to fill periods of silence while collecting their thoughts: "The . . . *uh* . . . best courses *you know* are offered by . . . *uh* . . . the speech department." False starts and disfluencies fall into this category: "I *thought we should, I mean* let's work together on this plan." Along with hedges, these phrases create the impression of indecisiveness.

Rising Intonation in Declarative Context

In the English language, when you ask a question, the pitch rises at the end of the sentence. If you read aloud the question, "Would you like to go out tonight?" you will notice that the word "tonight" is higher in pitch than the word "would." A powerless language style uses the same rising pitch pattern for some statements, making the speaker seem less self-assured.

Gestures

O'Barr used this term to indicate spoken indications of direction. Speakers who assume that their listeners can visualize an account of an event will not be as

---

20.   William O'Barr. *Linguistic Evidence: Language, Power, and Strategy in the Courtroom* (New York: Academic Press, 1982); See also Leigh Makay. "The Impact of Psychological Gender and Sex: Powerful/Powerless Language in the Face-to-Face Setting." Unpublished dissertation, The Ohio State University, 1992.

specific in their description of the event. When describing an accident, the powerful speaker will say, "The car turned west toward the cemetery and then the driver appeared to lose control, swerving first to his left, and then to his right." The powerless speaker is less specific, saying, "The car turned that way and then was all over the place."

Polite Forms

Excessive use of "please" and "thank you" reduces the force of a statement.

Use of "Sir"

Although this form of address is often used to show respect, it can also communicate unequal status. O'Barr found that a doctor or other person who held a professional position would be less likely to use "sir" when responding to the lawyer in court than a nonprofessional, such as a waitress or a truck driver. The statement, "Sir, I will try to be as accurate as possible," conveys less power than, "I will try to be as accurate as possible."

Direct Quotations

In a speech, one way to increase your credibility is to borrow it from an authority. However, when you report an event by repeatedly quoting the participants instead of paraphrasing them, your statements lose force. In reporting a fight, statements such as, "He said he would kill her. Then she said go ahead and try," convey less power than, "There was a fight in which he threatened to kill her."

To test the effect of powerful versus powerless speech, O'Barr constructed an experiment using edited versions of original testimony in which actors played the roles of witnesses and lawyers.[21] Four videotapes were constructed for each testimony: two powerful versions and two powerless versions. In the powerful versions, powerless speech patterns were absent while powerless versions were similar to actual court testimony.

Mock jurors were asked to listen to these testimonies and answer a questionnaire to assess their reactions. Powerful witnesses were believed more and seen as more competent and intelligent. O'Barr concluded that powerless speech variables are associated with social power including social class, educational background, and perhaps even courtroom experience. Those with lower social power tended to use powerless language.

Several other studies have used the courtroom setting to assess the impact of language. Researchers found that prosecutors who win cases use more powerful language than prosecutors who lose cases and that witnesses who use powerless speech are perceived as less competent, attractive, trustworthy, and dynamic than those who use a powerful style.

21. See J. J. Bradec, M. R. Hamphill, and C. H. Tardy, "Language Style on Trial: Effects of 'Powerful' and 'Powerless' Speech upon Judgements of Victims and Villains," *Western Journal of Speech* 45 (1981): 327–41; B. Danet, "Language in the Legal Process," *Law and Society Review* 14 (1980): 445–564; B. Erickson, E. A. Lind, B. C. Johnson, and W. M. O'Barr, "Speech Style and Impression Formation in a Court Setting: The Effects of "Powerful' and 'Powerless" Speech," *Journal of Experimental Social Psychology* 14 (1978): 266–79; W. O'Barr and B. Atkins, " 'Women's Language' or 'Powerless Language?'" in S. McConnell-Ginet, R. Borker, and N. Furman eds., *Women and Language in Literature and Society* (New York: Praeger, 1980): 93–110; K. Warfel, "Gender Schemas and Perceptions of Speech Style," *Communication Monographs* 51 (1984): 253–67; J. W. Wright and L. Hosman, "Language Style and Sex Bias in the Courtroom: The Effects of Male and Female Use of Hedges and Intensifiers on Impression Formation," *The Southern Speech Communication Journal* 48 (Winter 1983): 137–52.

Imagine listening to this for an entire speech. Even if the speaker has something valuable to say, it is virtually impossible to hear it through the clichés.

Clichés add unnecessary words to your speech. "By the same token" can be replaced by "also"; "at this point in time" by "now"; "game plan" by "plan," and so on.

Complete Your Thoughts and Your Sentences

Focus on completing every sentence you start. Although this may seem like common sense, many people don't follow this advice when speaking before groups. Although we accept the fact that many sentences trail off in conversational speech, we lose confidence in a speaker who has this habit. From the mouth of a public speaker, this language is disconcerting:

> In many states, your signature on your driver's license makes you a potential organ donor. If you are killed. . . . According to the laws in these states, if you are killed in an auto accident, the state has the right. . . . Your organs can be used to help people in need of organ transplants. There are sick people out there who need the kidneys, corneas, and even the hearts of people killed.
>
> Think about it. When you are dead, you can still give the gift of life.

Follow the Rules of Written English—Most of the Time

Most of us don't write sentence fragments, but most of us speak them. As you plan the language of your speech, keep in mind that carefully chosen sentence fragments can contribute to clear communication. Here is an example:

> Is Christmas too commercial? Well, maybe. It wasn't that long ago when the holiday season began after Thanksgiving. Now the first Christmas catalogs reach shoppers in September. Before summer is over. Before the temperature has dropped below 90 degrees. Even before Labor Day.

Don't confuse sentence fragments with the incomplete sentences we discussed earlier. In this case, the fragments are intentional and are used effectively to enhance meaning.

President George Bush often abbreviated sentences by dropping pronouns and eliminating verbs. In his 1990 State of the Union message he asked, "Ambitious aims? Of course. Easy to do? Far from it." In an address to the Academy of Television Arts and Sciences, to persuade his audience that Saturday cartoons were the right spot for antidrug messages, Bush said, "Twenty million kids. Impressionable. Just asking to be entertained." Before the Malta summit with the Russians, he was asked what the summit would mean for the world: "Grandkids. All of that. Very important." According to Kathleen Hall Jamieson, dean of the Annenberg School of Communication at the University of Pennsylvania, "George Bush is speaking a language that we do in fact recognize because it's a language we speak."

Avoid Sentences That Say Nothing

When asked at a news conference to comment on United States policy in the Middle East, President Bush made the following nonstatement:

> No we want to see that there's some follow on there. So the policy is set, I campaigned on what the policy is. . . . So the principles are there and I think we're you know, we've got to, now, flesh that out and figure out what we do specifically.[22]

Sentences that say nothing or, worse yet, communicate double or confusing messages damage a speaker's credibility. Listeners ask themselves what they're supposed to believe and whether the nonsense they are hearing is an indication of the speaker's competence. By the time listeners start asking these questions, the speech has almost certainly failed.

Speech tension can cause or contribute to these types of language pitfalls. Lack of preparation can also contribute. If you don't know as much as you should about your topic or if you are trying not to reveal your intentions, you may fall into the gobbledygook trap.

Avoid Using Profanity or Slang

Your goal is to convince your clients to adopt the advertising strategy you've devised to market their new shampoo-conditioner combination. The stakes are high—a $4 million advertising budget, the decision to be based on your formal presentation.

To prepare, you hold several information-gathering meetings with the clients. As in many informal settings, the language is casual and swearwords are common. Everyone seems confortable with this language, so you decide to pepper your presentation with it as well. What you do not realize—until it is too late—is that when used in a formal speech, these words seemed crude, ugly, and out of place. The same people who laughed along with you in your informal meetings look uncomfortable. Not surprisingly, the clients decide to give their business to another agency.

Listeners expect a degree of decorum in a formal speech, requiring that certain language be avoided. Profanity, of course, is the most obvious offender, but using the vernacular or slang can also be inappropriate. Terms like "ain't," and "you guys" should be used *only* for specific effect. In public discourse, they can violate an audience's sense of appropriateness—or propriety.

Avoid Phrases That Communicate Uncertainty

Language can communicate a sense of mastery of your subject, or it can communicate uncertainty. Compare the following paragraphs:

Version 1:
It seems to me that too many students choose a career solely on the basis of how much they are likely to earn. In my estimation, they forget that they also have to enjoy what they are going to spend the rest of their work lives doing.

---

22.   Tom Wicker, "Like Too Bad, Yeah," *The New York Times,* February 24, 1989, p. A33.

Version 2:
Too many students choose a career solely on the basis of how much they are likely to earn. They forget that they also have to enjoy what they are going to spend the rest of their work lives doing.

Version 1 contains weakening phrases: "it seems to me," and "in my estimation," add nothing but uncertainty to the speaker's message. If you have a position, state it directly without crutch words that signal your timidity to the audience.

USE LANGUAGE TO ENGAGE THE IMAGINATIONS OF YOUR LISTENERS

A carpenter uses a saw, hammer, and nails to construct a building. A speaker uses language to construct a speech. Words are literally the tools of a speaker's trade. When used effectively they can move an audience to action or tears; they can change minds or cement opinions; they can create a bond between you and your listeners or destroy a relationship. We examine next the ways language can be used to engage your listeners in your speech. Keep in mind that when your listeners are able to visualize what you are saying, they become active listeners.

Metaphors, Imagery, and Similes

Use metaphors and similes to create vivid images.

Metaphors.   The essence of a metaphor is understanding and experiencing one kind of thing in terms of another. Here are two examples from well known speeches:

⌘ "An iron curtain has descended across the continent." (Winston Churchill)

⌘ "Our democracy must not only be the envy of the world but also the engine of renewal." (Bill Clinton)

Imagery.   Imagery is the strength of the metaphor, as New York Governor Mario Cuomo demonstrated in his 1984 keynote address to the Democratic National Convention. In this address, Cuomo attacked a metaphor used by President Reagan that described America as a "shining city on a hill":

> President Reagan admitted that although some people in this country seemed to be doing well nowadays, others were unhappy, even worried, about themselves, their families and their futures.
>
> The president said he didn't understand that fear. He said. "Why, this country is a shining city on a hill."
>
> The president is right. In many ways we are "a shining city on a hill."
>
> But the hard truth is that not everyone is sharing in this city's splendor and glory.
>
> A shining city is perhaps all the president sees from the portico of the White House and the veranda of his ranch, where everyone seems to be doing well.
>
> But there's another part of the city, the part where some people can't pay their mortgages and most young people can't afford one, where students can't afford the education they need and middle-class parents watch the dreams they hold for their children evaporate.

This is despair, Mr. President, in faces you never see in the places you never visit in your shining city.

In fact, Mr. President, this nation is more a "Tale of Two Cities" than it is a "Shining City on a Hill"[23]

Similes.   Similes also create images as they compare the characteristics of two unlike things. (The comparison is made with the help of the words "like" or "as.") Here are two examples Ann Beattie uses in her novel *Picturing Will:* "Falling snow looked as solid as pearls. Tar could look like satin"; and "Wayne reacted like someone whose cat has proudly brought home a dead mouse."[24] Both metaphors and similes rely on concrete images as discussed early in the chapter. Although these can enliven your speech, guard against using images that are trite or too familiar.

Use Language To Create a Theme

A key word or phrase can reappear throughout your speech and carry your theme. Each time the image is repeated, it becomes more powerful and is likely to stay with your listeners after your speech is over. The chairman of a real estate investment company developed the "Amber Light Theory of Real Estate Investment" and used this metaphor as the theme of his speeches. His point was that the real estate market rarely gives investors strong signals to proceed or stop. Instead, its signal is always one of caution. By repeating the amber light image several times in his speech, the speaker delivered a message that was effective and memorable.[25]

HOW RONALD REAGAN IMPROVED THE LANGUAGE OF A PRESIDENTIAL SPEECH

All modern-day presidents rely on speechwriters to compose drafts of their speeches. But the most effective communicators among the presidents take the time to hone the language of these drafts. Here, for example, are some of the revisions former President Ronald Reagan made to a draft of a speech he gave to the U.S. Chamber of Commerce in 1982. In editing the draft, the president grafted his unique voice to the speech's language and rhythm.[26]

Speechwriter's draft:

The Chamber is celebrating an important milestone this week. You've almost caught up to me—almost, but not quite. From one who has been there already, may I just say: you're not getting older, but you sure are getting better. I never thought I'd be able to

---

23.   For an analysis of the use of metaphor in Mario Cuomo's address, see David Henry, "The Rhetorical Dynamics of Mario Cuomo's 1984 Keynote Address: Situation, Speaker, Metaphor," *The Southern Speech Communication Journal* 53 (Winter 1988): 105–20. For Cuomo's address, see Richard L. Johannesen, R. R. Allen, and Will A. Linkugel *Contemporary American Speeches,* 6th ed. (Dubuque, IA: Kendall/Hunt, 1988), pp. 307–15.

24.   Ann Beattie, *Picturing Will* (New York: Random House, 1989).

25.   Karen Berg and Andrew Gilman, *Get to the Point: How to Say What You Mean and Get What You Want* (New York: Bantam Books, 1989), p. 40.

26.   The following material is from James W. Robinson, *Better Speeches in Ten Simple Steps* (Rocklin, CA: Prima Publishing and Communications: 1989), pp. 58–61.

say this, but I've found something that can grow faster than the Federal Government—the membership of the Chamber of Commerce of the United States—and that makes me feel mighty good about our future.

Reagan draft:

The Chamber is celebrating an important milestone this week. Your 70th anniversary. I remember the day you started. Like good wine, you've grown better, not older. The membership of the Chamber of Commerce of the United States is the only thing that's grown faster than the Federal Government. Thank heaven!

Reagan's revisions tightened the language and made the age reference less personal.

Speechwriter's draft:

Well, if I could make a suggestion, our Administration still has a small problem on Capitol Hill we would love to have your help on.

Reagan draft:

Well, if I could make a suggestion, our Administration has a few small unfinished problems—about $400 billion worth—on Capitol Hill we would love to have your help on.

The concrete reference to the budget deficit had greater impact.

Speechwriter's draft:

We will never abandon our commitment to the needy.

Reagan draft:

We are meeting our commitment to the needy, even if that hasn't been the subject of a network documentary.

President Reagan rephrased the reference to the commitment to make it positive rather than negative and added a touch of humor.

Speechwriter's draft:

Yes, we have compassion for the needy. But how about a little compassion left over for the group Washington so often forgets—the wage earners and taxpayers of America? They are the heart and soul of the free enterprise system: They pay America's bills, they have been burned by higher inflation and taxes year after year, and they need help.

Reagan draft:

We are the most generous people on earth. I don't think any of us lack compassion for the needy. But isn't it time we had some compassion for those unsung heroes who work and pay their taxes and their bills while they struggle to make ends meet? They are the heart and soul of the free enterprise system. They need help too.

Reagan changed the language of the opening sentence to avoid a misunderstanding. In its original form, the sentence minimized the problems of the needy. His changes in the later sentences improved the rhythm of the speech and made the images more concrete.

"Of Poets and Word Processors"

In 1988, before the Democrats had chosen their nominee for president, Hugh Sidey, columnist for *Time,* described the language of three of the nation's best known political speakers. According to Sidey, while Jesse Jackson and Mario Cuomo take the language of public speaking to a higher plane, Michael Dukakis reduces it to mechanics. Sidey explains:

> Jesse is a poet. He looks and listens to America, to his aides and even to reporters. Their feelings, their moods, their words flow through his system. His lines come from his soul, and they have swirled around deep down in there, marinated in his special anger and ambition, sometimes for weeks. Then he speaks them into a tape recorder and hears them come back at him. And he tunes them and times them then lofts them to the misty-eyed worshippers who are swept with him into the clouds.
>
> Mario is a poet too. A man of immigrant parents, soaked in the American dream since birth. Man of the melting pot with big hands and arms and mind, who crouches and sweeps and roars in political iambic pentameter and some free verse. A man still surprised that he is Governor of New York and talked about for President of the U.S. It is the stuff of song.
>
> Mike is a word processor. Hmmmmmm. Click, click, click. Paragraphs from that fellow over there, thought from that woman opposite. Phrases from pleasant platitudes past and present. Committee review. Clip and paste. Put this up there, that down here. Reassemble it all in a white plastic machine and then read it.
>
> It took the practiced ear of Richard Nixon to tell us that. Give him his due. He's got a feel for the pols, and he can sum them up with a brutal line or two. [Asked if then presidential candidate Michael Dukakis was] "just too dull to be an effective nominee," Nixon was ready, dark flash from the eyes. "Let me answer that question this way. I've often said that the best politics is poetry rather than prose. Jesse Jackson is a poet. Cuomo is a poet. And Dukakis is a word processor." [27]

BE SURE YOUR LANGUAGE FITS YOUR PERSONALITY AND POSITION   As a classroom speaker, your choice of language should be tempered by the knowledge that you are a spokesperson for your cause. If you are delivering a speech on advances in microsurgery, a casual, flippant tone is inappropriate, though it might work for a speech on naming the family dog.

Audiences are perceptive. They know very quickly whether your are comfortable with your speaking style or whether you are trying to be something you are not. It is hard to fake an emotional presentation if you are a cool, nonemotional person. It you are naturally restrained, it is difficult to appear daring and impulsive. The language you choose mirrors who you are, so choose it carefully to reflect what you want others to know about you.

---

27.   Hugh Sidey, "The Presidency: Of Poets and Word Processors," *Time,* May 2, 1988, p. 32.

I N T E R V I E W

Curt Smith
Author, Journalist,
Political Speech Writer

We spoke with Curt Smith, a writer whose most recent book is *Voices of the Game: The First Full-Scale Overview of Baseball Broadcasting, 1921 to the Present.* Curt is also a political speechwriter who served President Bush as well as other public figures. The focus of our conversation was language. We also took the opportunity to ask Mr. Smith about working with a president on speeches and about his approach to preparing a speech for himself.

Question: When preparing a speech, what importance do you put on language in relation to the other factors of concern in speech preparation?

Answer: I believe language is extraordinarily important. Historically, language has been able to move, and public speakers that I admire value language as a way to inspire and move their audiences. I use language, whether as metaphor, anecdote, or punch line to evaluate and enrich a speech.

Question: When you wrote for the president or the other political figures you served, how did you adjust to particular audiences? In a previous conversation, for instance, you indicated to me that you particularly enjoyed preparing speeches for special occasions because of the opportunity you had to make words and ideas memorable.

Answer: What I enjoy especially are speeches of the emotions and principles by which we guide our lives. Often people in audiences are less intrigued by detailed matters of policy and programs than by basic ideals they like to see in a president. The speeches that I preferred tried to link that persona to the essence of the United States.

Question: When you were working with the president as member of a team of speechwriters, did the group circulate drafts to others in the White House before they arrived on the president's desk or were discussed with the president? Did the writers comment on the language of the presidential message?

Answer: At times. All speeches go through the process of being viewed by members of the administration's staff. Sadly, however, what I found in the Bush Administration is true of all politics generally: Very few people understand poetry, which is the essence of good writing. What I would do in writing speeches is make my first draft as emotional, instinctual, and as visceral as possible. I knew that at every stage between the time I wrote a speech and the time that it was delivered the staffing process would subdue, lessen, or downplay the fire and emotion of the first draft.

Question: Who among the staff would be most likely to bleach your message?

Answer: People with the souls of accountants and bookkeepers.

Question: I know of instances where President Reagan would really work over the language drafted by speechwriters, which indicates to me that he had a keen sense of the power of imagery in language. What is your view?

Answer: Ronald Reagan grasped the primacy of poetry. George Bush, on the other hand, is an honest, decent, thoughtful, and inspiring human being but with little appreciation for language in terms of rhetorical power. Politics is rhetoric conveyed to the American people that explains what you believe and plan to do. Language of political rhetoric is enormously important to a campaign. I wish the Bush Administration had grasped how politics and poetry cannot be divorced.

Question: I remember reading an article in a New York newspaper about a commencement speech you delivered to graduates of the high school you attended in Caledonia. How is preparing a speech for yourself different than for a public figure?

Answer: I show much less caution because I do not attempt to protect myself. I will take more chances when I deliver a speech because I am not concerned with whether people agree with me or not. I owe my audience what I feel and what I believe. I strongly believe in fidelity of the self and fidelity of principle and I owe it to the listeners to express that.

When you write for the president or other political figures, you have to think of the consequences of the words and ideas that will be shaped and delivered by that principal. When I prepare a speech for myself those consequences don't concern me.

Question: Can you summarize the steps you go through in preparing a speech?

Answer: I consider first the forum and the audience because they will guide what I talk about. For example, in the commencement speech at my high school I wanted to speak about what my hometown had meant to me and the lessons that I had learned. I usually sit down with a yellow legal pad to begin outlining the points I want to emphasize. I will look for research, anecdotes, one-liners, and applause lines that reinforce the issues I want to emphasize. The next step is to structure these parts into a mosaic that will make sense to my audience. After completing a first draft I think ahead to the next draft. I am different from most writers because I write every draft in longhand, which means I tend to write long. This means the stage after the first draft is especially important because only then does the real writing begin. I am my own best and toughest editor and I often ruthlessly edit my own copy. The better you become at editing your material, the more this process becomes fulfilling. This is the art form of writing a speech. Moving sentences, inverting words or paragraphs, and molding ideas as if you are using clay—shaping rhetoric to me is the craft of speech preparation.

Interview with Curt Smith, April 12, 1993.

HUMOR: HOW TO MAKE IT PART OF YOUR SPOKEN STYLE

Nothing brings you closer to your audience than humor. Language couched in humor relaxes listeners and makes them like you. Humor reveals your human side. Through a properly placed anecdote, you let your audience know that you are not taking yourself—or your subject—too seriously. Even in a serious speech, humor can be an effective tool to emphasize an important point.

Research has shown the favorable impact humor can have on an audience. According to Charles R. Gruner, a communication professor and recognized expert on the use of humor in public speaking, when appropriate humor is used in

Even in a serious speech, humor can be an effective tool for emphasizing an important point.

informative speaking, the humor enhances the speaker's image by improving the audience's perception of the speaker's character.[28] Research has also shown that humor can make a speech more memorable over a longer period of time. In one study, two groups of subjects were asked to recall lectures they heard six weeks earlier. The group who heard the lecture presented humorously had higher recall than the group who heard the same lecture delivered without humor.[29] In another experiment, students who took a statistics course given by an instructor who used humor in class lectures scored 15 percent higher on objective exams than did students who were taught the same material by an instructor who didn't.[30]

Humor works only if it is carefully used and only if it is connected to the theme of your speech.[31] Here are several guidelines for the effective use of humor in a speech.

---

28.   Charles R. Gruner, "Effect of Humor on Speaker Ethos and Audience Information Gain," *Journal of Communication* 17 (1967): 228–33: Charles R. Gruner, "The Effect of Humor in Dull and Interesting Informative Speeches," *Central States Speech Journal* 21 (1970): 160–66. Reported in Charles R. Gruner, "Advice to the Beginning Speaker on Using Humor—What the Research Tells Us," *Communication Education* 34 (April 1985): 142.
29.   R. M. Kaplan and G. C. Pascoe, "Humorous Lectures and Humorous Examples: Some Effects upon Comprehension and Retention," *Journal of Educational Psychology* 69 (1977): 61–65. Cited in Gruner, "Advice to the Beginning Speaker," p. 144.
30.   A. Ziv, "Cognitive Results of Using Humor in Teaching," paper presented at the Third International Conference on Humor, 1982 Washington, DC. Cited in Gruner, "Advice to the Beginning Speaker," p. 144.
31.   For a study showing the negative effects of irrelevant humor, see R. C. Youngman, "An Experimental Investigation of the Effect of Germane Humor vs. Non-germane Humor in an Informative Communication," unpublished Master's thesis, Ohio University, Athens, OH. Cited in Gruner, "Advice to the Beginning Speaker," p. 144.

Use Humor Only if You Can Be Funny

Some speakers don't know how to be funny in front of an audience. On a one-to-one basis they may be funny, but in front of a group, their humor leaves them. They stumble over punch lines, have no sense of timing, and look as if the humor is causing them pain. These people should limit themselves to serious speeches or "safe" humor. For example, former Maine Senator Ed Muskie made his audience laugh by describing the shortest will in Maine legal history—a will that was only ten words long: "Being of sound mind and memory, I spent it all."[32]

Laugh at Yourself, Not Others

Former California Governor George Deukmajian sometimes uses the following line to break the ice with his audience:

> I understand that you have been searching for a speaker who can dazzle you with his charm, wit, and personality. I'm pleased to be filling in while the search continues.[33]

Research has shown that speakers who make themselves the butt of their own humor often endear themselves to their listeners. In one study, students heard brief speeches from a "psychologist" and an "economist," both of whom explained the benefits of their professions. While half the speeches were read with mildly self-deprecating humor directed at the profession being discussed, the other half were read without humor. (Included among the humorous psychologist's lines was: "You know what a psychologist is. That's a guy who would father a set of twins, have one baptized, and keep the other for a control." Using a similar strategy, the economist told the audience: "You have probably heard that if all the economists in the world were laid end to end, they would still each point in a different direction.") Students rated the speakers with the self-deprecating humor higher on a scale of "wittiness" and "sense of humor," and no damage was done to the perceived character or authoritativeness of the speaker.[34]

It can be effective to tell a joke at your own expense, but it's in poor taste to tell a joke at the expense of others. Racial, ethnic, or sexist jokes are rarely acceptable, nor are jokes that poke fun at the personal characteristics of others. Although stand-up comics like Don Rickles, Joan Rivers, and Eddie Murphy may get away with such humor, public speakers cannot.[35]

---

32. Robert B. Rackleff, "The Art of Speech Writing: A Dramatic Event," delivered to the National Association of Bar Executives Section on Communications and Public Relations, September 26, 1987. Reprinted in *Vital Speeches of the Day,* March 1, 1988, p. 313.
33. James W. Robinson, *Better Speeches in Ten Simple Steps* (Rocklin, CA: Prima Publishing and Communications, 1989), p. 68.
34. M. Chang and C. R. Gruner, "Audience Reaction to Self-disparaging Humor," *Southern Speech Communication Journal* 46 (1981): 419–26. Reported in Gruner, "Advice to the Beginning Speaker," pp. 142–47.
35. For a study on the effects of "sick" jokes on both speech and speaker, see, William C. Munn and Charles R. Gruner, 'Sick' Jokes, Speaker Sex, and Informative Speech," *Southern Speech Communication Journal* 46 (Summer 1981): 411–18. The researchers found that the inclusion of these jokes generally caused negative evaluations of both the speech and the speaker.

Understated Anecdotes Can Be as Effective as Side-Splitting One-Liners

As an economist, you've been asked to give a speech to a group of your peers. You start with the following anecdote:

> I am constantly reminded by those who use our services that we often turn out a ton of material on the subject but we do not always give our clients something of value.
>
> A balloonist high above the earth found his balloon leaking and managed to land on the edge of a green pasture. He saw a man in a business suit approaching, and very happily said: "How good it is to see you. Could you tell me where I am?"
>
> The well-dressed man replied: "You are standing in a wicker basket in the middle of a pasture."
>
> "Well," said the balloonist, "You must be an economist." The man was startled. "Yes, I am, but how did you know that?"
>
> "That's easy," said the balloonist, "because the information you gave me was very accurate—and absolutely useless."[36]

This anecdote is funny—in an understated way. It works because it is relevant to the audience. Its humor comes from the recognition that the speaker knows—and shares—the foibles of the audience.

How to Find Appropriate Humor

The best humor comes from your own experiences. Although many books of jokes and stories for speakers are readily available, these are artificial compared to the humor you find all around you. You might want to start now to record humorous stories for your speeches so that you will have material when the need arises.

If you decide to use someone else's material, be sure to give the source credit. By telling your listeners that Woody Allen or Bob Newhart said it first, you make it clear that the line or story is meant as a joke. According to comedy expert, Professor Melvin Helitzer, "You'll get bigger laughs by using their names than if you tried to convince your audience that the humor was original."[37]

But No One Is Laughing

Although it is easy to recover from a one-liner no one thinks is funny, it is a lot harder to move ahead with grace after a three-minute story bombs. When your humor falls flat, try to take it in stride. Instead of standing in front of the group with egg on your face or admonishing your audience for being stupid, tell a joke about speakers who tell bad jokes. Be self-deprecating and your audience will love you for it.

Humorist and journalism professor Melvin Helitzer reminds us that we have "to understand the nature of humor. Humor is criticism. There's always a target. You're ridiculing somebody, something, some idea, some place. It's safe to ridicule

---

36.   Jack Valenti, *Speak Up with Confidence* (New York: William Morrow and Company, Inc., 1982), pp. 80–81.
37.   Interview with Professor Melvin Helitzer, January 17, 1990.

things you are sure the audience dislikes—the IRS for example. But you wouldn't do a Dan Quayle joke in front of the Indianapolis Rotary Club because he's their boy . . . the right way to use humor is to write out your speech straight then find humor that fits your points."[38]

When humor works and the audience responds with a spontaneous burst of applause or laughter, there is little that will make you feel better—or more relaxed—as a speaker. Its effect is almost magical. For more information on the use of humor in introductions and conclusions, see Chapter Nine.

SUMMARY   Spoken language differs from written language in several important ways. In many cases, spoken language requires redundancy; it affects the order of ideas, and it requires that the speaker pay attention to rhythm. Spoken language may also require that you signal your audience before you present important material.

The most effective language is simple, clear, and direct: Use short, common words instead of long unusual ones; avoid euphemisms and jargon; eliminate unnecessary words that pad your speech; be direct and concrete; and avoid exaggeration.

To improve your speaking style, avoid clichés, complete your thoughts, and use sentence fragments for specific effect. Avoid sentences that say nothing, as well as profanity, slang, and tongue twisters. Because certain phrases communicate uncertainty, avoid them during your presentation.

Try to engage the imaginations of your listeners through the use of metaphors and similes that paint memorable word pictures. Use language to create a theme. Regardless of the choices you make, be certain your language fits your personality, position, and the needs of your audience.

The effective use of humor requires that you have confidence in your ability to make people laugh (don't use humor if you have never been funny); that you laugh at yourself, not others; and that you use understated anecdotes as well as one-liners.

QUESTIONS FOR
STUDY AND
DISCUSSION

1. How can language contribute to or detract from the creation of meaning in a speech?
2. Why must language fit the needs of the speaker, audience, occasion, and message?
3. What guidelines can you use to choose the proper language in a speech?
4. Why is humor important in public speaking? How does it affect the speaker-audience relationship?

---

38.   Interview with Melvin Helitzer, January 17, 1990.

1. Read aloud a written report you wrote for another class, then analyze whether ACTIVITIES the report's language is appropriate as a speech. Analyze the changes necessary to transform the report into an effective oral presentation.
2. Select a speech from *Vital Speeches of the Day* or from another collection in your library. Study the language of the speech and write an assessment of its effectiveness, strengths, and weaknesses. Because the language was intended to be spoken, you might have to read the speech aloud during your evaluation.
3. Begin collecting humorous ideas, stories, and incidents for your next speech. As you develop your ideas, blend the humor into the speech, remembering to practice your delivery with a tape recorder.

"We will draw the curtain and show you the picture."

William Shakespeare

USING VISUAL AIDS

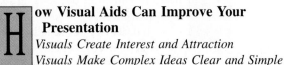

or the first time since your public speaking course began, you have chosen a speech topic that really excites you–one that you are sure will be provocative and controversial enough to excite your audience. Unlike many of the speeches you have heard recently, this one tells a story your classmates will find difficult to ignore–or so it seems.

It deals with the scandal of college football and basketball programs in which few athletes ever graduate—a scandal that looms large in your own school. Recent articles in the student newspaper have criticized your school's athletic department for emphasizing winning over education. As an editorial in last week's newspaper asks, how can student-athletes practice forty hours a week and still go to class, study, and complete their assignments? The answer is they cannot.

As you collect supporting material for your speech, you find statistics that tell a story of athletes not good enough for the pros and not prepared for anything more than menial work. Here is part of the speech your classmates hear:

> According to a recent study by the federal General Accounting Office, of the 97 colleges with Division 1-A basketball programs, considered the best in intercollegiate sports, 35—that's more than one third—graduate no more than 1 in 5 athletes; 33 graduate between 21 percent and 40 percent; 11 graduate between 41 percent and 60 percent; 10 graduate between 61 percent and 80 percent; and only 8 graduate between 81 percent and 100 percent.
>
> The graduation rates for football players on Division 1-A teams is little better. Of the 103 teams in this division, 14 graduate no more than 1 out of 5 players; 39 graduate between 21 and 40 percent; 31 graduate between 41 and 60 percent; 13 between 61 and 80 percent; and only 6 between 81 and 100 percent.[1]

Instead of startling your listeners, these statistics numb them. You see several people yawning, many doodling, a few whispering. You have no idea why until your classmates comment during the post-speech evaluation. The complaints are all the same: Your "can't miss" speech was boring and difficult to follow. Instead of stimulating your listeners, your long list of statistics put them to sleep.

Few of us think of speech making in visual terms—or find ways to reach our speaking goals by turning to visual aids. Here, for example, an appropriately constructed visual aid could have helped you avoid saying so much in words. Despite the interest your listeners had in your topic before your speech began, the number and complexity of your statistics made it difficult for them to pay attention. By presenting some of your data in visual form, you could communicate the same message more effectively. Consider the difference when the following speech text is substituted for the text above and combined with Figure 11.1.

> A recent study by the General Accounting Office, an arm of the federal government, shows that at some Division 1-A colleges, including those with the best intercollegiate athletic programs, no more than 1 out of 5 basketball and football players graduate. As

---

1. Irvin Molotsky, "No More Than 1 in 5 Athletes Graduating at Many Schools," *The New York Times,* September 10, 1989, pp. A1 and 46.

you can see, [speaker points to the figure] there are far fewer colleges with an 80 percent graduation rate than colleges graduating athletes at a rate of 20 percent or less. Although only 8 out of 97 colleges fit into the former group, 35 fit into the latter—and our college is one of them.

When a visual is well prepared, little can compete with it to capture—and hold—audience interest.

HOW VISUAL AIDS CAN IMPROVE YOUR PRESENTATION

Visuals Create Interest and Attraction

We live in a visual age. The images that surround us in the mass media make us more receptive, on a conscious and unconscious level, to visual presentations of all kinds. We are attuned to these presentations simply because they are visual—a phenomenon you can use to your advantage during a speech.

In recent years even the president of the United States has relied on visuals to create interest and attraction in speeches to the nation. Ronald Reagan, George Bush, and Bill Clinton have all used visual aids occasionally, but industrialist Ross Perot, made visuals a regular feature during his campaign against Bush and Clinton—and even afterward as he pressed the new administration about economic issues facing the nation.

Computers can generate visuals, companies are successful in producing visuals for professional presentations, and large organizations have graphics departments to produce visuals for speeches made by executives to internal or external audiences.

You can often enhance your communication by carefully choosing and using visuals for your speech assignments. For speeches in your classrooms you will not

GRADUATION RATE
FOR BASKETBALL PLAYERS FROM 97 COLLEGES

0 to 20%	21-40%	41-60%	61-80%	81-100%
35 colleges	33	11	10	8

FOR FOOTBALL PLAYERS FROM 103 COLLEGES

0 to 20%	21-40%	41-60%	61-80%	81-100%
14	39	31	13	6

FIGURE 11.1
A visual aid can be an effective way to present statistics.

need to have a graphics organization produce complicated and expensive visuals for your speeches. You can create your own visuals through careful planning and a minimal expense. Before you think about what visuals you might use in your next speech or about how you can prepare or obtain visuals, think about the ways in which visuals can serve your rhetorical needs.

Visuals Make Complex Ideas Clear and Simple

Visual aids have the power to clarify complex ideas. They are invaluable tools in explaining such mechanical functions as how a hot air balloon rises or how a computer stores information. They can help clarify complex interrelationships involving people, groups, and institutions. They can show, for example, the stages a bill must go through before it becomes a law and the role Congress and the president play in this process. Visuals reduce (but not eliminate) the need to explain verbally all the complex details in a process.

FIGURE 11.2
The audience listening to a speech that includes an explanation of where the oil spill took place needs to view a map with necessary detail included. In this figure, the words and the illustration work together to create meaning.

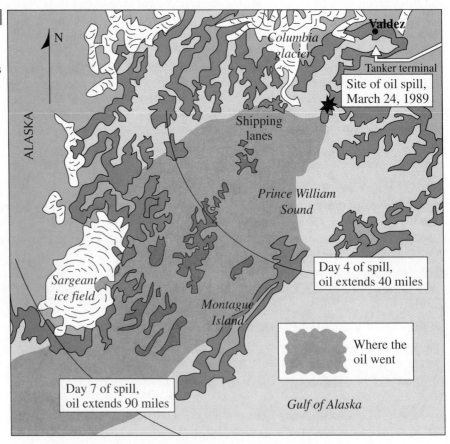

Visuals Make Abstract Ideas Concrete

Few of us are comfortable with abstractions. If, for example, you are delivering a speech on the effects of the 11 million gallon oil spill from the Exxon tanker *Valdez* into Alaska's Prince William Sound, it may not be enough to tell your audience that the spill was allowed to drift 470 miles in a period of fifty-six days. It is far more effective to refer to a map of the drifting spill that illustrates the extent of the spread on different days. Figure 11.2 shows the enormity of the disaster and eliminates any confusion audience members may have about its impact on the Alaskan coast. Along with this visual, you explain:

> For three days after the Exxon *Valdez* rammed into a reef on Alaska's Prince William Sound, the spill miraculously lingered near the ruptured hull. But officials were unable to take action. Instead they wasted this time—this precious time—arguing what to do. On day four, a powerful storm made their arguments academic as it spread the oil down the Alaskan coast where it drifted uncontrollably for 56 days and stained 470 miles of Alaska's pristine shore.[2]

Visuals Help Your Audience Remember Your Speech and Be Persuaded By Your Message

If you read the newspaper this morning, think of what you remember from it. Chances are a photo comes to mind—the picture of a fireman rescuing a child from a burning building or demonstrators protesting in front of a nuclear power plant. Although you may have read the articles that accompanied these pictures, the image is likely to have had the greatest impact.

The tendency of an audience to recall pictures longer than words can give speakers an important advantage. Research has shown, for example, that speakers who use overhead transparencies can increase audience retention of information. Without the visual, the retention of information can be as low as 10 percent, but with it the retention rate soars to 50 percent.[3]

Visuals have persuasive power. Business speakers, especially those in sales, have long realized that they can close a deal faster if they use visual aids. A recent study by the University of Minnesota and the 3M Corporation found that speakers who integrate visuals into their talks are 43 percent more likely to persuade their audiences than speakers who rely solely on verbal images.[4]

Visuals Help Your Audience Organize Your Ideas

The flow and connection of a speaker's ideas is not always apparent to an audience, especially if the topic is complicated or involves many steps. Flow charts, diagrams, graphs, and tables can help listeners follow a speaker's ideas.

---

2.   "Alaska after Exxon," *Newsweek,* September 18, 1989, p. 53.
3.   Eastman Kodak Company, "Kodak Introduces High-Resolution Datashow Products for 'MAC' and IBM," press release, January 16, 1988.
4.   Donald R. Vogel, Gary W. Dickson, and John A. Lehman, "Persuasion and the Role of Visual Presentation Support: The UM/3M Study," commissioned by Visual Systems Division of 3M, 1986.

F O C U S   O N   R E S E A R C H

THE ROLE OF VISUAL AIDS IN PERSUASION

Researchers from the Management Information Systems Research Center at the University of Minnesota and the 3M Corporation (Douglas R. Vogal, Gary W. Dickson, and John A. Lehman) conducted a study to discover whether visual support materials give presenters a persuasive edge.

They gathered nine groups of thirty-five undergraduate business students. The groups were shown a ten-minute speech to influence the audience to sign up for a series of time-management seminars. (The seminars involved two three-hour evening sessions at a cost of $15.) To make sure the quality of the speaker was consistent, each group watched the same presentation on videotape. The difference in the presentations was the use of visual support. While one group watched the presentation with no visual support, the other eight groups watched videotapes enhanced by some form of high quality visuals. (One of the researchers manually displayed the visual material for these presentations.) The variables in visual support treatments included color vs. black-and-white, plain text vs. text enhanced with "clip art" and graphs, and 35-mm slides vs. overhead transparencies.

At the conclusion of each videotape, researchers surveyed the subjects to learn their degree of interest in the time-management seminars (a questionnaire had been administered before the videotapes to determine initial attitudes) and to assess their comprehension of the videotape. Ten days later, a final questionnaire was administered to test how much of the videotaped information the students retained.

According to the researchers, compared to their pre-speech attitudes, the groups who had seen a speech supported by visuals were willing to spend 43 percent more time and 26.4 percent more money on the seminars than those who had seen the presenta-

tion without visual support. In addition, the various components of persuasion were improved by the presence of visual support. Action (the commitment to sign up for the course) improved by 43.1 percent; positive audience perception of the speaker by 11 percent; retention by 10.1 percent; comprehension by 8.5 percent; attention by 7.5 percent; and agreement with the presenter's position by 5.5 percent. When the speeches were delivered with visual support, the audiences perceived the presenter as more concise, clearer, a better user of supporting data, more professional, more persuasive, and more interesting.

Specific characteristics of the visuals also influenced the persuasive force of the presentation. Color overhead transparencies had the greatest positive impact on action. Also, color visuals aided comprehension and retention more than black-and-white. The researchers also found that 35-mm slides increased the audience's perception of speaker professionalism.

These findings were in response to an "average" or "typical" speaker. To determine the impact of visual support on the persuasive ability of a superior speaker, the researchers videotaped a second speaker with better skills. Both speakers read identical remarks. The researchers found that "typical" speakers who integrated visuals into their speeches were as effective as "better" speakers who used no visuals. They also found that the better presenters were most persuasive when they used high quality (machine-produced rather than hand-drawn) visual support. Audiences were less willing to commit their time or money to the seminar when the "better" speakers used inferior visual material.

This study demonstrates that visual support materials have the potential to add an important element of persuasion to a speaker's presentation.

Visuals Help Compress a Presentation

Visuals can take the place of many words and, in the process, shorten the length of a speech. Visuals do not replace words, and one or two statements are insufficient verbal support for a series of visual displays. But visuals and words in combination can reduce the amount of time you spend creating word pictures (see Figure 11.2).

Visuals Point the Audience to Action

In a persuasive speech, you frequently want the audience to act as a result of your presentation. A visual can help bring about this action. For example, in a speech urging listeners to give blood, you may want to include a visual of the university health office phone number where your listeners can call for an appointment. In an informative speech, if you are demonstrating how to stay fit while sitting in class, you may want to show, either in person or through a series of diagrams, the specific stomach, leg, and arm exercises students can do sitting in their seats. This type of visual "call to action" is likely to be remembered after your speech.

Visual aids fall into four general categories: actual objects, three-dimensional models, two-dimensional reproductions, and technology-based visual aids.

ACTUAL OBJECTS

A student who had been stricken with bone cancer as a child, a condition that required the amputation of her leg, demonstrated to her classmates how her prosthetic leg functioned and how she wore it. Not one of her listeners lost interest in her demonstration.

Another student, seeking to persuade her audience to pressure their members of Congress to support stricter toy safety regulations, brought to class a box filled with toys that could injure, maim, or even kill young children. As the audience watched in increasing horror, the speaker pulled out a pull-toy with parts small enough for a preschooler to swallow and lawn darts with points sharp enough to kill. Her demonstration was so persuasive that everyone signed the speaker's petition to encourage Congress to pass stronger toy safety legislation.

As these examples demonstrate, actual objects can be effective visual aids. Because you are showing your audience exactly what you are talking about, they have the power to inform or convince in a way no other visual aid can.

THREE-DIMENSIONAL MODELS

When you cannot display an actual object, a three-dimensional model, or prop, may be your best choice. Models are commonly used to show the structure of a complex object. For example, a student who watched his father almost die of a heart attack used a model of the heart to demonstrate what physically happened during the attack. Using a three-dimensional replica about five times the size of a human heart, he showed how the major blood vessels leading to his father's heart became clogged and how this blockage precipitated the attack.

Models are useful when you are explaining various steps in a sequence. A scale model of the space shuttle, the shuttle launch pad, and its booster rockets will help you describe what happens during the first few minutes after blast-off.

Some replicas are easier to find, build, and afford than others. If you are delivering a speech on antique cars, inexpensive plastic models are available in the hobby shop and take little time to assemble. But if you want to show through a model how proper city planning can untangle the daily downtown traffic snarl, you will have to build your own scaled-down version of downtown roads as they now are and as you would like them to be—a model that would be too time-consuming and expensive to be feasible.

TWO-DIMENSIONAL REPRODUCTIONS

Two-dimensional reproductions are the most common visual aids used by speakers. Among these are photographs, maps, tables and lists, diagrams and drawings, graphs, flow charts, organizational charts, competition brackets, and cutaways.

Photographs

Photographs are the most realistic of your two-dimensional visual choices and can have the greatest impact. If you are delivering a speech on animal rights, a photo of a fox struggling to free his leg from a trap will deliver your message more effectively than words. If you are speaking about forest fire prevention, a photo of a forest destroyed by fire is your most persuasive evidence.

To be effective, photos must be large enough for your audience to see. Magazine or newspaper photos won't do. If a photo is important to your presentation, consider having it enlarged by a professional printer or graphics service.

Maps

Weather reports on the TV news have made maps a familiar visual aid. Instead of merely talking about the weather, reporters show us the shifting patterns that turn sunshine into storms. The next time you watch a national weather report, pay attention to the kind of map being used. You will notice that details have been omitted because they distract viewers from what the reporter is explaining, the current and changing weather scene over a wide geographic area.

If you are talking about Europe's shrinking population, don't include in your map the location of the Acropolis or the Eiffel Tower. If you want to show the location of the national parks and protected wilderness areas in eleven western states, show the state boundaries and names as well as codes for these national recreational preserves but nothing more (see Figure 11.3). Additional details will only confuse your audience.

Because your map must be designed for a specific rhetorical purpose, you may have to draw it yourself. Start with a broad outline of the geographic area and add to it only those details that are necessary for your presentation.

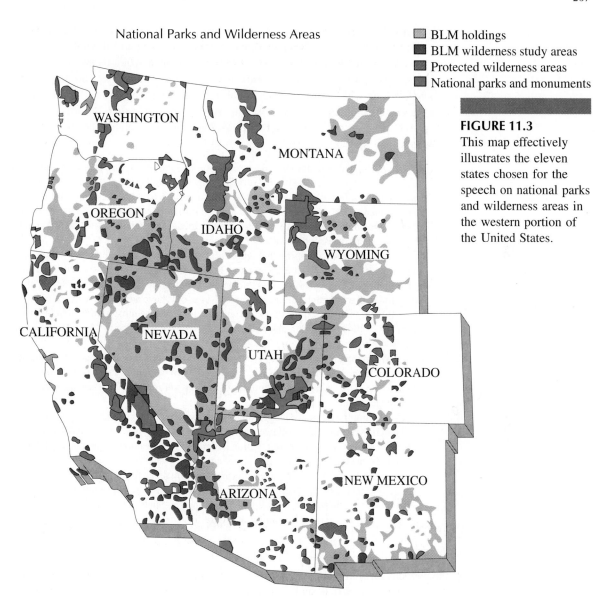

National Parks and Wilderness Areas

☐ BLM holdings
■ BLM wilderness study areas
■ Protected wilderness areas
■ National parks and monuments

FIGURE 11.3
This map effectively illustrates the eleven states chosen for the speech on national parks and wilderness areas in the western portion of the United States.

Lists

Even though a list is a collection of words without pictures, it can be an effective visual aid. If, for example, you are delivering a speech on the recreational attractions Americans enjoy best, you may want to include a visual that shows attractions in their order of popularity. The visual contains the outline of your speech: You will start with a discussion of amusement parks and end with a discussion of NBA basketball.

Visual lists help your listeners organize their thinking and follow the logic of your speech. If, for example, you are trying to persuade your listeners that our educational system is failing its students and the nation as a whole, you may want to include, along with your speech, a visual like the one in Figure 8.5. This list will help the audience focus on your most important points and retain the information when your speech is over. Look at Figure 11.4 as you read, noticing how it follows the logic of the speech:

> In 1988, the Department of Education issued a report to the president entitled "American Education: Making It Work." Using stunning language, the authors of the report condemned the performance of American schools as "unacceptably low." "Too many students do not graduate from our high schools." the report stated, "and too many of those who do graduate have been poorly educated. Our students know too little, and their command of essential skills is too slight."[5]
>
> At about the same time this report sent shock waves throughout the nation, an independent assessment group, known as the Nation's Report Card, studied the math performance of 17-year-olds across the nation. Terming the performance "dismal," the study found that although half the nation's 17-year-olds have no trouble with junior high school math, their reasoning skills fall apart in the face of multistep high-school level problems or those involving algebra or geometry; fewer than one in 15 students could supply the right answers.[6]
>
> When the same assessment group focused on performance in science, they found what they termed "a national disgrace." According to the report, most 17-year-olds do not have the skills to handle a technologically based job and only 7 percent are prepared for college science courses.
>
> The implications of these findings are staggering: In the not too distant future, the United States may be a follower rather than a leader in world scientific discovery— a fact that may jeopardize our national defense and economic health. And with technology becoming increasingly important in the way we live our lives, we may become a nation divided by scientific and mathematical literacy. Archie Lapointe, executive director of the Nation's Report Card, wonders whether young people "can understand the issues about the safety of nuclear power plants or the space-based missile system or the real dangers behind drug abuse or venereal disease."[7]

Tables

Tables focus on words and numbers presented in columns and rows. Tables are used most frequently to display statistical data. If, for example, you are delivering a speech on the fat content of food and are focusing on the types and percentage of fat in nuts, you could refer as you speak to a table like that shown in Figure 11.5. This single table should be divided into two parts because it contains too much information to

---

5. Edward B. Fiske, "Schools Fall Short Despite Drive for Improvements, Bennett Says," *The New York Times,* April 25, 1988, p. A1.
6. "In U.S. Schools, 2 + 2 =?" *U.S. News & World Report,* June 20, 1988, p. 14.
7. "U.S. Pupils Get Low Mark in Science," *The New York Times,* September 23, 1988, p. A24.

SYMPTOMS
1. Unacceptable low standards
2. Unacceptably high drop-out rate
3. "Dismal" performance in math
4. A "national disgrace" in science
IMPLICATIONS
Loss of world leadership
A nation divided by scientific and mathematical literacy

FIGURE 11.4
Our failing educational system.

present in one visual. Keep in mind your audience's information absorption threshold—the point at which a visual will cease to be useful because it says too much.

Charts

The three commonly used charts are flow charts, organizational charts, and competition brackets.

Flow Charts.   Flow charts are used to display the steps or stages in a process. Each step is illustrated by an image or label. If you are an amateur cartoonist, you might give a talk on the steps involved in producing an animated cartoon. As you can see in Figure 11.6, your speech will center on the role of the artist in creating the drawings, the completion of the artwork with ink and paint, the photography involved in putting the drawings on film, and the creation of a finished cartoon, with animation

	Saturated	Monosaturated	Polyunsaturated	Other
Chestnuts	18%	35%	40%	7%
Brazil nuts	15%	35%	36%	14%
Cashews	13%	59%	17%	11%
Pine nuts	13%	37%	41%	9%
Peanuts	12%	49%	33%	6%
Pistachios	12%	68%	15%	5%
Walnuts	8%	23%	63%	6%
Almonds	8%	65%	21%	6%
Pecans	6%	62%	25%	7%
Hazelnuts	6%	79%	9%	6%

FIGURE 11.5
The fat content of foods as measured in a single table.

FIGURE 11.6
A flow chart is a valuable way to present key steps in any process, such as producing an animated film.

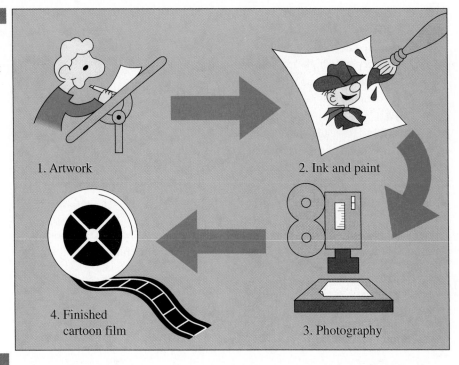

1. Artwork

2. Ink and paint

3. Photography

4. Finished cartoon film

FIGURE 11.7
Flow charts can use blocked boxes and words to show how a corporation delegates authority and responsibility to achieve its objectives.

and sound. This visual shows your audience that these steps occur in sequence and that one is dependent on the other.

Pictorial flow charts are also effective. You can draw the pictures yourself or, if your artistic ability is limited, you can use a series of carefully selected photographs from a variety of sources. Flow charts that depend on words alone should use short, simple labels that move the audience through the stages of a process. Figure 11.7

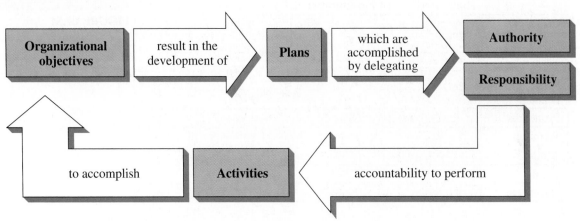

Organizational objectives   result in the development of   **Plans**   which are accomplished by delegating   **Authority**

Responsibility

to accomplish   **Activities**   accountability to perform

shows how authority and responsibility are delegated in a corporation to meet organizational objectives.

Organizational Charts. Organizational charts reflect our highly structured world. Corporations, government institutions, schools, associations, religious organizations, and so on are organized according to official hierarchies that determine the relationships of people as they work. You may want to refer to a hierarchy in a speech if you are trying to show the positions of people involved in a project. By looking at a chart like that shown in Figure 11.8, for example, your audience will know who reports to whom.

Competition Brackets. If you are delivering a speech on sports, you may need to refer to a competition bracket, a chart showing how competitors are paired at different stages. This type of visual can help you explain your favorites in a championship boxing tournament (see Figure 11.9).

Cutaways

In a speech you are delivering on why it is so difficult to build a concert hall with perfect acoustics, you decide to focus on the way architect I. M. Pei designed the Morton H. Meyerson Symphony Center in Dallas to maximize the beauty of the

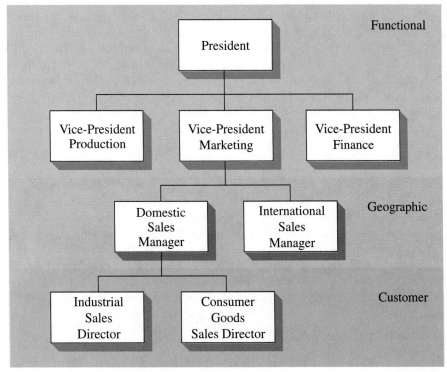

FIGURE 11.8
Almost every large group or company has an organization chart to illustrate the official hierarchy and lines of access.

FIGURE 11.9
Competition brackets can illustrate clearly the route to a championship. Only one name advances from each bracket pair.

sound. Pei, working with a team of acoustical consultants, equipped the hall with a series of construction innovations including a forty-two-ton canopy that lowers and tilts for optimum sound reflection. Although you explain these innovations in your speech, you also want to show them. Realizing that a picture of the completed hall won't help, because many of Pei's acoustical solutions are not visible, you use a cutaway like the one in Figure 11.10, a diagram that displays the relationship between the parts, elements, or sections of a structure that are not always visible to the eye.

Cutaways can be used for many different rhetorical purposes. A furniture sales representative may use one to demonstrate to clients his company's commitment to quality construction. A dentist delivering a lecture to schoolchildren on proper oral hygiene may use it to show the cross section of a tooth (see Figure 11.11). Cutaways differ in complexity depending upon the needs of your speech. When using a cutaway, the relationship of the parts to the whole may not be obvious to your listeners, so it is important to explain these relationships as you speak.

Drawings and Diagrams

When you cannot illustrate your point with a photograph—or would rather not use one—a drawing can be an adequate alternative. A drawing is your own representation of what you are describing. If you are demonstrating the difference between a kettledrum and a snare drum, a simple drawing may be all you need. If you want to extend your explanation to show how musicians are able to control the pitch of the sound made by a drum, your drawing must include more detail. The location of the screws used to tighten the skin of the drum must be shown as well as the relation between the size of the drum and the pitch of the sound. A drawing with detail

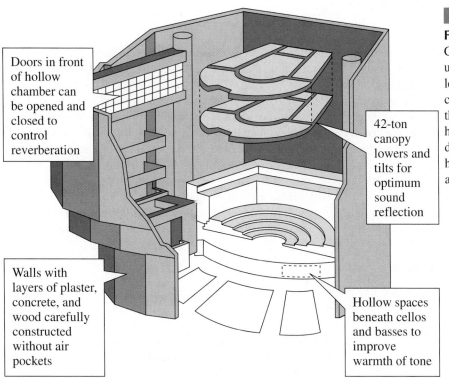

Doors in front of hollow chamber can be opened and closed to control reverberation

42-ton canopy lowers and tilts for optimum sound reflection

Walls with layers of plaster, concrete, and wood carefully constructed without air pockets

Hollow spaces beneath cellos and basses to improve warmth of tone

FIGURE 11.10
Cutaway figures can be used to show various levels of any type of construction, such as this illustration showing how architect I. M. Pei designed the concert hall to deliver the best acoustics possible.

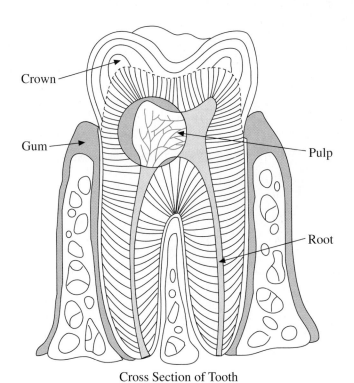

Crown

Gum

Pulp

Root

Cross Section of Tooth

FIGURE 11.11
Cross sections allow you to show all the layers of an object, in this case the internal structure of a human tooth.

showing the arrangement and relation of the parts to the whole is considered a diagram. Figure 11.12 is a simple diagram of a kettledrum. Labels are often used to pinpoint critical parts.

It is generally a mistake to attempt a complex drawing or diagram if you have little or no artistic ability. And it is a mistake to attempt to produce these drawings while your audience is watching. With time and patience, you may be able to prepare sketches in advance that are suitable for presentation or you can choose a sketch done by a professional artist that can be reproduced in a larger size for your speech. A book on drums, for example, may give you all the illustrations you need to show how drums work. Keep your audience's needs—and limitations—in mind when choosing sketches. Too much detail will frustrate your audience as they strain to see the tiniest parts and labels. And when people are frustrated, they often stop listening.

Graphs

Bar graphs, line graphs, pie graphs, and pictographs can be used to present complex statistical information.

Bar Graphs.   In a speech urging students to consider teaching the social sciences and humanities in college, you want to show, graphically, that our universities face a serious shortfall of liberal arts professors into the twenty-first century that may force many schools to redefine the nature of a liberal arts diploma. As part of your speech, you tell your audience:

> There were days back in the 1970s when having a Ph.D. in history or sociology or English literature or philosophy guaranteed little or nothing. Indeed, many people who

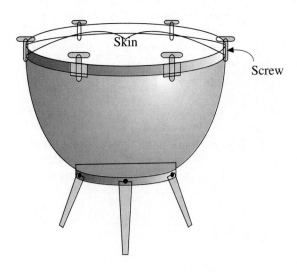

FIGURE 11.12
A simple diagram can show how the parts of objects such as this drum interact.

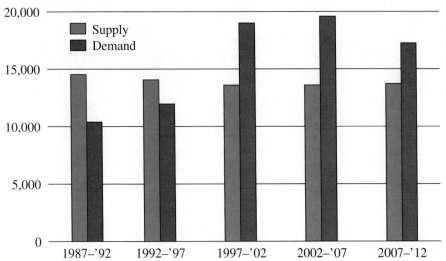

Faculty supply-and-demand projections in the social sciences and humanities

FIGURE 11.13
A speech to outline the projected need for a new faculty as we face the next century can be enhanced by a bar graph such as this.

aspired to teach the humanities and social sciences were forced into menial jobs just to survive. So great was the supply of potential faculty over the demand that a new phenomenon was created: the taxi-driving Ph.D.

Today the story is different. As you can see in this graph, by the year 1997, three out of ten faculty jobs in the humanities will remain unfilled and we'll have to wait to the year 2007 before the situation gets any better.[8]

The visual you refer to is shown in Figure 11.13, a bar graph of supply and demand projections for faculty members into the early part of the twenty-first century. The graph compares supply and demand figures for five five-year periods and measures these figures in thousands. This type of graph is especially helpful when you are comparing two or more items. In this case, one bar represents the supply of potential faculty while the other represents the potential demand for faculty. To make the trend clear, you may want to color code the bars.

Line Graphs.   When you want to show a trend over time, the line graph may be your best choice. When two or more lines are used in one graph, comparisons are also possible. In Figure 11.14, for example, we see not only how the number of yearly doctor visits per person has fluctuated year to year, but also that women aged eighteen to forty-four see the doctor far more often than men in the same age group.

---

8. "Remember the Ph.D. Glut? Colleges Will Go Begging," *U.S. News & World Report,* September 25, 1989, p. 55.

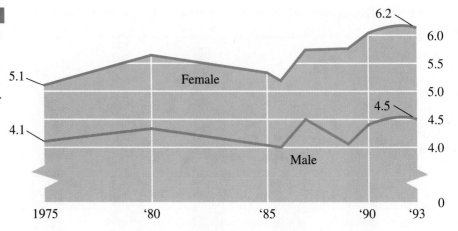

FIGURE 11.14
A line graph illustrates the fluctuations of certain factors—such as male/female ratio—over time.

Pie Graphs.   Pie graphs, also known as circle graphs, show your audience how the parts of an item relate to the whole. The most simple and direct way to demonstrate percentages graphically is with an accurate pie graph (see Figure 11.15).

Pictograph.   Pictographs are most commonly used as a variation of the bar graph. Instead of showing bars of various lengths comparing items on the graph, the bars are replaced by pictorial representations of the graph's subject. For example, if you are giving a speech on the effects of television on book sales, you can use a pictograph like that shown in Figure 11.16 to demonstrate the sales trend. The pictograph must include a scale explaining what each symbol means. In this case, each book represents 200 million books sold.

Displaying Two-Dimensional Visual Aids

Two-dimensional reproductions can be displayed in several different ways:

Mount Your Visual on Poster Board and Display It on an Easel.   If you choose this option, you have to be sure that an easel or similar stand is available. Many speakers come prepared with elaborate poster board mounted visuals only to find that they have no place to display them.

Use a Flip Chart.   Flip charts are among the most popular methods of display. These charts give speakers the ability to show a sequence of visuals. Flip charts can be prepared in advance or during your speech. Most speakers prefer advance preparation, because their work is likely to be neater and because they will avoid the long pauses associated with drawing in front of an audience. Studies indicate that listeners are more likely to retain information when the chart is not completed fully in advance. Instead of coming with finished visuals, leave out a few key lines or

Spending Pattern

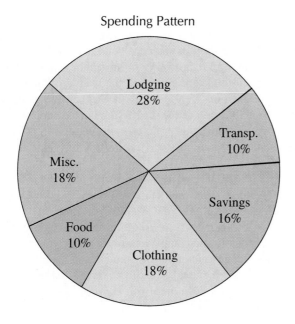

FIGURE 11.15
The pie chart is one of the most popular and effective ways to show how parts of a whole are divided. The pie is used frequently to display the division of expenses or resources a speaker wants an audience to see.

Books Sold —1985 vs. 1995

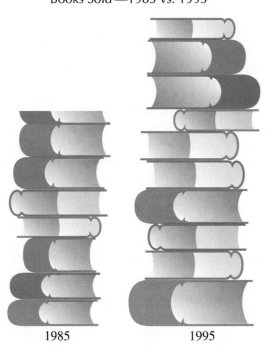

FIGURE 11.16
Pictographs provide a twist on the traditional bar graph by using pictures of the items discussed to illustrate as the "bar." The pictography should include an explanatory scale to explain what each symbol means, such as "each book represents 200 million sold."

words and fill them in as the audience watches. The process encourages listeners to perceive your visual as a product of your own expression—an identification important to developing the speaker-audience bond.

Although flip charts with heavy paper resembling poster board are more expensive than charts with light-weight paper, the weight of the paper can make a difference in your presentation. If you use the less expensive paper your audience will be able to see the marker pen on the page following the one you are showing—a distraction that can get in the way of your message. Because flip charts also require an easel for presentation, be sure that one is available for your talk.

Use the Blackboard With Care.   The blackboard is often the most logical way to present a visual concept, especially in class. However, it must be used with care because using it forces you to turn your back to your audience as you write and requires neat, legible handwriting. Try to write as little as possible during your speech (you may want to arrive early and complete most, or all, of your visual presentation in advance) and pay special attention to the neatness and legibility of your writing. If your chalkboard has a screen, and you write your notes on the board before your speech begins, pull the screen down until you are ready for your presentation.

TECHNOLOGY-BASED VISUAL AIDS

Depending upon the needs of your speech and the speaking situation, you may choose a visual aid requiring the use of projection equipment.

Slides

Slide presentations are more common in business and community meetings than they are in the classroom. A city planner may use a slide presentation to show plans for an urban renewal project; a businessperson may use slides to present an overview of a new advertising campaign.

If prepared and projected correctly, a slide presentation has the power to draw an audience into a speech even if the speaker falters. However, using slides has some drawbacks: A darkened room can disrupt your presentation, if you need to refer to detailed notes; mastery of the use of the projection equipment to avoid glitches during your speech is also a consideration. Although slide projectors are fairly standard, check the equipment before your speech to make sure you can operate it and that it is in good working order. Finally, slides require considerable setup time. The fastest way to label yourself a beginner is to project reversed or upside-down images or frames with nothing more than a blank screen.

Here are some suggestions for producing a successful slide presentation:

⌘ Use 2 × 2-inch 35-mm color slides, which are effective and inexpensive. In business, you may have access to microcomputer-generated graphics for use in a slide projector.

⌘ Use only the highest quality slides in a darkened room to increase visual readability.

⌘ Limit each slide to one main idea expressed in the simplest way and use as few words as possible.

⌘ If possible, use a machine with a remote control change button so that you are not forced to stay close to the projector.

⌘ Use a pointer rather than your finger to refer to details on a slide. It is more professional and exact.

⌘ Make sure the projection is large enough for your audience to see. According to Eastman Kodak, "One of the biggest mistakes speakers make is to think that legibility in one form means legibility in another. The picture you want to use from a book isn't going to be as easy to read on the screen as it is on the printed page. We ordinarily read printed material at a distance of 12 to 14 inches. The same image projected for presentation will be about 4×6 feet and the rear seats in a large room are often 70 feet from the screen. Reading the text of a 4-foot high image from 70 feet is like reading a 2-inch version of this page. You'd probably see only the title."[9]

Film, Videotape, and Audiotape

In certain situations, the most effective way to communicate your message is with a film, video, or audiotape. Of these three, films are rarely used because videos are more convenient and available. In a speech on tornadoes, showing a video of the damage done by a tornado is likely to be quite impressive. If demonstrating the influence of classical music on some forms of jazz, recorded excerpts can effectively serve your purpose. A speaker has to be cautious, however, about using a video or an audiotape, especially in a short speech, because the tapes can overshadow the oral presentation if they consume too much time. The inexperienced speaker using an audiotape often looks uncomfortably about the room while the audience attempts to listen to a muffled and hollow sound coming from a cassette player that is not appropriate for public speaking. The novice speaker with a five-minute speech for classmates may not edit the video carefully enough, the result being four of the five minutes is spent by the audience attending to the video, which leaves the speaker about a minute to talk. If you choose to use film, video, or audio tapes, you must plan how to use them and practice with them carefully.

Another reason to practice is that film and videotape can present technical problems similar to those you encounter with slides. But the problems are worse—especially with film—because the equipment is more complex. You have to know how to load, focus, and control the sound level on different machines—and you have to know what to do if the machine stops working.

You also face the possibility that you will be upstaged by your own film or video package. Your visual presentation—rather than your speech—will hold center stage. To avoid this program, prepare a careful introduction to support the video or

---

9.   Eastman Kodak Company, "Effective Lecture Slides," 1986.

film before it begins. Point your listeners to specific parts of the visual so they focus on what you want rather than on what happens to catch their interest. After the visual, continue your speech, building on its content with the force of your own words.

Incorporating an audiotape into your speech is a simpler task. If you are trying to describe the different messages babies send through their cries, an audiotape demonstration is all the support you need.

Overhead Projections

Many colleges and universities equip classrooms with an overhead projector that allows you to face your listeners and talk as you enlarge and project images onto a surface.

Using an overhead projector during your speech gives you greater flexibility than many other visual aids.

S P E A K   E A S Y

HOW TO MAKE YOUR OWN TRANSPARENCIES

If you have access to a plain-paper enlarging–reducing photocopier, you can make your own transparencies for use in an overhead projector following these four steps:[10]

Step 1: Create your visual, using an ordinary typewriter or word processor and whatever additional design elements you want. Use graphs, tables, diagrams, drawings, and so on, as well as typewritten labels. Design your visual by cutting out the various elements and pasting them in position on a clean sheet of paper. Then photocopy your final layout so that you will be working with a clean copy.

Step 2: If necessary, enlarge your visual with the use of an enlarging photocopier.

Step 3: Photocopy your visual onto transparent film. If you cannot find a photocopier that will print on this film, a local printer or graphics house will do it for you. Mount the visual in a cardboard frame for ease in handling.

Step 4: Customize the transparency as you speak by adding key words or underlining in color.

Computer technology is enabling speakers to streamline this process by going directly from computer to transparency. If you create a visual on your computer that you want to display on an overhead projector, you can transfer it directly onto computer transparency film by using a standard computer printer, eliminating the need to transfer the image from the computer memory to hard copy to transparency in Step 3 in the process above. In a system developed by Eastman Kodak, the Kodak Datashow, you can transfer sophisticated computer data and graphics from a personal computer onto a projection screen. These visuals are shown using an overhead projector. The Apple Desktop Media can be used with the Macintosh computer, an Apple scanner, and an Apple LaserWriter to create visuals in a variety of formats, sizes, and colors as overhead transparencies. The system can also be used to produce color slides.[11]

Overhead projectors can be used in normal light, which is an important advantage to the speaker. The fact that the room is lighted allows you to talk to your audience while near the screen rather than near the projector. You can face your listeners and use a pointer, just as you would if you were using any other visual. If you choose to remain near the projector instead, you run the risk of talking down to the transparency you are showing rather than looking up at your audience.

---

10.   N.R. Kleinfield, "Teaching the 'Sir Winston' Method," *The New York Times,* March 11, 1990, Section 3, p. 7.

11.   For more information on computer-generated visuals, see Leon Fletcher, "What's New in Audiovisual Aids? *The Toasatmaster* (February 1990): 4–5.

TABLE 11.1
A comparison of visual-aid formats. *Source: Burson-Marsteller, 230 Park Avenue South, New York, N.Y. 10003.*

Format	Audience	Advantages	Disadvantages
Slides	Medium to large	Flexible Modular Minimum equipment needs Type: Serves as outline Graphs: Show relationships Charts: Saves time conceptually	Do not show motion; lights must be dim
Overhead Transparencies	Medium to large	Portable No technician needed High flexibility	Can be distracting; Complex charts, graphs are ineffective
Flip Charts or Blackboards	Small	Help organize/summarize; High flexibility; low human error; informal	Low impact
Film	Medium to large	High emotional impact; takes audience where it can't go; works well with slides; provides stimulating change of pace Entertaining Portable	Availability may be limited Low flexibility
Video Cassettes	Small to medium	High impact Instant replay; flexible; easy assembly; supports other AV formats; provides change of pace	Requires equipment Availability
Models	Small	Audience can handle; leaves less to their imagination	Can be distracting

Unlike slides, transparencies displayed on an overhead projector can be altered as you speak. You can underline a phrase for emphasis or add a key word. Adding color can underscore your points.

Table 11.1 compares the uses of many visual aids including slides, overhead transparencies, flip charts and blackboards, film, video cassettes, and models.

Although no one in your audience expects you to produce professional quality visual aids, everyone expects an effective presentation that communicates your message in a clear, direct way. You can do this by focusing on simplicity, color, and size.

DESIGNING EFFECTIVE VISUAL AIDS

Simplicity

Keep your visuals simple. Speech consultants Karen Berg and Andrew Gilman explain, "When in doubt, simplify; eliminate extraneous material. If necessary, use an additional visual rather than burdening one with more information than it can efficiently transmit . . . . The art director of a television news broadcast team put it this way: A visual should contain no more information than what a motorist can absorb from a billboard driving past at forty miles an hour."[0]

In practical terms, limit each visual to one main point. Use the entire visual to make the point. Don't be afraid to fill the page. Leave details out. Use as few words as possible. Emphasize the crucial word or phrase by placing it at the top or bottom of the visual. Leave space between words and lines and don't crowd the images.

Color

With full color art standard in magazines and many books, audiences are accustomed to color and expect it in all types of presentations.

A study done by the Bureau of Advertising on color versus black-and-white ads found that the readership of color ads is 80 percent greater than the readership of black-and-white ads. Sales were 50 to 80 percent higher in response to the color ads. Reader memory of ad content increased 55 to 78 percent in response to the color.[13]

Rely on strong, bold colors that make your message stand out even in a large auditorium. Aim for contrast. Use blue lettering against a white background or vice versa. Or try vivid yellow images against a red background. The color wheel in Figure 11.17 will help you choose contrasting colors. You will achieve the strongest contrasts by using colors opposite one another. When these complements are combined, they produce distinct images. Blue and orange make an effective visual combination as do red and green, and so on.

---

12.   Karen Berg and Andrew Gilman, *Get to the Point: How to Say What You Mean and Get What You Want* (New York: Bantam, 1989), p. 73.

13.   Cited in Virginia Johnson, "Picture Perfect Presentations," *The Toastmaster* (February 1990): 7.

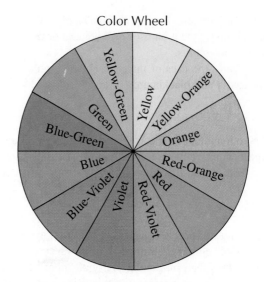

Color Wheel

Colors opposite each other on this wheel provide the most striking contrasts for visual displays.

You can emphasize important points on black and white flip charts and overhead transparencies by adding dashes of color. A word circled in red or an image underlined in green tells your audience the image is important.

Size

A student spent hours preparing a series of graphs and charts for use in her speech on low-impact aerobics. The problem was they were so small that no one beyond the third row could see them. She had forgotten the cardinal rule of visual aids: They have to be visible to add value.

To decide how large the lettering on a two-dimensional visual should be, measure the approximate size of the room in which you will be speaking. Use lettering one inch tall and 1/8 inch wide if the most distant member of your audience will be twenty feet away. For every ten feet the size of the room increases, double the size of your lettering. Thus, when your audience members are thirty feet away, use lettering two inches tall by 1/4 inch wide; when they are forty feet away, use lettering four inches tall by 1/2 inch wide, and so on. Use a felt-tip marker that makes thick, bold lines. To be certain your visuals can be read from the back of the room, take them in advance and see for yourself.

HOW TO GET THE MOST FROM YOUR VISUAL OR AUDIO-VISUAL AIDS

Decide the Points in Your Speech That Need Visual Support.   Link only the most important points in your speech with a visual aid and be sure the visual has a definite purpose. Focus on your core idea and main points and decide which are best displayed through a visual. Don't use visuals to illustrate unimportant features because the visuals themselves announce their own top billing.

I N T E R V I E W

Vickee Jordan Adams
Vice President, Director,
Ketchum Communications
Training Center

Vickee Jordan Adams, vice president and director of a communications training center, teaches corporate executives how to make lasting improvements in their personal communication skills. One area she emphasizes is the use of audiovisual (AV) materials. We asked Ms. Adams about her experiences in training executives in the proper use of AV materials.

Question: Are audiovisual materials always appropriate for an audience?

Answer: It depends on the materials you choose and your objective. For example, if you're speaking to a group of five or ten in a small conference room, slides can be distancing. They act as a barrier between you and your audience, making eye contact and other nonverbal reinforcement impossible. Unless you want the distance, I would not choose slides.

Question: When speakers begin to use audiovisual support, what is their most common mistake?

Answer: They let their AV support—rather than their message—become the focus of the presentation. At its worst, they stand and talk to the visual instead of the audience. I've seen speakers lean on the lectern standing sideways as they stare and talk to the slides. They're depending on the slides to do the communicating for them, rather than facing the audience and delivering the information themselves. Speakers get so wrapped up in having the right slide

at the right time and covering every point the slide is making that they forget the audience.

Question: What is the audience thinking when this happens?

Answer: They start staring at the slides and forget what is being said. They want to make sure that the speaker is telling them everything that's up there. They stop listening to the overall perspective, probably because it's not being given.

Question: Is delivering a speech with audiovisual aids harder than giving one without them? Is more practice required?

Answer: It is more of a challenge for someone who is just starting out. But the advantage is that the AV support can act as your guide, your speech outline. It also conveys a certain level of professionalism and provides built-in variety for both the speaker and audience.

Question: You brought up the word "professionalism." Do AV materials have to look like they came from an art studio to be acceptable?

Answer: No. But they have to be neat. There has to be a consistency of format. There has to be a consistency of style. You shouldn't mix vertical with horizontal slides. Flip charts should be predone and neatly printed with a variety of pen colors. Or if you have a good handwriting and want to use the flip chart as you speak, then that's fine too—just as long as the information is clear and simple.

Steer clear of anything that looks like it came out of a textbook. Interestingly, doctors use the worst AV materials. They take medical charts right from their books, make slides or overhead projections out of them, and ask the audience to decipher what they mean. It can't be done.

Question: How much should a speaker repeat what the audience can see?

Answer: The speaker's role is interpretation, not repetition. Tell your audience, "What you see here is . . .," not "We see this, this, this, and this." Always give individuals the credit they deserve for being able to read what's in front of them.

Question: Do you steer speakers away from multimedia presentations?

Answer: Without rehearsal, it's a lot for any inexperienced speaker to handle. The first thing to ask yourself is how long is the presentation. If all you've got is 15 minutes, you're asking for trouble if you use three different kinds of AV. If, on the other hand, you have an hour to fill and you want to break that hour up with different AV formats, go ahead.

But always rehearse in advance and have someone there to assist you to move video monitors to the front of the room, to turn on the slide projector, to make sure there is a remote cord for the projector, to change a burned out bulb, to make sure there are pens and adequate paper for the flip chart. So many things can go wrong. That's why you should never rely on the AV support to communicate your information. If the slide projector breaks you still have to be able to present your message.

Source: Interview with Vickee Jordan Adams, November 10, 1989.

Set Up in Advance.   Be sure your visuals and equipment are in place before you begin your speech.

Don't Let Your Visual Upstage You.   Keep in mind that your audience has come to see you, not your visual aid or video. If you create a situation in which your visual support is more important than you are or one in which you have to focus your attention on the visual itself rather than on the purpose of your speech, you will have defeated your purpose.

To establish yourself as the focus of the speech, avoid using any visual for the first few minutes. After you have set the tone of your speech and introduced your core idea you can turn to your first visual. Do not use a visual to end your speech. Doing so eliminates the person-to-person contact you have built to that point by shifting the focus away from you.

Use Multimedia Presentations Only With Careful Planning and Practice. Although multimedia presentations can be effective, they can challenge even professional speakers. Gracefully moving from a flip chart to a slide tray to an overhead projector while maintaining audience interest requires skill that comes from practice and experience. Mixing media increases your chance that something will go wrong. You can mix media successfully, but careful planning and preparation is essential.

Let Your Visuals Talk For Themselves.   Why display a visual if you repeat everything on it? Lead your listeners to the main points, and let them read the rest at their own pace.

Perfect Your Timing.   Display each visual only as you talk about it. Don't force people to make a choice between paying attention to you or paying attention to your visual. If you prepare your flip-chart in advance, leave a blank sheet between your visuals and turn the page. Cover your models with a sheet. Turn the slide or overhead projector off. Erase your diagram from the blackboard. Turn your poster board around. These actions tell your audience that you are ready to go on to another point.

Focus on Your Audience, Not Your Visual.   Many speakers make the mistake of turning their backs on the audience. They talk to their visual instead of looking at the audience. To avoid this tendency, become familiar with your visual so that you have little need to look at it during your talk.

Display Your Visual, Then Pause Two Or Three Seconds Before Talking.   This moment of silence gives your audience time to look at the display. You do not want to compete with your own visual aid.

Avoid Long Pauses As You Demonstrate the Steps in a Process.   To demonstrate to his class how to truss a turkey, a student brought in everything he needed including a turkey, string, and poultry pins. He began by explaining the procedure but stopped talking for about five minutes while he worked. Although many members of the class paid attention to his technique, several lost interest. Without a verbal presentation to accompany the visual, their attention drifted to other things. Long periods of silence are not a good idea. Because most audiences need help in maintaining their focus, keep talking.

Don't Let Your Visual Aids Leave the Lectern.   When you pass visual aids around the room, you will be competing with them as you speak. Your listeners will be reading your handouts, analyzing your models, studying your samples instead of listening to you. If handouts are necessary, distribute them at the end of the speech. When appropriate, invite people to take a close look at your displays after your speech.

Choose Appropriate Visuals or Audio-Visuals For the Audience.   Ask yourself whether the visual support is right for your listeners, considering their age, socioeconomic background, knowledge, and attitudes toward your subject. Consider people's sensibilities. Unintentionally, speakers may offend their listeners through visuals that are too graphic. Pictures of abused children, for example, can be disquieting to an audience not prepared for what they will see. If you have doubts about the appropriateness of a visual, leave it out of your presentation.

Choose Visuals Appropriate For the Occasion.   Certain situations are more serious or formal than others. Displaying a cartoon with little content or merit during a congressional hearing on the problems of the DC-10 aircraft would diminish the credibility of the speaker.

Rehearse, Rehearse, Rehearse.   Most speakers need practice blending their visual and oral presentations. They need the opportunity to rehearse moving from one visual to another, which is harder than it sounds, especially if you are tense. Too often, nervous speakers knock charts over, flip to the wrong page, or display the wrong slide because they never practiced with their visuals in advance.

SUMMARY   Visual aids, videos, and audio tapes serve many different functions in a speech. They help create interest in your subject; they simplify complex ideas and make abstract ideas concrete; they help make your message memorable; they help organize and shorten your presentation; and they help point your audience to action.

Visual aids fall into four general categories including actual objects, three-dimensional models, two-dimensional reproductions, and technology-based visual aids. Two-dimensional reproductions include photographs, maps, lists, tables, charts (flow charts, organizational charts, and competition brackets), cutaways, drawings and diagrams, and graphs (bar graphs, line graphs, pie graphs, and pictographs). Two-dimensional visual aids can be mounted on poster board and displayed on an easel or displayed on a flip-chart or chalkboard. Technology-based visual aids include slides, film, videotape and audiotape, and overhead projections.

Effective visual aids are simple; they use strong, bold contrasting colors; and they are large enough for everyone to read with ease. To present effective visuals, choose the points in your speech that need visual support; set up your presentation in advance; never let your visuals upstage you; use multimedia presentations only if they are well planned and rehearsed; avoid repeating what your audience sees in the visual; learn to display each visual only when you are talking about it; focus on your audience, not your visual; display your visual, then pause before talking; avoid long pauses during demonstrations; don't circulate your visuals around the room; choose visuals appropriate for the audience and occasion; and rehearse your presentation.

QUESTIONS
FOR STUDY AND
DISCUSSION

1. In what ways can visual aids help a speaker achieve the desired response from an audience?
2. Why are speakers who use visual support effectively likely to make a professional impression?
3. What guidelines would you include on your personal checklist for the proper use of visual aids or for mixing media?
4. Why is audience and situational analysis important in your choice of visual aids?

1. Plan to use visual aids in your next speech. Spend enough time designing and ACTIVITIES
   preparing the visuals so they will have the impact you want.
2. Contact several business or professional speakers in your campus community or
   hometown. Based on what you have learned in this chapter, interview them about
   using visual aids in their presentations. Report your findings to your class, paying
   special attention to the similarities and differences in their approaches.
3. Locate individuals on your campus or in your community who produce visual
   aids for speeches. Interview these specialists to learn the information they need
   to design effective visuals and how much these visuals cost. Consider both
   two-dimensional and technology-based visual aids and write a report on your
   findings.

"He spoke in Hell's and Heaven's name, Yet all he uttered seemed the same."

Anonymous

DELIVERING YOUR SPEECH

Choose A Delivery Style
Manuscript Speaking
Memorizing Your Speech
Extemporaneous Speaking
Impromptu Speaking
Find Your Best Voice
The Physiology of Speech
Loudness
Pitch
Rate
Pauses
Emphasis
Padding
Regional Dialects
Articulation and Pronunciation Problems

Mastering the Art of Body Language
Learn the Art of the Natural Gesture
Don't Be Afraid to Move
The Eyes Have It

Focus on Research: Can Delivery Make a Difference in Credibility and Persuasion?
The Unspoken Language of Clothes

Speakeasy—How to Handle a Question-and-Answer Period

hat do you remember most when a speech is over? Although you may walk away with the speaker's ideas buzzing through your head, it is often the quality of the performance that remains with you long after you have forgotten the content of the message. That is, the *how* of public speaking—the speaker's style of delivery—often makes the most lasting impression. Consider how these two orators earned their reputations:

> Everett McKinley Dirksen, the Republican U.S. Senate minority leader from 1959 to 1969, was known for his ability to captivate audiences with his baritone voice. A 1962 *Time* Magazine cover story described his eloquent delivery like this: "He speaks, and the words emerge in a soft, sepulchral baritone. They undulate in measured phrases, expire in breathless wisps. He fills his lungs and blows word-rings like smoke. They chase each other around the room in dreamy images of Steamboat Gothic." Dirksen's voice earned him the reputation as "the Silver Throated Senator."[1]
>
> Ti-Grace Atkinson is a political theorist and orator of the women's movement. She identified issues for the movement such as abortion, sex, and lesbianism, and she related these to the theory of women's oppression she espoused in her speeches. As an active participant in the National Organization for Women (NOW) since 1967 and the Feminists, a radical organization she helped found in 1968, she soon became disillusioned with the movement and was one of its most ardent critics. As a speaker, Atkinson exerted influence on the feminist movement rather than on the public. Using her knowledge and training as a writer and artist, she always thought about the rhetorical choices she made in developing her speeches. Although she wrote her speeches, she usually set aside her texts and extemporized. Her soft, well-modulated, clear, calm voice and genteel manner of speech were antithetical to her radical subject matter and her treatment of it.[2]

Everett Dirksen and Ti-Grace Atkinson had the ability to make audiences care about what they were saying—an accomplishment linked, in large part, to the quality of their delivery. Through the choices they made in using their voices and their overall physical presence, they communicated their messages to audiences interested in and attracted to their personae and their ideas. Through their eloquence they became spokespersons with devoted followings.

Words alone are not enough to make audiences want to listen to a speech. Many brilliant people—scientists, lawyers, politicians, engineers, environmentalists—never connect with their listeners, not for lack of trying, but for lack of ability to perform their speech. They are either too stiff, or they appear uninvolved. Or worse, they try to imitate other speakers and be something they are not.[3]

---

1. Edward L. Schapsmeier, "Everett McKinley Dirksen," in Bernard K. Duffy and Halford R. Ryan, eds., *American Orators of the Twentieth Century: Critical Studies and Sources* (New York: Greenwood Press, 1987), p. 103.

2. Beatrice Reynolds, "Ti-Grace Atkinson, Radical Feminist," in Bernard K. Duffy and Halford R. Ryan, eds., *American Orators of the Twentieth Century* (Westport: Greenwood Press, 1987), pp. 7 and 9.

3. The great British statesman Edmund Burke was one of these failed performers. Although he was known as a brilliant speechwriter, he was also known as the "dinner bell speaker." So uninspired was his presentation that when he rose to speak in the House of Commons, his colleagues rose to go to dinner, preferring to read rather than listen to his speeches. See "Edmund Burke," in Chauncey A. Goodrich, *Select British Eloquence* (Indianapolis, IN: Bobbs-Merrill Company, Inc.), pp. 206–40.

Delivery affects your credibility as a speaker. Your ability to communicate information, persuade, and entertain is influenced by the manner in which you present yourself to your audience. An effective delivery works *for* you, an ineffective delivery *against*—even when the content of your message is strong.

In this chapter, we address the two main factors that comprise delivery: voice and body language. We analyze their impact on communication and suggest ways to improve your presentation. First, we examine the four methods of speech delivery. Each method influences the quality of your spoken performance.

If you are delivering a prepared speech, you may choose to read your speech, memorize it word for word and recite it, or speak it extemporaneously, relying on carefully prepared notes. Speeches delivered without any advance notice or preparation are known as impromptu speeches. *The most appropriate mode of delivery for students of public speaking is extemporaneous speaking.* Occasionally, however, manuscript speaking or memorization is desirable.

CHOOSE A DELIVERY STYLE

Manuscript Speaking

President Harry S Truman was a terrible manuscript speaker. He could not read his speeches from a prepared text without speaking too quickly and using poor phrasing. Worse yet, he spoke in a monotone, never varying the pitch of his voice, and he often slurred and mispronounced words. Tied to a prepared text, Truman was a bland, ineffective speaker whose enthusiastic, energetic personality was hidden.[4]

The problems President Truman faced with manuscript speaking are typical. Bringing the printed page to life as you read a speech is difficult for most speakers. Most who try lose their connection with their listeners. They become readers instead of speakers, delivering a speech the audience would be better off reading.

But, sometimes manuscript reading is your best option. If, for example, you are making a controversial or sensitive speech, you may choose to read a carefully crafted statement word for word to avoid the possibility of misstating your position. You may also choose to read from a manuscript when addressing a hostile audience. When you know your listeners are ready—and waiting—to attack your statement, you want to be sure your communication is exact.

Performance Guidelines.   The key to successful manuscript reading is practice and more practice. Focus on expressing yourself naturally and communicating your personality. (You do not want to appear stiff or wooden.) Pronounce words as you would in normal speech and be conscious of speaking too quickly or too slowly. Think about what you want to emphasize and vary the pitch of your voice to avoid a monotone. Glance back and forth between your manuscript and your audience, taking care not to bob your head in the process. Pay special attention to preparing the written text. If you can't read what you've written, you will falter in your delivery.

---

4.   Halford R. Ryan, "Harry S Truman," in Bernard K. Duffy and Halford R. Ryan, eds., p. 402.

Memorizing Your Speech

It is every speaker's nightmare. You are in the middle of a ten-minute speech and you can't remember the next word. Because you memorized the speech (or so you thought), you have nothing to help you through the crisis. This nightmare comes to life on a regular basis in public speaking class. Nervous students who memorize their speeches find themselves without a clue as to what to say next. Even those who spend hours preparing for the presentation may forget everything when they face an audience.

Despite these serious drawbacks, in some instances, you should consider memorization. When you accept an award, deliver a commencement address, or speak regularly for a fee, memorization may be a useful delivery tool.

Memorization enables you to write the exact words you will speak without being forced to read them. It also makes it easier to establish eye contact with your audience and to deliver your speech skillfully.

To minimize the chance that you will forget your speech during the delivery, memorize small sections of your speech at a time. Jack Valente, president of the Motion Picture Association of America and former speechwriter for President Lyndon B. Johnson, explains: "Learn your lines piecemeal, enlarging what you have learned each time, so that eventually you will have captured in your memory cells what you need to say."[5]

Remember, too, that some people can memorize speeches more easily than others and that even experienced, professional speakers may have to work hard at remembering their lines. It may take a professional speaker eight to ten hours of concentrated practice to memorize a speech—an effort worth the time because they earn thousands of dollars in speaking fees. (Many also deliver the same message to various audiences, making this investment in time well worth it.)

But your classroom speech should not be delivered from memorization only.

Extemporaneous Speaking

As ineffective as Harry Truman was at reading his speeches, he was adept at delivering them extemporaneously. Freed from the burden of following a written manuscript, he spoke in a direct, conversational style that revealed his personality. Halford R. Ryan, an expert on presidential rhetoric, explains: During the presidential campaign, "Voters saw and heard a feisty, scrappy, and unpretentious president who talked with them in a . . . down-to-earth fashion and who earnestly and sincerely delivered his political remarks. They liked what they saw and heard."[6]

Performance Guidelines.   In extemporaneous speaking, you prepare the content of your speech with the same care you use when preparing a written report. You choose your purpose, develop your core idea, research your topic, organize your ideas, and

---

5. Jack Valente, *Speak with Confidence—How to Prepare, Learn, and Deliver Speeches* (New York: William Morrow, Inc. 1982), p. 57.
6. Ryan, "Harry S Truman," p. 403.

In extemporaneous speaking, you can glance around the room, looking occasionally at your notes without giving anyone the impression that you are reading your speech.

select the language and presentation style most appropriate to your audience. Then follow these steps:

1. Prepare a full content outline, according to the technique you learned in Chapter 8.

2. Prepare a key-word speaker's outline, also described in Chapter 8, and transfer the outline to 5 × 8, lined index cards. These cards are large enough to accomodate information from your key-word outline, yet small enough to be unobtrusive. You can place them, for example, on the lectern and refer to them as needed during your speech.

3. Place detailed facts, figures, and quotations on separate note cards for easy reference, always remembering your ethical responsibility not to misrepresent facts or opinions that require careful and precise explanations.

Think of your notes as a prompter—instead of the full text—that enables you to keep your ideas in mind without committing every word to memory. Notes also make it possible to maintain eye contact with your listeners. You can glance around the room, looking occasionally at your cards, without giving anyone the impression that you are reading your speech.

Your notes are useless if they cannot be read, so print your words boldly and, when necessary, highlight critical ideas with a colored marker. Remember, too, that your visual aids can serve as notes (see Chapter 11).

Extemporaneous speaking has many advantages. It enables you to maintain a personal connection with your listeners and to respond to their feedback. The most effective public speaking is often described as the speaker's response to the listener's reaction, both of which take shape in the communication transaction. The extemporaneous mode of delivery allows this interaction to occur as you adjust your choice of words and decide what to include—or exclude—in your speech. You can shorten a speech (you may want to follow the advice of the Reverend William Sloane Coffin who said about the length of an effective sermon, "No souls are saved after 20 minutes"[7]) or go into greater detail than you originally planned. The method provides flexibility.

Speaking extemporaneously means that your word choice is fresh. Although you know the intent of your message in advance, you choose your words as you are delivering your speech. The result is a spontaneous, conversational tone that puts you and your audience at ease. This is not to say that as you practice your speech, key words or phrases will not remain with you. On the contrary, the more you practice, the more likely you are to commit a particularly fitting word or phrase to memory.

Extemporaneous speech gives you the freedom to gesture as you would in conversational speech. With both hands free, you can move about and emphasize key points with forceful gestures.

Impromptu Speaking

Not everyone has the ability of African-American nationalist leader Marcus Garvey to speak on the spur of the moment. Dorothy L. Pennington, an expert in the rhetoric of African Americans, describes Garvey's oratorical style:

> He often spoke impromptu, gleaning his topic and remarks from something that had occurred during the earlier portion of the program. For example, in speaking before the conference of the Universal Negro Improvement Association in August 1937, Garvey showed how his theme emerged: "I came as usual without a subject, to pick the same from the surroundings, the environment, and I got one from the singing of the hymn 'Faith of our Fathers.' I shall talk to you on that as a theme for my discourse." This type of adaptation allowed Garvey to tap into the main artery of what an audience was thinking and feeling.[8]

Performance Guidelines.   Impromptu speaking forces you to think on your feet. With no opportunity to prepare a presentation in advance, you must rely on what you know. Here are several suggestions that will help you organize your ideas:

Focus Your Remarks on the Audience.   When called to speak unexpectedly, talk about the people who are present and the accomplishments of the group. You can

---

7. "How to Wow 'Em When You Speak," *Changing Times,* August 1988, p. 30.
8. Dorothy L. Pennington, "Marcus Garvey," in Duffy and Ryan, eds., p. 170.

praise the group leader ("She's done so much to solve the campus parking problem"), the preceding speaker, or the group as a whole.

Talk About the Occasion.   Remind your listeners of the purpose of the meeting. ("We have assembled to protest the rise in parking fines from $10 to $25.")

Use Examples.   Be as concrete as possible. ("I decided to become active in this organization after I heard about a student who was threatened with expulsion from school after accumulating $500 in unpaid parking fines.")

Talk About Something a Previous Speaker Has Said.   Whether you agree or disagree is not the point. The remarks give you a point of departure. ("The suggestion to organize a petition protesting the fine increase is a good one.")

  Starting with the here and now gives you time to think and organize your comments. Keep in mind that as an impromptu speaker, you are not expected to make a polished, professional speech (everyone knows you are not prepared). But you are expected to deliver your remarks in a clear, cogent way.

Don't Try to Say Too Much.   Instead of jumping from point to point in a vague manner, focus on your specific purpose. When you complete the mission of your speech, turn the platform over to another speaker.

Never Apologize.   Your audience is already aware that you are speaking impromptu, apologizing for the informality of your address is unnecessary.

  If you are in business, you may be called upon at the spur of the moment to express your ideas. At a sales meeting, your boss may ask you, without warning, to talk to the sales force about your latest project. With no chance to prepare, you must think as you speak. Though impromptu speaking is difficult, keep in mind that rarely will you be asked to talk about a subject you know nothing about. Start with the assumption that you are being asked to speak because of your expertise.

FIND YOUR BEST VOICE

When Franklin Delano Roosevelt became president, his wife, Eleanor, became a public figure along with him. In her role as first lady, Mrs. Roosevelt was invited to deliver speeches on a variety of issues—a task she willingly accepted. However, despite her willingness, her performance was terrible. She spoke in a falsetto voice that was difficult to listen to, and she used inflections and emphasis indiscriminately. Worse yet, she broke out in giggles for no apparent reason. After Elizabeth Fergeson von Hesse, a New York City speech teacher, heard Mrs. Roosevelt "lose an audience of 5,000 within ten minutes," she wrote to the first lady, telling her that she could help improve her voice. Mrs. Roosevelt agreed to a two-week crash course involving breath and diaphragm control, which eliminated the falsetto; and tone projection and placement, which succeeded in lowering her voice four major tones and giving her vocal depth. Hesse also gave Mrs. Roosevelt a card with the following message:

"The Creator has never as yet made a woman who can talk and laugh at the same time becomingly." The results were dramatic. Her voice became an effective communication tool instead of a barrier that obscured her message.[9]

Hesse was able to help Mrs. Roosevelt improve her voice by focusing on the basics of speech production.

The Physiology of Speech

Two separate but related mechanisms are involved in the production of speech: the voice-producing mechanism and the mechanism of articulation.

Voice Production.   As you can see in Figure 12.1, voice production involves the passage of air from the lungs, through the trachea, and into the larynx. As you relax and contract your diaphragm and abdominal and chest muscles, air is forced from the lungs into the larynx, which is connected above and below by muscles, which move it up and down. Sound is produced during exhalation when the vocal folds inside the larynx come together until there is only a slit between them. Air forced up the trachea and through the vocal folds causes the folds to vibrate and produce a weak sound.

This is not the sound others hear when you speak. The spoken voice first goes through a process of resonance in which qualities are added to the sound as it passes through a series of air chambers in the throat and head. The principal resonators of the voice are the upper part of the larynx, the throat, the nasal cavities, and the mouth. As the sounds produced by the vocal folds pass through these cavities, they are amplified and modified to produce the familiar qualities of your speaking voice. The role of these chambers can be understood by focusing on the role of the mouth to produce vowel sounds. As the mouth opens and closes, the size and shape of the oral cavity changes, and the vowel sound produced changes along with it. The sound of your vowels is determined, in part, by the size and functioning of these resonators.

Articulation.   The tongue, teeth, lips, jaw, and the hard and soft palates modify the resonated sound, enabling us to articulate it in the form of distinct speech. Through the movement of these articulators of speech, we change the size and shape of the oral cavity for the production of specific consonants and vowels. The quality of the spoken voice produced by these physiological mechanisms is expressed in terms of several different vocal characteristics that add variety to speech.

Loudness

If your audience cannot hear you, your speech serves little purpose. The loudness of your voice is controlled by how forcefully air is expelled through the trachea onto the vocal folds. This exhalation is controlled by the contraction of the abdominal

---

9.   Beth M. Waggenspack, "Anna Eleanor Roosevelt," in Bernard K. Duffy and Halford R. Ryan, eds., p. 339.

muscles. The more forcefully you use these muscles to exhale, the greater the force of the air, and the louder your voice.

Don't mistake projection for shouting. Shouting involves forcing the voice from the vocal folds, which is irritating to the folds, instead of projecting the sound from the abdominal area. When you have to be heard, increase the force of your abdominal exhalation to carry your voice. Straining at the throat will only make you hoarse. Instead, work on your posture and diaphragm.

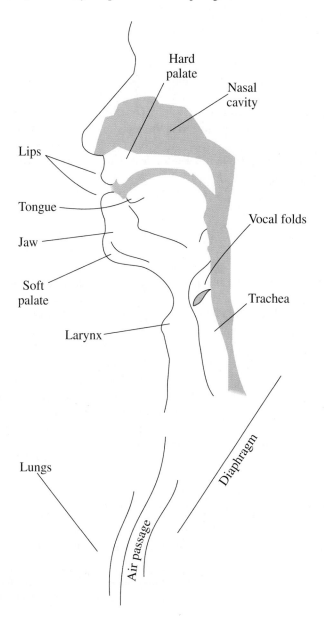

FIGURE 12.1
Voice production.

Improve your Posture.   Whether you are sitting or standing, poor posture limits the effect of abdominal breathing on voice production. When your body is erect, your lungs have more room to expand, making correct breathing easier. To improve your posture, follow the traditional advice to keep your chest up and your stomach in and to distribute your weight evenly.

Breathe From Your Diaphragm.   Sounds that originate in the diaphragm are more deeply supported than those originating in the throat.

Pitch

Pitch refers to your vocal range or key, the highness and lowness of your voice produced by the tightening and loosening of your vocal folds. Pitch is a problem when your voice is too high pitched (in men a high-pitched voice sounds childish and in women it sounds screechy) or when it is monotonous. When you don't vary the pitch of your voice, you risk putting your listeners to sleep. Variety adds interest to your presentation.

The range of most people's voices is less than two octaves. Instead of using a monotone, try to add variety by using your voice potential. To add color, lower the pitch of a word or phrase your want to emphasize. Resist the temptation to raise your voice at key points.

Rate

When Franklin Delano Roosevelt spoke to the nation in his fireside chats and addresses, he spoke in a slow, deliberate manner to communicate trust, authority, and control. Other presidents were known by their rate of speech. John F. Kennedy spoke so quickly that his listeners could hardly keep up, while Lyndon B. Johnson took so much time expressing his thoughts that he put his listeners to sleep.

Most of us speak between 120 and 160 words per minute. Speech tension may affect your normal pattern. Under the pressure of giving a speech, you may find yourself speeding up ("The faster I talk, the faster I'll finish") or slowing down ("If I don't take my time, no one will be able to follow me"). Rate is also affected by delivery style. If you read a manuscript rather than speak extemporaneously, you may find yourself running a verbal road race. It was no accident that Lyndon Johnson spoke so slowly. Like many other southerners (Johnson was from Texas), he had the tendency to take his time when he spoke. Northerners, in contrast, tend to speak at a much faster pace.

Follow these suggestions to adjust your rate of speech to your best advantage.

1. Choose a rate appropriate for the ideas being expressed and for the rhetorical setting. For example, it makes sense for a sportscaster announcing a basketball game to speak faster than a sportscaster at a golf match.

2. Vary your rate of speech to express different thoughts and feelings. You may want to speak slowly to emphasize an important point or to

communicate a serious or somber mood. A faster pace is appropriate when you are telling your audience something it already knows (many speeches include background information that sets the scene) or to express surprise, happiness, or fear. Use pauses to change the pace and add verbal variety.

3. Use a tape recorder to monitor your rate of speech while you read aloud a magazine article. Pay special attention to grouping words into phrases and to slowing down and speeding up at appropriate points. Play your speech back, then adjust your phrasing for a more effective delivery.

Pauses

Some speakers talk nonstop until, literally, they are out of breath. Others pause every three or four words in a kind of nervous verbal chop. Still others, particularly those who read their speeches, pause at the wrong times—perhaps in the middle of an important idea—making it difficult for their listeners to follow.

Pauses can get you into trouble, but they also can add power and control to your speech if used effectively. They can communicate self-confidence; they deliver the nonverbal message that you are relaxed enough to stop talking for a moment. Moreover, they help listeners digest what you are saying and anticipate what you will say next. A significant pause also helps you move from one topic to the next without actually telling your listeners what you are doing. Finally, they signal, *pay attention.* (This is especially true for long pauses lasting two or three seconds.) According to Don Hewitt, producer of "60 Minutes," "It's the intonation, the pauses, that tell the story. They are as important to us as commas and periods are to *The New York Times.*"[10]

Pauses add color, expression, and feeling to a speech. They should be used deliberately to achieve a desired effect. Here are a few suggestions:

1. Pause for a moment when you introduce a new idea or term to give your listeners time to absorb what you are saying.

2. Tie your pauses to verbal phrasing. To a speaker, a phrase has a different meaning than it does to a writer. It is a unit you speak in one breath in order to express a single idea.

   Each pause tells your listeners you are moving from one thought to the next. The effect is easy-to-follow short phrases. Here, for example, is how the opening lines of Abraham Lincoln's Gettysburg Address might be phrased:

   > Fourscore and seven years ago (*breath*)
   > Our Fathers brought forth on this continent (*breath*)
   > A new nation (*breath*)
   > Conceived in liberty (*breath*)
   > And dedicated to the proposition (*breath*)
   > That all men are created equal.[11]

---

10. Leon Fletcher, "Polishing Your Silent Languages," *The Toastmaster* (March 1990): 15.
11. Ibid.

3. Extend your pauses to two or three seconds when displaying a visual. This tactic enables your audience to read the information on the visual without missing your next thought. It is important to pause *after* the display, not before it.

Emphasis

Think about how many ways you can say "Come in." Depending on how they are said and how they are accented by nonverbal behavior, these words can be

1. A friendly invitation (from one friend to another)
2. A command (from a supervisor to an employee)
3. An angry growl (from a mother with a headache to her teenage son who has already interrupted her five times)
4. A nondescript response (to a knock at your office door)

These changes give meaning to a word or phrase. By singling out a few words for special attention, you add color to your speech and avoid monotony. Emphasis can be achieved by using these techniques and by adding emotion:

⌘ *Changing the volume of your speech.* Whether you choose to speak louder or more quietly, you draw attention to your speech through contrast. Sometimes, a quieter approach is often a more effective attention-grabber.

⌘ *Changing the pitch of your voice.* When you speak in a monotone, you tell your listeners you have nothing to emphasize. When you vary the pitch of your voice, you let them know that what you are saying is important.

⌘ *Changing the rate at which you speak and pause.* A change of pace—speeding up or slowing down your speech—draws attention to what will come next: Pausing can do the same.

⌘ *Adding emotion.* Emphasis comes naturally when you speak from the heart. When you have deep feelings about a subject—drug abuse, for example, or the need to protect the environment from pollution—you will express your feelings emphatically. Anything other than an impassioned delivery may seem inadequate.

You can practice adding emphasis to your speech by choosing sections of a famous speech and reading them aloud. The first time you read the speech, don't emphasize anything. Read it in a monotone, just as you would a telephone book. It's hard to get involved, isn't it? Now underscore the words or phrases that, if emphasized, would add meaning to the speech. Then read the speech a second time, adding the emphasis and emotion you think appropriate. You may find that the words seem to take a life of their own as they demand attention.

Padding

There is a difference between a meaningful pause and padding. While pauses work for you, padding can drive your listeners to distraction. Padding consists of annoying verbal tics that can ruin a speech. These include: "you know," "uh," "I believe," "that is," "so," "okay and uh," and "now." These are verbal debris, adding nothing to the content of your speech.

Your first step in eliminating padding is to become aware of the problem. (Many people don't realize they use these fillers.) You can start by recording your own phone conversation on a tape recorder. It is a good idea to record a business conversation rather than a conversation with friends because you are likely to experience some degree of anxiety during a speech and business conversations tend to be more formal. If you find you pad your natural speech, write the offending expression or expressions on a sticker and place it near the phone to act as a reminder during casual conversation. You can use stickers as well when you are practicing a speech. With practice, you will unlearn the annoying verbal habits.

You can also force yourself to be silent for a second or two after completing a phrase or other unit of thought. Because padding indicates, in part, a discomfort with silence, this approach will help you realize that pauses are an acceptable part of communication.

Padding can also take nonverbal forms. Giggling (remember Mrs. Roosevelt), throat clearing, and lip smacking serve the same function for the speaker as their verbal counterparts and are as annoying to the audience. To rid yourself of these habits, place boldfaced stickers, saying simply GIGGLE, or THROAT, or LIPS, in visible places when you practice your speech. Then monitor your performance with a tape recorder.

Regional Dialects

"Everybody says words different," said Ivy. "Arkansas folks says 'em different, and Oklahomy folks says 'em different. And we seen a lady from Massachusetts, an' she said 'em differentest of all. Couldn't hardly make out what she was sayin'."
John Steinbeck, *The Grapes of Wrath*

The mosaic that is U.S. culture brings with it a myriad of pronunciations for the same words. Even words as common as "yes," "aunt," and "third" are pronounced in many different ways depending on the part of the country you live in. Although the three principal speech patterns in the United States are tied to distinct regions of the country, there are many local variations:

   I. Eastern speech pattern
      A. Local variations
         1. New England
         2. New York City, Jersey City, Hoboken, etc.

        3. Pennsylvania
           a. Philadelphia
           b. Pennsylvania Dutch

  II.   Southern speech pattern
     A. Local variations
        1. Louisiana
        2. Sections of Delaware, Maryland, and Virginia
        3. East Texas
        4. Tidewater, including Southeastern Virginia, eastern North Carolina, and most of the coast of South Carolina.

  III.   Middle and Far West speech pattern (including upstate New York)[12]

Racial, ethnic, educational, and socioeconomic factors also may influence the way words are pronounced. Thus, African-Americans reared in the inner city may pronounce words differently from whites reared in suburbia. Polish-Americans from Chicago, Mexican-Americans from Los Angeles, and German-Americans from Milwaukee each have distinctive patterns of pronounciation.

Do you try to change a regional dialect? Not if you are easily understood. Dialect only becomes an issue when it stands in the way of communication, when your listeners do not understand you because of the way you speak. For most of us, this question is moot. After watching network television from the time we were children, we tend to talk like Tom Brokaw, Connie Chung, Bernard Shaw, and other notable newscasters. Because of television, regional dialects are losing their hold on the American tongue and being replaced by a "standard" dialect, similar to midwestern speech.

Sometimes speakers use regional dialects to endear themselves to their audiences—to be perceived as friends of the "common people." Alfred E. Smith, governor of New York during the 1920s, spoke with a New York East Side accent, which New Yorkers seemed to love. He said "rad-dio" for "radio," "foist" for "first," and "thoid" for "third." However, as professor of speech communication G. Jack Gravlee points out, the use of this distinctive dialect may have alienated him from people in other parts of the country. (Smith ran unsuccessfully for president in 1928.)[13]

Articulation and Pronunciation Problems

Although some pronunciation patterns stem from regional dialects, others are the result of mistakes in articulation and pronunciation.

---

12.   Dorothy Sarnoff, *Speech Can Change Your Life* (New York: 1970), pp. 89–90.
13.   G. Jack Gravlee, "Alfred Emanuel Smith," in Bernard K. Duffy and Halford R. Ryan, eds., *American Orators of the Twentieth Century: Critical Studies and Sources* (New York: Greenwood Press, 1987), p. 377.

Articulation Problems.   Articulation problems are failures to produce the sounds of words properly. Here are several examples:

Word or Phrase	How It Sounds When Spoken
let me	lemme
government	govmin
width	with
ask	ax
Saturday	Saddy
ought to	otta
how are you	harya

Some articulation problems are linked to regional dialects. In New York and New England, the "r" sound is added to many words. Thus, "idea" becomes "idear," "soda" becomes "soder," and so on. Many others, however, are the result of slurred sounds, dropped word endings, and sound substitutions.

The more formal the situation, the more our articulation needs to be precise. The more casual and relaxed we are, the more likely we are to be relaxed in our speech. Thus, when you are giving a speech in front of an audience, the sloppy or careless pronunciation patterns you use with your friends and family should not find their way into your presentation.

Mispronunciation.   In contrast to articulation problems, mispronunciation is the result of not knowing how to say a word and, as a result, *always* saying it the wrong way. Here are a few examples:

Word	Mispronunciation
mumbling	mumbuling
mischievous	mischeevious
extraordinary	extra-ordinary
nuclear	nucular
often	off-ten
library	libery
athletic	althaletic

Like problems with articulation, problems with pronunciation can leave listeners with an unfortunate impression of your abilities and may prevent them from hearing your message.

Start by becoming aware of your speech patterns. Tape record your voice and try to identify trouble spots. Ask a friend, relative, coworker, or classmate to critique your pronunciation. If you have questions about the way you are pronouncing a word, check the dictionary. Then practice the correct pronunciation. Then practice again. Read newspaper or magazine articles aloud several times a week, trying to pronounce each word with precision. Repeat this exercise over several months. If you still have trouble, consider working with a speech coach.

MASTERING THE ART OF BODY LANGUAGE

Appearance is no substitute for substance at the speaker's lectern. But the way you gesture, move, look at people, and dress say a great deal about you. More important, these elements leave a lasting impression that affects the speaker–audience connection. Although mastering the art of nonverbal communication will not guarantee your speaking success, it will help you convince your audience to pay attention.

Learn the Art of the Natural Gesture

Irene, an older student who had returned to school after five years of working for the loan department of a bank, gave a speech every one of her listeners wanted to hear. Her topic: how recent college graduates abuse credit cards and wind up owing thousands of dollars. She began:

> When you receive your first credit card, think of it as a loaded gun. If you don't use it properly you may wind up killing your credit for up to ten years.
>
> That means that no one will loan you money to buy a car, a VCR, or a house. You may not get the job you want because your credit is bad (prospective employers check applicants' credit ratings). And you'll go through a lot of torment while this is going on.
>
> Take my word for it. I've seen it happen dozens of times to people just like you.

Although Irene's message was effective, her delivery was stiff and uncomfortable. She grasped the lectern for dear life, as if she were afraid to move from her spot. She was a talking statue, and her listeners responded by becoming restless and uncomfortable themselves. During the post-speech criticism, one audience member explained what he was feeling: "You looked so wooden that I had trouble listening to what you were saying, which is amazing since I'm already in credit card trouble."

Irene's problem was a lack of gestures and body movement, which her audience could not ignore despite the inherent interest of her speech. Gestures tell an audience that you're comfortable and self-confident. As an outlet for nervous energy, they actually help you feel more at ease. Gestures encourage an enthusiastic presentation: If you put your body into your speech through movement and gestures, it is difficult to present a stilted speech. Gestures also have a positive effect on breathing, helping you relax the muscles that affect the quality of the voice.

Gestures are especially important when you are speaking to a large audience. People in the back rows may not be able to see the changes in your facial expressions, and gestures may be their only way of seeing your involvement with your speech.

Performance Suggestions.   Here are some suggestions for gesturing as you speak:

1. Try to make every gesture natural, appropriate, and consistent both with the ideas in the message and your own personality. If you are giving an impassioned plea to raise money for cancer research, gestures may seem more natural than if you are lecturing on the problems banks are having with loans to underdeveloped countries.

2. Stand straight with your arms bent at the waist and your hands relaxed, at the "ready" position. It is important not to clasp your hands together (this makes gesturing impossible except if you're willing to raise both hands at once); hug your body, as if you are trying to protect yourself from assault; hang your hands together at the crotch (another protective position); lock your hands behind your back, a position that may encourage you to rock back and forth; or grasp and lean into the lectern.

3. Pay attention to the position of your elbows. If they hang stiffly at your sides, your gestures will look shortened and artificial. To move your hands and forearms freely, make sure there's plenty of room between your elbows and your body.

You can tell if your gestures are effective by checking where your listeners are looking. If they are focusing on the movement of your arms and hands instead of your face, your gestures are a distraction rather than a help. If this situation occurs, stop gesturing or use only a few gestures during the rest of your speech. For the next speaking occasion, practice making your gestures appear more natural. Ask a friend or colleague to comment on your movement and gestures. Gestures should not draw attention to themselves and away from the ideas.

Deliver your speech in a spontaneous and conversational manner that puts both you and your audience at ease.

F O C U S   O N   R E S E A R C H

CAN DELIVERY MAKE A DIFFERENCE IN CREDIBILITY AND PERSUASION?

The role of *delivery* in public speaking has been given varied importance since antiquity, so D. F. Gunderson and Robert Hopper conducted a study to find out just how important delivery really is. Their research confirms that a speaker's delivery remains important in the perception of the audience but not as important as the content of the speech.[14] We all may, at one time or another, patiently concentrate on the content of a message being presented with lackluster delivery. We can also agree that an appropriately animated delivery fitting an occasion and a persuasive purpose is likely to help us listen more easily to the ideas of a speech presented to us. To investigate factors of delivery in relationship to credibility and persuasiveness, another team of researchers, Judee Burgoon, Thomas Birk, and Michael Pfau, more recently conducted research on nonverbal behaviors in public speaking.[15]

The researchers admit at the onset of their report that most studies of persuasion that include nonverbal communication usually relegate them to second-class status. However, the researchers argue that to consider nonverbal elements of speech as inconsequential is premature. The researchers were interested in looking at a variety of delivery factors in relation to the involvement listeners experienced in perceiving the persuader as well as the speech, the power or potency attributed to the speaker in terms of their perception of nonverbal behaviors, and the

arousal, or physiological and physical activity of the speaker as perceived by the audience. The research design linked these dimensions to constituents of credibility including the speaker's character, competence, composure, sociability, and dynamism. The dimensions also were viewed in relation to persuasiveness. The nonverbal behaviors considered in the study included variations in vocal projection related to fluency (repetitions, nonfluencies, sentence changes, incompletions, and stuttering), pleasantness (pitch variety, clarity, and voice quality), and potency (pitch, volume, rate, intensity). Weak intercorrelations of the vocal cues resulted in the researchers forming three composites: (1) fluency, voice quality, (2) clarity pleasantness, and (3) loudness/ intensity.

They also examined eye contact, facial expression, gestures, and body tension as well as other movements. Sixty undergraduate speakers (eighteen men and forty-two women) participated in five randomly selected sections of an introductory speech communication course. Listeners heard speakers deliver a required persuasive speech and they completed credibility and persuasiveness scales as part of the research procedures.

According to the findings: The sets of nonverbal behaviors we associate with a speaker's delivery can have substantial impact on source credibility and speaker persuasiveness. Their impact in terms of the perceptions of listeners can be understood more

---

14.   D. F. Gunderson and Robert Hopper, "Relationships Between Speech Delivery and Speech Effectiveness," *Communication Monographs* XLIII (June, 1976), 158–165.

15.   Judee K. Burgoon, Thomas Birk, and Michael Pfau, "Nonverbal Behaviors, Persuasion, and Credibility," *Human Communication Research* 17 (Fall, 1990), 140–169.

simply by grouping nonverbal behaviors according to the perceptions listeners experience. For example, nonverbal behaviors appropriate for creating pleasantness and immediacy contributed to the audience's perception of a speaker's competence, composure, sociability, and character. Fluency and pitch variety played a larger role in competence and composure judgments than did eye contact, facial expressions, or body movement, but the reverse was true for sociability and character judgments. Facial pleasantness affected perceptions of competence and composure, while vocal pleasantness affected sociability and pitch affected character. Essentially, the study suggests that the voice, gestures, and movement that connote pleasantness and immediacy foster credibility of the speaker in the eyes of the audience. Cues associated with a powerful voice apparently did not increase credibility, but other nonverbal cues such as eye contact and assertive gestures related positively to competence, composure, character, and sociability judgments.

The study supports the belief that animated nonverbal display supported by well managed visual directness and body language with minimal distracting cues can promote the speaker's credibility. Furthermore, the researchers found that the nonverbal behaviors they studied were associated with greater persuasiveness. Vocal pleasantness, physical relaxation, direct eye contact, and managed animated gestures had positive impact. Only vocal potency (rate, pitch, volume, variety) failed to affect persuasiveness. The overall result of this research confirms that indeed factors in delivery can contribute significantly to effectiveness in persuasion. The researchers suggest that "credibility and persuasiveness may be simultaneous outcomes, both of which are directly influenced by nonverbal variables."

Don't Be Afraid to Move

Remember Irene's second problem? She appeared glued to the lectern. After a while, her listeners got tired of watching her.

Irene's mistake is typical. Like many speakers, she failed to realize that an active speaker can encourage an active response from an audience, but an immobile speaker can leave listeners listless. When you move from one place to another while you speak your listeners are forced to keep their eyes on you, an involving activity in itself. Movement has the additional advantage of helping to reduce your nervous energy.

Performance Suggestions.   Here are some suggestions for effective movement:

1. Be natural, relaxed, and reasonable. Don't pace back and forth like a caged lion or make small darting movements that return you to the safety of the lectern.

2. Tie your movements to your use of visual aids. Walk over to the visual as you are presenting it and point to its relevant parts. Walk back to the lectern when you are through.

3. Circulate among your listeners (Phil Donahue does it), walking through the aisles as you talk. You'll involve your audience as you ease your own tension. In a small room, you can walk around without a microphone. In a large room, you'll need the help of a wireless electronic mike.

The Eyes Have It

No other aspect of nonverbal behavior is as important as eye contact—the connection you form with listeners through your gaze. Strong eye contact tells them:

⌘ You are confident.

⌘ You are open and honest—a person to be trusted.

⌘ You are a person of conviction.

⌘ You care what your listeners are thinking and you are eager for their feedback.

⌘ You want them to understand you.

When your eye contact is poor, you send these messages:

⌘ You are uncomfortable and nervous.

⌘ You are hostile. Your averted gaze sets you apart from your audience.

⌘ You have something to hide.

⌘ You have no interest in how your audience is responding.

When you turn on the nightly news, you see the anchor looking straight at you. After a while, as a result of TV, eye-to-eye contact is what you expect from every speaker; it is the norm. When a speaker looks away, we sense that something is wrong.

Performance Suggestions. Here are some suggestions for improving eye contact during a speech:

1. Don't keep your eyes glued to your notes.

2. Don't look just above the heads of your listeners. Although this advice is often given to speakers, it will be obvious to everyone that you are gazing into the air.

3. You will feel more comfortable during your presentation if you choose to look at people who are giving you positive feedback. There is no mistaking a friendly, sympathetic, or interested face.

4. Avoid the tendency to dart your eyes around the room or to sweep the room with your eyes. Instead, try to hold eye contact with a single person for a single thought. (This may be measured in a phrase or a sentence.)

5. Distribute your gaze evenly around the room. In your mind, divide the audience into several physical sectors. (The larger the room the greater the number of sectors you will need.) Then focus on a different person in each sector, rotating your gaze among the people and the sectors as you speak.

The Unspoken Language of Clothes

In a 1989 summit between Soviet President Mikhail Gorbachev and Chinese leader Deng Xiaoping, Gorbachev made a nearly fatal blunder: He wore a pair of beige loafers with his formal suit, a choice that offended the Chinese who believed that "holiday shoes" should not be worn on such a special occasion.

S P E A K   E A S Y

HOW TO HANDLE A QUESTION-AND-ANSWER PERIOD

With many speakers concluding their presentations by asking the audience for questions, it is important to know how to handle yourself in a question-and-answer period. Here are some suggestions.

1. Even though you have no way of knowing what will be asked, you can *anticipate* certain questions and prepare for them in advance. Keep in mind that most questions will be linked to audience concerns. That is, if you are an architect talking to a group of veterinarians, you may be questioned about designing office waiting rooms that are comfortable for pets. If you are giving the same speech to a group of school administrators, the questions are likely to focus on classroom design.

2. Listen carefully to questions so that you will correctly interpret the questioners' intent. If you are unsure about a question, ask for clarification.

3. Take questions from all parts of the room. If you repeatedly take questions from the front, for example, the rest of your audience will feel ignored.

4. Be conscious of your nonverbal behavior. Be composed and listen attentively—even if the question is difficult. Never show your nervousness—by rocking back and forth, for example, or wringing your hands. As you start your response, establish eye contact with the questioner. Then generalize the response to the entire audience by looking at other faces.

5. Repeat all positive questions so that everyone can hear them. Repetition will reinforce the positive tone of the questions and give you time to phrase your response.

6. When you are asked a loaded question (The language of the question gives away the intent; terms like "greed," "rip-off," "scandal," and "health hazard" are sure signs of trouble), try to defuse the confrontation. Rephrase the question, using less inflammatory language. For example, if you are asked, "Considering that your job as health commissioner is to head off a health emergency, how could you allow the dumping of tons of toxic waste in our community?", rephrase the question like this: "The gentleman has asked about the health department's policy in handling the dumping of toxic wastes. Well, I believe . . ." Your change in word choice helps neutralize the venom of the original question. Taking time as you answer helps as does pausing and remaining calm. Don't let yourself get pulled into an emotional, heated argument.

7. When you are asked a question you can't answer, admit it with an honest "I don't know." Everyone realizes that the question-and-answer period is impromptu, so you usually aren't penalized for honest ignorance. Whenever possible, promise to find out the information and get back to the questioner. This pledge will increase your credibility.

8. Don't feel pressed to answer questions. You may have reasons not to answer a question (the information is confidential; you believe it is best answered by someone else; the question is not relevant to your speech). In these cases, be direct ("I think Tom would be better equipped to answer that question," or "I'll be glad to answer

that question when I talk about that topic next week") or use finesse, ("You ask me what I think about the job our new college president is doing. Well, the demands of the job are such that more time is needed before judgment can be passed. Remember, she's only held the position six weeks").

9. Don't get bogged down in minutiae. When you encounter a questioner who quibbles with every fact and figure you mention, don't waste too much time trying to prove your point. Deal with the question quickly by suggesting a private conversation after the speech is over. If you take too much of the group's time dealing with minor points, you will lose the rest of your audience.

10. Prepare for questions through practice. Answer the questions you anticipate by talking into a tape recorder. Then analyze and improve your responses until they satisfy you.

It is important to view the question-and-answer period as an opportunity to clear up uncertainty andanswer objections. By keeping the specific purpose of your speech in mind, you will be reinforcing your message if you prepare to answer probable questions at the close of your formal presentation.

General Myrna Williamson offers some important advice about the question-and-answer period: "Let's say I am doing a forty-five minute presentation and I know that the ending I intend to use is a four-minute conclusion. I intend to conclude by summarizing my main ideas and end with an illustration along with my final thought. If I have a question-and-answer period I will build it into my planning and time. This means I take questions before my planned conclusion. I will never allow my speech to end with questions and answers. I have to leave my audience with my final thought because I do not want the audience to walk out with someone else's agenda on their minds. They will walk out after my presentation with my agenda on their minds."[16]

Your choice of shoes or suits or dresses should not isolate you from your listeners. Your clothes should make you look like you fit into the group. As rhetorical theorist Kenneth Burke reminds us, your clothes make a rhetorical statement of their own by contributing to your spoken message.[17]

Your appearance should always be in harmony with your message. Speech communication professor Leon Fletcher describes a city council meeting addressed by college students pleading for a clean-up of the local beaches. Although the speeches were clearly organized, well supported, and effectively presented, the unkempt physical appearance of the speakers conflicted with their message. They wore torn, filthy jeans and T-shirts and sloppy sandals. Their hair was long and ungroomed. The city council decided to take no action. Several months later, the same issue was brought before the council by a second group of students, all of whom wore ties and sport jackets—symbols of the neatness they wanted for the beaches. This time the proposal was accepted.[18]

16.   Interview with General Myrna Williamson, April 12, 1993.
17.   Kenneth Burke, *A Rhetoric of Motives* (Berkeley, CA: University of California Press, 1969), p. 119.
18.   Leon Fletcher, "Polishing Your Silent Languages," p. 14.

Although no one would tell you that wearing a certain suit or dress will make your listeners agree with your point of view, the image you create is undoubtedly important. Communication theorist Mark Knapp explains: "Although we are not able at this time to specify the exact influence of each aspect of one's physical appearance in any given social situation, it seems fair to conclude that [physical appearance] may be profoundly important in some situations."[19]

SUMMARY

The four methods of speech delivery are manuscript speaking, memorization, extemporaneous speaking, and impromtu speaking. We focus in this text on extemporaneous speaking, a method in which you prepare the content of your speech in advance, but speak from a key-word outline. Impromptu speaking requires that you speak without preparation.

The physiology of speech involves the mechanisms of voice production and articulation. Voice quality is determined by volume, pitch, rate, pausing, emphasis, padding (or annoying verbal tics that obstruct communication), and regional dialects. The quality of your voice is affected by patterns of articulation and mispronunciation.

Nonverbal behavior is an important part of delivery. Your gestures and movement affect your presentation, as does eye contact and the clothing you wear.

QUESTIONS FOR STUDY AND DISCUSSION

1. Why is extemporaneous speaking the most appropriate form of delivery? Under what circumstances is manuscript reading or memorization appropriate?
2. What steps can you take to improve the quality of your speaking voice?
3. How do your movements, gestures, eye contact, and clothing influence your relationship with your audience and the communication of your message?

ACTIVITIES

1. Select a film or video that contains a complete speech. With your classmates study the speaker's delivery style, examining strengths and weaknesses.
2. Prepare a two- to three-page report on an effective public speaker's delivery style (Mario Cuomo, Ronald Reagan, Barbara Jordan, and Jesse Jackson are four possibilities). Assess how the speaker's delivery contributes to or diminishes his or her power as a speaker.
3. Record several of your own speeches and make a written inventory of your strengths and weaknesses. Then list what you must do to improve your delivery.
4. Write twenty to thirty different topics on folded pieces of paper and place the papers in a bowl. With three or four other speakers, each speaker then pulls a topic from the bowl and delivers an impromptu speech lasting two to three minutes. Using the suggestions in this text, try to make your presentation as clear, organized, and fluent as possible.

---

19. Mark Knapp, "The Field of Nonverbal Communication: An Overview," *On Speech Communication*, Charles J. Stewart, ed. (New York: Holt, Rinehart, and Winston, 1972), p. 65.

"I only ask for information."

Charles Dickens

SPEAKING

TO

INFORM

As a young, professional single parent with a suburban home, Fran Williams is among the millions who must take precautions against burglary. Breaking and entering is a crime often perpetrated on the homes of individuals whose children are at school while they are at work during the day. Les McCreary is a law enforcement officer who devotes much of his evening time to speaking to neighborhood groups. He informs his listeners about what steps they can take to discourage burglary. Fran Williams was among the listeners gathered at a Parents Without Partners meeting to learn from Officer McCreary. Following is a sample of what they were told:

> The third point I want you to think about is the burglar in the neighborhood wants to break into a home where she or he can easily slip in without being noticed. The thief who visits a neighborhood such as the one where we are gathered this evening prefers to identify homes that have hidden access points that have been covered with lots of large shrubs and bushes. Certainly I suspect you all take pride in your landscaping and I am not suggesting you go home tonight and determine whether or not you should tear it out. You do need to know and think about whether or not your trees and bushes surrounding the outside of your homes are likely to offer a thief an opportunity to break into your house without being seen by anyone. Then determine whether or not appropriate trimming and lighting can lessen this opportunity. Earlier in my presentation I spoke about lighting your homes in the evening and I want to underscore the importance well-placed outdoor lighting can play in discouraging a burglar from entering your home.

According to Officer McCreary, responses to his presentations have been highly favorable and statistical reports show a decrease in the overall number of burglaries in communities he has addressed. Although his specific purpose for speaking is to inform his audiences, his efforts have had persuasive impact as well. Skeptical or ambivalent listeners have changed their attitudes after listening to one of his speeches. Most of his listeners use the information from Officer McCreary as knowledge about suburban security measures. Others find themselves persuaded that they need to take this problem seriously and to act on their need for improved home security.

PURPOSES OF THE INFORMATIVE SPEECH

Les McCreary's speeches are in demand by neighborhood audiences not only because they are timely and address a very important concern shared by homeowners, but also because his presentations are accurate, clear, meaningful, and memorable.

Accuracy: Informative speakers must be sure their facts are correct and current and their presentations fair. You cannot consider your speech objective if it takes a biased point of view or has a hidden persuasive agenda.

Clarity: For communication to take place, your listeners must be able to understand your information *at their level of knowledge.* The most effective informative speakers never assume knowledge, but find out, through audience assessment, how much is known before they begin speaking.

Meaningful: Even if a speech is accurate and clear, it may leave the audience behind if the speaker makes no attempt to relate the material to the interests, needs, and concerns of the audience. A meaningful informative speech focuses on what matters to the audience as well as on what matters to the speaker.

Memorable: The best informative speeches are those that remain with the audience. Your goal is to pass on information and to have your listeners remember it. Speakers who are enthusiastic, genuine, and creative and who can communicate their excitement to their listeners deliver memorable speeches.

Informative speaking involves sharing your own specialized knowledge about a subject with others. Just as Officer McCreary wants his audience to learn about home safety, all informative speakers are motivated by the desire to help listeners understand facts and their perspective on these facts.

Whether you are a nurse conducting CPR training for new parents at the local community center, a museum curator delivering a speech on impressionist art, or an auto repair manager lecturing to workers on the implications of a recent manufacturer's recall notice, when you deliver an informative speech you share Les McCreary's goals to communicate information and ideas in a way your audience will understand and remember.

When you deliver an informative speech, your intent is to enlighten your audience—to increase understanding or awareness and, perhaps, create a new perspective. Actions may be involved, but not necessarily actions related to choice. In contrast, when you deliver a persuasive speech, your intent is to move your audience to agree with your point of view—to change attitudes or beliefs, or to bring about a specific, desired action (see Chapter Fourteen). In theory, these two forms of rhetoric generally are distinct. In practice, the lines between them are often blurred.

THE FINE LINE BETWEEN INFORMATIVE AND PERSUASIVE SPEAKING

For example, if during an informative speech on the results of calling off a marriage, you suggest to the engaged couples in your audience that safeguards may have to be taken to prevent emotional or financial damage, you are implicitly being persuasive. If you suggest to the men in your audience that they obtain a written statement from their fiancées pledging the return of the engagement ring if the relationship ends, you have crossed the line between information and persuasion.

The key to informative speaking is intent. If your goal is to expand understanding, your speech is informational. If in the process you also want your audience to share or agree with your point of view, you may also be persuasive. Many times informational speeches also persuade. In describing the different kinds of assault rifles available to criminals, you may persuade your audience to support measures for stricter gun control. Some of your listeners may even write to Congress while others may send contributions to lobbying organizations that promote the passage of stricter handgun control legislation. Although your speech brought about these changes, it is still informational—because your intent is educational.

Some communication scholars assert that because all speeches start with a point of view, the line between persuasion and information is arbitrary, and that in communication, the potential for persuasion is inevitable. For example, the fact that you choose to talk about such an emotionally loaded subject as assault rifles implies that your intent is to convince your listeners of the need to pressure Congress for legislative change. For our purposes, we will tie the nature of persuasion and information to speaker intent and thus make the traditional distinction between speeches to inform and speeches to persuade.

To make sure your speech is informational rather than persuasive, start with a clear specific purpose signifying your intent. Here is an effective specific purpose for an informative speech:

> To inform my audience about the downfall of the Wall Street junk bond firm, Drexel Burnham Lambert.

Compare this statement with the following:

> To inform my audience that Drexel Burnham Lambert was the symbol of Wall Street greed, power, and corruption that marked the decade of the 1980s.

While the intent of the first statement is informational, the intent of the second is persuasion. The second statement should be redrafted, replacing the word "inform" with the word "persuade."

TYPES OF INFORMATIVE SPEECHES

The three types of informative speeches are: speeches of description, speeches of demonstration, and speeches of explanation.

Speeches of Description

A speech describing the circus to a group of youngsters is a speech of description as is a speech describing the effects of an earthquake or a speech describing the buying habits of teenagers. Speeches of description are speeches that paint a clear picture of an event, person, object, place, situation, or concept. The goal is to create images in the minds of listeners about your topic or to describe a concept in concrete detail. Here, for example, is a section of a speech describing the 1990 reenactment of the 1965 civil rights march on Selma, Alabama. We begin with the specific purpose and core idea:

> *Specific purpose.* To inform my audience of the 1990 and 1965 civil rights marches on Selma, Alabama.

> *Core idea.* Civil rights marchers returned to Selma, Alabama, in 1990 to commemorate the violence-marred march twenty-five years earlier.
>
> Five thousand civil rights marchers came together in Selma, Alabama, to walk slowly across the Edmund Pettus Bridge. The year was 1990 and the reason for the march was to commemorate the brutal and violent march that took place in Selma twenty-five years earlier. The first march awakened the country to the need to protect the civil liberties of African-Americans, but this one was a time of celebration and rededication to the cause of civil rights.

The 1990 march was peaceful. Only sound effects reminded participants of the billy club-wielding state troopers, of the screams and clomping horse hoofs, of the beatings and the inhumanity.[1]

In the following example, the speaker describes the buying power of teenagers:

There are roughly 13.4 million 12- to-15 year-olds in this country, a fact that marketers find interesting because each youngster spends an average of $13 a week—dollars that add up to a $10.5 billion-a-year market.

What do they spend it on? Here's a partial list: boom boxes, stereos, Levi and Guess? jeans, bubble gum, video games, Nikes and Reeboks, candy and potato chips.

When teenagers enter college, their spending increases to an average of $62 a week, making the college market a $20 billion a year market. Like their younger counterparts, college students spend their money on boom boxes, stereos, candy, potato chips and video games. But with more money in their pockets and with the privilege of age, they also buy cars, Walkmans, and VCR's.

The specific, concrete language in these examples conveys the information through vivid word pictures.

Speeches of Demonstration

Speeches of demonstration focus on a process by describing the gradual changes that lead to a particular result. These speeches often involve a "how" or a "how to" approach. Here are four specific purposes for speeches of demonstration:

⌘ To inform my audience of how to win at Nintendo

⌘ To inform my audience of how diabetes threatens health

⌘ To inform my audience of how to improve their tennis game

⌘ To inform my audience of the way college admissions committees choose the most qualified applicants

Speeches that take a "how" approach have as their goal audience understanding. They explain how a process functions without teaching the specific skills needed to complete a task. After listening to a speech on college admissions, for example, you may understand the process but not be prepared to take a seat on an admissions committee. In contrast, "how to" speeches try to communicate specific skills, like the best ways to play Nintendo. Let's look more closely at a small section of a "how" speech:

How are shows selected by the networks to be placed in prime-time for an upcoming television season? The answer to this question can lead to describing a complex process involving a host of people ranging from developers with an idea to advertising executives responsible for deciding whether or not to sponsor a program. When the

---

1. Information from Ronald Smothers, "A Selma March Relives Those First Steps of '65," *The New York Times,* March 5, 1990, p. B6.

proposed television programs are presented to advertisers the process engaged is one which can allow advertisers to have some influence over the content of programs they choose to sponsor. Before this sort of influence takes effect the network officials and advertising executives go through what is called "speculation season." In early spring those involved in the decision-making process may consider about 100 hours worth of programs. Usually no more than 23 to 25 hours of air time eventually make it. Thirty to forty projects may be developed by the networks while many more do not get past a one-page plot outline.[2]

Although the sample from this speech begins to explain how television programs are selected for the fall season, its primary goal is understanding, not application. Compare this to the following "how to" presentation geared to Nintendo players:

When you play the Nintendo game, "Spy Hunter," your goal as a CIA agent is to find and kill enemy spies on land and sea. Car races and boat chases are involved. Here are some winning strategies:

First focus on identifying your enemies. This step should be relatively easy since they are trying as hard as they can to destroy you. On land, guard against Tire Slashers, Bullet Proof Bullies, Limousines, and Helicopters. On water, learn to defend yourself against torpedo-equipped cruise boats and bomb-equipped speed boats.

You can improve the offensive and defensive capabilities of your vehicle by choosing the "power-up" option. To access this option, push the Start button. A Weapons Van will appear behind you. Drop your vehicle back and drive into the van. There you'll find the specific power-up options including a smoke screen that blinds your enemies, an oil slick that makes them lose control of their car, and missiles that destroy enemy helicopters.[3]

Speeches of demonstration often benefit from visual aids.

When your goal is to demonstrate a process, you may choose to complete the entire process—or only a part of it—in front of your audience. The nature of your demonstration and the constraints of time determine your choice. If you are giving CPR training, a partial demonstration will not give your listeners the information they need to save a life. However, if you are demonstrating how to cook a stew, your audience doesn't need to watch you chop onions—preparation in advance maintains audience interest and saves time.

Speeches of Explanation

Speeches of explanation deal with ideas, theories, principles, and beliefs, that is, more abstract subjects than speeches of description or demonstration. They also involve attempts to simplify complex topics. The goal of these speeches is audience under-standing. A psychologist addressing parents about the moral development of

---

2. Bill Carter, "Right of Spring in Assessing the Next Season's Hopefuls," *The New York Times* May 11, 1992. p. C6.
3. *Strategies for Nintendo Games* (Lincolnwood, IL: Publications International, Ltd. 1989), pp. 96–97.

The speech to demonstrate should be animated using well-selected visual aids that create interest as well as understanding.

children; a cabinet official explaining U.S. farm policy; a professor explaining the functionalist theory of sociology: These are examples of speeches of explanation.

To be effective, speeches of explanation must be connected to the real world. Avoid abstractions in favor of concrete images by using verbal pictures that define and explain. Here, for example, a speaker explains the concept of depression by telling listeners how patients describe it:

> Serious depression, a patient once said, is "like being in quicksand surrounded by a sense of doom, of sadness."
>
> Author William Styron described his own depression as "a veritable howling tempest in the brain" that took him down a hole so deep that he nearly committed suicide.
>
> In 1984 CBS correspondent Mike Wallace found himself unable to sleep, losing weight, and experiencing phantom pains in his arms and legs. "Depression is palpable," explained Wallace. "You begin to feel like a fake and fraud. You second guess yourself about everything."[4]

---

4.   Information from "Beating Depression." *U.S. News & World Report,* March 5, 1990, pp. 48–55.

Compare this presentation to the following more abstract version:

> Severe depression involves dramatic psychological changes that can be triggered by heredity or environmental stress. Depression is intense and long lasting and may result in hospitalization. The disease may manifest itself in agitation or lethargy.

This second explanation is much more effective when combined with the first. If the second is presented alone, listeners are limited in their ability to anchor the concept to something they understand.

Speeches of explanation may involve policies—statements of intent or purpose that guide or drive future decisions. The president may announce a new arms control policy. A school principal may announce the initiation of a school dress code. The director of human resources of a major corporation may discuss the firm's new flextime policy.

A speech that explains a policy should focus on the questions that are likely to occur to an audience. For example, as director of human resources for a major corporation about to deliver a speech on the company's decision to initiate flextime (the practice of allowing employees to vary their hours of work in order to accommodate the demands of their personal lives), you must anticipate that your listeners will probably want to know:

⌘ Will it change the number of hours I work?

⌘ Can I come in early or stay late?

⌘ Can I choose not to take a lunch hour and leave an hour early?

When organized logically, these and other questions form the basis of the presentation. As in all informative speeches, your purpose is not to persuade your listeners to support flextime, but to inform them about the policy.

HOW TO DELIVER A FOCUSED, EFFECTIVE INFORMATIVE SPEECH

The best informative speakers apply the techniques discussed throughout this text, techniques that focus on delivering a speech that meets audience needs—which implicitly acknowledges the reciprocal nature of public speaking. Let's review these techniques in the context of informative speaking.[5]

Link Your Speech to Audience Goals

The best informative speakers know what their listeners want to learn from their speech. While a group of weight watchers may be motivated to attend a lecture on dieting to learn how to lose weight, nutritionists drawn to the same speech may want

---

5. For a summary and bibliography on informative speaking and the informative speech, see, Charles R. Petrie, Jr. "Informative Speaking: Summary and Bibliography of Related Research," *Speech Monographs* (1963): 71–91.

to use the information to help clients. Audience goals are also linked to audience knowledge. When people feel ignorant about a topic they are often motivated to listen and learn. When they feel they already know all the answers, you must demonstrate that you have something valuable to add.

Some listeners are eager to hear your speech because your topic means so much to them (the weight watchers) while others can't imagine what you could say to interest them (people who never had a weight problem). Your job with the first group is easy; the audience is already motivated. The second group requires that you motivate them. Hold up pants in four sizes from the closet of a formerly overweight person to show that weight loss is possible. Make people who have no interest in your topic believe that your presentation has something to do with them. Tell them, for example, about metabolic changes that cause weight problems as people age.

The setting of your speech may tell you a lot about audience goals. Because many informative speeches take place in classroom lectures, community seminars, or business forums, audiences who attend these speeches come together because of their interest in the topic or because of a requirement to learn what you are teaching. For example, your speech may be part of an adult education mental health series at a local community college. If you are delivering a lifesaving lecture at a neighborhood YMCA as part of a series on preventive medicine and wellness, the nature of the series is conducive to your goal of communicating information. These settings tell you the specific reasons your audience has gathered. A group of middle-aged women attending the lifesaving lecture may be concerned about saving their husbands' live in the event of a heart attack, while a group of nursing students listening to the same lecture in a college classroom may be doing so as a requirement for graduation.

Avoid Telling the Audience What It Already Knows, but Don't Overestimate Audience Knowledge

As the Ping-Pong champion of your school, you decide to give your informative speech on the game of Ping-Pong. You begin by holding up the ball and paddle, declaring, "This little white ball is a Ping-Pong ball and this is a Ping-Pong paddle. Both are necessary to play the game." Plodding along, you describe the Ping-Pong table. "It's a rectangle with a net down the middle and lines drawn that divide it into sections." Your listeners start yawning—they don't want to hear what they already know. Although your presentation may be effective for an audience of extra-terrestrial aliens who have never heard of Ping-Pong, it is too simplistic for those with even a little knowledge of the game.

As you learned in Chapter 5, gauging your audience's level of information may require a prespeech questionnaire. Or you can select several individuals at random and ask what they know. If you are a professor teaching a course, this assessment is easy. If you are a guest lecturer addressing the group only once, more work is required.

Avoid Information Overload

When you're excited about your subject and you want your audience to know about it, you can find yourself trying to say too much in too short a time. Like a machine gun spraying bullets, you throw fact after fact at your listeners until you literally force them to stop listening. Saying too much is like touring London in a day: It can't be done if you expect to remember anything. As you recall from Chapter 3, our ability to absorb spoken information is limited. When an audience experiences information overload, it stops listening.

Your job as an informative speaker is to know how much to say and, just as importantly, how much not to say. If your goals are grand, plan a series of speeches rather than just one. For example, if you are delivering a speech on the changes in attitudes and habits that surround college drinking, you might break the following main points into two speeches.

I. Students who use mood-altering substances on campus usually prefer alcohol.

II. According to the tenth national survey conducted by the University of Michigan's Institute of Social Research, three of four students drink alcohol at least once a month, and two of five have five or more drinks in a row at least once every two weeks.

III. Students who abstain from drinking experience tremendous peer pressure.

IV. Many campuses across the country are instituting stricter alcohol policies.

V. Most students enter college as experienced drinkers.

VI. Students younger than twenty-one drink despite the fact that they are legally underage.

VII. By living off campus or sneaking alcohol into their dormitories, students hide their drinking from college administrators.

VIII. Although the percentage of light-to-moderate drinkers seems to be decreasing, students seem to be participating in the same amount of heavy binge drinking.[6]

Your first speech could focus on the use of alcohol (point I), the University of Michigan survey (point II), and the status of drinking patterns (point VIII). Your second speech could focus on student experience with alcohol before they enter college (point V), peer pressure (point III), the drinking patterns of underage students (points VI and VIII) and what colleges are doing to control the problem (point IV).

Be careful about overloading your audience with too many statistics. Long lists are numbing. Mention the high points and explain the details in a visual or in a hand-out distributed at the end of your speech. Technical information can also be

---

6. Information from Deirdre Carmody, "College Drinking: Changes in Attitude and Habit," *The New York Times,* March 7, 1990, p. B5.

daunting when given in large chunks. Let the fact that your audience is just learning the material guide you as you decide how much to say. In addition, be conscious of the relationship among time, purpose, and your audience's ability to absorb information. Tie key points to anecdotes and humor. Your goal is not to "get it all in" but to communicate your speech's message as effectively as possible.

Capture Audience Attention at the Start of Your Speech

Think for a moment of your primary goals as an informative speaker: You want to communicate what you know about a specific subject and you want your listeners to understand what you are saying. You must first convince your audience in your introduction that your topic has relevance to them. For example, a speech describing the accomplishments of the space program can begin by linking the launch of a telecommunication satellite to clear TV reception. You can provoke interest with the following title: "TV fuzz is gone—thanks to NASA." Similarly, if you are delivering a speech on white-collar crime, you can begin like this:

> Imagine taking part of your paycheck and handing it to a criminal. In an indirect way, that's what we all do to pay for white collar crime. Part of the tax dollars you give the federal government goes into the hands of unscrupulous business executives who pad their expenses and overcharge the government by millions of dollars. For example, General Dynamics, the third-largest military supplier, tacked on at least $75 million to the government's bill for such "overhead" expenses as country-club fees and personal travel for corporate executives.
>
> White collar crime is widespread because it pays. Unfortunately, the problem has no ready solutions.[7]

This approach is more likely to capture audience attention than a list of crimes detached from listeners' lives and pocketbooks.

Hold Audience Interest

To use a football analogy, once you're off and running, don't drop the ball until you're in the end zone. You can sustain audience interest in several ways:

Be Novel and Vivid.   You can enliven even the dullest topic if you are committed to trying something different: Use humorous visuals to display statistics. Demonstrate the physics of air travel by throwing paper airplanes across the room. Talk, as President Reagan did, about American heroes by pointing to actual heroes sitting for the occasion in the balcony of the House of Representatives.

Mold your images through concrete, animated language that creates pictures in listeners' minds. It is no accident that advertising campaigns are built around

---

7. Information from "Crime in the Suites," *Time,* June 10, 1985, pp. 56–57: "Stealing $200 Billion 'the Respectable Way,'" *U.S. News & World Report,* May 20, 1985, pp. 83–85; "Making Punishment Fit White-collar Crime," *Business Week,* June 15, 1987, pp. 84–85.

slogans, jingles, and other memorable language that people are likely to remember after a commercial is over. Your audiences also are more likely to remember vivid language than dull language. Futurist Alvin Toffler talks about the subject of "future shock," and John Naisbitt talks about "megatrends." We remember this language and along with it the underlying concepts.

Use Examples to Make Facts Come Alive.   Nothing elicits interest more than a good example—and nothing is better at clarifying difficult or technical topics. Here is an example:

> How common is noise-related hearing loss? The experts tell us that some 20 million Americans are affected by it. Let's look at a typical case.
>
> Joe is an electrician who works around heavy equipment including air hammers, pile drivers, drills and power saws eight hours a day. He commutes to work on the subway and, to make the time go faster, tunes in his stereo headset to hard rock music. Far from being a sanctuary free of noise, Joe's home is noisier than his job. Living right under the flight pattern for a runway of a large international airport, Joe is subjected to the noise of planes flying several hundred feet over his home every few minutes.
>
> The noises in Joe's life exceed the level of 80 decibels—the point at which hearing damage occurs after prolonged exposure. In addition to actual hearing loss, prolonged excessive noise is also linked to stress, strokes, and even suicide and murder.[8]

Humorous stories are effective in helping the audience remember the material. When attorney Sarah Weddington talks about the history of discriminatory practices in this country, she describes how a bank required her husband's signature on a loan even though she was working and he was in school. She also talks about playing basketball in school and being limited to three dribbles (men could dribble the ball as many times as they wanted). While these stories make the audience laugh, they also communicate the message that sex discrimination was pervasive when Weddington was younger.[9]

Use Visual Aids.   Using pictures, charts, models, slides, and other visual aids varies the pace of your speech, simplifies your presentation, and helps maintain audience interest. Professor Jo Sprague and Douglas Stuart explain: "Your message will be clearer if you send it through several channels. As you describe a process with words, also use your hands, a visual aid, a chart, a recording. Appeal to as many senses as possible to reinforce the message . . . . If a point is very important or very difficult always use one other channel besides the spoken word to get it across."[10]

---

8.   Information from Malcolm W. Browne, "Research on Noise Disappears in the Din," *The New York Times,* March 6, 1990, pp. C1 and C11.
9.   Interview with Sarah Weddington, March 19, 1990.
10.   Jo Sprague and Douglas Stuart, *The Speaker's Handbook,* 2d ed. (San Diego, CA: Harcourt Brace Jovanovich, 1988), p. 299.

I N T E R V I E W

Sarah Weddington
Feminist Attorney
and Advocate for Women

In 1973, at the age of twenty-six, Sarah Weddington argued the winning side of the landmark case of *Roe* v. *Wade* before the United States Supreme Court—a case that guaranteed to women the freedom of choice to continue or terminate an unwanted pregnancy. Since that time, Weddington has spent her career speaking out for equal rights, for ethics in government, and for individual involvement in public issues and leadership. Her voice has been heard as a three-term member of the Texas House of Representatives, as a special assistant to the president during the Carter administration, as an attorney, and as a senior lecturer at the University of Texas at Austin.

Weddington is now a writer, lecturer, and teacher. In 1990, she was named by the National Association for Campus Activities as the top lecturer on the college speaking circuit.

Weddington's focus as a lecturer is informational speaking. Her advice on handling information overload and reducing barriers between speaker and audience is especially valuable to speakers communicating complex or technical data. She also addresses the issue of women as public speakers and the link between public speaking and leadership.

Question: You say in your speeches that to be a leader, you have to feel comfortable being different. Would you also add, to be a leader, you have to feel comfortable speaking out? Is a willingness to speak in public necessary for leadership?

Answer: In most kinds of leadership it is. The higher you are in any organization, the more important your speech communication skills become. It's almost impossible to be in the public arena, trying to convince people to accept your point of view, without being an effective speaker.

Question: In the research you've done for your book, *Some Leaders Are Born Women,* have you found that women are comfortable in the role of public spokesperson or are women just beginning to develop that comfort?

Answer: When I talk to people who work with college students, they often tell me that even women in leadership positions need someone to tell them, "Yes, you're doing a good job. Just keep going." I think that as women learn that they *can* be leaders—and that they can do it well—they will develop more of the sense of confidence they need to be effective speakers. It's hard to be comfortable as a speaker without self-confidence.

Question: During your speeches, you give your audience a great deal of information about the background of *Roe* v. *Wade* and the entire abortion debate. Are you concerned about information overload?

Answer: I start with the assumption that the purpose of my speech is to give the audience more information than they have about the abortion issue. I want people to leave the auditorium with a greater understanding, with a knowledge of sources where they can learn more, and with the impetus to do further study. I also want them to be able to raise the complexities of the issue in other settings. I limit what I say, but I'm always conscious of my responsibility to communicate information, especially to college audiences.

I think of myself as an interpreter. I take very complex information and try to interpret it for very intelligent audiences who don't have the background on this issue that I do. But even though I speak to such intelligent groups, I still have to use word pictures and other traditional public speaking techniques to hold attention and increase the likelihood that people will remember what I say. For example, after talking about the complex legal issues involved in *Roe* v. *Wade,* I paint an elaborate picture of what it was like to walk into the Supreme Court chamber the day I pleaded the case. I describe everything about the chamber—the curtains, the marble, the people in the galleries, the justices in their robes, the "cheat sheet" I used to remember the justices' names. I'm always aware that people tend to remember word pictures and tie other points to them, especially if the descriptions are also humorous.

Question: You were nervous before arguing *Roe* v. *Wade.* Do you feel the same way before delivering a speech?

Source: Interview with Sarah Weddington, March 19, 1990.

Answer: I can think of very few instances where I was not nervous before a speech. It's important for me to be nervous because I feel it's a sign that my adrenaline is pumping in preparation for something important. To me, nervousness is a source of energy, so I try to concentrate it in the form of tension that works for me. I expect to be nervous and will almost work up a sense of that tension. If I'm not nervous, I'm convinced I won't do a good job. I'm convinced that my tension gives my speech greater impact.

Question: During a recent speech, you seemed purposefully to walk away from the lectern instead of standing behind it. Why?

Answer: I rarely use the lectern because I feel it acts as a barrier between me and the audience. I use it when I speak before very large groups of 5,000 to 7,000 people because I need the microphone. With smaller groups, I rely on it when I want to communicate authority. These are the exceptions. In most cases, I try to adopt a conversational, nonauthoritarian tone and the lectern seems out of place. My approach is never, "let me tell you what the real facts are," but, "let me tell you what I know about the subject."

Question: How do you account for your success with college audiences?

Answer: I always focus on audience motivation and interest—why they are there, what they know, and what they hope to get from my speech. Since I teach at the college level, I'm especially sensitive to the needs of college audiences and the kinds of speeches that work best with them.

Involve Your Listeners in Your Presentation.   Ask for help in assembling a three-dimensional kite. Ask for a show of hands on a pivotal question. ("How many of you think that a serious earthquake could hit the East Coast?") Ask listeners to take part in an experiment. (Hand out several stereo headsets and ask people to set the volume to the level at which they usually listen to music. Then show how this volume can affect hearing.)

Ask Rhetorical Questions to Move Your Speech From One Point to the Next and to Start the Audience Thinking.   The following question would leave many East Coasters scratching their heads, then listening intently to the rest of your speech: "What are the first things you should do to save your life in an earthquake?"

Change Your Pace.   One complex fact after another is difficult to remember—your audience does not have the luxury of reviewing your remarks after your speech is over. To help your audience absorb your message, mark your speech with intellectual changes of pace.

Be Animated in Your Delivery.   Talk about accounting principles, water filters, the phases of the moon, or corporate benefits with vigor and spirit and people will listen. When your subject is dry, your delivery can make a difference in the way your audience responds. Enthusiasm is infectious, even to those who have no interest in your subject.

Strive for Clarity

To be successful, your informative speech must communicate your ideas without confusion. This goal can be accomplished in the following ways:

Define Unfamiliar Words and Concepts.   Unfamiliar words, especially technical jargon, can defeat your purpose to inform your audience. When introducing a new word, define it in a way your listeners can understand. Because you are so close to your material, knowing what to define can be your hardest task. The best advice is to put yourself in the position of a listener who knows less about your topic than you do or ask a friend or colleague's opinion. Here are a few of the forms definitions can take:

⌘ *Logical definitions.* These definitions follow the pattern dictionaries use most often as they place the concept to be defined into a category and then describe the specific characteristics of the concept. For example, it is not enough to tell your listeners:

> Theory Y emphasizes self-control and direction instead of external control and constant supervision and is based on the premise that workers seek out responsibilities to feel good about themselves and their work.

This definition means more if it is not introduced like this:

> Theory Y is a theory of labor management that has gained popularity in recent years.

⌘ *Operational definitions.* These definitions explain how a concept works in a way the audience can understand. For example:

> Using a management-by-objectives plan, district sales managers set the goals that they and their sales force have to meet over the following year, thus letting the managers know in advance exactly how they will be evaluated.

⌘ *Definition through example.* Sometimes the best way to define a concept is through common examples. For example, here we learn who fits into the category of "white-collar criminal":

> White-collar criminals include the likes of former Wall Street financiers Ivan Boesky and Dennis Levine, both of whom served time in jail for insider trading.

⌘ *Definition by negation.* You can define something by telling your listeners what it is not, as in the following example:

> White-collar crime is neither violent nor dirty nor does it require criminals to associate with members of the mob nor take off their three-piece business suits.

Implicit in a clear definition is avoiding undefined technical language. If you persist in using jargon, no one will know what you are talking about—or care (see Chapter 10).

Enumerate.   Your audience may need help keeping track of the information in your speech. Separating one idea from another may be difficult for listeners when they are trying to learn all the information at once. You can help your audience understand the structure of your speech by creating oral lists. Simple "First, second, third, fourth . . ." or "one, two, three, four . . ." help the audience focus on your sequence of points. Here is an example:

> The U.S. divorce rate is so high for a number of reasons. First, divorce is now "permitted" by our society. It is no longer the shame it once was. Second, women are better educated and more independant than they have ever been. They no longer feel trapped in failed marriages. Third, liberalized laws make it easier to get a divorce. And fourth, men and women are no longer willing to sacrifice their lives for the sake of the children.

Each point is developed in the speech following this sequence.

Compare the New With the Familiar.   Informative speeches should introduce new information in terms of what the audience already knows. Analogies can be useful. Here is an example:

> A cooling-off period in labor management negotiations is like a parental imposed time-out. When we were children, our parents would send us to our rooms to think over what we had done. We were forbidden to come out for at least an hour in the hope that by the time we were released our tempers had cooled. Similarly, under the Taft-Hartley Act, the president can impose an 80-day cooling off period if a strike threatens to imperil the nation's health or safety.

References to the familiar help listeners assimilate new information.

Repeat Your Key Points.   Repetition is important when presenting new facts and ideas. You help your listeners by reinforcing your main points through summaries and paraphrasing. It is also helpful to review your material from a different perspective. For example, you can reinforce your point about noise pollution as you tie the problem of excessive noise to medical and emotional problems.

Show Trends.   Instead of talking only about the current population of Fort Worth, talk about the population in relation to what it was ten years ago and what the census bureau tells us it is likely to be in the year 2000. Instead of talking about the current cost of college tuition, show how the cost has risen in the last decade. Trends put individual facts in perspective as they clarify ideas in a larger context. The whole—the connection among ideas—gives each detail greater meaning.

Organize With a Focus on Clarity.   Logical, clear connections are imperative in informative speaking. Asking your audience to absorb new information presented in a disorganized fashion is asking too much.

Descriptive speeches are often arranged in spatial, topical, and chronological patterns. Speeches of demonstration often use a spatial, chronological cause-and-effect, problem-solution, and structure-function organizational pattern. Speeches of explanation are frequently arranged chonologically or topically or according to cause and effect, problem-solution or structure and function. Follow the organizational suggestions provided in Chapter Eight to link your ideas with clarity and precision.

MEET YOUR ETHICAL RESPONSIBILITY

Chapter Two introduces ethical responsibility in public speaking and Chapter Four discusses the ethical responsibilities speakers must assume. Too often the ethics of communication are linked solely with persuasive speaking but you also assume an ethical responsibility when preparing and delivering an informative speech. Please review Chapter Four for a careful review of communication ethics.

Remember, an informative speech requires you to assemble *accurate, sound, and pertinent* information that will enable you to tell your audience what you believe to be the truth. You must deliver your speech in a clear, concise, and meaningful way. Three decades ago the United States was involved in an escalating war in Vietnam. President Lyndon Johnson needed to keep his cabinet, the Congress, and the American people *informed* about the war and the level of U.S. involvement. Certainly wartime requires classifying certain information so that national security and the lives of men and women at war can be protected. But offering this protection does not justify withholding or disguising the truth at all costs. By 1968 U.S. intelligence was aware of a coming crisis in South Vietnam, one that could alter the course of the war at great expense to the our troops. Theodore White, a leading reporter of presidential campaigns, wrote about President Lyndon Johnson acting on information he withheld from a public that had the right to be informed. According to White, in 1968 as Mr. Johnson gathered information from his military advisers he:

> . . . found it unnecessary either to inform the American Cabinet (except for those directly concerned with security) or the American people. All through the fall, peaking in November, a series of happy stories was told the American people as first Ambassador

Bunker and then General Westmoreland reported to the nation that all was well. The opinion polls reflected these reports and, for the first time in over a year, Mr. Johnson's popularity and public confidence in the President began to climb.[11]

The communist forces launched the Tet offensive that proved to be a military disaster for both the North Vietnamese and the Vietcong troops. The cost, however, was considerable to American forces as well. Citizens across the U.S. realized that the nation was involved in a war it could not win and the confidence of millions of Americans was shaken. Three years after our commitment of ground, air, and sea forces, 35,000 of its sons and daughters had lost their lives in a war most of America did not understand. *Understanding comes from being clearly and thoroughly informed.*

The informative speeches you deliver in class and hear on your campus are not nearly as likely to affect the course of history as those delivered by high ranking public officials in a time of war. But the principles of ethical responsbility are similar for every speaker, whether the speaker is president of the United States or the president of your school. Each has an obligation to inform their constiuencies in nonmanipulative ways and provide them with information they need and have a right to know. Professors, doctors, police officers, and others engaged in informative communication ought to tell the truth as they know it and must not withhold information to serve personal gain. You, like others, should always rely on sources that can be proven credible and avoid what political scientists label as "calculated ambiguity." Calculated ambiguity is a speaker's planned effort to be vague, sketchy, and considerably abstract.

Ambiguity and high levels of abstraction are not speech behaviors practiced solely by politicians. A professor we know once boasted in a faculty lounge: "Only 5 percent of my students actually understand what I am saying in my lectures—but then I am only interested in reaching this 5 percent!" The professor is an informative speaker when he lectures—is he meeting his ethical responsibility by trying to inform only 5 percent of his audience while he apparently ignores the other 95 percent?

SAMPLE SPEECH ANALYSIS

Specific Purpose.   To inform my audience of parents about the results of studies conducted at the University of Minnesota's Center for Twin and Adoption Research.

Core Idea.   Identical twins separated at birth and reunited as adults show remarkably similar personalities, temperaments, and patterns of behavior—similarities that point to the importance of genetics in shaping who we are.

---

11.   Theodore H. White, *The Making of the President, 1968.* New York: Antheneum Publishers, 1969, p 11.

A provocative opener captures audience attention. Almost immediately, the link is made to the research done at the University of Minnesota. This establishes the serious nature and credibility of the topic.

The speaker tells the audience that the research will be explored. This statement acts as a preview. The core idea is then stated in a simplified form.

This paragraph also makes it clear to the audience that the speaker's message will help them.

The speaker briefly defines the nature of genes and their role in human development.

Instead of dry research data, findings are presented in terms of the stories of real people. The use of three separate stories reinforces the point and, at the same time, makes the audience feel that the findings are valid.

A picture shows the amazing resemblance between these men and reinforces the message that environment plays only a partial role in personality development.

Details are emphasized to make the stories real and to add interest. The more human the individuals seem, the easier it is for listeners to relate to them.

It is the stuff Hollywood "B" movies are made of: Twins separated soon after birth are reunited as adults only to learn that they like the same kind of food, have the same kinds of jobs, and even chose the same names for their children. Although this plot may stretch credibility as a Hollywood movie, it is real life for twins involved in a study conducted at the University of Minnesota's Center for Twin and Adoption Research.

I will explain these research findings because they tell us something about ourselves, our children, and the forces we deal with as we rear our children. What I hope will become clear is that we come into this world with a genetic inheritance that plays a large part in determining who we are.

Before I begin, I would like to explain in a very brief way what genes are. Even though we cannot see them, genes are segments within our chromosomes that contain the blueprint for our development. They determine the color of our hair, whether we can play the violin or have a tin ear, whether we are good at sports or at spectating, whether we are short or tall, shy or aggressive. Within each of our 46 chromosomes are 30,000 to 100,000 genes that determine what we will become in response to our environments.

Let's look at some specific cases from the University of Minnesota study to show the effect genes have. Judging from their life experiences, Oskar Stohr and Jack Yuke had little in common. Stohr grew up with his mother in Germany during World War II and was reared as a Nazi. Yuke, a Jew, spent his childhood in the Caribbean, California, and Israel with his father.

As you can see from this picture, these men are identical twins. Separated at birth and reunited for the first time as adults, they share some amazing similarities: Both wear rubber bands on their wrists, read magazines from back to front, flush the toilet before and after urinating, dunk their toast in coffee, and think that faking a sneeze in a crowded elevator is funny.

Or take the case of Jerry Levey and Mark Newman, another pair of identical, separated twins who were brought together by fate when they were in their early thirties. Both were volunteer firemen who never married; compulsive flirts with a raucous sense of humor; beer drinkers (Budweiser for both) who stretched their little fingers awkwardly beneath the beer bottle. A coincidence once again? The evidence is mounting that something else is involved.

The phrase, "one last case," acts as a signpost to listeners that the list will end and that another point will begin.

One last case. Jim Lewis and Jim Springer were only four weeks old when they were separated in 1940. When they were reunited in 1979 they discovered an eerie chain of similarities they could not explain, including the Salems they chain-smoked, their habit of biting their fingernails, and their choice of the same model blue Chevrolet. Both men also developed migraines at the same age, held the same job, and enjoyed woodworking—so much that they both built identical white wood benches around trees in their yards.

The core idea is echoed by identifying critical questions. Having set the stage with a series of anecdotes, the research is set forth. First, the general conclusion is stated.

These findings raise questions about how much of who we are is determined by heredity and how much by our surroundings. After testing 350 pairs of twins including 44 pairs of identical twins and 25 pairs of fraternal twins reared apart, the University of Minnesota researchers concluded that heredity and environment appear to play an equal role in the development of many traits, a finding that explains the similarity in behavior patterns in twins separated at birth.

Then the specific study results are analyzed.

After subjecting the twins to a battery of extensive physical and psychological tests, the researchers found striking similarities between the pairs in several major personality traits including leadership ability, the capacity for imaginative experiences, vulnerability to stress, alienation, and a desire to shun risks. These characteristics were determined more by heredity than environment.

One finding is presented in terms of another anecdote. The goal, once again, is to maintain audience interest.

The researchers also found that fears and phobias have a strong genetic link. Many of the separated twins shared phobias to water and height. One pair of twins dealt with their fear of the water in the same way—by wading into the ocean backward and never looking at the water.

The speaker then ties the findings to the concerns of the audience. Expert testimony is cited to make the point. The speaker uses the story of Chuck Yeager to accomplish this goal.

Does this mean that parents are totally powerless to shape the development of their children's personalities? Not so, says David T. Lykken, a member of the University of Minnesota team, pointing to daredevil test pilot Chuck Yeager as an example. Yeager, the ultimate risk taker with an uncanny ability to ignore danger and the eyesight and coordination to allow him to do just about anything, could have turned to a life of crime had his environment pointed him in that direction. According to Lykken, the same qualities that made Yeager a hero could also have made him the perfect criminal.

Testimony now takes the form of a direct quote, which increases the credibility of the statement.

Lykken sees the attempt to separate the impact of heredity from environment as a pointless exercise. "It's an endless circle. Your genes determine who you are, which in many respects determines the kind of environment you'll have, which determines who you are."

The conclusion restates the central message of the speech by relating it to the experiences of parents. When listeners are able to take your message personally, they are more likely to remember it. The conclusion also attempts to place the role of parenting in a broader perspective.

As parents, I'm sure most of you would agree with the University of Minnesota researchers that children do not start life with a blank slate. Although your first child may have been calm and serene, your second may have been active and aggressive and your third somewhere in between. Does this diminish your role as a parent to influence what your children will become? Certainly not. It only makes your job more interesting because you and everything else in your child's environment are only part of the equation.[12]

SUMMARY

As an informative speaker, you should strive to be accurate, clear, meaningful, and memorable. Usually a fine line exists between informative and persuasive speaking. The key to whether a speech is informative is speaker intent.

There are three types of informative speeches: Speeches of description paint a picture of an event, person, object, place, situation, or concept; speeches of demonstration focus on a process, describing the gradual changes that lead to a particular result; speeches of explanation deal with such abstractions as ideas, theories, principles, and beliefs.

Preparing and delivering an effective informative speech involves applying the techniques discussed throughout this text, such as linking your speech to audience goals, assessing audience knowledge, avoiding information overload, capturing and holding audience attention by using creative approaches, using examples and visual aids, involving your listeners in your presentation, asking rhetorical questions, changing your pace, and using an animated delivery style.

Remember: strive for clarity by defining all unfamiliar words and concepts; avoid technical language; enumerate your ideas; use analogies; repeat your key points; demonstrate trends; and use an effective pattern of organization.

---

12. "All about Twins," *Newsweek,* November 23, 1987, pp. 58–69; "The Eerie World of Reunited Twins," *Discover* (September 1987): 36–46; "Exploring the traits of twins," *Time,* January 12, 1987, p. 63; "Genes and Behavior: A Twin Legacy," *Psychology Today,* September 1987, pp. 18–19; "Genes: Little Things That Mean a Lot," *U.S. News & World Report,* December 15, 1986, p. 8; "Happiness Is a Reunited Set of Twins," *U.S. News & World Report,* April 13, 1987, pp. 63–66; "Sins and Twins," *The New Republic,* December 21, 1987, pp. 17–18; "To the Manner Born," *Rolling Stone,* November 19, 1987, pp. 56ff; Philip G. Zimbardo, *Psychology and Life,* 12th ed. (Glenview, IL: Scott, Foresman and Company, 1988), p. 66.

S P E A K   E A S Y

HOW TO HANDLE QUESTIONS AND COMMENTS THAT INTERRUPT YOUR SPEECH

In an informative speech you are likely to encounter questions and comments while you are speaking. It is hard for some people to resist raising their hands when they don't understand a point or when they want to contribute a fact or opinion. You can deal with these interruptions in two ways:

Tell Your Audience at the Start of Your Speech to Hold All Questions and Comments for the Question-and-Answer Period.

If you are scheduled to speak for thirty minutes, you can limit your prepared comments to twenty minutes and deal with the audience response in the remaining time. Audiences often appreciate this arrangement because it gives them enough time to focus on their interests and difficulties.

Acknowledge Raised Hands During Your Speech.

Many speakers choose to take time away from their prepared text to answer questions. This intra-speech interchange provides immediate feedback, enabling you to concentrate at least some of your remaining remarks on the topics that interest your audience.

If you decide to take questions during your speech, keep your responses short and, when appropriate, return to the point at which you left off. When too many hands are raised, you may have to tell your audience to save questions until the end.

Whichever method you choose, learn to direct your answers to the goals of your speech. That is, even if a question is only peripherally connected to your material, make the connections yourself. For example, if after listening to your speech about the Minnesota twin study, a listener raises her hand to ask how the separated twins reacted when brought together after so many years, you can describe the response and then explain how the twins were even more surprised when they realized they had so many things in common.

Always remember that even during the question-and-answer period, you are in charge of your own speech. Don't let a member of your audience lead the discussion in a direction you don't want to take. It takes nearly as much time and practice to learn how to handle questions you don't want to answer as to learn how to handle those you do.

QUESTIONS
FOR STUDY AND
DISCUSSION

1. What are the characteristics of an effective informative speech?
2. How can visual aids be used to enhance informative speeches?
3. Why does speaker intent differentiate informative from persuasive speaking?

ACTIVITIES

1. Attend an informative lecture on campus (not a class lecture). Assess whether the lecture was strictly informative or whether it was also persuasive. Describe and explain your findings in a written report.

2. Prepare a five-to six-minute informative speech that is primarily a description, an explanation, or a demonstration. Develop a planning and key-word outline, and practice the speech aloud.
3. Attend another informative lecture in your community. Take notes on the effectiveness of the speaker's message. Describe the techniques the speaker used to improve communication. Evaluate the speech on the message and the presentation.

"A time to keep silence, and
a time to speak.

Ecclesiastes, 3:7

INTRODUCTION TO PERSUASIVE SPEAKING

he power of free speech in our democratic society is most clear and vocal in speeches to persuade. Here is one example.

When Sarah Brady addressed Congress in support of the Brady Bill, a bill that would require a national seven-day waiting period for the purchase of handguns, she delivered a chilling message that appealed to the reason as well as to the emotion of her listeners. She spoke in her role as chairperson of Handgun Control, Inc. and as the wife of Jim Brady, former press secretary to Ronald Reagan who was partially brain damaged in John Hinckley's 1981 assassination attempt against the president. In part, here is what Mrs. Brady said:

> I am here today as Chair of Handgun Control, Inc., a national citizens' organization working to keep handguns out of the wrong hands. But today's hearing is very special for me. For the first time in an appearance before Congress, I have my husband Jim at my side. I cannot tell you how comforting that is.
>
> The fight for the Brady Bill has been going on for three long years. During that time, I have repeatedly urged policymakers to enact a national seven-day waiting period on handgun purchases so that local law enforcement may conduct background checks. And, I have tried to convey the devastating consequences that the lack of a waiting period has had on Jim, on our life together, and on the life of our son, Scott. Maybe with Jim's appearance here today, Congress will finally get the message . . . .
>
> Obviously, there is no substantive reason why the Brady Bill should not be enacted. The only reason to vote against the Brady Bill is because the gun lobby opposes it. But despite the National Rifle Association's opposition to waiting period legislation in the nation's capital, the NRA actively worked to pass a bill in Oregon this year extending that State's waiting period from five to fifteen days. This law not only lengthened the waiting period, it also required submission of thumbprints, a thorough background check, and user fees . . . .
>
> Handgun waiting periods do work. For example, the State of Illinois has a 72-hour waiting period for handgun purchases. The Governor of Illinois recently reported that his state's law caught 2,470 convicted felons attempting to purchase firearms in 1988 alone. In Maryland, which has a seven-day waiting period for the purchase of handguns, 838 prescribed purchasers were caught in 1988 because of their state's law . . . . According to the state police, Indiana's seven-day waiting period snared 939 persons attempting to illegally purchase handguns last year.
>
> It is time to do what every major law enforcement organization and 91 percent of the American people want. It is time to say enough to the gun lobby. It is time to stop the hedging, the vacillation, the delaying tactics. Last year, Congress passed the buck to the Attorney General. And now, the Attorney General has passed it back. Congress has no more excuses. It is time for Congress to enact the Brady Bill.[1]

Four years after Mrs. Brady delivered this speech her persuasive goal was reached when President Bill Clinton signed the Brady Bill into law. The U.S. Congress passed the legislation, and the president signed it in the presence of Jim and Sarah Brady.[2]

---

1. Testimony of Sarah Brady, chair Handgun Control, Inc., before the Senate Judiciary Subcommittee on the Constitution in support of S. 1236, November 21, 1989. Speech provided by Handgun Control Inc., 1225 Eye Street NW, Suite 1100, Washington, DC 20005.
2. Thomas C. Friedman, "Clinton Signs Handgun Bill, Calling It Victory for Public," *The New York Times* December 1, 1993, p. A14.

Sarah Brady's speech embodies the critical elements of persuasion that have been defined by generations of rhetorical scholars starting with Aristotle. Aristotle's views provide the underpinnings of our modern study of persuasion. Here is Aristotle's definition of persuasion:

ELEMENTS OF PERSUASION

> Of the means of persuasion supplied by the speech itself there are three kinds. The first kind reside in the character [*ethos*] of the speaker; the second consist in producing a certain [the right] attitude in the hearer; the third appertain to the argument proper . . . .

Aristotle believed that *ethos*, that is, or speaker credibility, makes speakers worthy of belief; audiences trust speakers they perceive as honest, especially "on points outside the realm of exact knowledge, where opinion is divided." In this regard, he believed, "we trust [credible speakers] absolutely . . . ."

Aristotle also believed in the power of speakers to persuade through emotional appeals. He explains: "Persuasion is effected through the audience, when they are brought by the speech into a state of emotion; for we give very different decisions under the sway of pain or joy, and liking or hatred . . . ."

Finally, Aristotle saw the power of persuasion as depending, in part, on logical arguments and sound reasoning.

He concluded:

> Such being the instruments of persuasion, to master all three obviously calls for a man who can reason logically, can analyze the types of human character, along with the virtues, and, thirdly, can analyze the emotions—the nature and quality of each several emotion, with the means by which, and the manner in which, it is excited.[3]

Since Aristotle, scholars have focused on these elements as the primary aspects of persuasion. They have added to these principles an emphasis on outcomes. Gary Woodward and Robert Denton, Jr., explain: "Persuasion is the process of preparing and delivering messages through verbal and nonverbal symbols to individuals or groups in order to alter, strengthen, or maintain attitudes, beliefs, values, or behaviors."[4]

Why Sarah Brady's Message Was a Message to Persuade

With these elements of persuasion in mind, we can understand Sarah Brady's speech as an example of persuasion:

⌘ Brady appealed to her audience through her own credibility as chairperson of Handgun Control, Inc. and as the wife of a shooting victim. She knew the consequences of unregulated handgun use because she lived them every day.

---

3.   Lane Cooper, trans., *The Rhetoric of Aristotle* (New York: Appleton-Century-Crofts, 1960), pp. 8–9.
4.   Gary Woodward and Robert Denton, Jr., *Persuasion and Influence in American Life* 2nd ed. (Prospect Heights, IL: Waveland Press, 1992), pp. 18–19; Wallace C. Fortheringham, *Perspectives on Persuasion* (Boston, MA: Allyn and Bacon, 1966), pp. 6–8; Carl I. Hovland, Irving L. Janis, and Harold H. Kelly, *Communication and Persuasion: Psychological Studies of Opinion Change* (New Haven, CT: Yale University Press, 1953).

⌘ Brady appealed to her audience's reasoning, presenting evidence in the form of statistics and examples to support her claim that handgun waiting periods work.

⌘ Brady appealed to the emotions of her listeners through the reference to "the devastating consequences that the lack of a waiting period have had on Jim, on our life together, and on the life of our son, Scott." Her most effective emotional appeal was nonverbal: the presence by her side of her handicapped husband, Jim.

⌘ The focus of Mrs. Brady's message was to change attitudes and motivate action: She spoke to show the inconsistency of the NRA's position, to prove the effectiveness of waiting periods on a state-by-state basis, and to urge the passage of the Brady Bill. The ultimate purpose of her speech was to motivate action.

In the following interview, Sarah Brady talks about the power of persuasion through public address. She also talks about other aspects of public speaking. A speaker's persuasive appeal derives from the audience's sense of the speaker's credibility as well as from appeals to an audience's emotion and logic.

At times, one persuasive element may be more important than others. Many speakers try to convince audiences based primarily on logical appeal, some use mainly emotional appeals, and others rely on their image and credibility as a speaker. The most effective speakers combine all three persuasive elements to meet a variety of audience needs.

Before we examine (in Chapter 15) the specific ways reason, emotion, and credibility are used in persuasion, we take a closer look at the goals of persuasion, the types of persuasive claims, and an effective method for organizing persuasive speeches. We also look at the link between persuasion and audience needs as defined by psychologist Abraham Maslow.

GOALS OF PERSUASION

Critical to the success of any persuasive effort is a clear sense of what you are trying to accomplish. As a speaker you must define for yourself your overall persuasive goals and the narrower persuasive aims.

Overall Persuasive Goals

The two overall goals of persuasion: to address attitudes and to move an audience to action.

Speeches that Focus on Attitudes.   In this type of speech, your goal is to convince an audience to share your views on a topic ("The tuition at this college is too high." "Too few Americans bother to vote.") The way you approach your goal depends on the nature of your audience.

When dealing with a negative audience, you face the challenge of trying to change your listeners' opinions. The more change you demand, the harder your

I N T E R V I E W

Sarah Brady
Advocate for
Handgun Control

Sarah Brady's life changed forever on March 30, 1981, when John Hinckley tried to assassinate President Ronald Reagan with an unlicensed handgun. One of Hinckley's bullets hit her husband, White House Press Secretary Jim Brady, leaving him permanently disabled.

Bearing personal witness to the devastation easy access to handguns can cause, Sarah Brady has chosen to use her tragically gained visibility to advocate a national seven-day waiting period for handgun purchases to allow for a criminal records check—a measure known in Congress as the Brady Bill. As chair of Handgun Control, Inc., Brady spoke nationwide to rally support for local and national legislative change. She has spoken before Congress, to law enforcement associations, college students, groups of Republicans and Democrats, and even to audiences filled with National Rifle Association (NRA) supporters. On November 30, 1993, President Bill Clinton signed the Brady Bill and it became a national law.

In this interview, Brady addresses the need to take a moderate, commonsense position with difficult audiences while never compromising her beliefs. She also talks about the separate roles that reason, emotion, and speaker credibility play in her persuasive message. Due, in large part, to the strength of her public voice, Sarah Brady is considered one of the hundred most powerful women in Washington.

Question: The organization you represent, Handgun Control Inc., lobbies, runs newspaper and magazine ads, and distributes print materials on the problems of unregulated handguns. What role does public speaking play in the persuasion equation? Does your singular voice—Sarah Brady speaking to an audience—reach people in ways these other forms of communication cannot?

Answer: Speaking to groups on behalf of handgun control is one of the most important tools we have. Although I never wanted to merchandise my position as Jim's wife, circumstances made me more visible than other victims' spouses. Because of that, I almost feel an obligation to speak out publicly, both on a political level and working within the Republican party.

Question: Is it difficult addressing audiences of NRA supporters?

Answer: I don't meet much hostility, even from the NRA, because I take a moderate, commonsense position. Speaking to NRA supporters has been very effective. Once they listen to me, they realize that we don't want to ban their guns or take away their right to bear arms. Instead, we're trying to find ways to keep guns out of the wrong hands.

I don't need to convince our supporters. I want to speak to people who don't share my views. Of course, there's always an element in any audience who doesn't believe what I'm saying.

Question: Have you ever been heckled?

Answer: Yes, but I try to ignore it as much as possible. I don't argue, but I do try to set the record straight. I tell the hecklers that gun control is an emotional issue that needs rational approaches. Interestingly, I find it is the audience that gets angry at the hecklers. I don't need to do it. It's done for me.

Question: Washington is a city where power is generally held by men. When you address Congress, is this a factor in your presentation?

Answer: It was when I first started speaking about gun control. I had the feeling that many people considered me the emotional spouse of someone who was injured. I had to work hard to convince them that I didn't want pity or sympathy. What I wanted was help in making sure that fewer gun-related tragedies occurred to other families. When I stick to the facts, offer commonsense solutions that work, and am unemotional, I give Congress what it needs to make a decision.

Question: Do you avoid emotion in all your speeches?

Answer: I always gear my speeches to the audience. Some audiences want a personal touch—they want to hear about Jim and our son Scott—while others want pure facts.

Question: Is there a place for outrage in your campaign against handguns, or must all your remarks be measured and political?

Answer: There is room for outrage, not hysterical outrage, but outrage at Congress for its inability to pass legislation that has such wide public support.

For the first few years, my role involved education and persuasion. Now that the country supports handgun control—85 percent of the people and even 70 percent of all gun owners back our position—it's clear that Congress is pandering to a very small minority of NRA supporters. Under these circumstances, I think outrage is reasonable.

Question: Is there a challenge you hold for yourself as a speaker?

Answer: I want to persuade the group. I want to know that when it's over people agree with me and are going to let their lawmakers know how they feel. When we first started working with local law enforcement agencies, our goal was to get them involved and united behind gun control. We've done that. On a national level, we want to get Congress to change its ways.

Question: Are you satisfied with your speech delivery?

Answer: I wish I knew what to do about the lights that shine in my face when I speak in a large auditorium. They blind me so I can't see faces. I like to pick out people as I talk to see if I have their attention. I also find it hard to speak in front of people I know. I feel as if they're judging my performance in a different way than strangers.

Question: Is it difficult to speak on television?

Answer: In one sense, it's easier to speak on television, in another it's harder. Since there's no audience, I'm not as self-conscious. But speaking in front of an audience helps get my adrenaline going.

Question: In a recent magazine article, you said, "Maybe that's what Jim and I are going to spend our lives doing—making people aware and saying this could happen to them." Are you planning to continue speaking out?

Answer: Absolutely, as long as people will listen. Because of what happened to Jim, we've had experiences that millions of others have gone through. Jim's visibility gives us the opportunity to help bring about change.

Question: What makes a successful speech?

Answer: You have to have a commitment to what you're saying; you have to feel strongly about it. It's the commitment that gives you the edge.

Source: Interview with Sarah Brady, March 13, 1990.

persuasive task. In other words, asking listeners to agree that U.S. automakers need the support of U.S. consumers to survive in the world market is easier than asking the same audience to agree that every American who buys a foreign car should be penalized through a special tax.

In contrast, when you address an audience that shares your point of view, your job is to reinforce existing attitudes. ("U.S. automakers deserve our support.")

When your audience has not yet formed an opinion, your message must be geared to presenting persuasive evidence (you may want to explain to your audience, for example, the economic necessity of buying U.S. products).

Speeches that Require Action.   Here your goal is to bring about actual change. You ask your listeners to make a purchase, sign a petition, attend a rally, write to Congress, attend a lecture, and so on. The effectiveness of your message is defined by the actions your audience take.

The Attitude-Behavior Connection.   Motivating your listeners to action is perhaps the hardest goal you face as a speaker, requiring attention to the connection between attitudes and behavior. Studies have shown that what people feel is not necessarily what they do; that is, little consistency exists between attitudes and actions.[5] Even if you convince your audience that you are the best candidate for student body president, they may not bother to vote. Similarly, even if you persuade them of the dangers of smoking, confirmed smokers will probably continue to smoke. Researchers have found several explanations for this behavior.

First, people say one thing and do another because of situational forces. If support for your position is strong immediately after your speech, it may dissipate or even disappear in the context in which the behavior takes place. For example, even if you convince listeners to work for your political campaign, if their friends ridicule that choice, they are unlikely to show up at campaign headquarters.

Researchers have found that an attitude is likely to predict behavior when the attitude involves a specific intention to change behavior, when specific attitudes and behaviors are involved, and when the listener's attitude is influenced by firsthand experience.[6] Firsthand experience is a powerful motivator. If you know a sun worshipper dying from melanoma, you are more likely to heed the speaker's advice to wear sun block than if you have no such acquaintance. An experiment by D. T. Regan and R. Fazio proves the point:

> A field study on the Cornell University campus was conducted after a housing shortage had forced some of the incoming freshmen to sleep on cots in the dorm lounges. All freshmen were asked about their attitudes toward the housing crisis and were then given an opportunity to take some related actions (such as signing a petition or joining a

5.   A. W. Wicker, "Attitudes Versus Actions. The Relationship of Verbal and Overt Behavioral Responses to Attitude Objects," *Journal of Social Sciences* 25, no. 4 (1969): 41–78.

6.   For a complete discussion of the attitude–behavior link, see Philip G. Zimbardo, *Psychology and Life,* 12th ed. Glenview, IL: Scott, Foresman and Company, 1988), pp. 618–19.

committee of dorm residents). While all of the respondents expressed the same attitude about the crisis, those who had had more direct experience with it (were actually sleeping in a lounge) showed a greater consistency between their expressed attitudes and their subsequent behavioral attempts to alleviate the problem.[7]

Therefore, if you were a leader on this campus trying to persuade freshmen to sign a petition or join a protest march, you would have had greater persuasive success with listeners who had been forced to sleep in the dorm lounges.

Persuasive Aims

Once you establish your overall persuasive goals, you must then decide the type and direction of the change you seek. You must define the narrower aims of your speech. Four persuasive aims define the nature of your overall persuasive goal.

Adoption.   When you want your audience to start doing something, your persuasive goal is to urge the audience to adopt a particular idea or plan. As a spokesperson for the American Cancer Society, you may deliver the following message: "I urge every woman over the age of forty to get a regular mammogram."

Continuance.   Sometimes your listeners are already doing the thing you want them to do. In this case, your goal is to urge continuance. For example, the same spokesperson might say:

> I am delighted to be speaking to this organization because of the commitment of every member to stop smoking. I urge all of you to maintain your commitment to be smoke free for the rest of your life.

Speeches that urge continuance are necessary when the group is under pressure to change. In this case, the spokesperson realized that many reformed smokers constantly fight the urge to begin smoking again.

Discontinuance.   You attempt to persuade your listeners to stop doing something:

> I can tell by looking around that many people in this room spend hours sitting in the sun. I want to share with you a grim fact. The evidence is unmistakable that there is a direct connection between exposure to the sun and the deadliest of all skin cancers—malignant melanoma.

Deterrence.   In this case, your goal is avoidance. You want to convince your listeners not to start something:

> We have found that exposure to asbestos can cause cancer twenty or thirty years later. If you have flaking asbestos insulation in your home, don't remove it yourself. Call in

7.   D. T. Regan and R. Fazio, "On the Consistency Between Attitudes and Behavior: Look to the Method of Attitude Formation, *Journal of Experimental Social Psychology* 13 (1977): 28–45. Cited in Philip G. Zimbardo, *Psychology and Life,* p. 618.

experts who have the knowledge and equipment to remove the insulation, protecting themselves as well as you and your family. Be sure you are not going to deal with an unscrupulous contractor who is likely to send in unqualified and unprotected workers likely to do a shoddy job.

Speeches that focus on deterrence are responses to problems that can be avoided. These messages are delivered when a persuasive speaker determines that an audience possesses something which the speaker sees as highly threatening or likely to result in disaster.[8] The speaker may try to bring about some sort of effective block or barrier to minimize if not eliminate the threat or danger. New homeowners, for example, in urban as well as suburban communities, frequently find themselves listening to persuasive presentations about the purchase of a home security system. The thrust of such a persuasive speech is the need of a homeowner to prevent burglary through use of an effective and economical security system.

TYPES OF PERSUASIVE CLAIMS

Within the context of these persuasive goals and aims, you must decide the type of persuasive message you want to deliver. Are you dealing with a question of fact, or value, or policy? To decide, look at your core idea, which expresses your judgment or point of view. In persuasive speeches, the core idea is phrased as a proposition that must be proved.

Propositions are necessary because persuasion always involves more than one point of view. If yours were the only way of thinking, persuasion would be unnecessary. Because your audience is faced with differing opinions, your goal is to present your opinion in the most effective way.

The three major types of propositions are those of fact, of value, and of policy.

Proposition of Fact

Because facts, like beauty, are often in the eye of the beholder, you may have to persuade your listeners that your interpretation of a situation, event, or concept is accurate. Like a lawyer in a courtroom, you have to convince people to accept your version of the truth. Here are two examples of facts that require proof:

- Water fluoridation is a potential cancer risk.
- American corporations are losing their hold on many world markets.

As we discussed in Chapter 13, informative speakers become persuasive speakers when they cross the line from presenting facts to presenting facts within the context of a point of view. The informative speaker lets listeners decide on a position based on their own analysis of the facts; the persuasive speaker draws the conclusion for them. Here are the same topics recast as informative speeches:

- Research on water fluoridation and cancer.

8. For more information on these persuasive speech forms, see Wallace C. Fotheringham, *Perspectives on Persuasion* (Boston: Allyn & Bacon, 1966), p. 32.

⌘ The changing role of American corporations on the world market.

When student orator Karen Kimmey had to deal with a proposition of fact regarding the dangers of riding a school bus, part of her approach was to convince her listeners of the safety hazards on the road:

> After a siege of serious accidents, the United States Department of Transportation investigated the structure of school buses, and found roofs and floors with little support, likely to tear apart—which proved to be fatal in a 1985 accident near Snow Hill, North Carolina. *Newsday* . . . reports that during a collision between a tractor and one such pre-standard bus, the floor of the bus had literally opened up, killing six children. According to *School Product News,* . . . the study also discovered nonshatter-resistant windows, seats which would separate from the floor on impact and flammable seat padding . . . .
>
> The Department of Transportation took action and insisted on numerous improvements. As of April 1, 1987, all vehicles used to transport school children must be built without the previously mentioned flaws, and, most importantly, built with protective metal baskets wrapped around the potentially explosive fuel tanks . . . .
>
> So realizing the danger of pre-standard buses the Department of Transportation also required that school districts dispose of such buses by the year 1992. And in 1989, they're nearly gone from our school districts.
>
> So you're all breathing a sigh of relief as it appears the school bus issue is over and this speech is simply superfluous. Actually, it has never been more necessary. For from this earlier situation, a bitter irony has arisen. The buses which we assume have quietly died in junkyards have returned to our nation's roads disguised as private and civic buses.[9]

When dealing with propositions of fact, you must convince your audience that your evaluation is based on widely accepted standards. In this example the audience looked for objective evidence that school buses are unsafe. Only when they were satisfied that these hazards were present and that the speaker was basing her contention on objective evidence was persuasion possible. To be effective, your objective evidence may have to be applied to a specific case. For example, you may need to show that the school bus involved in a recent accident was a safety hazard. By stating the standards first and then applying them to the unique situation, you strengthen your case.

Proposition of Value

Values are deep-seated beliefs that guide what we consider good or bad, moral or immoral, satisfying or unsatisfying, proper or improper, wise or foolish, valuable or invaluable, and so on. Persuasive speeches that deal with propositions of value are

---

9. Karen Kimmey, "The Bingity, Bangity School Bus," *Winning Orations of the Interstate Oratorical Association* (Mankato, MN: Interstate Oratorical Association, Mankato State University, Mankato, Minn 56001 1989), p. 8.

assertions based on these beliefs. The speaker's goal is to prove the worth of an evaluative statement, as in the following examples:

⌘ It is wrong for men to leave all the housework and childcare to their working wives.

⌘ My alma mater has the best biology department in the country.

⌘ Plagiarism is unacceptable.

Here Jeff Hudson, a student, talks about how the advantage incumbents hold over would-be challengers is inherently unfair:

> The flow of money almost exclusively to incumbents insures that we will have the same people representing us year after year. Incumbents are safer, they have more financial influence. They, therefore, make a much better bet for Political Action Committees, but not necessarily a better bet for an American that believes elections should be won by qualified candidates, and not automatons that can build up a veritable fortress of cash while serving in their own Congressional office . . . .
>
> Elections in this country used to be a joyous time, when colonists would revel in their newly found freedom and power. Today, I'm afraid that power has been lost. This country is based on the ability of people to make decisions. We may not always make the right ones, but if we have the choices, then we can be very safe in our assumption that our American electoral system is the best that it can be.[10]

Proposition of Policy

Propositions of policy are easily recognizable by their use of the word "should":

⌘ Campus safety should be the number one priority of the college administration.

⌘ Student-athletes should adhere to the same academic standards as other students.

Although the concept of "should" is not always stated in policy speeches, it is always implied. Action is advocated as the speaker presses his message. In the following policy address delivered in 1965, black activist leader Malcolm X advocated that the term "civil rights" be rejected in favor of "human rights" because civil rights confined blacks

> to the jurisdiction of Uncle Sam. No one from the outside world can speak out in your behalf as long as your struggle is a civil-rights struggle. Civil rights come within the domestic affairs of this country. All of our African brothers and our Asian brothers and our Latin-American brothers cannot open their mouths and interfere in the domestic affairs of the United States. And as long as it's civil rights, this comes under the jurisdiction of Uncle Sam. But the United Nations has what's known as the charter of human rights. It has a committee that deals in human rights . . . . When you expand the

---

10. Jeff Hudson, "The Incumbent Advantage . . . or Disadvantage," *Winning Orations of the Interstate Oratorical Association* (1989), pp. 56–59.

Persuasive speaking is effected through the listeners by keeping their interest with appeals to attitudes, beliefs, and values.

civil rights struggle to the level of human rights, you can then take the case of the black man in this country before the nations of the U.N. You can take it before the General Assembly. You can take Uncle Sam before a world court.[11]

11. Thomas W. Benson, "Malcolm X," in Bernard K. Duffy and Halford R. Ryan, *American Orators of the Twentieth Century: Critical Studies and Sources* (New York: Greenwood Press, 1987), pp. 319–20.

Policy Addresses Must Establish the Need For Change.   Your first task in a policy speech is to convince listeners of the need for change. This step gives people reason to continue listening and, in the end, to agree with your position and take action. To clarify the need in your own mind, organize your thoughts around a question:

⌘ Is there a need to increase funding to fight illiteracy?

⌘ Is there a need for Congress to pass child-care legislation?

⌘ Is there a need to limit which videos children can rent?

Here Dr. James S. Todd, spokesperson for the American Medical Association, talks about the need to strengthen the American health-care system:

> . . . . I'm unwilling to accept compromises in my country's health-care system, whose excellence is often taken for granted by most of us, and whose flaws draw all the attention, but can be corrected without radical reorganization.
>
> Our system is not perfect . . . but at its best, it is without comparison anywhere in the world.
>
> Where else would any of us go to receive treatment? . . .
>
> The research, technology, medical equipment, hospitals, and medical personnel in this country are substantially better, on average, than in any other nation in the world.
>
> I submit that our challenge is to strengthen our current system, not destroy it, or replace it with something totally foreign, and probably unacceptable to the American culture.
>
> H. L. Mencken once said that for every problem there is a solution that is simple, neat, and absolutely wrong.
>
> He could well have been referring to the centralized, monolithic health delivery mechanisms that some have promoted as a quick fix for our health-care system's flaws.
>
> The lessons of England, Canada, and other industrialized nations, bear testimony to the wisdom of Mencken's observation.
>
> The British system's problems have long been known and the government is working to move toward a system that is closer to our own . . . .
>
> And now the Canadian system, with its long lines for care, technology deprivation, temporal rationing of certain procedures, and serious underfunding, is receiving its fair share of scrutiny.[12]

The most effective satisfaction of needs statements focus on the audience. Here Nelson Mandela supplies his audience—the blacks of South Africa—with reasons for ending apartheid:

> Today the majority of South Africans, black and white, recognize that apartheid has no future. It has to be ended by our own decisive mass actions in order to build peace and security. The mass campaigns of defiance and other actions of our organizations and people can only culminate in the establishment of democracy.

---

12.   James S. Todd, "The American Health-Care System: Strengthen It, Don't Scrap It," speech delivered before the National Education Association 1989 Retirement and Benefits Forum, October 5, 1989. Reprinted in *Vital Speeches of the Day*, February 15, 1990, p. 276.

> The apartheid destruction in our subcontinent is incalculable. The fabric of family life of millions of my people has been shattered. Millions are homeless and unemployed . . . .[13]

The most effective needs statements are also specific, rather than abstract, leaving no room for misunderstanding or boredom. In a speech dealing with the problem of traffic congestion, C. Kenneth Orski, president of the Urban Mobility Corporation, provided specificity through several examples:

> Let me set the stage by relating a few anecdotes that will paint the dimensions of the traffic congestion problem.
> . . . In Orange County, California, freeway traffic reports are now a regular feature on the midnight radio newscasts . . . And in Santa Clara County they begin as early as 5 A.M. . . .
> In Los Angeles, the busiest freeway stretch is the Ventura Freeway in Encino, far from anyplace even remotely considered a "downtown . . . ."
> On the Washington Beltway police delivered more than a dozen babies last year to women who got stuck in traffic jams on the way to the maternity ward. . . .
> And on LBJ Freeway in Dallas, they say, the only way to change lanes is trade cars. . . .
> What these anecdotes suggest is that the very nature of traffic congestion has changed. Once a phenomenon confined in space and time, traffic congestion has become endemic and pervasive, affecting suburbs and central cities alike. . . .[14]

When formulating your statement of needs, remember the human tendency to hold onto the status quo. Your job is motivation. Supply the reason for change, be the advocate for change, and people will listen.

Policy Addresses Propose a Practical Solution.   Now your audience is ready to hear your solution, which is the core of your speech:

⌘ I propose that the local school board allocate resources to deal with adult illiteracy.

⌘ I propose that Congress pass the child-care legislation now before it, guaranteeing every American family affordable child care.

⌘ I propose that children under 16 not be allowed to rent "R"- or "X"-rated videos without adult permission.

For your proposal to be taken seriously, it should be practical. No one will listen, for example, if you suggest that the federal government supply every U.S. family with children with a full-time live-in nanny. Nor will they listen if you suggest

13.   Nelson Mandela, "Apartheid Has No Future: Africa Is Ours," speech delivered to the public, Cape Town, South Africa, February 11, 1990. Reprinted in *Vital Speeches of the Day,* March 1, 1990, p. 296.
14.   C. Kenneth Orski, "The Problem of Traffic Congestion: A Common Sense Look," speech delivered before the 22nd Anniversary Luncheon of the Traffic Improvement Association of Oakland County, November 3, 1989. Reprinted in *Vital Speeches of the Day,* January 1, 1990, p. 190.

that the federal government designate adult illiteracy as the nation's number one social problem. Although most people will agree that illiteracy is a major social ill, other problems such as drugs, AIDS, poverty, and homelessness generally are considered more pressing.

Here is Orski's solution for handling traffic congestion. Notice that the strength of his argument is in the evidence. He cites authorities and existing plans that work:

> How do we manage traffic congestion? Basically, by practicing three strategies:
>
> ✕ incrementally expanding road capacity
> ✕ reducing the growth of transportation demand; and
> ✕ controlling the intensity and pace of development (i.e. avoiding congestion) . . . .
>
> It goes without saying that we must do our best to keep expanding road capacity. The trouble is, as recent events in several jurisdictions have demonstrated, our distaste for higher taxes seems to outweigh our desire for road improvements.
>
> The good news is that a persistent imbalance between transportation demand and transportation supply is making highway facilities an attractive private investment. An official of Northern Virginia's Dulles Toll Road was recently quoted as saying that "The only thing that is more profitable than owning a private toll road is owning the government's printing press for currency." He knows whereof he speaks: the Dulles Toll Road earned $16.2 million in fiscal 1988, enough to pay the debt . . . and operating costs, and turn a small profit. And this, after only 5 years of operation. The surplus in the next 10 years is projected to exceed $10 million.
>
> There are signs that Wall Street is taking notice of the investment potential of commuter toll roads. Privately financed and operated tollways are no longer an arcane concept debated only by free market economists. They are being seriously considered in Denver (E-470), . . . in Orange County, CA (Foothills Freeway), and in Northern Virginia (Dulles Toll Road Extension). A bill to authorize up to four private toll roads in California has recently been signed by Governor Deukmejian. In sum, private toll roads offer us an opportunity to have our cake and eat it too; to expand highway infrastructure without raising the specter of new taxes or bigger budget deficits.[15]

The speech continues in this fashion, providing a practical solution to an identifiable problem. The speaker's argument is framed as an alternative to raising taxes. Recognizing that his audience would oppose a tax hike, Orski takes a different approach, attractive because it is feasible. Throughout your speech, your listeners may be comparing proposals—yours to the existing plan, yours to another proposal, and so on. You may have to prove that your plan has the best chance of success.

Policy Addresses Focus on the Individuals Or Groups Responsible For the Change.   One of the major differences between a proposition of policy and a proposition of value is that the proposition of policy makes clear what groups or individuals are responsible for the proposed action. According to Jo Sprague and Douglas Stuart, speeches that fail to supply this information are not policy speeches. "Although your thesis includes the word *should/should not,* it is really a disguised

---

15.   Ibid, p. 191.

proposition of value. Tax loopholes should be closed, for example, is only another way of saying: The present tax system is bad. To be a proposition of policy it must read: Congress should change the present tax structure to reduce oil depletion allowances, vacation home deductions, and home office deductions."[16]

Here student Jenelle C. Martin focuses on what students can do to make their campus safe:

> We as college students . . . must become involved. First of all, we must begin to report campus crimes whenever they occur; only when security personnel know about the problem can they begin to [deal with] it. Second, we must begin to take the necessary precautions—simple acts such as locking our doors and walking across campus in large groups can make a big difference. And finally, we must begin to make our concerns about campus safety known. Not only should it become a priority for ourselves, but a priority for the college as well. Speak with the Dean, the Director of Security or even the President himself. Talk to them and tell them of your concerns. Make it the topic of discussion in your classroom or appeal to your student government organization in assisting you in making your concerns about campus safety known.[17]

Propositions of Policy Always Involve Statements of Fact and Value.   Although for discussion purposes we have separated speeches dealing with propositions of fact, propositions of value, and propositions of policy, these propositions build on one another in the same speech. To convince an audience to take an action, you have to prove a proposition of value and establish a proposition of fact. For example, if your proposition of policy is that the television networks should reduce their coverage of sports, you must prove the proposition of value that the emphasis on sports in this country is extreme and inappropriate and establish the following propositions of fact:

⌘ In 1988, Americans spent about $61 billion on sports of every kind—an amount that roughly equals the total gross national product of Yugoslavia or Algeria.

⌘ Millions of Americans watch televised sports.

⌘ This activity reduces the amount of time American men spend with their families.[18]

ORGANIZING A PERSUASIVE SPEECH: THE MOTIVATED SEQUENCE   As emphasized throughout this text, communication is a transactional process connecting both speaker and audience. This awareness is particularly important in speeches to persuade, for without taking into account the mental stages your audience passes through, your persuasion may not succeed. Next we will examine the *motivated sequence,* a widely used method for organizing persuasive speeches developed by the late communication professor Alan H. Monroe. Professor Monroe

16.   Jo Sprague and Douglas Stuart, *The Speaker's Handbook,* 3d ed. (San Diego: Harcourt Brace Jovanovich, 1992), p. 264.

17.   Jenelle C. Martin, "Campus Safety: The Forgotten Priority," *Winning Orations of the Interstate Oratorical Association* (1989), p. 16.

18.   Data from Robert J. Samuelson, "The American Sports Mania," *Newsweek,* September 4, 1989, p. 49. Section based on Sprague and Stuart, *The Speaker's Handbook,* p. 308.

explained to his classes that the motivated sequence was rooted in traditional rhetoric and shaped by modern psychology.[19]

The method focuses on five steps to motivate your audience to act and, as Monroe would tell his students, they follow the normal pattern of human thought from attention to action: attention, need, satisfaction, visualization, and action.

Attention

Persuasion is impossible without attention. Your first step is to capture your listeners' attention in your introduction and convince them that you have something to say that is of genuine importance to them. Chapter 9 addresses several ways to do this, including making a startling statement, using an anecdote, and asking rhetorical questions. For example, in capturing her audiences' attention to address the listeners about the problem of injuries and deaths in youth baseball, Cherie Spurling began by saying:

> "Take me out to the ball game. Take me out to the crowd. Buy me some peanuts and Cracker Jack. I don't care if I ever get back . . ." Have you ever thought you might go to a ball game and never get back? Neither did nine-year-old Ryan Wojic. As his mother drove him to the ball field one day Ryan announced, "I am going to steal two bases, Mom . . ." His mother replied: "Ryan, you don't have to steal two bases; just do the best you can." We'll never know whether Ryan would have stolen two bases or done the best he could, because his first time up to bat was his last time up to bat. He sustained a lethal injury, and Ryan Wojic never got back.[20]

Need

In the need step, you describe the problem you will address in your speech. You hinted or suggested a need in your introduction, but now you state it in a way that accurately reflects your specific purpose. Your aim in the need step is to motivate your listeners to care about the problem by making it clear the problem affects them. You can illustrate the need by using examples, intensify it through the use of carefully selected additional supporting material, and *link* it directly to the audience. Too often the inexperienced speaker who uses the motivated sequence will pass through the need step too quickly in haste to get to the third step, the satisfaction step. Let's look at how Ms. Spurling described part of the need to recognize and eliminate a serious problem she asked her audience to face.

> Ryan Wojic was killed when one of these speeding balls struck his chest. His heart went into immediate cardiac arrhythmia and paramedics could not revive him. And Ryan is not alone, as I mentioned previously, a Consumer Product Safety Commission Report stated that in a single ten-year period 51 children have died from baseball injuries. Of

---

19. The motivated sequence was first explained to the author by Professor Alan H. Monroe in a 1965 seminar on "The Psychology of Speech" at Purdue University. For a current reference, see Bruce E. Gronbeck, Kathleen German, Douglas Ehninger, and Alan H. Monroe, *Principles of Speech Communication, 11th brief ed. (New York: Harper Collins, 1992),pp. 263–272.*

20. Cherie Spurling, "Batter Up—Batter Down," *Winning Orations of the Interstate Oratorical Association.* Mankato State University, The Interstate Oratorical Association, 1992.

these, 23 were caused by the impact of the ball to the chest. The players at greatest risk are the pitchers and batters, and every kid bats at some point.

The same holds true for the risk of head and facial injuries. Take the case of Daniel Schwartz for instance: as reported by ABC's Stone Phillips. Thirteen-year-old Daniel went up to bat. The first ball was pitched low; the second to the inside. The third nailed Daniel in the face, shattering his cheekbone and nearly destroying his left eye. According to the April 1988 issue of *American Health,* each year baseball produces thousands of stories like Daniel's.

Satisfaction

The satisfaction step presents a solution to the problem you just described. You offer a proposal in the form of an attitude, belief, or action you want your audience to adopt and act upon. Explanations in the form of statistics, testimony, examples, and other support ensure that your audience understands exactly what you mean. You clearly state what you want your audience to adopt and then explain your proposal. You certainly have to show your audience how your proposal meets the need you presented. To be sure everyone understands what you mean, you may wish to use several different forms of support accompanied by visuals or audio-visual aids. An audience is usually impressed if you can show the listeners where and how a similar proposal has worked elsewhere. Before you move to the fourth step you need to meet objections you predict that some listeners may hold. We are all familiar with the persuader who attempts to sell us a product or service and wants us to believe it is well worth the price and within our budget. In fact a considerable amount of sales appeal today aims at selling us a payment we can afford as a means to purchasing the product, whether it is an automobile, a vacation, or some other attractive item. If we can afford the monthly payment a major objection has been met. Here is how Ms. Spurling wanted to solve the problem she addressed:

> Well, "some sort" of protection has been developed. *American Health* reports that Home Safe Inc., has found an all-star solution. Teams like the Atlee Little Leaguers in Mechanicsville, Virginia, have solved many of their safety problems by wearing face shields like this one [shown]. This molded plastic shield snaps onto the ear flaps of the standard batter's helmet, which incidently, was invented in 1959 by none other than Creighton Hale. Most youth teams require the use of a batters helmet, but with this shield they could add complete facial protection, including the eyes, for a cost of under $15 per shield. Daniel Schwartz's injuries have cost $23,000 so far.
>
> Players could also be protected from chest impact death by wearing one of these padded vests [shown]. The vest may be a bit of a hindrance, that's true, but had Ryan Wojic been wearing one he would probably be stealing bases today.

Visualization

The visualization step encourages listeners to picture themselves benefitting from the adoption of your proposal. It focuses on a vision of the future if your proposal is adopted and, just as important, if it is rejected. It may also contrast these two visions, strengthening the attractiveness of your proposal by showing what will happen if no action is taken.

Positive visualization is specific and concrete. Your goal is to help listeners see themselves under the conditions you describe. You want them to experience enjoyment and satisfaction. In contrast, negative visualization focuses on what will happen without your plan. Here you encourage discomfort with conditions that would exist. Whichever method you choose, make your listeners feel part of the future. Ms. Spurling's speech did not include the visualization step but rather moved from satisfying the need to calling for action. Before moving to her strong call for the audience act she could have added persuasive appeal to this important message by saying:

> Imagine yourself on a quiet and lazy summer afternoon watching your own child, a niece, a nephew, a cousin or a neighborhood friend up to bat in an exciting youth-league baseball game. And think about the comfort you will experience when you see that she or he has the proper safety equipment on so that there is no possibility that a speeding baseball will take his or her life or result in any permanent disability. See for a moment the face and the form of a child enthusiastically awaiting the pitch and see as well this child effectively shielded from impact that could come from a missed pitch.

Action

The action step acts as the conclusion of your speech. Here you tell your listeners what you want them to do or if action is not necessary, the point of view you want them to share. You may have to explain the specific actions you want and the timing for these actions. This step is most effective when immediate action is sought.

Many students find the call to action a difficult part of the persuasive speech. They have difficulty when they are reluctant to make an explicit request for action. Can you imagine a politician failing to ask people for their vote? Such a candidate would surely lose an election. When sales representatives have difficulty in closing a deal because they are unable to ask consumers to buy their products they do not last long in sales. Persuasion is more likely to result when direction is clear and action is the goal. Ms. Spurling concluded her speech by asking her audience:

> We must realize, however, that it may be awhile before this equipment scores a home run, so now it is your turn up to bat. If you are personally interested in protecting these young ball players, spread the word about these injuries, especially to businesses that sponsor youth teams. Encourage them to purchase safety equipment for the teams and then to sponsor them only on the condition that the equipment be used.
>
> You can also write to Little League of America or any other youth league, requesting that they take their members' safety more seriously. And yes, do write to your congressional representative, because he or she may have a child or grandchild who plays on a youth team. Finally, if you happen to have a few extra dollars in your pocket, you could purchase some of this equipment and donate it to a local team as I'll do with this [equipment shown]."

Ms. Spurling provided effective closure to her persuasive speech and call for action when she told her audience:

> Now that we have discovered how children are being seriously injured and even killed while playing baseball, I know that you agree that given the children's lack of skill, we

need to mandate the use of face shields, padded vests, and safer balls. So take them out to the ball game, but make it one that children can play safely, because children may be dying to play baseball, but they should never die because of it."

In review, then, remember the five-step pattern that you can use as a persuader if you want to lead your audience from attention to action. As mentioned, the need step is often difficult for students to develop. The need step may require a difficult research undertaking. For some speakers a general statement about a need is made and, after a few additional comments, the speaker moves quickly to the satisfaction step. You should prove to your audience that indeed a significant need must be met. Because the need step is often difficult for speakers to complete we want to underscore the point that to be effective, persuasive speeches must be *motivational;* they must have the potential to propel the listeners to act or to change an attitude. A clear psychological perspective on *needs* can be understood by any of us if we examine and think carefully about how psychologist Abraham Maslow classified needs. You can find Maslow's theory helpful in creating in the audience's mind's eye the need to be satisfied.

MASLOW'S HIERARCHY OF NEEDS

Humanist psychologist Abraham Maslow classified human needs according to the hierarchy pictured in Figure 14.1. An analysis of these needs will help you understand audience motivation as you attempt to persuade. Maslow believed that our most basic needs—those at the bottom of the hierarchy—must be satisfied before we can consider those on the next levels. In effect, these "higher level" needs are put on "hold" and have little effect on our actions until the "lower level" needs are met.

Survival Needs.   At the bottom of the hierarchy are our biological needs for food, water, oxygen, rest, and release from stress. If you are delivering a speech in favor of a proposed new reservoir to a community experiencing problems with its water supply, it would be appropriate to appeal to the need for safe and abundant water.

Safety Needs.   Safety needs include the need for security, freedom from fear and attack, a home that offers tranquility and comfort, and a means of earning a living. If you are delivering the same speech to a group of unemployed construction workers, you might link the reservoir project to jobs and a steady family income.

Attachment Needs.   Attachment needs refer to our needs for affiliation, friendship, and love. Appealing to the need for social belonging, you may choose to emphasize the camaraderie that will emerge from the community effort to bring the reservoir from the planning stage to completion.

Esteem Needs.   Esteem needs include the need to see oneself as worthy and competent and to have the respect of others. In this case, an effective approach would be to praise community members for their initiative in helping to make the reservoir project a reality.

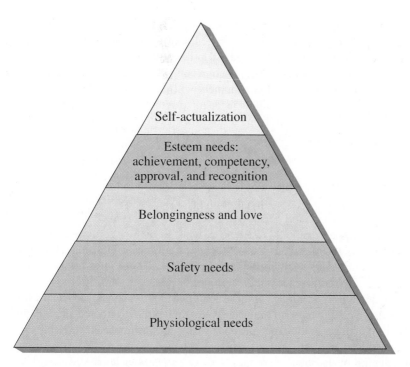

FIGURE 14.1
Maslow's Hierarchy of
Needs.

Self-Actualization Needs.   People who reach the top of the hierarchy seek to fulfill their highest potential through personal growth, creativity, self-awareness and knowledge, social responsibility, and responsiveness to challenge. Addressing this audience, you might emphasize the long-range environmental and ecological implications of the reservoir. Your appeal may include the need to safeguard the water supply for future generations.

Understanding the basis for Maslow's hierarchy is critical to your success as a persuasive speaker, for if you approach your listeners at an inappropriate level of need, you will find them unable or unwilling to respond.

Let's imagine you have a classmate Susan who is carefully considering several topics of interest to her. She faces making initial plans for two persuasive speeches that are class assignments. Certainly if Susan speaks about the need to manage and eliminate unhealthy stress in meeting academic, social, and family responsibilities she will ground her arguments in survival needs. However, if she chooses to speak about the need for increased lighting on campus accompanied by an effective escort service, she will have to address safety needs. If she speaks on behalf of her sorority during the rush period, she is likely to talk about everyone's need for friendship, common goals, and a sense of identification with others on campus. She will, of course, present the class with an attachment need.

Suppose that Susan chooses to persuade the members of the class to take part in campus activities such as student government, the school paper, or theatre productions. She is likely to argue that such participation results in a greater sense of self, new feelings of accomplishment, and an increase in respect from others. This persuasive speech, then, will be based on esteem needs. However, a speech in favor of selecting a major that each of you genuinely enjoys accompanied by a firm commitment to reach graduation is likely to be centered in self-actualization needs.

Once her classmates feel they share a compelling need, Susan must move her speech to a satisfaction step that genuinely will eliminate the need. She must also present a visualization step to allow listeners to actually picture the benefits—or the lack thereof—that will result from action—or inaction. The call to action must be powerful in telling the audience *what to do* and *how to do it.*

SUMMARY Persuasive speaking is rooted in the theories of Aristotle that define persuasion in terms of appeals to the reason and emotion of an audience and of the speaker's credibility. The two overall persuasive goals are to address audience attitudes and to move an audience to action. It is often difficult to motivate people to act—studies have shown there is little consistency between attitudes and actions. Four specific persuasive aims define the focus of your speech. These aims include adoption, continuance, discontinuance, and deterrence.

Within the broad context of these goals and aims, you must then define the type of persuasive claim you want to make. Your point of view, or core idea, is expressed in the form of a proposition that must be proved. Propositions take three basic forms: In propositions of fact, you attempt to convince your listeners to accept your interpretation of the facts; in propositions of value, your goal is to persuade your listeners to accept the worth of a value-based statement; in propositions of policy, you urge action first by convincing your listeners of the need for change and then presenting practical solutions.

An effective method for organizing a persuasive speech is Monroe's Motivated Sequence that includes five steps designed to motivate the audience to action. In the attention step, your goal is to convince your audience to listen to what you have to say. In the need step, you describe the problem you will address in your speech in a way that is consistent with the specific purpose of your speech. In the satisfaction step, you present a solution to the problem you described and support it with solid evidence. In the visualization step, you focus on visions of the future if your proposal is adopted or rejected. And in the action step, you point your listeners to the specific steps you want them to take, as well as to the timing of these actions. Understanding Abraham Maslow's hierarchy of human needs is helpful to persuasive speakers.

QUESTIONS FOR STUDY AND DISCUSSION
1. How would you define persuasion, persuasive goals, and persuasive aims? Illustrate your definitions with specific examples.
2. Why was Sarah Brady's speech to Congress a persuasive speech? What impact do Brady's comments in the chapter interview have on your evaluation of the speech?
3. Why is the motivated sequence audience centered? When using the sequence, why is it essential to understand audience needs as defined by Abraham Maslow?

1. List five persons you recognize as spokespersons on important public issues. In a written analysis, describe the *ethos* of each speaker.
2. Prepare a five- to six-minute persuasive speech, organizing it according to the motivated sequence. Prepare a written analysis of why the speech fits the requirements of the sequence. Then deliver the speech to your class.
3. Look through an anthology of speeches, such as *Vital Speeches of the Day,* or a video collection, to find an effective persuasive speech. Evaluate the persuasion used in the speech according to what you have learned in this chapter.

S A M P L E   S P E E C H E S

*I*n the speech that follows, Mindy Brewer, a student, talks about environmental racism characterized by industries that dispose of toxic waste and other garbage in inexpensive and poor residential areas populated primarily by minorities. Her persuasive speech is organized around a proposition of value: "Because of a push to dispose of garbage as quickly and as quietly as possible, a travesty known as environmental racism or environmental discrimination is becoming frighteningly prominent."

As you study and assess Mindy Brewer's speech, ask yourself: What are the persuasive ingredients of this speech? Can you identify and explain any strengths or weaknesses? Consider yourself a member of the audience for this speech and think about whether you find the message persuasive and why you think as you do about the speech. The notes to the left of this speech are there only to serve as a guide while you analyze the speech yourself.

DANCES WITH GARBAGE: THE TRAGEDY
OF ENVIRONMENTAL DISCRIMINATION

Mindy Brewer
Iowa State University

The contrast between celebrating the earth and the disappointing results are pointed out to capture the attention of the audience.

On April 22, 1990, much of the world paused to celebrate Earth Day. During the weeks directly before and after, more concern and attention was given to the environment than almost ever before. Sadly, over two years later, the trend is not necessarily continuing.

Statistics from a widely read magazine followed by a war metaphor reinforce the opener. The term "environmental racism" is introduced to create interest and provide a preliminary announcement of the topic.

In a poll published in the February 3, 1992, issue of *Time,* 45% of Americans thought we should go slow in spending money to clean up the environment, and a shocking 51% said environmentalists go too far in the demands they place upon businesses and the government. A battle between ecology and the economy has been raging for years—a battle which has left the environment and large portions of the population quickly losing. Because of a push to dispose of garbage as quickly and as quietly as possible, a travesty known as environmental racism or environmental discrimination is becoming frighteningly prominent.

An initial summary of the main ideas in the speech is provided as a preview.

In order to comprehend this tragedy, which has been obscured by a combination of economic worries and ignorance, we will first look at where environmental racism is found in our country and what it's doing to the people involved. Then we will examine why this disparity exists in the world's largest "democratic" nation. And finally, we will explore ways to fight the battle and bring equity to the distribution of the nation's waste.

This is a clear and vivid description of environmental waste as an act of racism.

According to the August 13, 1990, issue of *Time* magazine, the process of environmental discrimination is simple. Industries look for cheap land on which to build toxic waste incinerators and dispose of garbage. After they're shot down in suburban communities by active protest, they turn to land in poor areas, often with large populations of minorities. And because these people have other burdens to bear, like drugs, crime, and poverty, they are often too powerless or apathetic to prevent their neighborhoods from becoming the dumping ground for everyone else's waste.

These statistics and specific instances heighten the problem and point up a need.

A landmark study done in 1987 by the United Church of Christ's Commission for Racial Justice, and cited in the April, 1991, *Environment,* discovered that three out of every five African Americans and Hispanics live in neighborhoods with a hazardous waste site.

Business Week of May 20, 1991, details a civil rights lawsuit currently facing Chem Waste Management, Inc. The suit accuses the nation's largest waste disposal firm, the county, and the state of discrimination, when they chose to build a toxic waste incinerator in Kettleman City, CA—which is 95% Hispanic. Chem Waste also has several other sites around the nation that are currently under question, including Chicago's south side, and Port Arthur, TX. Both are places where the company has built incinerators in areas with large populations of blacks and Hispanics.

Here the speaker turns to another widely read source to point to a mean and mocking play on the title of the popular film "Dances With Wolves."

The problem, however, does not only affect minorities in urban areas, but also the poor of many races in rural areas, as well. According to *Newsweek* of April 26, 1991, economic pressures have driven a South Dakota Indian tribe to offer up their precious reservation land as the site for a proposed solid waste landfill—what some critics mockingly call, "Dances With Garbage."

One of the worst non-urban sites is a 75-mile stretch of land along the Mississippi River known as "Cancer Alley." According to *Time* of August 13, 1990, the poverty stricken strip is riddled with petro-chemical plants and oil refineries. And has such an abnormally high rate of cancer, one health expert called it a "massive human experiment."

By this point the speaker has moved from Western rural areas vulnerable to environmental discrimination to the East Coast to prove the problem is widespread.

The human experiments continue in working class Passaic, New Jersey, where one incinerator spills out over three tons of lead emissions a year—less than half a block from a county hospital. And in a poverty-stricken border town called Matamoros, which is struggling under the residue left by years of unchecked industrial pollution—pollution which is thought to be the cause of serious birth defects. According to the January 20, 1992 *Baltimore Sun,* over the past two years local hospitals have seen 12 infants born without brains.

Because the problem is so widespread, affecting poor and minorities in rural and urban areas from coast to coast, there are a variety of reasons why the disparity continues. In many neighborhoods with large populations of poor and minorities, there is, unfortunately, an inherent lack of the knowledge and resources necessary to successfully fight against huge corporations and disinterested government officials.

Dr. Robert Bullard, a Professor of Sociology at the University of California-Riverside, says circumstances like these make a neighborhood especially vulnerable. In the May 20, 1991, *Business Week* he said, "It's a pattern of picking the path of least resistance. Minority communities are the least likely to fight back." Unfortunately, some victims of environmental racism are actually there due to self-exploitation. In the case of the incinerator proposed on the Rosebud Sioux Indian Reservation, tribal leaders there were promised that their people would be given "preference" for the 80-100 jobs estimated at the site. This is almost impossible to pass up with an unemployment rate of 85%. The question being asked, however, is will these economic gains make a significant enough difference to make the environment ravages worthwhile. As critic Robert Valandro said in the April 26, 1991, *Newsweek,* "They say we have 85% unemployment. So we get a mega-dump and then what do we have? 84.5% unemployment."

By this point the audience has been confronted with a serious problem of discrimination that listeners have not been aware of, so the speaker's message moves to steps necessary to bring about change.

With such widespread scope, and so many elements working against them, the plight of the environmental refugee might seem hopeless. But, in fact, there are steps to be taken by groups and individuals to fight environmental discrimination, and bring more equity to the distribution of our waste.

First, perhaps the biggest barrier to overcome is the lack of knowledge and resources necessary to battle unwanted environmental hazards. In the May, 1991, issue of *Audubon* magazine, author Peter Reinhart suggests implementing programs of environmental education into poverty stricken and inner-city schools—to educate often forgotten children about the environment and what they, personally, can do to save it. Reinhart says that when children become more aware of the environmental status of their own neighborhoods, they become better equipped to keep unwanted waste out of their backyards.

Second, legislation should be passed making Indian Reservations subject to state and local environmental and business guidelines. This would keep the land from being manipulated, simply due to its vulnerability. Also, stricter enforcement of illegal dumping laws should be established—this would discourage unlicensed truckers from dumping in poor areas, thus taking advantage of people who are often too afraid to speak out. And implementation of already existing right-to-know laws would force the government and corporations to make people aware of the environmental hazards of a project proposed in their areas.

The audience is told what should be done by those with the power to act and what the listeners can do to empower themselves by acting in positive ways.

Finally, it is possible for each of us to create hope for the end of environmental discrimination. If you are not already a member of an environmental organization like the Sierra Club or the Environmental Defense Fund, become so. And encourage all groups to have an increased awareness of poverty and minority area problems. Groups which claim to embrace the environment should look into all endangered areas, regardless of the economic or racial status of its residents—and explore all issues, not just those of their special interest groups, or those that are popular.

The speech challenges the audience to extend themselves and to visualize areas such as the ones identified earlier in the speech.

Also, don't be afraid to look beyond your own backyard for environmental issues which demand your concern, money and action. Be willing to look beyond what only affects you, immediately, to what affects the environment as a whole. Chances are, you'll find many neighborhoods who are in dire need of your help.

This is a final summary or review to reinforce the main ideas and call for action: "Work now to eliminate the ignorance which fuels environmental discrimination."

Today, we have seen what environmental discrimination is, how if affects the people involved, why the disparity exists, and what can be done by each of us to fight it. Although we may not be personally involved now, in the end, a crippled environment will not discriminate against rich or poor, black or white. If we work now to eliminate the ignorance which fuels environmental discrimination, we drive home a victory for the residents of Kettleman City, California and Matamoros. Which, in the end, is a victory for all of us.

*T*he next speech by Kristen Schmidt is about suicide. Study the speech and look for her use of the motivated sequence. You should consider many elements in the speech, from supporting material, to language, to appropriateness for an audience of classmates. We offer it, *without identifying any strengths or weaknesses*, as an example of a persuasive speech you can analyze, evaluate, and discuss with others as you prepare your own persuasive speech and as you prepare to listen to the speeches of others in your class.

I LOST A FRIEND AND SO HAVE OTHERS: THE TRAGEDY OF SUICIDE

Kristen Schmidt
Bowling Green State University

The most tragic thing I have witnessed on a college campus was the suicide of a friend of mine, whose name was Jeffery. He hung himself after his fraternity had their biggest party of the year. The entire campus was affected. Everyone was confused and in a daze for weeks. The problem was that nobody understood why he did it, making it harder for them to cope with the situation. The weeks leading up to Jeff's suicide were the happiest we thought we saw him experience. I myself talked to him at that party about how good life was hours before the tragedy. There never seemed to be a problem. That was the blind mistake I and the rest of the campus who knew Jeff made.

Those that are left behind often blame themselves, wondering if there was anything they could have done to prevent a friend or family member from committing suicide. Chances are there were steps that could have been taken. This is the problem that is central in my speech. You and I must be fully aware of early warning signs of suicide and take effective action so we can help to prevent such a tragedy from taking place.

Suicide is a growing problem in the United States, and there are a multitude of reasons why people choose to take their lives. According to Wayne Dixon and Kimberly Rumford, whose findings are reported in *The Journal of Counseling*

Psychology in 1992, the most frequent and applicable reason and the best predictor of suicidal behavior for the majority of cases is *hopelessness.* Dixon and Rumford discussed a case they and others dealt with on the topic of suicide. "Hopelessness" in their view is defined as "negative future expectations," meaning a distraught person believes there is nothing for she or he to live for anymore. I learned from another university student who is a good friend of mine that "hopelessness" was a major reason for Jeffery's suicide. My friend closely monitored all of the reports surrounding his death and concluded that he believed the best years of his life were ending as he was about to graduate. Yet unlike others, he believed there was nothing else to look forward to after his finished college! He did not have a job lined up, he had a bad family life to face if he returned home, and he, unknown to others, became increasingly fearful and depressed. Recently I discovered in an issue of the magazine *The Family Circle* the case of another young student who was the class valedictorian at Pierson High School. He committed suicide in August, 1990, just two months after his graduation. His family and classmates, like those of us close to Jeff, were in shock and confusion followed by intense grief. No one understood why this bright young man with what appeared to be a rewarding future ahead would kill himself. He always seemed to be in good spirits and he had a great deal of good accomplishments going for himself. Apparently the pressure of being a role model in his community was pressure he could not cope with and it had a fatal price in his mind!

Do these stories have a ring of familiarity for any of you? The suicide rate among college students is shocking. Dixon and Rumford's study found that the estimated suicide rate for college students is 50% higher than the rest of the population of a comparable age. This figure suggests that the chances are probable that each of you in our class may encounter a suicide attempt sometime in your college lives. Even someone here in our room may have contemplated suicide.

You and I need to be aware of the warning signs of suicide and take the appropriate action when we believe they are present in someone we know, even ourselves. Nobody in the lives of the two young men I have cited apparently took the signs into account until after the two were gone. Hindsight is always 20/20 and it turns out that both guys were filled with a tremendous amount of stress and negative feelings. Whether the feelings combined to create hopelessness with life or reaction to the pressures they believed were being placed on themselves, they believed they could not continue life as the viewed it and took the fatal step that is irrevocable—suicide! We need to learn the signs to alert ourselves to a planned suicide and act. Experts claim that once a person reaches the point of hopelessness, her or his ability to perceive, generate, and implement effective coping responses to solve or overcome the crisis or problem is impaired. Therefore, people need to be aware of early warning signs so they can help the suicidal person before it is too late. What we can do? What can you and I do to prevent a suicide from taking place? First, pay attention to disclosures that indicate a growing state of hopelessness in someone. A suicidal person may be overstressed, overwhelmed, anxious, irritable, and is likely to demonstrate noticeable mood swings. A suicidal person may even begin to give personal items away as if she or he no longer wants to have them or as if she or he is going away and won't be able to take care of these items. We need to notice these behaviors, and not overlook or dismiss them too quickly. We must get the distressed individual to talk with us and to let out those destructive feelings and beliefs. Communication, conversation, genuine dialogue, this is what can prevent a person from taking their life. You could argue, "Well, if a person really wants to take their life that is their choice. Not much I can do about it." This line of argument is wrong! This is a choice the suicidal person should not make. Death not only ends their life but it impacts on the lives of all those who make up their community, their friends, and their family. We can make many, many choices in life that may be poor but certainly not fatal! There are always better alternatives for a distressed and overwhelmed person than suicide. Certainly life has its dark and down moments but they can be followed by uplifting events and brighter days. Do you want to return to your dorm or apartment to find someone you know and perhaps love has suddenly committed suicide, maybe hung himself, died through a self-inflicted wound, or jumped from the top of a campus tower? Or would you rather find yourself helping someone who is about to give up on life and talk them through to see hope and opportunity ahead? Learn about suicide. Read about it, and talk about it with others. Don't walk out of here today and think this is just another speech among many, simply a talk by me to earn a grade. Sure it is an assignment I have but I have also experienced the loss of a laughing friend who was crying behind his eyes and deep inside. And, I am very sorry. I won't miss the signs again. If you know someone who may be a candidate for suicide talk to this person. If you are down and out, look at the signs and seek positive alternatives. I have also written the phone number of a suicide hotline on the board behind me so please write it someplace in your notebook. The problem is severe and you and I can take positive steps to help reduce it.

"If people would dare to speak to one another unreservedly, there would be a good deal less sorrow in the world a hundred years hence."

Samuel Butler

PERSUASION: CREDIBILITY, ARGUMENT, AND EMOTION

s shown in Chapter 14, persuasion is communication intended to influence choice through appeals to the audience's sense of ethics, reasoning, and emotion. Ethical appeals are linked to speaker credibility, while appeals to reason and emotion provide the information and power necessary to convince. In this chapter, we examine each of these persuasive appeals. We also look at the role evidence plays in persuasion. We begin by focusing on speaker credibility.

SPEAKER CREDIBILITY AND PERSUASION

We introduced the concept of "source credibility" in Chapter Four. There our intent was to show the link between credibility and ethics. Here we focus on credibility and persuasion.

What your audience knows about you before you speak and what they learn about you and your point of view during your speech may influence your ability to persuade. Credibility is measured in terms of perceived competence, concern for the audience, dynamism, and ethics.

In many cases, your audience will decide whether your message has any value based on how competent they perceive you to be. Your listeners will ask themselves whether you have the background to speak (if your topic is crime, they are more likely to be persuaded by the Atlanta chief of police than by a postal worker delivering his personal opinions); whether the content of your speech has firm support (when it is clear that speakers have not researched their topic, they diminish their ability to persuade); and whether you communicate confidence and control of your subject matter through your delivery.

Persuasion is also influenced by concern for your audience. As you recall from Chapter 4, communication professor Richard L. Johannesen differentiated between speakers who engage in "dialogue" and those who engage in "monologue." A dialogue takes into account the welfare of the audience; a monologue focuses only on the speaker's self-interest.[1] Audiences sense a speaker's concern by looking at the actions the speaker has taken before the speech (if the group has been formed to protest the location of a highway through a residential community, the audience will consider what the speaker has already done to convince highway officials to change their minds); and by listening carefully to the strength and conviction of the speaker's message (does she promise to fly to Washington, if necessary, to convince federal officials to withhold funds until a new site is chosen, or is her approach less aggressive?). Persuasive speakers are able to convince their audiences they are on their side.

Your credibility and therefore your ability to persuade are also influenced by the audience's perception of you as a dynamic spokesperson. Your listeners will ask themselves whether you have the reputation for being a leader who gets the job done. They will listen for an aggressive, energetic style that communicates commitment

1. Richard L. Johannesen, "Attitude of Speaker Toward Audience: A Significant Concept for Contemporary Rhetorical Theory and Criticism," *Central States Speech Journal* (Summer 1974): 95.

David Duke ran for governor of Louisiana in 1991. He spoke of economic and social issues, but could not escape a racist image acquired in earlier years when he was an active spokesperson for the Ku Klux Klan.

to your point of view and for ideas that build on one another in a convincing, logical way.

Finally, your ability to persuade is influenced by the audience's perception of your ethics. If you come to the lectern with a reputation for dishonesty, few people will be persuaded to trust what you say. If your message is biased and you make little attempt to be fair or to concede the strength of your opponent's point of view, your listeners may question your integrity. They may have the same questions if you appear manipulative.[2]

When David Duke emerged as a serious candidate for the governorship of Louisiana his image was projected across the state and the nation. His ethos and credibility became a controversial issue because of his previous affiliation with the Ku Klux Klan. While he campaigned on economic issues, changing the welfare system, and combatting the drug problem, he could not escape his record of statements about Nazis, racial discrimination, and atheism. For example, in 1969 he said, "I am a National Socialist. You can call me a Nazi if you want to." In 1985 he announced, "Integration is absolutely unthinkable, because that will destroy our country as it has so many countries and so many civilizations." He questioned the Holocaust when he said, "I tend to believe it didn't happen . . . I think there's a lot of holes in the whole theory . . . It takes Jewish Hollywood to make crematoria into,

2. Discussion based on Jo Sprague and Douglas Stuart, *Speaker's Handbook,* 2d ed. (San Diego, CA: Harcourt Brace Jovanovich, 1988), pp 208–10.

F O C U S   O N   R E S E A R C H

THE EFFECTS OF STRONG ARGUMENTS AND SPEAKER EXPERTISE AND ATTRACTIVENESS ON PERSUASION

When trying to explain the ability to persuade, experts often mention three related factors: the strength of the argument, the perceived expertise of the speaker, and the attractiveness of the speaker. In the attempt to measure the impact of these factors on the ability to persuade, many studies have used what scientists call the *cognitive response model.* In this model, audience members are considered active participants in persuasion who produce thoughts— in the form of supporting and refuting arguments— in response to a persuasive message. Studies have found that these cognitive responses influence the relationship between the speaker's persuasive message and attitude change in the audience.

According to the cognitive response model, when speakers present strong arguments, backed by solid evidence and logical, clear reasoning, they increase the likelihood that the audience will respond favorably to their message. Listeners are more likely to generate reasons to support the speaker's position in the face of strong arguments than they are in the face of weak arguments. This favorable audience response has a positive effect on persuasion. The model also suggests that the more arguments a speaker presents, the more favorable the audience's response, and the more likely attitudes will change in response to persuasion.

Also, according to the cognitive response model, when listeners perceive speakers to be believable, they are more likely to agree with the persuasive message than when they have less trust in the source. Source credibility decreases the audience's motivation to disagree. However, the effect of credibility is strongest when the audience is not involved in the topic. In this circumstance, the audience is willing to take the word of the expert and be persuaded. In contrast, when the speaker's topic is important to listeners, they are less likely to be persuaded by a credible spokesperson than by the strength of the message. Thus, the less important and involving the topic is to the audience, the more likely the audience is to be influenced by speaker credibility.

Although the nature and quality of the argument and speaker credibility have been shown to affect the cognitive response of listeners, the influence of the speaker's physical attractiveness has not been thoroughly studied.

To test the effects of these three factors— argumentation, source credibility, and source attractiveness—on cognitive responses and persuasion, Benoit conducted the following study: Using 241 undergraduate students at a large midwestern public university, he introduced messages on the relationship between a knowledge of computer science and future job success. He used both strong and weak arguments and messages from four distinct sources (expert, nonexpert, attractive, and nonattractive). The strong arguments were logical and convincing as they established a link between studying computers in college and the availability of numerous, high-paying jobs after graduation. In contrast, the weak arguments referred to a single case in which a knowledge of computers resulted in a fairly good job.

Benoit identified the source's expertise by telling subjects that some messages came from an expert on the topic of computer education and business while others came from a nonexpert. The source's attractiveness was defined by attributing some messages to an attractive person, whose picture the subjects viewed, and others to an unattractive person.

The data from Benoit's study support previous findings on the relationship between argumentation, credibility, and attractiveness on persuasion. Although strong arguments produced favorable cognitive responses and attitude change in the context of a topic listeners were involved in, expertise and physical attractiveness had no similar effect. Benoit explains the significance of these results:

> These results are important because they confirm a limitation on the impact of source credibility; its effectiveness may well be restricted to uninvolving topics . . . . Expertise can be an important factor in social influence, but we must be careful not to overgeneralize the claims for persuasiveness of social credibility and we must delineate the conditions under which it is likely to be effective. Similarly, physical attractiveness cues can be very persuasive, but they do not appear to influence significantly the processing of persuasive messages on involving topics in any coherent manner.[3]

quote, ovens."[4] In 1991 Duke attempted to project a new public persona in his effort to defeat former governor Edwin Edwards but could not escape his past statements and their impact on the majority of the voters. Because of their perceptions of his ethics and lack of credibility he was not persuasive enough and Edwards was elected again.

Does credibility make a difference in your ability to persuade? Researchers have found that, in many cases, the most credible speakers are also the most persuasive.[5]

The Strategy of Identification: Seeking Common Ground

Your credibility and your ability to persuade may increase if you convince your audience that you share "common ground." Rhetorical theorist and critic Kenneth Burke explains: "You persuade a man insofar as you can talk his language by speech, gesture, tonality, order, image, attitude, idea, identifying your ways with his."[6]

Burke believes that the concept of identification broadens the definition of rhetoric to take into account unconscious as well as conscious persuasive experiences. When an Hispanic politician tells an Hispanic audience, "I know what it is like to be poor. I was born here and my roots will always be here," she is trying to create identification. Her words tell her listeners she is one of them in spirit and

3. William L. Benoit, "Argumentation and Credibility Appeals in Persuasion," *The Southern Speech Communication Journal* 52 (Winter 1987): 181–97.

4. Bill Nichols, "David Duke's Record at Odds With Public Persona," *USA Today* November 8, 1991, 2A.

5. E. Aronson, J. A. Turner, and J. M. Carlsmith, "Communicator Credibility and Communication Discrepancy as Determinants of Opinion Change," *Journal of Abnormal and Social Psychology* 67, (1963): 31–36.

6. Kenneth Burke, *A Grammar of Motives and a Rhetoric of Motives* (New York: Meridian Books, 1962) p. 579.

Cesar Chavez forged a common bond with his audience when he addressed a meeting of the National Association of Social Workers.

attitude. Her presence as an Hispanic talking to Hispanics delivers an unconscious message of sameness and unity. Burke believes persuasion can be achieved only through this process of identification.

In his classic work, *Public Speaking,* published in 1915, James A. Winans introduced the concept of "common ground." "To convince or persuade a man," he writes, "is largely a matter of identifying the opinion or course of action which you wish him to adopt with one or more of his fixed opinions or customary courses of action. When his mind is satisfied of the identity, then doubts vanish."[7]

Here is the way labor leader Cesar Chavez forged a common bond with his audience after a twenty-day fast in 1968 to call attention to the plight of California farm workers. (Chavez was the founder—and until his death in 1993, the leader—of the United Farm Workers, a union made up primarily of illiterate, indigent migrant workers.) After his fast, his speech was delivered to about 10,000 people attending a commemorative religious service. (Chavez, too weak to deliver the speech himself, had it read for him in both English and Spanish.)

Chavez proclaimed that the end of his fast was not the true reason for the gathering. Rather, people had come to observe that "we are a family bound together in a common struggle for justice. We are a Union family celebrating our unity and the nonviolent nature of our movement." Chavez explained why he had fasted: "My heart was filled with grief and pain for the suffering of farm workers. The Fast was first for me and then for all of us in this Union. It was a Fast for nonviolence and a call to sacrifice."

The rich and powerful opponents farm workers face can be defeated, he proclaimed at the conclusion of his speech: "We have something the rich do not own. We have our own bodies and spirits and the justice of our cause as our weapons. It is how we use our lives that determines what kind of men we are . . . . I am convinced that the truest act of courage, the strongest act of manliness is to sacrifice ourselves for others in a totally non-violent struggle for justice. To be a man is to suffer for others. God help us to be men."[8]

When Anwar el-Sadat journeyed to Israel in November 1977 to address the Israeli Parliament and explore the possibility of peace between the Arabs and Israelis, his success was based on his ability to establish common ground. Speech communication professor David Ross explains:

> With a backdrop of thirty years' hatred, war, and suffering, Sadat realized that he was addressing an adversary who would suspect his intentions. To allay suspicion about his motives, Sadat sought to project credibility by projecting shared religious values and by describing his personal risks. . . . Sadat also stressed the Egyptian and Israeli sharing of aversion to war and suffering. To counter Israeli reluctance to accept a plan originating in Egypt, Sadat attempted to make his proposal attractive by stressing mutual Arab-Israeli responsibility for peace. He implicitly offered Israel a positive self-image as "peace maker" and international recognition for sharing the burden to make a lasting peace.[9]

REASONING FOR LOGICAL APPEAL

Reasoning refers to the sequence of interlinking claims and arguments that, together, establish the content and force of your position. Although we believe the treatment of public speaking throughout this book promotes reasonableness, no aspect of our study is more instrumental in guiding you to improve your critical thinking than reasoning as logical appeal. Logical thought as critical thinking is intended to

7.   Cited in Dennis G. Day, "Persuasion and the Concept of Identification," paper delivered at the SAA Convention, Washington, DC 1959.

8.   John C. Hammerback and Richard J. Jensen, "Cesar Estrada Chavez," in Bernard K. Duffy and Halford R. Ryan, eds. *American Orators of the Twentieth Century: Critical Studies and Sources* (New York: Greenwood Press, 1987), p. 57.

9.   David Ross, "The Projection of Credibility as a Rhetorical Strategy in Anwar el-Sadat's Address to the Israeli Parliament," *The Western Journal of Speech Communication* 44 (Winter 1980): 79.

increase your ability to assess, analyze, and advocate ideas. As a persuasive speaker who appeals to an audience's sense of logic you will reason either inductively or deductively. Your responsibility as a speaker is to reason by offering your audience factual or judgmental statements based on sound inferences drawn from unambiguous statements of knowledge or belief.[10] *Think carefully about this responsibility* because reasoning or logical appeal in persuasive speaking is tremendously important for making good decisions. We believe that as a persuasive speaker you have an *ethical responsibility* to provide your audience with reasonable and well supported statements that you believe to be accurate and true.

To construct a sound, reasonable statement as a logical appeal for your audience you need to distill the essential parts of an argument: (1) the evidence in support of an idea you advocate; (2) a statement or contention the audience is urged to accept; and, (3) the inference linking the evidence with the statement. Here are two examples of statements that form the root of an argument:

⌘ Tests showed that the conductor had cocaine in his system, a finding that leads us to believe that the train crash was the result of his drug-induced impairment.

⌘ Rising malpractice fees, limited private practice opportunities, and increasing government control are responsible, in part, for students' declining interest in medical careers.

Of the three parts to an argument, the most difficult part to understand is often the inference. It may be an assumption that justifies using evidence as a basis for making a claim or drawing a conclusion. For example, let's suppose you take a big bite out of food you have taken for dinner in your cafeteria or apartment and you claim "this is the worst piece of meat I have ever put in my mouth." With this claim you are making a statement that you *infer* from tasting the meat.

What's the evidence? The meat before you. The statement or contention is: "The meat is awful." The relation of the evidence to the claim is made by an inference which may be an *unstated belief* that spoiled, old, or poorly prepared meat will taste bad. Stephen Toulmin, the British philosopher we acknowledge as an expert on argument, speaks of the inferential link between evidence and claim as the *warrant.* Toulmin points out that a warrant is the part of the argument that states or *implies* an inference.[11] When you reason with your audience by trying to persuade the listeners with an argument you want them to accept and act upon, you must use evidence, inferences, and statements as contentions the audience can understand and accept.

Sound reasoning is especially important when your audience is skeptical. Faced with the task of trying to convince people to change their minds or do something they might not otherwise be inclined to to do, your arguments must be impressive.

---

10.   Austin J. Freeley, *Argumentation and Debate: Critical Thinking for Reasonable Decision-Making.* 8th ed. Belmont, California: Wadsworth Publishing, 1993, 2.

11.   David L. Vancil, *Rhetoric and Argumentation* Boston: Allyn and Bacon, 1993: 120–124.

I N T E R V I E W

Joe Clark
Controversial Educator
and Public Speaker

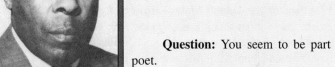

Controversy surrounds Joe Clark. It swirled around him when he was principal of Eastside High in Paterson, New Jersey, where he laid down the law in his army-reserve sergeant style. He chained doors, carried a baseball bat, and bellowed through a bullhorn in an attempt to bring education to a school that everyone considered an urban educational wasteland.

Today, Clark is still bellowing, but in another setting. He is one of the country's most controversial and charismatic lecturers who delivers a message of self-confidence in the face of controversy. Clark's comments underscore the importance of language and effective delivery. They also emphasize the role personal credibility plays in the power to persuade.

Question: You've said that when you're in front of an audience, you're "on fire," you're "buoyant." What happens to you during a speech?

Answer: People tell me that there are born orators who have the innate capacity to serve as a catalytic agent, as a galvanizing force for an audience. As far as I'm concerned, once I get up in front of an audience or a camera, there's a strange type of elation that seems to engulf the entire being of my mortal soul and catapults me into a state of ecstasy. I'm flamboyant, charismatic, well-endowed with all the traits of histrionics. It can be flammable; it can be volatile. It's not something that everyone has; it seems to be part of my overall philosophy, personality, and basic being.

Question: You seem to be part poet.

Answer: I read something every day, not for content necessarily. I look for potent phrases that will describe what I'm talking about . . . . The key to being an eloquent speaker is being able to speak extemporaneously, being quick of wit, and never being stymied by your audience. I tell my audiences that I have a lot of arrows in my quiver, and when I get an adversarial question, that there is a razor on my back. You have to be sharp as a razor when you speak—and your acumen and personal integrity must be flawless.

Question: You're a controversial speaker. Are you concerned about audience reaction?

Answer: I never worry what people say, or write, or what's on TV. You can't be thin-skinned. And I certainly never worry about my audience because I only talk about things I'm sure people want to hear. I talk about education and the fact that we need a voucher system in America. I talk about affirmative action. I talk about drugs. I talk about how I became a Republican. I talk about how, despite all the odds, I progressed from being a poor, black, welfare boy from Newark, New Jersey, to the pinnacle of success. I talk about how great a country America is. Who's going to be upset by that?

Question: In other words, you don't feel that at the end of your speech, half your audience hates you and half loves you?

Answer: Everyone stands up and claps. An epiphany resounds from the rafters. I don't know what motivates the applause, but it's there.

Question: Is personal credibility important, especially when you're controversial?

Answer: I have credentials that even my most virulent adversaries have to take note of. I have achieved more than anyone else they know. How many of them have been on the front cover of *Time* magazine? How many have been called by the President of the United States? How many had a movie made about them (*Lean On Me*)? How many have been profiled on "60 Minutes?" How many have written a book? All this gives me credibility as a speaker.

Question: What makes a successful speaker?

Answer: You have to have something to say; you have to stand for something and have a reputation for it. I can talk quickly and vociferously, eloquently, because I never go beyond the parameters of my supreme mastery. I talk about what I know. That's why it's so easy for me to go on for two hours. I have a repertoire of things from which I can draw. What you say should be tangible. It should be something individuals can relate to, something they're concerned about. And it should

be entertaining; that's especially important when you speak to college and corporate audiences. It also helps when you can use yourself as an example of having achieved the goals and objectives you speak of.

The best speakers also have a mastery of the language. Your speech should be melodious and use good vocabulary so that, if nothing else, you leave your listeners with a few words to ponder.

Next, your delivery should be one of power. I never look at the audience. I can look at them, but I don't see anything. You don't want to see grimaces; you don't want to see any of the emotions on people's faces because that affects your delivery. If you see someone scowling, that affects you. You have to make sure everything out there is in a state of oblivion. I don't want to see any vestiges of humanity.

A formidable, scintillating orator is never stationary. Don't stand behind a lectern. Those who do have an insipid, saturnine disposition as they relate to their audience.

And, finally, the most accomplished orators talk from the marrow of their bones. Their words come from the heart and the heart interacts with the soul and the soul lets a little of the marrow out and then you have one of the most powerful concoctions of oratorical genius.

Source: Interview with Joe Clark, March 8, 1990.

Supporters in an audience may require arguments in the form of reinforcement. You may have to remind a sympathetic crowd of the reasons your shared point of view is correct. This reminder is especially important if your goal is audience action. If you want a group of sympathetic parents to attend a board of trustees meeting to protest tuition increases, you must persuade them that a large turnout is necessary. It is up to you, through the presentation of an effective argument, to make action the most attractive course.

In persuasion, ethical and emotional appeals may be powerful factors, but reasoning or logical appeal can also be your most effective tool. Well developed reasons stated without exaggeration tell your listeners that you trust them to evaluate the facts on their merit, not on the basis of emotional appeal. Through the framework of a logical appeal we piece together important elements to persuade listeners to accept our position and respond to a call to action. The framework for logical appeal is based on inductive and deductive modes of reasoning, in particular on reasoning by analogy, reasoning from cause, reasoning from sign, and reasoning as an enthymeme.

With inductive reasoning, evidence leads to a conclusion that is probable; deductive reasoning claims that a conclusion is necessitated by the premises or statements that have been arrived at inductively. For example, suppose you travel to a village to visit a college campus in search of a place to work for your undergraduate degree. You enter the library and find it almost empty. You visit a dorm and discover very few books but lots of stereos and TVs. The student union is crowded with laughing students, many playing cards, while others are watching television soaps and game shows. At this point you declare, "I have seen enough! The students are this college are not committed to academic rigor." You arrive at this claim through an inductive process and you use your observations as evidence.

Now, further suppose you are in a town located next to the village with the campus. As you wait for a traffic light to turn green you see a student wearing a sweatshirt from the college you visited. "Aha," you think, "there is a student from the college. He is probably more interested in playing around and having a good time than hitting the books." This claim is made through deductive reasoning. You assume most (if not all) students at the campus are more committed to entertainment than education, so seeing a student as you sat waiting for the light to turn, you arrived at the conclusion that he is not a serious student. Of course, you cannot be absolutely certain that these students are not committed to academic rigor or that the student in town is not hardworking. Your reasoning can only arrive at statements that are probable. You can examine the inductive and deductive modes of reasoning continually, merely by observing human communication as you and your friends make statements about what you believe and how you intend to act.

To persuade your audience that a claim or conclusion is highly probable, you must have strong evidence and show that you have carefully reasoned in support of your points. Only when strong probability is established can you ask your listeners to make the inductive leap from specific cases to a general conclusion or to take the deductive move from statements as premises to a conclusion you want them to accept. We can look more closely now at inductive and deductive reasoning.

Inductive Reasoning

Aristotle spoke of inductive reasoning in his *Rhetoric*.[12] Through inductive reasoning, we generalize from specific examples and draw conclusions from what we observe. Inductive reasoning moves us from the specific to the general in an orderly, logical fashion.

---

12. Lane Cooper, *The Rhetoric of Aristotle* (New York: Appleton-Century-Crofts, 1960), p. 10.

When you argue on the basis of example, the inference step in the argument holds that what is true of specific cases can be generalized to other cases of the same class, or of the class as a whole. Suppose you are trying to persuade your audience that the disappearance of downtown merchants in your small village is a problem that can be solved with an effective plan you are about to present. You may infer that what has worked to solve a similar problem in a number of highly similar villages is likely to work in the small village that is the subject of your speech.

When we use inductive reasoning, we make assumptions that what we observe and know fit into a broader pattern. The child who won't eat anything green on her plate because of a bad experience with spinach, the television comic who after a trip to New York and four cab rides tells us that all New York City cabbies belong at the Indianapolis 500, the skeptic who claims that all politicians are crooks (he can name a dozen who went to jail) are all using inductive reasoning to make generalizations.

Here is an example of an inductive reasoning pattern:

⌘ Since the 1970s, membership in the United Steelworkers Union has dropped.

⌘ Since the 1970s, membership in the International Ladies Garment Workers Union has dropped.

⌘ Since the 1970s, membership in the bricklayers' union has dropped.

⌘ Since the 1970s, membership in the International Brotherhood of Electrical Workers has dropped.

⌘ Therefore, the membership of all unions has dropped since the 1970s.

The Specifics May Not Be Sufficient Proof.   This example demonstrates a problem associated with inductive reasoning—individual cases don't *always* add up to a correct conclusion. From four instances, the speaker concluded that *all* labor unions have suffered a drop in membership since the 1970s. Although true that these unions lost membership during this period, other unions grew stronger. (The Communication Workers of America, the National Association of Letter Carriers, and the American Federation of State, County, and Municipal Employees are three examples.) The speaker's sample was too small. He jumped to a conclusion based on limited information.

Here and in all other cases of inductive reasoning, you can never be sure that your conclusions are absolutely accurate. Because you are only looking at a sample, you must persuade your audience to accept a conclusion, that is probable—or maybe even just possible. The way you phrase your statement depends on how certain you are your generalization is correct. Certainty ranges from near absolute certainty ("all the broccoli I've ever seen is green: therefore all broccoli is green") to probable certainty ("as a reporter for a consumer magazine, I've tested 500 new Toasty toasters and found that their timing device is defective. I want to alert you that all Toasty toasters probably have this problem") to possible certainty ("I spoke to three people who recently applied for a car loan and all had more trouble than they expected; the banks may be tightening consumer credit").

Choose Your Words With Care.   When you develop your argument inductively, use language that indicates you are dealing in probabilities. Exaggerated conclusions based on a limited number of examples can create problems as in the following example:

> I've visited law schools, business schools, medical schools, dental schools and found that professional students care only about how much money they will earn when they finish their educations.

Few of your listeners will be convinced by such extreme language. Because most people realize that professional students are a varied group with different goals, your argument is likely to fail to persuade. With less extreme language, you can make your point:

> I've visited law schools, business schools, medical schools, dental schools and found that the primary concern of many students is how much they will earn when they graduate.

It is fair to argue that this type of hedging can be taken to an extreme. Even though we have not seen every sunrise, we can say absolutely that the sun rises in the east; even though we have no way of knowing whether the New York Stock Exchange will operate every workday, we can safely say that it will.

Back Your Reasoning With Solid Support.   To convince your audience that your conclusion is highly probable, you must show that your examples are relevant to your claim, that they are typical of what you are describing, and that they take place in the period of time critical to your argument. Only when a strong probability is established can you ask your listeners to make the inductive leap from specific cases to a general conclusion.

To encourage this leap, build your case with strong support. Make it difficult for your listeners to think of the instances you describe as isolated or unique. In the following example, we rely on several forms of support including statistics and individual examples to prove the point that a career in music may be hazardous to one's health:

> Many musicians are hurt while playing their instruments. According to a recent survey conducted by New York University researcher Dr. Fadi J. Bejjani and reported by Jane Brody in *The New York Times,* as many as three quarters of all musicians are affected by medical problems as a result of their playing. Sixty-nine percent of piano players, 73 percent of harp players, and 75 percent of cello players suffer back pain. Other injuries are common as well. Acclaimed pianists Leon Fleisher and Gary Graffman developed musculoskeletal problems affecting their right hands. In both cases, these injuries jeopardized their careers.[13]

---

13.   Jane E. Brody, "For Artists and Musicians, Creativity Can Mean Illness and Injury," *New York Times,* October 17, 1989, p. C1.

Reasoning by Analogy

As you learned in Chapter Seven, analogies establish common links between similar and not-so-similar concepts. They are effective tools of persuasion when you can convince your audience that the characteristics of one case are similar enough to the characteristics of the second case that your argument about the first also applies to the second. For example, during the 1964 presidential campaign, Democratic vice presidential candidate Hubert H. Humphrey used this analogy as he sought to inspire an audience:

> You have been taught that it is good to share, to be compassionate, to be friendly, to be charitable, to be considerate, that is what Sunday school and church and America and schools are all about. Now if it is all right for individuals to be that way, what's wrong with a government that represents those individuals, a government of the people, by the people and for the people to be that way?[14]

Figurative analogies can be used to persuade, but they must be supported with relevant facts, statistics, and testimony that link the dissimilar concepts you are comparing. Notice that the inference step in an argument from analogy holds that because two cases are known to be the same in certain basic regards they will also be the same in other basic steps. You may be trying to persuade your audience that the Greek Life Office on your campus not only will dramatically increase its efficiency but also extend its outreach to the community by implementing new procedures that have been effective elsewhere. The campus Greek Life Office on your campus plans to implement new procedures identical to those already being used with considerable success by the Greek Life Office on another campus comparable in size to yours. You *infer* that the similarities between the two campuses and the Greek Life Offices reveal conditions that make it highly probable that what works in one place will also work in another. Literal analogies, on the other hand, compare things with similar characteristics and therefore require less explanatory support. The distinction between literal and figurative analogies is important because only literal analogies are sufficient to establish a logical proof. Although figurative analogies can provide valuable illustrations, they will not prove your point. For example, before the United States entered World War II, President Franklin D. Roosevelt used the analogy of a "garden hose" to support his position that the United States should help England, France, and other European countries already involved in the war. In urging the passage of the Lend-Lease bill, he compared U.S. aid to the act of lending a garden hose to a neighbor whose house was on fire. Although this analogy supplied ethical and emotional proof, it did not prove the point on logical grounds. It is vastly different to lend a garden hose to a neighbor than it is to lend billions of dollars in foreign aid to nations at war.[15]

---

14.   L. Patrick Devlin, "Hubert Horatio Humphrey," in Duffy and Ryan, eds., *American Orators of the Twentieth Century,* p. 210.
15.   Austin J. Freeley, *Argumentation and Debate: Reasoned Decision-Making,* 5th ed. (Belmont, CA: Wadsworth, 1981), p. 119.

Let's look at three examples to see how analogical reasoning works. Remember that through the analogy you infer that what is true in one case is also true in another:

❀ Lee Brown was an effective police commissioner in Houston. There is every reason to expect that he will also be effective in New York City.

❀ The stadium is packed for every football game. If we attract a major league baseball team to the area, there's no reason to believe the stadium won't be packed for baseball as well.

❀ Look at the success of the Barbie and Ken dolls. All we need is another high fashion doll duo to repeat their marketing coup.

The degree to which an analogy works depends on the answers to the following questions:

1. *Are the cases being compared similar?* In the analogy comparing police commissioner Brown's performance in Houston and his expected performance in New York, the persuasiveness of your argument will depend on your audience's perception of the task Brown faced in Houston and the task he will face in New York: How do the crime rates compare? How about the population size and the size of the Houston and New York City police forces? Only if you convince your listeners of significant points of similarity will the analogy be persuasive.

2. *Are the similarities critical to the success of the comparison?* The fact that similarities exist may not be enough to prove your point. Persuasion occurs when the similarities are tied to critical points of the comparison. You can say, for example, that because Dr. Jones and Dr. Smith are both doctors, they are equally qualified to perform brain surgery. The analogy breaks down because Dr. Jones is a general practitioner while Dr. Smith is a highly trained neurosurgeon.

3. *Are the differences relatively small?* In an analogy, you compare similar, not identical, cases. Differences can always be found between the items you are comparing. It is up to you as an advocate for your position to decide how critical the differences are. For example, if you are delivering a proposal for a Ken and Barbie knockoff, your audience may think the differences are significant. Barbie and Ken were originals, and your idea is a copy. Barbie and Ken have been around for decades, with mothers passing them on to their daughters and reliving their own childhoods as they shop for new dolls at the toy store. Your version has no such tradition.

   Your audience may come to a different conclusion when it hears your analogy comparing football attendance to possible baseball attendance. You can argue that although the sports are different, the community shows indications that it would support baseball with the same enthusiasm as football. When differences raise questions in listener's minds, it is wise to address the questions directly in the hope of convincing people that their concerns are overblown.

4.   *Can you point to other similar cases?* Returning to our Barbie and Ken analogy, you have a better chance of convincing people that your new doll idea has a chance if you can point to other successful cases. Tell them about Maxie, a competing doll that has taken a share of Barbie's market. If you can show that the similarities between these additional comparisons are critical, you will help sway audience opinion.[16]

Reasoning from Cause

An advocate for the homeless delivered this message to a group of supporters.

We all know that money is allocated by the federal government, in part, according to the numbers of people in need. The census, conducted every ten years, is supposed to tell us how many farmers we have, how many blacks and Hispanics, how many homeless.

Unfortunately, in the 1990 census, many of the homeless were not counted. The government told us census takers would go into the streets, into bus and train station waiting rooms, and into the shelters to count every homeless person.

As advocates for the homeless, people in my organization know this was not done. Shelters were never visited. Hundreds and maybe thousands of homeless were ignored in this city alone.

A serious undercount is inevitable. This undercount will cause fewer federal dollars to be spent aiding those who need our help the most.

When you are reasoning from cause the inference step is that an event of one kind contributes to or brings about an event of another kind. The presence of a cat in a room when you are allergic to cats is likely to bring about a series of sneezes until the cat is removed. As the preceding example demonstrates, causal reasoning focuses on the cause-and-effect relationship between ideas:

cause—inaccurate count of the homeless for the 1990 census

effect—less money will be spent aiding the homeless

Let's look at two more examples:

Proposition: The chemicals suburbanites use to keep their lawns green have been responsible for illness and death.

cause—chemical lawn sprays

effect—illness and death

Proposition: October 19, 1987—the day Wall Street crashed—brought an end to the nothing-can-stop-me mentality on Wall Street. Jobs dried up as did the opportunity to make what was for many a seemingly unlimited amount of money.

---

16.   Questions from Austin J. Freely, *Argumentation and Debate: Reasoned Decision Making* 5th ed. (Belmont, CA: Wadsworth, 1981), pp. 119–20.

cause—the stock market crash on October 19, 1987

effect—limited opportunity to strike it rich

When used correctly, causal reasoning can be an effective persuasive tool. You must be sure that the cause and effect relationship is sound enough to stand up to scrutiny and criticism. To test the validity of your reasoning, ask yourself the following questions:

1. *Do the cause and effect you describe have anything to do with one another?* Some statements establish a cause-and-effect relationship between ideas when the relationship is at best questionable. For example:

   ✂ When a National Football Conference team wins the Super Bowl, the stock market is in for a good year.

   ✂ A stock price drop in January means the market will drop for the entire year.

   ✂ The stock market dropped fifty points because of the rumor that the president was having an extramarital affair.

   Before making any of these assumptions, ask yourself whether other factors contributed to the change. Even if the stock market dropped fifty points after a rumor of a presidential affair, the rumor may have had nothing to do with the drop. Did the Department of Labor issue unfavorable unemployment figures? Did IBM report record low earnings? Did a freeze hit the Northeast, sending the price of oil skyward? You may be attributing cause and effect where there is only coincidence.

   At their most extreme, unsubstantiated cause-and-effect relationships fall into the realm of superstition. The Super Bowl theory of the stock market rise is as much a superstition as the fear that breaking a mirror will bring bad luck.

2. *Is the cause acting alone or is it one of many producing the effect?* Even if the connection you draw is valid, it may be only one of several contributing factors that brings about an effect. To isolate it as solely responsible for an effect is to leave listeners with the wrong impression. For example, to suggest that the high divorce rate is the result of women's greater education is only partially true. Although independent women are less likely to remain in a bad marriage, other factors are involved. Here are a few:

   ✂ As products of the "me" generation, both men and women seek greater fulfillment in marriage.

   ✂ Divorce no longer carries the social stigma it once had. It is now acceptable for people to divorce.

   ✂ Women are not only better educated, they are also working beside men, earning an income that gives them the economic means to support themselves and their children if they choose.

✂ The liberalization of the divorce laws in many states has made it easier for couples to divorce.

Unethical public speakers misuse the cause-and-effect relationship to manipulate their listeners. A racist may say, for example, "Ever since blacks moved into this neighborhood there's been more crime," ignoring the effects crack cocaine and single-parent families—black and white—may have had on the increase in crime.

3. *Is the effect really the effect of another cause?*   To use a medical example, although fatigue and depression often occur simultaneously, it may be a mistake to conclude that depression causes fatigue when other factors may also be involved. Both conditions may be symptoms of other illnesses such as mononucleosis or the result of stress.

4. *Are you describing a continuum of causes and effects?*   Sociologists tell us that the only way we can look at our country's history of race relations is to see cause-and-effect occurring along a continuum:

discrimination → limited opportunities → poverty → crime → discrimination → limited opportunities → poverty

At one point on the continuum discrimination caused limited educational and job opportunities; at another point it was the result of the widespread perception that crime is race related. When you are dealing with an interrelated chain of causes and effects, it is wise to point out that you are looking at only one part of a broader picture.

5. *Are the cause and effect related but inconsequential?*   If you are delivering a speech on what causes many high school students to drop out, you may make the link between television viewing and the dropout rate when you conclude: "These kids don't go to school because they are watching too much television." Although television may play a minor role in the dropout problem, you are inflating the cause-and-effect relationship and ignoring the influence of other more important causal factors including drugs, the dissolution of families, poverty, teenage pregnancy, school violence, and feelings of hopelessness and despair. Ask yourself whether the cause you are presenting is sufficient to bring about the effect you claim.

Be Balanced, Fair, and Accurate in Your Claims.   To be an effective persuasive tool, causal reasoning must convince listeners that the link you claim is accurate. Because nonambiguous cause-and-effect relationships are rare outside the science laboratory (life is more complex than the lab) you may choose to show that your causal claim is true through a line of reasoning such as the following:

In the presence of X, Y occurred.
In the absence of X, Y did not occur.
When the amount of X is changed, there are changes in the amount of Y.
Therefore, it is probable that X causes Y.

Your listeners should be able to judge probability on the basis of your supporting evidence. They will ask themselves if your examples prove the point and if you explain or minimize conflicting claims.[17]

To be effective, causal reasoning should make an accurate claim but never overstate. By using phrases like, "This is one of several causes," or "The evidence suggests there is a cause-and-effect link," you are giving your audience a reasonable picture of a complex situation. Public speakers could learn from medical researchers who are reluctant to say flatly that one thing causes another. More often than not, researchers indicate that cause-and-effect relationships are not always clear and that links may not be as simple as they seem.

Reasoning from Sign

Suppose a person with whom you are romantically involved meets you in a local coffee shop, frowning, looking sad, dressed in messy clothes, apparently having gone without sleep the night before. Before even speaking to your friend you are likely to make an inference that something is drastically wrong. You notice *signs* of distress, and you arrive at your observation by making an inference based on these signs. We frequently reason from sign. Argumentation professor David Vancil tells us that "arguments from sign are based on our understanding of the way things are associated or related to each other in the world with them, [so] we conclude that the thing is present if its signs are present. The claim of a sign argument is invariably a statement that something is or is not the case."[18]

In the argument from sign, then, the inference step is that the presence of an attribute can be taken as the presence of some larger condition or situation of which the attribute is a part. As you step outside in the early morning to begin jogging, the gray clouds and moist air can be interpreted as signs that the weather conditions for the day are likely to result in a rainy day.

Among the ways to test the argument from sign are these four questions:[19]

1. Does a relevant relationship exist between the substance and the attribute under consideration? (His constant complaints about being persecuted provide evidence of paranoia.)

2. Is there an inherent (as opposed to mere incidental) relationship between the substance and the attribute? (Is the increasing presence of United States

17. Based on Sprague and Stuart, *The Speaker's Handbook,* pp. 165–166.
18. David L. Vancil, *Rhetoric and Argumentation.* Boston: Allyn and Bacon, 1993. p. 149.
19. Questions from Austin J. Freeley in *Argumentation & Debate.* 6th ed. Belmont, California: Wadsworth Publishing, 1986. pp. 145–146. We supplied the illustrations.

military forces near the borders of Iraq a sign of an imminent invasion, or is it a planned exercise to keep forces in a state of readiness?)

3.   Are there any constraints on what Freeley refers to as counter factors that disrupt the relationship? (Can we say that the increasing number of women who are working mothers is a sign of a deterioration of the American family?)

4.   Is the sign reasoning cumulative? (After Bill Clinton was elected President of the United States in 1992, economists and others looked at economic indicators as signs that the national economy was turning around, thereby signaling an end to the recession that was gripping the nation.)

The public speaker who reasons from sign must do so with caution. Certainly there are signs all around us to interpret in making sense of the world, but signs are easy to misinterpret. Therefore, the responsible speaker must carefully test any argument before offering using it to persuade an audience.

Deductive Reasoning

Aristotle also spoke of deduction as a form of reasoning in persuasive argument. Through deductive reasoning, we draw conclusions based on the connections between statements that serve as premises. Rather than introducing new facts, deductions enable us to rearrange the facts we already know, putting them in a form that will make our point. Deductive reasoning is the basis of police work and scientific research, enabling investigators to draw relationships between seemingly unrelated pieces of information.

At the heart of deduction reasoning is the syllogism, a pattern of reasoning involving a major and a minor premise and a conclusion. Syllogisms take this form:

$$a = b$$
$$b = c$$
$$c = a$$

Here is an example:

All basketball players can dribble the ball.
Anthony is a basketball player.
Anthony can dribble the ball.

Using this pattern of logic, the conclusion that Anthony can dribble the ball is inescapable. If your listeners accept your premise, they are likely to accept your conclusion. The major premise in this case is statement 1, "All basketball players can dribble the ball," while the minor premise is statement 2, "Anthony is a basketball player." Whether the deductive reasoning is stated in part or not, it leads us down an inescapable logical path: By knowing how two concepts relate to a third concept, we can say how they relate to each other. (Recognizing that people do not usually state every aspect of a syllogism as they reason deductively, Aristotle identified the *enthymeme* as the deductive reasoning used in persuasion. Because speakers and listeners often share similar assumptions, the entire argument may not be explicitly stated, even when the elements of a syllogism are all present. This truncated form of deductive reasoning is the enthymeme.) The inference step in reasoning with an enthymeme is that the audience, out of its judgment and values, must supply and accept the missing premises or conclusions. If a classmate in a persuasive speech makes the claim that a newly elected congressional representative will probably take unnecessary trips costly to the taxpayers, your classmate's claim is drawn from the major premise (unspoken) that most if not all congressional representatives engage in unnecessary and costly travel.

The interrelationships in a syllogism can be established in a series of deductive steps:

1. *Step One:*   Define the relationship between two terms.

     Major premise.   Plagiarism is a form of ethical abuse.

2. *Step Two:*   Define a condition or special characteristic of one of the terms.

     Minor premise. Plagiarism involves using the words of another author without quotations or footnotes as well as improper footnoting.

3. *Step Three:*   Show how a conclusion about the other term necessarily follows.[20]

     Conclusion: Students who use the words of another, but fail to use quotations or footnotes to indicate this, or who intentionally use incorrect footnotes, are guilty of an ethical abuse.

When support is used to buttress your premise, the conclusion becomes stronger:

> To plagiarize is to steal. It's not dirty or violent thievery in the same way robbing a bank is, but it is thievery nonetheless that crosses the line between what is ethically permissible and ethically wrong.
>
> It is easy to plagiarize—so easy that students do it all the time. In a recent study conducted at Miami University of Ohio, researchers found that 91.2 percent of the students admitted to plagiarizing their class work. They admitted to quoting information in a paper directly without noting or citing the sources and including misleading references in a bibliography or source page.
>
> According to Jerold Hale, the Miami University researcher who conducted the study, "The problem is that people don't see it as a problem so nobody has done anything to remedy it."
>
> I agree with Professor Hale that every time you write a paper and fail to give proper credit, you are guilty of an unethical act. Just because everyone around you is doing it doesn't lessen the seriousness of your crime.[21]

---

20.   Procedure described in Sprague and Stuart, *The Speaker's Handbook,* p. 160.
21.   Facts from "Miami of Ohio's Plagiarism is Rampant, A Survey Finds," *The New York Times,* April 1, 1990, p. 3.

Although here the deduction is inevitable (your logic gives your listeners little choice but to agree), persuasion is rarely that neat. Often, to the audience, your premises are probable rather than certain, placing you in the position of convincing your listeners to accept your conclusion. Because of this lack of 100 percent certainty, your appeal should take a different form:

> If you grant this premise as probable,
> and
> if you grant this other premise as probable,
> then it is logical to grant this conclusion as probable.[22]

Let's see how this works in the form of an actual argument:

> The practice of safe sex through abstinence is likely to reduce the spread of the AIDS virus throughout the country.
> Young people in America are increasingly practicing safe sex through abstinence.
> Therefore, it is likely that the spread of the AIDS virus among young people throughout the country will diminish.

Your ability to convince your listeners depends on their acceptance of your original premise and the conclusion you draw from it. The burden of proof rests with your evidence. Your goal is to convince your listeners through the strength of your supporting material to grant your premises and by extension your conclusion.

APPEAL TO AUDIENCE EMOTION

The third type of persuasive appeal focuses on the audience's emotion, or *pathos,* as Aristotle called it. Emotional appeals have the power to elicit the full range of human feelings including happiness, joy, pride, patriotism, fear, hate, anger, guilt, despair, hope, hopelessness, bitterness, and so on. George Kennedy, an authority on classical rhetoric, tells us, "Emotions in Aristotle's sense are moods, temporary states of mind, . . . and arise in large part from perception of what is publically due to or from oneself at a given time."[23]

The emotions we find in Aristotle's rhetoric appear as opposites. For example, anger is paired against patience and friendship is the opposite of enmity. Fear is opposed to confidence while shame is placed opposite of shamelessness. Contemporary persuasion theorists, Martha Cooper and William Nothstine, comment that "modern research into motivation and the passions moved beyond Aristotle's emphasis on the emotions themselves and moved extensively into broader theories of human psychology."[24] The persuader, they advise us, can influence their audiences by using appeals to create an emotional as well as a cognitive state of imbalance in listeners, which arouses feelings that something is wrong and something must be

---

22.   Sprague and Stewart, p. 162.
23.   George A. Kennedy, trans. *Aristotle's On Rhetoric — A Theory of Civic Discourse.* New York: Oxford Press, 1991. pp. 123–124.
24.   Martha D. Cooper and William L. Nothstine, *Power Persuasion — Moving from an Ancient Art Into The Media Age.* Greenwood, Indiana: The Educational Video Group, 1992. p. 74.

done. By taking the essential needs of an audience into consideration, the persuader can develop lines of reasoning that respond to pertinent needs. Yes, human needs can be described in terms of logic or what makes sense to a listener, but also, undoubtedly, needs are immersed in feelings or the emotional life of an individual as well.

Chapter Fourteen discusses Maslow's theory about human needs. His theory of needs can guide you in preparing a persuasive speech when you think about the feelings in your audience and how you can reach them in combination with the factors of credibility and sound argument. The constituents of persuasion, ethos or credibility, logos or logical appeal, and pathos or emotional appeal do not operate in a mutually exclusive fashion but instead are inherently bound together. One kind of appeal may have greater force in a persuasive argument than another. As a persuasive speaker you must be conscious of the persuasive potential of your appeals.

The Reverend Jesse Jackson has been (and continues to be) a featured speaker at Democratic National Conventions. Perhaps his strongest appeal to the emotions of his audience and the needs he perceived our nation must meet can be found in his 1984 address. This was a message climaxed by his repetitive and vocally powerful chant "Our time has come!"

> Young America, dream! Choose the human race over the nuclear race. Bury the weapons and don't burn the people. Dream of a new value system. Teachers who teach for life, and not just for a living, teach because they can't help it. Dream of lawyers more concerned about justice than a judgeship. Dream of doctors more concerned about public health than personal wealth. Dream of preachers and priests who will prophesy and not just profiteer. Preach and dream. Our time has come. Our time has come. Suffering breeds character. Character breeds faith. And in the end, faith will not disappoint. Our time has come. No graves can hold our body down. Our time has come. No lie can live forever. Our time has come. We must leave the racial battleground and come to economic common ground and moral higher ground. America, our time has come. We've come from disgrace to Amazing Grace, our time has come.[25]

By the time Reverend Jackson reached this point near the conclusion of his speech the majority of his immediate audience at the convention were cheering, many on their feet, and many with tears streaming down their faces. No one knows how the 90 million television viewers felt as they listened to this speech, but undoubtedly emotions were touched around the world as the speaker argued for the constituency he represented that evening: the poor, the disabled, the aged, and those discriminated against because of race, religion, or sexual preference.

Our emotions are powerful ingredients in our human composition. Your audience for a persuasive speech is a gathering of listeners who respond to a considerable extend according to how they feel (their emotions). You don't have to command the power of Jesse Jackson to appeal to an audience's emotions successfully. But you must be conscious of what feelings or emotions the members of the audience are likely to possess and you take them into consideration as you plan

---

25.   Jesse Jackson, "The Rainbow Coalition," *Vital Speeches of the Day* November 15, 1984, p. 81.

and present your speech. *You accept an ethical responsibility when you use emotional appeals. The ethically responsible speaker does not distort, delete, or exaggerate information for the sole purpose of emotionally charging an audience in order to manipulate their feelings for self-centered ends.*

Here is the way former congresswoman and presidential candidate Shirley Chisholm used an emotional appeal in her first speech as a freshman in Congress in 1969. Indicating the Nixon administration's claim that high levels of defense spending would be required for at least two more years of fighting in Vietnam, she said:

> Two more years, two more years of hunger for Americans, of death for our best young men, of children suffering the lifelong handicap of not having a good education when they are young . . . Two more years of high taxes . . . Two more years of too little being done to fight our greatest enemies—poverty, prejudice and neglect—here in this country. Two more years of fantastic waste in the Defense Department, of penny pinching social programs. Our country cannot survive two more years, or four, or these kinds of policies. It must stop—this year—now.[26]

Audience members moved by Chisholm's words would respond with feelings of anger and disgust—an emotional response that takes precedence over intellectual analysis.

Emotional appeals are often the most persuasive type of appeal because they provide the motivation listeners need to change their minds or take action. Instead of simply listing the reasons high fat foods are unhealthy, a more effective approach is to tie these foods to frightening consequences:

> Jim thought nothing could ever happen to him. He was healthy as an ox—or so he thought. His world fell apart one sunny May morning when he suffered a massive heart attack. He survived, but his doctors told him that his coronary arteries were blocked and that he needed bypass surgery.
>
> "Why me?" he asked. "I'm only 42 years old." The answer, he was told, had a lot to do with the high fat diet he had eaten since childhood.

Often, the only way to get an audience to act is to combine persuasive evidence with a strong emotional appeal.

To engage the emotions of your audience, use specific details and emotional language. Consider, for example, versions 1 and 2 of the same speech. In version 2 the speaker uses emotional rhetoric to urge the health committee of his state legislature to ban fragrance strips from magazines unless the strips are sealed, while in version 1 the same message is presented without any emotional overtones:

Version 1:

> It is not a good idea to include unsealed fragrance strips in magazines. I have gotten sick from them as have many other allergic people. My illnesses increase the premiums

---

26.   Susan Duffy, "Shirley Chisholm," in Duffy and Ryan, eds., *American Orators of the Twentieth Century: Critical Studies and Sources*, p. 64.

we all pay for health insurance. There is no way to predict allergic reactions and we all may be susceptible to these perfume fumes.

Version 2:

As you can see, I am here before you in an air mask to make the point that what I am about to say threatens my health. I cannot breathe when I open a magazine and am forced to inhale perfumes on unsealed fragrance strips. I have suffered asthmatic reactions so severe I have been rushed to the hospital gasping for air. I get migraine headaches and a rash all over my body.

I and thousands of others like me should have the right to decide whether or not we want to sample a chemical product. That decision should not be made for us by advertisers whose only concern is to sell perfume. Not when lives are at stake.

While you may not suffer as I do, your health insurance costs increase every time I'm forced to pay $500 or more for emergency room care . . . .

I want to leave you with one thought. While you are unaffected today, you may suffer as I do tomorrow. Anyone can develop sensitivities to the chemicals in perfumes and, let me assure you, these sensitivities will change your life.

Although version 1 contains the logical gist of the speaker's message, it fails to move the audience because of its lack of specificity and failure to use words with emotional impact. While version 2 talks of "gasping for air," version 1 talks about "getting sick." While version 2 described the problem as "life threatening," version 1 talks about the present practice as "not a good idea." While version 2 talks about hospital bills of $500 or more, version 1 talks about higher health insurance premiums, and so on.

Some subjects are more emotionally powerful than others and lend themselves to an emotional appeal. Stories of a personal health crisis, children in need, experiences with crime and deprivation, and the like, engage the emotions of listeners.

Delivery also has an impact. Your audience can tell if you are speaking from the heart or just mouthing words. They respond to the loudness of your voice, the pace and rhythm of your speech and to your verbal cues. In version 2 the air mask sends a chilling nonverbal message of life and death.

Finally, the placement of the appeal is important. Corporate speech consultant James Humes suggests using an emotional ending to motivate to action. In his view, the same emotions that stir people in their private lives motivate audiences. He explains: "C.E.O.s tell me, 'Listen, Jim, I'm not trying to save England, I'm just trying to get a message across to the company.' Well, you still want to ask the employees to join you in something. End on an emotional pitch. Work that audience up."[27]

Because of their power, emotional appeals can be tools of manipulation in the hands of unscrupulous speakers, racists, anti-Semites, and other extremists attempt to arouse audiences through emotion rather than logic. These speakers realize that

---

27.   N. R. Kleinfield, "Teaching the 'Sir Winston' Method," *The New York Times,* March 11, 1990, Section 3, p. 7.

fear and other negative emotions can be more powerful persuaders than reason when the audience is receptive to their emotional message. In 1985, for example, speakers in Kokomo, Indiana, preyed on the community's fear of AIDS as they urged the superintendent of schools to bar AIDS-victim Ryan White from attending class. (White, then 14 years old, had contracted AIDS through a blood transfusion. He died of the disease in 1990.) Ignoring the evidence that AIDS cannot be transmitted through casual contact, they helped create a discriminatory environment that ultimately forced White and his family to move to Cicero, Indiana—a town about twenty miles away. Not wanting to see the same thing happen there, the school board in Cicero held conferences about the disease, urging people to be guided by the facts, their common sense, and the positive emotion of compassion.

THE ROLE OF EVIDENCE IN PERSUASION

We address evidence throughout this chapter and we discuss evidence in detail in the chapters on researching your speech, using supporting material, and using visual aids. You should be highly familiar with the best ways to gather information, the kinds of support available, ways to assess the strength of evidence, and ways to present evidence effectively. To underscore the importance of evidence in persuasion you are reminded that *with the right amount and type of evidence, you can move your listeners to a natural and logical conclusion.* In contrast, weak or insufficient evidence gives your argument little power to persuade; your listeners are left wondering whether they should believe you or support your point of view[28].

As you plan your speech, think about the types of evidence most appropriate and persuasive. Review the chapters on finding and using information to support your points. Examples and extended anecdotes may be effective to support an important appeal in your speech, whether it is primarily an emotional appeal, ethical appeal, or logical appeal. It is easier to get involved in the stories of people's lives than in statistics. On the other hand, statistics can emphasize the severity of a problem for your audience when they follow an extended example that initially personalizes an important point.

The Occasion.   If you are delivering a speech that is part of a formal hearing—for example a campus meeting about the problem of parking for students—statistics and expert testimony might prove more suitable than examples or analogies. In an informal setting, say, a brief presentation in the lounge of your dorm, examples and analogies may be your most effective tools. Which occasion and which setting are likely to call for what kind of evidence for the purpose of persuasion?

The Audience.   If you are dealing with a resistant audience, use the testimony of experts. Force your listeners to disagree with recognized authorities rather than with

---

28.   Freeley, *Argumentation and Debate: Reasoned Decision Making,* p. 119.

only your opinion. If it is your position that children should never be spanked, quote experts like Drs. Benjamin Spock, David Elkind, and Burton White, all of whom oppose spanking as a form a child discipline.

A resistant audience also requires that you anticipate doubts and questions throughout your presentation with strong refuting evidence. When planning your speech, it is a good idea to list the opposing arguments and to marshal your evidence to deal with them.

In some ways a neutral audience is the most difficult audience to address because you have to focus much of your effort and evidence on capturing the audience's attention. Neutral listeners neither agree nor disagree with you, perhaps because they either know little or nothing about your subject or have no interest in it. To deal with either eventuality, start your speech with concrete examples that show a direct connection between your topic and the audience. If you use facts and statistics, make sure they are relevant and compelling. Once you have captured the attention of your audience, use your evidence to build a clear, precise case.

Finally, if you are dealing with a favorable audience, use evidence to reinforce your shared point of view. If possible, try to tell your listeners something they don't already know. You might present the testimony of a new authority or relate a personal experience you have not yet shared. Never take a favorable audience for granted by giving an off-the-cuff or poorly researched speech.

Ethics and Persuasive Speaking

The importance of ethics in public speaking is stressed both implicitly and explicitly throughout this book. Ethics provide standards for conduct that guide us, and persuasive speaking requires asking others to accept and act on ideas we believe to be accurate and true. So the ethics of persuasion merit particular consideration in our plans for persuasion. For example, do you want to be lied to—by anyone? Even when the truth hurts, we prefer it to deception. Telling the truth is the paramount ethical standard for the persuasive speaker.

Think for a few moments about rhetoric as persuasive speaking. Rhetoric is framed and expressed in language and presents ideas within a range of choice. As a speaker, when you make choices some degree of value is involved in your choosing, whether you speak about the quality of the environment or television programs to select. When choice is involved, ethics are involved; rhetoric and ethics are bound together.

The transactions between the speaker and audience are weighed in terms of a choice or choices involving something good or something bad or a mixture that includes both positive and negative consequences.

Citizens in 1993 had to decide what would be best for the country when the U.S. Congress debated whether or not to approve the North American Free Trade Agreement and the controversy was fierce. Many of our leaders, including the president, argued that NAFTA would be good for Americans and our economy while others argued quite the opposite. Ultimately a choice had to be made by our elected representatives and more legislators favored the treaty than opposed it. Those who were ethical persuasive speakers offered "good reasons" they believed confirmed the benefits likely to result if their stand on the agreement received the necessary votes. Advocates on both sides of the arguments over the treaty sought to persuade the general public and the legislators who represented various public constituencies that the benefits of their views certainly outweighed any disadvantages.

Citizens concerned about the truth of the persuasive speeches expected national decision-makers to base arguments on clear thinking, strong evidence, and the national public interest. The arguments offered a mixture of possible consequences if the treaty was passed or turned down. Any persuader who operated on the ethic of "tell them anything to win the argument" undermined the representatives who genuinely weighed information about the issues to arrive at premises and claims they believed to be true. The salesperson who will say anything to get the sale undermines the many honest persuaders who know and believe in the quality of the merchandise or services they are asking their customers to choose. There is, indeed, an ethical responsibility that must be assumed by persuasive speakers.

As members of an audience, many of the choices we make are largely inconsequential to us, such as which soft drink to buy in the local convenience store or which magazine to read while we wait for the dentist. Far more important, however, is the decision whether to reject our current religious beliefs to embrace new ones. Even the purchase of an expensive automobile is a considerable decision for us when weighed against the selection of a soft drink.

As a speaker you must decide not only what to tell your audience but also what you should avoid saying. In a persuasive speech you are asking listeners to think or act in ways called for to achieve your specific purpose, a desired response. Emotional appeals entail ethical responsibility, and this responsibility extends to other appeals as well. Consider again the four habits explained in Chapter Four.

The habit of search, in which we look for information to confirm or contradict a point of view, demands that we express genuine knowledge of our subject and an awareness of its issues and implications. As a persuasive speaker, you know that controversy exists in matters requiring persuasion. Your task, within the time constraints and resources you face, is to develop sound and good reasons for the response you desire from an audience. This task is centered in a careful search for the truth.

The habit of justice asks that you be fair in your search, selection, and presentation of facts for the audience to consider and accept. You should not distort ideas or hide information that an audience needs to properly evaluate your speech. Neither should you use loaded language or guilt-by-association tactics. In the 1988 presidential campaign George Bush labeled his opponent Michael Dukakis a card-carrying member of the American Civil Liberties Union, as if Dukakis should bear some guilt by association. In 1992 he called his opponents Bill Clinton and Al Gore a couple of "bozos."

The third habit of preferring public to private motivation stems from the fact that when you are involved in public speaking you act as public persons. As such you owe your audience the truth, which means you have a responsibility to disclose any special bias, prejudice, and private motivations in your sources and in your own motives. There are times in our society when political, religious, or economic spokespersons will articulate a public position that clearly indicates motives in the public interest when, in fact, their persuasive message is actually rooted in a private agenda that is self-serving. Popular films occasionally mirror this problem quite vividly. *Marjoe* is a dramatic documentary showing a popular traveling preacher who did not really believe in the Christian message he delivered. He enjoyed the money, the excitement, and other features from his success in holding revival and healing meetings for those who wanted to believe what he was willing to tell them. *Wall Street* is a film that portrays for viewers the tension between public messages and the private greed that can drive individuals obsessed by the pursuit of money and the power it buys.

In modern political persuasion, however, two films particularly point to the illusion of reality and the discrepancy between public motives and private motives: *The Candidate*, featuring Robert Redford as Bill McKay, a candidate for the U.S. Senate, and *Power* with Richard Gere as Pete St. John, a successful image-maker. In *The Candidate,* McKay is gradually transformed by image-makers into what the broader public expects from a popular senator at the expense of his own views and beliefs. In *Power,* the highly paid political consultant insists on complete control of a candidate/client's campaign in order to win an election. Both films dramatically underline and highlight how public figures choose not to disclose bias, prejudice, and private motives that could have a negative impact on the final vote.

Finally, *the habit of respect for dissent* requires that as a persuasive speaker you must recognize the legitimate diversity of positions that dissent from yours. As a persuader you are not compelled to sacrifice principle but, as Karl Wallace puts it, you should "prefer facing conflict to accepting appeasement." Leaders who serve as spokespersons from local community centers to the centers of power in Washington, D.C., are constantly being challenged about their opinions, policies, and actions. As a persuasive speaker you can ask with respect for dissent: "Can I freely admit the force of opposing evidence and argument and still advocate a position that represents my convictions?"[29]

The ethics of persuasion call for honesty, care, thoroughness, openness, and a concern for the audience without manipulative intent. The end does *not* justify the means at all costs. In a society as complex as ours, one marked in part by unethical as well as ethical persuaders, the moral imperative is to speak ethically.

Your credibility as a speaker is determined by the way the audience perceives you. SUMMARY Credibility is measured in terms of perceived competence, concern for the audience, dynamism, and ethics. According to rhetorical theorist Kenneth Burke, you can increase your credibility and ability to persuade if you convince your audience that you share "common ground" by indentifying with your listeners.

29.   Karl R. Wallace, "An Ethical Basis of Communication," *The Speech Teacher* January, 1955, p. 9.

Among the methods for reasoning are the inductive and deductive modes of reasoning. Inductive reasoning enables you to generalize from specific instances and draw a conclusion from your observations. Deductive reasoning draws a conclusion based on the connections between statements. Depending on your purpose for persuasion, you may choose to reason from examples, analogies, causal relations, or with enthymemes. Choosing the right amount of evidence, the most persuasive kind of evidence, and then reasoning carefully are essential for successful persuasion.

Emotional appeals can also provide powerful force in persuasion. Listeners respond to not only what they think but also how they feel. Through emotional appeals you can elicit the full range of human feelings in your listeners. Emotional appeals are persuasive because they provide the motivation for action and attitude change. To strengthen your appeal, use concrete detail and emotional language, and concentrate on delivering your speech effectively.

Persuasive speaking invites ethical responsbility. As a persuasive speaker you should be conscious of ethical standards and what the implications are of the choice you are asking your audience to make. The audience needs to be treated to the truth without manipulative intent to achieve an end guided by deception, trickery, gimmickery, or emotional ambiguity.

QUESTIONS FOR STUDY AND DISCUSSION

1. What are ethical, logical, and emotional appeals? How are these appeals distinct, yet interrelated?
2. After choosing a specific purpose for a persuasive speech, decide on the kind of reasoning that will provide the strongest argument. Why did you choose this reasoning form?
3. How important is evidence in a persuasive speech? How important are ethics in persuasive speaking? Does the importance depend on the audience and its shared needs and expectations? Is there a relationship among evidence, emotions, and credibility or is evidence simply a matter of cold, hard facts?

ACTIVITIES

1. Find transcripts, excerpts, or detailed news accounts of a well-known courtroom trial. Write a 500- to 750-word essay on the role of persuasive appeals in the attorneys' opening and closing arguments. Among the trials you may consider are the Lindbergh kidnapping trial and the more recent *Falwell* vs. *Flynt*, in which televangelist Jerry Falwell claimed he was defamed by pornographer Larry Flynt. Your focus should be on the strengths and weaknesses of the attorneys' persuasive appeals.
2. Select a persuasive political speech and analyze the reasoning used in the speech. Present an oral analysis to the class.
3. Develop and deliver a five- to six-minute persuasive speech on a controversial topic. Include in your persuasive strategy ethical, logical, and emotional appeals. Use a planning and key-word outline and strive to deliver your speech with power and animation.

S A M P L E   S P E E C H

*E*arlier in the chapter we discuss the persuasive power Cesar Chevas possessed with his constituency when he spoke. In his rhetoric he established common ground and inspired Latino farm workers to act to change their compensation and working conditions. In 1993 Chavez died, leaving behind a permanent legacy in human rights. His 1974 speech to citizens in Wooster, Ohio, is presented as an illustration of a persuasive speech for you to evaluate. He delivered this speech at a particularly important time for the union he founded, the United Farm Workers. His purpose was to persuade his audience that the UFWA was a necessary response to suffering and unfair labor practices by California Growers. He also wanted his audience to join the union's effort to get Americans to boycott California grapes, lettuce, and wine.

Study the speech carefully and assess what you perceive to be the ethical, logical, and emotional appeals in the speech. Think about the persuasive appeals, list them on paper, and form a critical opinion of the speech as a persuasive message.

April 7, 1974 Wooster, Ohio.

The value of a man is not what he has but what he is. We are confident; we have ourselves; we know how to work and to combat forces who fight us. Justice is on our side and will see us through. The farm workers must have a union. Children are workmen too, we estimate 800,000 of them. In past years the bakers, shoe men, carpenters, etc. have struggled and built unions. The farm workers have been going through unbelievable struggles, but have not made it. Not because they don't want a union.

California agribusiness is the biggest business in the state with $6 billion and one out of three jobs; it's bigger than aircraft and others. We are not fighting the family farmer, as you think or know him in Ohio. The number of family farmers has dropped in California. The corporations own 10,000 to 100,000 acres. In the lettuce industry there is no small family farmer left through the last 10–15 years. Who owns the corporate growers? South Pacific Railroad is the biggest, 200,000 acres; Prudential Life Insurance; *Los Angeles Times*, owners of Tjon Ranch, 168,000 acres, grapes; Kern Company, Land company, 35,000 acres; Ship Builders, Di Giorgia Fruit Corporation, 26,000 acres; Standard Oil, 218,000 acres; J.G. Boswell holdings, 108,200 acres; and others.

After five years struggling, with help of millions of people in the United States, Canada, and Europe who helped boycott table grapes, the farm workers broke the barrier with contracts being signed by growers in Coachella and San Joaquin valleys. For a short three years things were better for those families. Then, in April 1973, the contracts expired. In a very short time, without elections, nor warning, the corporations signed 200 contracts with the Teamsters Union leaving out the wishes of 58,000 members. We call this a "sweetheart agreement."

Well, remember, we have to organize in a different way because we are not covered by the National Labor Relations Act of 1935, which growers have successfully fought to exclude farm workers.

In California, years ago developed the sinister farm labor contractor who hires and exploits, often bringing Mexicans across the border. Our union wants to do away with this corrupt system, but the teamsters and corporations don't. We want a hiring hall, and work by seniority. They have the contract, but we have the people.

Why do the farm workers continue? They have given so much, been beaten, jailed. They want to be economically free like any other worker. But we are different from other groups because we are commited to nonviolence. We want to reach the men who oppress us, and teach them by example how to be human beings. Last summer was a most terrible time. Surely our workers would commit violence, with 200 beaten up by what we call hired "goons," 44 wounded, 2,000 arrests in jails; and when two were killed by officials and Teamsters, the picket lines were called off. Our workers do not believe in an eye for an eye, or death for a death. Violence does not bring victory. When you get violence, you can't extract yourself. We want to educate our enemies and win them to our side.

What we are asking of the employers? Nothing new. Wages are small, not much increase; it is not an issue. We need collective strength, independence, new-found dignity; regulations on pesticides; the sacred right to have a union forever; justice, and to determine for ourselves our rights.

In the lettuce industry, the workers are forced to use a short-handled hoe, which is crucifying. Workers may begin at 16, and in eight to ten years their lives are burned out, worn out, from the stooping, damaging permanently the spine. We want an end to the forced use of the short-handled hoe.

Some other things about migrants going from Texas to California or Florida north—they run all over the country to get a job. Their life expectancy is 49, while yours is 69. Forget the money, the suffering is taking our lives. TB is still around, it is 260 percent higher than the national rate, hundreds of cases. Infant mortality is 125 percent higher than the national rate.

Unregulated use of pesticides is terrible. They are the cause of 850 to 1,000 deaths, and 80,000 to 90,000 injuries, according to the Food and Drug Administration offical testifying before the Senate Subcommittee on Migratory Labor. Of course, in California the cause of death is never placed in the death certificate so it's hard to know how many deaths are caused in California alone. On the certificate it says heatstroke. We have 115 degrees when the work is being harvested. Or else it says weak heart. The chemical poisons most widely used on lettuce are chlorinated hydrocarbons or organic phosphates. Parathion is one of the most widely used, although it should not be. We want a 21-day re-entry onto fields after application. It is most dangerous, causing bleeding, convulsions, affecting the nerve impluses. The pesticide residues present serious hazards to you as the consumer. Residues do not deteriorate or disappear from our food, no does washing nor cooking, completely remove them. They are taken into our bodies and stored in our fatty tissues.

What we are asking is very simple. Don't eat iceberg lettuce from California. Or look for the black eagle on the packing box back in the store. When support keeps coming, we will force the companies to the bargaining tables. Boycott table grapes! We are also boycotting grapes used in wines. Gallo Company is the largest in the world. I thought the director was my friend. For seven years I had been meeting him every month on our Health Clinic Board. In 1967 Gallo signed a contract with the United Farm Workers of America, AFL-CIO, after the workers voted unanimously to be represented by UFWA. Wages improved, child labor was ended, and the dangerous pesticides were eliminated.

That contract expired on April 18, 1973, and for two and a half months the farm workers worked without a contract while negotiations with Gallo dragged on. Then, on July 26, 1973, Gallo announced that the workers would now be represented by the Teamsters and not the UFWA. That night the workers met and voted to strike. On July 27, 85 percent of the workers walked out of the fields and they have been on strike ever since. The issue in the Gallo strike is whether farm workers have the right to choose their own union, or whether Gallo will continue to impose his choice of a union on the workers. Please don't buy any Gallo wines!

Be instruments of love. When a man loses his cool, I will give you a fool. War trains men to kill. Being non-violent doesn't make the news, only violence. It takes training; and so does fasting. When you are in a fight with your wife, just fast, and by the second day you will be too weak to fight, and get over being mad. (Mr. Chavez closed with several jokes and took questions from his audience.)

Cesar Chavez, "Speech in Wooster, Ohio," printed in *Mexican American Anthology II*. ed. Joy Hintz, 500 E. Perry St., Tiffin, Ohio, 1976, pp. 304–306.

"It is generally better to deal by speech than by letter."

Francis Bacon

SPEECHES FOR SPECIAL OCCASIONS

ike all other forms of public speaking, a speech delivered on a special occasion can rise to the level of the extraordinary. Let's look at an example:

When Gale Sayers, the great running back for the Chicago Bears, accepted the Professional Football Writers' award for the most courageous player of the year in 1970 (Sayers had returned from knee surgery to lead the league in rushing), he used his speech to recognize the struggle of his teammate Brian Piccolo who was dying of cancer. In part, here is what Sayers said:

> He has the heart of a giant and that rare form of courage that allows him to kid himself and his opponent, cancer. He has the mental attitude that makes me proud to have a friend who spells out the word courage twenty-four hours a day.
>
> You flatter me by giving me this award but I tell you here and now that I accept it for Brian Piccolo. Brian Piccolo is the man of courage who should receive the George S. Halas award. It is mine tonight, it is Brian Piccolo's tomorrow . . . . I love Brian Piccolo and I'd like all of you to love him, too. Tonight, when you hit your knees, please ask God to love him . . . ."[1]

According to sports columnist Ira Berkow, Sayer's speech shocked the audience:

> [I had already begun to leave] as Sayers began to speak. He seemed serious, and he dispensed with the usual banter. He began talking about his teammate, Brian Piccolo.
>
> He talked about their friendship, and about how he, a black man, and Piccolo, who was white, roomed together on the road, highly unusual in those days, and not common today some 20 years later . . . .
>
> [After he finished], people in the banquet hall turned to each other and asked, "Did he say cancer?" Most people had been unaware of how seriously ill Piccolo was . . . .
>
> But Sayers had indeed said "cancer," and for the first time, it was out in the public about Piccolo . . . . It was all kind of unbelievable, and the "knees" and "God" and "love" were bunched together, but the sense of it was clear, and I had goose bumps, rooted there at the door.
>
> Piccolo died a few weeks later.[2]

Sayers used the vehicle of the acceptance speech to speak publicly about Piccolo's cancer for the first time. No one expected him to say what he did, yet his message was entirely fitting. Like all good acceptance speeches, the speech expressed Sayers' most sincere feelings about the award he had just received. He could not accept the award without telling his audience what weighed most heavily on his mind.

GENERAL GUIDELINES FOR CEREMONIAL SPEECHES

Acceptance speeches are one of the types of special occasion speeches we examine in this chapter. These speech forms are linked to ceremonies, delivered at occasions that require speeches to commemorate the event; speeches of introduction, speeches of presentation, speeches of acceptance, speeches of commemoration, keynote speeches, and after-dinner speeches. Whether you are introducing the new president

---

1. Gale Sayers with Al Silverman, *I Am Third* (New York: Viking Press, 1970), p. 77.
2. Ira Berkow, " 'Brian's Song' Reprise," *The New York Times,* November 2, 1988, p. B11.

of the freshman class, presenting an award honoring the volunteer of the year, or toasting the marriage of your sister, the following guidelines will help you decide what to say and how best to say it. Although there are differences among the types of special occasion speeches, these guidelines apply in most cases.

Make Sure Your Speech Meets Expectations

Ceremonies and the speeches that mark them are surrounded by sets of expectations. Mourners listening to a eulogy, graduates listening to a commencement address, members of a wedding party toasting the new couple expect certain words, gestures, and acts. Don't disappoint them. The words you choose to meet the occasion should remind people of the event they are commemorating. Even if you are sure everyone realizes the reason for your speech, explain it any way. For example, it is difficult to imagine an awards presentation speech that did not mention the background and purpose of the award and the reason the recipient was chosen. Similarly, a speech of acceptance that failed to say thank you would be less than appropriate.

Tailor Your Speech to the Person Being Honored and to the Occasion

Saying what people expect is not the same as delivering a canned speech. It isn't enough to change a few facts here and there and give the same speech of introduction at a parents' association meeting and at the meeting of a corporate board of directors. Your audience will realize that your speech has little to do with the specific reason for the gathering. Compare version 1 to version 2:

Version 1:

I am honored to introduce our Person of the Year, Ms. Elizabeth Steinberg. Thanks to her efforts, Elizabeth has helped make our community's dream of an art museum come true. She was a tireless worker in the cause and I urge you all to give her a round of applause as we honor her tonight.

Version 2:

I am honored to introduce our Person of the Year, Ms. Elizabeth Steinberg. Elizabeth is the sand in our community oyster that has produced an art museum that is a priceless pearl. She has worked tirelessly to give us this community treasure. While the rest of us were home relaxing on the weekends, Elizabeth was sweeping floors and working up financial support statements; fixing broken pipes and courting patrons. I can assure you that she did this for love, not money. Love of art and love of this community. I ask that we all honor her tonight as we celebrate the opening of this grand museum.

Version 1 is a much blander introduction. Mentioning Ms. Steinberg's specific contributions and using an appropriate metaphor enhances the effect of Version 2.

Use Personal Anecdotes and Appropriate Humor

The more you say about the people and occasion that are the reason for your speech, the more intimate and fitting your speech becomes. Personal anecdotes—especially humorous ones—help create the feeling that the speech was written for this event and no other. When Barbara Bush addressed graduating students at Wellesley College in 1990, she used humor to help defuse the bitterness that had erupted after she was chosen as commencement speaker. About 150 students had signed a petition against the choice of Mrs. Bush as commencement speaker because they believed she did not represent the career woman Wellesley sought to educate. Mrs. Bush first told the students what she thought about life's priorities:

> As important as your obligations as a doctor, a lawyer, or a business leader may be, your human connections with spouses, with children, with friends, are the most important investment you will ever make.
>
> At the end of your life, you will never regret not having passed one more test, not winning one more verdict or not closing one more deal. You will regret time not spent with a husband, a child, a friend or a parent.

She then softened her message with wit.

> Who knows, somewhere out in this audience may even be someone who will one day follow in my footsteps and preside over the White House as the President's spouse . . . And I wish him well.[3]

The 5,400 people in her audience roared with laughter as they cheered Mrs. Bush's remarks.

Avoid Clichés

Although speeches for special occasions should follow a predictable form, they should not be trite. To avoid delivering yet another tired introductory, presentation, acceptance, or commemorative speech, avoid the clichés that seem to be part of every speaker's vocabulary. These include:

1. "Ladies and gentlemen, heeeere's . . ." (use this line only if you're impersonating Ed McMahon).

2. "Without further ado . . ." (how many times have you heard this expression in ordinary conversation?).

3. "I don't know what to say" (don't believe it, most speakers plan their remarks well in advance).

4. "My friends, we are truly honored tonight" (is the audience filled with personal friends?).

5. "Ladies and gentlemen, here is a speaker who needs no introduction" (then why bother speaking?).

Clichés should be avoided, but appropriate metaphors can add texture and interest to your speech. Here, for example, is the way Paul Henmueller, then a senior

---

3. Fox Butterfield, "Family First, Mrs. Bush Tells Friend and Foe at Wellesley," *The New York Times,* June 2, 1990, p. A1

at the University of Illinois at Chicago, used the metaphor of diamonds of hope in his commencement address:

> Buried deep within the earth lie vast deposits of diamonds, the world's most precious gem. Although these stones are tremendously valuable, until they are mined they remain useless—glimmering pebbles hidden beneath the surface. Some day these jewels will be unearthed and the world will marvel at their brilliance.
>
> Just as there is a great storehouse of wealth hidden in the vaults of the earth, so is there tremendous wealth buried deep within the mind and soul of each individual. This wealth may be in the form of intelligence, personality, honor or a myriad of other abilities and attributes which comprise the spectrum of the human spirit.[4]

Be Aware that You Are Speaking for Others as Well as Yourself

Whether you are presenting a gold watch to commemorate a vice president's twenty-fifth year of employment or toasting the conference championship of your college football team, you are speaking as a representative of the group. Although your words are your own, your purpose is to echo the sentiments of those who have asked you to speak. In this capacity, you are the group spokesperson.

Be Sincere

You can't fake sincerity, so don't try. If you have been asked to give an award or introduce a person you have never met, don't pretend an intimate relationship. Instead of saying, "I've seen what Jim can do when he puts his mind to it," tell your listeners, "I've spoken to the people who know Jim best—his supervisors and coworkers. They told me how, single-handedly, he helped two dozen of his coworkers escape a fire-filled office and how he refused medical attention until he was certain everyone was safe. I'm proud to honor Jim as our employee of the year."

Bragging Is Inappropriate

Even when you are accepting an award or being honored as person of the year, resist the temptation to tell everyone how great you are. It is in poor taste. Be appropriately humble, remembering that your audience is aware of your accomplishments. Judge Sherman G. Finesilver demonstrates the grace of understatement in a commencement address he delivered in Boulder, Colorado:

> This is rather symbolic for me today, at the University of Colorado. In this very auditorium, I experienced somewhat of a victory for me personally. It occurred in December 1988. It was an occasion for me to receive an honorary doctorate from the University of Colorado. Yes, I had my bachelor's degree from the University of Colorado. My experience at law school was quite different. It marked a failure and a difficult time in my life.

---

4. Paul Henmueller, "Diamonds of Hope: The Value of a Person," speech delivered at commencement, University of Illinois, Chicago, June 11, 1989. Reprinted in *Vital Speeches of the Day,* September 1, 1989, pp. 680–81.

Going back a few years, a law school dean here at the University told my parents, "Sherm will never make a lawyer because of his low grades." I could have been destroyed at that time. In my mind in some respects I was a failure, but in the hearts and minds of my parents I was not a failure. With their support, encouragement, and yes, maybe with fierce determination on my part, I was able to attend and graduate from another law school—a night law school—holding down a full time job during the day.

Yes, I was able to become a lawyer, and was appointed a state judge at age twenty-eight. My law degree was a victory for me, and perhaps this is the touchstone of my remarks today. My failure, success, self-confidence, and committed work ethic all contributed to the fabric of my life and, yes . . . will also contribute to the lives of each of you.[5]

Through these words, the speaker creates an empathic bond with his audience. His failure—and subsequent victory—enable his listeners to identify with his struggle.

Be Accurate

Avoid embarrassing yourself with factual mistakes. If you are introducing a guest speaker, find out everything you need to know before the presentation by talking with the person or reading his or her résumé. If you are giving a commencement address, learn the names of the people who must be acknowledged at the start of your talk (as well as the correct pronunciation of the names). If you are toasting an employee for years of dedicated service, make sure you get the number of years right.

We will now turn to the specific types of special occasion speeches to see how these general guidelines apply and how other, more specific rules help define these speech forms.

SPEECHES OF INTRODUCTION

In a speech of introduction, you introduce the person who will give an important address. Keynote speakers are introduced, as are commencement speakers and speakers delivering inaugural remarks. When you deliver this type of speech, think of yourself as the conduit through which the audience learns something about the speaker. Research has shown that this speech is important because of its power to enhance the speaker's credibility.[6]

In many cases, your comments will follow written remarks about the speaker and his or her intended topic. When written descriptions are distributed in advance of a meeting, it is safe to assume that most people already know something about the speaker's background and perhaps even the title of the speech. It is your job to heighten the anticipation and to help your audience like and respect the speaker.

---

5. Sherman G. Finesilver, "The Tapestry of Your Life: Don't Be Afraid To Fail," speech delivered at the Front Range Community College commencement, University of Colorado Events Center, Boulder, Colorado, May 7, 1989. Reprinted in *Vital Speeches of the Day,* November 15, 1989, p. 82.
6. Tom Daniels and Richard F. Whitman, "The Effects of Message Introduction, Message Structure, and Verbal Organizing Ability upon Learning of Message Information," *Human Communication Research* (Winter 1981): 147–60.

You can accomplish these goals by describing the speaker's accomplishments in an appropriate way. Tell your listeners about the speaker's background and why he or she was invited to address the gathering:

> Rosita Hernandez is known to us all as president of the Hispanic students organization on campus and as the president of our college's chapter of Students Against Drunk Driving. What few of you know about Rosita is her untiring work with abused children. Rosita spends every Saturday afternoon at the Department of Social Service's shelter, playing games with and reading to children who are desperately in need of love. Please join me in welcoming Rosita Hernandez who will talk about how volunteering has changed her life.

Be Brief

If you are going to err in an introductory speech, err on the side of brevity. Never use an introduction to recite the speaker's résumé; it will embarrass you and the person you are introducing. Recently, we heard an introductory speaker make this mistake when introducing a congressman at a U.S. Naval retirement ceremony. Having received in advance a lengthy biography from the congressman's office including details of his education, military service, activities in community service organizations, campaigns for Congress, congressional committee assignments, and so on, the speaker went into great detail introducing the man. Overcome by information overload, members of the audience shifted restlessly, coughed, yawned, and even dozed off.

Be Personal

It is also wise to err on the side of personalization rather than generalization by adapting your remarks to address the occasion, the setting, and the main speaker. When Sondra was asked to introduce the main speaker at her college's Honor's Day Banquet, she made these connections:

> I am, of course, genuinely delighted to be here this evening to speak to all of you and, particularly, those of you who are honors students. As an honors alumnus of this college, I know how proud you must feel and how hard you worked to get to this point.
>
> As I walked around the campus earlier this afternoon, a campus I have not visited in a number of years, I found myself amazed at the new buildings—the Smith Library, the Porter Hall of Science, the Davidson Auditorium. I remember, fondly, as a student that Dorothy Smith was our chief librarian, Miles Porter a distinguished professor of biology, and John Davidson our president. How wonderful to see these great educators honored on our campus!
>
> One of the equally important graduates who rose from her undergraduate days on our campus to a level of great prominence in the field of broadcasting is our speaker tonight. Cheryl Simon, known to all of you for her work on the nightly news, had her professional beginnings delivering the news to college students at the campus TV station. The experience must have been a good one, for she has just celebrated her fifteenth anniversary on the air.
>
> Please join me in welcoming our honored guest, Cheryl Simon.

Additional Guidelines

The following guidelines will help you prepare appropriate introductory remarks:

- ⌘ *Be sure your remarks are consistent with the tone of the main speech.* It is a mistake to be funny if the main speaker's remarks are serious. Similarly, serious remarks will seem incongruous if the main speaker is a well known humorist. Your remarks will set the right tone if you consult the speaker before the presentation.

- ⌘ *Don't summarize the speaker's intended remarks.* Your job is to provide an enticement to listen, not a summary of the remarks to follow. If you have any questions, share your proposed comments with the main speaker before your presentation.

- ⌘ *Don't shift attention away from the main speaker onto yourself.* Your role is to introduce, not to be the star of the occasion. If you are too funny, if your remarks are too long, if you focus on yourself rather than on the person you are introducing, you may steal the limelight. Speeches of introduction are not the appropriate place to air personal opinions.

- ⌘ *Avoid creating expectations the speaker cannot meet.* By telling the audience, "This is the funniest speech you'll ever hear," or "This woman is known for being a brilliant communicator," you are making it difficult for the speaker to succeed. Few speakers can match these expectations.

- ⌘ *Listen carefully to the speaker's remarks because you may be mentioned.* When you return to your seat, don't sigh with relief and start thinking of other things. You may be caught off guard when the speaker mentions you during the presentation. If the speaker relates a humorous anecdote involving you, be ready to smile; if thanks are offered and the audience starts applauding, be ready to take a bow.

- ⌘ *Pronounce the speaker's name correctly and repeat it several times during the introduction.* After you have finished your introduction, face the audience and announce the speaker's name. Say something like: "I'm pleased to present the new head of the board of education . . . . Adriane Bernardo."

- ⌘ *End your remarks with a call to action.* You can encourage the audience to greet the speaker by closing your speech with the words: "Please join me in welcoming . . . ." Lead your audience in applause.

- ⌘ *Be willing to be spontaneous.* Spontaneous introductions are sometimes appropriate, as actor Dustin Hoffman can attest. When Hoffman was taking his curtain calls after completing a performance of Shakespeare's *The Merchant of Venice* on Broadway, he noticed that Arthur Miller, author of the critically acclaimed classic, *Death of a Salesman,* a play in which Hoffman had earned earlier accolades in his role of Willy Loman, was seated in the audience. Hoffman raised his hands, asked for quiet, and said:

  > When we were doing the play in London, we had the pleasure of playing one night to an audience that included Dame Peggy Ashcroft, who was introduced from the

stage. We do not have knights in America, but there is someone special in the audience tonight. He is one of the greatest voices and influences in the American theater—Mr. Arthur Miller.[7]

As Hoffman demonstrated that night, brevity and grace are the hallmarks of an effective introduction.

SPEECHES OF PRESENTATION

Each year, the nation honors five distinguished performing artists as recipients of the Kennedy Center Honors. In an award ceremony at a State Department dinner in Washington, each honoree received a gold medallion with rainbow-colored ribbons. Actor Gregory Peck, who presented the award citations, later admitted that his was an enviable job. "It's easy to throw roses at people," said Peck.[8]

Throwing roses is an apt description for the presentation speech, which is delivered as part of a ceremony to recognize an individual or group chosen for special honors.

Our personal and professional lives are marked, in part, by attendance at, or participation in, awards ceremonies to recognize personal achievement. We also witness these presentations in the public forum. Each of these ceremonies includes one or more presentation speeches. Here are some occasions for presentation speeches:

⌘ At commencement (high school, college, and graduate school) special presentations are made to students with exceptional academic and community service records.

⌘ Corporations routinely present employees with awards for twenty-five years of service.

⌘ The Heisman Memorial Trophy is presented each year to the nation's outstanding college football player.

⌘ In perhaps the most famous awards ceremony of all, the Academy of Motion Picture Arts and Sciences presents annual achievement awards: the Oscars.

Every speech of presentation should accomplish two goals: it should tell the audience why the award is being given to a particular person and it should state the importance of the award. When appropriate, the speech may also explain the selection process. Here is an example of a speech marking the presentation of the "Reporter of the Year" award for a student newspaper. Tom was asked to make the presentation to his fellow reporter, Kathryn Remm:

> I am pleased to have been asked by our editorial staff to present the "Reporter of the Year" award—the college's highest journalistic honor. This award was established six years ago by a group of alumni who place great value on maintaining our newspaper's high standard of journalism.

---

7.   Susan Heller Anderson, "Chronicle," *The New York Times,* January 18, 1990, p. B6.
8.   Barbara Gamarekian, "Performing Artists Honored in Words and Music," *The New York Times,* December 4, 1989, p. C17.

The award selection process is long and arduous. It starts when the paper's editorial staff calls for nominations and then reviews and evaluates dozens of writing samples. The staff sends its recommendations to a selection committee made up of two alumni sponsors and two local journalists. It is this group of four who determines the winner.

This year's honoree is Kathryn Remm, the community affairs reporter on the paper. Almost single-handedly, Kathryn reached out to noncollege community residents and established channels of communication that have never been open. In a series of articles, she told students about the need for literacy volunteers at the community library and for "Big Brothers" at the local Boys Club.

Please join me in recognizing this year's "Reporter of the Year," Kathryn Remm. Kathryn, please come forward to receive our applause and this plaque—symbols of recognition of your outstanding achievement.

Because many awards are established in the names and spirit of people—living and deceased—you may have to describe the achievements of the individual or individuals for whom the award has been established, as in the following example:

We are honored to present the Josephine McNeil award for community involvement in the field of adult literacy. Mrs. McNeil was a tireless worker who established this community's literacy volunteer program and personally tutored hundreds of young adults. She did this in the 1950s—well before the notion of helping the illiterate became popular. After her death, the community established this award in her name.

Your description is intended for both the audience and the award recipient. Your goal is to let them know the intent and meaning of the award in the view of those who initiated it. The speech may also explain the significance of the tangible symbol that marks the award. For example, it may be appropriate at the Academy Awards to explain the history of the Oscar.

Occasionally, it is appropriate to ask past recipients of the award to stand up and receive applause. This decision should be based, in part, on your conviction that this acknowledgement will magnify the value of the award to the current recipient as well as the audience. If the award is competitive, you may wish to mention the nature of the competition as long as you do not overemphasize the struggle for victory. You do not want to leave your listeners with the impression that the winner's achievement is at the expense of others.

Like speeches of introduction, the key to a successful presentation speech is brevity. Choose your words with care so that the power of your message is not diminished by unnecessary detail. Within this limited context, try to humanize the award recipient through a personal—perhaps humorous—anecdote.

SPEECHES OF ACCEPTANCE

When actress Katharine Hepburn received the Screen Actors' Guild award on January 27, 1980, she could not attend the awards ceremony. Instead, she sent a tape with the following message:

Good afternoon, everybody—I should say, fellow workers. That makes it sound revolutionary. This is the letter that I wrote Bill Schallert when he wrote me that you

I N T E R V I E W

Peter Davis
Award-Winning Writer,
Producer, and Director

The annual Academy and Emmy awards celebrate the best the motion picture and television industries have to offer. Not only do we watch these ceremonies to learn the industries' own top choices in various categories, we also watch to hear the winners say thank you. Millions of Americans care enough about these acceptance speeches to stay tuned to the ceremonies many hours at a time.

Saying thank you for an entertainment industry award is something Peter Davis knows well. As the producer and director of *Hearts and Minds,* Davis won an Academy Award in 1975 for best Documentary Film. As the writer and producer of *The Selling of the Pentagon,* he won an Emmy for best television documentary in 1971. He received the Peabody, Writers Guild of America, and the George Polk awards for the latter.

We asked Davis to reflect on the acceptance speeches he has given—and heard—over the years. His comments apply as much to acceptance speeches you might give as they do to the speeches of Hollywood stars.

Question: How do you define a good acceptance speech?

Answer: By its brevity and graciousness. Whether you're receiving an expected honor—if, for example, someone calls you in advance and tells you that you are going to be honored as man or woman of the year—or an unexpected honor, such as being nominated for an award and not knowing if you're going to win, the best speeches are brief, gracious, and let your audience know you do not regard yourself as having just become God.

Of course, some awards are presented expressly to give the honored person the opportunity to speak. Here brevity and perhaps even graciousness are secondary to the speaker's message. For example, if an organization presents an award to a Chinese dissident, the expectation is that he'll say more than, "Thank you. I couldn't have done it without the repression of Deng Xiaoping and his fellow Maoist thugs." Everyone expects to hear a good deal more about the current politics of China.

Question: If you are one of five people nominated for an Oscar or an Emmy, do you write your speech in advance?

Answer: No, but I have in mind what I would like to say. I remember when I was nominated for an Emmy for "The Selling of the Pentagon"— a television show that had its share of controversy— (CBS was threatened with a contempt of Congress citation and the government subpoenaed my notes) I felt it was necessary to send a message when I received the award. I told the audience that I was proud of what we did and, paraphrasing Harry Truman, I said, "If you can't stand the heat, get out of the kitchen. We do find it hot in here but our intention is to stay in the kitchen as long as we need to." My speech was that short, but it made the point. No doubt I was taking myself too seriously, but we all felt we were being viciously attacked by the government, so I decided to say we'd keep fighting as long as the government kept fighting.

Question: We've heard other speakers use the award ceremony to spout their political views on issues that have nothing to do with their work. How do you feel about this?

Answer: There are two things I object to in an acceptance speech. The first is when someone gets up and says, "Even as we sit here tonight, millions of Americans are starving." This doesn't focus attention on the plight of the hungry; it focuses on the speaker's own virtue. Demonstrations like this are odious.

I also object when the award winner gets up and says, "I've battled back from alcoholism or drug abuse and I never thought I'd be standing here tonight." That's okay when you're accepting an award in the privacy of your living room—among friends—but not before a national audience.

I used to cringe when Judy Garland would periodically announce, always to thunderous applause, her complete recovery from emotional and drinking problems—and it was never more than wishful thinking anyway.

Question: Are you saying that speakers should never say anything really personal?

Answer: When you receive an award—especially a nationally televised award—it's one thing to know your audience, it's another to know who you are. If a film editor or sound effects expert gives an intimate speech, we aren't very forgiving or patient because most of us never heard of him before.

We just want him to get up, say thank you, and sit down. When, on the other hand, major stars receive the best actor or actress awards, we want to hear more than a simple thank you. These are well known people to begin with and we want to know something about them. I remember one year how disappointing it was when, after receiving the best actor award, the actor simply said thank you and sat down. Everyone in the audience desperately wanted more, particularly after a whole evening of awards for obscure, if essential, filmmaking functions they had no real interest in.

Question: Whenever you turn on the Academy Awards, you hear the winners thanking everyone in sight—from Aunt Millie to the janitor who cleaned up the coffee cups on the movie set. Can you go too far with these kinds of thank yous, especially since the audience has no idea whom you're thanking?

Answer: Some people do go overboard in their thank yous, but there's nothing offensive about it. It's only boring.

Question: Is there any advice you have for students about to give their first acceptance speech?

Answer: I go back to grace and brevity. Part of what I mean by grace is the generosity of realizing that while this is your moment, and you should savor it, you should acknowledge that a number of others helped you get where you are. So even if you are giving a speech upon the acceptance of your diploma, which is a uniquely personal achievement, you can acknowledge that your parents and friends, professors and others contributed to your achievement. As I said earlier, you have not just become God, or even His first base coach.

Source: Interview with Peter Davis, October 14, 1989.

had chosen me: "I am dumbfounded, and at the same time, I am very proud to have been chosen by the Screen Actors' Guild as a good example, professionally and personally. It is always heartening to be told by one's fellows that one is first rate, and that they wish to say so publicly.

"Sitting here in my New York house, I enjoyed this news immensely. But if I had to go to California and accept this award, it would really make me a very miserable creature, as this sort of appearance is torture to me. I hope that they will understand how very, very happy I am they have made me their choice, and allow me the sweet privilege of enjoying it in private.

"With great many thanks to them and you for this great honor."

Now that's what I wrote to Bill Schallert. And now I am going to try to say to you what I feel secretly.

All the funny, the curious thoughts which assail one when a group of people, your own group, give you a pat on the back. And I thought of my family, my private family—I've been very lucky. I am one of six. I still live where I grew up. I am still friends with the man with whom I won the three-legged race in 1917. I have had community and I have had safety. Now I suddenly realize that I have a professional family. You. All my fellows. We all do the same things, more or less.

We have similar ambitions. We are traveling along the same road, so to speak. And I think: I am your sister. Well, I'm your mother, or I might be your grandmother more aptly. And you are mine and I am yours. And I am safe. Well, not safe. No one is safe. But I am protected by this union if I am sick or hopeless. And now you all get together and you give me the prize. That's very heartwarming.

And I think to myself, "You're too big a pig to go out there and accept it. You're just an old pig." And then I think to myself, "Yes, you are. But you're *their* old pig and they love you, and they gave you a prize, and they proved it." So I sit back. I'm touched and I'm very moved. You've done a lot for me. Thank you.[9]

This speech has many of the elements of the model eloquent acceptance speech. It is personal, gracious, and sincere and, as such, it is Hepburn's gift to her audience.

Ms. Hepburn understood that the main purpose of an acceptance speech is to express gratitude for the award. Most speakers develop this theme at the start of their speech, though its specific language may vary. One variation is, "I don't know what to say at this moment except that I am honored and thankful," while another is, "I am genuinely grateful for this award and I want to express my sincere thanks to everyone here."

Hepburn also recognized the support she received from others over the years by mentioning the people, including the members of her family and her fellow actors, who played a crucial role in her life. Recognition of others is a key element of an effective acceptance speech, for it is an expression of humility at having received the award.

You can also include in your speech a description of how you reached this point of achievement. Select with care the events you want to mention to avoid an endless chronology. When Joanne received an award for being the most valuable player on her soccer team, she said this:

Three events contributed to my success on the soccer field. The first occurred on Christmas four years ago when I found a soccer ball under the tree and a completed registration form to a soccer camp held in my hometown.

The second event was our final game during my senior year in high school when we won the city championship and I was fortunate enough to score the winning goal.

---

9. Speech reprinted in Steve Allen, *How to Make a Speech* (New York: McGraw-Hill Paperbacks, 1986), pp. 136–37.

I cannot tell you the great sense of satisfaction I felt when my kick took the ball past the goal tender and into the net.

The third event was the call I received from our coach inviting me to be part of this college team with its winning tradition and offering me an athletic scholarship.

Joanne then made the transition to what is often the final component of an acceptance speech: telling the audience what the award means to you:

I want everyone to understand how much I value this award. I have received other awards in my life, but none that means more to me than to be considered by my coaches and teammates as the team's most valuable player.

This honor will increase my motivation and my pride. And, while I know others in this room will receive the award in the future, I will always try to be a most valuable player. Thank you all very much.

An acceptance speech is built around the theme of thank you: You thank the person, group, or organization bestowing the award; you recognize the people who helped you gain it; you examine how you reached this point of recognition; and you tell your audience what receiving the award means to you.

In most cases, brievity is essential, as is grace and personal style. Instead of simply telling your listeners, "I am grateful to everyone who supported me in this project," share with them a personal anecdote. Like Katharine Hepburn, give something back to your audience as in the following example:

As everyone knows, I report directly to Ed Owens—a man who should be standing here along with me to receive this award. When I wanted to quit, when I thought the odds of ever finding a clue to this terrible mystery of cancer, were insurmountable, Ed urged me on. He never gave up on me—or my ideas. I remember one frustrating day, throwing all my notes in the garbage. If it weren't for Ed sifting through what I believed was a pile of useless data, I wouldn't have pursued the direction that eventually led me here. I thank Ed for his faith in me and his persistence.

COMMEMORATIVE SPEECHES

When we commemorate an event, we mark it through observation and ceremony. Public or private, these ceremonies are often punctuated by speeches appropriate for the occasion. Commencement speeches at college graduation, eulogies at the funeral of a loved one, speeches to celebrate the spirit of a special event or a national holiday like the Fourth of July, congratulatory toasts at a wedding or the birth of a baby or business deal, inaugural speeches, and farewell addresses all fit into this category.

Although commemorative speeches may inform, their purpose is not informational. Although they may persuade, their purpose is not persuasive. They are inspirational messages designed to stir emotions and make listeners reflect on what is being said through the use of rich language that lifts the audience to a higher emotional plane. More than in any other special occasion speech, your choice of words in the commemorative address will determine your success.

Many commemorative speeches express the speaker's most profound thoughts. As you talk about what it means to be graduated from college, be inaugurated to office, or lose a family member, your goal is to leave a lasting impression on your

An acceptance speech is built around the theme of "thank you"; Guns 'N' Roses accepted an award with that theme in mind.

audience. Although many commemorative speeches are short, they often contain memorable quotations that add strength and validity to the speaker's own emotion-filled message.

The following are four forms of commemorative speeches:

Commencement Speeches

No other speech offers a greater potential to achieve these aims than the commencement address delivered by an honored guest to a graduating class. Here is an example of a commencement speech delivered by Curt Smith, a speechwriter for President George Bush, to the 1989 graduating class at the State University of New York at Geneseo, his alma mater. Smith's carefully chosen language stirs thoughts, images, and memories. He starts with an expression of honor:[10]

> Let me thank all of you for your generous welcome. And say that to address these commencement ceremonies is, of course, among the greatest privileges of my life.
>
> Mark Twain once wrote: "In Boston, they ask: 'How much does he know?' In Philadelphia, 'Who were his parents?' In New York, 'How much is he worth?'"
>
> Well, from my perspective, you couldn't put a price tag on this morning. It is an honor to join you—especially my soon-to-be fellow graduates.
>
> Sixteen years ago, I sat where you do, as undergraduates, about to receive my degree.

10.   This and the following excerpts from Curt Smith, "Commencement Address: State University of New York at Geneseo," May 20, 1989.

At this point the speaker shifts from the honor of being invited to speak to a tribute to the college from which he was graduated. Vivid language conjures up images that have remained with him over the years:

> I loved bonfires, Indian summer, snow-flecked evenings, and the Boston Red Sox. But most of all, I loved tomorrow. Its possibilities were soaring, distant; they lay out ahead of us, like a day right behind the rain . . . .
>
> Yes, rhetoric, like perspective, can often be unclear. But as students in the early 1970s at Geneseo State University, our perspective—for better or worse—was perfectly clear . . .
>
> Even then, we inhaled the age's often brooding and quite wonderful songs—"Taxi" and "American Pie" and "Layla" and the classic "Maggie May." And we believed ours to be what retrospect proclaims it: The most tumultuous freshman class in the history of American education.
>
> We entered college in the fall of 1969; our first months were marked by Woodstock, moratoria, and talk of "impudent snobs." We left in the spring four years later—the Viet Nam conflict ending; our prisoners of war at home; and scandal searing—indelibly, tragically—an epochal American Presidency.
>
> It was a time to begin, of intolerance and, yet, of idealism—for in the cultural collision which marked the early 1970s, the university campus was its spiritual heart.

Then Smith pays tribute to the college as a place of excellence marked by enduring and important values:

> Mostly, though, Geneseo thrived in the early 1970s because of the Geneseo Experience, which is your experience: Excellence without elitism, Main Street values without facade.
>
> She knew, as you do, that those who burned buses and bombed buildings were not the voice of America's academic tradition. She knew that amid the tumult and the shouting, government at all levels must hear the voices of those who work and pay their taxes and who speak from conscience: Americans who ask government not to bless their lives, only to go their own way—gently, modestly—with the respect and dignity they deserve.

After his tribute, Smith offers counsel to the graduating members of his audience, urging them to strive for themselves and others. He concludes on a congratulatory note:

> In coming years, as alumni, you can reaffirm that voice. And as you do, remember how nearly a half-century ago Churchill said of a great battle of World War II: "Now this is not the end. It is not even the beginning of the end. But it is, perhaps, the end of the beginning."
>
> My friends, in the deepest personal sense, this Commencement marks the end of your beginning.
>
> Cherish the memories of your time at this university. Understand its joys, worries, and confessions of the heart. Care intensely, and give intensely of yourselves. Help spur that unity of purpose which benefits the nation as a whole.
>
> Your inheritance is America; treasure it. May your future be worthy of your dreams. And may you recall the penultimate words of a great film from my college

years, *Summer of '42:* "Life is made of comings and goings. And for everything we take with us, we leave a part of us behind."

Good luck, my heart-felt congratulations, and thank you so very much.

Although Smith's speech lasted only eighteen minutes, the strength of its emotional appeal endures.

Eulogies

Eulogies are perhaps the most difficult commemorative speeches to make. As you speak, you pay tribute to a family member, friend, colleague, or community member who died. It is a difficult time for the speaker as well as the audience. Here are several guidelines that will help you present this speech:

Deliver a Eulogy Only If You Can Control Your Emotions.   Composure is crucial. If you have any questions about your ability to control your grief, suggest that someone else be chosen. Your goal as a eulogist is to offer comfort to others, not to call attention to your own grief. While an expression of loss is appropriate, uncontrolled grief is out of place.

Start By Acknowledging the Special Loss Suffered By the Family.   Your first words should focus on the family of the deceased. Talk directly to them, taking care to acknowledge by name the spouse, children, and parents of the deceased.

Focus on a Celebration of Life Rather Than on Feelings of Loss.   Although it is appropriate to acknowledge shared feelings of sadness and even anger, the eulogy should focus on the unique gift the person brought to the world. Here is part of a eulogy a student might write for a friend killed in an auto accident:

> No one expected this. Andrew was so filled with life and hope. How could this happen? Why Andrew? Why now? These questions have tormented me since the accident, and I know they have filled your thoughts as well.
>
> It may sound silly, but I don't think Andrew would have wanted us to cry over him. He had too much joy to tolerate our tears. He would have urged us to remember what he accomplished in his twenty years—especially his music.
>
> What music! My soul soared everytime I heard him at the piano. We are so fortunate to have his recordings as tangible memories of his spirit and life.

You can continue the eulogy by focusing on such universal themes as the preciousness and fragility of life, the importance of family and friends at times of great loss, and the continuity of life:

> Andrew's death has forced us to look once more at how fragile and precious life is. I pray that his family can draw strength from all of us here. All of us who loved Andrew so deeply.

Use Anecdotes, Even Humor.   Nothing celebrates the spirit of the deceased better than a good story. A well chosen anecdote can comfort as it helps people focus on the memory of the person's life. Fitting anecdotes need not be humorless. On the contrary, according to professor of journalism Melvin Helitzer, euphemisms such as "a loving husband," "a loving father," "a wonderful person" mean far less to people than a humorous account of an incident in the person's life. Helitzer explains: "To say the deceased had a wonderful sense of humor and I remember the time . . . ., helps mourners get through the experience of attending the memorial as they recall pleasant memories and laugh along with you." [11]

Quote Others.   Turn to the remarks of noted public figures such as Winston Churchill, John F. Kennedy, and Mark Twain; to friends and family of the deceased; or even to the deceased to communicate the depth of your feelings. For example, Edward M. Kennedy used this quote from his brother Robert F. Kennedy at Robert's funeral:

> A few years back Robert Kennedy wrote some words about his own father which expresses the way we in his family felt about him. He said of what his father meant to him and I quote:
>
> "What it really all adds up to is love. Not love as it is described with such facility in popular magazines, but the kind of love that is affection and respect, order and encouragement and support.
>
> Our awareness of this was an incalculable source of strength. And because real love is something unselfish and involves sacrifice and giving, we could not help but profit from it . . ." [12]

Bring the Group Together Through Language.   People come together to mourn because they want to be part of a community; they want to share their grief with others. You can help them do this through your choice of language as in the following examples:

We all know how much Andrew loved his family.

I am sure we all agree that Andrew's determination and spirit left their mark.

I know all who mourn Andrew's death also celebrate his life.

Be Sincere and Be Brief.   Speak from the heart by shunning such bromides as "words cannot express our sorrow," "the family's loss is too much to bear," and "we were all privileged to know him." Rely instead on personal memories, anecdotes, and feelings. Focus also on your delivery for it too will affect the sincerity of your message. Eulogies need not be lengthy to be effective.

Speeches for National Holidays

Part of the way we celebrate national holidays is through oratory. We commemorate Independence Day, Memorial Day, and President's Day by delivering speeches—or

11.   Interview with Professor Melvin Helitzer, January 17, 1990.
12.   Edward M. Kennedy, "Eulogy to Robert F. Kennedy," *The New York Times,* June 9, 1968, p. 56.

being part of the audience marking the event. These speeches remind listeners why we celebrate the day and what we must do to carry on the tradition and spirit of the occasion.

The speech for Memorial Day usually revolves around the theme of sacrifice for country. Here is an excerpt from a Memorial Day speech delivered by college president William E. Hamm:

> Fellow citizens: Today is Memorial Day: The one day we set aside each year to remember those who gave their lives in service to their country in time of war. It is a noble thing we do in remembering those who have made so supreme a sacrifice, but not nearly so noble a thing as they have done . . . .
>
> The last two times I've been in Washington, I've visited the Vietnam Veterans Memorial. This must be one of the most powerful and moving places in the world. I found the names of two friends who gave their lives in that war . . . and I found myself absolutely drained both emotionally and physically when I left that place . . . .
>
> And so we build and visit monuments; we devote vast spaces in carefully groomed cemeteries for war dead, which become places on travel itineraries; we give memorials and build buildings as memorials; we remember. We remember.
>
> What do we remember? Why is it we do these things? Why don't we let these unpleasant memories pass from our consciousness? Why don't we put aside such draining and difficult memories? Perhaps it has to do with maintaining a sense of history. Or, as the title of the recent television movie about the effort to build a memorial to honor Vietnam veterans suggests, perhaps our purpose is partly "To Heal a Nation"; to heal our own wounds in the loss of loved ones and fellow citizens.

Hamm concludes his commemoration with a call for the audience to recommit itself to the defense of freedom.[13]

Toasts

You are more likely to be asked to deliver a toast than any other form of commemorative speech. Toasts are given at engagements, weddings, graduations, confirmations, births, the sealing of business deals, at dinner parties, and so on. They are brief messages of good will and congratulations.

It is thought that the custom of toasting began when the Norsemen, Vikings, and Greeks lifted their glasses in honor of the gods. But the newer "toast" derives from the seventeenth century British custom of placing toasted bits of bread in glasses to improve the taste of the drink. As the concept of the toast evolved, so did the customs surrounding it. In England, those proposing the toast got down on bended knee. In France, elaborate bows were required. In Scotland, the toast maker stood with one foot on a chair, the other on a table. Today, Western tradition dictates the clinking of glasses.[14]

---

13.   William E. Hamm, "Honoring the Noble Sacrifice: Once Again We Remember," speech delivered in Forest City, Iowa, May 30, 1988. Reprinted in *Vital Speeches of the Day*, August 1, 1989, pp. 626–27.
14.   R.J. Bayless, "Are You a Master of the Toast?" *The Toastmaster* (November 1988): 11.

Here are some guidelines for delivering a memorable toast:

Prepare a Short Inspirational Message and Memorize It.   If you are the best man at your brother's wedding, the mother of the new college graduate at her graduation dinner, a close associate of an executive just promoted to company president, you may be asked in advance to prepare a toast to celebrate the occasion. Even though most toasts are generally no more than a few sentences long, don't assume that you will be able to think of something appropriate to say when the glasses are raised. To avoid drawing a blank, write—and memorize—the toast in advance.

Choose your words with care. Depending on the situation, you may be humorous or serious, inspirational or practical. Here are two examples:

> Ken has been a tower of strength for all of us. When four partners were sick with the flu at the same time last year, Ken worked round the clock, seven days a week, to meet our deadlines. Here's to Ken—the best lawyer in town and the newest partner of our law firm.

Or:

> Here I am, the father of the bride, and all I can think of is Deborah at age three. A more self-assured, confident—and I must say stubborn—little girl never lived. When she wanted her way, she would look you straight in the eye and say, in the inimitable grammar of a preschooler, "A girl has to does what a girl has to does."
>
> Well twenty-five years later, we can look back at how Deborah has always done things her way—and, in the process, brought joy to us all. On this, her wedding day, I wish her and Bill a life of love, discovery, and adventure. I can guarantee Bill one thing: life won't be boring.
>
> Let's all raise our glasses in a toast to the new couple. Here's to Deborah and Bill.

Toasts provide an opportunity for a brief, meaningful speech.

Avoid Clichés.   Worn-out toasts like "Down the hatch," "Here's mud in your eye," "Cheers," and "Here's how" are a waste of the moment.

Be Appropriate to the Occasion.   There is a time to be frivolous and a time to be serious.

Be Positive.   Look to the future with hope. It is inappropriate to toast a college graduate like this: "If John does as poorly at work as he did at college, we may all be asked to help pay his rent."

Think of keynote speakers as cheerleaders and their speeches as cheers that set the tone for an event. Here, for example, is the way Ann Richards used the keynote address she delivered to the 1988 Democratic National Convention to rouse her audience to action. Richards spearheaded the race for the White House by attacking Republican policy and, specifically, the Republican presidential nominee, George Bush: ## THE KEYNOTE SPEECH

> Now we Democrats believe that America is still the country of fair play, that we can come out of a small town or a poor neighborhood and have the same chance as anyone else, and it doesn't matter whether we are black or Hispanic, or disabled or women . . . .
>
> We Democrats believe that America can overcome any problem, including the dreaded disease called AIDS. We believe that America is still a country where there is more to life than just a constant struggle for money. And we believe that America must have leaders who show us that our struggles amount to something and contribute to something larger, leaders who want us to be all that we can be . . . .
>
> We're not going to have the America that we want until we elect leaders who are going to tell the truth—not most days, but every day. Leaders who don't forget what they don't want to remember . . . .
>
> So when it comes right down to it, this election is a contest between those who are satisfied with what they have and those who know we can do better. That's what this election is really all about.
>
> It's about the American dream—those who want to keep it for the few, and those who know it must be nurtured and passed along.[15]

Richards is like a sales manager addressing a sales force at the launch of a new product. Her goal is to convince her listeners that their product is the best on the market and that the other brands pale in comparison.

Keynote addresses at political conventions are known for their tough approach and language. Although they may not be as tough in other settings—at academic or professional conventions, for example—they attempt to set the tone for the conference. A writer addressing the annual convention of the American Society of Journalists and Authors, for example, may choose to speak about the freedom to

---

15.   Ann Richards, "Keynote Address," delivered at the Democratic National Convention, July 18, 1988. Reprinted in *Vital Speeches of the Day,* August 15, 1988, pp. 647–49.

write—and publish—in the face of death threats from foreign powers. A lawyer delivering the keynote address at the annual convention of the American Bar Association may speak about how law has become a tool of the rich and powerful. Whatever the setting, the keynote address is usually anticipated as a highlight that has the potential to excite the audience to thought and action.

AFTER-DINNER
SPEECHES

If the keynote address is the meat-and-potatoes speech of a conference, the after-dinner speech is the dessert. It is a speech delivered, literally, after the meal is over and after all other substantive business is complete. Its purpose is to entertain, often with humor, although it may also convey a thoughtful message.

Do not make the mistake of delivering a ponderous talk filled with statistics and complex data. Talking about the national debt would probably be inappropriate as would a speech on what to do with the tons of garbage Americans produce each day. However, you can discuss these topics in a humorous way, relating, for example, how handling the national debt has become a growth industry for economists or how families are trying to cope with community rules to separate garbage by type. You can also be inspirational, filling your speech with stories from your own experiences that have changed your life. This approach is especially effective if you are well known or if the events you relate have meaning to others.

Former Chicago Bears running back Gale Sayers used this inspirational approach in the remarks he delivered at the annual prayer breakfast of the South Carolina Law Enforcement Officers Association. Sayers' reputation as a football player preceded him and made him a credible spokesperson when he began talking about athletic achievement. Although his speech is humorous at times, its intent is inspiration:

> When I was a student at Kansas I ran track in my sophomore and junior years. My track coach, Bill Easton, was a man who had a profound influence on my life. Bill Easton was the man who taught me about work and discipline . . . . The first time I went to Coach Easton's office during my sophomore year, I couldn't help but notice a small sign on his desk. It said simply, "I am third!" Coach Easton had an enviable record of success. He had won a couple of national championships, he always seemed to be winning. You can imagine I found that little sign puzzling at best. Coaches, as a rule, don't even want to know how to spell third. I was kind of shy at this time of my life. I was still trying to get the feel of things at Kansas so I said nothing. Coach Easton challenged me that year and the next.
>
> I remember once we were in a triangular meet. I was in the hurdles and broad jump and that day Easton said, "Why don't you run the 330-intermediate, too, just to keep in shape and get your wind up and everything?" So I ran it and, I tell you, I [felt like I was about to die]. I finished third—which is last really, but third sounds better. People were laughing at me. The first five hurdles I was ahead, then six got [gesture] *that* big, and seven got [gesture] *that* big, and I tried to go under the last two because I was real tired. I was so tired, and I struggled across the finish line and Easton came up to me and said, "Way to go, at least you finished the race." The one point I got finishing that race enabled us to beat out the third-place team by a point.

I never could get that little sign out of my mind, and, finally, after two years I asked Bill Easton about it. He said, "The Lord is first, my friends are second, and I am third." The more I thought about his adage the more sense it made and it continues to hold a lot of meaning for me.

I've tried to live by that motto and it is very hard to do. I haven't always been successful in living up to the standards of being third. Like everyone else I have my problems, but whenever I feel like my life is getting out of hand, I think of Bill Easton and "I am third," and it helps me get things back in order and it motivates me to try harder.[16]

SUMMARY

When delivering a speech for a special occasion, make sure it meets audience expectations. Tailor your speech to the honoree and the occasion, use personal anecdotes and appropriate humor, avoid clichés, be aware that you are speaking for others as well as yourself, be sincere, don't brag, and be accurate.

The purpose of a speech of introduction is to introduce the person who will deliver an important address. Your role is to heighten audience anticipation of the speaker through a brief, personal description of why he or she has been chosen to speak.

Speeches of presentation are delivered as part of special recognition ceremonies. These speeches tell the audience why the award is being given and state the importance of the award.

Marked by grace and sincerity, speeches of acceptance express gratitude for an award.

Commemorative speeches include commencement speeches, eulogies, speeches to celebrate the spirit of a special event or national holiday, and toasts. Commemorative speeches are inspirational messages designed to stir emotions and cause listeners to reflect.

Keynote speeches set the tone for an event often through the use of tough, direct language.

After-dinner speeches are speeches of entertainment and inspiration, generally delivered at the conclusion of substantive business.

QUESTIONS FOR STUDY AND DISCUSSION

1. How would you evaluate Curt Smith's commencement address in light of what you have learned about this speech form?
2. What are the elements of an effective toast?
3. What are the elements of an effective speech of introduction? What should speakers avoid?
4. Why are grace and brevity the key elements of an effective acceptance speech?

16. Gale Sayers, "Remarks of Mr. Gale Sayers," speech delivered at the South Carolina Law Enforcement Officers Association Annual Prayer Breakfast, February 22, 1989, Columbia, South Carolina.

ACTIVITIES   1.   Select a famous person from the past and prepare a three- to four-minute eulogy in his or her honor. Follow the guidelines presented in this chapter, and deliver the eulogy in front of your classmates. A sincere, thoughtful eulogy is difficult to prepare, so spend time developing and practicing your speech.

2.   Locate an individual in your community who is known as an effective special occasions speaker. Interview the speaker about how he or she selects materials, meets audience expectations, adapts to the occasion, and uses language and humor to influence the audience.

3.   Team up with a classmate for the purpose of presenting and accepting an award. Toss a coin to determine who will present and who will accept the award. Then join with other teams in your class for a round of speeches involving the presentation and acceptance of awards.

S A M P L E   S P E E C H

*P*rofessor John Kuo Wei Tchen is the historian and associate director of the Asian American Center at Queens College, City University of New York. He is also the cofounder of the New York Chinatown History Project. His publications include *Genthe's Photographs of San Francisco's Old Chinatown* (1984), and he was the editor and wrote the introduction for Paul C.P. Siu's *The Chinese Laundryman: A Study of Social Isolation* (1987). In January 1987 the Cultural Education Committee of the Smithsonian Institute in Washington, D.C., was inaugurated at the National Museum of History. Because the Committee is committed to partaking in ecumenism as espoused by Dr. Martin Luther King, it organized an annual Martin Luther King Jr. Holiday Celebration Program. Professor John Kuo Wei Tchen delivered this keynote address on January 16, 1989. This is the version of the speech printed for distribution.

"RACE" & CULTURAL DEMOCRACY
HISTORICAL CHALLENGES & FUTURE POSSIBILITIES*

by Dr. John Kuo Wei Tchen

"We must rapidly begin the shift from a 'thing-oriented' society to a 'person-oriented' society. When machines and computers, profit motives, and property rights are considered more important than people, the giant triplets of racism, materialism, and militarism are incapable of being conquered."

Martin Luther King, Jr.
Riverside Church, 4 April 1967

———————

*I have put the word "race" in quotations because it is not an objective, natural, biological term as commonly assumed. Biologists have long rejected its accuracy in describing differences among people. Instead, it is a culturally and historically constructed concept which is regularly under contention for its meaning.

The opening remarks combine the typical statement of gratitude for being asked to speak on a special occasion and a unique reference to cultural diversity by making reference to the new year as marked by several cultures. This is a speech that turns to the cultural struggles of separate individuals and groups necessitated by the discrimination due to self-centeredness, scape-goating, misunderstanding, distrust, and anger. The speech also calls for a renewed commitment to good cross-cultural relations and interdependency with respect, trust, and appreciation for cultural diversity. His purpose is to honor the memory of Martin Luther King, Jr. with a contemporary, reasoned, and positive commitment to healthy cultural democracy.

The remarks clearly reflect the speaker's knowledge as a historian with a strong commitment to cultural diversity, civil rights, and shared values with his audience. This audience is an educated group with a sense of history and a commitment to civil rights in a society marked by good cross-cultural relations.

Although much of his language is concrete and clear, his education and extensive vocabulary are reflected in terms such as "solstice," a reference to winter in the northern hemisphere.

The core idea for this keynote speech is his proposition that this time of commemoration is a time for reflection, reinvestment, and rededication to future struggles to provide equality, growth, and opportunity in cross-cultural relations.

Notice here that before proceeding with the development of his core idea, he pays tribute to those speakers who have addressed this occasion and its audiences before and he places himself in the context of the civil rights struggle that intensified during the 1960s. He lets his audience know that in his youthful days he was reasonably insulated from the struggle and arrived in the midst of the activity as a college student protestor and a student of profound authors on racial issues, DuBois, Wright, Sterling, and Fanon.

It is indeed an honor and a privilege to be commemorating Dr. Martin Luther King, Jr.'s birthday with friends, colleagues, and fellow citizens in our nation's museum. It occurred to me while working on this talk that Dr. King's birthday is nestled between January 1st, the Gregorian New Year, and February 6, this year's Chinese New Year, just after Kwanza and right during American Indian New Year. Despite our very different ways of marking this cultural timeshift, we all know that New Year's is a lot richer in meaning than the mechanical fact of the ball dropping from Times Square.

This is the period of the far Northern Hemisphere's winter solstice, that time in which days are short and nights are long, the time in which our wintered bodies begin to slow down. In our past, hunters and gatherers would disperse during the spring through fall and reunite in the winter. This was the time of communal activities, rituals, and a re-affirmation of identity. In our past, peasants and farmers would celebrate the harvest, reflect on the year's lessons, pay their material and spiritual debts, and prepare, with hope, for the new season to come.

Tonight is also the time for deep personal and communal reflection, a time to build and reinvest our identities with one another, and a time to rededicate ourselves for the coming struggles. As a historian, I want to reflect upon the past. As an activist, I want to imagine how we can visualize the future. And as an Asian American in this era of Howard Beach, Vincent Chin, Black boycotts of Asian businesses, and anti-African student protests in China, I want to explore strategies for bridging deteriorating cross-cultural relations.

I was particularly surprised and delighted to have been asked to speak tonight because I am but a child of the civil rights movement. Unlike Bernice Reagon, Sweet Honey in the Rock, and Frank Bonilla, my predecessors at this podium, all of whom have played important roles in the founding generation of civil rights activists, I have been part of the second generation, a child of these founders in a double sense.

I grew up in the '50s and '60s, not locked arm in arm in civil rights marches, but with my eyes glued to the television tube. The mail carrier brought the image and message of Dr. King through *Life* magazine, my father brought home the *Chicago Sun Times,* and Walter Cronkite presided over the film footage at six. All this information was received in an overwhelmingly white, middle-class, Protestant suburb of Chicago. Those horrifying sequences of German shepherds, fire hoses and Bull Connor intercut with the eloquence of Dr. King and other civil rights leaders somehow broke through the competing images of Hollywood, fallout shelters, baseball, and the space program.

Although I was born in Wisconsin and grew up in middle America, I was barraged with lots of: "My, you speak English so well!" and "Where do you come from?" (Somehow, Madison never seemed to be a sufficient answer.) At college, I became very much involved in protesting America's war in Vietnam primarily because on campus I, too, was called a "gook." I finally realized that Asians in the U.S. have been cast as perpetual foreigners, no matter how many generations we have been here.

I am also a child of the civil rights movement in a second sense. The growing Asian American student movement, which spawned Asian American studies, came out of the civil rights movement which gave impetus to African American studies. As I tried to understand myself, it was the history of W.E.B. DuBois, the writing of Richard E. Wright, the poetry of Sterling A. Brown, and the works of anti-colonialists such as the Tunisian Jew Albert Memmi and Martiniquean doctor Franz Fanon that gave me words, insights and alternatives. (My exposure to feminist writers was to come later.)

Tchen's background in history and his cultural awareness lead him to describe his own personal search for cultural meanings in terms of an archeological search. His reference to "shards" or fragments of pottery vessels of an ancient culture point to information to be gathered to uncover Chinese- and Asian-American history.

I began to find jags and riffs of my own buried deep down, in some pre-conscious, pre-verbal soul. Like uncovering the shards of some ancient forgotten culture, many of us began work to excavate and reconstruct Chinese and Asian American history.

Asians today **must** understand that African Americans and their creation of the civil rights movement are the elders of the Asian American movement to reclaim out lost history and to fight for our civil rights.

This passage into adulthood during the '60's and early '70's was a wondrous time for celebration of the possibility to be different. Years of socially conditioned self-hatred for not being like the people on television or in the Sears Roebuck catalogues could be shed, and new identities could be formed. Traditional boundaries between ourselves and others could be redefined. Those static dualisms, those rigid dichotomies of absolute good and absolute evil, male-female, black-white, proper-improper, modern-traditional, past-present could be re-examined, rejected, and re-envisioned. We could finally leave "Leave it to Beaver" behind.

He is pointing to intercultural interdependence particularly between African-American and Asian-American identities within the struggle for cultural identity and civil rights in America. "Free space" is the "moment in history" when society and its major institutions become open to cultural differences and group identity. In this "space," the speaker asserts, racial and cultural discrimination can be examined and assessed. The term "otherness" encapsulates this discrimination and victimization.

Sara Evans and Harry Boyte have called this moment in the '60's and '70's the creation of "free spaces" in which multiple democratic movements flourished. They define "free spaces" as moments in history in which environments open up between private lives and large-scale institutions where ordinary citizens act with dignity, independence, and vision—where folks learn a new self-respect and a deeper, more assertive group identity.

It is in such places where "a community of memory and hope" is nurtured that private identities cross over into public activity.

We should not be surprised, then, that the civil rights movement was one great nurturing free space, which in turn spawned other movements for the broadening of rights and freedom of women, Asians, Latinos, Native Americans, gays, and others in American society.[1]

It has been in this civil rights free space that many have labored to decode the workings and history of being cast into that never, never land of "otherness." What is this phenomenon of "otherness"?

It is what that great feminist Simone de Beauvoir began to articulate in Paris in 1952 when she wrote of male power relegating women to being the "other," the "second sex." It is what Edward Said has written about so instructively in his book *Orientalism.* The West created the image and mythos of the "Oriental" as everything the "Occidental" was not. The "Orient" was opulent, lustful, and artistic. The "Occident" was efficient, mechanical, and moral. "Otherness" is also what Lillian Breslow Rubin has described as the "worlds of pain" of the white, working class, "silent majority." (Those increasingly left behind by the American dream.) Let us not forget that "otherness" is also what, as Jean-Paul Sartre reminds us, the anti-Semite does to the Semite.

---

1. The 1960s and early 1970s was a special moment, but was not unique. Historians have often noted such "pregnant," conjectural periods in time and space. Special conditions have regularly produced a great outpouring of visionary leaders, creative thinkers, and committed activists—great renaissances changing individuals and groups. "Public culture" is a term scholars are using to describe this wondrous convergence of the efflorescence of criticism and creativity. Edinburgh, center of Scottish enlightment in the 18th century: Harlem and Shanghai in the late teens and '20s; the Jewish Lower East Side of New York City at the turn of the century were all such cultural moments which produced some of the world's greatest thinkers and transformative social movements. Like a great library, or even a great party, these moments have had an open architecture which was more accessible, more stimulating, and more joyful than business-as-usual.

And finally, "otherness" must be understood in Benjamin Ringer's terms. Having devoted 19 years of his adult life to writing his *magnum opus, "We the People" and Others,* Dr. Ringer has given us the gift of insight into the deep historical structures of U.S. racial relations. Analyzing five hundred years of legal history, we learn that American Indians, Africans, Asians, and Hispanics have been systematically not included in the people's domain as guaranteed in the Constitution.

"Others" are created by those who have the power to define the exclusivity of "we-ness." It is a means of identity formation by negative reference. It is a way to establish norms to control inside and outside. We are what they are not. We are not what they are. We are good, they are lesser. Power added to ethnocentrism creates a world in which the many shades of the rainbow are reduced, in a paranoid and unimaginative fashion, to white and non-white.

As we all know, like the dynamic of the *yin* and *yang* circle in the Taoist imagination, the victims are victimized, but so are the victimizers. Inhumanity imposed diminishes the humanity of the imposer.

Our civil rights free space has been able to nurture a fuller and fuller critique of what has been. The songs, the books, the new friendships we have forged these past decades give empowering strength to our resistance.

And yet, at the end of this millenium one hundred years after the Civil War, Reconstruction, and *Plessy vs. Ferguson* (the Supreme Court decision which sanctified "separate but equal"), we have been witnessing a backlash, a reaction of those in power who want to close this civil rights free space. The neo-conservative's battle cries are many: "English only," "cultural literacy," the lowering of standards, the "closing of the American mind," and "do you want to let Willie Horton loose on the street?" We know that mainstream fears of Blacks and non-white immigrants were cleverly and cynically manipulated to bring political victory this past Presidential election year. What is freedom for our multi-cultural diversity, appears to be anarchy to those threatened by a loss of control.[2]

---

2. Notions of "Western" purity deny Western civilization's very own history of borrowing and sometimes appropriating from foreign cultures, from sugar and spices to porcelains and moveable type, from Beethoven's use of Turkish marches in his Ninth Symphony to Picasso's African-influenced cubism. Why is the Western borrowing from ancient China via Marco Polo perfectly natural and acceptable, the stuff of great adventure stories (and television mini-series), but the Asian

Tchen intends to implicate not just the white power-brokers of the past as the doers-of-evil but the present company as well "for we too are irretrievably complicit." His support is contemporary through the use of illustrations of conflict between different cultural groups including African-Americans against Asian-Americans in New York and Chinese against Africans in China. This activity, he asserts, promotes "we" over "others" who serve as scapegoats. These clashes, in the view of the speaker, are but illustrations of racism rooted deeply in cultural misunderstanding and self-centered priorities.

But we would be wrong and naive to place all the evils of our time on those rulers above, or those ivory tower scholars who advocate a monocultural literacy—for we, too, are irretrievably complicit, whether we like it or not.

I am thinking here of two sets of deeply troubling racial clashes in Brooklyn, New York, and Nanjing, China. In Brooklyn, the largely Italian neighborhoods of Bensonhurst and Gravesend and the largely African American and West Indian community of Bedford-Stuyvestant have been boycotting Korean and Chinese small businesses. Some 100,000 legal-sized, single-spaced leaflets were distributed in Bensonhurst, decrying the Asian "invasion" and "takeover" of the neighborhood using drug and "Moonie" money to buy real estate. In Bed-Stuy, an incident between a Black woman customer and a Korean greengrocer ended with a community-wide boycott, posters depicting Koreans as vampires "sucking the blood out of the community," and calls for a city-wide boycott. In Nanjing, Chinese students have been rioting against African students, claiming they are raping Chinese women and complaining of the privileges given to foreigners. Racist cries of "Black Devils" and "Beat Blacks" seem to be springing out of nowhere. Police have been accused of using electric prods and have been beating African students.

In many respects both incidents appear parallel. We can detect certain similarities in the dynamics societies in which hyper-competitive economic values have been or are becoming pre-eminent. A legacy of limited mobility, impatience, and scrambling makes the two situations ripe to produce conditions seeking scapegoats. Both societies seem in a mad dash to promote individual success over collective well-being. The results are the same: desperate, ruthless struggles to form identities of "we-ness" at the sacrifice of scapegoated "others."

I fear these two deplorable instances are but manifestations of deeper, more profound national and international problems. We now know that racism is not just some troublesome remnant of slavery, nor is it simply the ignorant doings of "white trash" or racist students in China.

---

borrowing of American techniques and culture is imitation and unnatural, the source of discontent? The creative human spirit itself rebels against such solipsistic trickery. These artificial boundaries imprison, restrict, and strangle. They are the "iron cages" that Herman Melville wrote about and that scholar Ronald Takaki has elaborated on.

As the speech unfolds the audience can imagine a portrayal of Asian-American struggles that may be largely unnoticed because of the often more visible discrimination African-Americans have experienced in societies largely controlled by whites.

In the U.S., Asians have been regularly held up to be the upwardly mobile, Horatio Algeresque model minority. Despite regular rejection of such a portrayal by Asians themselves, publications like *The New York Times, Time* magazine, *U.S. News and World Report, ad infitinum* repeat endless variations of this story.

Asians who are already highly educated and middle class in Asia come as immigrants, work small businesses, and do well. This phenomenon is then used as confirmation that racial injustice has been exaggerated and inner city Blacks should be able to buckle down and do the same. It would take another talk to explore this new myth, but let me say here that Asian Americans are being misrepresented and manipulated by those at the very heights of American power who are grasping for some explanation of America's failure to eliminate inequality for Blacks.[3] To the degree that Asian Americans become complicit with such simplistic and politically manipulative explanations, we are making a pact with ghosts and demons.

Asian Americans are praised by those in power as the model for others to emulate; we are despised by those being left behind as the reason for their disenfranchisement. The rise of anti-Asian violence in this country is the flip side of the heightened use of the "model minority" ideology. Asians are becoming the all-purpose solution for keeping the powerful complacent and in control and the powerless embittered and even more out of control.[4]

Everyone is talking about our entering the "Asian Century." This may happen someday, but given the still overwhelming power of American and European multi-national corporations and our common-sense understanding that power is not given up without a fight, it seems much more likely that Asians will be used in the same way we always have been in this country—as a people put in the middle between the truly powerful and the powerless. In this regard, many overseas Asians occupy a position comparable to Jews in the diaspora. In point of fact,

3. For a fuller explanation of the "model minority" myth, see: John Kuo Wei Tchen, "Whiz Kids' and American Race Relations: Some Thoughts on the Model Minority Myth" in *Race, Gender and Eyeglasses,* Asian American Center Working Paper Series, Queens College, 1989.
4. See Michael H. Hunt, *Ideology and U.S. Foreign Policy* (1987) and Gil Loescher and John A. Scanlan, *Calculated Kindness* (1986).

Chinese have even been dubbed the "Jews of the East." As China increasingly enters the "free world's" neo-colonial economy, this middle position of overseas Chinese could easily become internationalized. The deplorable anti-Black racism expressed by elite Chinese students could be a dangerous harbinger of China's shifting attitudes towards non-white, non-aligned nations of the Third World.

Will this nation's stratified system of racial segmentation become the model that China, or even the Soviet Union, and developing nations increasingly buy into? In the coming centuries of the new millenium will the world's socio-economic reality be organized as but a variation of the racial and ethnic hierarchies we now have in New York City, Chicago, or Washington, D.C.?

Many neo-conservative critics are decrying a lack of core values to hold the nation together. They call for a return to a highly romanticized past in which purer, Western ideals were taught first and foremost without the pollution of morally inferior cultures. If this past ever did truly exist, a time machine has not yet been invented to carry out their wish. I, for one, do not want to return to an area in which "men" were white and "women" knew their place, and "coloreds" were neither to be seen, nor heard. I don't wax nostalgic for those days. Nor should these anorexic representations of American core values be defined as patriotic.

Tchen, in the spirit of the keynote speaker, points his audience toward the challenge of the future—"For it is in the civil rights free space that the practice and theory of truly multi-cultural core values can be pioneered." This forecasting is grounded in three concepts he sees as serving the foundation of multi-cultural democracy. These concepts of "identities" call for shared values within cultural diversity in society. There is, then, common ground on which to stand and shared interests in community life that includes cross-cultural expression.

But the problem remains: How do parts fit into wholes? What are the core values that can allow us to be different and at the same time bring us together? Acquisitive individualism, the right to "shop till we drop," should not be our primary exercise of democracy. We know the old tired notion of the "melting pot" never allowed us to be diverse; it was a demand for conformity. I wish I had the answers to give you from my privileged platform tonight. I don't, but we do. For it is in the civil rights free space that the practice and theory of truly multi-cultural core values can be pioneered. We must insist on protecting and militantly expanding this space, because we are finally on the verge of fresh multi-cultural ways of understanding our lived reality.

Dr. John Langston Gwaltney, the eminent anthropologist who is also African American, refers to the respect for diversity as a "poly-ocular" (many point-of-viewed) project, an important concept made all the more poignant because, as many of you know, Dr. Gwaltney is blind. He argues for the development of a post-colonial knowledge which is rooted in the core values of the communities we come from. John Gwaltney's reflections on the experience of blindness and blackness help us understand the lessons of power and powerlessness and the importance of appreciating fundamentally different perceptual frameworks.

We are just now beginning to sketch the outlines of some post-colonial, poly-ocular core values that can bridge these different frameworks and, while doing so, redefine what being an American is all about. Let me suggest but three concepts which should be components of the foundation of an inclusive multi-cultural democracy:

ONE: **Americans have shared histories which have created interwoven identities.** I've come to realize in my own historical work on Chinese laundry workers, it is fallacious to pull that laundry man from the street where he worked and the customers he served. He worked in a multi-cultural neighborhood setting and formed an important part of his identity in relation to the Chinese and non-Chinese with whom he came in contact.

Many of you know that in 1882, just three years before the Statue of Liberty was constructed, the Chinese Exclusion Act was passed. (A law which effectively lasted until 1965/68 when racial quotas were finally eliminated.) No convicts, no prostitutes, no "idiots," no Chinese. What we rarely realize is that the "Chinese Question" debate, which resulted in exclusion, was intimately tied to debates around African American freedom. And when politicians turned their backs on Reconstruction, they also turned their backs on the possibility of Chinese American civil rights.

We must also understand that it is not mere coincidence that the Voting Rights Act and Immigration Reform bills eliminating racial quotas were both signed in 1965. Without the civil rights movement's push to put anti-racism on the national agenda, most of the Asians living in this country today would simply not be here.

Our knowledge and our teaching does not reflect this truth. I am ashamed to say Asian Americans are largely ignorant of this debt and are, consequently, as racist as most Americans against Blacks. The conceptions we hold of ourselves as people cannot be simply Chinese American or Black American or whatever. That part of our identity may be very, very important, but it is not the whole story. We may have torn down the laws that have segregated the nation, but we still have the mental blinders which keep us from grasping that shared oppression also implies a shared freedom.[5]

TWO: **Human identities are not only shared cross-culturally but constructed and multi-faceted.** Any of us who love good novels or have done oral histories can but marvel at the delightfully layered complexity of the human experience. Witness, for example, the third-generation Peruvian Japanese man (whose grandfather worked on sugar plantations), who was sent to a WWII internment camp in Wyoming and then shipped to Seabrook, New Jersey's vegetable packing plant and is now living in New York. To simply identify that person as a Japanese American or as a New Yorker does grave violence to the multiplicity of his experiences and layers of his identity.

Outside powers, personal decisions, what we make of our lives, and the many cultures that we've lived in make us who we are as unique individuals, but more importantly these experiences form the basis of our shared community of interests with others.

Indeed, in this post-modern world in which frantic movement has become a prized value in-and-of-itself, we all have multi-faceted identities. Can we recognize that in each other? Can we learn to exercise qualities of empathy and insight, not to pigeon-hole, not to stereotype, and instead to look for the deeper "selves" and "othernesses" within our souls? Mutual respect and understanding, the ability to share experiences, and thus fight atomized, individualized alienation are all parts of multi-cultural core values.

THREE: **Citizenship is much more than individual and legal right; it is the affirmative cultural expression of community values and life.** In an era in which we increasingly define citizenship in technical and legal terms, the right to vote,

---

5. Asians today have to understand that in the early years of California, the anti-Chinese movement did not know quite how to classify Asians. Irish immigrants, trying desperately to demonstrate their right to belong to America, proved it by emphasizing their "whiteness" in leading the California efforts to exclude and evict those they branded "unassimilable foreigners"—Chinese. Classified as "Mongolians," Chinese children were judged to be from the same racial stock as American Indians, and, therefore, along with Blacks and Mexicans (who were there long before Anglo-Americans), could not go to public schools. This happened despite the disproportionate taxes Chinese miners paid to the State's coffers. Also, the U.S. could not mount a major anti-Communist human rights campaign to attract non-aligned, mostly non-white nations with such glaring racial injustice at home. In this light, it is not surprising that the Chinese Exclusion Law was not formally repealed until 1943, when the U.S. was an ally with China in fighting Japan. Even then, the law did not allow more than 105 Chinese per year until 1965/68.

or being born on U.S. soil, the term "cultural citizenship" places moral emphasis on a much broader and organic definition. The concept takes seriously the democratic ideals "of the people, by the people, and for the people" and gives value to the needs and interests of communities as the foundation for governing. When these needs and interests are denied, alternative "cultural citizenships" are forged which give us strength to fight for our rights.

When Native Americans in Maine make land claims related to territory taken from them illegally three hundred years ago, they are asserting their rights as citizens of the Algonquin Nation. When Japanese Americans demand redress for being put in camps during WWII, they are exercising their newly found power as Japanese American cultural citizens. When John Thompson, Black coach of the Georgetown University basektball team, protests the use of culturally biased exams as a basis for sports scholarships, he is exercising his rights as a cultural citizen of the civil rights movement. These are the cultures created when people are cast into "otherness," separated from "We the People." When excluded identities find a community of voices and act to affirm their rights, they have created a new sense of belonging, a new sense of being a citizen in a democracy.[6]

The most prized American concern with personal freedom needs to be balanced by our first core value of mutuality and interdependence. The notion that we are separate individuals needs to be understood with our second core value of self-knowledge cultivating our capacities to empathize and understand people very different from ourselves. And the heavy emphasis upon the mechanical act of American citizens voting on election day as our primary exercise of democracy has to be deepened by our third core value of active cultural citizenship.

---

6. "Cultural citizenship" is a concept pioneered by the Inter-University Program for Latino Research (IUP), a joint project of Latino scholars across the country. Let me quote from their work:

> Individuals and communities have 'cultural citizenships' that organize their sense of values, rights, and practices. Cultural citizenship is an identity that is formed not out of legal membership but out of a sense of cultural belonging. The definition of 'cultural' is broad and can include multiple and sometimes opposing determinations of nationality, ethnicity, gender, race, and class memberships. In this sense, it draws upon difference as well as commonality. This concept helps us understand the heterogeneity of constructed identities. It also reveals the multi-faceted nature of alternative responses to conditions that individuals and communities produce.

IUP Culture Studies Working Group. "Working Concept Paper on Cultural Citizenship" (unpublished, 1988), p. 2.

"In 1492, Columbus sailed the ocean blue" and "discovered" the "New World." Columbus' landing in the Caribbean signaled the beginning of Western culture on the shores of the old native cultures of the Americas. The Annales School of French scholars have taught us to look at these recent 500 years as a *longue durée* in which the marketplace-driven bourgeois revolution made unprecedented freedom possible for unprecedented numbers. This long, arduous, and never straightforward struggle for individual freedom is an achievement to be celebrated. But like the great pyramids of Egypt, such an achievement was not without cost—scholarship has clearly demonstrated this "New World" was built upon the ruins of many old worlds. It was built upon the unfreedom, the social death of millions of others. Lone bourgeois individuals triumphed over connective folk cultures.

The clock cannot be turned back. But can we be brave, daring, and civilized enough to gaze at what unfreedom has truly wrought and then imagine a world in which "otherness" is not invidious, does not divide and exploit us along lines of "race" and narrow nationalism, "race" and gender, or "race," gender and class? If indeed, the need for "otherness" to define **us** versus **them** is basic to human "nature," why can't our struggles be against those who promote ignorance, poverty, cruelty, or ecological violence?

The conclusion calls for cultural democracy and a multicultural new year as symbolized in the life and expressions of Martin Luther King, Jr. Invoking the image of "the solstice of the longest, darkest night" the speaker ties his message to a theme offered early in this speech.

Cultural democracy must be an individual and collective effort to constantly open and renew society for those left out and against those intent on conserving the exclusivity of power.

Martin Luther King, Jr.'s birthday should rightly serve as our multicultural new year. He is the symbol of a unifying dream which drives our struggles to be better and braver. As we are gathered tonight, may we give each other strength. May our houses be swept clean, our minds rededicated and our souls redeemed.

In this solstice of the longest, darkest night, we must fortify ourselves with good company, good conversation, and good food, for in the morning we must begin anew.

"Let thy speech be better than silence, or be silent."

*Dionysius the Elder
(circa 430–367 B.C.)*

SPEAKING IN SMALL GROUPS

et's start by acknowledging that a professional baseball team is a small group. Let's also agree that the team has regular meetings to discuss strategy and morale. Finally, let's agree that during these meetings, the team manager and players use their public speaking skills to iron out problems, develop plans of action, and present information.

The leading spokesperson is the team manager. Realizing that the way he handles the group may influence the number of games the team wins, the manager plans his remarks as if his job depended on what is said (it probably does). When he speaks to the group, he pays as much attention to the team's state of mind as he does to each player's skill on the field.

"The best managers know enough not to intrude on the players' talent," says Ira Berkow, sports columnist for *The New York Times*. "As far as I'm concerned, coaches can hurt more than they can help; they can overmanage and get in the way of players getting out there and doing their best.

"In the army the saying is that an uncomfortable soldier is a good soldier because he's on his toes," continued Berkow. "But it's different in sports. Players need to relax. You can't go up to bat worrying about your problems with the coach and do a good job. You have to concentrate on the pitcher and the ball."[1]

How does this insight translate into action during a team meeting? Here is a conversation that could take place in any team's locker room after a three-game losing streak:

> *First baseman:* We lost again tonight because Joe isn't doing his job at shortstop. He's letting balls go right past him, just like a Little Leaguer.

> *Shortstop:* Sure, I made a few fielding mistakes, but at least I'm hitting. I haven't seen you hit a ball out of the infield in weeks. You know we can't win unless you get some runs on the scoreboard.

> *Manager:* This type of name calling is going to get us into last place—fast. We all know what our problems are and it's up to each one of you take care of your own weaknesses. If you're having trouble with your hitting, get in an extra hour of batting practice every day. The same goes for guys making too many fielding errors.
>
> Am I going to tell you your job is on the line? No, but I will tell you that every game counts. Even though it's early in the season, the game we lose today is a game we'll never get back. So when we're two games out of first place in September with only two games to play, remember that how we played in May did us in.

Whether this small group discussion helped the team win ball games or not, we can be sure it helped the players focus on winning instead of on blaming each other for their past failures or proving something to the team manager.

---

1.   Interview with Ira Berkow, June 23, 1988.

Although the subject may be different, the type of small group communication that
characterized this post-game meeting is the same in all small groups. Group members
and leaders must communicate on an intellectual as well as a psychological level as
they attempt to move the group closer to its goals. They must learn to adapt their
public speaking skills to the small group setting that focuses attention on the
interactions among speakers rather than on a single speaker addressing a group of
listeners. Instead of standing up before a group and giving a speech, you are a group
member, along with your audience, as you express your point of view.

PUBLIC SPEAKING IN A SMALL GROUP

Are traditional public speaking skills used in small group discussions?
Although most of your interactions do not involve planned speeches, they do involve
the need for effective communication and an awareness of the reciprocal nature of
public speaking. Here are some of the ways public speaking skills are useful in small
groups:

- ⌘ You have to be aware of the needs of your fellow group members—why they
  are there and what they hope to accomplish.
- ⌘ You have to support your remarks with strong research.
- ⌘ You have to organize your thoughts effectively.
- ⌘ You have to use precise language to bring about your desired communication
  goal.
- ⌘ You have to know how to use visual aids in your talk.

You May Already Be a Member of a Small Group

If you are on the editorial board of your school newspaper or an organizer of the
community blood drive; if you are a member of a Great Books club or the captain
of an athletic team, you are a member of a small group. Your membership in small
groups may increase after you leave college. In business, academic life, government,
and civic affairs, tasks are defined and accomplished through small-group
communication. Many of the major decisions affecting your life are made by small
groups. College admissions departments, liquor control commissions, and zoning
boards are a few groups whose functioning depends on small-group communication.

Groups are characterized by their functions, which also define the nature of
intragroup communication. For purposes of discussion, we consider four types of
small groups.

TYPES OF SMALL GROUPS

Information-Gathering Groups

Suppose in your role as a hospital administrator, you have been assigned to a
committee to study patient-nurse relationships and to report your findings to the head
of the nursing staff. Early group meetings focus on developing a questionnaire for
patients and nurses; later meetings deal with analyzing the data and writing a report.

What is distinctive about this—and all information-gathering groups—is the focus on compiling data rather than on making decisions. Decisions are often made by nongroup members who have primary responsibility for dealing with the problem. In this case, the head of the nursing staff will decide what to do with the information.

Problem-Solving Groups

A group whose goal is to find a solution to a particular problem is a problem-solving group, as in the following examples:

- ⌘ A group is formed by the president of a large midwestern university to find ways to deal with racial tension on campus.
- ⌘ A group at the White House is asked by the president to find ways to slash the federal budget.
- ⌘ After the Challenger disaster, a group of scientists was given the goal of finding the cause of the explosion.

These groups make recommendations that will help alleviate a problem or solve it outright. The committee dealing with racial tensions on campus may recommend that a series of lectures on the subject be held in the college auditorium and that a dialogue be initiated in the student newspaper to deal with various sides of this emotionally charged issue.

Learning Groups

In a traditional classroom, the professor lectures while students listen. This is far different from the interactions in a learning group in which all group members have the opportunity to share information. According to professor John Brilhart, a specialist in small group communication, learning groups, such as student study groups, exist for the "personal enlightenment and growth of their members . . . . There is no need to reach accord on values, beliefs, or courses of action. What is sought is a fuller understanding, a wider grasp of information pertinent to a topic, or consideration of a problem from as many points of view as possible."[2]

Therapy Groups

Alcoholics Anonymous (AA) is a therapy group, as are Weight Watchers, Parents Without Partners, and SmokeEnders. These and other therapy groups are composed of members who share common problems in an attempt to overcome them. Members of AA, for example, talk about their reasons for drinking and their struggle to stay alcohol free. Many therapy groups are led by psychiatrists, psychologists, social workers, and other qualified counselors. Trained therapists help focus the discussion on analyzing behavior and on translating the insight gained from this analysis into behavioral change.

---

2.   John Brilhart, *Effective Group Discussion*, 5th ed. (Dubuque, IA: Wm C. Brown, 1986), p. 323.

Whether a group gathers information, solves problems, or is involved in learning or therapy, it shares with other groups characteristics affecting communication among group members.

CHARACTERISTICS OF SMALL GROUPS

Group Members Share a Purpose for Communication

Seven people waiting in line for tickets to the Los Angeles Lakers are not considered members of a small group as we have defined it here. Neither are five people sharing a taxi from the Dallas-Fort Worth airport or eight people in a dentist's waiting room. These collectives are not small groups because they lack a communication purpose. They have neither group goals nor an agenda for action. Can a collective of independent people turn into an organized group? If the ticket holders decide to form a cooperative so that only one out of seven members has to wait in line for tickets at subsequent games, they now have a purpose that will guide communication in all future meetings.

Communication Goals

Members of small groups usually have group-oriented and self-oriented goals.

Group-Oriented Goals.   Group-oriented goals center around specific tasks to be performed. If you are a member of a small group charged with the responsibility of determining policies of a new campus radio station, among the tasks you face are developing station operating policies, purchasing transmission equipment, and attracting advertisers. A meeting concerning these goals may include the following discussion:

> *Daniel:* We can't start contacting suppliers about equipment prices until the university firms up our budget. We need to know *exactly* how much we can spend before we start shopping.
>
> *Kathryn:* If we wait till the numbers are final, we'll have to scramble to find the equipment we need. And we won't have time to shop around for the best prices. I say we should begin pricing the equipment right now.
>
> *Chandra:* I agree with Kathryn. Even though our budget isn't final, we have a rough idea of how much we can spend. The two things I know for sure is that the university is not going to hand us a blank check and that we'll have to buy at the best prices—and that means starting to comparison shop right now.
>
> *Daniel:* You've convinced me.

The discussion remained centered on the goals of the group. All groups have similar goal-oriented discussions.

Self-Oriented Goals.   As group members work to achieve these group-oriented goals, they also interact in ways that reflect their personal needs and ambitions. For example, a group member may try to take charge of the group or in other ways influence the outcome of the discussion, thus reflecting a need for control. Or she may contribute very little, reflecting a desire to remain apart from the group. Here is an example of how a power struggle shifts the focus of the group away from the group's goals:

> *George:* I know we're here to discuss organizing a protest against the university's minority-hiring policy, but I would like to get something straight from the start. I know a lot more about protests than anybody in this room. As I'm sure you know, I ran last year's protests against tuition increases. I have a lot to offer if you let me take over.
>
> *Elizabeth:* I'm not sure any of us should be talking about taking over at this point. It's up to all eight of us to decide what we want to do and how best to do it. Right now, we're all equals.
>
> *Stephen:* Wait a minute. Maybe we can learn from George's protesting experience. We don't want to reinvent the wheel.
>
> *Elizabeth:* I'm not talking about having to learn the basics of protesting. I'm talking about keeping personal needs out of the discussion.

Here, George's bid for power sidetracked the work of the committee.

Group Size

The size of the group is one of the most important factors affecting communication. Speech communication professor Vincent DiSalvo defines small groups, in part, by the number of people involved. According to DiSalvo, "a small group is three or more individuals who are engaged in face-to-face interaction with one another in such a manner that each person influences and is influenced by each of the other individuals."[3] The ideal group size, says DiSalvo, is from five to seven members. These groups are large enough for individuals freely to express their feelings and thoughts even to the point of risking antagonizing other group members. At the same time, they are small enough for members to care about the feelings and needs of other group members.[4] The upper limit for a small group is about twenty people; however, at this size, the number of possible relationships is so great and the mechanics of running the group so unwieldy that the group accomplishes very little. Often, larger groups divide into subgroups to get work done.[5]

A two-person group, a dyad, is too small because the group falls apart if one member leaves. Dyads also tend to have high levels of tension and confrontation ("either you do what I say or I'm out of here"). When a group has three or more members, communication has certain distinctive characteristics.

---

3. Vincent DiSalvo, "Small Group Behavior," in John J. Makay, ed. *Explorations in Speech Communication* (Columbus, OH: Charles E. Merrill Publishing Co. 1973), pp. 111–12.
4. Philip E. Slater, "Contrasting Correlates of Group Size." *Sociometry* 21 (1958): 129–39.
5. A. Paul Hare, *Handbook of Small Group Research*, 2d ed. (New York: Free Press, 1976).

⌘ Coalitions are possible. Two or more group members may band together to express their point of view and determine group activity. As the group grows in size, so does the possibility of intragroup alliances. ("Adam, Tia, and I feel strongly that the group should focus its environmental cleanup efforts on getting rid of campus litter and not on organizing a newspaper recycling campaign.")

⌘ Disagreements with group members can be mediated by a third party. A group leader or a disinterested group member can help settle disputes. ("I know that Ramon and Bill disagree with this approach. Let's talk about how we can best use our resources to make a difference.")

⌘ The smaller the group, the harder it is for group members to hide from responsibility. Each member has a job to do, and the success of the group depends on each task being accomplished. ("Patricia, we can't continue until we hear your report. We're all disappointed that it isn't done. Brian, Alice, and I are depending on you to have the report by next week.")

Advantages and Disadvantages of Small-Group Communication

Advantages and disadvantages are inherent in small-group communication.[6]

Advantages of Group Communication

1. Different people bring to a group a wide range of knowledge and views that help complete the task.

2. Group discussion often produces creative approaches that no one would have thought of alone.

3. Group involvement through communication increases the likelihood that the group's decision will be accepted and supported by all group members and by the broader community. A decision that is the result of compromise among six people is often more acceptable than a decision from a single person, especially if the outcome affects group members personally. For example, if a college committee—made up of two members each from the college administration, faculty, and student body—decides to prohibit coed visits in dorm rooms after midnight, even dissident group members are likely to accept the majority rule. And although many students may feel that the restriction is unfair, the fact that it is the result of a consensus may make it easier to accept. Here is a sample of this consensus-forming discussion:

   Mark: I didn't come to college to be treated like a child. I'm twenty years old and want to be able to visit anyone I want at whatever time I want.

---

6. Discussion based on Raymond S. Ross and Jean Ricky Ross, *Small Groups in Organizational Settings* (Englewood Cliffs, NJ: Prentice-Hall, 1989), pp. 62–64.

Professor Anderson: I don't disagree with you—in principle. But we also have to consider the rights of the people who don't want their roommate's visitors bothering them after midnight.

Roberta: I agree. There are a lot of people who have no consideration for the privacy of others—who don't know when to go home unless someone tells them.

Mark: I still don't like being treated this way. But I can see what you mean. I'll go along with the rest of the group to restrict late-night visits.

Disadvantages of Group Communication

1. Social pressure has the power to produce bad group decisions. Group members have the tendency to conform to the views of others, even when they do not believe these views. Agreeing with other members of the group can seem more important than making the right decision.[7]

2. The ability to reach a consensus can be difficult if one or more group members is capable of manipulating group opinion.

3. Groups have the tendency to jump to obvious conclusions without critically evaluating the facts behind the decision. In the movie classic *Twelve Angry Men,* eleven members of a jury vote to convict the defendant—a minority slum dweller—of murder without even considering the possibility of his innocence. Had the twelfth juror not insisted that the evidence be examined and led the others through the flaws in the prosecution's case, the jury would have sentenced the man to death for a crime he did not commit.[8]

4. Because of the need of many groups to hear all opinions, group decisions generally take longer than decisions made by one person, especially if the group leader does not have the skill to bring the group to a consensus.

HOW GROUP
ROLES AFFECT
COMMUNICATION
When you become a group member, the way you communicate is shaped, in large part, by your role in the group. If you have been appointed leader or have a special expertise that sets you apart from the other members, you may be given more privileges and responsibilities than junior members. Junior members are often given the least desirable jobs—notetaking or photocopying, for example—and may be given little time to express their points of view.

---

7. For a landmark study of the effects of group pressure on decision making, see Solomon Asch, "Opinions and Social Pressure," *Scientific American*, vol. 193 (1955): 31–35.
8. Although one member of the group took charge in this case, he used reasoning rather than manipulation to influence the group decision. According to group communication researcher Norman Maier, groups can succeed under the pressure of a minority opinion if the opinion is constructive and logical. If it is self-serving and emotional, the result may be a poor decision. See Norman R. F. Maier, "Assets and Liabilities in Group Problem Solving: The Need for an Integrative Function," *Psychological Review* 74 (1967): 239–49.

Roles quickly appear in small groups. While one group member emerges as the leader, taking the initiative in setting the group's agenda, another is uncommunicative and plays a minor role in group discussions. Still other members of the group may try to dominate the discussion, oppose almost every point raised, close their minds before the discussion begins, or become scapegoats who are blamed for the group's failures. A group member may also take on a tension release role as a jokester to relieve the tension that builds as the group works to accomplish its goals.[9]

The role you assume determines how you will communicate in the group and how effective the group will be. Although there are many types of roles, we focus on two broad categories: your role as a group leader and your role as a group participant.

Leadership and Communication

The goal of the group leader is to exert a consistent, positive influence on group members by virtue of his or her personality and communication style. Whether an individual leads a grass roots community group or the United States, the leader's communication style defines the group.

Instrumental and Expressive Leadership.   As the leader of a small group, you can be an instrumental or expressive leader.

Instrumental leaders are goal-oriented leaders, and attempt to move group members to accomplish a specific mission. For example, Danny Billingsley, a captain on the Montgomery, Alabama, Police Department, loves children so much that he organized a church group to help children in Central and South America. In 1989, the group traveled to San Nicolas, Argentina, where they worked as many as sixteen hours a day to rebuild an orphanage.[10] Because they are so goal oriented, instrumental leaders may not be popular with group members who lack the leader's commitment.

Expressive leaders focus primarily on keeping morale high, reducing conflict, and motivating group members. After an automobile accident that resulted in the amputation of his right foot, Tom Whittaker formed C.W. HOG—the Cooperative Wilderness Handicapped Outdoor Group—which takes disabled adventurers on wilderness expeditions. Crucial to the group's success is Whittaker's ability to make group members feel "abled" rather than "disabled."[11]

An expressive leader guiding the cleanup of a shoreline oil spill may offer the following encouragement:

> *Group member:* There are so many birds covered with oil. We'll only be able to help a few of them. The rest will die.

---

9.   R. F. Bales, "The Equilibrium Problem in Small Groups," in T. Parson, R. F. Bales, and E. A. Shils, eds., *Working Papers in the Theory of Action* (Glencoe, IL: Free Press, (1953) pp. 111–61.
10.   Example from "A Salute to Everyday Heroes," *Newsweek*, July 10, 1989, p. 56.
11.   "Ibid., p. 46.

Group leader: We have hundreds of people working as hard as they can up and down the coast. If the weather holds—and it looks like it will—we'll be able to save thousands of birds who would have died without our help. We can't stop now.

Group member: But we won't be able to help them all.

Group leader: Every life makes a difference.

When groups are formed, they generally ask the same person to act as the group's instrumental and expressive leaders. Often, this combination fails, because it is difficult to be a taskmaster plus a source of emotional support. Small group research has shown that although a person may be perceived as an effective instrumental and expressive leader at the first group meeting, by the fourth meeting only 8 percent of the members said they still liked the leader.[12] When support drops off, leaders may have to choose between these two leadership roles.

Leadership Styles.   The three basic leadership styles are:

⌘ *Authoritarian leaders* give orders. They care little for group input or joint decision making. ("If you don't like my approach, you can resign from the group.")

⌘ *Democratic leaders* encourage the democratic process. They try to achieve consensus among group members before taking any action. ("After listening to how you feel, I think we are close to reaching a consensus. Andrea, let's talk again about your objections. If we can resolve them, we can move ahead.")

⌘ *Laissez-faire leaders* simply let things happen, intervening as little as possible in directing or organizing group activities. ("Let me know what you want to do.")

In a classic study of leadership styles, Kurt Lewin concluded that although authoritarian leaders are efficient, they often create discontent in the group. Democratic leaders, in contrast, are able to get the job done and at the same time motivate group members who feel part of a decision-making team. Lewin concluded that laissez-faire leadership is generally ineffective.[13]

To Be Effective, Leadership Must Fit the Needs of the Group.   You may find yourself called to leadership if your leadership style fits the needs of the group. To use an extreme example, "The pilot of a bomber crew may be an excellent leader for the group while the plane is in the air, but may be a most inadequate leader if the plane crashes and the crew is faced with the task of surviving or finding its way to safety."[14] The same principle applies to more conventional small groups. For

---

12.   Phillip E. Slater, "Role Differentiation in Small Groups," in A. Paul Hare et al., eds., *Small Groups: Studies in Social Interaction* (New York: Knopf, 1955).
13.   See Kurt Lewin, "A Research Approach to Leadership Problems," *Journal of Educational Sociology* 17 (March 1944), : 392–98.
14.   Dorwin Cartwright and Alvin Zander, eds., *Group Dynamics: Research and Theory*, 3d ed. (New York: Harper & Row, 1968).

instance, you may be able to motivate group members to plan a volunteer program to tutor underprivileged youngsters, but be unable to direct them in the hard-nosed tactics of fund-raising. Leadership change is possible at any given moment depending upon the needs of the group.

Although your leadership style is determined, in part, by your personality (if you are an aggressive, goal-directed person, you are more likely to adopt an authoritarian style than if you are an empathetic, people-oriented person), you can decide the form of leadership most likely to work with your group and adapt your personal style accordingly. Adaptation begins with analysis. Look analytically at the people in your group and decide the leadership style that will work best. Then look at your leadership style to see if it fits the group's needs. If you are normally an instrumental leader with an authoritarian style, try focusing on motivation and group decision making during one part of your meeting. See if group members respond and whether your new style translates into group action. Although no one can be effective in all situations, you can increase your chance of success by gearing your leadership style to what is needed to make the group work.

Leadership in Action.   Here are eight responsibilities of group leaders:

- ✂ *A leader should establish group procedures.* After the resignation of a division head, the company president appointed seven executives to find a replacement. At the first meeting, a leader was chosen to head the search group. Although she was a talented, action-oriented person, she did not understand the need to establish group procedures. As a result, group members never knew when meetings were scheduled, how long they would take, when reports were due, or even the criteria the group would use to analyze applicants' credentials. After several weeks of chaos a new leader was chosen who understood that nothing would get done without a procedural framework.

- ✂ *A leader should open the meeting with direction and purpose.* You may choose to open the meeting with action-directed comments ("We are here today to examine the charges of police brutality against a group of peaceful protesters") or to examine items on a written agenda. Once the discussion begins, others will contribute, but it is the leader's role to focus the meeting at the start.

- ✂ *A leader should keep the group on track.* Inevitably, the attention of group members will drift. Call a meeting to talk about organizing a volunteer fire department and you're likely to hear debates on the merits of different kinds of fire call boxes or on whether women are strong enough to be fire fighters. When side issues keep the group from its business, the leader must refocus the meeting.

- ✂ *A leader should make clarifying summaries when they seem necessary to group progress.* Groups, like the individuals who comprise them, can be confused by the information they hear. Warning signs include: questions asking for clarification, puzzled looks on listeners' faces, and drifting attention. When you sense confusion, one of the best ways to move forward is to provide a summary of what just occurred. ("In summary, there seems to be little doubt about the need for an effective volunteer fire department, but we're still grappling with the question of how to raise funds to support the effort. Although Jim suggests sending out an annual fund-raising letter, I think the rest of us agree that some form of face-to-face solicitation would be more effective.")

⌘ *A leader should try to keep group communication from being one-sided.* People rarely come to a group with completely open minds. We often have preconceived ideas of how a job should be done. Although these ideas are grist for debate, they may also be obstacles to group communication if the leader allows the discussion to become one-sided.

As a group leader, it is your job to recognize when one point of view is dominating the discussion. It is also your job to encourage other group members to express their opinions. A discussion can quickly turn one-sided if one or more members are aggressive and opinionated. If a single voice dominates, acknowledge the person's point of view but suggest that the problem be analyzed from other perspectives as well. Invite others into the discussion or provide a varying opinion yourself.

⌘ *A leader should try to maintain the cohesiveness of the group.* Nothing is inherently wrong with a heated discussion, especially when the issue is controversial. However, when the discussion turns into a shouting match, it is no longer productive. The group will fall apart if the anger is not controlled. It is the leader's job to intervene to defuse the argument and to refocus communication. You must act quickly and fairly to defuse the anger and, at the same time, encourage an open debate.

⌘ *A leader should draw information from participants.* Some people are hesitant to speak even when they have something valuable to contribute. Their reasons may range from speech tension to feeling they are junior members of the group. It is up to the leader to draw responses from these participants so that the group will reflect various points of view. A leader can:

Go around the table, asking every group member to speak.

Direct questions to those who remain silent, asking what they think about the subject in general or about the previous comment.

Be supportive when a normally quiet member makes a comment in the hope of encouraging additional responses at a later time.

Getting everyone to contribute is particularly important when one or more members of the group seem to dominate every discussion. It is up to the group leader to make sure the group benefits from the combined wisdom of all its members, not just a vocal minority.

⌘ *A leader should move people from self to task.* Many participants are so concerned with how others are evaluating them that they cannot concentrate on the purpose of the meeting. The leader's challenge is to divert attention from self to task by getting people involved, through a specific assignment or question, with the work of the group. If your meeting concerns setting up a new security system for the college dorms, assign one person the job of finding out how security is handled by nearby colleges, another the job of talking with the police, and so on. At the next meeting, ask participants to report what they have found. This technique will help focus *all* group members on the job to be done.

Be an Active Small-Group Participant

Group membership brings with it a set of roles and responsibilities that complement those of the group leader.

Make Group Goals Your #1 Priority.   Even when intragroup conflicts are justified, try to keep your focus on the group's mission. Here is the way a conflict over a missed deadline was handled successfully by a group member:

> *Lupe:* Bob, we've been waiting for your report for the last several weeks. We're all disappointed that it still isn't ready.

Group members should be able to adapt their public speaking skills to a small group setting.

Bob: Well, I was busy with other things.

Lupe: Since we really can't move ahead until we get your findings, we need this information as soon as possible. If you want to talk about your scheduling problems, I'm sure all of us would be willing to help you find the time to get the job done. We can take the next fifteen minutes of group time to do that if you want.

Bob: No, I don't think so. I just found out this morning that one of my classes was cancelled on Tuesday, so I can do the work then. Thanks anyway for your offer to help.

Although voices were never raised, Bob understood that the group would no longer tolerate his lack of participation. In the face of peer group pressure, he decided to comply. Making a commitment to the group means making a commitment to achieve group goals at each meeting.

Work to Find the Best Solution—Not Your Solution.   People often enter into group discussions with a preconceived notion of the necessary solution. The challenge this member perceives is not, "How can I help the group find the best possible answer?" but, "How can I get the others to see that my solution is best?"

A group needs a shared image of the group, in which individual aspirations are subsumed under the group umbrella that strives for the common good. When you feel strongly about your position, it is legitimate to try to convince the group you are correct. But if others disagree, it is important that you listen to their objections and try to find merit in them. You need an objective detachment from your own proposals to enable you to place the group's goals above your own.

Solve Interpersonal Conflicts Before They Sabotage Group Goals.   Group members can be dedicated to achieving the group's goals and, at the same time, be torn apart by in-group fighting. According to sports columnist Ira Berkow, interpersonal conflicts multiply on baseball teams that have lost too many games. "When the team is losing, the players start pointing fingers and accusing others of not doing their jobs. If this goes on too long, it could destroy a team."[15]

Here are some ways to avoid potentially destructive conflicts:

1.   *Have respect for other points of view, but don't capitulate unless you are convinced you are wrong.*   Use the following techniques to counter other points of view.[16]

      "I understand." When faced with an argument based on feelings rather than facts, you'll have a hard time changing the other person's mind. It is useless to argue with someone who says, "Your idea feels wrong."

---

15.   Interview with Ira Berkow, June 23, 1988.
16.   Techniques based on Eugene Ehrlich and Gene R. Hawes, *Speak for Success* (New York: Bantam Books, 1984), p. 133.

or "Your idea makes me uncomfortable." Instead, accept the person's feelings by saying something like, "I can see how you can feel that way," and move onto your next factual point. Here is an example:

"I can see how you can feel that way" (acknowledgement of feelings). "We're here to help students deal with the stress they feel around exam time and I think the best way to do this is to set up a phone line students can call when they feel too much pressure" (next factual point).

It is important to realize that your statement of understanding is not an agreement with the other person's point of view.

Calmly repeat your point. When another group member is openly hostile, when he or she pushes you to make a statement you don't want to make, counter by calmly repeating your point, thus emphasizing, in a nonargumentative way, that you have no intention of changing your mind. For example, if a group member is trying to force you to back down on the student help-line in favor of using the funds to hire a part-time school psychologist, calmly say, "When exam pressure is too great, students need to talk to someone who knows what they're going through." Although the idea is essentially the same, the words are different. The language change helps lessen the chance that the individual will be annoyed by your repetition.

Plead "no contest." Instead of arguing with a criticism that makes sense, accept it, but don't let a concession on a single point weaken your entire position. Change the direction of the argument and move on to the next point, as in the following example:

I can see what you mean that having a twenty-line system will be too costly. I think we can function with six lines as long as we can put the incoming calls on hold.

2. *Don't get personal.*   Comments like, "You have to be an idiot to believe that will work," or "My six-year-old cousin has better ideas than that," accomplish nothing. On the contrary, these comments are so antagonistic that they make it virtually impossible for people to work together. If you do not like an idea, say so directly by focusing on the idea, not the person. And try not to make your disagreement too negative. You can find a germ of promise in most ideas, if you try hard enough. Use that germ to compliment your fellow group member and to move on to a more effective approach.

3. *Look forward, not backward.*   Mistakes are inevitable—even with the best planning. Resist the temptation to spend too much time figuring out who was responsible for each group mistake. Instead, help redirect group energy to getting the job done.

4. *When you cannot settle a problem on your own, ask for help.*   The group leader or another disinterested party can act as a mediator to help settle your differences.

5. *Try to leave your personal problems at home.*   Group conflicts are often the result of personal problems brought to the group meeting. A fight with a family member, a poor test grade, an alarm clock that failed to ring, a near-accident on the highway, or school or work pressure can put you in a bad mood for the meeting and lessen your tolerance for other group members. Although an outburst of anger may make you feel better for the moment, it may destroy the relationships you have with the other members of the group.

6. *Learn how your fellow group members react.*   You know from your family and friends that different people take news in different ways. While one may start screaming, another may calmly ask a few questions, and another may raise an eyebrow and ask, "So what?" You may get the same range of reactions in a small group. Because most people are consistent in their reactions (for example, an overreactor is unlikely to take any crisis calmly), you can predict—and plan—for reactions, thus eliminating possible conflicts.

If you know that one group member gets nervous under too much time pressure, try to break the workload into realistic time frames. Then encourage focusing on one task at a time. "Instead of thinking about how much time the whole job will take you, focus on the work that's due next week. I know you can get that done in time.") If another group member sulks when feeling left out of the discussion, make an attempt to solicit her ideas. ("Abby, we all want to hear what you think.") Finally, if another group member jumps to conclusions and misunderstands your point of view, summarize your own statements and ask for questions. ("Ted, I know you *thought* I said that I support a campus-wide sit-in. What I meant was that if all else fails, a sit-in may be the only way to call attention to the problem. Do you see what I mean?")

MAKING THE MOST OF SMALL-GROUP COMMUNICATION

Here are some suggestions that will help you get your point across in the small group setting:[17]

Get People to Pay Attention.   After formal presentations are made, group members compete for the floor. With limited meeting time, it is important to know how to make people *want* to listen to what you have to say. The following suggestions will help:

Be ready with your comments as soon as the last speaker finishes. Take advantage of a lull in the group's momentum.

Acknowledge the comments of another group member and use this acknowledgement as a springboard for what you want to say, even if the topic has little to

---

17. Examples from "A Salute to Everyday Heroes," *Newsweek*, p. 60.

do with the direction you want to take. For example, in a meeting to determine the need for the student help-line, if the last comment related to increased student enrollment, you can say, "With more students on campus, we have an even greater need to provide psychological services at exam time. The best way to do this is through the student help-line."

Be Brief.   Make your point as briefly and clearly as possible and don't confuse your listeners with too many details. If you have more to say, save your comments for when the group starts discussing your idea and questions are asked.

Be Simple.   Because most small group discussions are informal and relaxed, keep your language simple and informal. Use humor when appropriate to make people more receptive to your ideas and to encourage a spontaneous discussion.

Watch for Nonverbal Clues.   When you see your listeners shifting in their seats, looking at their watches, yawning, shuffling papers, or doodling, chances are they're bored. Without realizing it, you may be repeating your point or presenting too much detail for your listeners to handle. Whatever the reason, these nonverbal clues tell you it is time to stop talking or to move on to another topic.

Some nonverbal clues are expressions of annoyance with what you are saying. When group members exchange quick, knowing glances with one another, tap their fingers on the table, or frown, be aware that tension is building and that you may face an argument. Nonverbal clues can also tell you when things are going well. When group members lean forward in their seats, watch you attentively, take notes, and nod their heads in agreement, you know that group sentiment is on your side.

Find the Right Place to Sit.   Choosing the right seat at a small group meeting may be more important than you think. Here is some advice on seating offered by Eugene Ehrlich and Gene R. Hawes:

> We tend to talk more with people we can see as well as hear. Translate this fact into seating arrangements in any small group of which you become a part: You will be more likely to speak after the person across from you or farthest from you has spoken. You will be least likely to speak after the person next to you speaks. So, to make an impact on a small group, you are probably best off distancing yourself from the person who is most likely to do a good deal of speaking.[18]

The exception, according to Ehrlich and Hawes, is the group leader. Despite the fact that he or she will probably have a lot to say, it is often a good idea to sit in the next seat. The leader's status and influence tends to "rub off" on people in the immediate area.

18.   Ehrlich and Hawes, *Speak for Success*, p. 134.

HOW GROUPS
WORK

Winning the down-to-the-wire election as student body president was easy compared to the job that lay ahead. During the campaign Deborah promised students she would work to make changes in the way college administrators handled complaints over dormitory assignments. Now that the election was over, she had to keep her word.

The dorm issue was the cause of so much friction on campus that it would take more than one person to come up with a solution everyone could accept. Realizing she needed the help of people who saw the issue from different perspectives, Deborah formed a committee to study the problem and recommend solutions. The group approached its task in eight different stages, all of which involve communicating ideas to others. These stages are based, in part, on the work of philosopher John Dewey who, in 1910, developed a theory of reflective thinking that is now applied to group communication.[19]

Stage 1: Choose Group Members

Small group members may be chosen by the group leader, elected to the group, or come to the group as a volunteer. In this case, Deborah designated two members of the student council and asked for two volunteers from the student body at large, thus making a five-person group.

Stage 2: Define the Problem and Set the Agenda

At the first meeting, Deborah defined the problem facing the group in terms of the following mission statement:

> It is the mission of this group to find a method for handling student complaints over dormitory assignments that will give students greater choice over where and with whom they live.

The group then set an agenda, creating a list of the issues they would have to consider to complete their mission. These items include the following:

1. Assess the current dorm complaint situation from the point of view of students to define the nature of the problem.

2. Assess the current dorm complaint situation from the point of view of the college administration.

3. Submit an internal report based on student responses detailing the advantages and problems of the system.

4. Submit an internal report detailing the advantages and problems of the system from the administration's point of view.

5. Debate the issues in order to decide an equitable solution for both sides.

---

19. John Dewey, *How We Think* (Boston: D. C. Heath, 1910).

6. Have a panel discussion open to the entire student body on committee findings.

7. Submit a formal report to the college administration.

Stage 3: Conduct the Inquiry and Analyze the Problem

Analysis begins with fact-finding. All relevant information must be gathered to find a solution that will work for both students and the administration. Items one and two on the group's agenda involve fact finding.

Deborah assigns two students to each item and gives both groups the following list to guide their research.

1. What is the nature of the dormitory problem?

2. Why are students dissatisfied with the current dormitory complaint system?

3. Are these students a vocal minority or does the problem involve a large number of students?

4. Why does the administration handle dorm complaints the way it does?

5. Has it considered the possibility of giving students greater choice in deciding where they will live?

6. Is this problem new or has it gone on for many years?

7. Suggest several feasible alternatives to the current system that will give students greater choice while maintaining administration control.

8. What are the merits and drawbacks of each proposed solution? Is the solution workable?

In addition to talking to students and members of the college administration about the dormitory problem, group members use other sources of information. They talk to students and administrators at neighboring colleges to see how the situation is handled there. And they check various periodical and book indexes at the library for published works on dormitory administration.

The fact-finding stage ends with the submission of the internal reports, detailing the advantages and problems of the current system from the point of view of students and the college administration.

Stage 4: Debate the Issues

Group members agree on a two-stage debate: First, they focus on establishing a set of standards upon which to base their recommendations. Second, they assess alternative solutions according to these standards. This careful approach is necessary to avoid mistakes that often occur when judgments are rushed. According to Dewey, *suspended judgment* is critical at this point in the decision-making process. The goal of group members is to maintain an intelligent state of doubts as they investigate the available options.[20]

Establish Problem-Solving Standards.   After an extended discussion, the group agrees on the following standards for evaluating the internal reports given by group members. These standards will also be used as a basis for the group's final recommendations:

1. The decision should consider both the needs of students for some control over where they live and the needs of the college for an administratively sound solution.

2. The decision will apply to all students living in dorms, not only entering freshmen.

3. The decision will not allow students to switch dorm assignments at will.

4. The decision will consider the fact that entering freshmen need to live in dormitories close to the center of campus.

5. The decision will be based on the fact that all dormitory rooms are considered of comparable quality.

6. The decision should recognize the need of entering freshmen to share a dorm with a compatible roommate.

7. Males and females shall not be allowed to share dorm rooms, although they will be allowed to have separate rooms on the same floor.

Assess the Alternatives.   Using these criteria, Deborah opens the debate. The conversation centers around the two fact-finding reports submitted earlier. Here is part of the discussion:

Deborah: Nick, after looking at this situation from the students' point of view, what is your recommendation?

Nick: Students need to feel that their complaints will be heard and acted upon by the administration. When they have a roommate who smokes or who plays loud music till two in the morning, they have a legitimate reason for a dorm room switch. I suggest setting up a clearinghouse for these complaints run by the administration but with an advisory board of students. This way students will make sure the administration doesn't let complaints slide and yet administration will maintain control.

Deborah: Anice, you heard the administration's point of view. How do you see things?

Anice: I think what Nick says has a lot of merit, but I'm not sure the administration will go for it. They're very comfortable letting the computer match students with dorms and with handling complaints in the same way. When a student brings up a problem, they

---

20.   Ross and Ross, *Small Groups in Organizational Settings*, p. 77.

really don't want to hear about it. But if they're pushed, I think they would agree to a clearinghouse—as long as they're the ones in charge.

Nick: How do we make sure that the students have real power?

Deborah: We have to set up a mechanism that enables the student advisory board to report problems to the dean of students. I think that would work.

Stage 5: Choose the Best Solution

The group can make its decision in three ways: It can seek a consensus, vote, or let the leader decide.

Consensus.   *Consensus* means an acceptance by all group members of the decision the group reaches. A consensus can occur when group members disagree as long as everyone in the group is willing to take part in carrying out the decision. To reach a consensus, all group members must be able to express their points of view. Although this process can be long and drawn out, as debate follows debate, the involvement of all group members ensures their commitment to the decision. According to Raymond S. Ross and Jean Ricky Ross, experts in small group communication, consensus decision making involves an awareness of four different factors:[21]

- ⌘ The need to be open-minded so that you can consider ideas different from your own.
- ⌘ The need to concentrate on the job to be done rather than personality issues that get in the way.
- ⌘ The need to guard against sudden opinion changes that result in a consensus. Group members may be swayed by an emotional appeal without weighing the consequences of their decision. Although they may be well-meaning, the decision may be poorly thought out.
- ⌘ The need for group members to embrace the decision and express a commitment to it.

Vote.   The second type of decision making involves voting. If your group has no policies governing voting, a simple majority will settle the decision. However, in established groups, voting procedures determine not only who will vote but also how the vote will be taken (a show of hands or ballot, for example) and whether each vote will be counted equally (in some groups, senior members have greater voting power than new members). Voting rules should be described at the group's first meeting to avoid confusion and delay later on.

Let the Leader Decide.   In order for groups to run efficiently, group leaders may make many decisions on their own. If they are democratic leaders, they will try to

---

21. Ibid., p. 70.

limit these decisions to minor issues (when to hold the next meeting; how to resolve a time conflict). If they are authoritarian leaders, they may make even major decisions without consulting the group.

In this case, the group seeks a consensus on its recommendations for handling dormitory complaints. After an extensive debate, group members agree that setting up a student advisory panel to oversee the administration is a workable, fair solution for everyone involved.

Stage 6: Submit the Preliminary Recommendations to a Broader Audience

Frequently, the efforts of a task-oriented group are not finished when a decision is made. The group must report its findings to a broader audience, which in this case is the entire student body. Although the audience may not have the power to vote down the recommendation, its comments are seriously considered by the committee and incorporated into the final report. Recommendations are most often submitted through a panel discussion, symposium, or colloquium.

Panel Discussion.   In a panel discussion, group members have an informal interchange on the issues in front of an audience. The positive and negative features of issues are debated, just as they were in the closed group meeting, but this time in front of an audience. When you are part of a panel discussion, it is important to keep in mind that you are talking for the benefit of the audience rather than for other group members. Although your responses are spontaneous, they should be thought out in advance, just as in any other public speaking presentation.

Panel discussions are directed by a moderator who attempts to elicit a balanced view of the issues and to involve all the group members. The role of the moderator is to encourage the discussion—he or she does not take part in the debate. Moderators coordinate and organize the discussion, ask pertinent questions, summarize conclusions, and keep the discussion moving. Once the discussion is over, the moderator often opens the discussion to audience questions.

Symposium.   A symposium is more formal and predictable than a panel discussion. Instead of focusing on the interaction among group members, it centers on prepared speeches on the same subject given by group members who are introduced by a moderator. These speeches may be followed by a panel discussion or an audience question-and-answer period. Although these panel discussions can be interesting because they involve people who know a great deal about the topic, they are often viewed as an afterthought and given little time.

Colloquium.   In a colloquium, group members respond to audience questions. Unlike a panel discussion or the second half of a symposium, a colloquium does not include interactions among group members. The success of the colloquium depends on how carefully the audience has thought about the topic (the topic is announced in advance) and the nature of their questions.

The following guidelines will help you be a successful participant in a panel discussion, symposium, or colloquium. Many of the guidelines apply to all three group forms, but others apply just to one:

1. *Since you will probably be given only about ten minutes to speak, limit your speech to a single point.*

2. *To avoid repetition, find out in advance what the other panelists will be covering in their speeches.*   The job of assigning topics should be the responsibility of the presentation organizer. If the organizer is negligent, you may want to get in touch with the other panelists yourself.

3. *Try to meet your fellow panelists in advance.*   When group members meet for the first time on stage, there is often an awkwardness in their interchange that comes from not knowing one another. This discomfort can be communicated to the audience.

4. *Restrict your speech to the allotted time.*   If speakers exceed the time limit, the audience will find it difficult to sit through the entire program, and little opportunity will remain for a panel interchange or a question-and-answer period.

5. *Prepare for audience questions.*   Because the question-and-answer period is often the most important part of the program, spend as much time preparing for the questions as you did your formal remarks. Make a list of the questions you are likely to be asked and frame your answers.

   During the question-and-answer period, be willing to speak up and add to someone else's response if none of the questions is being directed at you. When a fellow panel member finishes a response simply say, "I'd like to make one more point that . . ." If, on the other hand, a question is directed at you that you think would be better handled by another panel member, say, "I think that considering her background, Virginia is better able to answer that question."

6. *Consider enhancing your presentation with visual aids.*   Simple visual aids are as appropriate in group discussions as they are in single-person public speaking. The advantage of using them in this setting is that audiences don't expect them, since most panel members deliver "straight" talks.[22]

Stage 7: Present Final Recommendations

After a successful panel discussion on the dormitory complaint problem, Deborah presented the group's conclusions to the college administration. After submitting a formal written report, she was given the opportunity to speak before key members of the administration to present the group's findings and answer questions. After

---

22. For more information, see Bill Hennefrund, "Panel Power," *The Toastmaster* (January 1990): 8–10.

outlining the group's goals and its methods of analysis, she described in detail its recommended solution. Although the college administration did not agree at first on the need for an overseeing student committee, Deborah convinced them that this provision was necessary for student acceptance and that it still left control in the hands of the administration. During this stage traditional public speaking skills are most helpful as the speaker takes the role of spokesperson for the group.

Stage 8: Evaluate the Solution After Implementation

Six months after the dormitory complaint plan was put into effect, the group reconvened to assess the plan's success based on information from a questionnaire handed out to students before the spring break. Group members also collected information informally through discussions with individual students.

Although the plan seemed to be working, many students were upset because they had not heard about the changes in handling student complaints. Both the college administration and the student council had failed to inform students of their rights under the plan. Once the decision was made, little mention appeared in the student newspaper or on the student-run radio station. No posters had been distributed to inform students about the new complaint system. Based on these findings, the group recommended that the student council mount an extensive advertising campaign, which would be repeated every year for the benefit of entering freshmen.

SUMMARY When public speaking takes place in small group settings, attention is focused on the interactions among speakers rather than on a single speaker addressing a group of listeners. The four types of small groups are information-gathering, problem-solving, learning, and therapy groups.

Certain characteristics of small groups affect communication, including a shared sense of purpose, group-oriented versus self-oriented goals, and group size.

The way you communicate in a group is influenced by your role in the group. As group leader, you can be an instrumental or expressive leader. You can also choose an authoritarian, democratic, or laissez-faire leadership style. Your leadership style should fit the needs of the group.

Small group participants should center their communication around group goals, put their personal agendas aside, and avoid in-group fighting.

To communicate effectively in the small group setting, be conscious of the need to attract listener attention, be brief and simple in your presentation, watch for nonverbal cues from listeners, and understand the importance of where you sit.

Group functioning and its communication often occur in eight stages. In stage one, group members are chosen; in stage two, the problem is defined and an agenda set; in stage three, the problem is analyzed; in stage four, group members debate the issues; in stage five, the best solution is chosen through consensus, vote, or a decision by the leader; in stage six, preliminary recommendations are made to a broader audience. These recommendations may be submitted through a panel discussion, symposium, or colloquium. In stage seven, final recommendations are made; and in stage eight, the solution is evaluated after implementation.

QUESTIONS FOR STUDY AND DISCUSSION

1. Compare small group communication and traditional public speaking. What similarities and differences are evident? How can the development of strong public speaking skills serve the needs of small group communication?
2. What are the primary communication goals of group leaders? How do they compare to the goals of group members? How do different leadership styles affect group communication?
3. Review the eight stages of group problem solving. In which stages are communication problems common? How can groups measure the worth of their solutions? How are solutions and recommendations usually presented? How can a solution or recommendation be evaluated after it has been implemented?

ACTIVITIES

1. Select an actual small group on campus or in your community and obtain permission to observe several meetings. Take notes on what you observe, and write a 500- to 750-word paper comparing your observations to the guidelines presented in this chapter.
2. Join with four other class members to work on a common problem. Use a panel or symposium to present your analysis and recommendations. The group should move through all the stages of group activity, with the presentation stage conducted in your public speaking class.
3. Write a short paper in which you assess the above group's activities, drawing conclusions about the strengths and weaknesses of group communication.

A C K N O W L E D G M E N T S

For permission to reprint copyrighted material, the publisher is grateful to the following:

Aaronson, Robert, J., "Air Transportation: What is Safe and Needed," *Vital Speeches of the Day.*

Allen, Steve, *How to Make a Speech,* New York: McGraw-Hill Paperbacks, © 1986, pp. 136-137.

Bogue, E.G., "A Friend of Mine: Notes on the Gift of Teaching," *Vital Speeches of the Day,* August 1, 1988, p. 615.

Brady, Sarah, excerpt of speech by Sarah Brady courtesy of Handgun Control, Inc., Washington, D.C., Sarah Brady, Chair.

Chavez, Cesar, "Speech in Wooster, Ohio," printed in *Mexican American Anthology II,* ed. Joy Hintz, 500 E. Perry Street, Tiffin, OH 44883.

Chiu, Tony, "Whistle Blower," copyright © Tony Chiu, *Life,* March 1988, p. 19-22.

Duffy, Bernard K. and Ryan, Harold R., excerpts from *American Oratory of the Twentieth Century ,* edited by Bernard K. Duffy and Harold R. Ryan, reprinted by permission of Greenwood Publishing Group, Inc., Westport, CT (Greenwood Press, 1987).

Fimesliner, Sherman G., "The Tapestry of Your Life: Don't be Afraid to Fail," *Vital Speeches of the Day,* November 15, 1989, p. 82.

From *Winning Orations* 1988-1989, 1991-1992, Interstate Oratorical Association, Mankato State University: Siplon, Katie, "Children With AIDS;" Mouttet, Carolyn Sue, "Old Does Not Mean Stupid;" Clanton, Jenny, "Title Unknown;" Martin, Jenelle, "Campus Safety: The Forgotten Priority;" Kimmey, Karen, "The Bingity, Bangity School Bus;" Hudson, Jeff, "The Incumbent Advantage or Disadvantage;" Esslinger, Jonathan J., "National Parks: A Scenery of Destruction and Degradation;" Spurling, Cherie, "Batter Up-Batter Down;" Pankow, Paula, "Hours To Go Before I Sleep;" Wood, Andy, "America's Trauma Crisis;" Oehmen, Tisha R., "Not a Drop to Drink;" Jamison, Heather, "Do No Harm."

Gallwey, Timothy W. and Kriegel, Robert, excerpt from *Inner Skiing,* Copyright © 1977 by Timothy Gallwey. Reprinted by permission of Random House, Inc.

Geyer, Georgie Anne, Syndicated Columnist, Author, TV News Analyst; "Joy in Our Time: I Am Responsible for My Own Fight," *Vital Speeches of the Day,* August 15, 1989, p. 668.

Griffin, James, D., "To Snare the Feet of Greatness: The American Dream Is Alive," *Vital Speeches of the Day,* June 16, 1989, pp. 735-736.

Hamm, William E., "Honoring the Noble Sacrifice: Once Again We Remember," *Vital Speeches of the Day,* August 1, 1989, pp. 626-627.

Hearn, Thomas K., Jr., President, Wake Forest University, "Sports and Ethics: The University Response," *Vital Speeches of the Day,* October 15, 1988, p. 20.

Henmueller, Paul A., B.A. English. The University of Illinois at Chicago. "Diamonds of Hope: The Value of a Person," June, 1989 Commencement Address.

Hoff, Ron, *I Can See You Naked: A Fearless Guide to Making Great Presentations,* Kansas City: Andrews & McMeel © 1988, p. 189.

Jacob, John E., President & CEO, National Urban League, Inc., "The Future of Black America: The Doomed Generation," *Vital Speeches of the Day,* September 1, 1988, p. 616.

Johannesen, Richard L., *Ethics in Human Communication, Third Edition,* p. 256

(Copyright © 1990, 1983, 1975), published by Waveland Press, Inc., Prospect Heights, Ill.

Johnson, Virginia, "Picture Perfect Presentations," reprinted by permission of 3M Meeting Management Institute.

Kelly, Rex, "Speakers and the Bottom Line: The Character of the Speaker," *Vital Speeches of the Day,* November 1, 1987, p. 49.

Moyers, Bill, excerpts from *Bill Moyers: A World of Ideas* by Bill Moyers, © 1989 by Public Affairs Television, Inc. Used by permission of Doubleday, a division of Bantam Doubleday Dell Publishing Group, Inc.

Noonan, Peggy, excerpts from *What I Saw at the Revolution* by Peggy Noonan. Copyright © 1989 by Peggy Noonan. Reprinted by permission of Random House, Inc.

Orski, Ken C., President, Urban Mobility Corporation, "The Problem of Traffic Congestion: A Common Sense Look," *Vital Speeches of the Day,* January 1, 1990, p. 190.

Parnell, Charles, "Speech Writing: The Profession and Practice," *Vital Speeches of the Day,* January 15, 1990, p. 210.

Rackleff, Robert B., "The Art of Speech Writing: A Dramatic Event," *Vital Speeches of the Day.*

Robinson, James, *Better Speeches in Ten Simple Steps,* Rocklin: Prima Publishing and Communications, 1989, pp. 58-61.

Ross, Raymond S., *Small Groups in Organizational Settings,* © 1989, pp. 62-64. Reprinted by permission of Prentice Hall, Inc., Englewood Cliffs, New Jersey.

Sarnoff, Dorothy, *Speech Can Change Your Life* © 1970 Doubleday, Dell Publishing Group Inc.

Sayers, Gale, excerpts of speech to South Carolina Law Enforcement Association, February 22, 1989. Copyright © Gale Sayers.

Schanberg, Sydney H., "The Risk of Being Different: Stretch Yourself," *Vital Speeches of the Day,* September 1, 1989, pp. 700-702.

Sidey, Hugh, "The Presidency: Of Poets and Word Processors," from *Time,* May 2, 1988, p. 32. Copyright © 1988 Time Inc.

Sprague, Jo and Stuart, Douglas, excerpts from *The Speaker's Handbook, Third Edition* used with permission of Harcourt Brace and Company. Copyright © 1992.

Steil, Lyman K. et. al., *Effective Listening: Key To Your Success,* © 1983 Random House. Reproduced with permission of McGraw-Hill, Inc.

Tarver, Jerry, Professor of Speech Communication, University of Richmond, Richmond, Virginia, "Words in Time: Some Reflections on the Language of Speech," *Vital Speeches of the Day,* April 15, 1988, pp. 410-412.

Temple, Lieutenant General Herbert R., Jr., USA (Ret.), Former Chief National Guard Bureau, "The Nation's War on Drugs," *Vital Speeches of the Day,* June 15, 1989, p. 517.

Thompson, B.M., "Good Riddance: Solving America's Hazardous Waste Problem," *Vital Speeches of the Day,* September 1, 1989, p. 683.

Todd, James S., M.D., Executive Vice President, American Medical Association, "The American Health-Care System: Strengthen It, Don't Scrap It," *Vital Speeches of the Day,* January 1, 1990, p. 190.

Van Atta, Dale, speech excerpt reprinted by permission of the Keppler Associate, Washington, D.C.

Wyatt, Joseph B., "Is Professional Life Just a Game?" *Vital Speeches of the Day.*

Zimbardo, Philip G., figure from *Psychology and Life, 11/e* by Philip G. Zimbardo. © 1985 by Scott, Foresman and Company. Reprinted by permission of HarperCollins Publishers.

P H O T O S

INDEX

A

Aaronson, Robert J., 173–174
Abbreviations, 239
Abridged dictionaries, 146–147
Abstraction, 240–241, 334
Acceptance speeches, 414–418
Action step
    in conclusion, 221–222
    in persuasive speech, 359–360
Active listening, 65–66. *See also* Listening
Active versus passive voice, 241–242
Actual objects, 265
Adams, Randall Dale, 133
Adams, Vickee Jordan, 285–286
Adler, Mortimer J., 61
African Americans, 108, 115, 225, 304, 351–352, 428–430. *See also* specific persons
After-dinner speeches, 526–427
Ages of audience, 104–105
Ailes, Roger, 48
Allen, Woody, 255
Alliteration, 235
Almanacs, 154
Ambiguity
    in questionnaires, 120
    in speeches, 94–95, 333–334
American Authors, 151, 1600–1900
American Heritage Dictionary, 146
American Men and Women of Science, 152
American Political Dictionary, 147
Analogies
    figurative analogies, 179–180
    guidelines for, 180
    in informative speech, 332
    literal analogy, 180
    reasoning by analogy, 384–386
    reasoning supported by, 39
    as supporting material, 39, 179–180
Anaphora, 235
Anastrophe, 234
Anecdotes
    in eulogies, 421–422
    as humor, 255

in special occasion speeches, 407–408
    use of, in speeches, 9
Angelou, Maya, 114
Antithesis, 235
Apologies, 227, 297
Applause, 227
Applied Science and Technology Index, 153
Aristotle, 12, 75, 77, 78, 234, 343, 381
Arnot, Bob, 203–204
Art Index, 143, 153
Articulation, 48, 298, 304–305
Asian-Americans, 430–436
Atkinson, Ti-Grace, 292
Attention-getting devices, 8–9, 212–217, 236, 301, 327–328, 330–331, 357
Attitudes
    definition of, 111
    persuasive speech and, 344, 347–348
Attractiveness, of speaker, 374–375
Audience. *See also* Listening
    adaptation to, 126
    ages of, 104–105
    analysis of, 35–36, 102–111, 117–121
    appeal to audience emotion in persuasion, 392–396
    characteristics of, 102–111
    in communication transaction, 17, 21
    dialogue with, and ethical issues, 96
    expectations of, 115–117, 407
    feedback from, 47, 60, 125, 127
    gender role differences in, 105–106
    goals of, 324–325
    group affiliation of, 107–110
    informative speech and, 324–331
    interest in topic of speech, 116–117
    interruptions of informative speech of, 338

interviews of, 121
    knowledge of, 106–107, 117, 325
    knowledge of speaker, 117
    life-style choices of, 110–111, 111n
    observations of, 121
    and occasion of speech, 115–117
    occupational groups in, 108–109
    participation of, in speech, 124–125
    persuasive speech and, 396–397
    physical surroundings and, 123–124
    political affiliation of, 110
    questionnaires for, 118–121
    racial and ethnic backgrounds of, 108
    reasons audiences stop listening, 53
    religion of, 107
    room size and, 123
    seating arrangement of, 123–124
    size of, 123
    socioeconomic status of, 110
    and speaker-audience connection, 121–125, 147–148
    topic selection and, 30–31
    well-organized speech and, 184–185
    word choice and, 40
Audiotape, 279–280
Audio-visual aids. *See* Visual aids
Author Biographies Master Index, 150, 151
Authoritarian leaders, 450
AV materials. *See* Visual aids
Averages, 166–167

B

Bacon, Francis, 404
Baird, A. Craig, 77
Baird, John E., Jr., 220
Baker, Kristin M., 106
Bakker, Jim, 80
Bandwagoning, 92
Bar graphs, 274–275, 275
Barry, Marion, 91

Art Ability
(214) 741-9959